Lecture Notes in Computer Science 4444

Commenced Publication in 1973
Founding and Former Series Editors:
Gerhard Goos, Juris Hartmanis, and Jan van Leeuwen

Thomas Reps   Mooly Sagiv
Jörg Bauer (Eds.)

Program Analysis and Compilation, Theory and Practice

Essays Dedicated to Reinhard Wilhelm
on the Occasion of His 60th Birthday

 Springer

Volume Editors

Thomas Reps
University of Wisconsin-Madison
Computer Sciences Department
1210 West Dayton Street, Madison, WI 53706-1685, USA
E-mail: reps@cs.wisc.edu

Mooly Sagiv
Tel-Aviv University
School of Computer Science, Schreiber 317
Tel-Aviv, 69978, Israel
E-mail: msagiv@post.tau.ac.il

Jörg Bauer
Technical University of Denmark
Informatics and Mathematical Modelling
Building 322, 2800 Kongens Lyngby, Denmark
E-mail: joba@imm.dtu.dk

The illustration appearing on the cover of the book is the work of Sabrina Sperl, Saarbrücken.

The piece of art is in the possession of the International Conference and Research Centre for Informatics in Schloss Dagstuhl.

Library of Congress Control Number: 2007922986

CR Subject Classification (1998): D.3, F.3.1-2, D.2.8, F.4.2, D.1

LNCS Sublibrary: SL 2 – Programming and Software Engineering

ISSN   0302-9743
ISBN-10   3-540-71315-8 Springer Berlin Heidelberg New York
ISBN-13   978-3-540-71315-9 Springer Berlin Heidelberg New York

Springer is a part of Springer Science+Business Media

springer.com

© Springer-Verlag Berlin Heidelberg 2007
Printed in Germany

Typesetting: Camera-ready by author, data conversion by Scientific Publishing Services, Chennai, India
Printed on acid-free paper   SPIN: 12032570   06/3142   5 4 3 2 1 0

Preface

On June 9–10, 2006, a celebratory symposium in honor of Reinhard Wilhelm's 60th birthday was held at Schloß Dagstuhl. Many of his graduate students and research collaborators, as well as current and former colleagues, gathered for this celebration, and Schloß Dagstuhl was certainly the most appropriate location to honor its founder. During this day and a half of scientific discussions, there were 15 research presentations, as well as a group discussion on the topic "The Future of Static Analysis." The event consisted of the following talks:

1. *Christian Ferdinand*:
   "New Developments in WCET Analysis"
2. *Wolfgang J. Paul*:
   "Verification of Distributed Systems with Realistic Time Bounds"
3. *Dieter Maurer*:
   "Lazy Execution of Boolean Queries"
4. *Raimund Seidel*:
   "Ideally Distributed Dynamic Random Search Trees Without Using Extra Space"
5. *Andreas Zeller*:
   "Static and Dynamic Inference of Temporal Properties"
6. *Helmut Seidl*:
   "Verification of Cryptographic Protocols by Means of Tractable Classes of Horn Clauses"
7. *Neil Jones*:
   "The Flow of Data and the Complexity of Algorithms"
8. *Jaan Penjam*:
   "Deductive and Inductive Methods for Program Synthesis"
9. *Arnd Poetzsch-Heffter*:
   "Encapsulation Properties of OO-Programs Require New Heap Analyses"
10. *Bernhard Steffen*:
    "Service-Oriented Compiler Construction"
11. *Chris Hankin*:
    "Average Case Execution Times Matter Too"
12. *Robert Giegerich*:
    "Making Dynamic Programming Fun"
13. *Patrick Cousot*:
    "Grammar Abstract Interpretation"
14. *Yosi Ben-Asher*:
    "Source Level Merging of Programs for Embedded Systems"
15. *Mila Majster-Cederbaum*:
    "Ensuring Properties of Interaction Systems by Construction"

The articles of this volume serve roughly as a proceedings of this Dagstuhl symposium, although some of the contributors could not participate in the celebration, and not all of the participants managed to contribute an article. However, we are pleased to have been able to assemble this stimulating collection of research articles, which honor both Reinhard's 60th birthday and more broadly his contributions to computer science (some of which are summarized in the lead-off article, "An Appreciation of the Work of Reinhard Wilhelm").

The Dagstuhl symposium could not have been the success that it turned out to be without the help of Angelika Müller, Rosi Bardohl, Annette Beyer, and all of the Dagstuhl staff.

Following lunch on the second day, the participants traveled to Saarbrücken to attend a less scientific (and more alcoholic) 60th-birthday celebration, as is traditional for a German academic, given by the Computer Science Department at Saarland University. There, Reinhard endured another series of talks offered by his graduate students, his Dagstuhl colleagues, his colleagues from the department, his brother, and several close friends. Reinhard's closing speech in response provided insight into some of the events and influences—both personal and intellectual—that have shaped his career.

We would like to thank the local organizers of the afternoon/evening celebration, and in particular, Erich Reindel from the Computer Science Department at Saarland University and Volker Geiß from the Max Planck Institute for Computer Science.

We offer this volume to Reinhard as a token of the honor that he so richly deserves. It is fitting that the ideas in the articles found herein span such a broad range of Reinhard's research interests, from ones from very nearly the beginning of his career to current and—we hope!—future work to come.

December 2006   Thomas Reps
                                                                   Mooly Sagiv
                                                                   Jörg Bauer

Reinhard Wilhelm

Table of Contents

An Appreciation

Technical Papers

An Appreciation of the Work of Reinhard Wilhelm

Thomas Reps[1], Mooly Sagiv[2], and Jörg Bauer[3]

[1] Comp. Sci. Dept., University of Wisconsin
reps@cs.wisc.edu
[2] School of Comp. Sci., Tel-Aviv University
msagiv@post.tau.ac.il
[3] Fachrichtung Informatik, Univ. des Saarlandes
joba@cs.uni-sb.de

Reinhard Wilhelm's career in Computer Science spans more than a third of a century. During this time, he has made numerous research contributions in the areas of programming languages, compilers and compiler generators, static program analysis, program transformation, algorithm animation, and real-time systems; co-founded a company to transfer some of these ideas to industry; held the Chair for Programming Languages and Compiler Construction at Saarland University; and served since its inception as the Scientific Director of the International Conference and Research Center for Computer Science at Schloß Dagstuhl.

1 Research Activities

1.1 Foundations of Programming and Programming Languages

Reinhard's work in the area of programming languages is unusual in that he has had an interest in, and made contributions in, *all* styles of programming languages (imperative, functional, logic, parallel, object-oriented, and constraint-oriented) [14,15,16,17,20,19, 21,22,24,25,26,31,77].

1.2 Compilers, Compiler Generators, and Compilation Algorithms

Compilers convert a program or specification written in some language into a form that allows it to be executed on a computer or network of computers. *Compiler generators* are tools for creating compilers themselves (or components of compilers) from specifications. From the number of his publications on these subjects, and their distribution in time, it is easy to see that Reinhard's longest-held interest and deepest attachment in Computer Science has been to the area of compilers [32], including compiler generators [27,28,29,30] and the algorithms needed to accomplish the tasks required in various phases of compilation (see below).

Attribute Grammars. Attribute grammars are a language-description formalism that was introduced by Donald Knuth in 1968.[1] In an attribute grammar, a language and its properties are specified by giving

---

[1] D.E. Knuth: Semantics of context-free languages. Math. Syst. Theory 2(2): 127-145 (1968).

T. Reps, M. Sagiv, and J. Bauer (Eds.): Wilhelm Festschrift, LNCS 4444, pp. 1–11, 2007.

- a context-free grammar for the language,
- sets of "attributes" (annotations) to be attached to nodes of the grammar's derivation trees, and
- rules that describe how information from one node's attributes affects the attributes of other nodes.

Reinhard's research in this area concerned analysis and applications of attribute grammars [33,34,35,36,37,38,39,40,41,60,61]. Reinhard also spearheaded the implementation of three of the most influential compiler-generation systems that were based on attribute grammars: MUG1 [28], MUG2 [29,30], and OPTRAN [38,77,40,41,72].

Code Generation via Transformational Grammars/Tree Automata. The code-generation phase of a compiler turns an intermediate representation of a program into a sequence of machine-code instructions. One code-generation subtask is code selection— the actual selection of the instructions to be emitted. In a sequence of papers [44,46,48], Reinhard together with Helmut Seidl developed the connections between the code-selection problem and the theories of regular-tree grammars and finite tree automata. This work provided a sound theoretical basis for code selection, generalized and improved existing methods, and furthered the understanding of how to generate code-selection components of compilers from machine descriptions.

Other Compilation Algorithms. Other compilation issues with which Reinhard has been concerned include table compression [47], graph reduction [42], code optimization [43,49], and virtual machines [50,51].

1.3   Static Program Analysis

One of the areas in which Reinhard has worked for multiple decades, and made many important contributions, is *static program analysis* (also known as "dataflow analysis" or "abstract interpretation"). Static analysis is the basic technique used in optimizing compilers and other programming tools for obtaining information about the possible states that a program can reach during execution, but without actually running the program on specific inputs. Instead, static-analysis techniques explore a program's behavior for *all* possible inputs to determine (an approximation of) *all* possible states that the program can reach. To make this feasible, the program is "run in the aggregate"—i.e., on descriptors that represent collections of many states. The fundamental theory that provides the foundation for such techniques is that of *abstract interpretation*, enunciated in 1977 by Patrick and Radhia Cousot.[2]

Reinhard's work in the area of static analysis includes [52,53,54,55,56,57,58,61,59], as well as many other papers mentioned below.

Grammar Flow Analysis. In two papers with U. Möncke [60,61], Reinhard proposed the technique of "grammar flow analysis". This work generalized the concepts and

---

[2] P. Cousot, R. Cousot: Abstract interpretation: A unified lattice model for static analysis of programs by construction or approximation of fixpoints. POPL 1977: 238-252.

algorithms of (intraprocedural) dataflow analysis—which generally is applied to graph data structures—to a method for obtaining information about properties of derivation trees of the nonterminals in context-free grammars (but without actually building the grammar's derivation trees). Not only does this generalization have important applications in interprocedural dataflow analysis, but Möncke and Wilhelm also showed how grammar flow analysis has applications in many other areas of compilers—ranging from static-semantic analysis to code generation.

Shape Analysis. In a series of papers with M. Sagiv, T. Reps, and others, (e.g., [62, 63, 64, 65, 66, 67, 68, 69, 70, 71]), Reinhard has addressed one of the major remaining challenges in static analysis of program behavior—sometimes called *shape analysis*—namely, how to check properties of programs that manipulate linked data structures (i.e., programs that use dynamic allocation and freeing of storage cells, and destructive updating of structure fields—as happens pervasively in languages such as C, C++, and Java). In such programs, data structures can grow and shrink dynamically, with no fixed upper bound on their size or number. The analysis problem is complicated even more by the fact that such languages also permit fields of dynamically allocated objects to be destructively updated. In the case of thread-based languages, such as Java, the number of threads can also grow and shrink dynamically—again with no fixed upper bound on size or number. These features create considerable difficulties for any method that tries to check program properties, and this subject is considered to be one of the most challenging areas of program analysis.

A key issue when analyzing programs that use such features is how to create finite-sized descriptors of memory configurations, such that the descriptors

- abstract away certain details, but
- retain enough key information so that the analysis can identify interesting properties that hold.

One of the crucial obstacles is that dynamically-allocated storage cells have no static names, and the number of such objects is, in general, unbounded.

The Sagiv-Reps-Wilhelm approach [67] provides a solution to the problem of devising finite-sized descriptors of the infinite number of storage configurations that can arise at a point in the program. Moreover, it also provides a way to tune the precision of the descriptors in use, which is important both for reducing the time required to run an analysis, and for reducing the number of false positives that an analysis may report. From a static-analysis perspective, the work is novel because of the way that it uses 3-valued logic to address these issues.

1.4 Program Transformation/Rewriting

The heart of many compilation steps (such as optimization and code generation) is *tree transformation* or *rewriting*. Reinhard's work in this area has concerned systems for program transformation and optimization—originally formalized using attribute-grammar-based notations and implemented as rewriting of attributed abstract-syntax trees [72,73,74,75,77]. Later work addressed these problems using a specialized functional notation for specifying patterns and transformations [78].

1.5   Algorithm Animation and Visualization

Algorithm animation concerns how to create visual presentations of computations. This area has been another of Reinhard's long-term interests [79, 80, 81, 82, 83]. He has worked on such varied problems as the depiction of compilation steps [83], finite-state automata [82], and abstract interpretation [79, 80].

1.6   Timing Analysis for Real-Time Systems

In a series of papers with various authors (beginning with [84]), Reinhard spearheaded a new approach to predicting the timing behavior of processors that are equipped with cache memory. Because of the substantial differences exhibited by modern processors between the latency for an access that goes to main memory versus an access that can be resolved in the cache, cache behavior has to be taken into account to predict a program's execution time. Classical methods based on experimental measurement provide only soft guarantees: any measurement-based approach, via either hardware or software, only determines the execution time for the specific inputs of the test suite. Moreover, software-based monitoring alters the code, thereby influencing the cache behavior—and hence the performance—of the program whose performance one is trying to measure.

The behavior-prediction techniques that Reinhard has helped to devise make use of static program analysis, which (as noted above) provides a way to obtain information about the possible states that a program reaches during execution, but without actually running the program on specific inputs. Using this approach, Reinhard and his colleagues have shown that it is possible to determine the worst-case cache behavior (i.e., to identify what could be in the cache at each point in the program) [84,85,86,87,88,89], as well as to bound the worst-case running time of real-time programs and to check the program for the possibility of cache conflicts that could affect time-critical parts [90,91,92,93,94,95,96,97,98]. The advantage of their approach is that the predictions obtained using their techniques are valid for all inputs. From a static-analysis perspective, the work often combines "may" and "must" information in an unusual way.

An additional area of concern has been with processor models—e.g., with such issues as the semantics of processors and how to specify them—as well as with gaining an understanding of which real-time systems are time-predictable [99, 100, 101, 102, 103].

2   Technology Transfer

Reinhard has been successful in making the work on timing analysis for real-time systems accessible to the embedded-systems and real-time communities, thereby demonstrating how static program analysis can be applied to the problems that arise in these domains. This work also forms the basis for the products of a company that Reinhard co-founded (AbsInt Angewandte Informatik GmbH, Saarbruecken, Germany [104]). Their tool has been successfully used to certify time-critical subsystems of the Airbus A380 plane.

3   Pedagogical Activities

Reinhard Wilhelm holds the Chair for Programming Languages and Compiler Construction at Saarland University, where he has supervised twenty-five Ph.D. theses and nearly one hundred fifty Masters/Diploma theses.

Reinhard's textbook ("Compiler Design"), co-authored with D. Maurer and published in German [10], French [11], and English [12], is successfully used in many graduate and undergraduate compiler courses. The book is noteworthy for the way that it presents the problems of compiling imperative languages, functional languages, object-oriented languages, and logic-programming languages in a way that draws out their commonalities. The book covers in depth many difficult aspects of compilation, such as bottom-up parsing with error recovery, attribute grammars, and abstract interpretation. Compared with other textbooks, Reinhard's book provides the most theoretically well-grounded treatment of the problems that arise in writing compilers.

Recently, Reinhard also participated in an effort to design a graduate curriculum on embedded software and systems [13].

4   Schloß Dagstuhl

Reinhard has also performed a notable service to the international Computer Science community by having served since its inception as the Scientific Director of the International Conference and Research Center for Computer Science at Schloß Dagstuhl. Dagstuhl was set up in 1990 along the lines of the famous conference center for Mathematics at Oberwolfach. Dagstuhl hosts several kinds of activities, but predominantly "Dagstuhl Seminars", which are week-long intensive seminars involving lectures, group discussions, software demonstrations, etc. By now, Dagstuhl Seminars have been held in a large number of different subject areas of Computer Science. There are about forty of these every year, each with somewhere between twenty and sixty participants from all over the world.

Reinhard has been involved with Dagstuhl from the start, and as the founding Scientific Director, his imprint is to be found on all aspects of its operation, including not just the choice of seminar topics and attention to maintaining the highest scientific standards, but also the original renovation of Schloß Dagstuhl, the design and construction of a major second building, the solicitation of donations from industry and charitable foundations, the arrangement of a special funding program for junior researchers (young faculty and graduate students), and the list could go on and on. Many weeks, he even leads the traditional Wednesday mid-week hike.

Reinhard has made Dagstuhl a very special place for Computer Scientists by his quiet, but skillful, way of using his "bully pulpit" to nudge the Computer Science community into fruitful and interesting interactions:

- He has made seminars that bring together groups that have common interests, but that for one reason or another have had relatively limited contact, a Dagstuhl specialty.
- He attends at least one day of each Dagstuhl seminar to monitor progress and offer advice to that week's organizers about possible mid-course corrections.
- He actively solicits Seminars on new and promising topics.
- During the planning stages of Seminars, he keeps an eye out for potential attendees who might have been overlooked, but who would especially profit from and/or contribute to the activities of a Seminar.

Dagstuhl and its attendees have also benefited from Reinhard's careful—and tasteful—attention to detail, which goes far beyond the scientific aspects of the establishment: the choice of music scores and musical instruments in Dagstuhl's music room; the organizing of displays of modern art in the Dagstuhl buildings and on the Dagstuhl grounds; even the choice of wine in the famous Dagstuhl Wine Cellar, where participants are encouraged to repair for the evening for both technical and non-technical conversation.

5   A Partial List of Reinhard Wilhelm's Collaborators

L. Almeida, M. Alt, H.-J. Bach, M. Baston, J. Bauer, G. Becker, Y. Ben-Asher, A. Benveniste, C. Berg, J. Börstler, P. G. Bouillon, B. Bouyssounouse, B. Braune, F. Warren Burton, G. C. Buttazzo, P. Caspi, J. Ciesinger, V. Claus, I. Crnkovic, W. Damm, S. Diehl, J. Engblom, A. A. Evstiougov-Babaev, C. Fecht, C. Ferdinand, G. Fohler, F. Fontaine, N. Francez, N. Fritz, H. Ganzinger, M. García-Valls, R. Giegerich, I. Glasner, H. Hagen, R. Heckmann, E. Hoffmann, D. Johannes, D. Kästner, A. Kerren, H. Kopetz, B. Kuhn, W. Lahner, Y. Lakhnech, M. Langenbach, F. Laroussinie, L. Lavagno, T. Lev-Ami, G. Lipari, P. Lipps, J. Loeckx, P. Lucas, A. Lucks-Baus, F. Maraninchi, F. Martin, D. Maurer, K. Mehlhorn, J. Messerschmidt, U. Möncke, T. Müldner, F. Müller, R. Nollmann, H.-G. Oberhauser, M. Olk, O. Parshin, P. Peti, J. Antonio de la Puente, M. Raber, A. Rakib, F. Randimbivololona, T. Rauber, T. Remmel, T. Reps, N. Rinetzky, K. Ripken, B. Robinet, M. Rodeh, G. Rünger, M. Sagiv, G. Sander, A. L. Sangiovanni-Vincentelli, N. Scaife, M. Schmidt, J. Schneider, A. Schuster, R. Seidel, H. Seidl, M. Sicks, J. Sifakis, R. de Simone, J. Souyris, O. Spaniol, H. Theiling, S. Thesing, L. Thiele, W. Thome, M. Törngren, P. Veríssimo, B. Weisgerber, A.J. Wellings, D.B. Whalley, S. Wilhelm, T.A.C. Willemse, E. Yahav, W. Yi, G. Yorsh.

Acknowledgments

We would like to thank Angelika Müller, Rosi Bardohl, Annette Beyer, and all of the Dagstuhl staff for the splendid job they did organizing and hosting the Reinhard Wilhelm 60th-Birthday Celebratory Symposium. We would also like to thank Patrick

Cousot for furnishing us with the list of references to Reinhard's publications that he assembled for the presentation of Reinhard's work at the Saarland University celebration of Reinhard's birthday.

References

1. R. Wilhelm. *Informatics: 10 Years Back. 10 Years Ahead.* Lecture Notes in Computer Science 2000. Springer, Berlin, Germany, 2001.
2. R. Wilhelm: Compiler Construction, 10th International Conference, CC 2001 Held as Part of the Joint European Conferences on Theory and Practice of Software, ETAPS 2001 Genova, Italy, April 2-6, 2001, Proceedings Springer 2001
3. R. Wilhelm: Informatik: Grundlagen - Amwendungen - Perspektiven [Forum "Perspektiven der Informatik", Dagstuhl, November 1993] Verlag C. H. Beck 1996
4. R. Wilhelm: Generische und generative Methoden. Perspektiven der Informatik 1993: 84-85
5. R. Wilhelm, H. Hagen: Programmiersprachen. Perspektiven der Informatik 1993: 86-90
6. V. Claus, R. Wilhelm: Einleitung. Perspektiven der Informatik 1993: 9-12
7. R. Wilhelm, O. Spaniol: Parallele und verteilte Systeme. Perspektiven der Informatik 1993: 90-94
8. B. Robinet, R. Wilhelm: ESOP 86, European Symposium on Programming, Saarbrücken, Federal Republic of Germany, March 17-19, 1986, Proceedings, LNCS 213, Springer 1986
9. R. Wilhelm: GI - 10. Jahrestagung, Saarbrücken, 30. September - 2. Oktober 1980, Proceedings Springer 1980
10. R. Wilhelm and D. Maurer. *Übersetzerbau - Theorie, Konstruktion, Generierung.* Springer, Berlin, Germany, 1992, 2. Auflage Springer 1997
11. R. Wilhelm and D. Maurer. *Les Compilateurs, théorie, construction, génération.* Masson, Paris, France, 1994.
12. R. Wilhelm and D. Maurer. *Compiler Design: Theory, Construction, Generation.* Addison-Wesley, Reading, MA, 1996.
13. P. Caspi, A. L. Sangiovanni-Vincentelli, Luís Almeida, A. Benveniste, B. Bouyssounouse, G. C. Buttazzo, I. Crnkovic, W. Damm, J. Engblom, G. Fohler, M. García-Valls, H. Kopetz, Y. Lakhnech, François Laroussinie, L. Lavagno, G. Lipari, F. Maraninchi, P. Peti, J. Antonio de la Puente, N. Scaife, J. Sifakis, R. de Simone, M. Törngren, P. Veríssimo, A.J. Wellings, R. Wilhelm, T.A.C. Willemse, W. Yi: Guidelines for a Graduate Curriculum on Embedded Software and Systems. ACM Trans. Embedded Comput. Syst. 4(3): 587-611 (2005)
14. R. Wilhelm: Imperative, prädikative und funktionale Programmierung (Kurzfassung). GI Jahrestagung 1982: 188-193
15. J. Messerschmidt, R. Wilhelm: Constructors for Composed Objects. Comput. Lang. 7(2): 53-59 (1982)
16. R. Wilhelm: Symbolische Programmausführung - Das aktuelle Schlagwort. Informatik Spektrum 6(3): 170 (1983)
17. J. Loeckx, K. Mehlhorn, R. Wilhelm: Grundlagen der Programmiersprachen. Teubner, 1986
18. G. Becker, B. Kuhn, D. Maurer, R. Wilhelm: SiATEX - eine interaktive Arbeitsumgeubng für TEX. Innovative Informations-Infrastrukturen 1988: 162-169
19. J. Loeckx, K. Mehlhorn, R. Wilhelm: Foundations of Programming Languages. John Wiley, 1989
20. M. Baston, H.-J. Bach, A. Lucks-Baus, F. Müller, R. Wilhelm: Implementierung der funktionalen Programmiersprache HOPE mit Hilfe von Kombinatoren. Innovative Informations-Infrastrukturen 1988: 114-131

21. R. Wilhelm: Übersetzer für imperative, funktionale und logische Programmiersprachen: Ein Vergleich (eingeladener Vortrag). Software-Entwicklung 1989: 156-165
22. Y. Ben-Asher, G. Rünger, A. Schuster, R. Wilhelm: 2DT-FP: An FP Based Programming Language for Efficient Parallel Programming of Multiprocessor Networks. PARLE 1993: 42-55
23. Y. Ben-Asher, G. Rünger, R. Wilhelm, A. Schuster: Implementing 2DT on a Multiprocessor. CC 1994: 113-127
24. T. Rauber, G. Rünger, R. Wilhelm: An application specific parallel programming paradigm. HPCN Europe 1995: 735-740
25. R. Heckmann, R. Wilhelm: A Functional Description of TEX's Formula Layout. J. Funct. Program. 7(5): 451-485 (1997)
26. P. Lucas, N. Fritz, R. Wilhelm: The Development of the Data-Parallel GPU Programming Language CGiS. Int. Conf. on Computational Science, 2006: 200-203
27. H. Ganzinger, R. Wilhelm: Verschränkung von Compiler-Moduln. GI Jahrestagung 1975: 654-665
28. R. Wilhelm, K. Ripken, J. Ciesinger, H. Ganzinger, Walter Lahner, R. Nollmann: Design Evaluation of the Compiler Generating System MUGI. ICSE 1976: 571-576
29. H. Ganzinger, K. Ripken, R. Wilhelm: Automatic Generation of Optimizing Multipass Compilers. IFIP Congress 1977: 535-540
30. H. Ganzinger, R. Giegerich, U. Möncke, R. Wilhelm: A Truly Generative Semantics-Directed Compiler Generator. SIGPLAN Symposium on Compiler Construction 1982: 172-184
31. R. Wilhelm, M. Alt, F. Martin, M. Raber: Parallel Implementation of Functional Languages. LOMAPS 1996: 279-295
32. P. Lucas, N. Fritz, R. Wilhelm: The CGiS Compiler-A Tool Demonstration. CC 2006: 105-108
33. R. Giegerich, R. Wilhelm: Implementierbarkeit attributierter Grammatiken. GI Jahrestagung 1977: 17-36
34. R. Giegerich, R. Wilhelm: Counter-One-Pass Features in One-Pass Compilation: A Formalization Using Attribute Grammars. Inf. Process. Lett. 7(6): 279-284 (1978)
35. R. Wilhelm: Attributierte Grammatiken. Informatik Spektrum 2(3): 123-130 (1979)
36. R. Wilhelm: LL- and LR-Attributed Grammars. Fachtagung über Programmiersprachen 1982: 151-164
37. U. Möncke, B. Weisgerber, R. Wilhelm: How to Implement a System for Manipulation of Attributed Trees. Fachtagung über Programmiersprachen 1984: 112-127
38. P. Lipps, U. Möncke, M. Olk, R. Wilhelm: Attribute (Re)evaluation in OPTRAN. Acta Inf. 26(3): 213-239 (1988)
39. Winfried Thome, R. Wilhelm: Simulating Circular Attribute Grammars Through Attribute Reevaluation. Inf. Process. Lett. 33(2): 79-81 (1989)
40. R. Wilhelm: Attribute Reevaluation in OPTRAN. Attribute Grammars, Applications and Systems 1991: 507
41. P. Lipps, U. Möncke, R. Wilhelm: An Overview of the OPTRAN System. Attribute Grammars, Applications and Systems 1991: 505-506
42. M. Raber, T. Remmel, E. Hoffmann, D. Maurer, F. Müller, H.-G. Oberhauser, R. Wilhelm: Complied Graph Reduction on a Processor Network. ARCS 1988: 198-212
43. R. Wilhelm: Code-Optimierung Mittels Attributierter Transformationsgrammatiken. GI Jahrestagung 1974: 257-266
44. B. Weisgerber, R. Wilhelm: Two Tree Pattern Matchers for Code Selection. CC 1988: 215-229
45. C. Ferdinand, H. Seidl, R. Wilhelm: Tree Automata for Code Selection. Code Generation 1991: 30-50

46. R. Wilhelm: Tree Tranformations, Functional Languages, and Attribute Grammars. WAGA 1990: 116-129
47. J. Börstler, U. Möncke, R. Wilhelm: Table Compression for Tree Automata. ACM Trans. Program. Lang. Syst. 13(3): 295-314 (1991)
48. C. Ferdinand, H. Seidl, R. Wilhelm: Tree Automata for Code Selection. Acta Inf. 31(8): 741-760 (1994)
49. P. G. Bouillon, G. Sander, R. Wilhelm: Lokale Optimierung ausnahmebehafteter Programme durch Spuroptimierung. Inform., Forsch. Entwickl. 9(2): 72-81 (1994)
50. D. Maurer, R. Wilhelm: MaMa - eine abstrakte Maschine zur Implementierung funktionaler Programmiersprachen. Inform., Forsch. Entwickl. 4(2): 67-88 (1989)
51. M. Alt, G. Sander, R. Wilhelm: Generation of Synchronization Code for Parallel Compilers. PLILP 1993: 420-421
52. N. Rinetzky, J. Bauer, T. Reps, M. Sagiv, R. Wilhelm: A Semantics for Procedure Local Heaps and its Abstractions. POPL 2005: 296-309
53. T. Lev-Ami, T. Reps, M. Sagiv, R. Wilhelm: Putting Static Analysis to Work for Verification: A Case Study. ISSTA 2000: 26-38
54. F. Martin, M. Alt, R. Wilhelm, C. Ferdinand: Analysis of Loops. CC 1998: 80-94
55. M. Sagiv, N. Francez, M. Rodeh, R. Wilhelm: A Logic-Based Approach to Program Flow Analysis. Acta Inf. 35(6): 457-504 (1998) 1997
56. R. Wilhelm: Program Analysis: A Toolmaker's Perspective. SIGPLAN Notices 32(1): 120-121 (1997) 1996
57. R. Wilhelm: Program Analysis - A Toolmaker's Perspective. ACM Comput. Surv. 28(4es): 177 (1996)
58. M. Sagiv, N. Francez, M. Rodeh, R. Wilhelm: A Logic-Based Approach to Data Flow Analysis Problem. PLILP 1990: 277-292
59. R. Wilhelm: Computation and Use of Data Flow Information in Optimizing Compilers. Acta Inf. 12: 209-225 (1979)
60. U. Möncke, R. Wilhelm: Grammar Flow Analysis. Attribute Grammars, Applications and Systems 1991: 151-186
61. U. Möncke, R. Wilhelm: Iterative Algorithms on Grammar Graphs, 8th Conf. on Graphtheoretic Concepts in Comp. Sci. 1982: 177-194
62. M. Sagiv, T. Reps, R. Wilhelm: Solving Shape-Analysis Problems in Languages with Destructive Updating. POPL 1996: 16-31
63. M. Sagiv, T. Reps, R. Wilhelm: Solving Shape-Analysis Problems in Languages with Destructive Updating. ACM Trans. Program. Lang. Syst. 20(1): 1-50 (1998)
64. M. Sagiv, T. Reps, R. Wilhelm: Parametric Shape Analysis via 3-Valued Logic. POPL 1999: 105-118
65. R. Wilhelm, M. Sagiv, T. Reps: Shape Analysis. CC 2000: 1-17
66. R. Wilhelm, T. Reps, M. Sagiv: Shape Analysis and Applications. The Compiler Design Handbook 2002: 175-218
67. M. Sagiv, T. Reps, R. Wilhelm: Parametric Shape Analysis via 3-Valued Logic. ACM Trans. Program. Lang. Syst. 24(3): 217-298 (2002)
68. E. Yahav, T. Reps, M. Sagiv, R. Wilhelm: Verifying Temporal Heap Properties Specified via Evolution Logic. ESOP 2003: 204-222
69. T. Reps, M. Sagiv, R. Wilhelm: Static Program Analysis via 3-Valued Logic. CAV 2004: 15-30
70. E. Yahav, T. Reps, M. Sagiv, R. Wilhelm: Verifying Temporal Heap Properties Specified Via Evolution Logic. Logic Journal of the IGPL 14, 5 (Oct. 2006): 755-784
71. G. Yorsh, T. Reps, M. Sagiv, R. Wilhelm: Logical Characterizations of Heap Abstractions. ACM Trans. Comp. Logic 8, 1 (Jan. 2007)

72. I. Glasner, U. Möncke, R. Wilhelm: OPTRAN, a Language for the Specification of Program Transformations. Fachtagung über Programmiersprachen 1980: 125-142

73. R. Giegerich, U. Möncke, R. Wilhelm: Invariance of Approximate Semantics with Respect to Program Transformations. GI Jahrestagung 1981: 1-10

74. R. Wilhelm: A Modified Tree-to-Tree Correction Problem. Inf. Process. Lett. 12(3): 127-132 (1981)

75. R. Wilhelm: Inverse Currying Transformation on Attribute Grammars. POPL 1984: 140-147

76. F. Warren Burton, D. Maurer, H.-G. Oberhauser, R. Wilhelm: A Space-Efficient Optimization of Call-by-Need. IEEE Trans. Software Eng. 13(6): 636-642 (1987)

77. P. Lipps, U. Möncke, R. Wilhelm: OPTRAN - A Language/System for the Specification of Program Transformations: System Overview and Experiences. CC 1988: 52-65

78. M. Alt, C. Fecht, C. Ferdinand, R. Wilhelm: Transformation Development: TrafoLa-H Subsystem. PROSPECTRA Book 1993: 539-576

79. D. Johannes, R. Seidel, R. Wilhelm: Algorithm Animation Using Shape Analysis: Visualising Abstract Executions. SOFTVIS 2005: 17-26

80. R. Wilhelm, T. Müldner, R. Seidel: Algorithm Explanation: Visualizing Abstract States and Invariants. Software Visualization 2001: 381-394

81. B. Braune, R. Wilhelm: Focusing in Algorithm Explanation. IEEE Trans. Vis. Comput. Graph. 6(1): 1-7 (2000)

82. B. Braune, S. Diehl, A. Kerren, R. Wilhelm: Animation of the Generation and Computation of Finite Automata for Learning Software. WIA 1999: 39-47

83. G. Sander, M. Alt, C. Ferdinand, R. Wilhelm: CLaX - A Visualized Compiler. Graph Drawing 1995: 459-462

84. M. Alt, C. Ferdinand, F. Martin, R. Wilhelm: Cache Behavior Prediction by Abstract Interpretation. SAS 1996: 52-66

85. C. Ferdinand, R. Wilhelm: On Predicting Data Cache Behavior for Real-Time Systems. LCTES 1998: 16-30

86. C. Ferdinand, F. Martin, R. Wilhelm, M. Alt: Cache Behavior Prediction by Abstract Interpretation. Sci. Comput. Program. 35(2): 163-189 (1999)

87. C. Ferdinand, R. Wilhelm: Efficient and Precise Cache Behavior Prediction for Real-Time Systems. Real-Time Systems 17(2-3): 131-181 (1999)

88. H. Theiling, C. Ferdinand, R. Wilhelm: Fast and Precise WCET Prediction by Separated Cache and Path Analyses. Real-Time Systems 18(2/3): 157-179 (2000)

89. A. Rakib, O. Parshin, S. Thesing, R. Wilhelm: Component-Wise Instruction-Cache Behavior Prediction. ATVA 2004: 211-229

90. R. Wilhelm: Why AI + ILP Is Good for WCET, but MC Is Not, Nor ILP Alone. VMCAI 2004: 309-322

91. S. Thesing, J. Souyris, R. Heckmann, F. Randimbivololona, M. Langenbach, R. Wilhelm, C. Ferdinand: An Abstract Interpretation-Based Timing Validation of Hard Real-Time Avionics Software. Proc. Int. Performance and Dependability Symp.: 625-632

92. C. Ferdinand, D. Kästner, F. Martin, M. Langenbach, M. Sicks, S. Wilhelm, R. Heckmann, Nico Fritz, S. Thesing, F. Fontaine, H. Theiling, M. Schmidt, A. A. Evstiougov-Babaev, R. Wilhelm: Validierung des Zeitverhaltens von kritischer Echtzeit-Software. GI Jahrestagung (1) 2003: 335-339

93. C. Ferdinand, R. Heckmann, H. Theiling, R. Wilhelm: Convenient User Annotations for a WCET Tool. WCET 2003: 17-20

94. R. Wilhelm, J. Engblom, S. Thesing, D.B. Whalley: Industrial Requirements for WCET Tools - Answers to the ARTIST Questionnaire. WCET 2003: 39-43

95. R. Heckmann, M. Langenbach, S. Thesing, R. Wilhelm: The Influence of Processor Architecture on the Design and the Results of WCET Tools. Proc. of the IEEE 91(7): 1038-1054 (2003)

96. C. Ferdinand, R. Heckmann, M. Langenbach, F. Martin, M. Schmidt, H. Theiling, S. Thesing, R. Wilhelm: Reliable and Precise WCET Determination for a Real-Life Processor. EMSOFT 2001: 469-485

97. C. Ferdinand, D. Kästner, M. Langenbach, F. Martin, M. Schmidt, J. Schneider, H. Theiling, S. Thesing, R. Wilhelm: Run-Time Guarantees for Real-Time Systems - The USES Approach. GI Jahrestagung 1999: 410-419

98. R. Wilhelm: Timing Analysis and Validation for Real-Time Systems - Guest Editor's Introduction. Real-Time Systems 17(2-3): 127-129 (1999)

99. R. Wilhelm: Timing Analysis and Timing Predictability. FMCO 2004: 317-323

100. R. Wilhelm: Formal Analysis of Processor Timing Models. SPIN 2004: 1-4

101. L. Thiele, R. Wilhelm: Design for Timing Predictability. Real-Time Systems 28(2-3): 157-177 (2004)

102. R. Wilhelm: Run-Time Guarantees for Real-Time Systems. FORMATS 2003: 166-167

103. R. Wilhelm: Determining Bounds on Execution Times. In R. Zurawski, editor, Handbook on Embedded Systems, pages 14-1,14-23. CRC Press, 2005.

104. http://www.absint.com/

New Developments in WCET Analysis

Christian Ferdinand[1], Florian Martin[1], Christoph Cullmann[1],
Marc Schlickling[1,2], Ingmar Stein[1], Stephan Thesing[2],
and Reinhold Heckmann[1]

[1] AbsInt Angewandte Informatik GmbH
Science Park 1, D-66123 Saarbrücken, Germany
info@absint.com
http://www.absint.com

[2] Universität des Saarlandes, Postfach 15 11 50, D-66041 Saarbrücken, Germany
{schlickling,thesing}@cs.uni-sb.de
http://rw4.cs.uni-sb.de

Abstract. The worst-case execution time analyzer aiT originally developed by Saarland University and AbsInt GmbH computes safe and precise upper bounds for the WCETs of tasks. It relies on a pipeline model
that usually has been handcrafted. We present some new approaches aiming at automatically obtaining a pipeline model as required by aiT from
a formal processor description in VHDL or Verilog. The derivation of the
total WCET from the basic-block WCETs requires knowledge about upper bounds on the number of loop iterations. We present a new method
for loop bound detection using dataflow analysis to derive loop invariants. A task may contain infeasible paths caused by conditionals with
logically related conditions. We present a static analysis that identifies
and collects conditions from the executable, and relates these collections
to detect infeasible paths. This new analysis uses the results of a novel
generic slicer on the level of binary code.

1 Introduction

Many tasks in safety-critical embedded systems have hard real-time characteristics. A schedulability analysis has to be performed in order to guarantee that
all timing constraints will be met [1]. It requires the worst-case execution time
(WCET) of each task in the system to be known prior to its execution. The
worst-case execution time analyzer **aiT** originally developed by Saarland University and AbsInt GmbH computes safe and precise upper bounds for the WCETs
of tasks (see Section 2).

Input of the analyzer is an executable. After decoding it, value analysis computes upper and lower bounds for the values in the registers and memory cells.
Then a microarchitecture analysis computes the WCETs of basic blocks taking
into account cache and pipeline behavior. It relies on a pipeline model that usually has been handcrafted. In Section 6, we present some new approaches aiming
at automatically obtaining a pipeline model as required by **aiT** from a formal
processor description in VHDL or Verilog.

T. Reps, M. Sagiv, and J. Bauer (Eds.): Wilhelm Festschrift, LNCS 4444, pp. 12–52, 2007.

The derivation of the total WCET from the basic-block WCETs requires knowledge about upper bounds on the number of loop iterations. We present a new method for loop bound detection using dataflow analysis to derive loop invariants in Section 3.

A task may contain infeasible paths caused by conditionals with logically related (weaker, stronger, or even equivalent) conditions. Including such infeasible paths in the global WCET computation may lead to a huge overestimation of the WCET. In Section 4, we present a static analysis that identifies and collects conditions from the executable, and relates these collections to detect infeasible paths. This new analysis uses the results of a novel generic slicer on the level of binary code that is presented in Section 5.

2   Worst-Case Execution Time Prediction by aiT

The determination of the WCET of a task is a difficult problem because of the characteristics of modern software and hardware [2]. Caches, branch target buffers, and pipelines are used in virtually all performance-oriented processors. Consequently the timing of the instructions depends on the execution history. Hence, the widely used classical methods of predicting execution times are not generally applicable. Software monitoring and dual-loop benchmark change the code, which in turn changes the cache behavior. Hardware simulation, emulation, or direct measurement with logic analyzers can only determine the execution time for some fixed inputs.

In contrast, abstract interpretation [3] can be used to efficiently compute a safe approximation for all possible cache and pipeline states that can occur at a program point in any program run with any input. These results can be combined with ILP (Integer Linear Programming) techniques to safely predict the worst-case execution time and a corresponding worst-case execution path.

The overview paper [4] describes different approaches to the WCET problem and surveys several commercially available tools and research prototypes. Here we concentrate on **AbsInt**'s **aiT** WCET analyzer tools. These tools get as input an executable, user annotations, a description of the (external) memories and buses (i.e. a list of memory areas with minimal and maximal access times), and a task (identified by a start address). A task denotes a sequentially executed piece of code (no threads, no parallelism, and no waiting for external events). This should not be confused with a task in an operating system that might include code for synchronization or communication. Effects of interrupts, IO and timer (co-)processors are not reflected in the predicted runtime and have to be considered separately (e.g., by a quantitative analysis).

aiT operates in several phases (see Figure 1). First a *decoder* reads the executable, identifies the instructions and their operands, and reconstructs the control flow [5]. The reconstructed control flow is annotated with the information needed by subsequent analyses and then translated into CRL (Control-Flow Representation Language).

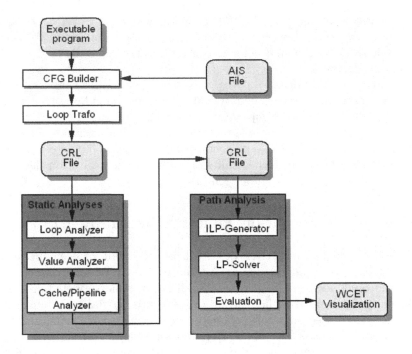

Fig. 1. Phases of WCET computation

The original control-flow graph is modified by the so-called *loop transformation*, which turns loops into separate routines that call themselves recursively. The purpose of this loop transformation is to enhance the precision of timing analysis in presence of loops. Note that loop transformation only concerns the graphs used as internal representation; the executable itself is not affected.

Figure 2 shows the effect of loop transformation on a simple loop. The picture on the left shows the control-flow graph of routine F that contains such a simple loop. The routine is entered at b0 and left at the special *exit node* end. In a kind of pseudo source code, this routine could be specified as

```
routine F {
  b0;
  while (b1)  b2;
  b3;
}
```

The picture on the right hand side of Figure 2 shows the result of loop transformation. The loop has been turned into a separate *loop routine* named F.L1 that is called from F at loop call F.L1; the calling relationship is indicated by the arrow from routine F to routine F.L1.

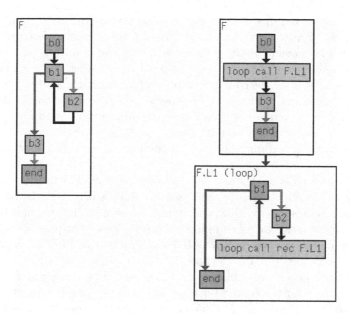

Fig. 2. Loop transformation

In pseudo source code, the transformed program could be specified as

```
routine F {
  b0;
  loop_call_F.L1:  call F.L1;
  b3;
}
routine F.L1 {
  if (b1) {
    b2;
    loop_call_rec_F.L1:  call F.L1;
  }
}
```

Thus, iteration has been replaced by recursion: the loop routine calls itself at
loop call rec F.L1, indicated by the arrow from loop call rec F.L1 to b1.
The loop routine is left if b1 is false, which is depicted by the arrow from b1 to
end.

The loop-transformed control-flow graph serves as the input for all further
analyses. *Value analysis* tries to determine the values in the processor registers
for every program point and execution context. Often it cannot determine these
values exactly, but only finds safe lower and upper bounds, i.e. intervals that are
guaranteed to contain the exact values. The results of value analysis are used to
determine possible addresses of indirect memory accesses—important for cache
analysis—and in loop bound analysis.

WCET analysis requires that upper bounds for the iteration numbers of all loops be known. Previous versions of **aiT** tried to determine the number of loop iterations by a *loop bound analysis*, that relied on a combination of value analysis and pattern matching, which looks for typical loop patterns. In general, these loop patterns depend on the code generator and/or compiler used to generate the code that is being analyzed. There are special **aiT** versions adapted to various generators and compilers. In Section 3, we present a new method for loop bound analysis that is entirely based on data-flow analysis and therefore provides a more generic approach since it does not rely on compiler-specific or generator-specific code patterns.

Cache analysis classifies the accesses to main memory. The analysis in our tool is based upon [6], which handles analysis of caches with LRU (Least Recently Used) replacement strategy. However, it had to be modified to reflect the non-LRU replacement strategies of common microprocessors: the pseudo-round-robin replacement policy of the ColdFire MCF 5307, and the PLRU (Pseudo-LRU) strategy of the PowerPC MPC 750 and 755. The modified algorithms distinguish between sure cache hits and unclassified accesses. The deviation from perfect LRU is the reason for the reduced predictability of the cache contents in case of ColdFire 5307 and PowerPC 750/755 compared to processors with perfect LRU caches [7].

Pipeline analysis models the pipeline behavior to determine execution times for a sequential flow (basic block) of instructions. It takes into account the current pipeline state(s), in particular resource occupancies, contents of prefetch queues, grouping of instructions, and classification of memory references as cache hits or misses. The result is an execution time for each instruction in each distinguished execution context.

Pipeline analysis relies on a pipeline model that usually has been handcrafted, using mainly the processor documentation as input. A more reliable and complete source of information about the timing behavior of the processor pipeline is given by formal processor descriptions in VHDL or Verilog (if available). In Section 6, we present some new approaches aiming at automatically obtaining a pipeline model as required by **aiT** from such a formal processor description.

Using the results of the micro-architecture analyses, *path analysis* determines a safe estimate of the WCET. While the analyses described so far are based on abstract interpretation, integer linear programming is used for path analysis. The program's control flow is modeled by an integer linear program [8] so that the solution to the objective function is the predicted worst-case execution time for the input program.

Detailed information about the WCET, the WCET path, and the possible cache and pipeline states at any program point are visualized in the aiSee tool [9].

The predicted WCET is in general an upper bound of the real WCET. Some imprecision may be caused by the presence of infeasible paths not noticed by **aiT**. Consider for instance code such as

```
if (x > 0) b1;   b2;   if (x < 0) b3;
```

where x may hold any positive or negative value depending on the inputs and is not modified in any of the three blocks. Then the path b1 → b2 → b3 that includes both b1 and b3 is infeasible because b1 and b3 cannot be executed together in the same run through this code snippet. Yet each of the three blocks is feasible since there are runs that execute b1 and other runs that execute b3. aiT's traditional path analysis does not track conditions and will display the infeasible path b1 → b2 → b3 as the worst-case execution path. This is a safe but imprecise approximation of the real WCET since the infeasible path b1 → b2 → b3 needs more time than the feasible paths b1 → b2 and b2 → b3. In Section 4, we present a static analysis that identifies and collects conditions from the executable, and relates these conditions to detect implications and equivalences among them that cause infeasible paths. This new analysis uses the results of a novel generic slicer on the level of binary code that is presented in Section 5.

3 Loop Bound Detection by Data-Flow Analysis

To calculate the WCET for a program, safe upper bounds for the iterations of all included loops must be known. To get a high precision WCET estimation, lower bounds should be known, too.

As programs tend to contain many loops with bounds depending on the call sites of the surrounding routine, relying on user annotations for loop bounds would cause too much work for the user. Beside that, there is also the inherent danger that user-annotated bounds could contain errors. Therefore aiT aims at deriving safe loop bounds automatically by using a static analysis.

Until now, a solely pattern-based approach for loop bound detection is used. This method needs adjustments for all supported compilers and in some cases even different optimization levels. While experience has shown that this works well for many simple loops, no bounds are detectable for more complex loops with multiple modifications of the loop counter inside one iteration.

To overcome these restrictions, we introduced a new method for loop bound detection that uses an interprocedural data-flow analysis to derive loop invariants from the semantics of the instructions. This new analysis does not depend on the compiler used or optimization level but only on the semantics of the instruction set for the target machine. It is able to handle loops with multiple exits and multiple modifications of the loop counter per iteration including modifications in procedures called from the loop.

In this section, we describe the techniques behind the old and new loop analyses, compare their results, and provide insight on how the new analysis will be used in aiT. First we start in Section 3.1 with introducing the common basis of both analyses. In Section 3.2 two small examples for loops are shown that will be used later as running examples to illustrate the application of both analyses. Section 3.3 will cover the pattern-based approach. Then we introduce the new data-flow based approach in Section 3.4 and compare both analyses in Section 3.5. Finally we show how the new analysis is integrated into the WCET Analyzer aiT in Section 3.6.

3.1 Common Basis for Both Analyses

As both loop analyses have been developed to be used as part of the WCET Analyzer **aiT**, they are using the **aiT** framework presented in Section 2. In particular, they operate on loops that have been transformed to tail-recursive routines by the loop transformation. The next section will show two example loop routines, which are used in the subsequent description of both analyses. A loop iteration equals one execution of the loop routine.

To avoid code duplication, the analyses use the existing value analyzer of the framework to query the addresses of memory accesses and to obtain knowledge about the contents of accessed registers and memory cells. As the value analysis produces integer intervals as approximations for addresses and memory contents, both loop analyses use intervals for their calculations, too. Beside this, the loop analyses query the value analysis for infeasible control-flow edges, i.e. edges that are not taken in any run of the program. This information is used in both analyses to exclude unreachable loops from loop bound detection. For more details about the value analysis please refer to [10].

The analyses take into account that programs often contain nested loops for which the iteration bounds of the inner loops depend on the iteration bounds of outer loops. Therefore both analyses sort the loops by their nesting depth and analyze them from the outside to the inside. After handling one nesting depth, value analysis is restarted with the new derived loop bounds as input to get more precise information while looking for the bounds of the inner loops.

As value analysis gets more precise if it also knows the lower bound of a loop, both analyses output not only the safe upper bounds needed to calculate any WCET, but intervals that are guaranteed to contain all possibilities for the number of loop iterations.

3.2 Running Examples

To illustrate the working of the two loop analyses, two simple loops found in programs for the *PowerPC* architecture are chosen as examples. Figures 3 and 4 show the corresponding loop routines.

Both loops use machine register 31 as their loop counter. We assume for the upcoming calculations and analyses that this register contains the value zero before the first loop iteration.

The loop in Figure 3 is a simple loop incrementing its loop counter in each iteration by exactly one. The loop is first entered with counter value 0, then with value 1, etc. until it reaches 16. When it is entered with counter value 16, the test r31 < 16 fails for the first time so that there are no further loop iterations. Therefore, there are exactly 17 loop iterations. The loop analysis should thus return the interval [17, 17] (the most precise answer) or any larger interval containing 17 (correct, but imprecise).

The loop in Figure 4 is similar, but a counter increment of one or two is possible, as the control flow forks into two branches inside the loop routine. The

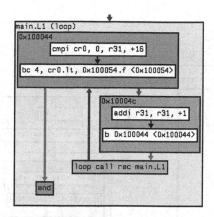

Fig. 3. A loop with one loop test and single increment

safe upper bound is still 17 like in the first example, but the lower bound is now only 9. The result of the loop analysis should thus be [9, 17] or any larger interval.

3.3 The Pattern-Based Approach

The current loop analysis in **aiT** uses fixed patterns to detect the loop bounds for common loop variants. These patterns are handcrafted for the supported compilers and their different optimization levels. Some intraprocedural analyses are used to handle the matching, like intraprocedural slicing and dominator/postdominator analysis.

A typical loop pattern to detect loops generated by C compilers from for-loops consists of the following conditions:

- The loop is only left by one conditional branch;
- a compare of a register with a constant sets the condition for this branch;
- the register that is compared is incremented by a constant value at the same instruction in each iteration;
- the start value of the register is known by the value analysis.

To match even such a simple pattern, multiple internal subanalyses must be performed. For this example pattern, the following steps would be needed:

- Check for a conditional branch instruction that dominates and postdominates the recursive call of the loop routine;
- slice backwards from the branch inside the loop routine to find the compare instruction modifying the condition flag evaluated by the branch instruction;
- test whether it is a compare of a register with a constant;
- slice backwards from the compare instruction to find all instructions modifying the registers/memory cells used in the compare instruction;

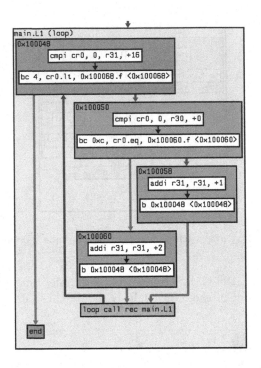

Fig. 4. A loop with one loop test and two different increments

- test whether only one instruction is found in the last step and whether it is a constant addition/subtraction;
- test whether this one instruction dominates and postdominates the compare instruction;
- query the value analysis for the start value of the used register;
- calculate the bounds by using the now known start/end value and increment.

If we apply this pattern to our example loop of Figure 3, we get a match, as this loop is left only by a conditional branch after the compare of the loop counter with some constant and the loop counter is incremented in each round by one. The resulting bound would be [17, 17], which is in this case the optimal solution.

The slightly more complex loop of Figure 4 is not matched by this pattern, as the loop counter is not incremented in each iteration by the same instruction, but by two different `addi` instructions in two different control-flow branches. Therefore no loop bound can be determined and thus no WCET is obtained.

Given how many steps are already needed for this simple pattern and that all this needs to be done by handwritten code, it is clear that bigger patterns to handle more complex loops, like the one shown above, are hard to implement correctly and to maintain. This illustrates the need for a new kind of loop analysis, which will be presented in the next section.

3.4   Improved Loop Analysis Based on Data-Flow Analysis

To enhance the loop bound detection for more complex loops and to avoid the dependencies on compiler versions and optimization levels, a new loop bound analysis based on data-flow analysis was designed. The following provides a brief introduction to this new method. More information can be found in [11].

A run of the new analysis consists of the following phases:

1. Classification of all loops;
2. Detection of possible loop counters;
3. Data-flow analysis to derive the invariants;
4. Analysis of the loop tests to calculate the loop bounds.

Loop classification. In the first phase, loops are classified using information obtained from value analysis. Loops that can never be reached are excluded from further analysis and get the safe bound $[0, 0]$ as the corresponding loop routines are never called. For the remaining loops, the algorithm checks whether value analysis already knows after how many recursive calls their loop routine cannot be called again. If this number is known, it can be taken as a safe upper bound for the loop, even if the further stages fail to produce results.

Search for possible loop counters. For the loops that still need to be analyzed, a simple intraprocedural analysis is run to search all registers and memory cells accessed inside the loop routine. Then it is checked whether value analysis knows their start value, i.e. their value before the first call of the loop routine. The registers and memory cells with known start value are considered as potential loop counters. They are further examined by a data-flow analysis to derive loop invariants (see below).

Our first example loop (Figure 3) only accesses register 31. For our second example (Figure 4), the intraprocedural analysis would find registers 30 and 31. Assuming that value analysis only knows the start value of register 31, this register would be the only potential loop counter in both loops.

Invariant analysis. This data-flow analysis is the core of the improved loop analysis. For each potential loop counter detected in the previous phase, it calculates for each program point of the loop routine a set of expressions, called invariants, that indicate how the counter is modified from the entry of the loop routine to this point in each iteration.

The analysis uses a special language for the expressions, $IVALA$. Variables in $IVALA$ expressions describe registers or memory cells, including information about the register number or memory address and the data size in bytes. The loop counter in our examples would be expressed in $IVALA$ as $(register, 31, 4)$, as it is register 31, which is 4 byte wide.

The language allows to express assignment between variables, assignment of a constant integer interval to a variable, and modification of a variable by adding a constant integer interval. This seems to be very restrictive, as other modifications like non-constant addition or any kind of multiplication are not supported, but the evaluation in the next section will show that it is sufficient to detect most loop bounds in a program, as the most common loops are counting loops. Besides, this restriction serves to keep the complexities of invariant analysis and of the subsequent bound calculation within reasonable bounds.

For the loop routine of our first example shown in Figure 3 the analysis would e.g. calculate the following expression set for the ingoing edge of the recursive call of the loop routine:

$$\{(register, 31, 4) = (register, 31, 4)^\circ + [1, 1]\}$$

where $(register, 31, 4)^\circ$ is a placeholder for the value of $(register, 31, 4)$ at the beginning of the loop iteration. The expression indicates that register 31 is incremented by exactly one in each iteration. For the example in Figure 4 the analysis would calculate:

$$\{(register, 31, 4) = (register, 31, 4)^\circ + [1, 2]\}$$

This provides the information that the register is incremented by one or two.

Evaluation of the loop tests and bound calculation. In this phase, for each loop all existing loop tests will be evaluated. A loop test is a basic block with a conditional branch leaving the loop routine. For each test a bound will be calculated. All these bounds are then combined to one bound for the whole loop. The following steps are needed to calculate the bound for a loop test:

- The branch type is determined;
- the compare instruction evaluating the condition used by the branch is searched;
- the variables used in the compare instruction are detected;
- the flow-analysis results are used to get expressions for the found variables;
- an equation system is built and solved to get the concrete loop bound.

A detailed description of this process can be found in [11].

For our first example, this process would look as follows:

- Inspection of the branch in basic block 0x100044 yields that the loop is left on greater-equal.
- A search for the corresponding compare instruction finds the first instruction in the block.
- As variable $(register, 31, 4)$ and the constant integer 16 are used, the exit expression is $(register, 31, 4) \geq 16$.
- The flow-analysis will yield that $(register, 31, 4)$ is incremented by one in each iteration.
- The solver will compute the concrete bound [17, 17], which is the optimal solution.

The handling of the second example is analogous, except that the flow-analysis delivers an increment of [1, 2] and therefore the solver would calculate the bound [9, 17].

3.5 Evaluation of Both Methods

While the new analysis is more generic by design, we still need to demonstrate that it is applicable to real-world programs. Therefore an extensive evaluation with both code from a compiler benchmarks suite and with real software from the embedded-system world was performed in [11].

The results show that the new analysis method works for most loops equally well or better than the pattern-based method. Only in some corner cases, the old analysis takes the lead, as it has special patterns for them. The runtime costs of both analyses are comparable: the new analysis is slower than the pattern-based approach only by a constant factor of at most three for some tests.

To show that the new analysis is compiler-independent, Tables 1 and 2 present the results of both analyses for code generated by the *DiabData* and *GNU* C compiler, respectively. While both analyses work reasonably well for the Diab-Data compiler, only the data-flow based analysis works for the GNU C compiler without adjustments. To obtain comparable results, the pattern-based analysis would require additional effort to develop loop patterns adapted to the code generated by the GNU C compiler.

Table 1. Synthetic tests with one single loop, *DiabData*

test	optimal bound	old analysis	new analysis
do_char_001	$[1, \infty]$	$[1, \infty]$	$[1, \infty]$
do_char_008	$[16]$	$[16]$	$[16]$
do_char_009	$[16]$	$[16]$	$[1, \infty]$
do_char_010	$[1, 16]$	$[1, 16]$	$[1, \infty]$
for_char_001	$[17]$	$[1, \infty]$	$\mathbf{[17]}$
for_char_017	$[17]$	$[17]$	$[17]$
for_char_049	$[1]$	$[1, 17]$	$[1, 17]$
for_char_058	$[17]$	$[1, \infty]$	$\mathbf{[17]}$
for_char_061	$[9]$	$[1, \infty]$	$\mathbf{[9]}$
for_char_062	$[17]$	$[1, \infty]$	$\mathbf{[17]}$
for_int_001	$[17]$	$[1, \infty]$	$\mathbf{[17]}$
for_int_017	$[17]$	$[17]$	$[17]$
for_int_049	$[1]$	$[1, 17]$	$[1, 17]$
for_int_058	$[17]$	$[1, \infty]$	$\mathbf{[17]}$
for_int_061	$[9]$	$[1, \infty]$	$\mathbf{[9]}$
for_int_062	$[17]$	$[1, \infty]$	$\mathbf{[17]}$

3.6 Integration in aiT, and Outlook

As the evaluation has shown, both analyses have some benefits in their own areas. While the pattern-based analysis can keep the lead for special cornercases where handcrafted patterns can play out their strength, the data-flow based analysis works best for typical loops occurring in standard programs.

Table 2. Synthetic tests with one single loop, *GNU*

test	optimal bound	old analysis	new analysis
do_char_001	$[1, \infty]$	$[1, \infty]$	$[1, \infty]$
do_char_008	$[16]$	$[1, \infty]$	$[\mathbf{16}]$
do_char_009	$[16]$	$[1, \infty]$	$[\mathbf{16}]$
do_char_010	$[1, 16]$	$[1, \infty]$	$[\mathbf{1, 16}]$
for_char_001	$[17]$	$[1, \infty]$	$[\mathbf{17}]$
for_char_017	$[17]$	$[1, \infty]$	$[\mathbf{17}]$
for_char_049	$[1]$	$[1, \infty]$	$[\mathbf{1, 17}]$
for_char_058	$[17]$	$[1, \infty]$	$[\mathbf{17}]$
for_char_061	$[9]$	$[1, \infty]$	$[\mathbf{9}]$
for_char_062	$[17]$	$[1, \infty]$	$[\mathbf{17}]$
for_int_001	$[17]$	$[1, \infty]$	$[\mathbf{17}]$
for_int_017	$[17]$	$[1, \infty]$	$[\mathbf{17}]$
for_int_049	$[1]$	$[1, \infty]$	$[\mathbf{1, 17}]$
for_int_058	$[17]$	$[1, \infty]$	$[\mathbf{17}]$
for_int_061	$[9]$	$[1, \infty]$	$[\mathbf{9}]$
for_int_062	$[17]$	$[1, \infty]$	$[\mathbf{17}]$

As **aiT** is aimed to provide the best loop bound detection possible, both analyses will be used in combination. First the fast pattern-based analysis is applied, and only for the loops it is not able to handle, the more generic new analysis is run. This avoids any slow down for the analysis of programs for which the old analysis already detected all bounds, and enables the calculation of the WCET for programs with more complex loops.

This combined strategy is already in use for the *PowerPC* and *M32* architectures, with plans to extend it to the *VAMP* architecture in the near future.

4   Detecting Infeasible Paths by Analyzing Conditions

The result of an ILP-based path analysis is a path that represents a safe upper bound of the execution time. However, it is possible that this path can never occur at runtime. At a fork in the control-flow graph, the decision which of the successor nodes will be executed next often depends on the path that leads to the fork. Depending on the execution history, only one of two successors might be feasible. Those dependencies are not accounted for in the ILP, and the path analysis views both nodes as possible successors. This situation can lead to a drastic overestimation of the real WCET.

In this section, we introduce an extension of the **aiT** analyzer that incorporates those dependencies into the ILP, which in turn improves the WCET prediction. The analysis produces additional ILP constraints that can exclude several classes of infeasible paths.

The example in Figure 5 illustrates how flow facts can be beneficial for the WCET computation. In this example, the path analysis has to select the successor nodes with the highest costs for both of the branches A and D. The resulting

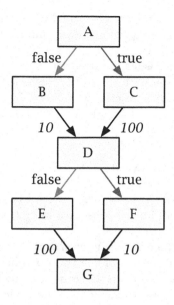

Fig. 5. A control flow graph

WCET is the sum of the costs associated with the edges constituting the critical path, i.e. $100 + 100 = 200$.

However, if the analysis finds out that a positive outcome of the branch condition at A implies a positive outcome of the branch condition at D, it creates a flow fact which allows only the paths $ACDFG$ and $ABDEG$. As a result, the new critical path has a WCET of $100 + 10 = 110$.

Such constructs as in the example often occur in code generated by code-generators such as SCADE or in mode-driven code where many execution paths are controlled via relatively few flags.

4.1 Overview

The input for the flow-constraint analysis is the control-flow graph of the program. While traversing this graph, each conditional branch is visited and an expression describing the branch condition is built. This step is trivial for high-level programming languages where the conditions are given in the source code, but as we are facing machine code, we have to reconstruct this information. Using the slicing component presented in the next section 5, we find a set of instructions and variables that contribute to the branch conditions. If all instructions contained in that set can be mapped to arithmetic or comparison operations, we can build a boolean expression representing the branch condition.

In a second step, the expressions are transformed into another representation suitable for a solver library (Omega). The solver is used to compare two expressions, i.e. to check whether one expression implies the other or whether they are even equivalent. Beforehand, we test whether the two expressions can actually occur on the same path because not every implication allows for a sensible statement about the program.

The results of the comparisons are used to create new ILP constraints that are added to the ILP for the path analysis. This leads to a higher precision of the WCET prediction, i.e. a predicted worst-case execution time that is lower than the predicted WCET without the flow-constraint analysis, but still is a safe upper bound of the real WCET.

4.2   The Flow-Constraint Analysis

The flow-constraint analysis traverses the control-flow graph and inspects all conditional branches, i.e. all inner nodes with more than one successor that are not call nodes.

If value analysis finds the exact (singleton) value of the condition register at a conditional branch, it marks one of the two outgoing edges as infeasible, and additional flow facts cannot improve the situation any more. Hence, only those branches where value analysis cannot deduce the value of the condition register are relevant for the flow-fact generation; the ones whose outcome is already determined by the value analysis are skipped.

A backward slice is computed for each considered conditional branch using the condition register as the initial target. A slice is a set of program points that directly or indirectly participate in the computation of the slicing criterion. A method how to compute slices is presented in the next section 5.

Definition 1. *A slice is called* linear *iff the program points contained in the slice can be ordered such that each program point is dominated by its predecessor. A linear slice that is ordered like that is called an* ordered slice.

Example 1 (Linear slice). Figure 6 shows two control-flow graphs. The instructions that constitute two different slices are highlighted using a bold border. The left graph represents a linear slice because the two basic blocks can be ordered as A, D and block A dominates block D. In contrast, the right graph is non-linear because block C dominates neither D nor A.

We now restrict the analysis to linear slices. This excludes exactly those conditions that are built up on several different paths. The ordered slices are then transformed into slice trees. The inner nodes of a slice tree represent instructions while the leaves are either registers, memory cells, or constants (see for instance Figure 7).

Slice trees containing memory accesses whose target addresses cannot be determined statically cannot be used for the following comparisons and are therefore discarded.

A slice tree is an intermediate representation that can be transformed into other formats for different theorem provers. This process is described in the following for the Omega library.

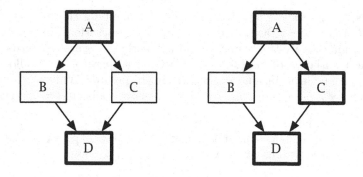

Fig. 6. Linear slice (left) and non-linear slice (right)

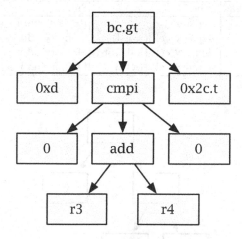

Fig. 7. A slice tree

The Omega Project is a collection of "Frameworks and Algorithms for the Analysis and Transformation of Scientific Programs" by William Pugh and the Omega Project Team [12]. In particular, Omega offers a tautology test for Presburger formulas that we will use to compare the branch expressions.

Definition 2. Presburger arithmetic *is defined as an arithmetic with the constants* 0 *and* 1, *a function* $+$, *a relation* $=$ *and the axioms*

1. $\forall x\colon \neg(0 = x + 1);$
2. $\forall x \, \forall y\colon \neg(x = y) \Rightarrow \neg(x + 1 = y + 1);$
3. $\forall x\colon x + 0 = x;$
4. $\forall x \, \forall y\colon (x + y) + 1 = x + (y + 1);$
5. *If* $P(x)$ *is a formula consisting of the constants* $0, 1, +, =$ *and a single free variable* x, *then the following formula is an axiom*

$$(P(0) \wedge \forall x\colon P(x) \Rightarrow P(x + 1)) \Rightarrow \forall x\colon P(x).$$

Slice trees are translated into Omega trees by mapping the semantics of the individual instructions to arithmetic or comparison operations. Instructions with unknown semantics are treated as symbolic functions. Several patterns are used during the translation of instructions into Omega operators that allow for the combination of multiple instructions into a single operator. While the inner nodes of Omega trees represent operations, the leaves are translated as follows:

- Integer constants remain constants.
- Registers and memory cells become free variables. A prefix of the variable name encodes the type of the variable as shown in Table 3.

Table 3. Omega tree leaves

Prefix	Type	Suffix
r	Register	Register number
m	Memory cell (word)	Memory address
h	Memory cell (halfword)	Memory address
b	Memory cell (byte)	Memory address

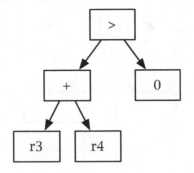

Fig. 8. An Omega tree

Figure 8 shows the Omega tree resulting from the slice tree of Figure 7 using a simplified notation.

If all conditional branches are annotated with Omega trees, we can compare the branch conditions of two basic blocks A and B by testing several boolean expressions using Omega: $A \Rightarrow B$, $A \Rightarrow \neg B$, $\neg A \Rightarrow B$, $\neg A \Rightarrow \neg B$ and the same expressions with A and B swapped. If Omega determines one of the expressions to be a tautology, we can derive the flow constraints according to Table 4. The names a_t, a_f, b_t, and b_f stand for the *true* and *false* successors of the two basic blocks a and b, and $c(x)$ the execution count of basic block x. The table includes expressions that are logically equivalent to cover those cases where some of the successors a_t, a_f, b_t, and b_f are unavailable.

Table 4. Implications and corresponding flow constraints

Expression	Flow constraint
$A \Rightarrow B$	$c(a_t) \leq c(b_t)$
$A \Rightarrow \neg B$	$c(a_t) \leq c(b_f)$
$\neg A \Rightarrow B$	$c(a_f) \leq c(b_t)$
$\neg A \Rightarrow \neg B$	$c(a_f) \leq c(b_f)$
$B \Rightarrow A$	$c(b_t) \leq c(a_t)$
$B \Rightarrow \neg A$	$c(b_t) \leq c(a_f)$
$\neg B \Rightarrow A$	$c(b_f) \leq c(a_t)$
$\neg B \Rightarrow \neg A$	$c(b_f) \leq c(a_f)$

4.3 Evaluation

In order to evaluate the effectiveness of the analysis, we have analyzed a set of test programs. All tests were performed using **aiT** for MPC755. Table 5 illustrates how the WCET changes if path analysis is run without or with the flow constraints (WCET$_{fc}$). The last column shows the number of generated flow facts.

Table 5. Results for several test programs

Program	WCET	WCET$_{fc}$	Improvement	Constraints
Synth. example 1	1440 cycles	1154 cycles	19.9 %	4
Synth. example 2	1140 cycles	819 cycles	28.2 %	5
avionic 1	1480 cycles	1420 cycles	4.1 %	1
avionic 2	3178 cycles	3050 cycles	4.0 %	8
zlib	6706 cycles	5242 cycles	21.8 %	2

Table 6. Sizes of the test programs

Program	Instructions	Basic Blocks	Size [Bytes]	Type
Synth. example 1	44	13	912	Mach-O
Synth. example 2	38	13	792	Mach-O
avionic 1	764	40	26232192	ELF
avionic 2	523	14	433472	ELF
zlib	163	40	1700	Mach-O

4.4 Outlook

With the main work done, we now look at possible future enhancements and additional uses of the flow-constraint analysis.

Portability. We plan to implement the analysis for further microarchitectures besides the PowerPC platform. The ARM platform is a natural extension since the slicing component already exists for it.

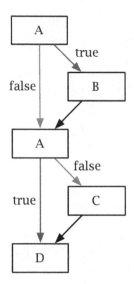

Fig. 9. Implication that cannot be described as a simple flow constraint

Nonlinear slices. Furthermore, it seems worthwhile to examine nonlinear slices to find out whether new opportunities for optimization arise if the linearity constraint is dropped. Nonlinear slices may be handled by using a data-flow analysis that propagates the node conditions and subsequently combines all conditions associated with a node. However, the risk is very high that the resulting expressions grow too large for the Omega library and that the runtime increases by several orders of magnitude.

Theorem-prover interface. In addition to this, other theorem provers could be evaluated by providing an interface to the flow-constraint analysis. An alternative prover could provide a performance superior to Omega in some cases or offer more functionality such as floating-point support.

Context-sensitive flow constraints. Version 2 of **AbsInt**'s Control-Flow Representation Language (CRL2) offers several advantages over the CRL1 language that is used in the PowerPC implementation of the analysis. One of them is the possibility to formulate flow constraints valid in a single context in contrast to CRL1 where constraints have to be valid either for each context in a uniform way or for the sums of the execution counts over all contexts. It can be beneficial to create flow constraints for individual contexts in order to handle loops that are not completely unrolled.

Linear combinations. Some implications cannot be accounted for by a simple flow constraint. Figure 9 illustrates such a situation. The control-flow graph contains two conditional branches with complementary branch conditions. Both have only one successor that is not a post-dominator. The constraint that node

C cannot be reached if node B was taken cannot be expressed as a simple flow constraint. One needs a constraint that represents a linear combination of the execution counts of several basic blocks. Which implications result in which linear combinations is shown in Table 7.

Table 7. Implications and associated linear combinations

Expression	Linear combination
$A \iff \neg B$	$c(a) = c(a_t) + c(b_t)$
	$c(a) = c(a_f) + c(b_f)$
$A \iff B$	$c(a) = c(a_t) + c(b_f)$
	$c(a) = c(a_f) + c(b_t)$

Elimination of unreachable code. With a simple extension, flow-constraint analysis is able to detect some cases of unreachable code and to exclude the respective code blocks from the subsequent analyses, e.g., pipeline analysis. For that, a condition of a child node is compared to that of its direct parent. If they are equivalent or complementary, one of the two successors of the child node can be marked as infeasible.

PAG. Unreachable code elimination as described above is an example how the information gathered by flow-constraint analysis can be used for additional purposes. Another use case is PAG-generated analyzers whose precision can be improved by path exclusions.

5   Generic Slicing of Binary Code

The complexity of software used in embedded systems grows rapidly whereas the development cycle is getting shorter and shorter. Furthermore, embedded software often is subject to strict timing and resource constraints.

While guaranteeing the safeness of an application, the developer needs knowledge about targets of indirect call and branch instructions, which often depends on values stored in memory. Yet finding the program point(s) where the values were written to memory may be hard. Slicing may help the developer to find these point(s).

Another application of slicing has already been introduced in Section 4, where slicing is used for restricting the set of possible execution paths through a program to detect infeasible paths.

This section introduces the idea of a generic slicing tool for binaries. The proposed approach computes slices in an interprocedural, context-sensitive manner as defined in [13]. First, we briefly introduce program dependency based slicing in Section 5.1. In Section 5.2 we present some challenges in computing data dependencies. Section 5.3 introduces a new dynamic solution for modeling memory accesses, and Section 5.4 describes the resulting slicing algorithm. Experimental results are presented in Section 5.5. Section 5.6 concludes.

5.1 Slicing Using Program Dependencies

A program slice according to [14,15,16] consists of all parts of a program that potentially affect the values computed at a point of interest. This point is called the *slicing criterion*. It will be written as $C = (n, V)$, where n denotes a node in the control-flow graph and V is a subset of the program's variables. In [17], Ottenstein and Ottenstein presented a slicing approach based on a program dependency graph. Horwitz, Reps, and Binkley [13] extended this approach to compute interprocedural, context-sensitive slices.

Let $def(i)$ denote the set of all variables defined at node i and $ref(i)$ be the set of all variables referenced at node i. Using these notations, several types of *data dependence* can be defined, such as flow dependence, output dependence and anti-dependence. For slicing, only flow dependence is taken into account:

A node j is *flow dependent* on a node i if there exists a variable x such that:

- $x \in def(i)$,
- $x \in ref(j)$,
- there exists a path from i to j without any redefinition of x.

Furthermore, it is necessary to define *control dependency* between two nodes. This is usually done in terms of *postdominance*:

A node j is *postdominated* by a node i if all paths from j to the exit node of the control-flow graph contain the node i.
A node j is *control dependent* on a node i if

- there exists a path π from i to j such that for any $u \in \pi$, $u \neq i$, node u is postdominated by j, and
- i is not postdominated by j.

As mentioned in the overview section 2, the annotated control-flow graph obtained from the executable serves as input for slicing. The annotations include information on used and defined resources, but do not provide any relation between instructions and registers. Thus, it is necessary to reconstruct the control and data dependencies.

The reconstruction of control dependencies is analogous to the two-level definition. It can be computed by two successive standard data-flow analyses, namely a dominator and a postdominator analysis. The nodes on which a specific node n of the control-flow graph is control dependent are computed by combining the data-flow values of these two analyses:

$$CtrlDep(n) = \{m \in \mathit{dfi}_{dom}(n) \mid n \notin \mathit{dfi}_{pdom}(m)\},$$

where $\mathit{dfi}_{dom}(n)$ and $\mathit{dfi}_{pdom}(n)$ return the data-flow values of the dominator and the postdominator analyses for node n respectively.

Reconstruction of data dependencies, or, to be more precise, of flow dependencies, can be easily formulated as a data-flow problem by computing the reaching definitions for each node in the control-flow graph. A definition *reaches* a program point if there is a path from the definition to this point without any redefinition. This data-flow problem computes a superset of the flow dependencies (a proof can be found e.g., in [18]).

Computing reaching definitions on binaries requires a mapping f defined on the set $\mathcal{R}$ of processor resources such that $f(r)$ is the set of nodes in the control-flow graph defining resource r. The domain for reaching-definitions analysis consists of these functions plus additional least and greatest elements $\bot$ and $\top$:

$$dom_{rd} \equiv \{f \mid f : \mathcal{R} \to \mathcal{P}(N)\} \cup \{\bot, \top\}$$

Here, the order of the functions is pointwise, i.e. $f \sqsubseteq g$ iff $f(r) \subseteq g(r)$ for all r in $\mathcal{R}$. At control-flow joins the union of the incoming information is formed.

5.2   Challenges in Computing Data-Dependencies

On many architectures, assembly instructions can be executed with an optional guard. The value of such a guard often cannot be determined by static analysis so that it is not known whether the instruction is executed or not. To be correct, guarded instructions have to be treated in a different way than the others.

If it is statically not decidable whether an instruction is executed, the incoming data-flow value has to be preserved and the actual program point has to be added to the set of defining points for the changed resources. This way of updating the data-flow value is called a *may-update*. In the other case (the instruction is definitively executed), the changes of resources are definitive, and thus, the incoming value has to be updated by removing all previously existing defining points for the changed resources. This update is called a *must-update*.

Another characteristic of hardware architectures are *composed registers*. These registers are composed of smaller subregisters that can be accessed with different names at the assembly level. Figure 10 shows an example for a composed register. The reaching-definition analysis has to deal with these special registers. For this, a *register tree* as shown in Figure 11 has been introduced. An assignment to register $R1$ in Figure 10 does not change the content of register $R2$, but a part of the content of R changes. Thus, in case of a must-update of $R1$, a may-update of R has to be performed. On the other hand, a change of R definitively affects the registers $R1$ and $R2$. In general, all hierarchy ranks below the changed register have to be updated, whereas all hierarchy levels higher than the changed one may change their value.

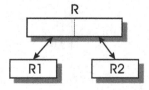

Fig. 10. Example for a composed register

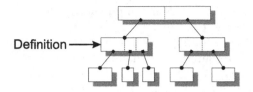

Fig. 11. Example for a register tree

5.3 Modeling Memory Accesses

The dependencies computed so far are sufficient for the computation of slices on programs using only registers for computation, but this approach is not suitable for programs using the memory.

Looking at the example program in Figure 12(a), a slice for the criterion $C = (5, R_1)$ will be wrong if the memory is handled like a normal register (Figure 12(b)). To be correct, changes of memory cells have to be always handled like may-updates. This leads to the conservative slice displayed in Figure 12(c), but this is often unsatisfactory. To take the best benefit from a slice, it has to contain as few statements as possible. The minimal slice for criterion C is shown in Figure 12(d).

$0 : M[0] = 1;$		$M[0] = 1;$	$M[0] = 1;$
$1 : M[1] = 2;$	$M[1] = 2;$	$M[1] = 2;$	
$2 : R_1 = M[0];$	$R_1 = M[0];$	$R_1 = M[0];$	$R_1 = M[0];$
$3 : R_2 = M[1];$			
$4 : R_1 = R_1 + R_2;$	$R_1 = R_1 + R_2;$	$R_1 = R_1 + R_2;$	$R_1 = R_1 + R_2;$
$5 : M[0] = R_1;$			
(a)	(b)	(c)	(d)

Fig. 12. (a) Example sequence, (b) wrong slice, (c) conservative slice, and (d) minimal slice for criterion $(5, R_1)$

To get high-quality slicing results, it is necessary to model the memory in more detail. Thus, a *memory function* $\Xi : \mathcal{A} \to \mathcal{P}(N)$ has to be determined on the set $\mathcal{A}$ of memory addresses of an architecture such that $\Xi(a)$ is the set of program points at which the memory cell with address a has been last modified. The update functions $must : (\mathcal{A} \to \mathcal{P}(N)) \times N \times \mathcal{P}(\mathcal{A}) \to (\mathcal{A} \to \mathcal{P}(N))$ and $may : (\mathcal{A} \to \mathcal{P}(N)) \times N \times \mathcal{P}(\mathcal{A}) \to (\mathcal{A} \to \mathcal{P}(N))$ are defined as:

$$must(f, n, I)(a) = \begin{cases} \{n\}, & \text{if } a \in I, \\ f(a), & \text{if } a \notin I. \end{cases}$$

and

$$may(f, n, I)(a) = \begin{cases} f(a) \cup \{n\}, & \text{if } a \in I, \\ f(a), & \text{if } a \notin I. \end{cases}$$

With these two update functions, it is possible to set up an analysis that calculates an approximation of the memory function Ξ.

Unfortunately, a direct implementation of the domain of functions $\mathcal{A} \to \mathcal{P}(N)$ and the update functions as presented above is too inefficient. Also a partitioning of the memory in disjoint parts separating different accesses from each other is generally not computable in static analysis. Thus, there is a need for a model handling memory accesses and their access widths dynamically. The approach presented here uses a binary tree structure where each node is labeled with an interval denoting the boundaries of the memory cells it represents. A leaf is also labeled with a set of points denoting the program points defining the memory cells represented by the leaf.

So, the set $\mathcal{M}$ of memory trees can be recursively defined as:

A tuple $(x_1, x_2, A) \in \mathcal{L} \equiv \mathbb{N} \times \mathbb{N} \times \mathcal{P}(N)$ is called a *leaf*.
A tuple $(x_1, x_2, t_1, t_2) \in \mathcal{I} \equiv \mathbb{N} \times \mathbb{N} \times \mathcal{M} \times \mathcal{M}$ is called an *inner node*.
An element $m \in \mathcal{M}$ is called a *memory tree* if in case of $m = (x_1, x_2, t_1, t_2) \in \mathcal{I}$ and w.l.o.g. $t_1 = (y_1, y_2, ...) \wedge t_2 = (w_1, w_2, ...)$

$$x_1 < x_2 \wedge y_2 = w_1 - 1$$
$$\wedge \, y_1 = x_1 \wedge w_2 = x_2$$
$$\wedge \, y_1 \leq y_2 < w_1 \leq w_2$$
$$\wedge \, t_1, t_2 \in \mathcal{M}$$

and in case of $m = (x_1, x_2, A) \in \mathcal{L}$

$$x_1 \leq x_2$$
$$\wedge \, A \subseteq N$$

holds.

An example memory tree is shown in Figure 13. It carries the information that the memory cells between a and b have been last modified at program point n_1, the cells from $b + 1$ to c have been modified at program points n_2 or n_3, whereas the cells from $c + 1$ to d have not been modified since program start.

Assuming that there is a function returning the address range of a memory access, there are 10 different transformations to transform a memory tree into a new one. Each case must also be treated differently for may-updates and must-updates (see Section 5.2 for more details). Thus two functions $may : \mathcal{M} \times \mathcal{P}(N) \times$

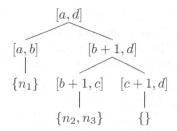

Fig. 13. Example for a memory tree

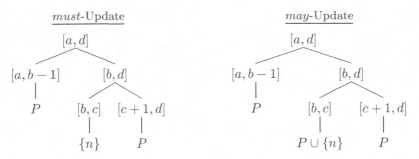

Fig. 14. Transformation of a leaf (a, d, P) for access address $[b, c]$ at program point n

$\mathbb{N} \times \mathbb{N} \to \mathcal{M}$ and $must : \mathcal{M} \times N \times \mathbb{N} \times \mathbb{N} \to \mathcal{M}$ have to be defined. One example transformation for a leaf is shown in Figure 14.

[19,20] shows that analyzing values of registers and the memory is possible within a data-flow analysis. Moreover, [21] describes a format to exchange the computed data-flow values between different analyses. Thus, it is possible to use information about the access range of load and store instructions of an external value analysis within the analysis of the memory. In addition, the results of the external value analysis contain a flag indicating whether the access range of an instruction could be determined exactly.

Using the results of value analysis, it is possible to define the memory access problem as a data-flow problem on the domain $\mathcal{M} \cup \{\top, \bot\}$. Whenever a memory access cannot be uniquely determined, the old data-flow values for the affected memory cells have to be preserved, i.e. the data-flow values have to be updated using the may-update function. Otherwise, the must-update function can be used.

So, considering the example control-flow graph in Figure 15 composed of ARM assembly instructions, and assuming a stack pointer value $r13 = 0x80$, the memory tree displayed in Figure 16 can be constructed.

By construction, the data-flow value at a program point always represents the whole memory. To access the calculated value for a specific node n, the data-flow value needs to be restricted to the interval the instruction n accesses. Thus, an access function $MemDep(n)$ for a node n can be defined.

5.4   Computing Slices

Interprocedural slices for arbitrary criteria can be computed by means of reachability along control- and flow-dependence edges as described in [17]. Furthermore, the dependence introduced by memory accesses has to be gathered.

The general slicing algorithm is shown in Figure 17. The input for the algorithm is the control-flow graph and the result of the value analysis. Thus, the slicing tool perfectly fits into the tool chain described in Section 2. After the computation of the data-flow problems introduced in the Sections 5.1 and 5.3, slices can be computed arbitrarily often until abort is requested.

For computation, the algorithm holds two sets. One set is the working set (*wset*) containing tuples of nodes and resources that still have to be considered.

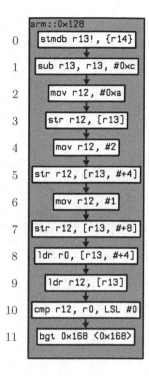

Fig. 15. Example control-flow graph

The visited set (*vset*) contains all tuples that have already been treated guaranteeing termination of the algorithm. A third set (*tset*) is employed as temporary storage. While the working set is not empty, the slice is not yet completely computed. In this case, an element (m, w) is selected from the working set and added to the visited set, together with all "control nodes" c on which the current node m is control-dependent. All data and memory dependencies of the current node m and also the data and memory dependencies of the control nodes are intersected with the visited set and then added to the working set. This guarantees the termination of the algorithm in $\mathcal{O}(|N| \times |\mathcal{R}|)$ where $|N|$ is the number of nodes in the analyzed program.

The slice for the specified criterion C can be calculated as the projection of the visited set to the nodes of the given control-flow graph.

5.5 Evaluation

The usability of the described slicing algorithm depends on two criteria: the time required for the computation and the quality of the results. The first point can be split in different parts:

− Initialization time,
− time for executing the analyses,
− and time for the computation of slices for arbitrary slicing criteria.

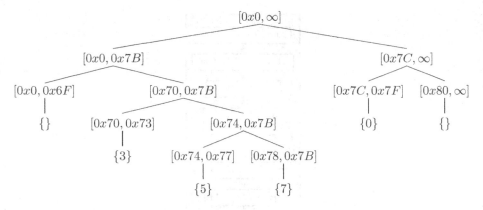

Fig. 16. Memory tree for example graph in Figure 15

Input : control flow graph (N, E, s, x) ,
         results of a value analysis

compute D_{rd}, D_{pdom}, D_{dom} and D_{mem} for (N, E, s, x)

while (no abort) {
   wait for new slicing criterion $C = (n, V)$
   $wset = \{(n, v) \mid v \in V\}$
   $vset = \emptyset$
   while $(wset \neq \emptyset)\{$
      let $(m, w) \in wset$
      $vset = vset \cup \{(m, w)\} \cup \{(c, \_) \mid c \in CtrlDep(m)\}$
      $tset = \{m\} \cup CtrlDep(m)$
      $wset = wset\backslash\{(m, w)\} \cup$
$$\Big(vset \cap \bigcup\nolimits_{o\in tset,\, u\in def(o)\backslash\{Mem\}}$$
$$\big(\{(x, u) \mid x \in DataDep(o, u)\} \cup \{(x, Mem) \mid x \in MemDep(o)\}\big)\Big)$$
   }
   $slice = \{m \mid (m, w) \in vset\}$
}

Fig. 17. The slicing algorithm

Especially the last point depends only on the chosen slicing criterion, thus, a general statement is impossible. For the example programs being analyzed, this computation time for arbitrary criteria was always smaller than 1 second.

But for a practical usage, the first two points were also very interesting. These two times can be summarized as the precomputation time.

The example programs chosen are typical applications to guarantee the quality of software projects. They are chosen because of their characteristics: minmax is a rather simple program containing no loops and no recursion, whereas `fac` contains a recursive implementation of the factorial function called within a loop. `prime` is chosen for testing loops, `dry2_1` is a real benchmark program. The usability in real world software projects is shown with `automotif`, a program for controlling the pressure of wheels in automobiles. The characteristics are shown in Table 8. All example programs are compiled for the ARM-architecture family.

The measurement of the precomputation times has been performed on an Intel Pentium III 1200 MHz CPU with 256 MB SD-RAM and a Debian Woody OS. Each test was run several times and the average execution time was computed. These times are shown in Table 9. The columns show the times for building up the internal data structure (*pre*) and to execute the analyses.

A measure for the quality of a computed slice is the relative deviation Δ of its size to the size of a minimal slice. Since minimal slices are not computable [14,15,16], the relative deviation cannot be determined automatically. Nevertheless, minimal slices for certain slicing critera in the example executables have been determined by hand. The Δ-values for the corresponding computed slices were always smaller than 25%, and their average was less than 9%. More details can be found in [18].

Table 8. Characteristics of the example programs

program	minmax	fac	prime	dry2_1	automotif
routines	4	2	4	17	163
instructions	114	24	119	773	3820
calls	5	2	4	32	309
loops	0	1	2	9	50
loads	4	2	20	296	984
stores	4	2	10	140	877

Table 9. Precomputation times for the example programs

program	pre	D_{rd}	D_{pdom}	D_{dom}	D_{mem}	$\sum$
minmax	0.03 s	0.02 s	< 0.01 s	< 0.01 s	< 0.01 s	0.07 s
fac	0.02 s	0.03 s	< 0.01 s	0.02 s	0.02 s	0.10 s
prime	0.03 s	0.04 s	< 0.01 s	0.02 s	0.02 s	0.13 s
dry2_1	0.17 s	0.25 s	0.07 s	0.10 s	0.32 s	0.82 s
automotif	0.50 s	173.20 s	0.40 s	0.40 s	1.20 s	177.50 s

5.6   Conclusion

This section has shown how to slice binaries with only a minimum of hardware-specific knowledge. Besides the reconstruction of data and control dependencies, we introduced a dynamic solution for modeling memory accesses efficiently.

The results of the various analyses have been used to design an efficient slicing algorithm. They are all combined to a tool, which has been successfully integrated in the **aiT** framework. Moreover, an interface was designed to display the computed slices in the interactive graph viewing software `aiSee3`.

Several experiments have also shown that the precomputation times can be considered as moderate and furthermore the computed slices are precise enough to legitimate their usage in software development environments. Moreover, the proposed slicing technique has been successfully used for restricting the set of possible execution paths through a program. A similar approach at a different level to speed up WCET analysis using slicing techniques has been presented in [22].

6   From VHDL to Timing Models

All the sections so far dealt with certain parts of **aiT**. In contrast, this section deals with a method to *generate* some part of **aiT**, namely the timing model used in the pipeline analysis, which models the effects of the pipeline including related features such as out-of-order evaluation or branch prediction.

Timing models are used as the basis for WCET analysis, describing the system's behavior at cycle granularity. Abstract interpretation of the timing model is guaranteed to give upper WCET bounds for the execution of an instruction sequence [23]. The guarantee, however, is relative to the model itself. If the model fails to correctly describe the system's behavior, the computed WCET bound may be incorrect.

To ensure correctness of the model it is highly desirable to derive it from an authoritative specification of the system. Such specifications are available as system descriptions written in a hardware description language such as VHDL or Verilog HDL. Nowadays the system hardware itself is synthesized from these descriptions.

Unfortunately, a VHDL description of a typical system component, e.g., CPU or system controller, is much too large to serve as the basis for a WCET analysis. Furthermore, the component itself can only handle concrete data, while the WCET analysis has to handle abstract data, e.g., address intervals instead of addresses for unknown data accesses. Therefore, a VHDL model has to be reduced and abstracted until it reaches a compatible and sufficiently efficient form and size [24].

In this section, we describe a semi-automatic framework that can be used to perform this task. First, we briefly introduce VHDL and its semantics in Section 6.1. Then, we present the semantics of the timing analysis and how the final timing model fits into the whole framework. Section 6.3 presents the steps necessary to transform a VHDL model into a timing model suitable to be plugged into the **aiT** timing analysis.

6.1   VHDL and Its Semantics

VHDL is an IEEE Standard (IEEE 1076) [25,26]. The focus of the language ranges from specifying circuits at the physical timing/wavefront level to describing them with high-level language constructs. Therefore, the language and the

standard are quite huge. For our purposes, we only have to look at the so called
synthesizable subset of VHDL, which is defined in the 1076.3 substandard. The
goal of this subset is to restrict the language to constructs that can easily be
synthesized into actual hardware (mostly by translating them into netlists and
mapping those via design libraries to actual layouts).

A VHDL description of a circuit is given by a *declaration* of the *interfacing* of
the circuit and then by one (or more) *implementation(s)* for the circuit. In VHDL
parlance, the first is called an *entity*, the second an *architecture*. An example for
a simple bit counter can be seen in Figure 18.

```
ENTITY ctr IS
   PORT( clk: IN std_logic; reset: IN std_logic;
         val: OUT std_logic_vector(2 downto 0) );
END;
ARCHITECTURE rtl OF ctr IS
   SIGNAL cnt: std_logic_vector(2 downto 0);
   work: PROCESS(reset, clk) IS
      IF (reset='1') THEN
         cnt<="000";
      ELSIF (rising_edge(clk)) THEN
         cnt<=cnt+'1';
         val<=cnt;
      END IF;
   END;
END;
```

Fig. 18. A simple 3-bit counter in VHDL

Here, the implementation of the circuit is given in terms of a *process* called
`work`. The code of this process is executed, whenever one of the signals in its
sensitivity list (`clk` and `reset`) changes its *value*. In the example, the process
first checks whether the reset signal is asserted and sets the internal 3-bit signal
`cnt` back to the initial value in that case. If the circuit is not reset, the process
then checks for the rising edge of the clock signal `clk` and then increments the
internal counter if the event occurs. Afterwards, the internal `cnt` is driven to the
output signal `val`.

Another way to specify the circuit is to compose it from (smaller) circuits:
the architecture gives the components (entities) and defines the wiring of input
and output signals among them. Figure 19 gives an example for this style.

Here, a circuit for the logical implication $a \rightarrow b$ for two inputs a and b and the
output c is built from a logical-or gate **or** and a negation gate **not**, implementing
the implication by the formula $c = \neg a \lor b$. Note that or0 is an *instance* of the
generic entity **or**, as not0 is one of the entity **not**.

When one has a definition of a circuit as a collection of entities and architectures that realize them, one has to perform *elaboration* in order to get one

```
ENTITY implies IS
  PORT(a: IN std_logic; b: IN std_logic;
       c: OUT std_logic);
END;
ARCHITECTURE struct OF implies IS
BEGIN
  SIGNAL int_neg: std_logic;
  not0: ENTITY not PORT MAP(a, int_neg);
  or0:  ENTITY or  PORT MAP(int_neg, b, c);
END;
```

Fig. 19. A structural VHDL architecture

flat definition for the circuit. Elaboration performs all the wiring in structural definitions, does the necessary renaming so that the names of locally declared signals do not clash, etc. The result can be seen as one big entity with a number of processes that define the behavior of the circuit and a set of locally defined signals (i.e. signals not occurring in the external interface of the circuit).

A process consists of a set of local *variables* that are only accessible from the process itself. Local signals, on the other hand, can be accessible from two or more processes. The only restriction is that no two distinct processes can drive (i.e. assign to) the same signal[1].

VHDL makes a distinction between assignments to a variable and to a signal. Assigning a value to a variable takes effect immediately, and the next reference to that variable results in the new value to be returned. Assigning a value to a signal, however, only *schedules* the new value to be the future value of the signal. E.g., in Figure 18 the signal assignment cnt<=cnt+'1'; schedules the next value of cnt to be the current value plus one. However, the next assignment, val<=cnt;, schedules the next value of val to be the *current* value of cnt. These 'future' values scheduled by signal assignments take effect as soon as the process *suspends* its execution. A process suspends if it executes a wait S instruction, where S is a set of signal names. The process resumes execution as soon as a signal $s \in S$ changes its *value*. In full VHDL, the wait instruction may also contain a timeout, after which the process resumes even if no signal from S changed its value in the meantime. However, timeouts are not allowed in the synthesizable subset of VHDL.

The signals from the sensitivity list of a process are automatically waited for when the process finishes its execution. That means that we can transform a process p : PROCESS $(s_1, \ldots, s_n)$ IS body END; to an equivalent process without a sensitivity list, namely: p' : PROCESS IS body; wait $s_1, \ldots, s_n$; END;. The

---

[1] In full VHDL, one can use the construct of *resolution functions* to compute the value that wins if two processes assign to the same signal. This construct can be modeled in the reduced subset of VHDL we are looking at by introducing new signals with new names for each occurrence of the signal, and another process that uniquely assigns to the original signal and has the new signals in its sensitivity list.

only place where a `wait` instruction may occur within a process is at the end of the body of the process.

The instructions that can occur within a process are either assignments to signals (`<=`) or variables (`:=`), sequences of instructions, the conditional (`IF-THEN-ELSE`), bounded loops (`WHILE`), or procedure calls. Expressions may contain the expected set of operators on integers and bit values (arithmetic, logical operators, shifts, etc.) and function calls.

The semantics of the VHDL program, i.e. a set of processes, can then be described as follows:

1. Execute any process until it suspends (i.e. it reaches a `wait` statement).
2. If all processes are suspended, perform all scheduled signal assignments at once.
3. If any signal s changes its value by this and it occurs in a set S from a `wait` S instruction of a process, resume all such processes and go to step 1.
4. Otherwise, an external signal must change its value for the execution to resume. If this happens, resume all processes waiting for the changed external signal and go to step 1.

Note that this semantics is different from the usual semantics for full VHDL: because synthesizable VHDL does not allow to specify timeouts in `wait` statements, time can only pass if an external signal (i.e. a signal that is input to the circuit and is not driven by any process in the program) changes its value.

As we are only interested in *synchronous* designs, i.e. designs where actions are triggered by the rising (and/or falling) edge of a global *clock*, the clock and the reset signal are most often the only signals being waited for in a process.

It is noteworthy that the semantics of signal assignment and the process locality of variables mean that the order in which we execute processes until they suspend is arbitrary: the resulting values for variables (which depend only on the process' execution itself) and the scheduled values for signals (only at most one process is allowed to drive a signal) are always the same, no matter what the order of execution was. We can, when defining a semantics, thus choose a fixed ordering. However, a process is only executed if a signal in its sensitivity list changed. Nevertheless, we can transform a set of processes into *one* sequential program by introducing new conditionals that check whether a signal changed its value since the last time the process was executed. To support this construct and to handle the signal assignment semantics in terms of the more commonly met instant assignment semantics, we furthermore introduce for each signal s two variants of the signal, s^{old} and s^{new}, representing its values before the last assignment and the future value, resp. Thus, we can replace every occurrence $s<=e$ of a signal assignment by $s^{\text{new}}:=e$.

The check at the start of a process p whether any of the signals $s_1, \ldots, s_n$ in its sensitivity list changed its value can then be written as

$$\text{SCH}(s_1, \ldots, s_n) \equiv \bigvee_{1 \leq i \leq n} s_i \neq s_i^{\text{old}}$$

When all processes have been executed, the synchronization phase (i.e. the copying of the future signal values to the current ones) can then be simply a short piece of code $\text{COPY}(s_1, \ldots, s_n)$, where $s_1, \ldots, s_n$ are all signals:

$$\text{COPY}(s_1, \ldots, s_n) \equiv$$
$$s_1^{old} := s_1;$$
$$s_1 := s_1^{new};$$
$$\ldots$$
$$s_n^{old} := s_n;$$
$$s_n := s_n^{new};$$

Now we can express the semantics of VHDL's simulation algorithm by giving an equivalent piece of a sequential program with only simple, well known, constructs. So let $p_1, \ldots, p_n$ be the bodies of the n processes in the design. The equivalent sequential program is then as shown in Figure 20.

```
Init; SIMUL
where
SIMUL  ≡  DO
                IF  SCH(s₁¹,...,sₘ₁¹)  THEN
                    p₁
                FI
                ...
                IF  SCH(s₁ⁿ,...,sₘₙⁿ)  THEN
                    pₙ
                FI
                IF  SCH(e₁,...,eₖ)  THEN
                    e
                FI
                COPY(s₁¹,...,sₘₙⁿ , e₁,...,eₖ)
            WHILE  (SCH(s₁¹,...,sₘₙⁿ , e₁,...,eₖ))
```

Fig. 20. Transforming VHDL processes into a sequential program

There, $s_1^i, \ldots, s_{m_i}^i$ are the signals from process i's sensitivity list, $e_1, \ldots, e_k$ are the external signals of the design and e is a code piece (not in VHDL) that performs the actions of the external circuits, acting upon the external signals. Init is the initialization code, which assigns initial values to the variables and signals in a way that $\text{SCH}(s)$ is true for any signal s in the first iteration of the loop. The external piece e will often be used to drive the clock signal and provide the reactions of the external circuit to outputs driven by the design.

This representation allows us to easily apply standard data-flow techniques, as the whole VHDL semantics is represented in a standard imperative language. However, our aim is to derive *timing information* from the design in terms of processor cycles spent on program execution. The notion of time at this level

```
Init
DO
    clk:=1; clk^old:=0; clk^new:=1;
    SIMUL
    clk:=0; clk^old:=1; clk^new:=0;
    SIMUL
WHILE(true);
```

Fig. 21. Transforming VHDL processes into a sequential program with a clock

is present only for synchronous designs, which act upon the rising edge of a *clock*. Thus, we want to introduce as basic notion how the design evolves during one processor cycle, i.e. what action is triggered by a rising edge of the system clock. Thus, we first have to identify the system clock signal, say `clk`. As clocks cannot be modeled in synthesizable VHDL, `clk` has to be an external signal of the design. We make the clock transition from low to high (the rising edge) explicit in our representation of the design as a sequential program and arrive at the code in Figure 21.

Here, we basically perform the VHDL simulation twice, for the rising edge of the clock and the falling edge in an infinite loop. If no process acts upon the falling edge, then naturally the second occurrence of SIMUL can be omitted.

With this construct, we can simulate one clock cycle as one iteration of the outermost loop. This simulation serves as the basis for our timing analysis. An abstracted and reduced version of this code will be plugged into the timing analysis in order to simulate the processor's behavior. The next section will further explain the abstract cycle-wise simulation used in the timing analysis.

6.2 Timing Models and Analysis Framework

A timing model is at the heart of the pipeline analysis in Figure 1. A timing model describes how the processor state changes during one processor cycle. The pipeline analysis can then, for each instruction in the CFG, simulate this model, until the instruction leaves the pipeline. The number of simulation cycles, which correspond to one processor cycle each, then gives the execution time of that instruction from the given start state of the processor. A sequence of instructions can be simulated in the same way: the states where an instruction leaves the pipeline mark the start of the next instruction—for the purposes of counting processor cycles; at this point, the next instruction usually is already in the pipeline for some time. This overlapping of instructions means that the number of simulation cycles is usually smaller than the sum of the execution times for instructions simulated separately.

Because we are performing a static analysis, some parameters in the processor states and some inputs will not be known exactly. One example is the contents of memory cells, another one is inputs read from peripherals. Furthermore, for practical reasons it is impossible to represent even information that we may know exactly in full detail in the analysis. If we were to exactly record e.g., the contents of all memory cells or registers, the space required for the analysis would be prohibitive. Luckily, in many cases the exact knowledge about these things is not important as far as timing is concerned: an addition always takes the same amount of time, no matter what the arguments are. In other cases, the timing does depend on such information, but we may choose to lose the exact timing knowledge in order to make the analysis more efficient, or even to make it possible at all. One example for this are multiplications on some architectures, which are faster if one argument has many leading zero bits. By not keeping track of the arguments exactly, we have to assume an entire range of execution times for multiplication. The loss in precision is acceptable in this case, as the difference is usually only a few processor cycles and multiplications are rare.

The framework of abstract interpretation [3] gives a useful methodology, where one can trade precision of the analysis against efficiency by choosing different abstractions and concretization relations between the concrete domain (set of processor states) and an abstract one (set of abstract processor states). Abstract processor states in our case are simply processor states where some components are left out (memory cells, registers) and others are approximated, e.g., the addresses of data accesses in an access queue. The details can be found in [23].

When we go to abstract processor states by leaving out components or approximating others, the evolution of one processor state to another given by the timing model is no longer deterministic. This is obvious since decisions in the state transition depend on information that is no longer represented exactly in the state. What we obtain is then a non-deterministic state evolution for one processor cycle starting from an abstract processor state: one abstract processor state can have several successor states for one cycle evolution.

The pipeline analysis is now simply an abstract simulation on abstract processor states. For each instruction in the CFG and a set of abstract processor states present at the start of execution of that instruction[2] we take each abstract state and simulate it for one cycle, giving a set of result states. For the states in this result, we repeat the simulation until the instruction has finished execution in the resulting states. The highest number of simulation cycles we encounter for the whole simulation is then an upper bound for the WCET of that instruction.

For our purposes, what is important is that the pipeline analysis does a processor cycle-wise simulation that receives as input an abstract processor state and outputs a set of result states. Furthermore, it requires that we can decide when an instruction has finished execution (i.e. left the pipeline) given an abstract processor result state at the end of a simulation cycle. More precisely, the simulation cycle function must provide, for each result state, a *status*, which can be one of:

Finished: The current instruction has finished its execution.
Busy: The current instruction is still executing in the result state.

---

[2] Or, more precisely, after the predecessor instruction has finished execution. In pipelined processors, a successor instruction has often already begun to execute when its predecessor instruction finishes.

Stopped: The processor has stopped in this state. This may happen, e.g., because of special instructions that halt the processor or because an exception occurred in that state. The WCET for this program will be unbounded.

Deleted: This means that the result state represents an impossible state in the processor, e.g., the state propagated to the target of a conditional branch whose condition evaluated to false. Such a state can arise because of our approximation or as artifact of the data-flow framework. It will not contribute to the WCET computation and will not be simulated further: it is simply dropped.

Remembering the VHDL simulation per clock cycle from Figure 21, we can now see how to integrate that into the timing framework with simulation function detailed above. The values of the VHDL variables and signals will form our processor state. Abstraction of unnecessary and expensive components will give the abstract processor state, consisting of abstract VHDL signals and variables, together with the signals and variables that are kept precisely.

An adapted version of the VHDL simulation from Figure 21 will then give the simulation function for the timing analysis framework. To obtain status information for each state, we have to define predicates on the VHDL signals and variables that determine when an instruction has left the pipeline, etc. The next section presents the necessary steps for obtaining the abstract states and predicates from the concrete VHDL design.

6.3   Transformation of VHDL to a Timing Model

When we transform a VHDL design into a timing model as described in the previous section, the first thing we have to do is to identify the clock and reset signals of the VHDL design, a trivial task. Because we are interested in execution times for an instruction, we then have to identify the place in the VHDL design, where an instruction leaves the pipeline, i.e. it finishes execution. Here, we add an artificial bit variable `isfinished` into the design that is asserted via an assignment `isfinished:=1;` when the instruction finishes. Furthermore, we reset this variable at the start of each processor cycle simulation cycle by `isfinished:=0;`[3]. Note that instruction retirement may be performed at more than one place in the VHDL design. E.g., branches may be removed from the instruction stream by a fetch unit and never reach the execution stages of the pipeline. Then, we must insert code at all these places and handle multiple retirement.

Because our timing analysis is a data-flow analysis on the control-flow graph of the program, when a branch instruction is encountered, we have to know which abstract states correspond to executions along which outgoing edges of the branch. For this, we may have to add variables to the design that keep track of the direction of branches encountered (taken, not-taken). Then we can decide which state is propagated along which branch successor edge: a state with the taken bit set for the oldest branch is propagated along the taken edge of the

---

[3] For processors with multiple retirement, we simply add an array of such variables and additionally an array of the *addresses* of the retired instructions.

branch but not along the fall-through edge. Additionally, we have to keep the number of branches encountered but not handled (i.e. passed during propagation in the CFG). Finally, so that we know which instruction should be worked on in the CFG, we add a component that holds the address of that instruction. With this, we can decide when a state has to be deleted: if its address in the CFG does not match the component address.

As noted earlier, a VHDL design is too large to be used directly for timing analysis: we have to throw away things not influencing timing and abstract other parts to reduce size (thereby losing precision and introducing non-determinism). To determine the components that influence timing, we look again at the places where an instruction is retired. We determine all variables and code sections in the design that may influence this retirement. For this, we determine a *backwards slice* (cf. Section 5) for the variable isfinished at the end of the design code from Figure 21. This backwards slice determines all code sequences in the design that may influence the retirement of an instruction and thus its timing. All places not in this backwards slice can be removed from the design without influencing the timing behavior. Only external variables or signals or those being *assigned to* in the slice can influence timing. All others can be removed from the design, without influencing timing behavior.

Signals and variables that are *used* (i.e. read) but not assigned to never change their values during execution. Their value thus stays at the value they had after initialization of the system, i.e. after reset handling had been finished. To determine those fixed values, we analyze the reset behavior. Reset normally means that the reset signal is asserted for a given number of cycles and when it is deasserted again, the components have their initial values. We can obtain these values by simply performing a *forward slice* with reset=1[4] as input and look at all code sections that are activated by this configuration. Then, we perform a constant propagation analysis [27] on that slice and record the values of the variables and signals at the end of the design code: they are the initial values we can substitute into all read-only places in the backward-sliced design, removing these variables/signals completely.

Furthermore, the timing analysis makes some assumptions about the behavior of the system and the code itself, e.g., that no exceptions are caused by instructions or that no interrupts occur, etc. To utilize these assumptions in the reduction of the design, one has to identify the signals that trigger e.g., interrupts. Then, by asserting that these always remain unasserted, one can perform a forward slice and remove unreachable code (the interrupt handling code of the design) and unreachable components.

Even after removing all components that do not influence timing, the design will most probably be too large to be handled efficiently. Especially large memory arrays like main memory, caches or register files blow up the design. If the execution time of an instruction is data dependent, e.g., a multiplication with shortcuts for operands with many leading zeros, memory arrays will still be in the design after the first removal phase. In order to have an efficient analysis, we need

---

[4] Or reset=0 for low-active reset lines.

to introduce *abstractions* for large components. Abstraction is done in the sense of abstract interpretation theory [3] by giving an abstract domain with abstract components that approximate concrete components but are smaller in size. In general, this loses precision because one abstract component may describe a set of concrete components, which are then indistinguishable under the abstraction. One example is the approximation of a cache by an abstract cache as described in [6]. One abstract cache describes a set of concrete ones. If a memory block is in the abstract cache, then it is guaranteed to be in all concrete caches thus represented by the abstract cache.

Abstraction can happen in a wide range of choices: on the one extreme we can abstract a component by itself, thus not losing any information at the cost of not obtaining any size reduction. At the other extreme, we can abstract a component by a single symbol, $\top$, which represents *all* concrete components. This variant retains no information, because all concrete components are indistinguishable, but needs no space for representation, thus is most compact. Our abstractions for the components in the VHDL design will be somewhere in this range. Memory arrays and register files will be abstracted by $\top$, while signals that trigger process reevaluation will often be represented exactly.

Another reason why we need abstraction anyway is that some data is never available exactly. Most notably, the data access addresses of instructions are only known as safe intervals, not as single addresses, computed by the value analysis, cf. Section 2. Thus, we have to adapt the VHDL design to utilize this information instead of the real computation of addresses. For this, we have to identify the places where data access memory addresses are generated by instructions. At these places, pseudo VHDL code has to be added that interfaces with the value analysis to retrieve the previously computed intervals. Hence, we abstract addresses by intervals.

Using abstraction in the VHDL design leads to a significant change in the VHDL code semantics. Removing unreachable components and code did not change anything w.r.t. the simulation of the VHDL code. Introducing abstractions makes it impossible to directly simulate the VHDL code because now conditions in expressions, if-then-else, and loop statements may depend on abstracted components whose exact value is no longer known but only approximations are available. This means that we no longer get one result state from our simulation, but we have to go over to a set of result states: whenever a condition depends on an abstracted component, and we cannot evaluate the condition exactly under the abstraction used[5], we introduce a new state by copying the current one. We then simulate the remaining VHDL code once with the old state assuming that the condition evaluates to true and once with the new state assuming that the condition is false. For expressions that contain abstracted components, e.g., in the assignment c:=a AND b;, where c and b are represented exactly as 1-bit variables and a is abstracted, we continue with one state, where c is '1' and

---

[5] Note that sometimes it is possible to evaluate an abstracted condition exactly. E.g., the condition a>0x1000 for an address a is false if a is abstracted by the interval [0x0000, 0x0080].

one state where it is '0'. This handling of multiple states can automatically be generated by a compiler that takes the VHDL code with abstractions and outputs C code for the processor cycle simulation. It uses a work list to keep track of the states currently being worked on.

The process of abstraction may make some components superfluous because they no longer influence other components (they are 'shadowed' by the abstraction). Thus, we can repeat the elimination process described previously. The introduction of abstractions is an iterative process that terminates when the abstract processor state has reached a size that can be efficiently handled.

Finally, the analysis simulates the VHDL semantics of process reevaluation triggered by changes of the signals in sensitivity lists. This reevaluation is in principle not bounded, thus the ordering and number of reevaluations of process code is not static in general. However, most synchronous designs have a fixed depth and clear conditions when processes can be reevaluated. If the abstraction did not destroy the reevaluation conditions, a static analysis of the processes can find a *fixed* finite ordering of the process reevaluation, thus replacing the DO-WHILE loop from Figure 21 by a number of process evaluations.

Finally, the transformed (pseudo) VHDL code is passed to a code generator that generates C code that simulates the VHDL effects on the (abstracted) signals and variables, inserting abstract versions for things like additions on addresses that are now abstracted as intervals, and handles the non-determinism as described above. This code can then be invoked by the pipeline analysis, finishing the transformation process.

6.4   Outlook and Conclusions

We described a way to generate authoritative timing models for WCET analysis from the VHDL code of a processor/system design. The method is highly automated and requires only minor manual actions, namely in the identification of the places where an instruction leaves the pipeline and performs data accesses. The design of suitable abstractions also remains to be done manually, although the "standard" abstractions like intervals for addresses or caches could be performed automatically, too. The effects of the abstractions are handled automatically. The generation of code suitable to be plugged into the pipeline analysis is automatized, too. This methodology utilizes a number of sophisticated analyses in order to reduce the VHDL design to a size that can be handled efficiently.

A framework based on the tools and intermediate formats of **aiT** is being developed in the context of the AVACS SFB of the German Science Foundation (DFG). The current research foccusses on a generator producing efficient C code that simulates the abstracted VHDL. Furthermore, first versions of the forward and backward slicing algorithms are currently being developed. A first target will be the Leon SPARC processor. Future work includes the optional usage of designs written in Verilog, the second-most popular HDL.

References

1. Stankovic, J.A.: Real-Time and Embedded Systems. ACM 50th Anniversary Report on Real-Time Computing Research. (1996) http://www-ccs.cs.umass.edu/sdcr/rt.ps
2. Wilhelm, R.: Determining bounds on execution times. In Zurawski, R., ed.: Handbook on Embedded Systems. CRC Press (2005) 14-1 – 14-23
3. Cousot, P., Cousot, R.: Abstract Interpretation: A Unified Lattice Model for Static Analysis of Programs by Construction or Approximation of Fixpoints. In: Proceedings of the 4th ACM Symposium on Principles of Programming Languages, Los Angeles, California (1977)
4. Wilhelm, R., Engblom, J., Ermedahl, A., Holsti, N., Thesing, S., Whalley, D., Bernat, G., Ferdinand, C., Heckmann, R., Mueller, F., Puaut, I., Puschner, P., Staschulat, J., Stenström, P.: The worst-case execution time problem - overview of methods and survey of tools. Under revision for ACM Transactions on Embedded Computing Systems (2007)
5. Theiling, H.: Extracting safe and precise control flow from binaries. In: Proceedings of the 7th Conference on Real-Time Computing Systems and Applications, Cheju Island, South Korea (2000)
6. Ferdinand, C.: Cache Behavior Prediction for Real-Time Systems. PhD Thesis, Universität des Saarlandes (1997)
7. Heckmann, R., Langenbach, M., Thesing, S., Wilhelm, R.: The influence of processor architecture on the design and the results of WCET tools. Proceedings of the IEEE **91**(7) (2003) 1038–1054 Special Issue on Real-Time Systems.
8. Theiling, H., Ferdinand, C.: Combining abstract interpretation and ILP for microarchitecture modelling and program path analysis. In: Proceedings of the 19th IEEE Real-Time Systems Symposium, Madrid, Spain (1998) 144–153
9. AbsInt Angewandte Informatik GmbH: aiSee Home Page. http://www.aisee.com. (2006)
10. Sicks, M.: Adreßbestimmung zur Vorhersage des Verhaltens von Daten-Caches. Diploma Thesis, Universität d. Saarlandes (1997)
11. Cullmann, C.: Statische Berechnung sicherer Schleifengrenzen auf Maschinencode. Diploma Thesis, Universität d. Saarlandes (2006)
12. Pugh, W.: The Omega Test: A Fast and Practical Integer Programming Algorithm for Dependence Analysis. In: Proceedings of the 4th International Conference on Supercomputing. (1991)
13. Horwitz, S., Reps, T., Binkley, D.: Interprocedural slicing using dependence graphs. In: Proceedings of the ACM SIGPLAN '88 Conference on Programming Language Design and Implementation. Volume 23., Atlanta, GA (1988) 35–46
14. Weiser, M.: Program Slicing. IEEE Transactions on Software Engineering **SE-10**(4) (1984) 352–357
15. Weiser, M.: Program Slices: Formal, Psychological, and Practical Investigations of an Automatic Program Abstraction Method. PhD thesis, The University of Michigan (1979)
16. Weiser, M.: Programmers Use Slicing When Debugging. Communications of the ACM **25(7)** (1982) 446–452
17. Ottenstein, K.J., Ottenstein, L.: The program dependence graph in a software development environment. ACM SIGPLAN Notices **19**(5) (1984) 177–184
18. Schlickling, M.: Generisches Slicing auf Maschinencode. Diploma Thesis, Universität des Saarlandes (2005)

19. Ferdinand, C., Kästner, D., Langenbach, M., Martin, F., Schmidt, M., Schneider, J., Theiling, H., Thesing, S., Wilhelm, R.: Run-Time Guarantees for Real-Time Systems — The USES Approach. In: Proceedings of Informatik '99 – Arbeitstagung Programmiersprachen. (1999)
20. Ferdinand, C., Kästner, D., Langenbach, M., Martin, F., Schmidt, M., Schneider, J., Theiling, H., Thesing, S., Wilhelm, R.: Run-Time Guarantees for Real-Time Systems - The USES Approach. Proceedings of the ATPS (1999)
21. Theiling, H., Martin, F., Schneider, J., Schmidt, M.: Specification of the Standard for a File Format used for Exchanging Results of Different Parts of a Run-Time Analysis (ERD). Technischer Bericht, Universität des Saarlandes, AbsInt Angewandte Informatik GmbH (2003)
22. Sandberg, C., Ermedahl, A., Gustafsson, J., Lisper, B.: Faster WCET flow analysis by program slicing. In: ACM SIGPLAN Conference on Languages, Compilers and Tools for Embedded Systems (LCTES2006), Ottawa, Canada, ACM (2006)
23. Thesing, S.: Safe and Precise WCET Determination by Abstract Interpretation of Pipeline Models. PhD thesis, Saarland University (2004)
24. Thesing, S.: Modeling a System Controller for Timing Analysis. In: Proceedings of the 6th ACM Conference on Embedded Software, EMSOFT'06. (2006) to appear.
25. Institute of Electrical and Electronic Engineers New York: Draft IEEE Standard P1076 2000/D3 VHDL Language Reference Manual. (2000)
26. Ashenden, P.J.: The Designer's Guide to VHDL. 2nd edn. Morgan Kaufmann Publishers, Academic Press (2002)
27. Callahan, D., Cooper, K.D., Kennedy, K., Torczon, L.: Interprocedural Constant Propagation. ACM SIGPLAN Notices **21**(7) (1986) 152–161 Proceedings of the ACM SIGPLAN '86 Symposium on Compiler Construction, Palo Alto, USA.

Realistic Worst-Case Execution Time Analysis in the Context of Pervasive System Verification

Steffen Knapp* and Wolfgang Paul

Saarland University, Computer Science Dept., 66123 Saarbrücken, Germany
{sknapp,wjp}@wjpserver.cs.uni-sb.de

Abstract. We describe a gate level design of a FlexRay-like bus interface. An electronic control unit (ECU) is obtained by integrating this interface into the design of the verified VAMP processor. We get a time triggered distributed real-time system by connecting several such ECU's via a common bus. We define a programming model for such a system at the instruction set architecture (ISA) level and prove that it is correctly implemented at the gate level. The proof combines theories of processor correctness, communication systems, program correctness and realistic worst-case execution time (WCET) analysis into a single unified mathematical theory.

1 Introduction

1.1 Pervasive Verification and Unified Theory

The results of this paper were obtained under the German Verisoft project that aims at the development of tools and methods for the pervasive formal verification of computer systems. Pervasive correctness theorems argue simultaneously about the correctness of several system components like: Processors, I/O devices and programs. For real-time systems the correctness proofs are also based on the fact that certain computations are performed within certain time bounds.

Here we consider a distributed real-time system. In the pervasive correctness proof of this system we combine theories of processor correctness, communication systems, program correctness and realistic worst-case execution time (WCET) analysis [Abs06] into a single unified mathematical theory in the following sense:

Concepts shared between theories must not only be defined using the same formalism (this can be done easily using e.g. set theory) they must be defined *literally* in the same way in all theories concerned. Hardware correctness proofs of processors, I/O-devices and networks must use the same hardware- and the same instruction set architecture (ISA)[1] model. Correctness proofs of communicating assembler programs must use literally the same ISA model, too.

---

* Work partially funded by the International Max Planck Research School for Computer Science (IMPRS) and the German Federal Ministry of Education and Research (BMBF) in the framework of the Verisoft project under grant 01 IS C38.
[1] In a nutshell the ISA is an assembler semantic with interrupts visible, i.e. syntactic sugar for the machine language.

T. Reps, M. Sagiv, and J. Bauer (Eds.): Wilhelm Festschrift, LNCS 4444, pp. 53–81, 2007.

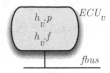

Fig. 1. Electronic Control Units

WCET analysis done for hardware models with real-time timers must clearly be based on cycle counts of the hardware. Yet in a pervasive theory of real-time systems this execution time analysis must be *formally* combined with program correctness proofs based on the ISA model, where caches are invisible and hence argumentation about the exact cycle count is impossible.

1.2   System Overview

The distributed real-time system considered here is very similar to systems used in the automotive industry: A fixed number p of electronic control units ECU_v for $v \in \{0, \ldots, p-1\}$ are connected via a FlexRay-like bus; applications run with a fixed schedule under an OSEKtime-like [OSE06] real-time operating system.

FlexRay is a communication protocol for safety critical real-time automotive applications, which has been developed by the FlexRay Consortium [Fle06]. It is a static time division multiplexing network protocol that supports clock synchronization. In this paper we do not deal with fault tolerance regarding the inter ECU communication.

The hardware of each ECU is clocked by an oscillator with a nominal clock period of say τ_{ref}. For all v the individual clock period τ_v of ECU_v is allowed to deviate from the nominal period by $\delta = 0.15\%$:

$$| \tau_v - \tau_{ref} | \leq \tau_{ref} \cdot \delta$$

This limitation can be easily achieved by current technology.

With $\Delta = 2\delta/(1 - \delta)$ we easily bound for all u and v the relative deviation of individual clock periods among each other by:

$$| \tau_v - \tau_u | \leq \tau_v \cdot \Delta$$

The assembler programmer sees such a system *mostly* at the ISA level. An ECU configuration $d_v = (d_v.p, d_v.f)$, see Fig. 1, is a pair consisting of a DLX processor configuration $d_v.p$, as defined in [DHP05], and a configuration of a FlexRay-like interface (f-interface) $d_v.f$.

From an interface configuration $d_v.f$ it is easy to define two user-visible buffers: A send buffer $sb(d_v)$ and a receive buffer $rb(d_v)$. Each buffer is capable of holding a message of ℓ bytes.

In the distributed system all communications and computations proceed in rounds r where $r \in \mathbb{N}$. As depicted in Fig. 2 each round is divided into an even[2] number of slots s where $s \in \{0, \ldots, ns - 1\}$. The tuple (r, s) refers to slot s in round r.

---

[2] In Sect. 4.1 we will argue why an even number of slots is required.

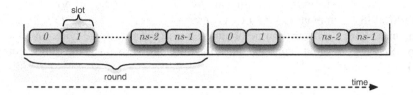

Fig. 2. Slots and Rounds

On each ECU, boundaries between slots are determined by local timer interrupts every T hardware cycles. At the beginning of each round, the local timers are synchronized.

Given a slot (r, s) we define the predecessor $(r, s) - 1$ and the successor $(r, s) + 1$ according to the lexicographical order of slots. We denote by $d_v(r, s)$ the first and by $e_v(r, s)$ the last ISA configuration of ECU_v during slot (r, s).

ECUs communicate according to a fixed schedule that is identical for each round: The function $send$ specifies for all rounds r the ECU that owns the bus during slot (r, s):

$$send : \{0, \ldots, ns - 1\} \rightarrow \{0, \ldots, p - 1\}$$

During slot (r, s) the content of the send buffer of $ECU_{send(s)}$ at the end of the previous round $(r, s) - 1$ is broadcast to the receive buffers of all units ECU_u and becomes visible there at the beginning of the next round $(r, s) + 1$:

$$\forall u, r, s : sb(e_{send(s)}((r, s) - 1)) = rb(d_u((r, s) + 1)).$$

1.3 Results

We present the following results:

1. We describe a gate level design of a FlexRay-like bus interface and elaborate the sketchy correctness proof from [BBG⁺05] in a distributed hardware model (Theorem 1). To the best of our knowledge this is the first detailed *gate level* correctness proof of an I/O device.
2. An ECU is obtained by integrating the f-interface into the verified VAMP processor [BJK⁺03, DHP05]. We develop an ISA model for such an ECU. This model is necessarily nondeterministic, because f-interfaces contain timers that interrupt the processor every say T hardware cycles; but cache misses (and hence hardware cycles) are invisible at the ISA level. We then prove the correctness of its hardware implementation (Theorem 2). To the best of our knowledge this is the first hardware correctness proof for a processor *together* with a device capable of generating timer interrupts.
3. Combining the first two results we obtain a correctness proof for the hardware of an entire distributed real-time system (Theorem 3). Again, to the best of our knowledge no such proof has been presented in the literature before.

4. The last result (Theorem 4) is technical. We show how pervasive correctness proofs for local ISA computations with timer interrupts (which are nondeterministic) and the underlying hardware can be obtained from i) conventional correctness proofs for ISA programs that cannot be interrupted ii) hardware correctness theorems and iii) WCET analysis.

2   Overview and Related Work

Consider a situation, where a sending ECU puts a bit on the bus and this bit is sampled into registers of receiving ECUs. Then, due to the clock drift between ECUs, we cannot guarantee that the set up and hold times of the receiving registers are obeyed at all clock edges. This problem occurs whenever computers without a common clock exchange data. It is solved by serial interfaces using a nontrivial protocol. Section 3 deals with the hardware correctness proof of a serial interface as prescribed by the FlexRay standard.

The main arguments have already been published in [BBG+05], so we only summarize the results. We cannot completely argue on the digital levels. Certain lemmas concerning the data transmission on the bus argue about continuous time. Formal proofs for these arguments have already been obtained [Sch06]. Beautiful automatic correctness proofs for abstract versions of protocols for serial interfaces using k-induction are reported in [BP06]. It would be highly desirable to use results of this nature as lemmas in overall correctness proofs for serial interface hardware. However, this would require to formally justify the abstractions being used in [BP06] within a hardware model with set-up and hold times.

In Sect. 4 we deal with f-interfaces that are constructed with the help of serial interfaces. The interfaces have local timers that are synchronized at the start of each round. Using arguments from classical clock synchronization [WL88] we derive conditions on the number of cycles T of each slot, such that for all slots (r, s) the following holds: The send buffer of the sending unit $ECU_{send(s)}$ can be broadcast to the receive buffers of all units in a transmission window, when according to their local timers all ECUs are in slot (r, s). This section provides the crucial arguments of lemmas sketched without proof in [BBG+05]. Detailed hardware constructions and proofs for the results of Sects. 3 and 4 can be found in the lecture notes [Pau05].

The ISA processor configuration is sketched in Sect. 5. Furthermore the semantics of the processor's DLX instruction set are defined by specifying the next state functions of the processor. Details regarding this function are to be found in [HP96, MP00]. Here we focus on the semantics of load / store instructions and on the interrupt mechanism.

In Sect. 6 we introduce an ISA model of a processor together with a f-interface. The next state function of the processor gets two new arguments. One of them is the input sampled by the device on the bus. The second new argument is an oracle input for the ISA computation of the ECU indicating whether a timer interrupt is generated or not. At first sight this looks odd because after all the ECU hardware is completely deterministic. But here we are not looking at the hardware, we are only looking at its ISA model. As pointed out above, in the ISA model, cache hits and misses are not visible. Hence the occurrence of timer interrupts is inherently nondeterministic at the ISA level.

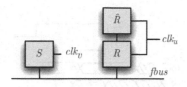

Fig. 3. Serial Interface

In Sect. 7 we show the hardware correctness theorems: The hardware of the entire distributed system simulates the ISA model for a particular choice of the oracle inputs (the latter is specified in Sect. 6.2). We first review the concept of scheduling functions and proof strategies from [SH98, MP00, BJK$^+$03, DHP05]. The scheduling functions enable us to determine the interrupted ISA instructions in a straightforward way. This determines the oracle inputs and thus resolves the nondeterminism present in the pure ISA model.

Section 8 starts with fairly plain computation theory for uninterrupted ISA computations as well as for hardware computations. In particular we formally define the run time and the result of such computations. The definition of run times of hardware computations is again based on the scheduling functions. Then we formally combine the results of WCET analysis, of program correctness proofs for uninterrupted ISA computations and of the hardware correctness proofs into a single result: At the end of slots, the post conditions for memories and registers (but not for program counters) stated for the uninterrupted local ISA computation also hold for their counter parts in the hardware configuration.

3   Serial Interface

In this section we deal with the implementation and the correctness proof of a serial interface as prescribed by the FlexRay standard.

3.1   Hardware Model with Continuous Time

In the standard digital hardware model a computation proceeds in cycles i. The hardware configuration of ECU_v during cycle i of ECU_v is denoted by h_v^i.

Configurations h have components $h.R$ where R is a register content or the content of a memory. Circuits compute signals S from register contents or memory contents. The value of such a signal S is therefore –in well designed hardware– a function $S(h)$ of the hardware configuration.

We denote the clock enable signal, which triggers the update of registers R, by Rce. Then $Rce(h^i)$ is the value of the clock enable of register R in cycle i.

The problems solved by serial interfaces can by their very nature not be treated in the standard digital hardware model with a single digital clock clk. Nevertheless, we can describe each ECU_v in a standard digital hardware model having its own hardware configuration h_v.

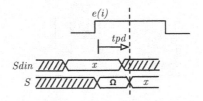

Fig. 4. Sender Register

In order to argue about a 1-bit sender register S of a sending unit ECU_v that is transmitting data via the FlexRay-like bus ($fbus$) to a 1-bit receiver register R of a receiving ECU, as depicted in Fig. 3, we have to extend the digital model.

For the 1-bit registers –and only for these registers– connected to the $fbus$ we extend the hardware model such that we can deal with the concepts of propagation delay (tpd), set-up time (ts), hold time (th) and metastability of registers from hardware data sheets. In the extended model used near the $fbus$ we therefore consider time to be a real valued variable t. The clock edge $e_v(i)$ starting cycle i on ECU_v is defined by

$$e_v(i) = c_v + i \cdot \tau_v \tag{1}$$

for some offset $c_v < \tau_v$. In this continuous time model the content of the sender register S at time t is denoted by $S(t)$.

Now we have enough machinery to define in the continuous time model the output of a sender register S_v on ECU_v during cycle i of ECU_v, i.e. for $t \in (e_v(i), e_v(i+1)]$. If in cycle $i-1$ the digital clock enable $Sce(h_v^{i-1})$ signal was off, we see the old digital value $h_v^{i-1}.S$ of the register during the whole cycle. If the update enable signal was on, then during some propagation delay $tpd < \tau_v - ts$ we cannot predict what we see, which is denoted by Ω. When the tpd has passed, we see the new digital value of the register, which is given by the digital input $Sdin(h_v^{i-1})$ during the previous cycle (see Fig. 4):

$$S_v(t) = \begin{cases} h_v^{i-1}.S & \neg Sce(h_v^{i-1}) \\ \Omega & Sce(h_v^{i-1}) \wedge t \le e_v(i) + tpd \\ Sdin(h_v^{i-1}) & Sce(h_v^{i-1}) \wedge t > e_v(i) + tpd \end{cases}$$

The $fbus$ is an open collector bus modeled for all time t by:

$$fbus(t) = \bigwedge_v S_v(t)$$

Now consider a receiver register R_u on ECU_u whose clock enable is continuously turned on; thus the register always samples from the $fbus$. In order to define the new digital value $h_u^j.R$ of register R during cycle j on ECU_u we have to consider the value of the $fbus(t)$ in the time interval $(e_u(j) - ts, e_u(j) + th)$, i.e. from the clock edge minus the set-up time until the clock edge plus the hold time. If during that time the $fbus$ has a constant digital value x, the register samples that value:

$$\exists x \in \{0, 1\} \; \forall t \in (e_u(j) - ts, e_u(j) + th) : fbus(t) = x \rightarrow h_u^j.R = fbus(e_u(j))$$

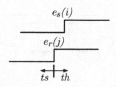

Fig. 5. Clock Edges

Otherwise we define $h_u^j.R = \Omega$. Thus we still have to argue how to deal with unknown values Ω as input to digital hardware. We use the output of register R only as input to a second register $\hat{R}$ whose clock enable is always turned on, too. If Ω is clocked into $\hat{R}$ we assume that $\hat{R}$ has an unknown but digital value:

$$h_u^j.R = \Omega \rightarrow h_u^{j+1}.\hat{R} \in \{0,1\}$$

Indeed, in industrial systems the counterpart of register $\hat{R}$ exists. The probability that R becomes metastable for an entire cycle *and* that this causes $\hat{R}$ to become metastable too is for practical purposes zero. This is exactly what has been formalized above.

Note that the above model uses different but fixed individual clock periods τ_v. There is no problem to extend the model to deal with jitter. Let $\tau_v(i)$ denote the length of cycle i on ECU_v, then we require for all v and i:

$$\tau_v(i) \in [\tau_{ref} \cdot (1 - \delta), \tau_{ref} \cdot (1 + \delta)]$$

The time $e_v(i)$ of the i-th clock edge on ECU_j is then defined as:

$$e_v(i) = \begin{cases} c_v & i = 0 \\ e_v(i-1) + \tau_v(i-1) & \text{otherwise} \end{cases}$$

This does not complicate the subsequent theory significantly.

3.2 Continuous Time Lemmas for the Bus

Consider a pair of ECUs, where ECU_s is the sender and ECU_r is a receiver in a given slot. Let i be a sender *cycle* such that $Sce(h_s^{i-1}) = 1$, i.e. the output of S is not guaranteed to stay constant at time $e_s(i)$. This change can only affect the value of register R of ECU_r in cycle j if it occurs before the sampling edge $e_r(j)$ plus the hold time th: $e_s(i) < e_r(j) + th$. Figure 5 shows a situation where due to a hold time violation we have $e_s(i) > e_r(j)$. The first cycle that is possibly being affected is denoted by:

$$cy_{r,s}(i) = \min\{j \mid e_s(i) < e_r(j) + th\}$$

In what follows we assume that all ECUs other than the sender unit ECU_s put the 'idle' value 1 on the bus (hence $fbus(t) = S_s(t)$ for all t under consideration) and we consider only one receiving unit ECU_r. Because the indices r and s are fixed we simply write $cy(i)$ instead of $cy_{r,s}(i)$.

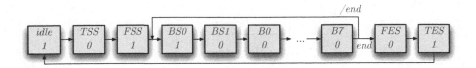

Fig. 6. Frame Encoding

There are two essential lemmas whose proof hinges on the continuous time model. The first lemma considers a situation, where we activate the clock enable Sce of the sender ECU in cycle $i - 1$ but not in the following seven cycles[3]. In the digital model we then have $h_s^i.S = \ldots = h_s^{i+7}.S$ and in the continuous time model we observe $x = fbus(t) = S_s(t) = h_s^i.S$ for all $t \in [e_s(i) + tpd, e_s(i + 8)]$. We claim that x is correctly sampled in at least six consecutive cycles.

Lemma 1 (Correct Sampling Interval). *Let the clock enable signal of the S register be turned on in cycle $i - 1$, i.e. $Sce(h_s^{i-1}) = 1$ and let the same signal be turned off in the next seven cycles, i.e. $Sce(h_s^j) = 0$ for $j \in \{i, \ldots, i + 6\}$ then:*

$$h_r^{cy(i)+k}.R = h_s^i.S \quad \text{for } k \in \{1, \ldots, 6\}$$

The second lemma simply bounds the clock drift. It essentially states that within 300 cycles clocks cannot drift by more than one cycle; this is shown using $\delta \leq 0.15\%$.

Lemma 2 (Bounded Clock Drift). *The clock drift in the interval $m \in \{1, \ldots, 300\}$ is bounded by:*

$$cy(i) + m - 1 \leq cy(i + m) \leq cy(i) + m + 1$$

Detailed proofs of very similar lemmas are to be found in [Pau05, BBG+05, Sch06].

3.3 Serial Interface Construction and Correctness

For natural numbers n and bits y we denote by y^n the string in which bit y is replicated n times, e.g. $0^4 = 0000$. For strings $x[0 : k - 1]$ consisting of k bits $x[i]$ we denote by $8 \cdot x$ the string obtained by repeating each bit eight times:

$$8 \cdot x = x[0]^8 \cdots x[k - 1]^8$$

Our serial interface transmits messages $m[0 : \ell - 1]$ consisting of ℓ bytes $m[i]$ from a send buffer sb of the sending ECU to a receive buffer rb of the receiving ECU.

The following protocol is used for transmission (see Fig. 6). A frame $f(m)$ is created from a message m by inserting falling edges between the bytes and adding some bits at the start and the end of the frame:

$$f(m) = 0110m[0] \cdots 10m[\ell - 1]01$$

---

[3] This particular interval of 8 cycles is taken from the FlexRay standard [Fle06].

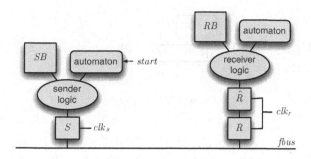

Fig. 7. Send and Receive Buffer

In $f(m)$ we call the first zero the transmission start sequence (*TSS*), the first one the frame start sequence (*FSS*), the last zero the frame end sequence (*FES*) and the last one the transmission end sequence (*TES*). The two bits producing a falling edge before each byte are called the byte start sequence (*BS0, BS1*).

The sending ECU broadcasts $8 \cdot f(m)$ over the *fbus*. For each bit of the frame the update-enable signal is on for 1 cycle and then off for 7 cycles. All serial interfaces that are not actively transmitting put by construction the idle value (the bit 1) on the bus.

Figure 7 shows a simplified view of the hardware involved in the transmission of a message. On the sender side, there is an automaton keeping track of which bit of the frame is currently being transmitted. This automaton inserts the additional protocol bits around the message bytes. Hardware for sending each bit eight times and for addressing the send buffer is not shown.

On the receiver side there is the automaton from Fig. 6 trying to keep track of which bit of the frame is currently being transmitted (the automaton on the sender side is very similar). That it does so successfully requires proof.

The bits sampled in register $\hat{R}$ are processed in the following way. The voted bit v is computed by applying a majority vote to the last five sampled bits. These bits are given by the $\hat{R}$ register and a 4-bit shift register as depicted in Fig. 8.

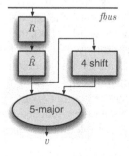

Fig. 8. Receiver Logic

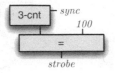

Fig. 9. Strobe Signal

According to Lemma 1 for each bit of the frame a sequence of at least six bits is correctly sampled. The filtering essentially maintains this property. If the receiver succeeds
to sample that sequence roughly in the middle, he wins. For this purpose the receiver
has a modulo-8 counter trying to keep track of which of the eight identical copies of a
frame bit is currently being transmitted. When the counter value equals four the *strobe*
signal is turned on (see Fig. 9). For frame decoding the voted bit is sampled with this
strobe signal. The automaton trying to keep track of the protocol is also clocked with
the *strobe* signal.

Clocks are drifting, hence the hardware has to perform a low level synchronization.
The counter is reset by a *sync* signal in two situations: At the beginning of a transmission or at an expected falling edge during the byte start sequence. Abbreviating
signals $s(h_r^i)$ with s^i we write:

$$sync^i = (idle^i \lor BS1^i) \land (\neg v^i \land v^{i-1})$$

The crucial part of the correctness proof is a lemma arguing simultaneously about
three statements by induction over the receiver cycles:

1. The state of the automaton keeps track of the transmitted frame bit.
2. The *sync* signal is activated at the corresponding falling edge of the voted bit v
   between *BS1* and *BS0*.
3. Sequences of identical bit are sampled roughly in the middle.

We sketch the proof of this lemma. Statement 1 is clearly true in the *idle* state.
From statement 1 follows that the automaton expects the falling edges of the voted
signal exactly when the sender generates them. Thus the counter is well synchronized
after these falling edges. This shows statement 2. Immediately after synchronization
the receiver samples roughly in the middle. There is a synchronization roughly every 80
sender cycles. By Lemma 2 and because $80 < 300$, the sampling point can wander by at
most one bit between activations of the *sync* signal. This is good enough to stay within
the correctly sampled six copies. This shows statement 3. If transmitted frame bits are
correctly sampled, then the automaton keeps track of them. This shows statement 1.

Let t_0 be the time (not the cycle) when the *start* signal of the sender is activated.
Let t_1 be the time, when all automata have reached the *idle* state again and all write
accesses to the receive buffer have completed. Let the number of 'transmission cycles'
be defined by:

$$tc = 45 + 80 \cdot \ell$$

Intuitively, the product $80 \cdot \ell$ in the definition of tc comes from the fact that each byte
produces 10 frame bits and each of these is transmitted 8 times. The four bits added at

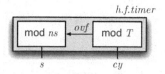

Fig. 10. Hardware Timer

the start and the end of the frame contribute $4 \cdot 8 = 32$. The remaining 13 cycles are caused by delays in the receiver logic, in particular by delay in the shift register before the majority voter. The correctness of message transmission is stated as follows:

Lemma 3 (Correct Message Transfer With Time Bound). *Messages are correctly transmitted, and the transmission does not last longer than tc sender cycles:*

$$rb(t_1) = sb(t_0)$$
$$t_1 - t_0 \leq tc \cdot \tau_s$$

4   FlexRay-Like Interfaces and Clock Synchronization

In this section we outline the implementation and the correctness proof of FlexRay-like interfaces (f-interfaces).

4.1   Hardware Components

Recall that we denote hardware configurations of ECU_v by h_v. If the index v of the ECU does not matter, we drop it. The hardware configuration is split into a processor configuration $h.p$ and an interface configuration $h.f$. In addition to the registers of the serial interface, the essential components of the hardware configuration $h.f$ of our (non fault tolerant) f-interface are

- double buffers $h.f.sb(par)$ and $h.f.rb(par)$, where $par \in \{0,1\}$, implementing the user-visible send and receive buffers,
- the flipflops of a somewhat non trivial timer $h.f.timer$,
- configuration registers.

   The organization of the hardware timer $h.f.timer$ is depicted in Fig. 10. The low-order bits $h.f.timer.cy$ count the cycles of a slot. Unless the timer is synchronized, slots have locally T cycles, thus the low-order bits are part of a modulo-T counter. The high-order bits $h.f.timer.s$ count the slot index s of the current slot (r, s) modulo ns. The timer is initialized with the value $(ns - 1, T - 1)$.

   The timers on all ECUs but $ECU_{send(0)}$ stall when reaching the maximum value $(ns-1, T-1)$ and wait for synchronization. The timer on $ECU_{send(0)}$ always continues counting. Details regarding the synchronization mechanism are given in Sect. 4.2.

The overflow signal $ovf(h)$ between the low-order and the high-order bits of the counter can essentially serve as the timer interrupt signal $ti(h)$ generated by the interface hardware[4]:

$$ti(h^i) = ovf(h^i) \wedge \neg ovf(h^{i-1})$$

The low-order bit of the slot counter keeps track of the parity of the current slot and is called the hardware parity signal:

$$par(h) = h.f.timer.s[0]$$

In general the *fbus* side of the interface sees the two buffers $h.f.sb(par(h))$ and $h.f.rb(par(h))$. Messages are always transmitted between these buffers. The processor on the other hand writes to $h.f.sb(\neg par(h))$ and reads from $h.f.rb(\neg par(h))$. This does not work at boundaries of rounds unless the number of slots ns is even.

The configuration registers are written immediately after reset / power-up. They contain in particular the locally relevant portions of the scheduling function. Thus if ECU_v is (locally) in a slot with slot index s and $send(s) = v$ then ECU_v transmits the content of the send buffer $h.f.sb(par(h))$ via the *fbus* during some transmission interval $[ts(r, s), te(r, s)]$.

If we can guarantee that during the transmission interval *all* ECUs are locally in slot (r, s), then transmission is successful by Lemma 3. The clock synchronization algorithm together with an appropriate choice of the transmission interval guarantees exactly that.

4.2   Clock Synchronization

The idea of clock synchronization is easily explained: Imagine one slot is one hour and one round is one day. Assume different clocks drift by up to $drift = 5$ minutes per day. ECUs synchronize to the first bit of the message transmission due between midnight and 1 o'clock. Assume adjusting the clocks at the receiving ECUs takes up to $adj = 1$ minute. Then the maximal deviation during 1 day is $off = drift + adj = 6$ minutes. $ECU_{send(s)}$, which is the sender in hour s, is on the safe side if it starts transmitting from s o'clock plus off minutes until off minutes before $s + 1$ o'clock, i.e. somewhen in between $s : 06$ o'clock and $s + 1 : 54$ o'clock.

At midnight life becomes slightly tricky: $ECU_{send(0)}$ waits until it can be sure that everybody believes that midnight is over and hence nobody is transmitting, i.e. until its local time $0 : 06$. Then it starts sending. All other ECUs are waiting for the broadcast message and adjust their clocks to midnight + $off = 0 : 06$ once they detect the first falling bit. Since that might take the receiving ECUs up to 1 minute it might be $0 : 07$ o'clock on the sender when it is $0 : 06$ o'clock at the receiver; thus after synchronization the clocks differ by at most $adj = 1$ minute.

We formalize this idea in the following way: Assume without loss of generality that $send(0) = 0$. All ECUs but ECU_0 synchronize to the transmission start sequence (*TSS*) of the first message of ECU_0. When ECU's waiting for synchronization

---

[4] In general one needs to keep an interrupt signal active until it is cleared by software; the extra hardware is simple.

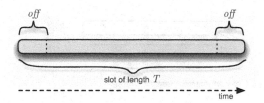

Fig. 11. Slots

$(d.f.timer = (ns - 1, T - 1))$ receive this *TSS*, they advance their local slot counter to 0 and their cycle counter to *off*. Analysis of the algorithm implies that for all $v \neq 0$, ECU_v is waiting for synchronization, when ECU_0 starts message transmission in any slot $(r, 0)$.

First we define the start times $\alpha_v(r, s)$ of slot (r, s) on ECU_v. This is the start time of the first cycle t in round r when the timer in the previous cycle had the value:

$$h^{t-1}.f.timer = ((s - 1 \bmod ns), T - 1)$$

These are the cycles immediately after the local timer interrupts. For every round r, we also define the cycles $\beta_v(r)$ when the synchronization is completed on ECU_v. Formally this is defined as the first cycle $\beta > \alpha_v(r, 0)$ such that the local timer has value:

$$h^{\beta}.f.timer = (0, off)$$

Timing analysis of the synchronization process in the complete hardware design shows that for all v and y adjustment of the local timer of ECU_v to value $(0, off)$ is completed within an adjustment time $ad = 15 \cdot \tau_y$ after $\alpha_0(r, 0)$:

$$\beta_0(r) = \alpha_0(r, 0) + off \cdot \tau_0$$
$$\beta_v(r) \leq \beta_0(r) + 15 \cdot \tau_y$$

For $s \geq 1$ no synchronization takes place and the start of new slots is only determined by the progress of the local timer:

$$\alpha_v(r, s) = \begin{cases} \beta_v(r) + (T - off) \cdot \tau_v & s = 1 \\ \alpha_v(r, s - 1) + T \cdot \tau_v & s > 1 \end{cases}$$

ECU_0 synchronizes the other ECUs. Thus the start of slot $(r, 0)$ on ECU_0 depends only on the progress of the local counter:

$$\alpha_0(r, 0) = \alpha_0(r - 1, ns - 1) + T \cdot \tau_0$$

An easy induction on s bounds the difference between start times of the same slot on different $ECUs$:

$$\begin{aligned} \alpha_x(r, s) - \alpha_v(r, s) &\leq 15 \cdot \tau_v + (s \cdot T - off) \cdot (\tau_x - \tau_v) \\ &\leq 15 \cdot \tau_v + (ns \cdot T \cdot \Delta \cdot \tau_v) \\ &= \tau_v \cdot (15 + (ns \cdot T \cdot \Delta)) \\ &= \tau_v \cdot off \end{aligned} \tag{2}$$

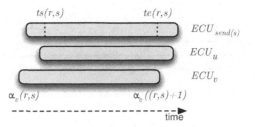

Fig. 12. Schedules

Thus we have $off = ad + drift$ with $ad = 15$ and $drift = ns \cdot T \cdot \Delta$.

Transmission is started in slots (r, s) by $ECU_{send(s)}$ when the local cycle count is off. Thus the transmission start time is:

$$ts(r, s) = \alpha_{send(s)}(r, s) + off \cdot \tau_{send(s)}$$

By Lemma 3 the transmission ends at time:

$$\begin{aligned} te(r, s) &= ts(r, s) + tc \cdot \tau_{send(s)} \\ &= \alpha_{send(s)}(r, s) + (off + tc) \cdot \tau_{send(s)} \end{aligned}$$

The transmission interval $[ts(r, s), te(r, s)]$ must be contained in the time interval, when all ECUs are in slot (r, s), as depicted in Fig. 12.

Lemma 4 (No Bus Contention). *For all indices v and u of ECUs:*

$$\begin{aligned} \alpha_v(r, s) &\leq ts(r, s) \\ te(r, s) &\leq \alpha_u((r, s) + 1) \end{aligned}$$

Proof. The first inequality holds because of (2). Let $x = send(s)$:

$$\begin{aligned} \alpha_v(r, s) &\leq \alpha_x(r, s) + \tau_x \cdot off \\ &= ts(r, s) \end{aligned}$$

The second inequality determines the minimal size of T:

$$\begin{aligned} te(r, s) &\leq \alpha_x(r, s) + (off + tc) \cdot \tau_x \\ &\leq \alpha_u(r, s) + off \cdot \tau_u + (off + tc) \cdot (1 + \Delta) \cdot \tau_u \\ &\leq \alpha_u((r, s) + 1) \\ &= \alpha_u(r, s) + T \cdot \tau_u \end{aligned}$$

Further calculations are necessary at the borders between rounds. Details can be found in [Pau05]. $\qquad \Box$

From the local start times of slots $\alpha_v(r, s)$ we calculate the numbers of local start cycles $t_v(r, s)$ using (1)

$$\alpha_v(r, s) = c_v + t_v(r, s) \cdot \tau_v$$

and then solving for $t_v(r, s)$. Trivially the number $u_v(r, s)$ of the locally last cycle on ECU_v is:

$$u_v(r, s) = t_v((r, s) + 1) - 1$$

Consider slot (r, s). Lemma 3 and Lemma 4 then imply that the value of the send buffer of $ECU_{send(s)}$ on the network side ($par = s \bmod 2$) at the start of slot (r, s) is copied to all receive buffers on the network side by the end of that slot.

Theorem 1 (Message Transfer With Cycles). *Let* $x = send(s)$. *Then for all* v:

$$h_x^{t_x(r,s)}.f.sb(s \bmod 2) = h_v^{u_v(r,s)}.f.rb(s \bmod 2)$$

This theorem talks only about digital hardware and hardware cycles. Thus we have shown the correctness of data transmission via the bus *and* we are back in the digital world.

5 Specifying an Instruction Set Architecture

In this section we sketch the DLX instruction set architecture (ISA).

5.1 Configurations and Auxiliary Concepts

Processor configurations d have the following components:

- $d.R \in \{0, 1\}^{32}$: The current value of register R. For this paper, the relevant registers are: The program counter pc, the delayed PC dpc (which is used to specify the delayed branch mechanism detailed in [MP00]), the general purpose registers $gpr[x]$ with $x \in \{0, 1\}^5$, the status register sr (it contains the mask bits for the interrupts) as well as a exception cause register eca (to be explained later on).
- The byte addressable memory $d.m : \{0, 1\}^{32} \rightarrow \{0, 1\}^8$. The content of the memory at byte address a is given by $d.m(a)$.

For addresses a, memories m, and natural numbers x we denote by $m_x(a)$ the concatenation of the memory bytes from address a to address $a + x - 1$ in little-endian order:

$$m_x(a) = m(a + x - 1) \ldots m(a)$$

The instruction executed in configuration d is the memory word addressed by the delayed PC:

$$I(d) = d.m_4(d.dpc)$$

The six high-order bits of the instruction word constitute the opcode:

$$opc(d) = I(d)[31 : 26]$$

Instruction decoding can easily be formalized by predicates on $I(d)$. In some cases it suffices to inspect the opcode only. The current instruction is for instance a 'load word' (lw) instruction if the opcode (opc) equals 100011:

$$lw(d) \Leftrightarrow opc(d) = 100011$$

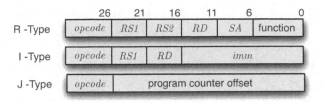

Fig. 13. Instruction Types

DLX instructions come in three instruction types as shown in Fig. 13. The type of an instruction defines how the bits of the instruction outside the opcode are interpreted. The occurrence of an register-type (R-type) instruction, e.g. a add or a subtract instruction, is for instance specified by:

$$rtype(d) \Leftrightarrow opc(d) = 000000$$

Definitions of immediate-constant-type (I-type) instructions and jump-type (J-type) instructions are slightly more complex.

Depending on the instruction type, certain fields have different positions within the instruction. For the register 'destination' operand (RD) we have for instance:

$$RD(d) = \begin{cases} I(d)[20:16] & itype(d) \\ I(d)[15:11] & \text{otherwise} \end{cases}$$

The effective address (ea) of load / store operations is computed as the sum of the content of the register addressed by the $RS1$ field $d.gpr(RS1(d))$ and the immediate field $imm(d) = I(d)[15:0]$. The addition is performed modulo 2^{32} using two's complement arithmetic. Formally, the sign extension of the immediate constant is defined by:

$$sxt(imm(d)) = imm(d)[15]^{16}imm(d)$$

This turns the immediate constant into a 32-bit constant while preserving the value as a two's complement number. It is like adding leading zeros to a natural number. Denoting ordinary binary addition modulo 2^{32} by $+_{32}$ we define:

$$ea(d) = d.gpr(RS1(d)) +_{32} sxt(imm(d))$$

This works because n bit two's complement numbers and n bit binary numbers have the same value modulo 2^n. For details see e.g. Sect. 2 of [MP00].

5.2   Basic Instruction Set

With the above few preliminary definitions in place we easily specify the next configuration d', i.e. the configuration after execution of $I(d)$. This obviously formalizes the instruction set. In the definition of d' we split cases depending on the instruction to be executed. As an example we specify the next configuration for a load word instruction.

The main effect of a load word instruction is that the general purpose register addressed by the RD field is updated with the memory word addressed by the effective address ea:

$$d'.gpr(RD(d)) = d.m_4(ea(d))$$

The PC is incremented by four in 32-bit binary arithmetic and the old PC is copied into the delayed PC:

$$d'.pc = d.pc +_{32} 0^{30}10$$
$$d'.dpc = d.pc$$

This part of the definition is identical for all instructions except control instructions. One also must specify what is not changed:

$$d'.m = d.m$$
$$d'.gpr(x) = d.gpr(x) \quad \text{for} \quad x \neq RD(d)$$
$$d'.sr = d.sr$$
$$d'.eca = d.eca$$

The main effect of store word instructions is that the general purpose register content addressed by RD is copied into the memory word addressed by ea:

$$d'.m_4(ea(d)) = d.gpr(RD(d))$$

Completing this definition for all instructions, we get the definition of a DLX next state function:

$$d' = \delta_D(d)$$

5.3   Interrupts

Interrupts are triggered by interrupt event signals that might be internally generated (like illegal instruction, misalignment, or overflow) or externally generated (like reset and timer interrupt). Interrupts are numbered with indices $j \in \{0, \dots, 31\}$. We classify the set of these indices in two ways:

1. maskable / not maskable. The set of indices of maskable interrupts is denoted by M.
2. external / internal. The set of indices of external interrupts is called E.

We denote external event signals by $eev[j]$ with $j \in E$ and we denote internal event signals by $iev[j]$ with $j \notin E$. We gather the external event signals into a vector eev and the internal event signals into a vector iev.

Formally these signals must be treated in a very different way. Whether an internal event signal $iev[j]$ is activated in configuration d is determined only by the configuration d. For instance if we use $j = 1$ for the illegal instruction interrupt and $LI \subset \{0,1\}^{32}$ is the set of bit patterns for which d' is defined if $I(d) \in LI$, then:

$$iev(d)[1] \Leftrightarrow I(d) \notin LI$$

Thus the vector of internal event signals is a function $iev(d)$ of the current processor configuration d. In contrast, external interrupts are external inputs for the next state function. We therefore get a new next state function:

$$d' = \delta_D(d, eev)$$

The cause vector ca of all event signals is a function of the processor configuration d and the external input eev:

$$ca(d, eev)[j] = \begin{cases} eev[j] & j \in E \\ iev(d)[j] & \text{otherwise} \end{cases}$$

The masked cause vector mca is computed from ca with the help of the interrupt mask stored in the status register: If interrupt j is maskable and $sr[j] = 0$, it is masked out:

$$mca(d, eev)[j] = \begin{cases} ca(d, eev)[j] \wedge d.sr[j] & j \in M \\ ca(d, eev)[j] & \text{otherwise} \end{cases}$$

If any one of the masked cause bits is on, the jump to interrupt service routine ($JISR$) bit is turned on:

$$JISR(d, eev) = \bigvee_j mca(d, eev)[j]$$

If this occurs, many things happen. We mention only a few: The PCs are forced to point to the start addresses of the interrupt service routine (ISR). We assume it starts at the (binary) address 0:

$$d'.dpc = 0^{32}$$
$$d'.pc = 0^{30}10$$

All maskable interrupts are masked:

$$d'.sr = 0^{32}$$

The masked cause register is saved into the exception cause register:

$$d'.eca = mca(d, eev)$$

For a complete definition see Chap. 5 of [MP00].

6   ISA of Processors with f-Interfaces

In this section we integrate our f-interface into the ISA model of the processor.

6.1   I/O Ports and Message Buffers

As already mentioned earlier an ISA configuration d of a processor with an f-interface is a pair $(d.p, d.f)$, where $d.p$ is a processor configuration as described in the previous section. It has registers $d.p.R$ and a memory $d.p.m$. The range of the function m is however restricted to a subset $A \subset \{0, 1\}^{32}$ of the entire address range:

$$d.p.m : A \rightarrow \{0, 1\}^8$$

Identifying bit strings a with their value if they are interpreted as a binary number, we define A to be in the range of addresses below a certain address D:

$$A = \{a \mid a < D\}$$

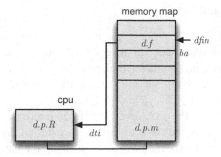

Fig. 14. Memory Mapped IO

Addresses from address D on are called I/O ports. They are reserved for I/O devices. Every device dv is assigned a base address $ba(dv)$ in the range of I/O ports (see Fig. 14):

$$ba(dv) \in \{D, \ldots, 2^{32} - 1\}$$

Here we only consider a single device and a single base address ba.

When a processor accesses a device with K I/O ports, then for $k = \lceil \log K \rceil$ the device configuration (here $d.f$) must contain a memory:

$$d.f.m : \{0,1\}^k \to \{0,1\}^8$$

In our case the memory of the device contains the send buffer, the receive buffer –each with ℓ bytes where ℓ is a multiple of 4– and say c configuration registers. Thus

$$K = 2 \cdot \ell + 4 \cdot c$$

We use the first ℓ bytes of this memory for the send buffer, the next ℓ bytes for the receive buffer and the remaining bytes for the configuration registers. We formalize this by defining for all indices of message bytes $y \in \{0, \ldots, \ell - 1\}$:

$$sb(d)(y) = d.f.m(y)$$
$$rb(d)(y) = d.f.m(\ell + y)$$

The semantics of accesses of the processor to the I/O ports are simply defined by a slight change of the semantics of lw and sw instructions. If the effective address[5] lies in the address range assigned to the device in the memory map, i.e. if

$$ea(d.p) = ba + x \quad \text{with} \quad 0 \leq x \leq K - 4$$

the essential effect of a load word instruction is

$$d'.p.gpr(RD(d.p)) = d.f.m_4(x)$$

and the essential effect of a store word instruction is:

$$d'.f.m_4(x) = d.p.gpr(RD(d.p))$$

---

[5] We require the effective address be word aligned.

6.2 Timer Interrupt and I/O

So far we have covered a single processor with a device but we have not considered timer interrupts. The consequences for integrating those in the processor construction and processor correctness proofs have already been outlined (e.g. for a hard-disk) in [HIP05]. In the remainder of this section we extend these results with timer interrupts generated by an f-interface.

As pointed out earlier, at the ISA level the timer interrupt must be treated as an oracle input dti. Furthermore we have to deal with external data input $dfin$ from the f-interface. Thus –ignoring reset– the next state function for the device has on the ISA level the format:

$$d' = \delta_D(d, dti, dfin)$$

If we denote by dti^i and $dfin^i$ the oracle input and the input from the $fbus$ for the i-th executed instruction, then we get computations $d^0, d^1, \ldots$ by defining (straight from the automata theory textbooks):

$$d^{i+1} = \delta_D(d^i, dti^i, dfin^i)$$

In our distributed system we have configurations d_v from many ECUs. Within this programming model we now introduce names, e.g. $j_v(r, s)$, for certain indices of local *instructions* on ECU_v.

Intuitively, the timer interrupts the instruction executed in the local configuration $d_v^{j_v(r,s)}$ of ECU_v, and this locally ends slot (r, s).

Based on these indices we can define some more useful concepts purely within the ISA model:

- $i_v(r, s) = j_v((r, s) - 1) + 1$: The index of the first local instruction in slot (r, s)
- $d_v(r, s) = d_v^{i_v(r,s)}$: The first local ISA configuration in slot (r, s)
- $e_v(r, s) = d_v^{j_v(r,s)}$: The last local ISA configuration in slot (r, s)

We can even define the sequence $dti(r, s)$ of oracle timer inputs dti^i where $i \in \{i_v(r, s), \ldots, j_v(r, s)\}$. It has the form

$$dti(r, s) = 1^a 0^b 1$$

where the timer interrupt is cleared by software instruction $i_v(r, s) + a - 1$ and $a + b + 1 = j_v(r, s) - i_v(r, s) + 1$ is the number of local instructions in slot (r, s).

Indeed we can complete, without any effort, the entire ISA programming model. The effect of an interrupt on the processor configuration has been defined in the previous section, thus we get for instance:

$$d_v(r, s).dpc = 0^{32}$$
$$d_v(r, s).pc = 0^{30}10$$

Also for the transition from $e_v(r, s)$ to $d_v((r, s) + 1)$ and only for this transition we use the external input:

$$dfin^{j_v(r,s)} \in \{0, 1\}^{8 \cdot \ell}$$

Thus we assume that it consists of an entire message and we copy that message into the user-visible receive buffer:

$$rb(d_v((r, s) + 1)) = dfin^{j_v(r,s)}$$

Of course we also know what this message is supposed to be: The content of the user-visible send buffer of $ECU_{send(s)}$ at the end of slot $(r, s) - 1$:

$$dfin^{j_v(r,s)} = sb(e_{send(s)}((r, s) - 1)$$

Thus

$$rb(d_v((r, s) + 1)) = sb(e_{send(s)}((r, s) - 1)) \tag{3}$$

This completes the user-visible ISA model. And with Theorem 1 we essentially already completed the hardware correctness proof of the implementation of (3). The non-determinism is completely encapsulated in the numbers $j_v(r, s)$ as it should be, at least if the local computations are fast enough. All we need to do is to justify the model by a hardware correctness theorem and to identify the conditions under which it can be used.

7 Hardware Correctness

In this section we outline a hardware correctness proof that establishes a relationship between an ISA configuration and a hardware configuration.

7.1 Scheduling Functions

The processor correctness proofs considered here hinge on the concept of scheduling functions s. The hardware of pipelined processors consists of many stages k, e.g. fetch stage, issue stage, reservation stations, reorder buffer, write back stage, etc. (see Fig. 17). Stages can be full or empty due to pipeline bubbles. The hardware keeps track of this with the help of full bits $full_k$ for each stage as defined in [MP00]. Recall that $full_k(h^t)$ is the value of the full bit in cycle t. We use the shorthand $full_k^t$. Note that the fetch state is always full, i.e. $\forall t : full_0^t = 1$.

For hardware cycles t and stages k that are full during cycle t, i.e. such that $full_k^t$ holds, the value $s(k, t)$ of the scheduling function is the index i of the instruction that is in stage k during cycle t. If the stage is not full, it is the index of the instruction that was in stage k in the last cycle before t when the stage was full. Initially $s(0, 0) = 0$ holds.

The formal definition of scheduling functions uses an extremely simple idea: Imagine that the hardware has registers that can hold integers of arbitrary size. Augment each stage with such a register and store in it the index of the instruction currently being executed in that stage. These indices are computed exactly as the tags in a Tomasulo scheduler. The only difference is that they have unbounded size because we want to count up to arbitrarily large indices. In real hardware this is not possible and not necessary. In an abstract mathematical model there is no problem to do this.

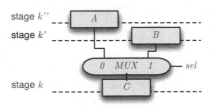

Fig. 15. Scheduling Functions

Each stage k of the processors under consideration has an update enable signal ue_k. Stage k gets new data in cycle t if the update enable signal ue_k was on in cycle $t-1$. We fetch instructions in order and hence define for the instruction fetch stage IF:

$$s(IF, t) = \begin{cases} s(IF, t-1) + 1 & ue_{IF}^{t-1} \\ s(IF, t-1) & \text{otherwise} \end{cases}$$

In general, a stage k can get data belonging to a new instruction from one or more stages k'. Examples where more than one predecessor stage k' exists for a stage k are i) cycles in the data path of a floating point unit performing iterative division or ii) the producer registers feeding on the common data bus of a Tomasulo scheduler. In this situation we must define for each stage k a predicate $trans(k', k, t)$ indicating that in cycle t data are transmitted from stage k' to stage k. In the example of Fig. 15 we use the select signal sel of the multiplexer and define:

$$trans(k', k, t) = ue_k^t \wedge sel^t$$

If $trans(k', k, t-1)$ holds for some k', then we set $s(k, t) = s(k', t-1)$ for that k'. Otherwise $s(k, t) = s(k, t-1)$.

7.2   Simple Simulation Relations

For ECUs we first consider a 'naive' simulation relation $sim(d, h)$ between ISA configurations d and hardware configurations h. We require that the user-visible registers R have identical values:

$$h.p.R = d.p.R$$

Furthermore we require that the send and receive buffers on the processor side (indexed in the hardware by $\neg par(h)$) of the hardware have the same value as the user-visible buffers. Thus, we require for all indices $y \in \{0, \dots, \ell - 1\}$ of message bytes:

$$h.f.sb(\neg par(h))(y) = sb(d)(y)$$
$$h.f.rb(\neg par(h))(y) = rb(d)(y)$$

For the addresses a in the processor we would like to make a similar definition, but this does not work, because the user-visible processor memory is simulated in the hardware by a memory system consisting e.g. of an instruction cache $icache$, a data

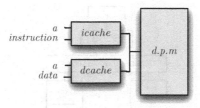

Fig. 16. Memory System

cache $dcache$ and a user main memory $mainm$. Thus there is a quite nontrivial function $m(h.p) : A \rightarrow \{0,1\}^8$ specifying the memory simulated by the memory system. We can define this functions in the following way: Imagine you apply in configuration h at the memory interface (either at the $icache$ or at the $dcache$) address a. Considering a hit in the instruction cache, i.e. $ihit(h.p, a) = 1$, the $icache$ would return $icache(h.p, a)$. Similarly, considering a hit in the data cache $dhit(h.p, a) = 1$ the $dcache$ would return $dcache(h.p, a)$. Then we can define[6]:

$$m(h.p)(a) = \begin{cases} icache(h.p, a) & ihit(h.p, a) \\ dcache(h.p, a) & dhit(h.p, a) \\ h.p.mainm(a) & \text{otherwise} \end{cases}$$

Using this definition we can require in the simulation relation for all addresses not being I/O ports, i.e. $a \in A$:

$$m(h.p)(a) = d.p.m(a)$$

In a pipelined machine this simulation relation almost never holds, because in one cycle different hardware stages k usually hold data from different ISA configurations; after all this is the very idea of pipelining. There is however an important exception: When the pipe is drained, i.e. all hardware stages except the instruction fetch stage are empty:

$$drained(h) \Leftrightarrow \forall k : k \neq IF \rightarrow full_k^t = 0$$

This happens to be the case after interrupts, in particular initially after reset and at the boundaries between slots when a timer interrupt is being generated.

7.3 Processor Correctness Theorem

Figure 17 shows in simplified form the stages of a processor with out of order processing and a Tomasulo scheduler.

Each user-visible register $d.R$ of the processor has a counter part $h.R$ belonging to the stage in the hardware specified by $stage(R)$. If the processor would have only

---

[6] In the processors under consideration the caches snoop on each other; data of address a is only in at most one cache [Bey05, BJK$^+$03].

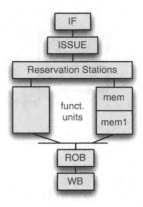

Fig. 17. Processor Pipeline

registers R and no memory, we could show by induction over t for all cycles t and stages k:

If $k = stage(R)$, then the value $h^t.p.R$ of the hardware register R in cycle t is the value $d^{s(k,t)}.p.R$ of the ISA register R for the instruction scheduled in stage k in cycle t:

$$h^t.p.R = d^{s(k,t)}.p.R$$

For the memory we have to consider the memory unit of the processor consisting of two stages mem and $mem1$. Stage mem contains hardware for the computation of the effective address. The memory $m(h^t.p)$ that is simulated by the memory hierarchy of the hardware in cycle t, is identical with the ISA memory $d^{s(mem1,t)}.p.m$ for the instruction scheduled in stage $mem1$ in cycle t:

$$m(h^t.p) = d^{s(mem1,t)}.p.m$$

In the hardware the send and receive buffers are 'parallel' to the memory system, so we can reuse the scheduling functions. For the copy of the buffers on the processors side we get:

$$h^t.f.sb(\neg par(h^t)) = sb(d^{s(mem1,t)})$$
$$h^t.f.rb(\neg par(h^t)) = rb(d^{s(mem1,t)})$$

We summarize this by stating for all ECUs the correctness statement for the processor and the processor side of the interface for slot (r, s). It is proven by induction over the cycles of the slot. Recall from Sect. 4.2 that we know already the start *cycles* $t_v(r, s)$ for all ECUs. The statement of the theorem is identical for all ECU_v. Thus we drop the subscript v.

The theorem assumes that at the start of a slot the pipe is drained (e.g. by the timer interrupt that ended the previous slot) and that the simulation relation holds between the first hardware configuration $h(r, s) = h^{t(r,s)}$ and the first ISA configuration $d(r, s) = d^{i(r,s)}$ of the slot.

Theorem 2 (Hardware Correctness for One Slot). *Assume that* $drained(h(r,s))$
and $sim(d(r,s), h(r,s))$ *holds. Then for all* $t \in \{t(r,s), \ldots, t((r,s)+1) - 1\}$, *for
all stages* k *and for all registers* R *with* $stage(R) = k$:

$$h^t.p.R = d^{s(k,t)}.p.R$$
$$m(h^t.p) = d^{s(mem1,t)}.p.m$$
$$h^t.f.sb(\neg par(h^t)) = sb(d^{s(mem1,t)})$$
$$h^t.f.rb(\neg par(h^t)) = rb(d^{s(mem1,t)})$$

The theorem is proven by induction over the cycles of the slot. Using the above theorem
we can show:

Theorem 3 (Hardware Correctness for System)

$$\forall (r,s), v : drained(h_v(r,s)) \wedge sim(d_v(r,s), h_v(r,s))$$

Theorem 3 is proven by induction over the slots (r,s) using additional assumptions
about registers not visible at the ISA level. In order to argue about the boundaries between two slots Theorem 2 and Lemma 4 must be applied on the last cycle of the
previous slot.

7.4 The Interrupted Instruction

To support precise interrupts the cause signals of internal as well as of external interrupts are sampled in the write back stage (WB). The instruction interrupted by an active
cause signal in cycle t is therefore the instruction scheduled in the writeback stage during cycle t. Thus the index $j(r,s)$ of the interrupted instruction, which resolves the
nondeterminism and makes the proof work, is:

$$j(r,s) = s(WB, t(r,s))$$

For detailed processor correctness proofs dealing with sequences of internal and external interrupts (but without devices) see [Bey05, Dal06].

8 Pervasive Correctness Proofs

Finally, we show how pervasive correctness proofs for computations with timer interrupts can be obtained from i) correctness proofs for ISA programs that cannot be
interrupted ii) hardware correctness theorems and iii) WCET analysis. As one would
expect, the arguments are reasonably simple, but the entire formalism of the last sections is needed in order to formulate them.

We consider only programs of the form[7]:

```
{P;    a : jump a;    a+4 : NOP }
```

The program does the useful work in portion P and then waits in the idle loop for the
timer interrupt. P initially has to clear and then to unmask the timer interrupt, which is
masked when P is started (see Sect. 6.2).

---

[7] Note that we have a byte addressable memory and that in an ISA with delayed branch the idle
loop has two instructions.

8.1   Computation Theory

We have to distinguish carefully between the transition function $\delta_D(d, dti, fdin)$ of the interruptible ISA computation and the transition function $\delta_U(d)$ of the non interruptible ISA computation, which we define as follows:

$$\delta_U(d) = \delta_D(d, 0, *)$$

Observe that this definition permits the non interruptible computation to clear the timer interrupt bit by software. Non interruptible computations starting from configuration d are obtained by iterated application of δ_U:

$$\delta_U^i(d) = \begin{cases} d & i = 0 \\ \delta_U(\delta_U^{i-1}(d)) & \text{otherwise} \end{cases}$$

For the ISA computation

$$d(r, s) = d^{i(r,s)}, d^{i(r,s)+1}, \ldots, d^{j(r,s)} = e(r, s)$$

that has been constructed in Theorem 2 we get:

Lemma 5. *For all instructions in a given slot, i.e.* $t \in [0 : (j(r, s) - i(r, s))]$:

$$d^{i(r,s)+t} = \delta_U^t(d(r, s))$$

This lemma holds due to the definition of $j(r, s)$ and the fact that the timer is masked initially such that the instructions of the interruptible computation are not interrupted.

We define the ISA run time $T_U(d, a)$, i.e. the time until the idle loop is reached, simply as the smallest i such that δ_U^i fetches an instruction from address a:

$$T_U(d, a) = \min\{i \mid \delta_U^i(d).p.dpc = a\}$$

Furthermore we define the result of the non interruptible ISA computation as:

$$res_U(d, a) = \delta_U^{T_U(d,a)}(d)$$

Correctness proofs for non interruptible computations can be obtained by classical program correctness proofs. They usually have the form $d \in E \to res_U(d, a) \in Q$ or, written as a Hoare triple $\{E\}P\{Q\}$.

We assume that the definition of Q does not involve the PC and the delayed PC. Because the idle loop only changes the PC and the delayed PC of the ISA computation we can infer on the ISA level that property Q continues to hold while we execute the idle loop:

$$\forall i \geq T_U(d, a) : \delta_U^i(d) \in Q$$

8.2   Pervasive Correctness

Assume $sim(d, h)$ holds. Then the ISA configuration d can be decoded from the hardware configuration by a function:

$$d = decode(h)$$

Clearly, in order to apply the correctness statement $\{E\}P\{Q\}$ to a local computation in slot (r, s), we have to show for the first ISA configuration in the slot:

$$d(r, s) \in E$$

In order to apply the processor correctness theorem the simulation relation must hold initially:

$$sim(d(r, s), h(r, s))$$

Now consider the last hardware configuration $g(r, s) = h^{t((r,s)+1)-1}$ of the slot. We want to conclude

Theorem 4. *The decoded configuration obeys the postcondition Q:*

$$decode(g(r, s)) \in Q$$

This only works if portion P is executed fast enough on the pipelined processor hardware.

8.3   Worst-Case Execution Time

We consider the set $H(E)$ of all hardware configurations h encoding an ISA configuration $d \in E$:

$$H(E) = \{h \mid decode(h) \in E\}$$

While the decoding is unique, the encoding is definitely not. Portions of the ISA memory can be kept in the caches in various ways.

For a hardware configuration $h = h^0$ we define the hardware run time $T_H(h, a)$ until a fetch from address a as the smallest number of cycles such that in cycle t an instruction, which has been fetched in an earlier cycle $t' < t$ from address a, is in the write back stage WB. Using scheduling functions this definition is formalized as:

$$T_H(h, a) = \min\{t \mid \exists t' : s(WB, t) = s(IF, t') \wedge h^{t'}.dpc = a\}$$

Thus for ISA configurations satisfying E we define the worst-case execution time $WCET(E, a)$ as the largest hardware runtime $T_H(h, a)$ of a hardware configuration encoding a configuration in E:

$$WCET(E, a) = \max\{T_H(h, a) \mid h \in H(E)\}$$

As pointed out earlier such estimates can be obtained from (sound!) industrial tools based on the concept of abstract interpretation [Abs06]. AbsInt's WCET analyzer does not calculate the "real" worst-case execution time $WCET(E, a)$, but an upper bound $WCET'(E, a) \geq WCET(E, a)$. Nevertheless this is sufficient for correctness since $WCET'(E, a) \leq T - off \Rightarrow WCET(E, a) \leq T - off$. Assume we have:

$$WCET(E, a) \leq T - off$$

Within slot (r, s) we look at the ISA configuration $d(r, s) = d^{i(r,s)}$ and a local computation starting in hardware configuration $h(r, s) = h^{t(r,s)}$. Considering the computation after hardware run time many cycles $T_H(h(r, s), a) < T - \textit{off}$ we can conclude that the computation is not interrupted and the instruction in the write back stage (at the end of the computation) is the first instruction being fetched from a. By the definition of the ISA run time this is exactly instruction $i(r, s) + T_U(d(r, s), a)$, thus:

$$s(WB, t(r, s) + T_H(h(r, s), a)) = i(r, s) + T_U(d(r, s), a)$$

Let $h' = h^{t(r,s)+T_H(h(r,s),a)}$ be the hardware configuration in this cycle and let $d' = d^{i(r,s)+T_U(d(r,s),a)} = res_U(d(r, s), a)$ be the ISA configuration of the instruction in the write back stage.

In this situation the pipe is almost drained. It contains nothing but instructions from the idle loop. Thus the processor correctness theorem $sim(d', h')$ holds for all components of the configuration but the PC and the delayed PC. Therefore we weaken the simulation relation sim to a relation $dsim$ by dropping the requirement that the PCs and delayed PCs should match:

$$dsim(d', h')$$

Until the end of the slot in cycle $t(r, s) + T$ and instruction $j(r, s)$, only instructions from the idle loops are executed. They do not affect the $dsim$ relation, hence:

$$dsim(e(r, s), g(r, s))$$

Since $res_U(d(r, s), a) \in Q$ and Q does not depend on the program counters we have $e(r, s) \in Q$. We derive that $decode(g(r, s))$ coincides with $e(r, s)$ except for the program counters. And again, because this does not affect the membership in Q, we get the desired Theorem 4.

References

[Abs06]   AbsInt Angewandte Informatik GmbH. Worst-Case Execution Time Analyzers. http://www.absint.com/, December 2006.

[BBG⁺05]   S. Beyer, P. Böhm, M. Gerke, M. Hillebrand, T. In der Rieden, S. Knapp, D. Leinenbach, and W.J. Paul. Towards the formal verification of lower system layers in automotive systems. In *23nd IEEE International Conference on Computer Design: VLSI in Computers and Processors (ICCD 2005), 2–5 October 2005, San Jose, CA, USA, Proceedings*, pages 317–324. IEEE, 2005.

[Bey05]   Sven Beyer. *Putting It All Together: Formal Verification of the VAMP*. PhD thesis, Saarland University, Computer Science Department, March 2005.

[BJK⁺03]   Sven Beyer, Christian Jacobi, Daniel Kröning, Dirk Leinenbach, and Wolfgang Paul. Instantiating uninterpreted functional units and memory system: Functional verification of the VAMP. In D. Geist and E. Tronci, editors, *Proc. of the 12th Advanced Research Working Conference on Correct Hardware Design and Verification Methods (CHARME)*, volume 2860 of *LNCS*, pages 51–65. Springer, 2003.

[BP06]   Geoffrey M. Brown and Lee Pike. Easy parameterized verification of biphase mark and 8N1 protocols. In *Proceedings of the 12th International Conference on Tools and the Construction of Algorithms (TACAS'06)*, volume 3920 of *LNCS*, pages 58–72. Springer, 2006.

[Dal06]   Iakov Dalinger. *Formal Verification of a Processor with Memory Management Units*. PhD thesis, Saarland University, Computer Science Department, July 2006.

[DHP05]   Iakov Dalinger, Mark Hillebrand, and Wolfgang Paul. On the verification of memory management mechanisms. In D. Borrione and W. Paul, editors, *Proceedings of the 13th Advanced Research Working Conference on Correct Hardware Design and Verification Methods (CHARME 2005)*, volume 3725 of *LNCS*, pages 301–316. Springer, 2005.

[Fle06]   FlexRay Consortium. http://www.flexray.com, December 2006.

[HIP05]   Mark Hillebrand, Thomas In der Rieden, and Wolfgang Paul. Dealing with I/O devices in the context of pervasive system verification. In *ICCD '05*, pages 309–316. IEEE Computer Society, 2005.

[HP96]   John L. Hennessy and David A. Patterson. *Computer Architecture: A Quantitative Approach*. Morgan Kaufmann, San Mateo, CA, second edition, 1996.

[MP00]   Silvia M. Müller and Wolfgang J. Paul. *Computer Architecture: Complexity and Correctness*. Springer, 2000.

[OSE06]   OSEK/VDX. http://www.osek-vdx.org, December 2006.

[Pau05]   Wolfgang Paul. Lecture Notes from the lecture Computer Architecture 2: Automotive Systems. http://www-wjp.cs.uni-sb.de/lehre/vorlesung/rechnerarchitektur2/ws0506/temp/060302_CA2_AUTO.pdf, 2005.

[Sch06]   Julien Schmaltz. A formal model of lower system layer. In Aarti Gupta and Panagiotis Manolios, editors, *Formal Methods in Computer-Aided Design, 6th International Conference, FMCAD 2006, San Jose, CA, USA, November 12–16, 2006, Proceedings*. IEEE Computer Society, 2006. To appear.

[SH98]   Jun Sawada and Warren A. Hunt. Processor verification with precise exceptions and speculative execution. In Alan J. Hu and Moshe Y. Vardi, editors, *CAV '98*, pages 135–146. Springer, 1998.

[WL88]   J. Lundelius Welch and N. Lynch. A new fault-tolerant algorithm for clock synchronization. *Information and Communication*, 77(1):1–36, April 1988.

Lazy Execution of Boolean Queries

Dieter Maurer

Eichendorffstr. 23, D-66385 St. Ingbert
dieter@handshake.de

Abstract. Lazy evaluation, the technique to build special data structures allowing to perform an evaluation at a later time, has many uses in functional programming languages [1,2,3]. This article shows a use in imperative (object oriented) languages: the lazy execution of boolean queries. Applying lazy index lookup can result in drastic gains in search speed and reduce the amount of required main memory.

1 Introduction

Functional programming languages and especially lazy evaluation have been a focal point of Reinhard's research for some time. The lazy evaluation technique builds special data structures, so called closures, allowing to postpone evaluations until the result is known to be required. Hughes [1] demonstrates how this feature can be used to increase modularity. Especially, he applies it to searching using quadtrees. More recently, Nordin&al [3] exploited lazyness to modularize a set of algorithms for contraint satisfaction problems.

Obviously, delaying work may be advantageous in non-functional and especially imperative contexts, too. It may prevent doing work which ultimately would turn out to be irrelevant for the final task or to collect additional information allowing to perform the work more efficiently.

The next section introduces boolean queries. Such queries are often used by search engines. The result set of such queries is usually large but in almost all cases, only a few hits will be examined. It therefore seems promising to execute the search lazily or incementally: rather than determining the complete result set as a whole, determine only a few hits at a time and continue the search when the user calls for more hits. Even when the complete final result is called for, large parts of intermediate results may be irrelevant. This holds especially for specific "and" queries. Lazy execution can partly avoid the computation of those parts.

The following section demonstrates how lazy query execution can be implemented in an object oriented language. Even when the complete result set must be determined, the technique can often reduce search costs both in terms of time and main memory needs as the construction of irrelevant intermediate results is avoided. Some experimental results are shown in section 4.

2 Boolean Queries

Queries supported by most search engines usually consist of a set of search terms with an indication whether the documents in the result set may, must or must not

T. Reps, M. Sagiv, and J. Bauer (Eds.): Wilhelm Festschrift, LNCS 4444, pp. 82–96, 2007.

contain a given term. Such queries form a subset of the boolean queries. Boolean queries are constructed from elementary queries with the boolean operators $\wedge$ ("and"), $\vee$ ("or") and $\neg$ ("not").

Search engine search results are often large, so large that usually only a tiny part of the result set is examined. Therefore, it seems promising to execute the search lazily or incrementally.

We first define the boolean queries formally and exhibit the standard interpretation as a document set (the search result).

2.1 Abstract Syntax

Boolean queries are constructed from elementary queries with the boolean operators $\wedge$ ("and"), $\vee$ ("or") and $\neg$ ("not"). We are not interested in the elementary queries and treat them as terminals. Boolean queries are defined by the abstract syntax in table 2.1.

Table 1. Abstract Syntax of Boolean Queries

Terminals

$\qquad e \in E \quad$ Elementary query

Nonterminals

$\qquad b \in B \quad$ Boolean query

Structure

$\qquad b = e$
$\qquad | \;\; \wedge(b_1, ..., b_n) \quad$ "and" query
$\qquad | \;\; \vee(b_1, ..., b_n) \quad$ "or" query
$\qquad | \;\; \neg(b) \quad$ "not" query

2.2 Standard Interpretation

Boolean queries are usually interpreted over a finite domain D of documents as a subset of D, the set of query *hits*. $\wedge$, $\vee$ and $\neg$ are interpreted as set intersection, union and complement of D subsets, respectively. The evaluation of an elementary query e over D yields the set of documents in D matching e.

Note that the evaluation result is obtained as a whole and that the evaluation of an "and" query may involve much larger intermediate sets than the final result. If set operations are performed in main memory this may lead to high memory consumption.

Elementary queries are usually implemented by means of indexes. In realistic applications indexes are large and maintained on secondary storage. A naive implementation could touch large index parts not relevant for the final result with the potential to significantly increase search time due to larger amounts of slow IO operations.

3 Lazy Execution

Our lazy execution of boolean queries will not determine the result set as a whole but instead will incrementally determine the elements in the result set one at a time. The size of any intermediate result is linear in the size of the final result and the complexity of the query (as measured by the sum of the complexities of the elementary queries). It will try to optimize access to the results of elementary subqueries.

Of course, most optimization potential comes from the "and" queries as they have the potential to drasticly reduce the result set.

We will use the name *hit* for an element in the result set of a (given) query. In order to get a concise notion for terms like "the first hit" and the "next hit", we impose a total order $\leq$ on D. In order to later avoid boundary cases, we extend D to a domain $\bar{D}$ by adding new minimal and maximal elements BOT and TOP, respectively. As the order does not need to have any semantic meaning, such an order always exists. In fact, real implementations do not handle documents (and sets thereof) directly but instead persistent document ids, mapped to the real documents as late as possible. These document ids usually have a natural complete order and induce an adequate order on the document set.[1]

Relevance ranking becomes vital when the result sets get large. In a ranked result list, the first hits are the most relevant ones. This drasticly increases the probability that only the first few hits need to be examined and therefore the profits to determine the result incrementally. If relevancy is based on query independent document properties (only), then it can be used to define the order mentioned above.[2] In this case, the lazy execution will incrementally generate the hits ordered by relevancy. The link connectivity of a document is an example for a query independent relevance criteria. If the relevance criteria depends on the query, then the approach described in this article cannot directly generate hits in relevance order.

Dealing not with the complete result set as a whole but instead with one hit at a time is widely used in query processing. The standard device for such incremental hit processing is called a *cursor*. Its current state represents one hit. It has a method to advance to the next hit (if any). In some sense the imperative cursor corresponds to the closure notion in the functional world in that it encapsulates the state necessary to continue execution at a later time. We, too, use a form of cursor, a so called HitCursor. Our cursors, however, provide more versatile advancing methods to efficiently skip hits deemed irrelevant based on environmental knowledge.

HitCursor is an abstract object class. The lazy interpretation of boolean queries maps each query to a HitCursor instance. It takes over the role of the "subset of D" in the standard interpretation. We use subclasses to represent the various query types, among others AndCursor, OrCursor and NotCursor to represent the result of an "and", "or" and "not" query, respectively. Their constructors are used as the lazy interpretation of the $\wedge$, $\vee$ and $\neg$ query operators.

---

[1] The document order induced by the id order often has no semantic meaning. If, however, ids are assigned consecutively, then this order implies age.

[2] Relevancy will define only a preorder: there may be different documents with the same rank. This can easily by fixed by combining the relevance order with an artificial total order in a lexicographic way.

Each `HitCursor` has an associated set it traverses. We call the elements in this set the *hits* of the cursor. We will define `AndCursor`, `OrCursor` and `NotCursor` in such a way that their associated sets are the intersection, union and difference of the associated sets of their children, respectively.

`HitCursor` instances c have attributes `value` $\in \bar{D}$, the current cursor value, and `classification`, an indication whether the current value is a hit, and methods

- `advanceTo(to` $\in D$`) -> Classification`
- `advanceFrom(from` $\in \bar{D}$`, limit` $\in \bar{D}$`) -> Classification`
- `asSet() -> Subset of` D

Derived `HitCursor` classes may of course have additional attributes (and methods). In particular, most of the classes described in this article will have the attribute `subcursors`. Its value is a list of hit cursors which represents the operand[s] for the given hit cursor.

`Classification` has the following values

HIT: `c.value` is in the associated set
NOHIT: `c.value` is not in the associated set
CANDIDATE: `c.value` may or may not be in the associated set
END: the cursor is exhausted, `c.value` is TOP

A newly constructed `HitCursor` c has `c.value` = BOT and `c.classification` = NOHIT.

Informally, `advanceTo(to)` moves forward to `to` or, if that is not a hit, further to the next potential hit (called a *candidate*), provided a candidate can be efficiently determined.

Informally, `advanceFrom(from, limit)` moves forward to the smallest hit between `from` and `limit` (both exclusive) or, if there is no hit in this range, to the next candidate beyond `limit`.[3]

The parameters `to` and `from`/`limit`, respectively, pass environmental knowledge down into the methods. `to` and `from` indicate that any hit below the given value is irrelevant and can be skipped/needs not be computed. `limit` is used to tell the method that there is no need to put in effort at the moment to determine a hit above `limit`.

The distinction between NOHIT and CANDIDATE is an optimization. It is used primarily by `advanceTo`. `advanceTo(to)` will return CANDIDATE when `to` is not a hit but the next potential hit (the next candidate) could be efficiently determined. The calling environment can use this candidate to optimize the overall search for the next hit. If, on the other hand, the next potential hit can not be efficiently determined, then NOHIT will be returned. In this case, the calling environment must continue its search without additional information from this hit cursor.

---

[3] It can use `limit`, but if it can efficiently determine a value c > `limit` with no hit between `limit` (inclusive) and c (exclusive), then c is a better (more efficient) choice.

A `HitCursor` is called *initial* when its value is BOT and its (potentially 0) subcursors are initial. `asSet` called on an initial `HitCursor` returns its associated set.

There is a notion of *consistency* which plays an essential role for the algorithm correctness proof. For a cursor to be consistent, its `value` and `classification` must relate as given above in the classification values definition and all subcursors must be consistent. We call this *base consistency*. Moreover, consistency relates the value of a `HitCursor` to that of its subcursors. We call this *child consistency*. The various subclasses define child consistency differently. A cursor is consistent if it is both base and child consistent. An initial cursor is consistent. The advancing methods must maintain consistency.

As the names suggest, a `HitCursor` c behaves like a cursor over its associated set. `c.value` is the current cursor value which may or may not be in the set depending on `c.classification`. `advanceTo` and `advanceFrom` move the cursor forward over the set. It is *illegal* to call `advanceTo` or `advanceFrom` on an inconsistent cursor or with a first parameter d smaller than the cursor's value. A call to `advanceFrom` is also illegal when `limit` is not larger than `from`. A concrete implementation may raise an exception for an illegal call or may show undefined behaviour.

A legal call of `c.advanceTo(to)` must satisfy the following restrictions.

To0 c remains consistent.
To1 If `to` is a hit, then the call will return HIT and will set `c.value` to `to`.
To2 If the call returns CANDIDATE, then the call has set `c.value` to a value $d \in D$ larger than `to` and there are no hits between `to` (inclusive) and d (exclusive). `c.value` is in this case the next possible hit candidate.
To3 If the call returns NOHIT, then the call has set `c.value` to `to`. As a consequence of To1 `to` is not a hit.
To4 If the call returns END, then there are no hits at or above `to`. `c.value` is set to TOP.

A legal call of `c.advanceFrom(from, limit)` must satisfy the following1 Vreak restrictions.

Fr0 c remains consistent.
Fr1 If there is a hit between `from` (exclusive) and `limit` (exclusive), then the call must return HIT and set `c.value` to the smallest such hit.
Fr2 If the call returns CANDIDATE, then the call has set `c.value` to a value $d \in D$ not smaller than `limit` and there are no hits between `from` and d (both exclusive). `c.value` is in this case the next possible hit candidate.
Fr3 The call does not return NOHIT.
Fr4 If the call returns END, then there are no hits above `from`. `c.value` is set to TOP.

In all these cases, `c.classification` is set to the return value of `advanceTo` or `advanceFrom`.

Below is the definition of the `asSet` method (in the programming language Python [4]). Fr1 ensures that this method called on an initial `HitCursor` indeed returns its associated set. All `advanceFrom` calls are obviously legal.

asSet Definition

```
def asSet(self):
  s = set()
  while self.advanceFrom(self.value, TOP) == HIT:
    s.add(self.value)
  return s
```

3.1   AndCursor

An `AndCursor` implements the lazy execution of a (non-empty) "and" query
It derives from `HitCursor` and adds to it an additional attribute `subcursors`
containing the (non-empty) list of `HitCursors` which implement the subqueries
that are "and"ed together.

An `AndCursor` is *child consistent*, when no subcursor value is larger than its
value.

AndCursor. advanceTo Definition

```
def advanceTo(self, to):
  # Note: 'self.subcursors' is not empty
  for subcursor in self.subcursors:
    cl = subcursor.advanceTo(to)
    if cl != HIT: break
  self.value = subcursor.value
  self.classification = cl
  return cl
```

AndCursor. advanceFrom Definition

```
def advanceFrom(self, from_, limit):
  self.value = from_
  # Note: 'self.subcursors' is not empty
  subcursor0 = self.subcursors[0]
  while True:
    # chose a candidate from the first subcursor
    cl = subcursor0.advanceFrom(self.value, limit)
    self.value = subcursor0.value
    self.classification = cl
    # if the first subcursor does not have a hit, there is None
    if cl != HIT: return cl
    # verify the candidate with all subcursors
    verified = False
    while not verified:
      verified = True
      for subcursor in self.subcursors:
        cl = subcursor.advanceTo(self.value)
```

```
          self.value = subcursor.value
          self.classification = cl
          if cl == HIT: continue
          elif cl == END: return END
          # the verification failed, the candidate is not a hit
          # we return, in case we have advanced enough
          if self.value >= limit: return CANDIDATE
          # we leave the verification loop,
          # when we did not get a new candidate
          if cl == NOHIT: break
          # otherwise, we continue verification with the new candidate
          verified = False
      # get a new candidate from the first subquery when
      # we have no current candidate
      if cl == NOHIT: break
  if verified: return HIT
```

As we move the cursor value when we move one of its subcursor values, any legal cursor method call of a cursor maintains child consistency. A direct verification also shows that a legal cursor method call on a cursor results in only legal subcursor method calls.

Let c be a consistent `AndCursor` with subcursors $c_1 \ldots c_n$ ($n >= 1$), $S_1 \ldots S_n$ their associated sets. We want to compute the set associated with c. With $S := \bigcap_{i=1}^{n} S_i$ a legal call to `advanceFrom(from, limit)` fulfills:

And-Fr1 If there is $d \in S$ between `from` (exclusive) and `limit` (exclusive), then the call returns HIT and sets c.value to the smallest such d.

And-Fr2 If the call returns CANDIDATE, then the call sets c.value to a value $d \in D$ not smaller than `limit` and there are no $d' \in S$ between `from` and d (both exclusive).

And-Fr3 The call does not return NOHIT.

And-Fr4 If the call returns END, then there are no $d \in S$ above `from`. c.value is set to TOP.

As a consequence, c.asSet() returns S for an initial c and the associated set of an `AndCursor` is indeed the intersection of the associated sets of its subcursors. Moreover, `advanceFrom` fulfills Fr0 to Fr4 and `advanceTo` fulfills To0 to To4.

As a simple example, lets take a look at the (initial) `AndCursor` c with subcursors c1 and c2 and associated sets $\{1, 5, 9, 10\}$ and $\{6, 8, 9, 15\}$, respectively. The first hit is determined by c.advanceFrom(BOT, TOP). This call will start with a call c1.advanceFrom(BOT, TOP) and get HIT with a value of 1. This value is then verified with c2 by calling c2.advanceTo(1). The call will return CANDIDATE with a value of 6. 6 is our new candidate which will be checked with c1.advanceTo(6), skipping 5. This returns CANDIDATE with a value of 9. c1.advanceTo(9) and c2.advanceTo(9) both return HIT: we have found 9 as the first hit for c. The next hit could then be computed by c.advanceFrom(9, TOP).

3.2 OrCursor

An OrCursor implements the lazy execution of an "or" query. It derives from
HitCursor and adds to it two additional attributes, a heap candidates of subcursors ordered by their value and a list noncandidates of subcursors. Initially,
candidates is empty and noncandidates is the list of HitCursors which implement the subqueries that are "or"ed together. As the names suggest, candidates
contains the subcursors for which candidates with respect to the cursor's current value are known while noncadidates contains the remaining subcursors.
candidates is a heap to efficiently determine the smallest candidate.

An OrCursor c is child consistent if for all subcursors c' in c.noncandidates
we have c'.value $<=$ c.value and for all subcursors c' in c.candidates we have
c'.value $>=$ c.value and there is no $d \in D_{c'}$ with c.value $< d <$ c'.value.

OrCursor. advanceTo Definition

```
def advanceTo(self, to):
  heap = self.candidates
  nohits = []
  # advance the heap until we either find a hit
  # or all values are > to
  cl = NOHIT
  while heap:
    subcursor = heap[0]
    if subcursor.value > to: break
    if subcursor.value == to and subcursor.classification == HIT:
      cl = HIT; break
    clt = subcursor.advanceTo(to)
    if clt in (HIT, CANDIDATE):
      heapreplace(heap, subcursor) # replace top by subcursor
      if clt == HIT: cl = HIT; break
    else:
      heappop(heap) # remove top element
      if clt == NOHIT: nohits.append(subcursor)
      # "clt == END"; thus we can forget this subcursor now
  if cl == NOHIT: # no hit found so far
    # check non-candidates
    noncandidates = self.noncandidates
    for i,subcursor in enumerate(noncandidates[:]):
      del noncandidates[i]
      cl = subcursor.advanceTo(to)
      if cl in (HIT, CANDIDATE):
        heappush(heap, subcursor)
        if cl == HIT: break
      elif cl == NOHIT: nohits.append(subcursor)
      # "cl == END": we can forget about this subcursor
  self.noncandidates.extend(nohits)
```

```
  if cl != HIT: # no hit found
    if nohits:
      # we have "nohits" and cannot provide a candidate
      self.value = to; self.classification = NOHIT
      return NOHIT
    elif heap:
      subcursor = heap[0]; cl = CANDIDATE
    else:
      # no candidates and no noncandidates -- at the end
      self.value = TOP; self.classification = END
      return END
  # we found at least a candidate
  self.value = subcursor.value
  self.classification = cl
  return cl
```

OrCursor.advanceFrom Definition

```
def advanceFrom(self, from_, limit):
  heap = self.candidates
  cl = NOHIT
  # advance the heap until its first (lowest) value is > "from_"
  # and is a hit
  while heap:
    subcursor = heap[0]
    if subcursor.value > from_:
      if cl == NOHIT and subcursor.value >= limit:
        cl = CANDIDATE; break
      # either: cl == HIT (i.e. "limit" already found to be a hit)
      # or:     subcursur.value < limit
      # in both cases: subcursor.value <= limit
      # ensure, this is indeed a hit (and not only a candidate)
      clt = subcursor.classification
      if clt != HIT:
        clt = subcursor.advanceTo(subcursor.value)
        if clt == NOHIT:
          # it is not a hit of this subcursor
          # we may need to get rid of it
          if subcursor.value == limit:
            # "limit" is a hit (see above)
            clt = HIT
          else:
            # note: subcursor.value < limit
            clt = subcursor.advanceFrom(subcursor.value, limit)
    else: clt = subcursor.advanceFrom(from_, limit)
    if clt in (HIT, CANDIDATE):
```

```
   heapreplace(heap, subcursor)
   if clt == HIT:
     # any hit is better than a previous one
     limit = subcursor.value; cl = HIT
  else: heappop(heap) # END
 # process noncandidates
 for subcursor in self.noncandidates:
   clt = subcursor.advanceFrom(from_, limit)
   if clt in (HIT, CANDIDATE):
     heappush(heap, subcursor)
     if clt == HIT:
       # any hit is better than the previous one
       limit = subcursor.value; cl = HIT
     elif cl == NOHIT: cl = CANDIDATE
   # else: END -- we can forget the exhausted cursor
 self.noncandidates = []
 if cl == NOHIT:
   # we are at the end
   self.value = TOP; self.classification = END
   return END
 self.value = heap[0]
 self.classification = cl
 return cl
```

A direct verification shows that a legal call to advanceTo and advanceFrom maintains child consistency and causes only legal calls for subcursors.

Let c be a consistent OrCursor with subcursors $c_1, \ldots c_n$, S_i the associated set of c_i $(i = 1 \ldots n)$ and $S := \bigcup_{i=1}^{n} S_i$, then a legal call c.advanceFrom(from, limit) satisfies:

Or-Fr1 If there is $d \in S$ between from (exclusive) and limit (exclusive), then the call returns HIT and sets c.value to the smallest such d.

Or-Fr2 If the call returns CANDIDATE, then the call sets c.value to a value $d \in D$ not smaller than limit and there are no $d' \in S$ between from and d (both exclusive).

Or-Fr3 The call does not return NOHIT.

Or-Fr4 If the call returns END, then there are no $d \in S$ above from. c.value is set to TOP.

As a consequence, S is the set associated with c and advanceFrom satisfies Fr0 to Fr4. A direct verification shows that advanceTo satisfies To0 to To4.

As a simple example, lets take a look at the (initial) OrCursor c with subcursors c1 and c2 and associated sets $\{1, 5, 9, 10\}$ and $\{6, 8, 9, 15\}$, respectively. After the construction of c, the heap candidates is empty and noncandidates contains [c1, c2]. The call c.advanceFrom(BOT, TOP) to compute the first hit finds an empty heap and calls c1.advanceFrom(BOT, TOP). This returns HIT with value 1. This hit is used as new limit. There is no need for another hit cursor to invest effort in computing hits above 1. `c1` is put onto the heap. `c2.advanceFrom(BOT, 1)` is called and returns `CANDIDATE` with value 6. `c2` is put onto the heap. We now have two candidates and no noncandidates and the heap top gives us the first hit: 1. `c.advanceFrom(1, TOP)` is called to determine the next hit. It finds `c1` on the heap top with a too small value. Therefore, it calls `c1.advanceFrom(1, TOP)`, gets `HIT` with value 5 and replaces the heap top. The heap top is now larger than `from`, it is a hit and we have no noncandidates. Thus, 5 is the next hit.

3.3   NotCursor

A `NotCursor` implements the lazy execution of a "not" query. In order to define it, we need another class: a `DocumentEnumerator`.

A `DocumentEnumerator` for D has a single method `next` returning for $d \in \bar{D}$ the next smallest element in D or `TOP` (if no next smallest element exists). `E` denotes a `DocumentEnumerator` for D.

A `NotCursor` derives from `HitCursor` and adds the additional attribute `subcursor`. Initially, `subcursor` is set to the `HitCursor` describing the subquery of which we want to determine the "not".

A `NotCursor` is child consistent when its subcursor value is not smaller than its value and there are no subcursor hits between the cursor's and the subcursor's value (both exclusive).

NotCursor.advanceTo Definition

```
def advanceTo(self, to):
  self.value = to
  subcursor = self.subcursor
  if to < subquery.value: cl = HIT
  else:
    cl = subcursor.advanceTo(to)
    cl = cl == HIT and NOHIT or HIT
  self.classification = cl
  return cl
```

NotCursor.advanceFrom Definition

```
def advanceFrom(self, from_, limit):
  subcursor = self.subcursor
  self.value = from_; cl = CANDIDATE
  while self.value < limit:
    self.value = E.next(self.value)
    if self.value == TOP: cl = END; break
    if self.value < subcursor.value: cl = HIT; break
    cl = subcursor.advanceTo(self.value)
    if cl != HIT: cl = HIT; break
    cl = CANDIDATE
  self.classification = cl
  return cl
```

Let c be a consistent `NotCursor` with subcursor c', S' the set associated with c' and $S := D - S'$, then a legal call c.`advanceFrom(from, limit)` satisfied:

Not-Fr1 If there is $d \in S$ between `from` (exclusive) and `limit` (exclusive), then the call returns `HIT` and sets c.`value` to the smallest such d.

Not-Fr2 If the call returns `CANDIDATE`, then the call sets c.`value` to a value $d \in D$ not smaller than `limit` and there are no $d' \in S$ between `from` and d (both exclusive).

Not-Fr3 The call does not return `NOHIT`.

Not-Fr4 If the call returns `END`, then there are no $d \in S$ above `from`. c.`value` is set to `TOP`.

As a consequence, S is the set associated with c and ows that `advanceTo` satisfies To0 to To4.

As a simple example, assume that the document enumerator enumerates documents $1, 2, 3 \ldots$ and that the (initial) NotCursor c contains a subcursor c1 with associated set $\{1, 5, 9, 10\}$. The call c.`advanceFrom(BOT, TOP)` to determine the first hit will get 1 from the document enumerator. It will check with c1.`advanceTo(1)` and get a `HIT`. Therefore, 1 is not a hit of the NotCursor and the document enumerator is asked for the next value: 2. This time, c1.`advanceTo(2)` returns `CANDIDATE` with its value set to 5. This implies that there are not c1 hits between 2 (inclusive) and 5 (exclusive). c.`advanceFrom(BOT, TOP)` returns `HIT` with its value set to 2. When the next hit is determined by c.`advanceFrom(2, TOP)`, the enumerator will return 3 and as this is smaller than c1.`value`, the call will return `HIT` with `value` set to 3.

3.4   IndexLookupCursor

Search engines perform queries over very large document sets. Indexes are used to speed up queries. The most elementary indexes map a search term to the set of documents that are matched by this term. More complex indexes are often composed of one or more elementary indexes.

As documents can usually be modified and such a modification may change the search terms matching the document, the set implementation used for elementary indexes must efficiently support dynamic insertion and removal of documents. Some variant of B+ trees are an often used implementation for such sets. The leaf nodes of such trees contain a non-empty (usually) ordered set of keys. The keys of all leaf nodes together form the represented set. The inner nodes contain $c_1, k_1, c_2, k_2, \ldots, c_n$ where the c_i are the child nodes and $k_1 < k_2 < \ldots k_{n-1}$ are keys. With $k_0 := BOT$ and $k_n := TOP$, all keys k in c_i satisfy $k_{i-1} <= k < k_i$. A comparison with the k_i can thus determine in which child a given key k might be found. If these trees are balanced, then lookup, insertion and removal of a key all have logarithmic time complexity.

It is easy to define a `HitCursor` for such a tree. We call it an `IndexLookup-Cursor`. It derives from `HitCursor` and adds the attribute `tree` holding the tree iterated over. Its `advanceTo(to)` informally locates the leaf l of `tree` that may contain `to` together with the key k separating this leaf from the next leaf. If l

indeed contains `to`, then we found a hit. If l contains a key larger than `to`, then the smallest of these keys is a candidate. Otherwise, k is a candidate, unless it is `TOP` in which case the cursor is exhausted. Similarly, the implementation of `advanceFrom(from, limit)` is informally given by: locate the leaf that may contain `from` and the leaf following it (if any). Combine the keys from these leaves. If there are no keys above `from` in this set, the cursor is exhausted. Otherwise, the smallest such key is either a hit or a candidate depending of whether it is smaller than `limit` or not, respectively. The associated set obviously is the set represented by `tree`.

This implementation uses constant space but requires logarithimic time per `advanceTo` and `advanceFrom` call. We may use the fact that the overall algorithm only performs legal `advanceTo` and `advanceFrom` calls to speed up typical calls (e.g. by caching the path from the tree root to the most recently accessed leaf) but the worst case will remain unchanged.

4   Experimental Results

I implemented a (slightly optimized) variant of the above algorithm as `IncrementalSearch2` [5]. This section describes two series of measurements demonstrating the performance of `IncrementalSearch2`.

All measurements were performed with empty caches to analyse especially the IO reduction, which heavily dominates the search time. When all objects are already cached, the searches only take a few milliseconds.[4] To be fair, the `asSet` method is measured for the lazy execution. This means that the lazy and non-lazy execution both determine the same result. The lazyness gain only comes from the more efficient handling of intermediate results.

The first series measures subpath queries. Sometimes documents may have an associated hierachical classification, e.g. their location in a hierarchical file system or their location in a hierarchical classification structure. We call such a hierarchical classification a path. A path query determines for a given query path the documents the path of which contains the query path as subpath. Usually, the query specifies where the query path can occur as a subpath, e.g. at the start, at the end, at a fixed level or anywhere.

Path queries are supported by specialized path indexes. If a document has path $s_1 \ldots s_n$, then the path index indexes the document under all pairs s_i, i for $1 \leq i \leq n$. In order to determine e.g. the documents the path of which starts with $s_1 \ldots s_n$, it can use an "and" query over the documents indexed under s_i, i for $1 \leq i \leq n$. We study this type of queries. We observe that the number of "and" operands is equal to the path length. Table 4 shows the results for a series of path queries with increasing path length against a dataset of about 270.000 documents.

Path searches represent one of the query types that can best be optimized by lazy query execution. Pure "or" queries on the other hand cannot be optimized and are a bit slower than with eager search. Table 4 shows measurements for the

---

[4] Whether or not we execute the query lazily or eagerly.

Table 2. Search/Load Time and Number of Objects Loaded for Path Queries depending on Path Length ("len")

len	# hits	search time (ms)			# loads			load time (ms)		
		eager	lazy	%	eager	lazy	%	eager	lazy	%
1	262233	10089	10075	99	3153	3153	100	8176	8180	100
2	32909	11930	11695	98	3550	3555	100	9239	9194	100
3	10964	11874	11431	96	3680	3580	97	9537	9286	97
4	935	12125	4559	37	3770	1394	37	9736	3623	37
5	9	12097	342	3	3773	78	2	9778	210	2
6	3	12582	357	3	3912	79	2	10135	207	2
7	1	13250	341	3	4128	80	2	10692	210	2

execution of queries of the form $\mathrm{Ge}(\mathtt{created}, 2004 - 01 - 01) \wedge \mathrm{Eq}(\mathtt{forum}, \mathtt{fid}) \wedge$ $\mathrm{Eq}(\mathtt{reply}, '')$. They locate not too old threads in the forum $\mathtt{fid}$. The Ge ("GreaterOrEqual") subquery is in fact a large or with about 600 elementary subqueries. The total number of documents is about 35.000.

Table 3. Search/Load time and Number of Objects Loaded for specific queries with large "or" component

# hits	search time (ms)			# loads			load time (ms)		
	eager	lazy	%	eager	lazy	%	eager	lazy	%
1851	2630	2156	82	828	669	81	2210	1801	81
1570	2557	2076	81	806	643	80	2154	1741	81
1475	2585	2089	81	822	648	79	2188	1748	80
365	2393	1740	72	755	542	72	2012	1458	72
246	2353	1637	70	742	493	66	1987	1357	68
174	2792	1620	58	738	503	68	2419	1356	56
13	2310	1584	69	732	493	67	1947	1327	68
10	2510	1598	63	732	496	68	2151	1335	62

5 Conclusion

We have presented an algorithm for the execution of boolean queries. The algorithm was motivated by the lazy evaluation of funtional programming languages. Indexes as well as subqueries are interpreted as cursor like data structures accessing the indexes in a lazy fashion. Main memory consumption is linear in the number of final hits and query complexity (as measured by the number of elementary indexes involved). Lazy index access can often drasticly reduce the number of loaded objects and thereby query time as IO dominates the complete search process. The gain is especially high for specific "and" queries (up to two orders) but slightly negative for pure "or" queries. Typical quite specific queries involving a large "or" query can still expect gains in the order of 20 to 40 percent.

References

1. John Hughes: Why Functional Programming Matters. Internal report, Programming Methodology Group, Chalmers Institute of Technology, Gothenburg, Sweden, 1985
2. R. Bird and P.Wadler: Introduction to Functional Programming. Prentice Hall, 1988
3. Thomas Nordin and Andrew Tolmach: Modular Lazy Search for Constraint Satisfaction Problems. Pacific Software Research Center, Oregon Graduate Institute & Portland State University, 1999
4. Guido van Rossum: Programming Language Python. http://www.python.org
5. Dieter Maurer: IncrementalSearch2.
   http://www.dieter.handshake.de/pyprojects/zope#IncrementalSearch2

Cryptographic Protocol Verification Using Tractable Classes of Horn Clauses

Helmut Seidl and Kumar Neeraj Verma

Institut für Informatik, TU München, Germany
{seidl,verma}@in.tum.de

Abstract. We consider secrecy problems for cryptographic protocols modeled using Horn clauses and present general classes of Horn clauses which can be efficiently decided. Besides simplifying the methods for the class of flat and one-variable clauses introduced for modeling of protocols with single blind copying [7,25], we also generalize this class by considering k-variable clauses instead of one-variable clauses with suitable restrictions similar to those for the class $\mathcal{S}^+$. This class allows to conveniently model protocols with joint blind copying. We show that for a fixed k, our new class can be decided in DEXPTIME, as in the case of one variable.

1 Introduction

Cryptographic protocols are today widely deployed for securing communication in various applications notably electronic commerce. These protocols are rules for exchanging messages, and rely on certain cryptographic algorithms like encryption and decryption of messages using keys. Experience has shown that even very simple protocols can have subtle flaws which are hard to detect by manual analysis. The classic example is that of the Needham-Schroeder public key protocol [19], which was considered to be correct until a bug was found 15 years after its publication [17]. Such experiences have recently led to considerable work on techniques for automatic verification of cryptographic protocols.

An important point in the example cited above is that the attack does not consist in breaking any underlying cryptographic algorithm like encryption or decryption. These algorithms are assumed to be perfect, and the attack only involves simple techniques like replaying intercepted messages, encrypting and decrypting messages with known keys, etc. Such considerations have led to the use of the so-called Dolev-Yao model [10] which essentially consists in treating cryptographic algorithms as black boxes, and assuming agents to be communicating over a completely hostile network, in the sense that any message passing through it can be intercepted or deleted by an all-powerful adversary. Further, new messages known to the adversary could be sent to agents, for example with the aim of impersonating as another honest agent. These assumptions allow us to treat messages as terms and allow us to design symbolic techniques, e.g. those based on automata and logic, for analyzing these protocols.

The complexity of verifying such protocols is due to several factors, like potentially infinite number of sessions of the same protocol between different agents, possibly in

T. Reps, M. Sagiv, and J. Bauer (Eds.): Wilhelm Festschrift, LNCS 4444, pp. 97–119, 2007.

parallel with complex interactions between them, possibly infinite number of agents, infinite possibilities for messages etc. Several kinds of restrictions are considered in order to have efficient algorithms for the verification problem. For example if the number of sessions is bounded, then checking for the presence of an attack is NP-complete [24]. This may be helpful for detecting some simple attacks during the design phase, considering that most known attacks involve very small number of sessions. However we are often interested in *certifying* protocols, i.e. guaranteeing that there are no attacks involving any number of sessions. This is a difficult problem, and remains undecidable even with serious restrictions [5]. This class of problem is often modeled using Horn clauses of first order logic [2,7,25,26] and related formalisms like automata and set constraints [5,16,18]. In order to obtain tractable problems, one often uses *safe* abstractions, i.e. those that detect all attacks, but can possibly introduce false attacks. Further, algorithms are also designed for specific classes of protocols which can be efficiently treated.

In this paper we present several interesting classes of Horn clauses which can be efficiently treated. We consider secrecy questions about cryptographic protocols modeled as satisfiability problems about Horn clauses. Our goal is to have as general classes of clauses as possible, which can be decided in single exponential time. We consider single exponential time to be the feasibility limit for this class of protocol verification problems, as in [25]. For our modeling, we typically use a unary predicate known that represents the set of messages that the adversary can know after arbitrary many sessions of the protocol. The secrecy question is then whether known(t) does not hold for a certain message t. In particular we adopt the approach of normalization of Horn clauses, i.e. given a set of clauses we transform it to a set of simpler clauses on which various kinds of queries, e.g. whether some ground $P(t)$ holds, can be easily evaluated (in polynomial time). The classes we deal with are interesting in the sense that they are all general classes which still allow exponential time normalization, and further, no decidable generalizations of these classes seem to be evident.

Compared to related work on verification of cryptographic protocols, note that our interest is in certifying protocols, whereas approaches dealing with a bounded number of sessions [24] only help to find some attacks involving small number of sessions. Approaches involving general classes of Horn clauses [2] seem to work well in practice, but no termination guarantees are offered for the algorithm. Most similar to our approach are works like [5,26,7] which try to find decidable classes of automata or clauses which however may not model all protocols. In these approaches, the infinitely many nonces (random numbers), generated in different protocol sessions, are typically abstracted to finitely many nonces. This is a safe abstraction. A more precise modeling may represent these nonces not as constants but as functions of the history (all previous sessions). But this leads to clauses which are difficult to treat efficiently. Another possibility is to use linear logic instead of classical logic [3]. Finally, certain decidability results have been obtained for general classes of protocols with infinitely many sessions, by putting certain tagging constraints on the protocols [4,21,22].

In the rest of the section we describe the classes dealt with in the paper. We start with the class $\mathcal{H}_1$ [20] which generalizes uniform Horn clauses [12] and further allows us to express operations on relations like Cartesian products of relations, transitive closures and permutations of components, still allowing exponential time normalization. This also shows that despite their generality, $\mathcal{H}_1$ describes only (Cartesian products of) regular tree languages. We then consider the related class of flat clauses which models various extensions of tree automata like two-wayness and alternation, permutations and duplications of components, but also equality constraints between brothers which is disallowed by $\mathcal{H}_1$. Compared to the various classes of flat clauses considered in the literature, we allow maximal generality. In particular different functional terms may contain different sets of variables. We show that this class can still be normalized in exponential time.

While these two classes have very general features, they do not easily model specific kinds of actions occurring in cryptographic protocols. In particular, we consider cryptographic protocols in which each step involves copying of at most one piece of unknown message. This class was considered in [7,9] and was modeled using flat clauses and clauses involving at most one variable. The original upper bound provided in [7,9] for this class of clauses and protocols was triply exponential. We introduced new techniques like on-the-fly decomposition of one-variable terms to show that this class can in fact be decided in single exponential time, giving us the optimal complexity for the class of protocols as well as of clauses [25]. The proof in [25] used resolution and dealt only with the satisfiability problem (in the Horn as well as non-Horn cases).

The main contribution of the present paper therefore is to simplify the algorithm for the Horn case as well as to obtain a normalized set of clauses. Furthermore, we consider protocols where, instead of just one piece of unknown message, several pieces of unknown messages can be copied in a protocol step. Multiple blind copying, however, easily leads to undecidability. We show here, though, that multiple blind copying can be dealt with given that copying is always *joint*, i.e., all copied parts always occur in every non-ground functional subexpression of the protocol. For that, we introduce a generalization of the class of flat and one-variable Horn clauses. The new class allows k-variable instead of one-variable clauses, but with some restriction, similar to those for the class $\mathcal{S}^+$ [11]. We show that our ideas for the one-variable case can be suitably generalized to give an exponential normalization procedure also for the k-variable case.

Several proofs have been ommitted in order to keep the paper readable. They can be found in a longer version available from the authors and at http://www2.in.tum de/ verma.

2   Horn Clauses and Cryptographic Protocols

A *Horn clause* is of the form $A \Leftarrow A_1 \wedge \ldots \wedge A_n$ where $n \geq 0$ and A, A_i are atoms of the form $P(t_1, \ldots, t_k)$ where P is a k-ary predicate for $k \geq 0$ and t_i are terms built up from variables and function symbols of fixed arities. A is called the *head*, and the remaining part the *body* of the clause. *Substitutions* map variables to terms. Application of a substitution σ to a term, atom, clause or substitution M is denoted $M\sigma$ and is defined as usual. Composition of substitutions is defined as usual: $M(\sigma_1 \ldots \sigma_k)$ should be read as $(\ldots((M\sigma_1)\ldots)\sigma_k$. The *least Herbrand model* H of a set S of clauses is a set of ground atoms (i.e. those without variables) inductively defined as: if σ is a ground substitution (mapping variables to ground terms), if clause $A \Leftarrow A_1 \wedge \ldots \wedge A_n \in S$

and if each $A_i\sigma \in H$ then $A\sigma \in H$. Further we are interested in considering clauses as representing generalizations of tree automata. Accordingly if $P(t_1, \ldots, t_n)$ is in the least Herbrand model of a set of clauses then we also say that the *state P accepts* the tuple $(t_1, \ldots, t_n)$. We also say that $P(t_1, \ldots, t_n)$ *holds*. Hence given a set of Horn clauses, we can talk of questions like *membership* (is a given tuple accepted at a given state), *non-emptiness* (does a given state accept at least one tuple) or *intersection-non-emptiness* (do two given states of the same arity accept at least one common tuple?). Another approach is to treat these questions as questions about satisfiability of a set of clauses. For example a term $P(t_1, \ldots, t_n)$ holds iff the set of clauses, together with the clause $\bot \Leftarrow P(t_1, \ldots, t_n)$ is *unsatisfiable*, i.e. $\bot$ is present in the least Herbrand model, where $\bot$ is a special zero-ary predicate representing a contradiction. Our approach to dealing with these questions is to convert the set of clauses into another equivalent set of simple clauses, which we call normal clauses, on which such queries can be easily evaluated (in polynomial time). Hence our emphasis in this paper is to give normalization algorithms for the clause sets that we consider.

For modeling of cryptographic protocols, we assume at least the binary functions $\{\_\}\_$ and $\langle\_,\_\rangle$ denoting encryption and pairing. Here is the Needham-Schroeder protocol, mentioned in the introduction, in standard notation. Message $\{\langle x, y\rangle\}_k$ is abbreviated as $\{x, y\}_k$.

$$A \to B : \{A, N_A\}_{K_B}$$
$$B \to A : \{N_A, N_B\}_{K_A}$$
$$A \to B : \{N_B\}_{K_B}$$

The meaning of the protocol is as follows. The notation $A \to B : M$ denotes agent A sending message M to agent B. Inside messages, A and B represent the identities of respective agents, K_A and K_B their public keys. Public keys are known to everyone and messages encrypted with the public key are decrypted with the corresponding private keys (which are known only to the respective agents), and vice-versa. In the first step, A starts a session with B by sending his identity and a nonce (a random number) N_A that he generates, both encrypted with the public key of B. B decrypts the message and sends back the received nonce with a nonce that he generates, both encrypted again appropriately. This can be considered as a proof that B got the original message and sent this message as a reply. A sends back the received nonce, again encrypted, as a confirmation. Such a protocol is usually executed to establish authenticity of the communicating parties before going ahead with some further transaction. For example B could be a bank which is contacted by client A for some monetary transaction. Hence they may execute this protocol at the beginning to agree on secret values N_A and N_B which is expected to remain unknown to third parties. Further encrypted messages dealing with some financial transactions would then include these secret values as proof that these messages have really been generated by A and B and not by some adversary pretending to be A or B. While it may not be apparent at first glance, we have mentioned that the protocol has a flaw discovered 15 years after its publication. The attack involves two parallel sessions, one in which the adversary plays the role of B and another in which he plays the role of A but impersonating as the agent playing A's role in the first session. This kind of attack is also known as a *man-in-the-middle attack*.

We present here a modeling of this protocol using Horn clauses. Our modeling will only deal with the secrecy problem, i.e. whether some message is known to the adversary or not. Note however that other security questions are also interesting. For example authenticity talks about questions like whether some message received by a given agent was actually sent by another given agent. When we restrict ourself to the secrecy problem then we only need to consider three agents in our model for finding whether the above protocol is secure. This is a consequence of a result [8,7]) stating that under some mild assumptions on the protocol and for many security properties including secrecy, we need to consider a very small number (which is calculable from the protocol and the security property) of agents in our modeling in order to find whether there exists an attack. For the example protocol we need to consider two honest and one dishonest agent. We now need to consider all possible sessions between these bounded number of agents. For every two agents u and v in our model, we have infinitely many sessions in which u is the initiator (i.e. plays the role of A) and v is the responder (i.e. plays the role of B). In each of these sessions we have a fresh nonce. We choose two nonces n_{uv}^1 and n_{uv}^2 to represent these infinitely many nonces. This modeling using only finitely many nonces is a safe abstraction. Corresponding to the three steps in the protocol we have the following clauses for all agents u and v. Our intention is that known(m) should hold exactly for messages m which the adversary can know.

$$\mathsf{known}(\{\langle u, n_{uv}^1\rangle\}_{k_v})$$
$$\mathsf{known}(\{\langle x, n_{uv}^2\rangle\}_{k_u}) \Leftarrow \mathsf{known}(\{\langle u, x\rangle\}_{k_v})$$
$$\mathsf{known}(\{x\}_{k_v}) \qquad \Longleftarrow \mathsf{known}(\{\langle n_{uv}^1, x\rangle\}_{k_u})$$

Note that we write such clauses for all (finitely many) pairs of agents in our system, whether they are honest or dishonest agents. The above clauses correspond to our assumption that all messages received by agents are sent by the adversary, and hence should be known to the adversary, and that all messages sent by agents become known to the adversary. For example the second clause represents the fact that v, on receiving a message of the form $\{\langle u, x\rangle\}_{k_v}$, sends a message of the form $\{\langle x, n_{uv}^2\rangle\}_{k_u}$. We use a variable x in place of the nonce sent by u, since this is an unknown for the recipient v, and the adversary could send to him any message of this form, provided he knows such a message. Implicit in this modeling is the fact that we may have arbitrary many sessions between u and v. Note that we can apply the clauses as many times as we like for different values of concerned variables. The essential abstraction is in our modeling here is that infinitely many nonces from different sessions are represented by finitely many nonces. This is a safe abstraction and insecure protocols remain insecure in our modeling. It is possible to make less severe abstractions at the cost of introducing more complex clauses, and we will see some examples in Sections 5 and 7.

We need further clauses to express adversary capabilities. The clauses

$$\mathsf{known}(\{x\}_y) \Leftarrow \mathsf{known}(x) \wedge \mathsf{known}(y)$$
$$\mathsf{known}(x) \qquad \Leftarrow \mathsf{known}(\{x\}_k) \wedge \mathsf{known}(k')$$
$$\mathsf{known}(\langle x, y\rangle) \Leftarrow \mathsf{known}(x) \wedge \mathsf{known}(y)$$
$$\mathsf{known}(x) \qquad \Leftarrow \mathsf{known}(\langle x, y\rangle)$$
$$\mathsf{known}(y) \qquad \Leftarrow \mathsf{known}(\langle x, y\rangle)$$

express the ability of the adversary to perform encryption, decryption, pairing and un-pairing, where k' is the private key corresponding to public key k. We have considered k and k' to be constants, although there exist other methods of modeling public and private keys, e.g. letting the term $sk(x)$ represent the private key corresponding to the public key x.

The adversary's knowledge of other data m like agents' names, public keys, etc. are expressed by clauses known(m). For example if w is some dishonest agent then we have the clause known(k'_w) to say that private key of w is known to the adversary. Further we have clauses known(n^1_{wu}) and known(n^2_{uw}) for every other agent u, to say that nonces generated by dishonest agents are known to the adversary. Then the secrecy question, whether some message m is known to the adversary is translated to the membership question, whether known(m) holds. More precisely, our modeling involves safe abstraction, so that if m is known to the adversary then known(m) holds. Further checking whether known(m) holds is equivalent to checking whether the clause set together with the clause $\perp \Leftarrow$ known(m) is unsatisfiable.

In the above particular example, our modeling requires two honest agents a and b and a dishonest agent c. Each of these can be the initiator of a session or the responder of a session. We don't consider the cases where the same agent can be the initiator as well as the responder, though some models and tools allow this possibility, and this can easily be allowed in our Horn clause modeling. After writing the necessary clauses and running a suitable solver, e.g. a solver for the class $\mathcal{H}_1$, we find that known(n^1_{ab}) does not hold. As our modeling involves safe abstraction, we are then sure that the nonce generated by an honest initiator for an honest responder is never leaked to the adversary. On the other hand, known(n^2_{ab}) holds. This suggests the possibility that the nonce created by an honest responder for an honest initiator can be leaked to the adversary. Indeed such a leak happens in the man-in-the-middle attack mentioned above. More precisely, in this attack, the nonce n^2_{ab} is generated by the agent b because he is fooled into believing that the agent a has started a session with him.

3 $\mathcal{H}_1$ and Strongly Recognizable Relations

A relation on ground terms is called *strongly recognizable* if it can be described as finite union of Cartesian products of recognizable languages (i.e. languages accepted by tree automata). In case of unary relations, strongly recognizable relations are just the recognizable languages. The class $\mathcal{H}_1$ presented in this section allows general forms of clauses which still describe only strongly recognizable relations. Although $\mathcal{H}_1$ is not specifically meant for modeling some particular class of protocols, the advantage of this class is that we have a systematic way of safely abstracting arbitrary clauses to clauses in this class [14].

With a clause we associate a *variable dependence graph* whose vertices are the atoms in the body of the clause, and two atoms are neighbors if they have a common variable. Two variables are called *connected* if they occur within connected atoms. In particular two variables in the same atom are connected. A clause has property $H1$ if

1. the head is linear (i.e. no variables occur twice in it).
2. if variables x and y occur in the head and are connected in the body then they are siblings in the head.

Here we call two variables as siblings if they occur as arguments of a common father. Hence x, y are connected in $P(x, y)$ and in $Q(f(x, a, y))$. The class $\mathcal{H}_1$ consists of finite sets of $H1$ clauses. $\mathcal{H}_1$ allows clauses which can express various operations on relations, like arbitrary projections through constructors, permutations of components, and compositions of relation [20]:

$$P(x, y) \quad \Leftarrow Q(f(x, y, z))$$
$$Q(x, y, z) \Leftarrow Q(y, z, x)$$
$$P(x, z) \quad \Leftarrow Q(x, y) \wedge R(y, z)$$

However they still describe only strongly recognizable relations. To show this we give a procedure that converts the set of clauses into a new set of simple clauses, that we call *normal clauses*. *Normal* $H1$ clauses are $H1$ clauses of the form

1. $P(f(x_1, \ldots, x_n)) \Leftarrow P_1(x_1) \wedge \ldots \wedge P_n(x_n)$.
2. $P(x_1, \ldots, x_n) \Leftarrow P_1(x_1) \wedge \ldots \wedge P_n(x_n)$ where $n \neq 1$.

where $x_1, \ldots, x_n$ are pairwise distinct variables. Here we allow $n = 0$ to take care of nullary symbols and predicates. Clearly a set of normal $H1$ clauses can describe only strongly recognizable relations, and conversely every strongly recognizable relation can be described by a set of normal $H1$ clauses. We now show that any set of $H1$ clauses can be normalized, i.e. converted to an equivalent set of normal $H1$ clauses, implying that $\mathcal{H}_1$ describes exactly strongly recognizable relations.

Theorem 1 ([20,14]). *A set of clauses in $\mathcal{H}_1$ can be normalized in DEXPTIME.*

Proof: First we ensure that all variables in the head occur also in the body, by adding atoms $P(x)$ in the body where P is a fresh predicate defined to accept all terms. Then we ensure that every head is of the form $P(f(x_1, \ldots, x_n))$ or $P(x_1, \ldots, x_n)$. For example the clause $P(f(x, y), z) \Leftarrow P_1(x, x') \wedge P_2(x', y) \wedge P_3(z, z')$ is replaced by clauses $P(x, z) \Leftarrow P'(x), P_3(z, z')$ and $P'(f(x, y)) \Leftarrow P_1(x, x') \wedge P_2(x', y)$ where P' is a fresh predicate. Now it remains to simplify the bodies of clauses.

We use sets $\{P_1, \ldots, P_n\}$ of unary predicates to represent intersections of the unary predicates. P_1 is identified with the set $\{P_1\}$. The normalization procedure essentially consists of using a non-normal clause and a normal clause to produce a new simpler clause and continuing this process until the non-normal clauses are redundant. The following kinds of steps are involved.

- Clauses $T_i(f(x_1, \ldots, x_n)) \Leftarrow S_i^1(x_1) \wedge \ldots \wedge S_i^n(x_n)$ produce clause $T(f(x_1, \ldots, x_n)) \Leftarrow S_1(x_1) \wedge \ldots \wedge S_n(x_n)$ where $T = \bigcup_i T_i$ and $S_j = \bigcup_i S_i^j$.
- Clauses $h \Leftarrow \mathcal{B} \wedge S(f(t_1, \ldots, t_n))$ and $S(f(x_1, \ldots, x_n)) \Leftarrow S_1(x_1) \wedge \ldots \wedge S_n(x_n)$ produce the clause $h \Leftarrow \mathcal{B} \wedge S_1(t_1) \wedge \ldots \wedge S_n(t_n)$, where $\mathcal{B}$ is used here and elsewhere to denote a conjunction of atoms.
- Clauses $h \Leftarrow \mathcal{B} \wedge S(t_1, \ldots, t_n)$ and $S(x_1, \ldots, x_n) \Leftarrow S_1(x_1) \wedge \ldots \wedge S_n(x_n)$ produce the clause $h \Leftarrow \mathcal{B} \wedge S_1(t_1) \wedge \ldots \wedge S_n(t_n)$ where $n \geq 1$.
- Clause $h \Leftarrow \mathcal{B} \wedge S_1(x) \wedge S_2(x)$ produces the clause $h \Leftarrow \mathcal{B} \wedge (S_1 \cup S_2)(x)$.

- Clause $S(x) \Leftarrow S'(x)$ and $S'(f(x_1, \ldots, x_n)) \Leftarrow S_1(x_1) \wedge \ldots \wedge S_n(x_n)$ produce $S(f(x_1, \ldots, x_n)) \Leftarrow S_1(x_1) \wedge \ldots \wedge S_n(x_n)$.
- Clause $h \Leftarrow \mathcal{B} \wedge S(x)$ produces the clause $h \Leftarrow \mathcal{B}$ if x does not occur in $h \Leftarrow \mathcal{B}$, and if S accepts at least one term using only the normal predicates.

The essential idea in the above and other normalization algorithms is that if at all the clause set contains a non-normal clause which is not redundant, then we consider a minimal derivation which uses some non-normal clause C of the form $A \Leftarrow A_1 \wedge \ldots \wedge A_n$. This clause allows us to derive the atom $A\sigma$ by applying some ground substitution σ. Now we consider the reason why C is not normal. If some A_i is of the form $P(f(t_1, \ldots, t_n))$, then we know that the atom $A_i\sigma$ is derivable using only normal clauses, because of the minimality assumption. The last clause D used in the latter derivation is of the form $P(f(x_1, \ldots, x_n)) \Leftarrow S_1(x_1) \wedge \ldots \wedge S_n(x_n)$. But then a normalization step involving C and D can produce a "simpler" clause which could instead be used for deriving $A\sigma$. A similar argument holds for the case where the body of C contains a non-unary predicate. On the other hand, if C is not normal because two of the atoms in the body are of the form $S_1(x)$ and $S_2(x)$ then we can replace these two atoms by the atom $(S_1 \cup S_2)(x)$. The first rule above intuitively defines the meaning of the fresh predicates $\{P_1, \ldots, P_n\}$. The intuition behind the last two rules is simple, and they remove some other clauses which are not normal. □

Note that $\mathcal{H}_1$ allows for example the modeling of the Needham-Schroeder protocol described above, and more [13]. As our approach always involves safe abstractions, all attacks, in particular the man-in-the-middle attack on the Needham-Schroeder protocol, are found. The normalization procedure further means that for example the secrecy question, whether some term is not accepted at some predicate, can be evaluated in time polynomial on the resulting clause size. Further, subclasses of $\mathcal{H}_1$, for example the class $\mathcal{H}_3$ [20] can be normalized in polynomial time and suffice for the above example protocol. $\mathcal{H}_1$ has also been successfully used to verify real implementations of cryptographic protocols in the C language [15].

4   General Flat Clauses

The class $\mathcal{H}_1$ allows us to represent tree automata, as well as their extensions like alternating tree automata and two-way tree automata [6]. Alternation is described by clauses of the form

$$P(x) \Leftarrow P_1(x) \wedge \ldots \wedge P_n(x)$$

whereas two-way tree automata contain clauses like

$$P(x) \Leftarrow Q(f(x, y, z)), Q_1(y), Q_2(z)$$

The clauses in Section 2 describing abilities of the adversary to perform encryption, decryption, pairing and unpairing are clauses of two-way tree automata, upto some details. Despite its generality, $\mathcal{H}_1$ does not allow for example the clause

$$P(f(x, y, x)) \Leftarrow Q(x) \wedge R(y)$$

Such clauses describe tree automata with equality constraints between brothers [6]. In fact, it may be verified that allowing such clauses will make the class $\mathcal{H}_1$ undecidable.

We now consider a class which is specially suited for describing such features, e.g. tree automata with alternation, two-wayness and equality constraints between brothers. A *general flat clause* is one that contains only atoms of the form $P(x)$ and $P(f(x_1, \ldots, x_n))$. We put no restrictions on the occurrences and repetitions of variables. An example clause is

$$P(f(x, y, x)) \Leftarrow Q(g(y, y, z)) \wedge R(y)$$

Note that we consider only unary predicates. This class of clauses is more general (in the Horn case) than the flat clauses considered in [25]. The complexity for this class is however still DEXPTIME, as for the class in [25]. Among other things, these clauses can model the ability of the adversary to perform operations like encryption, decryption, pairing, unpairing, hashing etc. But we have tried throughout this paper to obtain maximal classes which can be efficiently decided. A general flat clause is called *normal* if it is of the form

$$P(f(x_1, \ldots, x_n)) \Leftarrow P_1(x_{i_1}) \wedge \ldots \wedge P_k(x_{i_k})$$

where $\{x_1, \ldots, x_n\} = \{x_{i_1}, \ldots, x_{i_k}\}$ and $x_{i_1}, \ldots, x_{i_k}$ are pairwise distinct. Define *trivial* terms, atoms or clauses to be those in which no function symbols appear.

Theorem 2. *A set of general flat clauses can be normalized in DEXPTIME.*

Proof: We proceed exactly as in the case of $H1$ clauses, by trying to simplify the body. However since the heads can be non-linear, the variables in the non-trivial atoms in clauses can get unified. E.g. clauses $P_1(f(x, y)) \Leftarrow P_2(g(x, y, z)) \wedge P_3(h(x, x))$ and $P_2(g(x, x, z)) \Leftarrow P_4(x) \wedge P_5(z)$ produce $P_1(f(x, x)) \Leftarrow P_3(h(x, x)) \wedge P_4(x) \wedge P_5(z)$. Similarly clauses $P(f(x, y, y)) \Leftarrow P_1(x) \wedge P_2(y)$ and $Q(f(x, x, y)) \Leftarrow Q_1(x) \wedge Q_2(y)$ produce the $\{P, Q\}(f(x, x, x)) \Leftarrow \{P_1, P_2, Q_1, Q_2\}(x)$. Hence in general arbitrary sequences of variables can occur in the non-trivial atoms in a clause. However the number of such atoms is always linearly bounded and the number of variables in clauses is also linearly bounded. Hence only exponential number of clauses are possible.   □

5 One Variable Clauses

One-variable clauses are defined to be clauses in which at most one variable occurs. Note that we put no restriction on the number of occurrences of this variable. The following is an example of a one-variable clause.

$$P(f(x, g(h(x), i(x, x)))) \Leftarrow Q(g(x, x)) \wedge R(x)$$

Having dealt with general flat clauses, our next goal is to allow general flat clauses in the presence of one-variable clauses. However we will restrict the form of general flat clauses that we consider. This is done in the next section. In this section we show how to deal with just one-variable clauses. The main motivation is that this allows us to naturally encode a very interesting class of cryptographic protocols, namely cryptographic protocols with *single blind copying*, introduced in [7]. As we saw in Section 2, each protocol step involves copying certain unknown parts of the received message into the sent message. In the example we discussed, an agent always copies only one unknown (the nonce created by the other participant) into the sent message. This is precisely the restriction imposed by the restriction of single blind copying. Although in our example, this unknown occurs exactly once in the received and sent messages, we may allow more than one occurrences thereof. As a consequence of this restriction, the clauses required for modeling the protocol steps are one-variable clauses, as we can see for our example protocol. The other clauses which are independent of the protocol steps, e.g. encryption and decryption abilities of the adversary, are modeled using general flat clauses of Section 4 or their restrictions introduced in the next section.

The modeling described in Section 2 of the Needham-Schroeder protocol is based on abstraction of an infinite set of nonces by a single constant. This is secure in the sense that no attacks are missed. However this may sometimes lead to too many false attacks. Hence we could adopt a less severe abstraction in which a nonce is not necessarily a constant, but a function of some previous messages exchanged in the protocol. Hence nonces in two distinct sessions may still be the same. This kind of abstraction leads to the following clauses for the steps of the Needham-Schroeder protocol. Note that the second nonce n_{uv}^2 is now a function of the first nonce n_{uv}^1 which is a constant. These clauses are still one-variable clauses, although they do not belong to the class $\mathcal{H}_1$.

$$\mathsf{known}(\{\langle u, n_{uv}^1 \rangle\}_{k_v})$$
$$\mathsf{known}(\{\langle x, n_{uv}^2(x) \rangle\}_{k_u}) \Leftarrow \mathsf{known}(\{\langle a, x \rangle\}_{k_v})$$
$$\mathsf{known}(\{x\}_{k_v}) \qquad\qquad \Leftarrow \mathsf{known}(\{\langle n_{uv}^1, x \rangle\}_{k_u})$$

We restrict ourselves to only unary predicates. For one-variable clauses, this causes no loss of generality as we can encode atoms $P(t_1, \ldots, t_n)$ as $P(c(t_1, \ldots, t_n))$ by choosing a fresh symbol c. *Normal* one-variable clauses are one-variable clauses of the forms

1. $P(t) \Leftarrow Q(x)$ where t is non-ground and non-trivial.
2. $P(t)$ where t is ground.
3. $P(x)$.

To restrict the form of unifiers of one-variable terms required during normalization, we decompose these terms, similar to decomposing a string into symbols. If t is a one-variable term (i.e. one containing at most one variable) which is non-ground and s is any other term, then $t[s]$ denotes the effect of replacing the variable in t by s. This notation is extended to sets of terms in the expected manner. A non-ground one-variable term $t[x]$ is called *reduced* if it is not of the form $u[v[x]]$ for any non-ground non-trivial one-variable terms $u[x]$ and $v[x]$. The term $f(g(x), h(g(x)))$ for example is not reduced because it can be written as $f(x, h(x))[g(x)]$. The term $f'(x, g(x), a)$ is reduced. Unifying it with the reduced term $f'(h(y), g(h(a)), y)$ produces ground unifier $\{x \mapsto h(y)[a], y \mapsto a\}$ and both $h(y)$ and a are strict subterms of the given terms. Indeed we find:

Lemma 1. *Let $s[x]$ and $t[y]$ be reduced, non-ground and non-trivial terms where $x \neq y$ and $s[x] \neq t[x]$. If s and t have a unifier σ, then $x\sigma, y\sigma \in U[V]$ where U is the set of non-ground (possibly trivial) strict subterms of s and t, and V is the set of ground strict subterms of s and t.*

In case both terms (even if not reduced) have the same variable:

Lemma 2. *Let σ be a unifier of two non-trivial, non-ground and distinct one-variable terms $s[x]$ and $t[x]$. Then $x\sigma$ is a ground strict subterm of s or of t.*

The intuition behind Lemma 2 is that the variable x could not be mapped to a non-ground non-trivial term because that term itself would contain x. Similarly the intuition behind Lemma 1 is that if x (resp. y) is not immediately mapped to a ground term, then x (resp. y) is mapped to a non-ground subterm of $t[y]$ (resp. $s[x]$) and then y (resp. x) could only be mapped to a ground term.

Hence in the following one-variable clauses are simplified to involve only reduced terms.

Lemma 3. *Any non-ground one-variable term $t[x]$ can be uniquely written as $t[x] = t_1[t_2[\ldots[t_n[x]]\ldots]]$ where $n \geq 0$ and each $t_i[x]$ is non-trivial, non-ground and reduced. This decomposition can be computed in time polynomial in the size of t.*

Proof: We represent $t[x]$ as a DAG by doing maximal sharing of subterms. If $t[x] = x$ then the result is trivial. Otherwise let N be the position in this graph, other than the root node, closest to the root such that N lies on every path from the root to the node corresponding to the subterm x. Let t' be the strict subterm of t at position N and let t_1 be the term obtained from t by replacing the sub-DAG at N by x. Then $t = t_1[t']$ and t_1 is reduced. We then recursively decompose t'.

Uniqueness of decomposition follows from Lemma 1.   □

Above and elsewhere, if $n = 0$ then $t_1[t_2[\ldots[t_n[x]]\ldots]]$ denotes x. Now if there is an atom $P(t[x])$ occurring in some clause, with $t[x]$ being non-ground, and if $t[x] = t_1[\ldots[t_n[x]]\ldots]$ where each t_i is non-trivial and reduced, then we create fresh predicates $Pt_1\ldots t_i$ for $1 \leq i \leq n-1$ and replace this atom by the atom $Pt_1\ldots t_{n-1}(t_n[x])$. Also we add clauses $Pt_1\ldots t_i(t_{i+1}[x]) \Leftarrow Pt_1\ldots t_{i+1}(x)$ and $Pt_1\ldots t_{i+1}(x) \Leftarrow Pt_1\ldots t_i(t_{i+1}[x])$ for $0 \leq i \leq n - 2$ to our clause set.

Hence now we assume that non-ground atoms in clauses involve only reduced terms or trivial terms as arguments of predicates. Let Ng be the set of these terms, w.l.o.g. containing also the trivial term. Let Ngs be the set of non-ground subterms of terms in Ng. Let G be the ground terms occurring in the clauses. During normalization we are only going to produce atoms $P(t)$ with $t \in$ Ng $\cup$ Ng[Ngs[G]]. As before we consider sets of predicates to represent intersections of individual predicates. If a clause has a non-ground head and a ground body then we add the atom $P(x)$ in the body, where $P(x)$ is a fresh predicate. We add the clause $P(x)$ to the set to say that P accepts all terms. Here are the possible normalization steps.

- We have clause $h \Leftarrow B \wedge S(t[x])$ and normal clause $S(s[y]) \Leftarrow S'(y)$ where $s, t \in$ Ng are non-trivial. The normalization step produces $h\sigma \Leftarrow B\sigma \wedge S'(y\sigma)$ where σ unifies s and t. If $s[x] = t[x]$ then σ is a renaming. Otherwise $x\sigma, y\sigma \in$ Ngs[G] by Lemma 1. Further Ngs[G] $\subseteq$ Ng[Ngs[G]]. Ground atoms $S''(g)$ are removed from the body by checking that g is accepted at S'' using the normal clauses only.
- We have clauses $h \Leftarrow B \wedge S(t[y])$ and $S(s)$ where $t \in$ Ng is non-trivial and $s \in$ Ng[Ngs[G]]. The normalization step produces $h\sigma \Leftarrow B\sigma$ where σ unifies t and s.

The ground atoms from the body are removed as before. If $s \in \mathsf{Ngs}[\mathsf{G}]$ then the clause is clearly of the right form. Otherwise $s = u[g]$ where $u \in \mathsf{Ng}$ is non-trivial, and $g \in \mathsf{Ngs}[\mathsf{G}]$. Hence σ is also a unifier of non-trivial reduced terms t and u. If $s[x] = t[x]$ then the result is easy. Otherwise by Lemma 1, $x\sigma \in \mathsf{Ngs}[\mathsf{G}]$, and the result is again easy. The last argument is crucial: the unifier is independent of g hence the ground terms in clauses don't grow arbitrarily.

- Clause $S(x) \Leftarrow S'(x)$ and normal clause $S'(t) \Leftarrow \mathcal{B}$ produce $S(t) \Leftarrow \mathcal{B}$ where $\mathcal{B}$ may be possibly empty.
- The case of normalization steps involving clause $P(x)$ is easy.
- Clause $h \Leftarrow \mathcal{B} \wedge S_1(x) \wedge S_2(x)$ produces $h \Leftarrow \mathcal{B} \wedge (S_1 \cup S_2)(x)$.
- Normal clauses $S_1(s) \Leftarrow T_1(x)$ and $S_2(t) \Leftarrow T_2(x)$ produce $(S_1 \cup S_2)(t\sigma) \Leftarrow (T_1 \cup T_2)(x\sigma)$ where σ unifies s and t. Similarly a normal non-ground and a normal ground clause can produce a new clause. The unifications involved are as considered above.

Hence we produce only polynomially many terms during normalization and hence only exponentially many clauses. While [25] uses resolution techniques to decide satisfiability for these clauses, we further show here that the clauses can even be put into normal form.

Theorem 3 ([25]). *A set of one-variable clauses can be normalized in DEXPTIME.*

6   One Variable Clauses and Flat Clauses

We now return to our goal of having both general flat clauses and one-variable clauses, in order to be able to model cryptographic protocols with single blind copying. However instead of the general flat clauses considered before, we consider *flat clauses* which are those general flat clauses in which every non-trivial atom contains all variables of the clause. The clause

$$P(f(x, y)) \Leftarrow Q(g(y, z))$$

is a general flat clause but not a flat clause. The set of variables in one atom is $\{x, y\}$ and in the other is $\{y, z\}$. The following clause is a flat clause.

$$P_1(f(x, y, x, z)) \Leftarrow P_2(g(y, z, x)) \wedge P_3(h(y, y, x, z, z)) \wedge P_4(x)$$

This class of flat clauses is what is considered in [25] and also suffices for modeling cryptographic protocols with single blind copying. Recall that the one-variable clauses model the protocol steps involving single blind copying, as explained in Section 5 and the flat clauses model the additional capabilities of the adversary to perform encryption, decryption etc. This restriction simplifies the interaction between flat and one-variable clauses. *Normal* clauses are now defined to be clauses which are either normal one-variable clauses or normal flat clauses. Note that the definition of normal flat clauses is same as in the case of general flat clauses. Our goal in this case is to obtain a set of normal flat clauses and normal one-variable clauses.

We will now have three kinds of normalization steps. Normalization steps between two flat clauses or between two one-variable clauses are as in Sections 4 and 5. The third kind of normalization step is between a one-variable clause and a flat clause, and this always produces a one-variable clause. As a typical example a normalization step between the following two clauses

$$C_1 = \qquad P_1(f(x,y)) \Leftarrow P_2(g(y,x)) \wedge P_3(x)$$
$$C_2 = P_2(g(x,h(h(x)))) \Leftarrow P_4(x) \wedge P_5(x)$$

produces the clause

$$P_1(f(h(h(x)),x)) \Leftarrow P_3(h(h(x))) \wedge P_4(x) \wedge P_5(x)$$

Further the term $f(h(h(x)),x)$ is reduced. However $h(h(x))$ is not reduced and hence this term needs to be further decomposed. We replace this clause by the following clauses where $P_3h(x)$ is a fresh predicate. In general we require new predicates corresponding to original predicates and a sequence of one-variable terms. The variables occurring in the terms in these sequences are not important, and these new predicates are identified upto replacements of these variables by other variables.

$$P_1(f(h(h(x)),x)) \Leftarrow P_3h(x)(h(x)) \wedge P_4(x) \wedge P_5(x)$$
$$P_3h(x)(x) \Leftarrow P_3(h(x))$$
$$P_3(h(x)) \Leftarrow P_3h(x)(x)$$

Let Ngs be the set of non-ground (subterms of) terms in the one-variable clauses, Ngr $= \{\{s[x_{r+1}] \mid s$ is non-ground and reduced,and for some $t, s[t] \in$ Ngs$\}$. Define Ngrr $= \{s_1[\ldots[s_m]\ldots] \mid s_1[\ldots[s_n]\ldots] \in$ Ngs, $m \leq n$, and each s_i is non-trivial and reduced$\}$. The reason we need these new sets is that during resolution we create subterms of reduced terms which need to be then further decomposed, as in the above example. We further define the set Ngr$_1 = \{f(s_1,\ldots,s_n) \mid g(t_1,\ldots,t_m) \in$ Ngr$, \{s_1,\ldots,s_n\} = \{t_1,\ldots,t_n\}\}$. These terms are reduced but are exponentially many. These are produced as instances of the non-trivial terms in the flat clauses as in the above example. However, the number of such terms in a clause is linear in the initial clause size. Further a normalization step of this clause with a normal flat clause can only produce strict subterms of these terms (in Ngrr) which can then be further decomposed. Readers may consult [25] for precise details about the form of clauses produced during normalization.

The other important observation is that we need only polynomially many fresh predicates for performing decompositions, because the trivial atoms in the flat clause C_2 above can never involve the auxiliary predicates. This is because when we introduce auxiliary predicate as above, the clause becomes a one-variable clause. No further steps can transform this atom into a trivial atom in a non-trivial flat clause.

Theorem 4 ([25]). *A set of flat and one-variable clauses can be normalized in DEXP-TIME.*

While only the satisfiability problem is considered in [25] (for Horn and non-Horn clauses), we have here presented a simpler procedure which further produces a set of normal clauses in the Horn case.

Example 1. Consider the set $S = \{C_1, \dots, C_5\}$ of clauses where

$$
\begin{aligned}
C_1 &= & P(a) \\
C_2 &= & Q(a) \\
C_3 &= P(f(g(\mathbf{x}_1, a), g(a, \mathbf{x}_1), a)) \Leftarrow P(\mathbf{x}_1) \\
C_4 &= P(f(g(\mathbf{x}_1, a), g(a, \mathbf{x}_1), b)) \Leftarrow P(\mathbf{x}_1) \\
C_5 &= & R(\mathbf{x}_1) \Leftarrow P(f(\mathbf{x}_1, \mathbf{x}_1, \mathbf{x}_2)) \wedge Q(\mathbf{x}_2)
\end{aligned}
$$

We first get the following normal clauses.

$$
\begin{aligned}
C_1' &= & \{P\}(a) \\
C_2' &= & \{Q\}(a) \\
C_3' &= \{P\}(f(g(\mathbf{x}_1, a), g(a, \mathbf{x}_1), a)) \Leftarrow \{P\}(\mathbf{x}_1) \\
C_4' &= \{P\}(f(g(\mathbf{x}_1, a), g(a, \mathbf{x}_1), b)) \Leftarrow \{P\}(\mathbf{x}_1)
\end{aligned}
$$

The clause

$$ C_5' = \{R\}(\mathbf{x}_1) \Leftarrow \{P\}(f(\mathbf{x}_1, \mathbf{x}_1, \mathbf{x}_2)) \wedge \{Q\}(\mathbf{x}_2) $$

is not normal. A normalization step with C_3' gives the clause

$$ \{R\}(g(a, a)) \Leftarrow \{P\}(a) \wedge \{Q\}(a) $$

As a is accepted at $\{P\}$ and $\{Q\}$ using the normal clauses C_1' and C_2', hence we get a new normal clause

$$ C_6 = \{R\}(g(a, a)) $$

Resolving C_5' with C_4' gives

$$ \{R\}(g(a, a)) \Leftarrow \{P\}(a) \wedge \{Q\}(b) $$

But b is not accepted at $\{Q\}$ using the normal clauses hence this clause is rejected. Finally C_1' and C_2' also give the normal clause

$$ C_7 = \{P, Q\}(a) $$

The resulting set of normal clauses is $\{C_1', \dots, C_4', C_6, C_7\}$.

For protocols this gives us the following complexity of the verification problem, which is also optimal [25].

Theorem 5 ([25]). *Secrecy for cryptographic protocols with single blind copying can be decided in DEXPTIME.*

7 k-Variable Clauses and Flat Clauses

Now we consider a further generalization by allowing not just one-variable clauses but also k-variable clauses, i.e. clauses having at most k variables. Our goal is to be able to model protocols in which more than one unknown data may be blindly copied. We are interested in the case where k is small, hence we assume it is bounded by some constant. Further, to obtain decidability, we impose restrictions on the occurrences of variables. A term or literal is called *covering* if every non-ground functional term occurring in it contains all variables of the term or literal. A clause is called *covering* if every literal in it is covering and every non-ground literal involving a n-ary predicate for $n \geq 2$ contains all variables of the clause. We are interested in covering k-variable clauses together with flat clauses. Note that every flat clause can also be considered as covering k-variable clauses for a suitable k, however we allow the flat clauses to have arbitrary many variables. Further as in the one-variable case, we could restrict covering k-variable clauses to have only unary-predicates. However during normalization, we are going to introduce new predicates of arity at most k. Hence w.l.o.g. we assume that our k-variable clauses always involve predicates of arity at most k. Flat clauses of course involve only unary predicates. Our definitions are inspired by that of the class S^+ [11]. Flat clauses belong to the class S^+. Our definition of covering k-variable clauses is essentially the same as that of S^+ clauses, except for the fact that we have restricted the number of variables, and we allow arbitrary ground subterms unlike in the case of S^+.

As example for protocols modeled by such clauses, consider the Yahalom protocol [1] below. Participants A and B use a trusted server S to compute a common key K_{AB}. N_A and N_B are nonces chosen by A and B respectively. K_{AS} and K_{BS} are long term shared keys between A and S and between B and S respectively.

$$A \longrightarrow B : A, N_A$$
$$B \longrightarrow S : B, \{A, N_A, N_B\}_{K_{BS}}$$
$$S \longrightarrow A : \{B, K_{AB}, N_A, N_B\}_{K_{AS}}, \{A, K_{AB}\}_{K_{BS}}$$
$$A \longrightarrow B : \{A, K_{AB}\}_{K_{BS}}, \{N_B\}_{K_{AB}}$$

To model the protocol, as before we use constants n_{uv}^1 and n_{uv}^2 to represent the two respective nonces chosen by u and v for sessions among themselves. For every pair (u, v) of agents, the clauses corresponding to the protocol steps as as follows. For the first step we have the clause

$$\mathsf{known}(\langle u, n_{uv}^1 \rangle)$$

For the second step we have clauses, using the fact that the adversary knows a pair of message iff he knows the individual messages.

$$\mathsf{known}(v) \qquad\qquad \Leftarrow \mathsf{known}(\langle u, x \rangle)$$
$$\mathsf{known}(\{\langle u, x, n_{uv}^2 \rangle\}_{k_{bs}}) \Leftarrow \mathsf{known}(\langle u, x \rangle)$$

By similar reasoning we obtain the following clauses for the third step.

$$\mathsf{known}(\{\langle v, k_{uv}, x, y \rangle\}_{k_{uS}}) \Leftarrow \mathsf{known}(v), \mathsf{known}(\{\langle u, x, y \rangle\}_{k_{vS}})$$
$$\mathsf{known}(\{\langle u, k_{uv} \rangle\}_{k_{vS}}) \qquad \Leftarrow \mathsf{known}(v), \mathsf{known}(\{\langle u, x, y \rangle\}_{k_{vS}})$$

For the fourth step we have the following clause, where the body has only the first component of the message received by u, because the second component is copied without any checks, hence has no impact on the adversary's knowledge.

$$\mathsf{known}(\{x\}_y) \Leftarrow \mathsf{known}(\{\langle v, y, n_{uv}^1, x \rangle\}_{k_{uS}})$$

Here we consider $\langle \_, \_, \_ \rangle$ and $\langle \_, \_, \_, \_ \rangle$ to be 3-ary and 4-ary functions respectively, instead of considering them to be built up by compositions of the binary function $\langle \_, \_ \rangle$. With this choice, the clauses we obtain are covering 2-variable clauses. Further, if we adopt a milder abstraction, as in Section 5 for the Needham-Schroeder protocol, then we have the following covering k-variable clauses. n_{uv}^2 is now a function of n_{uv}^1 and k_{uv} is a function of both of them.

$$
\begin{aligned}
&\mathsf{known}(\langle u, n_{uv}^1 \rangle) \\
&\mathsf{known}(v) && \Leftarrow \mathsf{known}(\langle u, x \rangle) \\
&\mathsf{known}(\{\langle u, x, n_{uv}^2(x) \rangle\}_{k_{vS}}) && \Leftarrow \mathsf{known}(\langle u, x \rangle) \\
&\mathsf{known}(\{\langle v, k_{uv}(x, y), x, y \rangle\}_{k_{uS}}) && \Leftarrow \mathsf{known}(v), \mathsf{known}(\{\langle u, x, y \rangle\}_{k_{vS}}) \\
&\mathsf{known}(\{\langle u, k_{uv}(x, y) \rangle\}_{k_{vS}}) && \Leftarrow \mathsf{known}(v), \mathsf{known}(\{\langle u, x, y \rangle\}_{k_{vS}}) \\
&\mathsf{known}(\{x\}_y) && \Leftarrow \mathsf{known}(\{\langle v, y, n_{uv}^1, x \rangle\}_{k_{uS}})
\end{aligned}
$$

In case of k-variable clauses, we define normal clauses to be those of the form

1. $P(t_1, \ldots, t_n) \Leftarrow Q(x_1, \ldots, x_m)$ where $x_1, \ldots, x_m$ are exactly the (pairwise distinct) variables in the head, and $(t_1, \ldots, t_n)$ is not a permutation of $(x_1, \ldots, x_m)$.
2. $P(t_1, \ldots, t_n)$.

It is easy to check that given a set of normal clauses of the above form, we can verify in polynomial time whether some ground atom $P(t_1, \ldots, t_n)$ holds (membership test). First we show how to normalize a set of k-variable covering clauses. As in the case of one-variable clauses, we need to rely on decompositions of terms. But as we have more than one variable, it is more convenient to talk of decompositions of substitutions. In this section, we consider substitutions σ to be always over a finite domain $dom(\sigma)$ of variables and $\mathsf{fv}(\sigma)$ denotes the set of free variables of the terms in the range $range(\sigma)$ of σ, also called the variables *occurring* in σ. If X is the domain of σ and $Y \subset X$ then $\sigma|_X$ denotes as usual the restriction of σ to the domain Y. We define a k-*variable* term, literal, or substitution to be one in which at most k variables occur. A substitution is called *covering* if every non-ground functional term occurring in the range contains all variables in the range. A term or literal is called *simple* if it contains only variables or ground terms. A substitution is *simple* if it maps variables to variables and ground terms. A covering k-variable substitution σ is called *fat* if it maps every variable to a non-ground term and $x\sigma = y\sigma$ only when $x = y$. The only substitutions which are both fat and simple are renamings. The substitution $\{x \mapsto a, y \mapsto f(x, y)\}$ is neither fat nor simple. Composition of two fat covering k-variable substitutions is a fat covering k-variable substitution. A non-renaming fat covering k-variable substitution σ is called *reduced* if it cannot be written as composition of two non-renaming fat covering k-variable substitutions. A term t is called *reduced* if the substitution $\{x \mapsto t\}$ is reduced. We will consider tuples $(t_1, \ldots, t_n)$ interchangeably as substitutions $\{x_1 \mapsto t_1, \ldots, x_n \mapsto t_n\}$ for convenience. Hence if substitution σ has a domain of size n and P is a n-ary predicate then $P(\sigma)$ denotes an atom as expected.

The extra problem in the k-variable case is that reduced terms may become non-reduced after application of some simple substitutions which unify two subterms. E.g. the substitution $\{x \mapsto f(x_1, g(x_1, x_2, a), g(x_1, a, x_2))\}$ is reduced. However the instance $\{x \mapsto f(x_1, g(x_1, a, a), g(x_1, a, a))\}$ is not reduced and can be written as

$\{x \mapsto f(x_1, x_2, x_2)\}\{x_1 \mapsto x_1, x_2 \mapsto g(x_1, a, a)\}$. Indeed the only way to unify two distinct k-variable covering terms, which have the same set of free variables, is by mapping variables to variables and to ground subterms of the two terms.

Lemmas 4 and 5 below are generalizations of Lemmas 1 and 2 to the k-variable case. Given two substitutions σ_1 and σ_2 over disjoint domains $\sigma_1 \oplus \sigma_2$ denotes as expected the substitution over the union of the two domains.

Lemma 4. *Consider two non-renaming reduced fat covering k-variable substitutions σ_1 and σ_2, over the same domain, and which are not renamings of each other. Let G be the set of ground subterms of terms in the range of σ_1 and σ_2 and $\mathsf{fv}(\sigma_1) \cap \mathsf{fv}(\sigma_2) = \emptyset$. Let σ be the mgu of σ_1 and σ_2. Then one of the following cases occur.*

- *$\sigma = \sigma_3 \oplus \sigma_4$ where $dom(\sigma_3) = \mathsf{fv}(\sigma_1)$, $dom(\sigma_4) = \mathsf{fv}(\sigma_2)$. σ_3 maps variables in $dom(\sigma_1)$ to variables in $dom(\sigma_1)$ and to terms in G. σ_4 is of the form $\theta\rho\sigma_3$ where θ maps variables in $dom(\sigma_2)$ to variables in $dom(\sigma_2)$ and to terms in G, ρ and is a fat substitution. Further, either θ or σ_3 is non-renaming.*
- *The symmetric case, with roles of σ_1 and σ_2 exchanged.*

Essentially non-renaming unification involves a fat substitution preceded and succeeded by simple substitutions. One of these two simple substitutions has to be non-renaming because of the reducedness condition. For example consider

$$\sigma_1 = \{x \mapsto f(h(x_1, a, y_1), h(x_1, y_1, a), g(x_1, y_1)), y \mapsto g(x_1, y_1)\}$$
$$\sigma_2 = \{x \mapsto f(x_2, x_2, y_2), \qquad\qquad\qquad y \mapsto y_2\}$$

We have $\sigma_3 \oplus \sigma_4$ as the mgu of σ_1 and σ_2 where

$$\sigma_3 = \{x_1 \mapsto x_1, y_1 \mapsto a\}$$
$$\theta = \{x_2 \mapsto x_2, y_2 \mapsto y_2\}$$
$$\rho = \{x_2 \mapsto h(x_1, a, y_1), y_2 \mapsto g(x_1, y_1)\}$$
$$\sigma_4 = \theta\rho\sigma_3$$

Here the first two arguments of $\sigma_1(x)$ had to be unified which led to y_1 being mapped to a. In case the sets of free variables in the ranges are the same, then we have the following generalization of Lemma 2.

Lemma 5. *Consider two covering k-variable substitutions σ_1 and σ_2 over the same domain. Let G be the set of ground subterms of terms in the range of σ_1 and σ_2 and $\mathsf{fv}(\sigma_1) = \mathsf{fv}(\sigma_2)$. Let σ be the mgu of σ_1 and σ_2. If σ_1 and σ_2 are not renamings then σ maps variables to variables and to terms in G.*

For example the mgu of the substitutions $\{x \mapsto f(x, g(x, y, z), h(a))\}$ and $\{x \mapsto f(y, g(x, y, z), z)\}$ is $\{x \mapsto x, y \mapsto x, z \mapsto h(a)\}$. The point is that a variable x cannot be mapped to a non-ground functional term since that term itself must contain the variable x. Lemma 3 is generalized as follows. We decompose covering substitutions as $\sigma = \theta\rho_1 \ldots \rho_n$ where θ is simple and ρ_i are fat and reduced. Intuitively θ tells us exactly which variables should be made equal to each other, and which variables should be made ground. The uniqueness of the choice of the ρ_i follows from Lemma 4.

Lemma 6. *1. Every non-ground covering k-variable substitution can be uniquely written as $\theta\sigma$ where θ is simple and σ is a fat covering k-variable substitution.*
2. *Every fat covering k-variable substitution σ can be uniquely written as $\sigma = \rho_1 \ldots \rho_n$ where $n \geq 0$ and each ρ_i is a reduced fat covering k-variable substitution.*

For example the substitution $\{x_1 \mapsto f(x,y), x_2 \mapsto f(x,y), x_3 \mapsto f(y,x), x_4 \mapsto x, x_5 \mapsto h(a)\}$ can be written as $\theta\sigma$ where $\theta = \{x_1 \mapsto y_1, x_2 \mapsto y_1, x_3 \mapsto y_2, x_4 \mapsto x, x_5 \mapsto h(a)\}$ is simple and $\sigma = \{y_1 \mapsto f(x,y), y_2 \mapsto f(y,x), x \mapsto x\}$ is fat covering. The fat covering substitution $\{x_1 \mapsto f(h(x), g(y)), x_2 \mapsto f(g(y), h(x)), x_3 \mapsto h(x)\}$ can be written as $\rho_1\rho_2$ where $\rho_1 = \{x_1 \mapsto f(y_1, y_2), x_2 \mapsto f(y_2, y_1), x_3 \mapsto y_1\}$ and $\rho_2 = \{y_1 \mapsto h(x), y_2 \mapsto g(y)\}$ are reduced fat covering. If $k = 1$ then the substitution $\{x_1 \mapsto f(g(x), h(x))\}$ is reduced. But if $k \geq 2$ then we can decompose it as $\{x_1 \mapsto f(y_1, y_2)\}$ and $\{y_1 \mapsto g(x), y_2 \mapsto h(x)\}$.

Hence given a set $\mathbb{S}$ of k-variable covering clauses, let G be the set of all ground terms occurring in $\mathbb{S}$. We add to $\mathbb{S}$ all possible instances of clauses by mapping variables to variables and terms from G. This means that now we never need to consider instances of these clauses which unify two distinct subterms occurring in a term or which unify some non-ground term in a clause with a term in G.

Next we decompose the terms occurring in the clauses, as in the one-variable case. An atom of the form $P(\theta\rho_1 \ldots \rho_n)$, with $n \geq 1$, in a clause is replaced by the atom $P_{\theta,\rho_1,\ldots,\rho_n}(\boldsymbol{x})$ and we add clauses

$$P_\theta(\boldsymbol{x}) \Leftarrow P(\theta)$$
$$P(\theta) \Leftarrow P_\theta(\boldsymbol{x})$$
$$P_{\theta,\rho_1}(\boldsymbol{x}) \Leftarrow P_\theta(\rho_1)$$
$$P_\theta(\rho_1) \Leftarrow P_{\theta,\rho_1}(\boldsymbol{x})$$
$$\cdots$$
$$P_{\theta,\rho_1,\ldots,\rho_n}(\boldsymbol{x}) \Leftarrow P_{\theta,\rho_1,\ldots,\rho_{n-1}}(\rho_n)$$
$$P_{\theta,\rho_1,\ldots,\rho_{n-1}}(\rho_n) \Leftarrow P_{\theta,\rho_1,\ldots,\rho_n}(\boldsymbol{x})$$

where in each clause, $\boldsymbol{x}$ represents a sequence of mutually distinct variables of appropriate length, $P_{\theta,\rho_1,\ldots,\rho_i}$ are fresh predicates, θ is a simple covering k-variable substitution and ρ_i are non-renaming reduced fat covering k-variable substitutions. In case θ is a renaming then $P\theta$ is the same as P and the first two clauses are omitted. If $n = 0$ then the atom is replaced by $P\theta(\boldsymbol{x})$. This means that now predicates are only applied to simple or reduced fat substitutions. As an example the literal $P(f(h(x), g(y)), f(g(y), h(x)), h(x))$ is written as $P(\sigma)$ where $\sigma = \{x_1 \mapsto f(h(x), g(y)), x_2 \mapsto f(g(y), h(x)), x_3 \mapsto g(x)\}$. σ can be written as $\rho_1\rho_2$ where $\rho_1 = \{x_1 \mapsto f(y_1, y_2), x_2 \mapsto f(y_2, y_1), x_3 \mapsto y_1\}$ and $\rho_2 = \{y_1 \mapsto h(x), y_2 \mapsto g(y)\}$. Hence this literal can be replaced by the literal $P\rho_1\rho_2(x,y)$ and additionally we have the following clauses. Further if in the original clause x and y never needed to be unified then in the new clauses also x and y never need to be unified, and y_1 and y_2 never need to be unified.

$$\begin{aligned}
P\rho_1(y_1, y_2) &\Leftarrow P(f(y_1, y_2), f(y_2, y_1), y_1) \\
P(f(y_1, y_2), f(y_2, y_1), y_1) &\Leftarrow P\rho_1(y_1, y_2) \\
P\rho_1\rho_2(x, y) &\Leftarrow P\rho_1(h(x), g(y)) \\
P\rho_1(h(x), g(y)) &\Leftarrow P\rho_1\rho_2(x, y)
\end{aligned}$$

Let $\mathbb{S}_1$ be the new set of clauses. Even after these transformations, we never need to consider instances of our clauses which unify two distinct subterms occurring in a term or which unify some non-ground term in a clause with a term in G. This property is going to be preserved during all stages of our normalization procedure. Further we preserve the property that at most one atom in a clause has a predicate applied to a non-renaming substitution. Let Ng be the set of non-ground terms occurring in $\mathbb{S}_1$, and Ngs the set of their subterms, as well as non-ground subterms of terms occurring in $\mathbb{S}$ (not $\mathbb{S}_1$). Let F be the set of fat covering k-variable substitutions with domain of size at most k and range containing (renamings of) terms from Ngs. Let S be the set of simple k-variable substitutions with domain of size at most k and the ground terms in the range being only from G. Compositions of sets of substitutions are defined as expected. During normalization, we are only going to produce atoms in which the predicate has an argument of one of the following forms.

- $\theta \in$ S.
- some non-renaming reduced $\rho \in$ F.
- $\theta_1 \rho_1 \rho_2 \theta_2$, where $\theta_1, \theta_2 \in$ S, θ_2 is ground, $\rho_1, \rho_2 \in$ F and ρ_1 is non-renaming and reduced.

The normalization procedure now consists of the following kinds of steps, quite similar to the one-variable case. Because of our assumptions about the kinds of instantiations that need to be made of clauses, we are going to avoid unnecessary unifications between the atoms involved. Further the assumptions will continue to hold after each normalization step. We further maintain the invariant that every clause has at most two literals, one of which is a renaming. This is true of the auxiliary clauses produced above. The clauses produced by replacing original clauses have only renamings as arguments in literals. To them we apply the following transformation. For every n-ary predicate and permutation π over n variables, we introduce predicate $P\pi$ which is supposed to accept tuples σ such that $\sigma\pi$ is accepted at P. We further introduce n-ary predicates $\{P_1, \ldots, P_i\}$, where P_i are n-ary predicates, with the usual meaning. Given n-ary predicate S and unary predicates $S_1, \ldots, S_n$ we introduce predicate $S[S_1, \ldots, S_n]$ which accepts tuples $(x_1, \ldots, x_n)$ accepted at S such that x_i is accepted at S_i. Given a permutation π, $S[S_1, \ldots, S_n]\pi$ is defined to be a state of the same form as expected. $S[S_1, \ldots, S_n] \cup T[T_1, \ldots, T_n]$ is defined to be $(S \cup T)[S_1 \cup T_1, \ldots, S_n \cup T_n]$. $S[\emptyset, \ldots, \emptyset]$ is same as S. $\emptyset[\emptyset, \ldots, \emptyset, S_i, \emptyset, \ldots, \emptyset](x_1, \ldots, x_n)$ is same as $S_i(x_i)$. Then a conjunction $S(x_1, \ldots, x_n) \wedge T(x_1, \ldots, x_n)$ in the body is replaced by $(S \cup T)(x_1, \ldots, x_n)$.

- We have a non-normal clause $C_1 = h \Leftarrow S(\sigma_1)$ and a normal clause $C_2 = S(\sigma_2) \Leftarrow \mathcal{B}$ and the normalization step produces $C = h\sigma \Leftarrow \mathcal{B}\sigma$ where σ is mgu of σ_1 and σ_2. $\mathcal{B}$ has at most one atom. The following cases are possible. In our case analysis below, we frequently need to forbid steps where two variables need to be made equal or where a variable needs to be instantiated to a term in G. We will do this without stating the reason explicitly.
  - σ_1 is a renaming. We consider this step only if the substitution occurring as argument in the head is also a renaming since we have assumed C_1 to be

non-normal. Then C is trivially of the required form. In the remaining subcases below, we assume that σ_1 is not a renaming. Hence the head of C_1 must have a renaming as argument.

- $\sigma_1 \in S$ is not a renaming. If $\sigma_2 \in F$ then this step is not performed. If $\sigma_2 \in S$ then this step is performed only if σ_2 is a renaming of σ_1, and then C is of the required form. If σ_2 is of the third form above then C is a ground clause with literals of the required form. Any ground atom from the body is removed by a membership test on the normal clauses.

- $\sigma_1 \in F$ is not a renaming and σ_2 is a renaming. Then $\mathcal{B}_2$ is empty and C is trivially of the required form.

- $\sigma_1 \in F$ is not a renaming and $\sigma_2 \in S$ is not a renaming. Then then this step is not possible.

- $\sigma_1 \in F$ is not a renaming and $\sigma_2 \in F$ is not a renaming. If σ_2 is a renaming of σ_1 then C is of the right form. Otherwise this normalization step is not considered because of the substitutions involved according to Lemma 4.

- $\sigma_1 \in F$ is not a renaming and σ_2 is of the form $\theta_1 \rho_1 \rho_2 \theta_2$ where $\theta_1, \theta_2 \in S$, θ_2 is ground, $\rho_1, \rho_2 \in F$ and ρ_1 is non-renaming and reduced. θ_1 must be a renaming for this normalization step to be allowed. Hence σ is also a unifier of σ_1 and ρ_1. By Lemma 4, σ is of the form $\rho_3 \theta_3$ where $\theta_3 \in S$ is ground and $\rho_3 \in F$. Hence the resulting clause is a ground clause of the right form.

- Two normal clauses $S_1(\sigma_1) \Leftarrow \mathcal{B}_1$ and $S_2(\sigma_2) \Leftarrow \mathcal{B}_2$, where S_1 and S_2 have the same arity, produces a clause $(S_1 \cup S_2)(\sigma_1 \sigma) \Leftarrow \mathcal{B}_1 \sigma \wedge \mathcal{B}_2 \sigma$ where σ unifies σ_1 and σ_2. The unifications involved are as above. A possible ground literal from the body is removed as before. A possible conjunction of two literals (with renamings as arguments) in the body is replaced by a single literal as before.

- Normal clause $S[S_1, \ldots, S_n](t_1, \ldots, t_n) \Leftarrow \mathcal{B}$ produces normal clause $S[S_1, \ldots, S_{i-1}, S_i \cup T, S_{i+1}, \ldots, S_n](t_1, \ldots, t_n) \Leftarrow \mathcal{B} \wedge T(t_i)$ if t_i is a variable. The conjunction in the body is replaced by a single literal as before.

- Given normal clauses $S[S_1, \ldots, S_n](t_1, \ldots, t_n) \Leftarrow \mathcal{B}_1$ and $T(t) \Leftarrow \mathcal{B}_2$ (t cannot be a variable) we consider the mgu σ of t_i and t. We generate the clause $S[S_1, \ldots, S_{i-1}, S_i \cup T, S_{i+1}, \ldots, S_n](t_1, \ldots, t_n)\sigma \Leftarrow \mathcal{B}_1 \sigma \wedge \mathcal{B}_2 \sigma$. Ground literals from body are again removed by membership tests.

- Normal clause $S(\sigma) \Leftarrow \mathcal{B}$ produces clause $S\pi(\sigma\pi^{-1}) \Leftarrow \mathcal{B}$ where π^{-1} is the inverse of the permutation π.

In other words we have polynomially many possible tuples occurring as arguments of predicates and consequently exponentially many clauses.

Theorem 6. *For a fixed k, a set of covering k-variable clauses can be normalized in DEXPTIME.*

For practical implementations, the systematic instantiations and decompositions could be wasteful. Hence it is better to do them as required. Firstly it is only necessary to decompose the arguments in heads but not in the body. Secondly the instantiations followed by decomposition should be done before a normalization step as needed, and not in advance. This avoids unnecessary instantiations. Hence given clauses

$$h \Leftarrow P(g(h(x)), g(h(x))))$$
$$P(g(x), g(y)) \Leftarrow Q(x, y)$$

we apply the substitution $\{x \mapsto x, y \mapsto x\}$ on the second clause and the new clause can then be decomposed to produce the following clauses

$$P'(x) \Leftarrow Q(x, x)$$
$$P(x, x) \Leftarrow P''(x)$$
$$P''(x) \Leftarrow P(x, x)$$
$$P''(h(x)) \Leftarrow P'(x)$$
$$P'(x) \Leftarrow P''(h(x))$$

Hence a normalization step then produces the new clause

$$h \Leftarrow P''(g(h(x)))$$

When we further allow flat clauses together with k-variable clauses, then the situation is again analogous to the case of one-variable clauses with flat clauses. Normalization steps between a covering k-variable clause and a flat clause produces a covering k-variable clause, which may again need to be decomposed.

Theorem 7. *For a fixed k, a set of covering k-variable clauses and flat clauses can be normalized in DEXPTIME.*

As we have considered k to be a constant, this upper bound does not apply to the class S^+. However letting k be a variable in our algorithm still allows us to show:

Theorem 8. *Satisfiability for the class S^+ can be decided in double exponential time in the Horn case.*

As far as we know no upper bound was previously known for this class. DEXPTIME lower bound for this class is obvious, and tightening the complexity bounds further remains to be done.

8   Conclusion

We have considered several general classes of Horn clauses. For each of them, we provided a normalization procedure which runs in exponential time but practically may be much faster. In particular, our methods can be used to decide satisfiability for these classes. Moreover, these classes provide flexible tools for modeling and certifying secrecy of protocols.

Beyond simplifying the methods from [25], we also generalized the class of flat and one-variable clauses to allow (restricted) k-variable clauses. For fixed small k, normalization and thus satisfiability still is in DEXPTIME. For unbounded k, we have provided a new double exponential time upper bound, which thus also holds for the full Horn fragment of the class S^+. It remains as a challenging problem whether this upper bound can be significantly improved.

References

1. Spore: Security protocol open repository. Available at http://www.lsv.ens-cachan.fr/spore/.
2. B. Blanchet. An efficient cryptographic protocol verifier based on Prolog rules. In *14th IEEE Computer Security Foundations Workshop (CSFW'01)*, pages 82–96. IEEE Computer Society Press, Cape Breton, Nouvelle-Écosse, Canada, 2001.
3. B. Blanchet. Security protocols: From linear to classical logic by abstract interpretation. *Information Processing Letters*, 95(5):473–479, 2005.
4. B. Blanchet and A. Podelski. Verification of cryptographic protocols: Tagging enforces termination. *Theoretical Computer Science*, 333(1-2):67–90, 2005.
5. H. Comon and V. Cortier. Tree automata with one memory, set constraints and cryptographic protocols. *Theoretical Computer Science*, 331(1):143–214, 2005.
6. H. Comon, M. Dauchet, R. Gilleron, F. Jacquemard, D. Lugiez, S. Tison, and M. Tommasi. Tree automata techniques and applications. http://www.grappa.univ-lille3.fr/tata, 1997.
7. H. Comon-Lundh and V. Cortier. New decidability results for fragments of first-order logic and application to cryptographic protocols. In R. Nieuwenhuis, editor, *14th International Conference on Rewriting Techniques and Applications (RTA'03)*, volume 2706 of *LNCS*, pages 148–164, Valencia, Spain, June 2003. Springer-Verlag.
8. H. Comon-Lundh and V. Cortier. Security properties: Two agents are sufficient. In *12th European Symposium on Programming (ESOP'03)*, volume 2618 of *LNCS*, pages 99–113, Warsaw, Poland, Apr. 2003. Springer-Verlag.
9. V. Cortier. *Vérification Automatique des Protocoles Cryptographiques*. PhD thesis, ENS Cachan, France, 2003.
10. D. Dolev and A. C. Yao. On the security of public key protocols. *IEEE Transactions on Information Theory*, IT-29(2):198–208, March 1983.
11. C. Fermüller, A. Leitsch, U. Hustadt, and T. Tammet. *Resolution Decision Procedures*, chapter 25, pages 1791–1849. Volume II of Robinson and Voronkov [23], 2001.
12. T. Frühwirth, E. Shapiro, M. Y. Vardi, and E. Yardeni. Logic programs as types for logic programs. In *6th Annual IEEE Symposium on Logic in Computer Science (LICS'91)*, Amsterdam, The Netherlands, July 1991. IEEE Computer Society Press.
13. J. Goubault-Larrecq. Une fois qu'on n'a pas trouvé de preuve, comment le faire comprendre à un assistant de preuve? In V. Ménissier-Morain, editor, *Actes des 12èmes Journées Francophones des Langages Applicatifs (JFLA'04)*. INRIA, collection didactique, 2004.
14. J. Goubault-Larrecq. Deciding $\mathcal{H}_1$ by resolution. *Information Processing Letters*, 95(3):401–408, 2005.
15. J. Goubault-Larrecq and F. Parrennes. Cryptographic protocol analysis on real C code. In R. Cousot, editor, *6th International Conference on Verification, Model Checking and Abstract Interpretation (VMCAI'05)*, volume 3385 of *LNCS*, pages 363–379. Springer-Verlag, 2005.
16. J. Goubault-Larrecq, M. Roger, and K. N. Verma. Abstraction and resolution modulo AC: How to verify Diffie-Hellman-like protocols automatically. *Journal of Logic and Algebraic Programming*, 64(2):219–251, Aug. 2005.
17. G. Lowe. An attack on the Needham-Schroeder public-key protocol. *Information Processing Letters*, 56(3):131–133, 1995.
18. D. Monniaux. Abstracting cryptographic protocols with tree automata. In A. Cortesi and G. Filé, editors, *6th International Static Analysis Symposium (SAS'99)*, volume 1694 of *LNCS*, pages 149–163, Venice, Italy, September 1999. Springer-Verlag.
19. R. M. Needham and M. D. Schroeder. Using encryption for authentication in large networks of computers. *Communications of the ACM*, 21(12):993–999, 1978.

20. F. Nielson, H. R. Nielson, and H. Seidl. Normalizable Horn clauses, strongly recognizable relations and Spi. In *9th Static Analysis Symposium (SAS'02)*, volume 24477 of *LNCS*, pages 20–35. Springer-Verlag, 2002.
21. R. Ramanujam and S. P. Suresh. A decidable subclass of unbounded security protocols. In *Workshop on Issues in the Theory of Security (WITS'03)*, 2003.
22. R. Ramanujam and S. P. Suresh. Tagging makes secrecy decidable with unbounded nonces as well. In *23rd Conference on Foundations of Software Technology and Theoretical Computer Science (FSTTCS'03)*, volume 2914 of *LNCS*, pages 363–374. Springer-Verlag, 2003.
23. J. A. Robinson and A. Voronkov, editors. *Handbook of Automated Reasoning*. North-Holland, 2001.
24. M. Rusinowitch and M. Turuani. Protocol insecurity with finite number of sessions is NP-complete. In P. Pandya and J. Radhakrishnan, editors, *14th IEEE Computer Security Foundations Workshop (CSFW'01)*, Cape Breton, Nova-Scotia, Canada, June 2001. IEEE Computer Society Press.
25. H. Seidl and K. N. Verma. Flat and one-variable clauses: Complexity of verifying cryptographic protocols with single blind copying. In F. B. ad Andrei Voronkov, editor, *11th International Conference on Logic for Programming Artificial Intelligence and Reasoning (LPAR'04)*, volume 3452 of *LNCS*, pages 79–94. Springer-Verlag, 2005.
26. C. Weidenbach. Towards an automatic analysis of security protocols. In H. Ganzinger, editor, *16th International Conference on Automated Deduction (CADE'99)*, number 1632 in LNAI, pages 378–382. Springer-Verlag, 1999.

Infering Ownership Types for Encapsulated Object-Oriented Program Components

Arnd Poetzsch-Heffter*, Kathrin Geilmann, and Jan Schäfer**

Technische Universität Kaiserslautern, Germany
{poetzsch|geilmann|jschaefer}@informatik.uni-kl.de

Abstract. Modular analyses of object-oriented programs need clear encapsulation boundaries between program components. The reference semantics of object-oriented languages complicates encapsulation. Ownership type systems are a way to guarantee encapsulation. However, they introduce a substantial and nontrivial annotation overhead for the programmer. This is in particular true for type systems with an access policy that is more flexible than owners-as-dominators. As we want to use ownership disciplines as basis for modular analyses, we need the flexibility. However, to keep it practical, the annotation overhead should be kept minimal.

In this paper, we present such a flexible ownership type system together with an inference technique to reduce the annotation overhead. Runtime components in our approach can be accessed via the interface of the owner as well as via other boundary objects with explicitly declared interface types. The resulting type system is quite complex, however, the programmer only has to annotate the interface types of a component. The ownership type information for the classes implementing the components is automatically inferred by a constraint-based algorithm. We proved the soundness of our approach for a Java-like core language.

1 Introduction

The practical application of global program analyses is limited by the size of the program. The goal of modular program analysis is to make analyses scalable to very large programs. The basic idea is to partition the program into components and to analyse the components separately such that the results of the analysis of one component C can be exploited in the analysis of components that use C. Modularity is in particular important for costly analysis and verification techniques like for example shape analysis, making these techniques even more powerful and effective than they are today.

Modularity needs clear encapsulation boundaries between components. In object-oriented programming, encapsulation is endangered by the reference semantics and subtyping. References to objects implementing the state of a runtime component C could be passed out to C's clients giving them direct access

---

* Partially supported by the Rheinland-Pfalz cluster of excellence "Dependable Adaptive Systems and Mathematical Modelling" (DASMOD).

** Supported by the Deutsche Forschungsgemeinschaft (German Research Foundation).

T. Reps, M. Sagiv, and J. Bauer (Eds.): Wilhelm Festschrift, LNCS 4444, pp. 120–144, 2007.

to the internal state. This breach of encapsulation is usually called *representation exposure* (cf. [13]). For programming and program analysis, representation exposure has two main disadvantages:

- It allows clients to read internal secrets and to break implementation invariants.
- It prevents modular program analysis, because such analyses can only be sound if all accesses to a component can be statically controlled.

In the last years, a number of techniques have been developed to prevent representation exposure (see Sect. 5). In particular, a variety of ownership type systems have been designed and studied ([11, 29, 3, 8, 2, 25, 39]). They statically control references going into a runtime component. The basic idea is that only the owner *ow* of a component C is allowed to hold references to C's internal objects (extensions are discussed below). Thus, access to C is completely controlled by *ow*'s interface. By ownership type systems, the programmer can in particular express which objects should be confined to a representation.

The static encapsulation guarantees of ownership type systems are not for free. Ownership type systems that are sufficiently expressive for common programming patterns are complex and create a heavy annotation burden for the programmer. She or he has to extend the normal type information by parametric ownership annotations. This is more than challenging for the ordinary programmer and diverts the development focus. Furthermore, the additional annotations can lead to less readable programs.

Our approach to encapsulated object-oriented components is based on two goals:

1. It should allow access to a component via several references or ports. This is needed to handle common programming patterns like iterators and observers. In addition, this avoids to develop wrappers or facades for composed components which is important for scalability.
2. The annotation should be restricted to component interfaces. This reduces the annotation overhead and simplifies the applicablility as well as the reuse of existing components.

In this paper, we present the techniques to achieve these goals, namely a generalized ownership discipline and a new technique for ownership type inference.

Our programming and component model is based on interface-oriented programming: Like a class, a component can be instantiated. A component instance is called a *box*. Like an object, a box has an identity and a local state. However, in general, a box may consist of several objects and inner boxes. To provide flexible access to a box and to simplify the composition of boxes, a box can be accessed via multiple read-write references generalizing the owners-as-dominators discipline. In particular, a box B_0 that is composed of boxes $B_1, \ldots, B_n$ can make the services of the B_i's directly available to its clients and need not to reimplement all their methods as part of the interface of the owner of B_0. The programmer has to declare all interface types that provide access to a box. That is, only references of these types are allowed to be passed out of the box. We call this the *encapsulation property*. The implementation of components consists of a set of classes some of which implement the component interfaces.

Our ownership type system is used to statically check the encapsulation property. It distinguishes between three kinds of objects, namely objects outside the box, objects in the box that are not allowed to be accessed from the outside, so-called *local* objects, and objects in the box accessible from the outside, so-called *boundary* objects. The programmer has to provide ownership annotations only for the interfaces of the box, the ownership annotations of the classes are automatically inferred. Thus, the programmer is freed from annotating the implementation, but remains in control to define the encapsulation. In particular, she controls which references are allowed to be passed into and out of a component. This is different from [3, 30] where explicit component interfaces are not supported (cf. Sect. 5) and where the goal of inference essentially is to discover potential encapsulation in given code. This can end up with almost no encapsulation, whereas in our approach the encapsulation structure is given by the box interfaces and the inferred type information is only used to statically check the encapsulation property. As we have more predetermined knowledge, we are less dependent on heuristics.

Overview. In Sect. 2, we illustrate and explain the approach by an example. We substantiate the approach by presenting an object-oriented core language for interface-oriented programming with an appropriate ownership type system (Sect. 3). The type system adapts the one described in [39] to boxes. Section 4 presents the new inference algorithm based on constraint solving. Section 5 discusses related work, Section 6 contains our conclusions.

2   Encapsulated Object-Oriented Components

In this section, we illustrate the goals of our approach from a programmer's perspective. First, we describe how box implementations look like. Then, we show which ownership information is derived by our approach.

Programming with Boxes. The box model builds on the general object-oriented model with interfaces, classes, objects, (object) references, object-local state, and methods to define behavior. The following brief description of the model is merely to motivate our type inference approach. A more detailed description including the discussion of design decisions and showing the use of the model for modular specification can be found in [36].

Boxes are described by modules. Figure 1 shows a module implementing simple list boxes with iterators. It provides two interfaces and three classes. In our simple language, a module defines exactly one box interface and one box class, indicated by the keyword **box**. The box class has to implement the box interface. Like in Java, we assume default constructors for classes. In addition, box interfaces have a default constructor. Calling the constructor of a box interface

```
module list;                        class Node {
                                      Node next;
box interface List<d> {               Object value;
   void add(d Object o);              Node(Node n, Object o) {
   boundary Iterator<d> iter();         next = n;
}                                       value = o;
interface Iterator<d> {               }
   d Object next();                 }
}
                                    class LIterator
box class ListImp                     implements Iterator {
   implements List {                  Node current;
   Node head;                         LIterator(Node n) {
   void add(Object o) {                 current = n
      head = new Node(head,o);        }
   }                                  Object next() {
   Iterator iter() {                    Node t = current;
      return new LIterator(head);       current = current.next;
   }                                    return t.value;
}                                     }
                                    }
                                  }
```

Fig. 1. The list module

B calls the constructor of the class implementing B. An application of box constructor **List** is demonstrated in Fig. 2 in the body of method do. A box is a runtime entity that is created together with an object of a box class. That is, the mentioned constructor call creates a ListImp object, say l, and a box; l is called the owner of the box. Objects of normal classes are usually created in the box of the this-object. E.g. the **Node** and **LIterator** objects created in class **ListImp** belong to the List box owned by the current this-object. In general, our type system allows to create objects in all boxes that are accessible at the creation site (for details see Sect. 3).

```
module client;                      box class ClientImp
import list;                          implements Client {
                                      void do(){
                                        List l = new List();
box interface Client {                l.add(new Object());
   void do();                         Iterator it = l.iter();
}                                     Object o = it.next();
                                      }
                                    }
```

Fig. 2. Client module using the list module

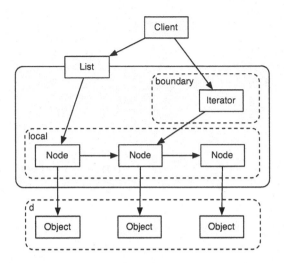

Fig. 3. A list box at runtime showing the different objects and their domains. Objects are represented by rectangles, arrows are references, the box is indicated by a solid rounded rectangle, the different domains are shown as dashed rounded rectangles. The box owner resides on the edge of the box.

Every box has two domains – a local and a boundary domain. Each object of a box resides in one of these domains. Local objects are encapsulated and cannot be referenced from the outside, boundary objects are accessible from the outside. Figure 3 shows a list box at runtime. The client object can only access the `List` object itself or `Iterator` objects in the boundary domain. As `Node` objects are in the local domain, they cannot be accessed. Data objects referenced by `Node` objects reside in an external domain `d`, which is a parameter of the box.

Ownership Annotations. A box can only be accessed via the interfaces given in the module. E.g. a List box can only be accessed via the reference of its owner or via `Iterator` references. In particular, the implementation must not pass out references to `Node` objects. E.g. method `next` in Fig. 1 is not allowed to return `t` instead of `t.value`. However, it can return references of outside objects that are captured earlier (e.g. `next` returns a reference captured earlier in a call to `add`). To statically check this encapsulation property, we use an ownership type system. Types can be annotated with `local`, `boundary` and `global`, representing the domain of the referenced objects. In addition, we allow genericity parameters. E.g. the `List` module is generic w.r.t. the owner of objects entered into the list. This is indicated by the parameter `<d>` in Fig. 1. In our approach, the programmer only has to annotate the interfaces with ownership information. Classes need not to be annotated. The ownership information is automatically inferred. Figure 4 shows the list module with inferred ownership types to illustrate the gain of our inference technique. For more complex examples, the gain is even bigger. The type system underlying the annotations is described in the next section.

```
module list;                          class Node<d> {
                                        local Node<d> next;
box interface List<d> {                 d Object value;
   void add(d Object o);                Node(local Node<d> n, d Object o) {
   boundary Iterator<d> iter();           next = n;
}                                         value = o;
interface Iterator<d> {                 }
   d Object next();                    }
}
                                      class LIterator<d>
box class ListImp<d>                     implements Iterator<d> {
   implements List<d> {                  local Node<d> current;
   local Node<d> head;                   boundary LIterator(
   void add(d Object o) {                           local Node<d> n) {
      head =                                current = n
        new local Node<d>(head,o);       }
   }                                    d Object next() {
   boundary Iterator<d> iter() {           local Node<d> t = current;
      return new boundary                  current = current.next;
        LIterator<d>(head);                return t.value;
   }                                     }
}                                     }
```

Fig. 4. The list module with inferred ownership annotations

3   Ownership Domains for Boxes

The basic idea of Ownership Domains for Boxes is to group objects into distinct domains. Every box has two domains, a *local* domain and a *boundary* domain. Every object belongs to exactly one domain. A box belongs to the domain to which its owner object belongs to. The ownership relation of domains and objects forms a hierarchy rooted at the special domain *global*. Encapsulation is defined by the accessibility relation of objects in different domains. Objects in the local domain of a box are encapsulated and cannot be accessed by the outside. Objects in the boundary domain can be accessed by the outside of a box and have access to objects in the corresponding local domain. The owner object of a box has a special role as it can access the local domain, even though the object itself belongs to the surrounding domain. In order to statically guarantee the encapsulation property at runtime, types are parameterized with domain annotations. Like ordinary types, the additional domain annotations restrict the possible values that a variable or field can hold.

This section presents a formalization of the language and the ownership type system. To shorten the presentation, the language is a slight simplification of the language that we used in Sect. 2 to illustrate our approach. The formalization is inspired by several existing formal type systems for Java, namely Featherweight

$$
\begin{array}{llll}
\mathsf{P} & ::= \overline{\mathsf{L}}_i\ \overline{\mathsf{L}}_b\ \overline{\mathsf{L}}_m\ e & \text{programs} \\
\mathsf{L}_i & ::= \text{interface } \mathsf{I}\langle\alpha,\overline{\beta}\rangle\ \{\ \overline{\mathsf{M}}_h\ \} & \text{interfaces} \\
\mathsf{L}_b & ::= \text{box interface } \mathsf{B}\langle\alpha,\overline{\beta}\rangle\ \{\ \overline{\mathsf{M}}_h\ \} & \text{box interfaces} \\
\mathsf{L}_m & ::= \text{module } \{\ \mathsf{K}_b\ \overline{\mathsf{K}}_i\ \} & \text{modules} \\
\mathsf{K}_b & ::= \text{box class } \mathsf{C} \text{ implements } \mathsf{B}\ \{\ \overline{\mathsf{T}}\ \overline{\mathsf{f}};\ \overline{\mathsf{M}}\ \} & \text{box classes} \\
\mathsf{K}_i & ::= \text{class } \mathsf{C} \text{ implements } \mathsf{I}\ \{\ \overline{\mathsf{T}}\ \overline{\mathsf{f}};\ \overline{\mathsf{M}}\ \} & \text{classes} \\
\mathsf{M}_h & ::= \mathsf{T}\ \mathsf{m}(\overline{\mathsf{T}}\ \overline{\mathsf{x}}) & \text{method headers} \\
\mathsf{M} & ::= \mathsf{M}_h\ \{e\} & \text{methods} \\
\mathsf{N} & ::= \mathsf{C}\ |\ \mathsf{I}\ |\ \mathsf{B} & \text{type names} \\
\mathsf{T},\mathsf{U} & ::= \mathsf{N}\langle\overline{\mathsf{d}}\rangle & \text{types} \\
\mathsf{d},\mathsf{g} & ::= \alpha\ |\ \mathsf{b}.\mathsf{c}\ |\ \text{global} & \text{domain annotations} \\
\mathsf{b} & ::= \text{box}\ |\ \mathsf{x}\ |\ \underline{\text{null}}\ |\ \underline{?} & \text{domain owners} \\
\mathsf{c} & ::= \text{boundary}\ |\ \text{local} & \text{domain kinds} \\
e & ::= & \text{expressions} \\
& \quad \mathsf{x} & \text{local variables} \\
& \quad |\ \text{new } \mathsf{C}\langle\overline{\mathsf{d}}\rangle & \text{object creation} \\
& \quad |\ \text{new } \mathsf{B}\langle\overline{\mathsf{d}}\rangle & \text{box creation} \\
& \quad |\ e.\mathsf{f} & \text{field access} \\
& \quad |\ e.\mathsf{f} = e & \text{field update} \\
& \quad |\ e.\mathsf{m}(\overline{e}) & \text{method call} \\
& \quad |\ \text{let } \mathsf{x} = e \text{ in } e & \text{variable binding} \\
& \quad |\ (\mathsf{C}\langle\overline{\mathsf{d}}\rangle)\ e & \text{cast} \\
& \quad |\ \text{null} & \text{null constant} \\
\mathsf{I} & \in \text{interface names} \\
\mathsf{B} & \in \text{box interface names} \\
\mathsf{C} & \in \text{class names} \\
\mathsf{m} & \in \text{method names} \\
\alpha,\beta & \in \text{domain parameters}
\end{array}
$$

Fig. 5. Abstract syntax

Java (FJ) [22] and CLASSICJAVA [17], and by several flavors of these type systems which already incorporate ownership information [11, 10, 2, 37, 25].

3.1   Language Syntax

The object-oriented core language supports interface-oriented programming with the box model described in [36] and an adapted version of the Simple Loose Ownership Domains type system described in [39]. The abstract syntax of our formal language is shown in Fig. 5. We use similar notations as FJ [22]. A bar indicates a sequence: $\overline{\mathsf{L}} = \mathsf{L}_1, \mathsf{L}_2, \ldots, \mathsf{L}_n$, where the length is defined as $|\overline{\mathsf{L}}| = n$. Similar, $\overline{\mathsf{T}}\ \overline{\mathsf{f}}$; is equal to $\mathsf{T}_1\ \mathsf{f}_1; \mathsf{T}_2\ \mathsf{f}_2; \ldots; \mathsf{T}_n\ \mathsf{f}_n$. If there is some sequence $\overline{\mathsf{x}}$, we write x_i for any element of $\overline{\mathsf{x}}$.

A program consists of interfaces, box interfaces, modules and an expression, which acts as the main procedure of the program. Every module contains one box class implementing a box interface and normal classes implementing other interfaces.

For simplicity, we assume that every class has a companion interface that it implements. In our simple language, an interface essentially lists the publicly available methods of the class. The syntactic separation of interfaces and classes also simplifies the presentation of our inference technique. We do not consider inheritance in this paper. Subtyping is only supported between classes and interfaces. It is straightforward to extend our language with subtyping of interfaces. Our language has no constructors; new objects are created by setting all fields to null. Note that we can simulate constructors by ordinary method calls. For example, we could demand that methods named init are always called directly after an object has been created and can never be called directly. Classes and box classes can declare fields and methods. As we do not support abstract classes, a class has to implement all methods declared in its interface.

For conciseness of the formalization, we have streamlined the notation of ownership annotations used in Sect. 2. Instead of writing the owning domain in front of the type, we now write it as the first parameter of the type. Furthermore, we make the owning domain of the current receiver object explicit by adding an additional domain parameter (this follows notations of similar systems, see e.g. [10]). With this modifications, a domain annotation can either be a domain parameter α, the global domain, or is of the form b.c, where the first part defines the owner of the domain, and the second part defines the domain kind, that is, whether it is the boundary or local domain.

The keyword box denotes the owner of the current box. The name of a local variable x is used for objects of box classes and denotes the box owned by x. For example, x.local denotes the local domain of the box owned by x. Owners null and ? do not belong to the user syntax (indicated by an underline), but can appear during reduction. ? as owner represents an invalid domain annotation, and null is the owner of the global domain. In fact, all occurrences of global are treated as null.local.

The domain kind c can either be boundary or local. For example, consider an object x with field f of type $N\langle box.local, box.boundary\rangle$ and let b be the box to which x belongs. Then, f can hold references to objects y in the local domain of b, such that the second domain parameter of y's type is instantiated by the boundary domain of b.

In our language we have the usual set of expressions. Just the creation expressions need some explanations. To create a new box we use the interface name of the box, for classes we use their class name. As in our language classes are only visible inside their module, this implies that within a module M only boxes or objects for classes declared in M can be created.

3.2 Auxiliary Functions

To define the type system for our language we need some helper functions. To retrieve the type name and the domains from a type, we use the functions raw and doms.

$$\mathrm{raw}(N\langle\overline{d}\rangle) \triangleq N$$
$$\mathrm{doms}(N\langle\overline{d}\rangle) \triangleq \overline{d}$$

To save space we only give informal descriptions for the following auxiliary functions.

$$
\begin{aligned}
\mathsf{intfNames}(\mathsf{P}) &\triangleq \text{the set of interface names defined in P} \\
\mathsf{boxNames}(\mathsf{P}) &\triangleq \text{the set of box interface names defined in P} \\
\mathsf{classNames}(\mathsf{L}) &\triangleq \text{the set of class names defined in module L} \\
\mathsf{implBox}(\mathsf{L}) &\triangleq \text{the name of the implemented box interface in L} \\
\mathsf{boxClass}(\mathsf{B}) &\triangleq \text{the class that implements box B} \\
\mathsf{isBoxClass}(\mathsf{C}) &\triangleq \text{class C is a box class} \\
\mathsf{isBoxType}(\mathsf{N}\langle \overline{\mathsf{d}} \rangle) &\triangleq \text{N is either a box class or a box interface}
\end{aligned}
$$

The function owner returns the owner part of a domain annotation. Its first parameter N is the type in which the domain annotation is interpreted. It is used to make the case distinction between objects of box and non-box types. If N is not a box type, we know that box is a representation of the owner. Otherwise, we do not have a syntactic representation of the owner. Thus, function owner returns ?, leading to an invalid type.

$$
\mathsf{owner}(\mathsf{N}, \mathsf{d}) \triangleq \begin{cases} \mathsf{b} & \text{if } \mathsf{d} = \mathsf{b}.\mathsf{c} \\ \mathsf{box} & \text{if } \mathsf{d} = \alpha \wedge \neg \mathsf{isBoxType}(\mathsf{N}) \\ ? & \text{if } \mathsf{d} = \alpha \wedge \mathsf{isBoxType}(\mathsf{N}) \end{cases}
$$

params just returns the domain parameters of a class or an interface.

$$
\frac{\ldots \text{interface } \mathsf{N}\langle \overline{\alpha} \rangle \ldots}{\mathsf{params}(\mathsf{N}) = \overline{\alpha}} \qquad \frac{\ldots \text{class C implements N} \ldots}{\mathsf{params}(\mathsf{C}) = \mathsf{params}(\mathsf{N})}
$$

The function field looks up the type of a field in a class. Analogous for the method function which returns the method definition of m.

$$
\frac{\ldots \text{class C} \ldots \mathsf{T}' \mathsf{f}; \ldots}{\mathsf{field}(\mathsf{C}\langle \_ \rangle, \mathsf{f}) = \mathsf{T}'}
$$

$$
\frac{\ldots \text{class C} \ldots \mathsf{T} \, \mathsf{m}(\overline{\mathsf{T}} \, \overline{\mathsf{x}})\{\mathsf{e}\} \ldots}{\mathsf{method}(\mathsf{C}\langle \_ \rangle, \mathsf{m}) = \mathsf{T} \, \mathsf{m}(\overline{\mathsf{T}} \, \overline{\mathsf{x}})\{\mathsf{e}\}} \qquad \frac{\ldots \text{interface } \mathsf{N}\langle \_ \rangle \ldots \mathsf{T} \, \mathsf{m}(\overline{\mathsf{T}} \, \overline{\mathsf{x}}) \ldots}{\mathsf{method}(\mathsf{N}\langle \_ \rangle, \mathsf{m}) = \mathsf{T} \, \mathsf{m}(\overline{\mathsf{T}} \, \overline{\mathsf{x}})}
$$

The function $\mathsf{boxOwner}$ checks whether an expression denotes a valid owner representation. Only variables and null can be used as owners.

$$
\mathsf{boxOwner}(\mathsf{e}) \triangleq \begin{cases} \mathsf{e} & \text{if } \mathsf{e} = \mathsf{x} \text{ or } \mathsf{e} = \mathsf{null} \\ ? & \text{else} \end{cases}
$$

For method call and field selection sites, the declared generic type of parameters and fields has to be translated to the domain in which it is used. This translation takes the type annotation $\mathsf{N}\langle \overline{\mathsf{d}} \rangle$ of the actual method parameter or of the selected expression and uses it to adapt the domain parameters and box owner of the declared formal parameter or field type. A domain parameter α is replaced by

$\Gamma; T; b \vdash \diamond$	environment Γ is valid
$\Gamma; T; b \vdash d_1 \rightarrow d_2$	domain d_1 can access domain d_2
$\Gamma; T; b \vdash d$	domain d is valid
$\Gamma; T; b \vdash T$	type T is valid
$\Gamma; T; b \vdash e : T$	expression e has type T
$\Gamma; T; b \vdash M_h$	method header M_h is well-typed
$\Gamma; T; b \vdash M$	method M is well-typed
$T <: U$	type T is a subtype of type U
$L_m \vdash N$	type name N is valid in module L_m
$L_m \vdash K_i$	class K_i is well-typed in module L_m
$L_m \vdash K_b$	box class K_b is well-typed in module L_m
$\vdash P$	program P is well-typed
$\vdash L_m$	module L_m is well-typed
$\vdash L_i$	interface L_i is well-typed
$\vdash L_b$	box interface L_b is well-typed

Fig. 6. Judgments used by the type system

the corresponding actual domain, the box keyword is replaced depending on whether N is a box type or not.

(TRANS-C)
$$\frac{\neg \text{isBoxType}(N) \qquad params(N) = \overline{\alpha}}{\text{trans}(N\langle \overline{d}\rangle, e, d') = [\overline{d}/\overline{\alpha}, owner(N, d_1)/\text{box}]d'}$$

(TRANS-B)
$$\frac{\text{isBoxType}(N) \qquad params(N) = \overline{\alpha}}{\text{trans}(N\langle \overline{d}\rangle, e, d') = [\overline{d}/\overline{\alpha}, boxOwner(e)/\text{box}]d'}$$

(TRANS-TYPE)
$$\frac{}{\text{trans}(T, e, N\langle \overline{d}\rangle) = N\langle \text{trans}(T, e, \overline{d})\rangle}$$

3.3 Type System

We now present the rules of our type system. The used judgments are shown in Fig. 6. Some judgments are of the form $\Gamma; T; b \vdash \dots$. This means, that the right hand side is evaluated under the context $\Gamma; T; b$, where Γ is the type environment, T is the current context type, i.e. the type of this, and b represents the current box. T is important as it defines the valid domain parameters and whether the current context is a box class or a normal class. b is needed for the accessibility relation.

By the type of box we refer to the class name of the box class of the current module, which is left implicit, parameterized by the parameters of the implemented interface.

$$\frac{L_m \vdash C \qquad \text{box class } C \dots \qquad params(C) = \overline{\alpha}}{\text{type}(\text{box}) = C\langle \overline{\alpha}\rangle}$$

Subtyping. The subtype relation is the reflexive closure of the relation between classes and their implemented interfaces. Note that the subtype relation on types require that the domain parameters must be the same.

$$\text{(T-SUB-REFL)} \qquad\qquad \frac{\text{(T-SUB-DIRECT)}}{\text{... class C implements N ...}} \qquad\qquad \text{(T-SUB-TYPE)}$$

$$\frac{}{N <: N} \qquad\qquad \frac{}{C <: N} \qquad\qquad \frac{N_1 <: N_2}{N_1\langle\overline{d}\rangle <: N_2\langle\overline{d}\rangle}$$

Valid Type Names. Interfaces are visible everywhere, but class names can only be used in their corresponding module.

$$\text{(V-CLASS)} \qquad\qquad \text{(V-INTERFACE)} \qquad\qquad \text{(V-BOX)}$$

$$\frac{C \in \text{classNames}(L_m)}{L_m \vdash C} \qquad \frac{I \in \text{intfNames}(P)}{L_m \vdash I} \qquad \frac{B \in \text{boxNames}(P)}{L_m \vdash B}$$

Environment. The environment Γ is a map from variables to types. It records the type information of free variables.

$$\Gamma ::= \varnothing \mid \Gamma, x : T \qquad \text{environment}$$

The following rules ensure that valid environments can only be extended by variables not already existing in the domain of Γ, i.e. $\Gamma, x : T; T'; b \vdash \diamond \Rightarrow x \notin \text{dom}(\Gamma)$, and that all variables are well-typed.

$$\text{(V-ENV-EMPTY)}$$
$$\frac{\text{owner}(N, d_1) = b \lor \text{type}(b) <: N\langle\overline{d}\rangle}{\varnothing; N\langle\overline{d}\rangle; b \vdash \diamond}$$

$$\text{(V-ENV-VAR)}$$
$$\frac{\Gamma; T'; b \vdash \diamond \qquad x \notin \text{dom}(\Gamma) \qquad \Gamma; T'; b \vdash T}{\Gamma, x : T; T'; b \vdash \diamond}$$

Accessibility Relation. The key element of our type system is the accessibility relation on domains which is shown in Fig. 7. It is the basis of the encapsulation property. The judgment $\Gamma; T; b \vdash d_1 \rightarrow d_2$ tells us that domain d_1 can access domain d_2 in the given context. That is, objects in domain d_1 can access all objects in domain d_2. The relation formalizes the informal accessibility between domains that we explained above, which depends on the ownership hierarchy of boxes.

The accessibility relation is reflexive (A-REFL), that is, every domain can access itself. Note however that it is not transitive. For example in the program scenario of Fig. 1 and 2, a client object can access an iterator object, iterator objects can access the nodes of their list, but client objects may not access node objects. Rule (A-OWNER) tells us that two domains with the same owner, i.e. domains belonging to the same box, can access each other. The following four rules relate the domains of the current context type and the domains of the current box. The domains of the current box can access all parameter domains (A-PARAM); this is mirrored by type rule (V-TYPE) that regulated the instantiation of domain parameters (see below). Furthermore, the first parameter domain, that is, the owner domain of this, has access to all other parameter domains (A-PARAM-2). If the current context class is not a box class, then the first parameter domain can access the domains of the current box (A-PARAM-3). If it is a box class then it can only access the boundary domain of the current box (A-PARAM-4). A domain can always access the boundary domain of a box, which it can access (A-BOUNDARY). The boundary domain of a box has access to the owning domain of its box (A-BOUNDARY-2). Every domain can access the global domain, i.e. domains owned by null (A-NULL).

$$(\text{A-REFL})$$
$$\overline{\Gamma; T; b \vdash d \rightarrow d}$$

$$(\text{A-OWNER})$$
$$\overline{\Gamma; T; b \vdash b.c_1 \rightarrow b.c_2}$$

$$(\text{A-PARAM})$$
$$\overline{\Gamma; N\langle \overline{d} \rangle; b \vdash b.c \rightarrow \overline{d}}$$

$$(\text{A-PARAM-2})$$
$$\overline{\Gamma; N\langle \overline{d} \rangle; b \vdash d_1 \rightarrow \overline{d}}$$

$$(\text{A-PARAM-3})$$
$$\frac{\neg isBoxType(N)}{\Gamma; N\langle \overline{d} \rangle; b \vdash d_1 \rightarrow b.c}$$

$$(\text{A-PARAM-4})$$
$$\frac{isBoxType(N)}{\Gamma; N\langle \overline{d} \rangle; b \vdash d_1 \rightarrow b.\text{boundary}}$$

$$(\text{A-BOUNDARY})$$
$$\frac{\Gamma; T; b \vdash b' : N\langle \overline{d} \rangle \qquad \Gamma; T; b \vdash d \rightarrow d_1}{\Gamma; T; b \vdash d \rightarrow b'.\text{boundary}}$$

$$(\text{A-BOUNDARY-2})$$
$$\frac{\Gamma; T; b \vdash b' : N\langle \overline{d} \rangle}{\Gamma; T; b \vdash b'.\text{boundary} \rightarrow d_1}$$

$$(\text{A-NULL})$$
$$\overline{\Gamma; T; b \vdash d \rightarrow \text{null}.c}$$

Fig. 7. Accessibility relation

Valid Domains and Types. Figure 8 shows rules to ensure the validity of domains and types. Valid domains have neither ?, nor variables as owners that are not of a box type. The (V-TYPE) rule is very important, because it ensures that it is not possible to break encapsulation by passing domains as parameters which are not accessible by the first domain parameter. In addition, all domain parameters must be accessible by the domains of the current box. The rule is implicitly parameterized by the module L_m.

Programs, Interfaces, Modules and Classes. Figure 9 shows the typing rules for programs, interfaces, modules and classes. The (T-PROG) rule requires some explanation. The initial expression e is typed under the context type Global⟨null.local⟩. We just assume that Global is some predefined interface without any methods. In addition, all other elements of the program must be well-typed, and some sanity conditions must hold. A module is correctly typed if its classes are correctly typed. Classes and box classes are correctly typed if their methods and fields are correctly typed under the corresponding context.

(V-DOMAIN-BOX)   (V-DOMAIN-BOX)   (V-DOMAIN-BOX)

$$\frac{}{\Gamma;T;b \vdash box.c} \qquad \frac{}{\Gamma;T;b \vdash null.c} \qquad \frac{}{\Gamma;N\langle\overline{d}\rangle;b \vdash d_i}$$

(V-DOMAIN-VAR)

$$\frac{\Gamma;T;b \vdash x : T_x \qquad isBoxType(T_x)}{\Gamma;T;b \vdash x.boundary}$$

(V-TYPE)

$$\frac{L_m \vdash N \quad \Gamma;T;b \vdash \overline{d} \quad \Gamma;T;b \vdash \diamond \quad \Gamma;T;b \vdash d_1 \rightarrow \overline{d} \qquad \Gamma;T;b \vdash b.c \rightarrow \overline{d} \quad |params(N)| = |\overline{d}|}{\Gamma;T;b \vdash N\langle\overline{d}\rangle}$$

Fig. 8. Valid domains and types

Methods are typed as usual. The types appearing in the method signature must be valid in the current context, and the type of the body expression must be a subtype of the declared return type.

Expressions. The expression type rules are shown in Fig. 10. The non-standard rules are (T-FIELD) and (T-INVK). In both rules the function trans from above is used to adapt the declared type to the application context.

3.4   Properties

This subsection summarizes the central properties of our type system.[1] We proved Subject Reduction, that is, that during the execution of a well-typed program all dynamic types are subtypes of their declared static types.

Theorem 1 (Subject Reduction). *If an expression is typed by the type system, then the type of the evaluated expression is a subtype of the original type.*

Proof. By defining an operational semantics for our language and using induction on its rules.

The Subject Reduction Theorem is a central prerequisite to prove that objects during runtime can only access other objects according to their declared static domains.

Theorem 2 (Accessibility Invariant). *Objects can only access other objects which are*

1. *in the same box,*
2. *in the boundary domain of a box which they can access,*
3. *in a surrounding box of their own box.*

---

[1] The operational semantics and the proofs of the theorems can be obtained from the authors.

(T-PROG)

$$\vdash \overline{L}_i \qquad \vdash \overline{L}_b \qquad \varnothing; \text{Global}\langle \text{null.local}\rangle; \text{null} \vdash e : T \qquad \vdash \overline{L}_m$$
$$\forall B \in \text{boxNames}(\overline{L}_b).\ \exists L_m \in \overline{L}_m.\ \text{implBox}(L_m) = B$$
$$\forall L_m, L'_m \in \overline{L}_m.\ \text{implBox}(L_m) = \text{implBox}(L'_m) \Rightarrow L_m = L'_m$$
$$\overline{\qquad\qquad\qquad\qquad \vdash \overline{L}_i\ \overline{L}_b\ \overline{L}_m\ e \qquad\qquad\qquad\qquad}$$

(T-INTERFACE)
$$\frac{\text{this} : T; T; \text{box} \vdash \overline{M}_h}{\vdash \ldots \text{ interface } T \{ \overline{M}_h \}}$$

(T-METHOD-HEADER)
$$\frac{\Gamma; T_i; b \vdash T \qquad \Gamma; T_i; b \vdash \overline{T}}{\Gamma; T_i; b \vdash T\ m(\overline{T}\ \overline{x})}$$

(T-MODULE)
$$\frac{L_m = \text{module } \{ K_b\ \overline{K}_i \} \qquad L_m \vdash K_b \qquad L_m \vdash \overline{K}_i}{\vdash L_m}$$

(T-CLASS)
$$\frac{\overline{\alpha} = \text{params}(C) \qquad \varnothing; C\langle \overline{\alpha}\rangle; \text{box} \vdash \overline{T} \qquad \text{this} : C\langle \overline{\alpha}\rangle; C\langle \overline{\alpha}\rangle; \text{box} \vdash \overline{M}}{\text{All methods of interface } N \text{ are implemented in } \overline{M}}$$
$$\overline{L_m \vdash \text{class } C \text{ implements } N \{ \overline{T}\ \overline{f};\ \overline{M} \}}$$

(T-METHOD)
$$\frac{\Gamma; T_c; b \vdash T, \overline{T} \qquad \Gamma, \overline{x} : \overline{T}; T_c; b \vdash e : T_e \qquad T_e <: T}{\Gamma; T_c; b \vdash T\ m(\overline{T}\ \overline{x})\{e\}}$$

Fig. 9. Program, interface, module, class and method typing

Note that an object can access a box if it can access its owner object. The negation of the Accessibility Invariant is the Encapsulation Invariant:

Corollary 1 (Encapsulation Invariant). *Objects in the local domain of a box cannot be accessed by objects of surrounding boxes.*

4   Domain Inference

In the previous section we presented a language which statically guarantees object encapsulation. The type system ensures this by checking the domain annotations of types. However, the domain annotations are a significant syntactical overhead and an additional burden to the programmer. As we believe that the programmer wants to express the domain restrictions in the interfaces, but wants to leave them out in the implementation, we present an inference algorithm that infers all domain annotations within a module, but requires fully annotated interfaces. That is, our inference algorithm is intra-module but inter-class. As within a module, only classes of the same module or interfaces can be used as types, we can modularly infer the types of a single module. The algorithm also only infers domain annotations, all other type information, like class or interface names

(T-NULL)

$$\frac{\Gamma; T_c; b \vdash T}{\Gamma; T_c; b \vdash \mathsf{null} : T}$$

(T-VAR)

$$\frac{\Gamma; T_c; b \vdash T \qquad x : T \in \Gamma}{\Gamma; T_c; b \vdash x : T}$$

(T-FIELD)

$$\frac{\Gamma; T_c; b \vdash e : T \qquad T_f = \mathsf{trans}(T, e, \mathsf{field}(T, f)) \qquad \Gamma; T_c; b \vdash T_f}{\Gamma; T_c; b \vdash e.f : T_f}$$

(T-FIELD-UP)

$$\frac{\Gamma; T_c; b \vdash e_1.f : T_f \qquad \Gamma; T_c; b \vdash e_2 : T \qquad T <: T_f}{\Gamma; T_c; b \vdash e_1.f = e_2 : T}$$

(T-INVK)

$$\frac{\Gamma; T_c; b \vdash e : T_e \quad \overline{\Gamma; T_c; b \vdash \overline{e} : \overline{T}_e} \quad \mathsf{method}(T_e, m) = T_m \ m(\overline{T}_m \ \_) \ \dots \quad T = \mathsf{trans}(T_e, e, T_m)}{\overline{T} = \mathsf{trans}(T_e, e, \overline{T}_m) \qquad \overline{T}_e <: \overline{T} \qquad \Gamma; T_c; b \vdash T \qquad \Gamma; T_c; b \vdash \overline{T}}{\Gamma; T_c; b \vdash e.m(\overline{e}) : T}$$

(T-NEW-CLASS)

$$\frac{\Gamma; T; b \vdash C\langle\overline{d}\rangle \qquad \neg\mathsf{isBoxClass}(C)}{\Gamma; T; b \vdash \mathsf{new} \ C\langle\overline{d}\rangle : C\langle\overline{d}\rangle}$$

(T-NEW-BOX)

$$\frac{\Gamma; T; b \vdash B\langle\overline{d}\rangle}{\Gamma; T; b \vdash \mathsf{new} \ B\langle\overline{d}\rangle : B\langle\overline{d}\rangle}$$

(T-LET)

$$\frac{\Gamma; T; b \vdash e_1 : T_1 \qquad \Gamma, x : T_1; T; b \vdash e_2 : T_2 \qquad \Gamma; T; b \vdash T_2}{\Gamma; T; b \vdash \mathsf{let} \ x = e_1 \ \mathsf{in} \ e_2 : T_2}$$

(T-CAST)

$$\frac{\Gamma; T_c; b \vdash e : T' \qquad T <: T' \ \vee \ T' <: T}{\Gamma; T_c; b \vdash (T)e : T}$$

Fig. 10. Expression type rules

must be given by the programmer. There are other inference algorithms that can infer such kind of type information for object-oriented languages e.g. [33, 35, 15].

4.1 Overall Inference Algorithm

Figure 11 describes the tasks and the overall procedure of our inference algorithm. The input is an unannotated module and the set of all interfaces. The preparation step adds type annotations to the type names occurring in the classes. More precisely: Let N be a type occurring in some class C.

- If N is a parameter or return type of a method m declared in the implemented interface, N gets the annotation it has in the interface.
- Otherwise, it gets an annotation of the form $\langle X_1, \dots, X_n \rangle$ where the X_is are fresh constraint variables (see below) and n equals $|\mathsf{params}(N)|$. By fresh we mean here that all constraint variables added to the module are distinct.

Furthermore, to simplify the presentation of the algorithm, preparation renames all parameters and variables introduced in let expressions so that they are unique in the module.

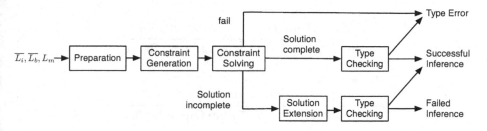

Fig. 11. Inference algorithm

In the second step, a set of constraints is generated for the module. The third step solves the constraints by a unification algorithm. There are three possible results of the third step. If it fails, then the constraints are contradictory, and we know that there are no type correct annotations for the module. If it does not fail, it returns a solution for the constraint set. A solution is a map from constraint variables to concrete domain annotations. If all constraint variables are covered by the solution, we call the solution complete, otherwise we call it incomplete. In both cases we have to check the solution by the type system, because our constraint inference algorithm only considers a subset of the typing rules, and the resulting constraint set may be under-determined. Before checking an incomplete solution we extend it by setting all unsolved variables to box.local to obtain a complete solution. Note that this extension may be type incorrect as the contraints ignore the accessability rules of the type system. Therefore, if in the case of an incomplete solution the type check fails we do not know whether a correct annotation exists or not, because the failure may be caused by the extension or may have already existed in the input. In summary, the algorithm has three possible *outcomes*:

1. Type Error: The program cannot be typed.
2. Successful Inference: A type correct annotation is inferred.
3. Failed Inference: There might be a correct annotation, but it is not found.

4.2   Constraint Generation

For the constraint system we extend the syntax for domain annotations (see Fig. 12). We add constraint variables, standing for unknown annotations. In addition, we need a delayed substitution and $\omega(N, d).c$, where ω is later reduced to the *owner* function. The set of possible types is extended by a type Null to type the null constant.

Auxiliary Functions. Due to the syntax extension of the domain annotations we redefine the trans rule of the normal type system in order to use the delayed substitution $\lfloor\ \rfloor$ instead of an ordinary substitution and to use ω instead of *owner*.

(TRANS-C)

$$\frac{\neg\mathsf{isBoxType}(\mathsf{N}) \qquad \mathsf{params}(\mathsf{N}) = \overline{\alpha}}{\mathsf{trans}(\mathsf{N}\langle\overline{d}\rangle, e, d') = \lfloor\overline{d}/\overline{\alpha}\rfloor[\omega(\mathsf{N}, d_1)/\mathsf{box}]d'}$$

(TRANS-B)

$$\frac{\mathsf{isBoxType}(\mathsf{N}) \qquad \mathsf{params}(\mathsf{N}) = \overline{\alpha}}{\mathsf{trans}(\mathsf{N}\langle\overline{d}\rangle, e, d') = \lfloor\overline{d}/\overline{\alpha}\rfloor[\mathsf{boxOwner}(e)/\mathsf{box}]d'}$$

The cgen function generates constraints for two given types. If one of the types is the Null type, which matches every type, cgen returns the empty set.

$$\frac{T_1 \neq \mathsf{Null} \qquad T_2 \neq \mathsf{Null}}{\mathsf{cgen}(T_1, T_2) = \{\mathsf{doms}(T_1) = \mathsf{doms}(T_2)\}} \qquad \frac{T_1 = \mathsf{Null} \ \vee \ T_2 = \mathsf{Null}}{\mathsf{cgen}(T_1, T_2) = \{\}}$$

Inference Rules. The constraint inference rules are of the form

$$\Gamma \vdash e : T \mid R$$

read: "expression e has type T under environment Γ, whenever constraints R are satisfied". The constraints in R are equations of extended domain annotations.

The inference rules are given in Fig. 13. Note that the preparation step already has replaced all missing domain annotations by unique constraint variables, and that all local variables are renamed so that they are unique in the regarded module.

As we do not take the accessibility relation into account, new constraints are only created for field updates, method declarations and method calls. For a field update the type on both sides of the assignment has to be the same. In method calls the argument types have to match the declared parameters and for method declarations the declared return type has to match the type of the implementing expression.

Properties. If there is a substitution of constraint variables by domain annotations, such that the resulting program is type correct by our type system, then such a substitution will fulfill the constraint set generated by the inference rules. Note, however, that the solution for some constraint sets, generated by our inference rules, can lead to a type incorrect program. This is due to the fact, that the inference rules ignore the accessibility relation. Taking the accessibility relation into account complicates the algorithm. In the examples that we studied, the gain in precision was too small to justify the additional technical complexity.

X, Y, Z		constraint variables
d	$::= \ldots \mid d^x$	extended domain annotations
d^x	$::= X \mid \rho\, d \mid \omega(\mathsf{N}, d).c$	augmented domain annotations
ρ	$::= \lfloor d_1/d_2 \rfloor$	delayed substitution
T	$::= \ldots \mid \mathsf{Null}$	extended types

Fig. 12. Extended syntax for the inference algorithm

(CT-VAR)   (CT-NULL)   (CT-CAST)   (CT-NEW-C)

$x : T \in \Gamma$ $\Gamma \vdash e : T \mid R$

$\overline{\Gamma \vdash x : T \mid \{\}}$ $\overline{\Gamma \vdash null : Null \mid \{\}}$ $\overline{\Gamma \vdash (T_1)e : T_1 \mid R}$ $\overline{\Gamma \vdash new\ C\langle\overline{d}\rangle : C\langle\overline{d}\rangle \mid \{\}}$

(CT-NEW-B)   (CT-LET)

$\Gamma \vdash e_1 : T_1 \mid R_1 \qquad \Gamma, x : T_1 \vdash e_2 : T_2 \mid R_2$

$\overline{\Gamma \vdash new\ B\langle\overline{d}\rangle : B\langle\overline{d}\rangle \mid \{\}}$ $\overline{\Gamma \vdash let\ x = e_1\ in\ e_2 : T_2 \mid R_1 \cup R_2}$

(CT-FIELD)

$\dfrac{\Gamma \vdash e : T \mid R \qquad T' = trans(T, boxOwner(e), field(T, f))}{\Gamma \vdash e.f : T' \mid R}$

(CT-FIELDUP)

$\dfrac{\Gamma \vdash e_1.f : T_1 \mid R_1 \qquad \Gamma \vdash e_2 : T_2 \mid R_2 \qquad R' = R_1 \cup R_2 \cup cgen(T_1, T_2)}{\Gamma \vdash e_1.f = e_2 : T_2 \mid R'}$

(CT-CALL)

$\Gamma \vdash e_1 : T \mid R_1 \qquad method(T, m) = T_m\ m(\overline{T}_m\ \_) \ldots$

$T_r = trans(T, boxOwner(e_1), T_m) \qquad \overline{T}_p = trans(T, boxOwner(e_1), \overline{T}_m)$

$\dfrac{\Gamma \vdash \overline{e}_2 : \overline{T}_2 \mid \overline{R}_2 \qquad R' = R_1 \cup \overline{R}_2 \cup cgen(\overline{T}_2, \overline{T}_p)}{\Gamma \vdash e_1.m(\overline{e}_2) : T_r \mid R'}$

(CT-METHOD)

$\dfrac{\Gamma, \overline{x} : \overline{T}_p \vdash e : T_e \mid R_e \qquad R = R_e \cup cgen(T_e, T_r)}{\Gamma \vdash T_r\ m(\overline{T}_p\ \overline{x})\{e\} \mid R}$

(CT-CLASS)   (CT-BOX)

$\dfrac{params(I) = \overline{\alpha} \qquad this : C\langle\overline{\alpha}\rangle \vdash \overline{M} \mid \overline{R}}{\vdash class\ C\ implements\ I\ \{\overline{Tf}; \overline{M}\} \mid \overline{R}}$ $\dfrac{params(B) = \overline{\alpha} \qquad this : C\langle\overline{\alpha}\rangle \vdash \overline{M} \mid \overline{R}}{\vdash box\ class\ C\ implements\ B\ \{\overline{Tf}; \overline{M}\} \mid \overline{R}}$

(CT-MODULE)

$\dfrac{\vdash K_b \mid R_b \qquad \vdash \overline{K}_c \mid \overline{R}_c \qquad R' = \bigcup \overline{R}_c \cup R_b}{\vdash module\ \{K_b \overline{K}_c\} \mid R'}$

Fig. 13. Constraint inference rules

4.3   Constraint Solving

In this subsection we present the algorithm to solve the generated constraint set.

Domain Reduction. To eliminate the delayed substitutions ρ and the owner terms ω in domain annotations, we define a reduction relation $\hookrightarrow$ on domains. A delayed substitution is reduced to a normal substitution if neither the domain, which is to be replaced, nor the domain on which the substitution is applied, contains a constraint variable. ω is only reduced to *owner* on unextended domains, because otherwise $owner$ would not be defined. The function $FV(d)$ returns the set of constraint variables appearing anywhere in d.

$$\frac{FV(d_2) \cup FV(d) = \varnothing}{\lfloor d_1/d_2 \rfloor d \hookrightarrow \lfloor d_1/d_2 \rfloor d} \qquad \frac{d \neq d^x}{\omega(N, d).c \hookrightarrow owner(N, d).c}$$

We write $\mathcal{D}$ for a domain annotation with a hole [] somewhere inside the domain annotation. $\mathcal{D}[d]$ means that the hole is replaced by d. E.g. if $\mathcal{D} = \lfloor d_1/[] \rfloor d$ then $\mathcal{D}[d_2] = \lfloor d_1/d_2 \rfloor d$. With $\mathcal{D}$ we extend the reduction relation to subterms.

$$\frac{d \hookrightarrow d'}{\mathcal{D}[d] \hookrightarrow \mathcal{D}[d']}$$

$\hookrightarrow^*$ is the transitive, reflexive closure of $\hookrightarrow$. A domain that cannot not be further reduced by $\hookrightarrow^*$ is called a normal form and denoted by $\downarrow d$. The normal form of a domain is unique as the reduction relation $\hookrightarrow$ is confluent, i.e. it is congruent and terminating.

Unification. To find a solution for the constraint set R, we use the unification algorithm given in Fig. 14. It is similar to the one presented in [34, Chap. 22.4]. The input is a set R of constraints, and the output is a unifier for R which is a map from constraint variables to domains. The inverse delayed substitution $\lfloor d_1/d_2 \rfloor^{-1}$ used in the formulation of the algorithm can be expressed as $\lfloor d_2/d_1 \rfloor$ in concrete domain annotations.

The algorithm uses three sets: R is the constraint set we try to find a solution for, Q stores constraints which cannot be fully processed at the moment and Q' stores the set Q of the previous recursive call and is needed to ensure termination. As long as R contains constraints we try to calculate a part of the solution and call unify recursively. If the chosen constraint d = g cannot yet be processed because an inverse of the delayed substitution ρ cannot be calculated, or the single constraint variable of one side occurs also on the other side, d = g is stored in Q and therefore it will be processed again later. The algorithm halts if R and Q are empty, or if R is empty and Q has not changed in the last call; that is, if no new information has been gathered, but there are still unsolved constraints left. This happens e.g. if fields are declared but never used, so nothing is known about their annotations.

Properties. The unification algorithm has three important properties. First, $unify$ always terminates and either returns a solution or fails. Second, if the solution is complete then it is the most general unifier for the input constraints. And third, if there exists a unifier for R then $unify$ will find a solution, i.e. it will not fail.

4.4   Properties of the Overall Inference Algorithm

As described in Subsect. 4.1, the overall inference algorithm has three possible outcomes. We proved the following properties:

1. If, for a given unannotated module, there exists a type correct annotation, then the outcome is either "Successful Inference" with a correctly inferred type annotation or "Failed Inference".

$unify(R) = unify_r(R, \{\}, \{\})$
$unify_r(R, Q, Q') =$
   if $(R \neq \{\})$ then
     choose $(d' = g')$ in R in
     let $R' = R \setminus \{d' = g'\}$ in
     let $d = \downarrow d', g = \downarrow g'$ in
       if $d = g$ then
         $unify_r(R', Q, Q')$
       else if $d = X$ and $X \notin FV(g)$ then
         $unify_r([X \mapsto g]R', [X \mapsto g]Q, [X \mapsto g]Q') \circ [X \mapsto g]$
       else if $g = X$ and $X \notin FV(d)$ then
         $unify_r([X \mapsto d]R', [X \mapsto d]Q, [X \mapsto d]Q') \circ [X \mapsto d]$
       else if $d = X$ and $X \in FV(g)$ then
         $unify_r(R', \{d = g\} \cup Q, Q')$
       else if $g = X$ and $X \in FV(d)$ then
         $unify_r(R', \{d = g\} \cup Q, Q')$
       else if $d = \rho X$ and $FV(\rho) = \{\}$ and $X \notin FV(g)$ then
         $unify_r([X \mapsto \rho^{-1}g]R', [X \mapsto \rho^{-1}g]Q, [X \mapsto \rho^{-1}g]Q') \circ [X \mapsto \rho^{-1}g]$
       else if $g = \rho X$ and $FV(\rho) = \{\}$ and $X \notin FV(d)$ then
         $unify_r([X \mapsto \rho^{-1}d]R', [X \mapsto \rho^{-1}d]Q, [X \mapsto \rho^{-1}d]Q') \circ [X \mapsto \rho^{-1}d]$
       else if $d = \rho d''$ or $g = \rho g''$ then
         $unify_r(R', \{d = g\} \cup Q, Q')$
       else if $d = \omega(N, d'').c$ then
         $unify_r(R', \{d = g\} \cup Q, Q')$
       else if $g = \omega(N, g'').c$ then
         $unify_r(R', \{d = g\} \cup Q, Q')$
       else fail
   else if $Q \neq \{\}$ then
     if $Q' = Q$ then $[]$
     else
       $unify_r(Q, \{\}, Q)$
   else $[]$

Fig. 14. Unification algorithm

2. Otherwise, if there exists no type correct annotation, then the outcome is either "Type Error" or "Failed Inference".

Thus, a type error is always a fault in the input program and needs to be fixed by the progammer. So far our experience showed that in practical program examples the algorithm only rarely terminates with "Failed Inference".

5 Related Work

We focus the discussion of related work to techniques for object encapsulation and type inference. For related work on the use of the box model, we refer the reader to [36].

Object Encapsulation. The first systems encapsulating objects were proposed by Hogg with Islands [21] and by Almeida with Balloons [4]. Both solution needed a different assignment semantics to ensure encapsulation.

Ownership Types are a static way to guarantee encapsulation of objects during runtime. The notion of ownership types stems from Clarke [11, 12, 9] to formalize the core of Flexible Alias Protection [31]. Ever since, many researchers investigated ownership type systems [29, 3, 8, to name a few]. Ownership type systems have been used to prevent data-races [6], deadlocks [7, 5], and to allow the modular specification and verification of object-oriented programs [28, 14]. Lately, ownership types have been combined with type genericity [37].

All the mentioned ownership type systems have one thing in common: They have problems with multi-access ownership contexts like our boxes. In particular, they cannot handle the iterator pattern properly. Recently several more or less powerful solutions have been proposed. The first allows the creation of dynamic aliases to owned objects [10], that is, aliases stored in the stack. The second approach [9, 7] is to allow Java's inner member classes [18] to access the representation objects of their parent objects. Both solutions do not provide the full power to generalize the owners-as-dominators property. *Ownership Domains* (OD) [2] has been the first approach which could handle the iterator problem properly. Objects are not owned directly by other objects anymore, but are owned by domains, which are in turn owned by objects. Every object can have an arbitrary number of domains, which can either be *private* or *public*. Objects in the private domain are encapsulated, and objects in the public domain can be accessed by the outside. This is similar to our local and boundary domains. The difference is that we only allow two domains per object, where OD allows an arbitrary number of domains. In addition, the accessibility between domains is hard-wired in our approach, where in OD the programmer has the possibility to define which domains can access which other domains by *link* declarations. Our system presented in the paper can be completely encoded in the OD approach. However, our system can be extended by so called *loose* domains, not presented here, which allow programming patterns that are not possible in OD [39]. OD have been combined with an effects system [40]. A more general version of OD has been formalized in System F [23].

Lu and Potter [25] presented a type system which separates object ownership and accessibility. Instead of only giving the owner of a type, types are also annotated by their possible accessibility. This introduces a very flexible system, which allows programming patterns not possible with our type system. However, this flexibility comes with the price of a higher annotation overhead, as both the owner and the accessibility must be given. This effectively doubles the number of parameters needed for classes and interfaces.

A previous system [26] considers the encapsulation of effects instead of objects. This allows, for example, to access internal representation objects from the outside, but disallows their direct modification. This mechanism is similar to the read-only mechanism of the Universes approach [29], where it is allowed to have read-only references to representation objects. However, this approach forbids programming patterns where boundary objects should be able to directly change the state of representation objects without using the owner object.

Confined Types [41, 42] is a lightweight mechanism that allows the encapsulation of objects within the boundary of a Java package. Confined types can be relatively easily inferred from unannotated programs [19].

Beside type systems there are other possibilities to statically ensure object encapsulation. In Boogie [24] a theorem prover is used to prove the absence of illegal accesses to representation objects. This is, for sure, the most flexible approach that is statically possible, however, it is also very heavy compared to a type system.

Type Inference. Robinson introduced the unify algorithm [38], Hindley [20] and Milner [27] introduced the notion of polymorphic type inference.

Aldrich et al. [3] present a constraint-based inference algorithm for AliasFJ, a capability-based alias annotation system. The annotations in their system not only define, which objects can access some other objects but also specify which aliases to an object may exist. Their inference algorithm first constructs a directed graph, consisting of a node for every entity in the program, to which a type can be assigned, i.e. fields, variables, expressions, etc., and different types of edges, representing different types of constraints, then propagation rules are used to determine annotations for all nodes. In contrast to our approach, their algorithm is supposed to infer alias information for completely unannotated programs. The found annotations can be refined by the programmer. But as the inference often leads to an unmanageable number of alias parameters, this is difficult. They have no proof that their algorithm terminates.

Agarwal and Stoller [1] present a runtime inference algorithm to infer type annotations for an ownership type system. During runtime, information about the accesses to some objects is collected, which is analyzed afterwards and leads to an annotated program. The runtime analysis is combined with a static analysis about the uniqueness of references. A small number of program executions suffice to gather enough information to infer a meaningful annotation for the whole program. For some type systems this approach is more effective, i.e. it can infer more annotations than type inference algorithms just based on static analysis.

In [6], Boyapati and Rinard use an ownership type system to guarantee that programs are free of data races. They presented a constraint-based intra-method algorithm to infer annotations for method-local variables. Because their constraints are simpler then ours, they can use a standard union-find algorithm to solve them. Like we do, they extend incomplete solutions with a default value.

Flanagan et al. [16] present an inference algorithm to verify automicity. In their approach the type rules generate a set of constraints, which is later solved by a fix-point iteration. Similar to our approach, they use a delayed substitution, delaying the application of a substitution on a constraint variable until the variable is resolved to some value.

6   Conclusions

We draw the conclusions in connection with the event that caused us to write up the presented boxes, namely Reinhard Wilhelm's birthday. Boxes cannot only be used as containers for birthday presents, they can as well encapsulate other objects and boxes. Although – like in the birthday scenario – ownership transfer is very important, we focussed here on a simpler box model in which the owner is determined at box creation time. In the present [ation], we adapted an ownership type system to the box model and developed an algorithm for inferring ownership annotations.

What might not be directly obvious from the small present [ation], is the fact that it causes new work for researches like Reinhard Wilhelm who are interested in heap analysis. The semantic-based structuring and encapsulation techniques for heaps can be used to localize and modularize heap analyses. Another interesting goal would be to use heap analyses to support type or structure inference in more complex encapsulation models, e.g. in models that support ownership transfer.

References

[1] Rahul Agarwal and Scott D. Stoller. Type inference for parameterized race-free Java. In *Proceedings of the Fifth International Conference on Verification, Model Checking and Abstract Interpretation (VMCAI)*, volume 2937 of *LNCS*, pages 149–160. Springer, January 2004.

[2] Jonathan Aldrich and Criag Chambers. Ownership domains: Separating aliasing policy from mechanism. In Odersky [32], pages 1–25.

[3] Jonathan Aldrich, Valentin Kostadinov, and Craig Chambers. Alias annotations for program understanding. In *Proc. OOPSLA 2002*, pages 311–330. ACM Press, November 2002.

[4] Paulo Sérgio Almeida. Balloon Types: Controlling sharing of state in data types. In *Proc. ECOOP'97*, volume 1241 of *LNCS*, pages 32–59. Springer, June 1998.

[5] Chandrasekhar Boyapati. *SafeJava: A Unified Type System for Safe Programming*. PhD thesis, Massachusetts Institute of Technology, February 2004.

[6] Chandrasekhar Boyapati and Martin Rinard. A parameterized type system for race-free java programs. In *Proc. OOPSLA 2001*, pages 56–69. ACM Press, October 2001.

[7] Chandrasekhar Boyapati, Robert Lee, and Martin Rinard. Ownership types for safe programming: Preventing data races and deadlocks. In *Proc. OOPSLA 2002*, pages 211–230. ACM Press, November 2002.

[8] Chandrasekhar Boyapati, Barbara Liskov, and Liuba Shrira. Ownership types for object encapsulation. In *Proc. POPL '03*, pages 213–223. ACM Press, January 2003.

[9] Dave Clarke. *Object Ownership and Containment*. PhD thesis, University of New South Wales, July 2001.

[10] Dave Clarke and S. Drossopoulou. Ownership, encapsulation, and the disjointness of type and effect. In *Proc. OOPSLA 2002*, pages 292–310. ACM Press, November 2002.

[11] Dave Clarke, John Potter, and James Noble. Ownership types for flexible alias protection. In *Proc. OOPSLA '98*, pages 48–64. ACM Press, October 1998.

[12] Dave Clarke, James Noble, and John M. Potter. Simple ownership types for object containment. In J. Lindskov Knudsen, editor, *Proc. ECOOP 2001*, volume 2072 of *Lecture Notes in Computer Science*, pages 53–76. Springer, June 2001.

[13] David L. Detlefs, K. Rustan M. Leino, and Greg Nelson. Wrestling with rep exposure. Research Report 156, Digital Systems Research Center, July 1998. SRC-RR-156.

[14] Werner Dietl and Peter Müller. Universes: Lightweight ownership for JML. *Journal of Object Technology*, 4(8):5–32, 2005.

[15] Alan Donovan, Adam Kiežun Matthew S. Tschantz, and Michael D. Ernst. Converting java programs to use generic libraries. In *OOPSLA '04*, pages 15–34. ACM Press, 2004.

[16] "Cormac Flanagan, Stephen N. Freund, and Marina Lifshin". Type inference for atomicity. In *In Proc. TLDI '05*, pages 47–58. ACM Press, 2005.

[17] Matthew Flatt, Shriram Krishnamurthi, and Matthias Felleisen. A programmer's reduction semantics for classes and mixins. *Formal Syntax and Semantics of Java*, 1523:241–269, 1999.

[18] James Gosling, Bill Joy, Guy Steele, and Gilad Bracha. *The Java^{TM} Language Specification – Second Edition*. Addison-Wesley, June 2000.

[19] Christian Grothoff, Jens Palsberg, and Jan Vitek. Encapsulating objects with confined types. In *Proc. OOPSLA 2001*, pages 241–253. ACM Press, October 2001.

[20] J. Roger Hindley. The principal type-scheme of an object in combinatory logic. *Transactions of the American Mathematical Society*, 146:29–60, December 1969.

[21] John Hogg. Islands: Aliasing protection in object-oriented languages. In *Proc. OOPSLA '91*, pages 271–285. ACM Press, November 1991.

[22] Atsushi Igarashi, Benjamin C. Pierce, and Philip Wadler. Featherweight Java: A minimal core calculus for Java and GJ. *ACM Transactions on Programming Languages and Systems (TOPLAS)*, 23(3):396–450, May 2001.

[23] Neel Krishnaswami and Jonathan Aldrich. Permission-based ownership: Encapsulating state in higher-order typed languages. In *Proc. PLDI'05*, pages 96–106. ACM Press, June 2005.

[24] K. R. M. Leino and P. Müller. Object invariants in dynamic contexts. In Odersky [32], pages 491–516.

[25] Yi Lu and John Potter. On ownership and accessibility. In Dave Thomas, editor, *Proc. ECOOP 2006*, volume 4067 of *LNCS*, pages 99–123. Springer, July 2006.

[26] Yi Lu and John Potter. Protecting representation with effect encapsulation. In *In Proc. POPL '06*, pages 359–371. ACM Press, 2006.

[27] Robin Milner. A theory of type polymorphism in programming. *Journal of Computer and System Sciences*, 17(3):348–375, 1978.

[28] Peter Müller. *Modular Specification and Verification of Object-Oriented Programs*, volume 2262 of *LNCS*. Springer, 2002.

[29] Peter Müller and Arnd Poetzsch-Heffter. A type system for controlling representation exposure in Java. In Drossopoulou et al., editor, *Formal Techniques for Java Programs*. Technical Report 269–5, Fernuniversität Hagen, 2000.

[30] Matthias Niklaus. Static universe type inference using a sat-solver. Master's thesis, Software Component Technology Group, Department of Computer Science, ETH Zurich, 2006.

[31] James Noble, Jan Vitek, and John Potter. Flexible alias protection. In Eric Jul, editor, *Proc. ECOOP'98*, volume 1445 of *LNCS*, pages 158–185. Springer, July 1998.

[32] Martin Odersky, editor. *Proc. ECOOP 2004*, volume 3086 of *LNCS*, June 2004. Springer.

[33] Jens Palsberg and Michael I. Schwartzbach. Object-oriented type inference. In *OOPSLA '91*, pages 146–161. ACM Press, 1991.

[34] Benjamin C. Pierce. *Types and programming languages*. MIT Press, 2002. ISBN 0-262-16209-1.

[35] John Plevyak and Andrew A. Chien. Precise concrete type inference for object-oriented languages. In *OOPSLA '94*, pages 324–340. ACM Press, 1994.

[36] Arnd Poetzsch-Heffter and Jan Schäfer. Modular specification of encapuslated object-oriented components. In Frank S. de Boer, Marcello M. Bonsangue, Susanne Graf, and Willem-Paul de Roever, editors, *Formal Methods for Components and Objects, Fourth International Symposium, FMCO 2005*, volume 4111 of *LNCS*, pages 313–341. Springer, 2006.

[37] Alex Potanin, James Noble, Dave Clarke, and Robert Biddle. Generic ownership for generic java. In *Proc. OOPSLA 2006*. ACM Press, 2006.

[38] J. Alan Robinson. Computational logic: The unification computation. *Machine Intelligence*, 6:63–72, 1971.

[39] Jan Schäfer and Arnd Poetzsch-Heffter. Simple loose ownership domains. In *ECOOP Workshop on Formal Techniques for Java-like Programs (FTfJP)*, July 2006.

[40] Matthew Smith. Towards an effects system for ownership domains. In *ECOOP Workshop - FTfJP 2005*, July 2005.

[41] Jan Vitek and Boris Bokowski. Confined types in Java. *Software - Practice and Experience*, 31(6):507–532, 2001.

[42] Tian Zhao, Jens Palsberg, and Jan Vitek. Lightweight confinement for featherweight Java. In Ron Crocker and Guy L. Steele Jr., editors, *Proc. OOPSLA 2003*, pages 135–148. ACM Press, October 2003.

ViDoC- Visual Design of Optimizing Compilers

Tiziana Margaria[1], Oliver Rüthing[2], and Bernhard Steffen[2]

[1] Universität Potsdam
`margaria@cs.uni-potsdam.de`
[2] Universität Dortmund
`{Oliver.Ruething,Bernhard.Steffen}@udo.edu`

Abstract. Designing optimizing compilers is a challenging task that involves numerous mutually interdependent transformations. Often, these interdependencies are only captured in an ad-hoc manner, relying on the ingenuity and experience of the compiler engineers. ViDoC is a tool-kit for the specification-driven, interactive development of program optimizers in a service oriented way. In particular, ViDoC facilitates the specification of dependencies between transformations in terms of modal logic properties and requirements. These specifications can be used for checking, as well as synthesizing, suitable optimization sequences , which are expressed in terms of a workflow (graph) model. ViDoC also offers various kinds of visual support, like the display of flow graphs, call graphs and analysis information, and the visualization and even manipulation of the graphs expressing the optimization workflows. These features make Vi-DoC especially appropriate for rapid prototyping. ViDoC is constructed on top of the Soot infrastructure project, that targets the manipulation of Java byte code and offers powerful engines for realizing the specified analyzes and transformations. The visualization and workflow handling are designed according to the paradigm of Lightweight Process Coordination, realized in the jABC environment.

1 Introduction

Generating high-quality optimized code is a difficult and laborious task, that is occupying tool and environment builders since the inception of high-level coding. Even with a set of optimizations at disposal, it is often impossible to reliably predict their run-time behaviour, and how they perform together. Although coupling effects (feature interactions) among optimizations have been studied already long ago [3] exploring interactions systematically is restricted to settings with a few, mutually enhancing transformations [12,2]. In a real optimizing compiler, however, one is faced with numerous interdependent transformations including also destructive coupling effects. This hampers already the platform-independent optimization level. Nowadays, hardware-targeted optimizations are becoming common, thus predictions become even more difficult because of the impact of machine characteristics, like cache sizes and register limitations on the foreseen optimizations. Up to now, the potential space of optimization combinations is not adequately explored: Usually, the order of applications among a set

T. Reps, M. Sagiv, and J. Bauer (Eds.): Wilhelm Festschrift, LNCS 4444, pp. 145–159, 2007.

of program transformations is chosen in an ad-hoc manner, capturing only some of the most obvious interactions recognized by compiler engineers.

Addressing these issues systematically requires an advanced tool-set for the specification of and experimentation with complex optimization scenarios, and for their analysis prior to enactment. ViDoC provides such a platform, that exploits for the management and coordination of heterogeneous optimizations the paradigm of Lightweight Process Coordination, as realized in METAFrame's ABC, and now in the *java Application Building Center* (jABC) [11,14]. This enables enables the rapid prototyping and context/platform-specific evaluation of complex optimizations.

The paper is organized as follows. In Sect. 2 we provide an overview of ViDoC's structure, followed, in Sect. 3, by a sketch of its relation with the underlying jABC coordination framework. In Sect. 4 we illustrate its capabilities in detail by means of a running example. Finally, Sect. 5 discusses related work and Sect. 6 presents our conclusions and plans for future work.

2   ViDoC

ViDoC provides a platform for the design, analysis, and implementation of compiler optimizations. Its focus is on rapid prototyping and experimental evaluation of the optimizations, and on the analysis of the impact of their interdependencies. For this purpose, ViDoC supports the

- easy integration of functionalities of existing compiler infrastructures,
- coordination of different compiler functionalities to complex solutions beyond the boundaries of individual compiler platforms
- visual analysis of the coordination graph, representing the complex solutions, as well as of the analysis and optimization results.

The general structure of ViDoC is shown in Figure 1.

ViDoC heavily exploits the *Soot* Java optimization framework [6] for analyzing and transforming Java bytecode. It is implemented in Java and provides a set of Java APIs for different functionalities that are needed for optimizing or transforming Java bytecode. Soot is particularly suitable for our project since it

- allows users to automatically generate customized control-flow representations of Java byte code which are more adequate for flow analysis and transformations than Java byte code itself. In the ViDoC project the intermediate format Jimple [6], a Soot specific 3-address format, rendered most convenient as a starting point.
- offers a strong engine to create analyzes and transformations automatically from specifications. This supports compiler developers to design their own analyzes and transformations in an easy and rapid way.
  In order to implement a new flow analysis Soot only requires to implement a new subclass of the Java class `FlowAnalysis`. This is essentially accomplished by implementing the standard ingredients of the data flow framework

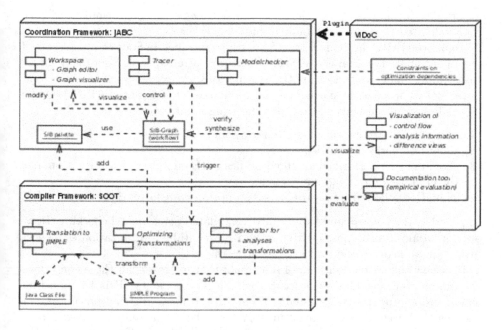

Fig. 1. Structure of ViDoC

like the underlying abstract domain, the local transfer functions and the merge operator. Likewise Soot also facilitates the integration of customized transformations which are specified by implementing a `BodyTransformer` or `SceneTransformer`.

- provides a rich selection of standard analyzes and transformations that can readily be used with or without further enhancements.
- gives a good handle to import transformation descriptions as building blocks into the ViDoC's coordination environment, and to export the optimization workflows back to Soot.

3 The Coordination Framework

The *java Application Building Center* (jABC) [11,14] provides the technology concerning workflow modelling and coordination, ViDoC means to express compositions of analyzes, optimizations, and transformations.

Essentially, the jABC is an application-independent framework for the analysis, verification, and synthesis of services, and more generally of component-based systems. Technically, such component-based systems are modelled in terms of workflow graphs whose nodes are units of functionality called *service independent building blocks* (SIBs). The construction and manipulation of SIB graphs is supported by a flexible graphical editor that in particular supports the drag-and-drop construction and configuration of workflows on the basis of collections of SIBs. Vital system constraints on the workflows like causality or eventuality properties are specified in terms of *temporal logic* formulas, and are then validated by means of a built-in model checker [15].

To use the jABC, individual transformations specified in Soot can be imported via an automated mechanism as SIBs of an application-specific Soot SIB palette. Constraints among optimization transformations are expressed in terms of temporal logic. For instance, correct partial redundancies elimination (PRE) [4] can be easily formalized by requiring that the transformation:

1. must always be preceded by a removal of critical edges;
2. should be performed at least once;
3. should not be performed again without a PRE-enabling transformation, like the elimination of dead assignments;
4. should be followed by a variable subsumption transformation.

In practice, these constraints are typically validated using model checking. However, it would also be possible to synthesize executable optimization sequences using our tableaux-based synthesis feature [16].

It is easy to construct a temporal formula that expresses all these conditions as conjunction of subformulas for the single requirements. This is important as numerous program transformations require specific additional preconditions, such as the program being given in SSA form, having a reducible flow graph, or having no critical edges. Moreover, the preconditions differ, influencing the quality of the obtained optimization, and they may be destroyed during some of the transformations. ViDoC's coordination facility is tailored to deal with the structures required for this enterprise. It supports hierarchy, which is necessary to reason at different levels of abstraction, and it is typed, allowing to elegantly characterize the required preconditions for the transformations.

In order to complete the cycle the information on a satisfying optimization schedule has to be transfered back to Soot. Since Soot's transformation package which implements the selection of transformations cannot cope with cycles in the transformation orderings, the transformations are executed using the jABC Tracer. This is a SIB graph interpreter, which traverses the graph and at each SIB delegates its execution to the Soot environment, if it is a Soot SIB, or to its jABC functionality if it is a jABC SIB.

4   Using ViDoC

In the following, we illustrate ViDoC's capabilities in detail by means of a running example. After presenting the concrete optimization example in Section 4.1, we focus on illustrating the visual support by ViDoC. First, for the design of complex optimizations, second, for visualizing program representations, and third, for visualizing analysis and transformation results.

4.1   Example: Partial Dead Code Elimination

Partial dead code elimination (PDCE) [5] is a powerful program transformation composed of two mutually enhancing transformations. Essentially, its idea is to

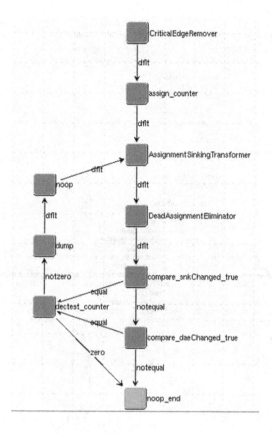

Fig. 2. The SIB graph of the PDCE complex optimization

utilize *assignment sinking* in order to increase the potential for the *elimination of dead assignments*, which is a standard transformation for removing assignments to variables that are not subsequently used. Furthermore, as almost any transformation involving code movement, PDCE benefits from the *removal of critical edges*, i.e., edges in the flow graph that connect nodes with multiple successors with nodes with multiple predecessors. The remainder of this section will illustrate ViDoC using this example.

4.2 Visual Aids for Designing Optimizations

Workspace and SIBs. Since ViDoC is constructed as a jABC-plugin it uses jABC's graphic interface for displaying and manipulating workflows processing SIB graphs. Figure 2 shows the SIB graph of the PDCE transformation. Nodes are SIBs representing elementary transformations contributing to the PDCE transformation. The SIBs are connected by directed edges which model

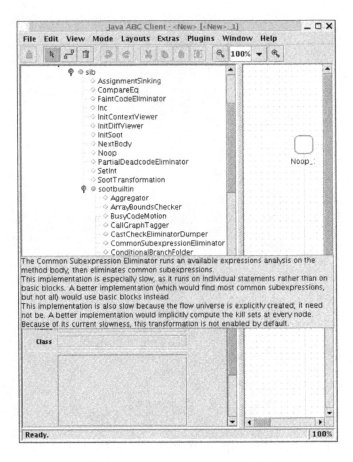

Fig. 3. ViDoC's workspace with SIB palettes and available Soot SIBs

their order of execution. The set of possible edge labels is provided by the implementation of the source SIB. In this example, most SIBs only allow single outgoing edges with default-labels.

In the graph of Figure 2, the `CriticalEdgeRemover` and the `DeadAssignmentEliminator` are part of Soot's standard transformation package. SIBs corresponding to each transformation of this package have been automatically generated and are thus readily available within ViDoC. Figure 3 shows how to access them from a drop-down menu in the main workspace of ViDoC. Here we see on the left the palette of available transformations. The `Sootbuiltin` palette is directly imported from the Soot environment, while the SIBs `AssignmentSinking` and `FaintCodeEliminator` in Fig. 2 represent specific transformations which have been created within Soot. Finally, some SIBs like `CompareEq` and `assign_counter` are generic SIBs available in the jABC environment. They have simply been appropriately parameterized and renamed for this application.

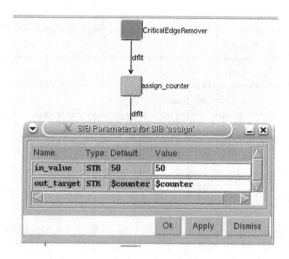

Fig. 4. Setting the parameters of the `assign_counter` SIB

A short description of each SIB pops up in a tooltip when moving the cursor on the entry. In Figure 3 we see this illustrated by means of the Soot SIB `CommonSubexpressionEliminator`.

In addition to the two basic Soot SIBs, in the PDCE graph we see the `AssignmentSinkingTransformer` SIB, a new transformation that has been built using Soot's data flow analysis and transformation engines. Moreover, two `compare` SIBs are used for checking whether the loop over the main transformations reaches stability. Finally, a `counter` SIB is introduced, to force termination of the transformation cycle if a preset value is reached. Figure 4 shows how to initialize the SIB parameters in the corresponding SIB inspector of the jABC.

The Context Viewer. Tracing the execution of SIB workflows is facilitated by means of an integrated context viewer that is started from the workspace, as shown in Figure 5. The context viewer gives information on the state of variables and their changes during the execution of the transformation, as in Fig. 6.

The effects of the execution of the SIBs on the code are displayed by other ViDoC modules. For program representations, like the JIMPLE intermediate format and certain flow graph representations (see Section 4.3), various *difference viewers* are available, emphasizing the structural changes to the code under optimization. The design of ViDoC makes it easy to profit here from functionality provided by other tools.

Model Checking. Vital constraints concerning both the correctness of the transformation as well as the correctness of the general workflow can be expressed

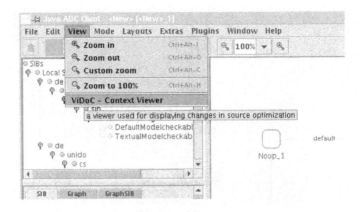

Fig. 5. Starting the *Context Viewer* from the workspace

Fig. 6. Context viewer window with context information

in terms of modal logics, and model checked automatically for the underlying SIB graph.

As an example consider the following constraint concerning a correct use of a counter, which occurs in the PDCE graph:

```
//: CounterCheck
// Every counter must be assigned before it can be used
//(e.g., read, incremented, decremented).

constraint CounterCheck{
Forall X in model ('Start =>
AWU_F(~('UseCounter[ name == X ]),
      'AssignCounter[ name == X ]) )
               }
```

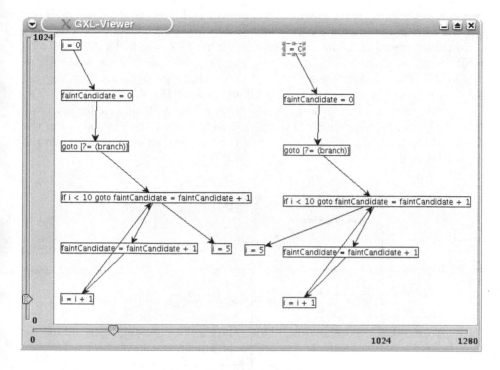

Fig. 7. Flow graph visualization

ViDoC uses the counter example facility of the jABC to highlight runs violating these kinds of constraints.

4.3   Visualizing Program Representations

ViDoC provides flexible access to the control flow visualization of the programs that are manipulated, with flexible access to views of distinct granularity. For instance, users can interactively explode nodes in the call graph representation of a program to basic block flow graphs of their corresponding methods, and then further refine the presentation to an instruction-wise representation. Displaying corresponding fragments of the flow graphs in a common panel emphasizes the effects of the transformations.

Our implementation uses GXL (the *Graph eXchange Language*) as graph specification language and *JGraphpad*, a versatile free graph editor, as layout tool. We are still improving and extending ViDoC's visualization capabilities, with main focus on integrating visual support for documenting the impact of analyzes and transformation.

Figure 7 shows the visualization of the control flow graph in terms of a single instruction representation. In this figure, an example flow graph is subjected to an extension of partial dead code elimination called *partial faint code elimination*.

Since no assignment is found eliminable on this code, the initial flow graph (on the left side) is not altered (on the right side).

In this representation the source code is "inlined" in the node. Alternatively, a SIB graph representation can be chosen in the jABC, with the actual code as label (SIB name) below a generic SIB icon. In this representation the program assumes a look very similar to the workflow graph of Fig. 2.

Finally, Figures 8 and 9 show the *JGraphpad* layout of call graphs and basic block flow graphs, respectively. The inlined basic blocks can be explored in the large canvas, while a miniature picture of the whole program is available in the right inspector.

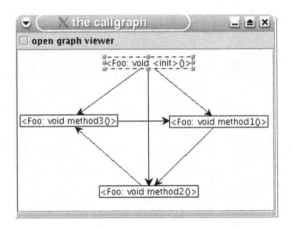

Fig. 8. Call graph visualisation

4.4   Visualizing Transformation Results

As mentioned, ViDoC's difference viewers provide a means to relate the results of optimizations with the underlying original program (see Section 4.2). However, this can only give a rough picture on the impact of the transformation. In order to evaluate the quality of optimization orders and to compare different orders ViDoC integrates a documentation tool that automatically runs benchmark suites and summarizes the results in graphical reports. The documentation tool is based on the JVM profiling tool *HPROF* and the Java chart library *JFreeChart*.

Figure 10 gives an impression on the documentation tool's GUI: several views collect and condense data concerning several runs on the single benchmarks and on benchmark suites. This enables the comparison of the effects of different transformations, in particular of different complex transformations realized in ViDoC).

Figure 11 shows as example a histogram evaluation of a benchmark set against several transformations. Representations like this help engineers tuning the transformations and refining the own intuition about interactions.

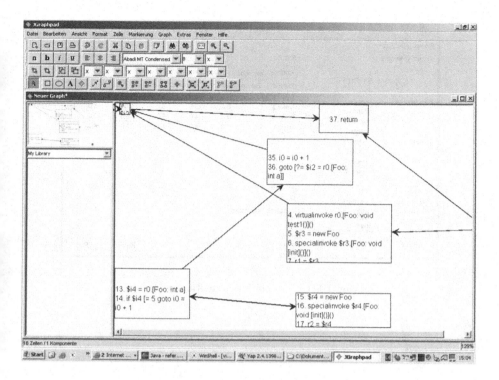

Fig. 9. Basic block graph visualisation

5 Related Work

Dependencies among optimizing program transformations as a research issue has been pioneered by the work of Giegerich, Möncke and Wilhelm [3]. In particular, the idea of flexibly combining enabling analyzes and transformations was later further generalized [2]. However, these approaches focus on a small set of mutually enabling transformations.

Most closely related to ViDoC are two approaches dealing with a broader set of optimizing transformations and their dependencies. Soffa and Whitfield proposed a framework for reasoning on transformation orders [19] which integrates a specification mechanism for transformations called *Gospel* and a tool called *Genesis*. However, only enabling and disabling properties between transformations are discovered. Hence this framework does not resolve transformation orders where parts have to be iterated. Moreover, their tool Genesis is less flexible than ViDoC in managing transformation orders and thus not as suited for rapid prototyping. Vista is another tool focussing on transformation orders [20]. However, this tool targets more on the generation of low-level embedded code. Moreover, its usage is highly interactive requiring the user to guide through the whole transformation process where single transformations can be committed or undone.

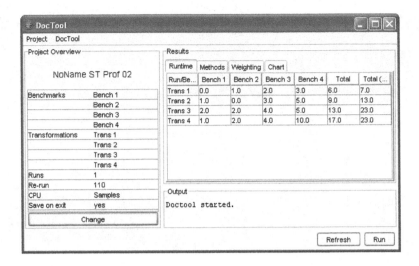

Fig. 10. GUI of the documentation tool

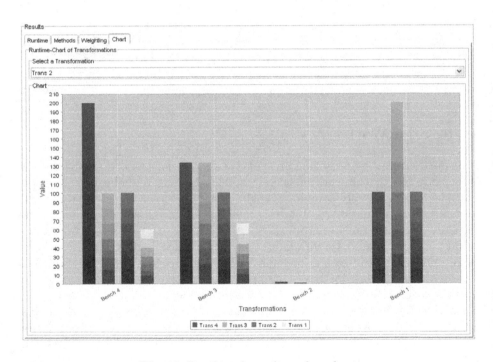

Fig. 11. Benchmark results as bar charts

Lerner et al. have proposed domain specific languages for specifying analyzes and transformations and proving them automatically correct [8,9]. Basically,

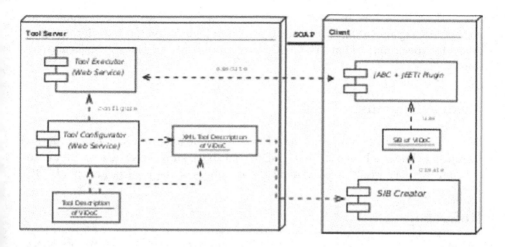

Fig. 12. Remote access to ViDoC via jETI

their approach checks a specification based on an abstract interpretation against the programs full semantics and mainly targets on proving one individual transformation or analysis correct. Although they also address the problem of combining analyzes and transformations [7] their approach is essentially based on checking the effect of all possible combinations exhaustively. In contrast, our approach focusses on capturing the interactions between the different transformations.

6   Conclusion and Future Work

We have presented ViDoC, a flexible platform for supporting the visual, library-based design of optimizing compilers. ViDoC offers (semi-)automatic support for validating vital constraints of compilation and transformation schedules and for evaluating and relating the quality of different schedules. Moreover it supports systematic experimentation and rapid prototyping, and is therefore an ideal means for the context/platform-specific evaluation of complex optimizations.

We plan to make ViDoC available on the world wide web in order to open it for third parties for all purposes of research, teaching, development, and experimentation. This will be done on top of the *Electronic Tool Integration Platform jETI* [1,13,10], which supports the flexible integration of remote tools into complex, heterogeneous optimization solutions. As sketched in Figure 12, ViDoC and its functionality will be specified as a web-service running on a jETI-server. This service can be accessed from any jABC-client with a corresponding jETI-Plugin. According to jETI's philosophy researchers can contribute to the project by releasing additional tool components on a jETI-server as well.

Finally, an ambitious future goal is to globalize and automate correctness arguments for program transformations. Focussing on the underlying analyzes the work on data flow analysis as model checking [17,18] gives a good handle for correctness arguments. In this setting temporal logic is used as a declarative language for specifying "what" the analysis computes rather "how" this is actually done.

Acknowledgement

We are grateful to Lenore Zuck and Harald Raffelt for discussions and valuable comments. The implementation of ViDoC has been supported by a one-year student project. We would like to thank the members of the project group VIDOC.

References

1. T. Margaria A. Arenas, J. Bicarregui. The FMICS view on the verified software repository. *Proc. Integrated Design and Process Technology, IDPT-2006, San Diego (USA), 26-29.6.2006, Society for Design and Process Science*, 2006.
2. C. Click and K. D. Cooper. Combining analyses, combining optimizations. *ACM Transactions on Programming Languages and Systems*, 17(2):181 – 196, 1995.
3. Robert Giegerich, Ulrich Möncke, and Reinhard Wilhelm. Invariance of approximate semantics with respect to program transformations. In *11. GI Jahrestagung. In conjunction with Third Conference of the European Co-operation in Informatics (ECI)*, number 50 in Informatik-Fachberichte, pages 1–10, Heidelberg, Germany, 1981. Springer-Verlag.
4. J. Knoop, O. Rüthing, and B. Steffen. Optimal code motion: Theory and practice. *ACM Trans. Prog. Lang. Syst.*, 16(4):1117–1155, 1994.
5. Jens Knoop, Oliver Rüthing, and Bernhard Steffen. Partial dead code elimination. In *SIGPLAN Conference on Programming Language Design and Implementation*, pages 147–158, 1994.
6. Patrick Lam, Feng Qian, and Ondrej Lhoták. Soot: a java optimization framework. See http://www.sable.mcgill.ca/soot/.
7. Sorin Lerner, David Grove, and Craig Chambers. Combining dataflow analyses and transformations. In *In Conferernce Record of the 29th ACM SIGPLAN-SIGACT Symposium on Principles of Programming Languages (POPL 2002)*, pages 270–282, 2002.
8. Sorin Lerner, Todd Millstein, and Craig Chambers. Automatically proving the correctness of compiler optimizations. In *SIGPLAN Conference on Programming Language Design and Implementation*, pages 220–231, 2003.
9. Sorin Lerner, Todd Millstein, Erika Rice, and Craig Chambers. Automated soundness proofs for dataflow analyses and transformations via local rules. In *In Conferernce Record of the 32nd ACM SIGPLAN-SIGACT, Symposium on Principles of Programming Languages (POPL 2005)*, pages 364–377, 2005.
10. T. Margaria. Web services-based tool-integration in the ETI platform. *SoSyM, Int. Journal on Software and System Modelling, Vol. 4, N. 2,pp. 141 - 156, Springer Verlag*, May 2005.
11. T. Margaria and B. Steffen. Service engineering: Linking business and IT. *IEEE Computer*, 2006. (To appear), Cover feature of IEEE Computer, (invited), issue for the 60th anniversary of the Computer Society.

12. O. Rüthing. *Interacting Code Motion Transformations: Their Impact and Their Complexity*. PhD thesis, Institut für Informatik und Praktische Mathematik, Christian-Albrechts-Universität zu Kiel, Kiel, Germany, 1997. Lecture Notes in Computer Science, vol. 1539, Springer-Verlag, Heidelberg, 1998.

13. B. Steffen, V. Braun, and T. Margaria. The electronic tool integration platform: Concepts and design. *Int. Journal on Software Tools for Technology Transfer (STTT)*, 1(1/2):9–30, 1997. See also http://eti.cs.uni-dortmund.de.

14. B. Steffen and T. Margaria. Metaframe in practice: Intelligent network service design. In B. Steffen E.-R. Olderog, editor, *Correct System Design – Issues, Methods and Perspectives*, volume 1710 of *Lecture Notes in Computer Science (LNCS)*, pages 390 – 415, Heidelberg, Germany, 1999. Springer-Verlag.

15. B. Steffen, T. Margaria, R. Nagel, S. Jörges, and C. Kubczak. Model-driven development with the jABC. *Proc. HVC'06, IBM Haifa Verification Conference, Haifa (Israel), (to appear in LNCS), Springer Verlag*, October 2006.

16. B. Steffen, T. Margaria, and M. von der Beeck. Automatic synthesis of linear process models from temporal constraints: An incremental approach. In *Proc. ACM Int. Workshop on Automated Analysis of Software (AAS'97) - affiliated to POPL'97*, pages 127–141, 1997.

17. Bernhard Steffen. Data flow analysis as model checking. In A.R. Meyer T. Ito, editor, *Theoretical Aspects of Computer Science (TACS'91), Sendai (Japan)*, volume 526 of *Lecture Notes in Computer Science (LNCS)*, pages 346–364, Heidelberg, Germany, September 1991. Springer-Verlag.

18. Bernhard Steffen. Generating data flow analysis algorithms from modal specifications. *International Journal on Science of Computer Programming*, 21:115–139, 1993.

19. Deborah L. Whitfield and Mary Lou Soffa. An approach for exploring code improving transformations. *ACM Transactions on Programming Languages and Systems*, 19(6):1053–1084, 1997.

20. W. Zhao, B. Cai, D. Whalley, M. Bailey, R. van Engelen, X. Yuan, J. Hiser, J. Davidson, K. Gallivan, and D. Jones. Vista: a system for interactive code improvement. In *In Proceedings of the joint conference on Languages, compilers and tools for embedded systems (LCTES)*, pages 155–164. ACM Press, 2002.

Abstract Interpretation for Worst and Average Case Analysis

Alessandra Di Pierro[1], Chris Hankin[2], and Herbert Wiklicky[2]

[1] Dipartimento di Informatica, University of Pisa, Italy
[2] Department of Computing, Imperial College London, UK

Abstract. We review Wilhelm's work on WCET for hard real-time applications and also recent work on analysis of soft-real time systems using probabilistic methods. We then present Probabilistic Abstract Interpretation (PAI) as a quantitative variation of the classical approach; PAI aims to provide close approximations – this should be contrasted to the safe approximations studied in the standard setting. We discuss the relation between PAI and classical Abstract Interpretation as well as average case analysis.

1 Introduction

This paper has been written as a contribution to the Festschrift to celebrate the sixtieth birthday of Reinhard Wilhelm. As befits such an occasion, we have sought to relate some of our current interests to Reinhard's canon of work. Given such an illustrious career, there is no shortage of possible topics. We have taken Reinhard's relatively recent work on worst case execution times (WCET) as our inspiration. This combines abstract interpretation, the topic about which the middle author and Reinhard first met 21 years ago, with quantitative issues – an area which is the topic of much of our recent work.

Reinhard's approach, which is surveyed in [1], concentrates on WCET for hard real-time problems – examples include safety-critical systems such as control software in automobiles. It is not difficult to see traditional approaches to WCET, for example those based on Timing Schemata [2], as abstract interpretation. States are abstracted to upper bounds on execution times and language constructs abstracted to work with these. For example a suitable interpretation for the conditional construct might be the function $\lambda xyz.x + max(y, z)$. The complexities of modern processors mean that WCET is much less predictable than this; cache performance and pipelines can have a dramatic impact and timing anomalies [3] can have counter-intuitive effects. As a consequence, Reinhard's approach is much more sophisticated: the first phase extracts a control flow graph – for some classes of language this may already involve an abstract interpretation or program analysis; he then performs some abstract interpretation to predict cache and pipeline behaviour; the result of this is upper bounds on the execution times for basic blocks and these are combined and integer linear programming is used to produce an upper bound on WCET for the whole

T. Reps, M. Sagiv, and J. Bauer (Eds.): Wilhelm Festschrift, LNCS 4444, pp. 160–174, 2007.

program. The paper [1] analyses the sources of unpredictability in these bounds and is actually a manifesto for "Design for Predictability".

In safety-critical embedded systems it is essential to work with worst case execution times. In systems with softer real-time constraints average case execution times can be a useful design tool in analysing power/performance trade-offs. Example application areas are multi-media and mobile devices. Approaches based on stochastic modelling have become popular in recent years. Stochastic Petri Nets [4,5], Stochastic Automata Networks [6] and Stochastic State Machine Languages have all been used. Kwiatkowska [7] and co-workers have used the latter with PRISM and MAPLE to optimise average energy usage whilst bounding the average number of requests waiting to be served. PRISM is used to generate the generator stochastic matrix for systems and MAPLE is used for formulating and solving the linear optimisation problem. As an alternative to model-checking, we have developed an approach to abstract interpretation of such stochastic matrices [8]. In this paper we explore how our framework can be used to study average case behaviour.

2   Probabilistic Abstract Interpretation

Without doubt, static program analysis is a fascinating and interesting area from a purely theoretical point of view – but it is done for a practical reason: In order to protect oneself against nasty surprises when software is run, the idea is to predict in advance what will happen when a program is executed. Unfortunately, well known fundamental results, like the Halting problem, tell us that it is in principle impossible to know everything about the behaviour of every program. The solution to this obstacle of undecidabilty is to aim for partial answers to some of the questions.

However, different applications and users have different priorities and interests and therefore accept different kinds of imprecision. When it comes, for example, to systems which are critical for life and limb of humans one might be cautious and attempt to determine absolute limits on what can go wrong in the worst case – like in the case of safety critical systems in cars, air planes, etc. If, on the other hand, the possible damage is only in terms of lost money, time or other resource one might be inclined to accept an estimate in order to forecast average profits or losses – as in the context of speculative threading, power consumption of mobile devices, etc.

There is no one-size-fits-all approach to this issue: While the cliché of a German engineer will aim to protect his "Vorsprung durch Technik" by accommodating for a worst case catastrophe, the caricature of a British speculator might gamble on an average case scenario – and both approaches can be justified in certain circumstances.

Abstract Interpretation [9,10,11] provides a general methodology for constructing static analyses which is, to some extent, independent of the particular style used to specify the program analysis. Thus, it applies to any formulation of a (data/control flow or type/effect-system) analysis.

One common theme behind all traditional approaches to program analysis (data and control flow analysis, type and effect systems, abstract interpretation) is that in order to remain computable, one can only provide *approximate answers* [11]. As a consequence an analysis does not usually give precise information; moreover, in order for this information to be useful, the analysis must be *safe*, that is the information obtained from the analysis must be proved to be correct with respect to a semantics of the programming language.

Quantitative approaches to program analysis aim at developing techniques which provide approximate answers (in a way similar to the classical program analysis) together with some numerical estimate of the approximation introduced by the analysis.

One useful source of numerical information for a quantitative program analysis is a probabilistic semantics and in particular the use of vector space or linear algebraic structures for modelling the computational domain. By exploiting the probabilistic information resulting from a probabilistic program analysis one can quantify the precision of the analysis and obtain as a result answers which are for example "approximate up to 35%".

As a quantitative approach to program analysis we have developed Probabilistic Abstract Interpretation (PAI) [8,12] which recasts classical Abstract Interpretation in a probabilistic setting where linear spaces replace the classical order-theoretic domains, and the notion of the so-called *Moore-Penrose pseudo-inverse* of a linear operator replaces the classical notion of a Galois connection. The abstractions we get this way are *close* approximations of the concrete semantics. Thus, closeness is a quantitative replacement for classical safety which does not require any approximation ordering.

The application of operator algebraic methods instead of order theoretic ones makes the framework of probabilistic abstract interpretation essentially different from approaches which apply classical abstract interpretation to probabilistic domains [13,14]. Although classical AI techniques can also be used in a probabilistic context, e.g. to approximate distributions, as was demostrated for example in a number of papers by D.Monniaux [13,14], this will always result in safe, i.e. worst case analysis. In contrast, our PAI approach allows to construct averages and other statistical information which are more in the spirit of an average case analysis.

The definition of a probabilistic abstract interpretation is given in terms of *probabilistic domains*. We define a probabilistic domain as a suitable vector space with a inner product $\langle ., . \rangle$, namely as a Hilbert space.

Probabilistic Abstract Interpretation is defined in general for infinite dimensional Hilbert spaces. We recall here the general definition, although in this paper we will only consider the finite dimensional case. Given two probabilistic domains $\mathcal{C}$ and $\mathcal{D}$, a *probabilistic abstract interpretation* is defined by a pair of linear maps, $\mathbf{A} : \mathcal{C} \mapsto \mathcal{D}$ and $\mathbf{G} : \mathcal{D} \mapsto \mathcal{C}$, between the concrete domain $\mathcal{C}$ and the abstract domain $\mathcal{D}$, such that $\mathbf{G}$ is the *Moore-Penrose pseudo-inverse* of $\mathbf{A}$, and vice versa. Let $\mathcal{C}$ and $\mathcal{D}$ be two Hilbert spaces and $\mathbf{A} : \mathcal{C} \mapsto \mathcal{D}$ a bounded linear map between them. A bounded linear map $\mathbf{A}^\dagger = \mathbf{G} : \mathcal{D} \mapsto \mathcal{C}$ is the Moore-Penrose pseudo-inverse of $\mathbf{A}$ iff

$$\mathbf{A} \circ \mathbf{G} = \mathbf{P}_A \quad \text{and} \quad \mathbf{G} \circ \mathbf{A} = \mathbf{P}_G$$

where $\mathbf{P}_A$ and $\mathbf{P}_G$ denote orthogonal projections (i.e. $\mathbf{P}_A^* = \mathbf{P}_A = \mathbf{P}_A^2$ and $\mathbf{P}_G^* = \mathbf{P}_G = \mathbf{P}_G^2$) onto the ranges of $\mathbf{A}$ and $\mathbf{G}$.

Alternatively, if $\mathbf{A}$ is Moore-Penrose invertible, its Moore-Penrose pseudo-inverse, $\mathbf{A}^\dagger$ satisfies the following:

$$\text{(i) } \mathbf{A}\mathbf{A}^\dagger\mathbf{A} = \mathbf{A}, \qquad \text{(iii) } (\mathbf{A}\mathbf{A}^\dagger)^* = \mathbf{A}\mathbf{A}^\dagger,$$
$$\text{(ii) } \mathbf{A}^\dagger\mathbf{A}\mathbf{A}^\dagger = \mathbf{A}^\dagger, \qquad \text{(iv) } (\mathbf{A}^\dagger\mathbf{A})^* = \mathbf{A}^\dagger\mathbf{A},$$

where $\mathbf{M}^*$ is the adjoint of $\mathbf{M}$. The adjoint $\mathbf{M}^*$ of a linear operator $\mathbf{M}$ on a Hilbert space $\mathcal{H}$ is uniquely defined via the condition $\langle \mathbf{M}(x), y \rangle = \langle x, \mathbf{M}^*(y) \rangle$, for all $x, y \in \mathcal{H}$. In matrix terms, $\mathbf{M}^*$ corresponds to the transpose complex conjugate matrix $\overline{\mathbf{M}^T}$ of the matrix $\mathbf{M}$.

It is instructive to compare these equations with the classical setting. For example, if (α, γ) is a Galois connection we similarly have $\alpha \circ \gamma \circ \alpha = \alpha$ and $\gamma \circ \alpha \circ \gamma = \gamma$.

Please note that we identify linear maps and operators with their matrix representation. This implies that for two linear maps or operators represented by matrices $\mathbf{M}$ and $\mathbf{N}$ their composition $\mathbf{M} \circ \mathbf{N}$ (if it is well-defined) corresponds to the matrix product $\mathbf{N} \cdot \mathbf{M} = \mathbf{NM}$, i.e. in the reverse order. Similarily, the application of $\mathbf{M}$ to a (row) vector, i.e. $\mathbf{M}(x)$, corresponds to a vector/matrix multiplication $x \cdot \mathbf{M} = x\mathbf{M}$. This notation is consistent with the one for the octave tool [15] which was used by us to compute the examples in this paper.

As in the classical framework, given a concrete semantics we can always construct a *best correct approximation* for this semantics, although the notions of correctness and optimality assume a different connotation in our linear setting as explained in the following.

If Φ is a linear operator on some vector space $\mathcal{V}$ expressing the probabilistic semantics of a concrete system, and $\mathbf{A} : \mathcal{V} \mapsto \mathcal{W}$ is a linear abstraction function from the concrete domain into an abstract domain $\mathcal{W}$, we can compute the (unique) Moore-Penrose pseudo-inverse $\mathbf{G} = \mathbf{A}^\dagger$ of $\mathbf{A}$. An abstract semantics can then be defined as the linear operator on the abstract domain $\mathcal{W}$:

$$\Psi = \mathbf{A} \circ \Phi \circ \mathbf{G} = \mathbf{G}\Phi\mathbf{A}.$$

In the case of classical abstract interpretation the abstract semantics constructed in this way (called the *induced semantics in* [16]) is guaranteed to be the best correct approximation of the concrete semantics, meaning that it is the most precise among all correct approximation (the relative precision being left unquantified). In the linear space based setting of PAI where the order of the classical domains is replaced by some notion of metric distance, the induced abstract semantics is the *closest* one to the concrete semantics. This "closeness" property expresses both the "safety" of the approximation and its optimality, which comes from the following properties of the Moore-Penrose pseudo-inverse.

The theory of the least-square approximation [17,18] tells us that if $\mathcal{C}$ and $\mathcal{D}$ are two finite dimensional vector spaces, $\mathbf{A} : \mathcal{C} \mapsto \mathcal{D}$ a linear map between them, and $\mathbf{A}^\dagger = \mathbf{G} : \mathcal{D} \mapsto \mathcal{C}$ its Moore-Penrose pseudo-inverse, then the vector $x_0 = y\mathbf{G}$ is the one minimising the distance between $x\mathbf{A}$, for any vector x in $\mathcal{C}$, and y, i.e.

$$\inf_{x \in \mathcal{C}} \|x\mathbf{A} - y\| = \|x_0\mathbf{A} - y\|,$$

where $\|.\|$ denotes the usual *Euclidean* or *2-norm*.

In other words, if we consider the equation $x\mathbf{A} = y$ we can identify a (exact) solution x_* as a vector for which $\|x_*\mathbf{A} - y\| = 0$. In particular, in the case that no such solution vector x_* exists we can generalise the concept of a exact solution to that of a "pseudo-solution", i.e. we can look for a x_0 such that $x_0\mathbf{A}$ is the *closest* vector to y we can construct. This closest approximation to the exact solution is now constructed using the Moore-Penrose pseudo-inverse, i.e. take $x_0 = y\mathbf{A}^\dagger$.

Returning to our program analysis setting, suppose that we have an operator Φ and a vector x. We can apply Φ to x and abstract the result giving $x\Phi\mathbf{A}$ or we can apply the abstract operator to an abstract vector giving $x\mathbf{A}\mathbf{A}^\dagger\Phi\mathbf{A}$. Ideally, we would like these to be equal. If $\mathbf{A}$ is invertible then its Moore-Penrose pseudo-inverse is identical to the inverse and we are done. As in program analysis abstract domains are usually smaller (i.e. in our setting vector spaces of smaller dimension) than the concrete ones, $\mathbf{A}$ is never a square matrix and thus $\mathbf{A}\mathbf{A}^\dagger$ in $x\mathbf{A}\mathbf{A}^\dagger\Phi\mathbf{A}$ will lead to some loss of precision. The Moore-Penrose pseudo-inverse is as close as possible to an inverse if the matrix is not invertible and thus for the particular choice of $\mathbf{A}$, $\mathbf{A}^\dagger\Phi\mathbf{A}$ is the best approximation of Φ that we can have. Moreover, by choosing an appropriate notion of distance we can measure this closeness to get a quantitative estimate of the information lost in the abstraction process [12].

3   Approximations: A Classical Example

Classical abstract interpretation and probabilistic abstract interpretation provide "approximations" for completely different mathematical structures, namely partial orders vs vector spaces. In order to illustrate and compare their features we therefore need a setting where the domain in question in some way naturally provides both structures. One such situation is in the context of classical function interpolation or approximation.

The set of real-valued functions on real interval $[a, b]$ obviously comes with a canonical partial order, namely the point-wise ordering, and at the same time is equiped with a vector space structure, again the point-wise addition and scalar multiplication. Some care has to be taken in order to define an inner product, e.g. one could consider only the square integrable functions $L^2([a, b])$. In order to avoid mathematical (e.g. measure-theoretic) details we simplify the situation by just considering the step functions on the interval $[a, b]$.

For a (closed) real interval $[a, b] \subseteq \mathbb{R}$ we call the set of subintervals $[a_i, b_i]$ with $i = 1, \ldots, n$ the *n-subdivision* of $[a, b]$ if $\bigcup_{i=1}^n [a_i, b_i] = [a, b]$ and $b_i - a_i = \frac{b-a}{n}$ for all $i = 1, \ldots, n$. We assume that the subintervals are enumerated in the obvious way, i.e. $a_i < b_i = a_{i+1} < b_{i+1}$ for all i and in particular that $a = a_1$ and $b_n = b$.

Definition 1. *The set of* n-step functions $\mathcal{T}_n([a,b])$ *on* $[a,b]$ *is the set of real-valued functions* $f : [a,b] \to \mathbb{R}$ *such that* f *is constant on each subinterval* (a_i, b_i) *in the n-subdivision of* $[a,b]$.

Note that since L^2 is the set of equivalence classes of functions with respect to the equivalence relation $\sim$ defined by $f \sim g$ iff $\int |f(x) - g(x)|^2 dx = 0$, we can identify functions if they differ in only finitely many points. Thus, the values $f(a_i)$ and $f(b_i)$ are irrelevant for our purpose.

We define a partial order on $\mathcal{T}_n([a,b])$ in the obvious way: for $f, g \in \mathcal{T}_n([a,b])$:

$$f \sqsubseteq g \text{ iff } f(\frac{b_i - a_i}{2}) \leq g(\frac{b_i - a_i}{2}), \text{ for all } 1 \leq i \leq n$$

i.e. iff the value of f (which we obtain by evaluating it on the mid-point in (a_i, b_i)) on all subintervals (a_i, b_i) is less or equal to the value of g.

It is also obvious to see that $\mathcal{T}_n([a,b])$ has a vector space structure isomorphic to $\mathbb{R}^n$ and thus is also provided with an inner product. More concretely we define the vector space operations $\ldots : \mathbb{R} \times \mathcal{T}_n([a,b]) \to \mathcal{T}_n([a,b])$ and $. + . : \mathcal{T}_n([a,b]) \times \mathcal{T}_n([a,b]) \to \mathcal{T}_n([a,b])$ pointwise as follows:

$$(\alpha \cdot f)(x) = \alpha f(x)$$

$$(f + g)(x) = f(x) + g(x)$$

for all $\alpha \in \mathbb{R}$, $f, g \in \mathcal{T}_n([a,b])$ and $x \in [a,b]$. The inner product is given by:

$$\langle f, g \rangle = \sum_{i=1}^{n} f(\frac{b_i - a_i}{2}) g(\frac{b_i - a_i}{2}).$$

In this setting we now can apply and compare both the classical and the quantitative version of abstract interpretation as in the following example.

Example 1. Let us consider a step function f in $\mathcal{T}_{16}$ (the concrete values of a and b don't really play a role in our setting) which can be depicted as:

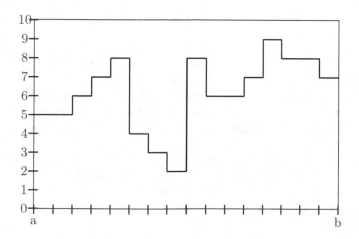

We can also represent f by the vector in $\mathbb{R}^{16}$:

$$(5\ 5\ 6\ 7\ 8\ 4\ 3\ 2\ 8\ 6\ 6\ 7\ 9\ 8\ 8\ 7)$$

We then construct a series of abstractions which correspond to coarser and coarser sub-divisions of the interval $[a, b]$, e.g. considering 8, 4 etc. subintervals instead of the original 16. These abstractions are from $\mathcal{T}_{16}([a, b])$ to $\mathcal{T}_8([a, b])$, $\mathcal{T}_4([a, b])$ etc. and can be represented by 16×8, 16×4, etc. matrices. For example, the abstraction which joins two sub-intervals and which corresponds to the abstraction $\alpha_8 : \mathcal{T}_{16}([a, b]) \to \mathcal{T}_8([a, b])$ together with its Moore-Penrose pseudo-inverse is represented by:

$$\mathbf{A}_8 = \begin{pmatrix} 1&0&0&0&0&0&0&0 \\ 1&0&0&0&0&0&0&0 \\ 0&1&0&0&0&0&0&0 \\ 0&1&0&0&0&0&0&0 \\ 0&0&1&0&0&0&0&0 \\ 0&0&1&0&0&0&0&0 \\ 0&0&0&1&0&0&0&0 \\ 0&0&0&1&0&0&0&0 \\ 0&0&0&0&1&0&0&0 \\ 0&0&0&0&1&0&0&0 \\ 0&0&0&0&0&1&0&0 \\ 0&0&0&0&0&1&0&0 \\ 0&0&0&0&0&0&1&0 \\ 0&0&0&0&0&0&1&0 \\ 0&0&0&0&0&0&0&1 \\ 0&0&0&0&0&0&0&1 \end{pmatrix} \quad \mathbf{G}_8 = \begin{pmatrix} \frac{1}{2}&\frac{1}{2}&0&0&0&0&0&0&0&0&0&0&0&0&0&0 \\ 0&0&\frac{1}{2}&\frac{1}{2}&0&0&0&0&0&0&0&0&0&0&0&0 \\ 0&0&0&0&\frac{1}{2}&\frac{1}{2}&0&0&0&0&0&0&0&0&0&0 \\ 0&0&0&0&0&0&\frac{1}{2}&\frac{1}{2}&0&0&0&0&0&0&0&0 \\ 0&0&0&0&0&0&0&0&\frac{1}{2}&\frac{1}{2}&0&0&0&0&0&0 \\ 0&0&0&0&0&0&0&0&0&0&\frac{1}{2}&\frac{1}{2}&0&0&0&0 \\ 0&0&0&0&0&0&0&0&0&0&0&0&\frac{1}{2}&\frac{1}{2}&0&0 \\ 0&0&0&0&0&0&0&0&0&0&0&0&0&0&\frac{1}{2}&\frac{1}{2} \end{pmatrix}$$

With the help of $\mathbf{A}_j$, $j \in \{1, 2, 4, 8\}$, we can easily compute the abstraction of f as $f\mathbf{A}_j$, which in order to compare it with the original f we can then again concretise using $\mathbf{G}$, i.e. computing $f\mathbf{AG}$. In a similar way we can also compute the over- and under-approximation of f in $\mathcal{T}_i$ based on the above pointwise ordering and its reverse ordering. The result of these abstractions is depicted geometrically in Figure 1.

The individual diagrams in this figure depict the original, i.e. concrete step function $f \in \mathcal{T}_{16}$ together with its approximations in $\mathcal{T}_8$, $\mathcal{T}_4$, etc. On the left hand side the PAI abstractions show how coarser and coarser interval subdivisions result in a series of approximations which try to interpolate the given function as closely as possible, sometimes below, sometimes above the concrete values. The diagrams on the right hand side depict the classical over- and under-approximations: In each case the function f is entirely below or above these approximations, i.e. we have safe but not necessarily close approximations. Additionally, one can also see from these figures not only that the PAI interpolation is in general closer to the original function than the classical abstractions (in fact it is the closest possible) but also that the PAI interpolation is always between the classical over- and under-approximations.

Probabilistic Abstract Interpretation   Classical Abstract Interpretation

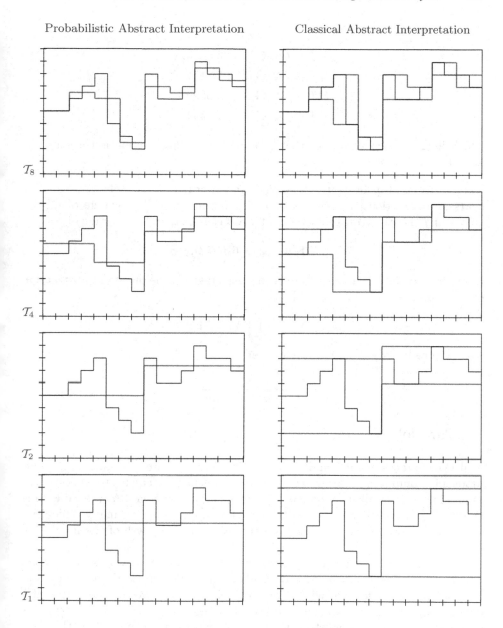

Fig. 1. Average, Over- and Under-Approximation

The vector space framework also allows us to judge the quality of an abstraction or approximation via the Eucledian distance between the concrete and abstract version of a function. We can compute the *least square error* as

$$\|f - f\mathbf{AG}\|.$$

In our case we get for example:

$$\|f - f\mathbf{A}_8\mathbf{G}_8\| = 3.5355$$
$$\|f - f\mathbf{A}_4\mathbf{G}_4\| = 5.3151$$
$$\|f - f\mathbf{A}_2\mathbf{G}_2\| = 5.9896$$
$$\|f - f\mathbf{A}_1\mathbf{G}_1\| = 7.6444$$

which illustrates, as expected, that the coarser our abstraction is the larger is also the mistake or error.

This example also illustrates how PAI and averages are closely related. The coarsest abstraction $\alpha_1 : \mathcal{T}_{16} \rightarrow \mathcal{T}_1$ computes in effect the average of all the values of f, i.e. the (constant) value of $f\mathbf{A}_1\mathbf{G}_1$ is exactly the average of

$$5, 5, 6, 7, 8, 4, 3, 2, 8, 6, 6, 7, 9, 8, 8, 7.$$

In general, we can always compute such an average via the one point abstraction of an n-dimensional space given by

$$\mathbf{A}^T = \begin{pmatrix} 1\ 1\ 1 \ldots 1 \end{pmatrix}$$

with Moore-Penrose pseudo-inverse given by

$$\mathbf{A}^\dagger = (\frac{1}{n}, \frac{1}{n}, \ldots, \frac{1}{n}).$$

4   Parallel Systems

Multi-core processors and multi-threaded applications are emerging as the new models in computing. This makes the development of adequate tools and techniques for code parallelisation one of today's major challenges. At the same time the study of parallel systems and their performance also poses many difficulties due to their complexity deriving from the exponential growth of the number of states.

Automatic tools such as compilers must provide code that works in all cases. Therefore, when a compiler has to parallelise two pieces of code it has to consider all potential dependencies. Current techniques are over-conservative: if a dependency cannot be proved, the compiler assumes that it does occur. As a consequence, many opportunities for parallelisation are missed in the code generation.

Contrary to this "worse-case" conservative approach, speculative threading is an emerging technique which allows for some incorrect thread parallelisation by postponing the check to some later time. In the following example we will show how this "optimistic" approach can be justified via PAI. We will also show how

PAI can be used to face the state space explosion problem in the performance evaluation of parallel systems.

4.1   Tensor Models

We will now discuss how to abstract or simplify dynamical systems described by iterations of linear maps, in particular stochastic systems, i.e. Discrete Time Markov Chains (DTMCs).

There exist numerous formalisms to describe the semantics or dynamics of discrete as well as continuous time (stochastic) systems like, for example, Stochastic Petri Nets (SPNs) [4,5], Stochastic Automata Networks (SANs) [6], etc.

In practice, in most of these models, as well as in the authors' Probabilistic Chemical Abstract Machine (pCHAM) [19] and the linear semantics of Probabilistic KLAIM (pKLAIM) [20], the operation which combines the semantics of individual components of the system (nodes, etc.) in order to describe the global structure (network, etc.) is the *tensor product*. The tensor or Kronecker product $\mathbf{A} \otimes \mathbf{B}$ of an $n \times m$ matrix $\mathbf{A}$ and a $k \times l$ matrix $\mathbf{B}$ is an $nk \times ml$ matrix:

$$\mathbf{A} \otimes \mathbf{B} = \begin{pmatrix} a_{11}\mathbf{B} & \dots & a_{1n}\mathbf{B} \\ \vdots & \ddots & \vdots \\ a_{1m}\mathbf{B} & \dots & a_{nm}\mathbf{B} \end{pmatrix}$$

This construction has the advantage of a clean separation of local and global aspects, i.e. of the micro and macro dynamics of a system. However, the price to pay for this is the (exponential) state explosion introduced by the tensor product. The issue we discuss next is how to control this explosion, at least partially, by simplifying the model using the PAI framework.

Before we look at an example of such an abstraction, let us first present the basic elements of "tensor models". The basic entities of these models are simple counters, which could be interpreted as "token stores" (as in pKLAIM) or to indicate the "multiplicity of molecules" (as in the pCHAM model).

The basic local operations we allow for are essentially just counting operations in steps of $+1$ and -1. These are represented by so called shift operators:

$$(\mathbf{C})_{ij} = \begin{cases} 1 \text{ for } j = i+1 \\ 0 \text{ otherwise} \end{cases} \quad \text{and} \quad (\mathbf{D})_{ij} = \begin{cases} 1 \text{ for } j = i-1 \\ 0 \text{ otherwise} \end{cases}$$

or more concretely:

$$\mathbf{C} = \begin{pmatrix} 0 & 1 & 0 & \dots & 0 & 0 \\ 0 & 0 & 1 & \dots & 0 & 0 \\ 0 & 0 & 0 & \dots & 0 & 0 \\ \vdots & & & \ddots & & \vdots \\ 0 & 0 & 0 & \dots & 0 & 1 \\ 0 & 0 & 0 & \dots & 0 & 0 \end{pmatrix} \quad \mathbf{D} = \begin{pmatrix} 0 & 0 & 0 & \dots & 0 & 0 \\ 1 & 0 & 0 & \dots & 0 & 0 \\ 0 & 1 & 0 & \dots & 0 & 0 \\ \vdots & & & \ddots & & \vdots \\ 0 & 0 & 0 & \dots & 0 & 0 \\ 0 & 0 & 0 & \dots & 1 & 0 \end{pmatrix}$$

Additionally we need to provide for testing operations which determine whether a certain "counter" is below or above a certain threshold. We represent these by projection operators:

$$(\mathbf{T}_m^{\min})_{ij} = \begin{cases} 1 \text{ for } i = j \geq m \\ 0 \text{ otherwise} \end{cases} \quad \text{and} \quad (\mathbf{T}_m^{\max})_{ij} = \begin{cases} 1 \text{ for } i = j \leq n \\ 0 \text{ otherwise} \end{cases}$$

or more concretely again:

$$\mathbf{T}_m^{\min} = \begin{pmatrix} 0\,0\,0\,\ldots\,0\,0 \\ 0\,0\,0\,\ldots\,0\,0 \\ 0\,0\,0\,\ldots\,0\,0 \\ \vdots \quad \ddots \quad \vdots \\ 0\,0\,0\,\ldots\,1\,0 \\ 0\,0\,0\,\ldots\,0\,1 \end{pmatrix} \quad \mathbf{T}_n^{\max} = \begin{pmatrix} 1\,0\,0\,\ldots\,0\,0 \\ 0\,1\,0\,\ldots\,0\,0 \\ 0\,0\,1\,\ldots\,0\,0 \\ \vdots \quad \ddots \quad \vdots \\ 0\,0\,0\,\ldots\,0\,0 \\ 0\,0\,0\,\ldots\,0\,0 \end{pmatrix}$$

To simplify our treatment we assume in the following that all operators have the right dimension, e.g. are all $s \times s$ matrices. It could also be noted that by moving from finite dimensional matrix algebras to infinite dimensional operator algebras, e.g. C* algebras, one can drop limits for the counting operations, i.e. $s = \infty$.

Due to the huge size of "tensor models" it is necessary to simplify them in some way in order to extract certain global behavioural properties. The underlying idea is somewhat similar to the approach in statistical mechanics, where macroscopic parameters like pressure or temperature are explained or aggregated from the statistics of the microscopic features of individual molecules, such as their momentum, mass, velocity, etc.

The simplification of tensor product models using probabilistic abstract interpretation can drastically reduce the complexity of the analysis while we can still guarantee that the obtained results are as close as possible to the exact values. It also allows a kind of compositional analysis as Moore-Penrose pseudo-inverse and tensor product are compatible in the following sense: Given two (bounded) linear operators $\mathbf{A}_1$ and $\mathbf{A}_2$ on a Hilbert space, then

$$(\mathbf{A}_1 \otimes \mathbf{A}_2)^\dagger = \mathbf{A}_1^\dagger \otimes \mathbf{A}_2^\dagger.$$

Therefore, by exploiting the algebraic properties of the tensor product, we can abstract tensor models component wise, i.e.

$$(\mathbf{A}_1 \otimes \mathbf{A}_2)^\dagger (\mathbf{T}_1 \otimes \mathbf{T}_2)(\mathbf{A}_1 \otimes \mathbf{A}_2) = (\mathbf{A}_1^\dagger \mathbf{T}_1 \mathbf{A}_1) \otimes (\mathbf{A}_2^\dagger \mathbf{T}_2 \mathbf{A}_2)$$

This is illustrated in the following example where we only abstract one part of the system while another one stays unchanged, i.e. we use an abstraction of the form $\mathbf{I} \otimes \mathbf{A}$ with $\mathbf{I}$ the identity.

4.2   Average Running Time

A simple example which relates to the issue of speculative threading or scheduling we discussed before concerns the parallel execution of two processes with the following constraint: If thread A finishes before thread B then B has to be restarted. The reason could be, for example, the following scenario: process A puts its final result into some storage area or memory which is used by process B to store intermediate results: as long as process A does not finish, the results/computations in thread B are correct, but if process A finishes too early than we have to redo all its work again. The problem is to estimate the maximal and average chance that this happens.

Let us consider a slightly simplified version where we are interested in analysing the behaviour of A in parallel with B until a restarting is needed. Concretely we have two processes: A just executes three steps and then stops; B counts up to some number n, e.g. $n = 100$, and then terminates. However at every step B can also terminate immediately; the chances for continuing counting or for termination are $50 : 50$. The tensor model for this example is simply given by:

$$\mathbf{T}_n = \mathbf{A} \otimes \mathbf{B}_n$$

with A being represented simply by a creation operator in four dimensions:

$$\mathbf{A} = \mathbf{C}_4 = \begin{pmatrix} 0 & 1 & 0 & 0 \\ 0 & 0 & 1 & 0 \\ 0 & 0 & 0 & 1 \\ 0 & 0 & 0 & 0 \end{pmatrix}.$$

The representation of B_n is a bit more complicated:

$$\mathbf{B}_n = \frac{1}{2} \cdot \mathbf{C}_n + \frac{1}{2} \cdot \left(\sum_{i=0}^{n-1} \mathbf{T}_i^{\min} \mathbf{T}_i^{\max} (\mathbf{C}_n)^{n-i} \right).$$

In other words, this process either continues counting from i to $i + 1$, or if has already reached exactly i (for which we have a min and a max test) then by applying the $(n - i)$-th power of the creation operator produces the n which leads to the termination of the whole process. More concretely, for $n = 4$ we have:

$$\mathbf{B}_4 = \begin{pmatrix} 0 & \frac{1}{2} & 0 & 0 & \frac{1}{2} \\ 0 & 0 & \frac{1}{2} & 0 & \frac{1}{2} \\ 0 & 0 & 0 & \frac{1}{2} & \frac{1}{2} \\ 0 & 0 & 0 & 0 & 1 \\ 0 & 0 & 0 & 0 & 0 \end{pmatrix}$$

The worst case analysis of these processes needs, in effect, to determine the longest running time of both process. That means we have to determine the *nilpotency* of $\mathbf{T}_n$ or at least of $\mathbf{A}$ and $\mathbf{B}_n$. It is easy to see that the longest possible running time, i.e. the nilpotency, for $\mathbf{A}$ is 3 steps, while for $\mathbf{B}_n$ is n. If we look at $\mathbf{T}_n = \mathbf{A} \otimes \mathbf{B}_n$, then it is easy to see that (for $n > 3$) the maximal running time is also as n.

There are a few problems with this analysis: firstly, in complexity theoretic terms, it requires to analyse a rather large $4n \times 4n$ matrix (and with more processes the tensor product will cause a huge explosion in the dimension of the exact model); secondly, for unbounded counting in B we don't get any meaningful result; and thirdly, the results are somewhat meaningless as the chances that B counts to n stepwise, instead of terminating early are rather small such that the average running time of B is much smaller than n, i.e. in the scenario discussed earlier it is rather unlikely that we have to restart B.

In order to see this we can compute an abstracted version of B and compare this to the worst case estimates and the exact results. For this we identify all intermediate states except for the terminating state n. We can use the following simple abstraction represented by the $n \times 2$ matrix

$$(\mathbf{K})_{ij} = \begin{cases} 1 \text{ for } i < n \text{ and } j = 1 \\ 1 \text{ for } i = n \text{ and } j = 2 \\ 0 \text{ otherwise} \end{cases} \quad \text{e.g. } \mathbf{K}_4 = \begin{pmatrix} 1 & 0 \\ 1 & 0 \\ 1 & 0 \\ 1 & 0 \\ 0 & 1 \end{pmatrix} \quad \mathbf{K}_4^\dagger = \begin{pmatrix} \frac{1}{4} & \frac{1}{4} & \frac{1}{4} & \frac{1}{4} & 0 \\ 0 & 0 & 0 & 0 & 1 \end{pmatrix}$$

It is particular easy to compute $\mathbf{K}^\dagger$ for abstractions like $\mathbf{K}$ where every concrete state is uniquely classified, i.e. where every row of $\mathbf{K}$ contains only one non-zero entry equal to 1: $\mathbf{K}^\dagger$ is in this case obtained by transposing $\mathbf{K}$ followed by a row-normalisation. With this we can construct abstract versions $\mathbf{B}_n^\# = \mathbf{K}^\dagger \mathbf{B} \mathbf{K}$ of $\mathbf{B}_n$ which are given by only 2×2 matrices, i.e. the combination of the concrete A process and the abstract process $B_n^\#$ is represented by just a 6×6 matrix.

If we compare the concrete average running time of $\mathbf{B}_n$, which means we have to iterate a $n \times n$ matrix, with the average running times of its abstract 2×2 version we get the following numerical results.

	avg	avg$^\#$	$P(3)$	$P(3)^\#$	max
$\mathbf{B}_5^\# = \begin{pmatrix} 0.38 & 0.62 \\ 0.00 & 0.00 \end{pmatrix}$	1.8750	1.6000	0.8750	0.9473	5
$\mathbf{B}_{10}^\# = \begin{pmatrix} 0.44 & 0.56 \\ 0.00 & 0.00 \end{pmatrix}$	1.9961	1.8000	0.8750	0.9122	10
$\mathbf{B}_{25}^\# = \begin{pmatrix} 0.48 & 0.52 \\ 0.00 & 0.00 \end{pmatrix}$	2.0000	1.9200	0.8750	0.8750	25
$\mathbf{B}_{100}^\# = \begin{pmatrix} 0.49 & 0.51 \\ 0.00 & 0.00 \end{pmatrix}$	2.0000	1.9800	0.8750	0.8750	100

Here we present the simplified 2×2 systems and give the exact average running time 'avg', the abstract average running time (of the simplified system) 'avg$^\#$', the exact and abstract probabilities for terminating after three steps $P(3)$ and $P(3)^\#$, and finally the maximal, i.e. worst case running time max.

This example illustrates a number of important technical issues, e.g.: (i) how PAI can be used to reduce the complexity of a model, in this case from $4n \times 4n$ to just 6×6 matrices; and (ii) the small difference between the concrete properties and the PAI approximated values, e.g. of the average running time or the probability of stopping after a certain number of steps.

This example also demonstrates a case where worst case analysis, although correct, is practically nearly useless: The worst case running time of 100 steps for the process B_{100} is much larger than the 3 steps for A. This would suggest in a speculative threading situation that it would be pointless to execute A and B_{100} in parallel as B_{100} would finish too late and thus have to be restarted anyway. However, the average case analysis and in particular the value for $P(3)$ tells us that B_{100} will terminate with nearly 90% chance before A, and that it would therefore make sense to schedule these two processes in parallel.

5 Conclusions

We started by reviewing Reinhard's work on WCET analysis. Knowledge of worst case execution times is absolutely essential in many applications. The field is quite mature and Reinhard's work provides an excellent example of a semantics-based approach to this problem. In the body of this paper, we have argued for the equal importance of average case execution times. The need for such analyses is well-recognised by the soft real-time community where average values are much more useful in the optimisation of designs (average power consumption, average heap usage, . . .).

We have shown how Probabilistic Abstract Interpretation may be used to support average case analysis; this contrasts with classical abstract interpretation where safety constrains us to work with worst cases. This paper presents first tentative steps in this direction. There are many open problems; one of the most fundamental is how to present operator algebra semantics in a compositional way. This is a necessary development to allow us to construct automatic tools for analysis as alternatives to the model checking approaches discussed in the Introduction.

References

1. Wilhelm, R.: Timing analysis and timing predictability. In de Boer, F., Bonsangue, M., Graf, S., de Roever, W.P., eds.: Formal Methods for Components and Objects. Volume 3657 of Lecture Notes in Computer Science. Springer (2004) 317–323
2. Shaw, A.: Reasoning about time in higher-level language software. IEEE Transactions on Software Engineering **15** (1989) 875–889
3. Lundquist, T., Stenström, P.: Timing anomalies in dynamically scheduled microprocessors. In: 20th IEEE Real-Time Systems Symposium. (1999)
4. Balbo, G.: Introduction to stochastic Petri nets. In: Springer Lectures on Formal Methods and Performance Analysis. Springer (2002) 84–155
5. Bause, F., Kritzinger, P.S.: Stochastic Petri Nets – An Introduction to the Theory. second edn. Vieweg Verlag (2002)
6. Plateau, B., Atif, K.: Stochastic automata network of modeling parallel systems. IEEE Transactions on Software Engineering **17** (1991) 1093–1108
7. Norman, G., Parker, D., Kwiatkowska, M., Shukla, S., Gupta, R.: Formal analysis and validation of continuous time Markov chain based system level power management strategies. In Rosenstiel, W., ed.: Proc. 7th Annual IEEE International Workshop on High Level Design Validation and Test (HLDVT'02), IEEE Computer Society Press (2002) 45–50

8. Di Pierro, A., Wiklicky, H.: Concurrent Constraint Programming: Towards Probabilistic Abstract Interpretation. In Gabbrielli, M., Pfenning, F., eds.: Proceedings of PPDP'00 – Priciples and Practice of Declarative Programming, Montréal, Canada, ACM SIGPLAN, Association of Computing Machinery (2000) 127–138
9. Cousot, P., Cousot, R.: Abstract Interpretation and Applications to Logic Programs. Journal of Logic Programming **13** (1992) 103–180
10. Abramsky, S., Hankin, C., eds.: Abstract Interpretation of Declarative Languages. Ellis-Horwood, Chichester, England (1987)
11. Nielson, F., Nielson, H.R., Hankin, C.: Principles of Program Analysis. Springer Verlag, Berlin – Heidelberg (1999)
12. Di Pierro, A., Wiklicky, H.: Measuring the precision of abstract interpretations. In: Proceedings of LOPSTR'00 – 10th International Workshop on Logic-Based Program Synthesis and Transformation, London, UK. Volume 2042 of Lecture Notes in Computer Science., Berlin – New York, Springer Verlag (2001) 147–164
13. Monniaux, D.: Abstract interpretation of probabilistic semantics. In: Proceedings of SAS'00. Volume 1824 of Lecture Notes in Computer Science., Springer Verlag (2000)
14. Monniaux, D.: Abstract interpretation of probabilistic semantics. In: Seventh International Static Analysis Symposium (SAS'00). Number 1824 in Lecture Notes in Computer Science, Springer Verlag (2000) 322–339
15. Eaton, J.: Gnu Octave Manual. www.octave.org (2002)
16. Cousot, P., Cousot, R.: Systematic Design of Program Analysis Frameworks. In: Symposium on Principles of Programming Languages (POPL), San Antonio, Texas (1979) 269–282
17. Deutsch, F.: Bet Approximation in Inner Product Spaces. Volume 7 of CMS Books in Mathematics. Springer Verlag, New York — Berlin (2001)
18. Ben-Israel, A., Greville, T.: Generalised Inverses — Theory and Applications. second edn. Volume 15 of CMS Books in Mathematics. Springer Verlag, New York — Berlin (2003)
19. Di Pierro, A., Hankin, C., Wiklicky, H.: Probabilistic chemical abstract machine and the expressiveness of linda languages. In de Boer, F., Bonsangue, M., Graf, S., de Roever, W.P., eds.: Proceedings of FMCO 2005, 4th International Symposium on Formal Methods for Components and Object. Volume 4111 of Lecture Notes in Computer Science., Springer Verlag (2006) 388–407
20. Di Pierro, A., Hankin, C., Wiklicky, H.: Quantitative static analysis of distributed systems. Journal of Functional Programming **15** (2005) 1–47

Grammar Analysis and Parsing by Abstract Interpretation

Patrick Cousot[1] and Radhia Cousot[2]

[1] École Normale Supérieure, 45 rue d'Ulm, 75230 Paris cedex 05 (France)
Patrick.Cousot@ens.fr
www.di.ens.fr/~cousot
[2] CNRS & École polytechnique, 91128 Palaiseau cedex (France)
Radhia.Cousot@polytechnique.fr
www.enseignement.polytechnique.fr/profs/informatique/Radhia.Cousot/

Abstract. We study abstract interpretations of a fixpoint protoderivation semantics defining the maximal derivations of a transitional semantics of context-free grammars akin to pushdown automata. The result is a hierarchy of bottom-up or top-down semantics refining the classical equational and derivational language semantics and including Knuth grammar problem, classical grammar flow analysis algorithms, and parsing algorithms.

1 Introduction

Grammar flow problems consist in computing a function of the [proto]language generated by the grammar for each nonterminal. This includes Knuth's grammar problem [1,2], grammar decision problems such as emptiness and finiteness [3], and classical compilation algorithms such as FIRST and FOLLOW [4]. For the later case, Ulrich Möncke and Reinhard Wilhelm introduced *grammar flow analysis* to solve computation problems over context-free grammars [5,6,7], [8, Sect. 8.2.4]. The idea is to provide two fixpoint algorithm schemata, one for bottom-up grammar flow analysis and one for top-down grammar flow analysis which can be instantiated with different parameters to get classical iterative algorithms such as FIRST and FOLLOW.

More generally, we show that grammar flow algorithms are abstract interpretations [9] of a hierarchy of bottom-up or top-down grammar semantics refining the classical (proto-)language semantics.

Then, we apply this comprehensive abstract-interpretation-based approach to the systematic derivation of parsing algorithms.

2 Languages and Context-Free Grammars

A *sentence* $\sigma \in \mathcal{A}^\star$ *over the alphabet* $\mathcal{A}$ of length $|\sigma| \triangleq n \geqslant 0$ is a possibly empty finite sequence $\sigma_1 \sigma_2 \ldots \sigma_n$ of letters $\sigma_1, \sigma_2, \ldots, \sigma_n \in \mathcal{A}$. For $n = 0$, the empty sentence is denoted ϵ of length $|\epsilon| = 0$. A *language* Σ *over the alphabet* $\mathcal{A}$

T. Reps, M. Sagiv, and J. Bauer (Eds.): Wilhelm Festschrift, LNCS 4444, pp. 175–200, 2007.

is a set of sentences $\Sigma \in \wp(\mathcal{A}^\star)$. We represent concatenation by juxtaposition. It is extended to languages as $\Sigma\Sigma' \triangleq \{\sigma\sigma' \mid \sigma \in \Sigma \wedge \sigma' \in \Sigma'\}$. For brevity, σ denotes the language $\{\sigma\}$ so that we can write $\Sigma\sigma\Sigma'$ for $\Sigma\{\sigma\}\Sigma'$. The *junction* of languages is $\Sigma \mathbin{\S} \Sigma' \triangleq \{\sigma_1\sigma_2\ldots\sigma_m\sigma'_2\ldots\sigma'_n \mid \sigma_1\sigma_2\ldots\sigma_m \in \Sigma \wedge \sigma'_1\sigma'_2\ldots\sigma'_n \in \Sigma' \wedge \sigma_m = \sigma'_1\}$. Given a set $\mathscr{P} \triangleq \{[_i \mid i \in \Delta\} \cup \{]_i \mid i \in \Delta\}$ of matching parentheses and an alphabet $\mathcal{A}$, the *Dyck language* $\mathbb{D}_{\mathscr{P},\mathcal{A}} \subseteq (\mathscr{P} \cup \mathcal{A})^\star$ over $\mathscr{P}$ and $\mathcal{A}$ is the set of well-parenthesized sentences over $\mathscr{P} \cup \mathcal{A}$. It is *pure* if $\mathcal{A} = \varnothing$. The *parenthesized language* over $\mathscr{P}$ and $\mathcal{A}$ is $\mathbb{P}_{\mathscr{P},\mathcal{A}} \triangleq \{[_i\sigma]_i \mid i \in \Delta \wedge \sigma \in \mathbb{D}_{\mathscr{P},\mathcal{A}} \setminus \{\epsilon\}\}$.

A context-free grammar [10,11] is a quadruple $\mathcal{G} = \langle \mathcal{T}, \mathcal{N}, \overline{S}, \mathscr{R} \rangle$ where $\mathcal{T}$ is the alphabet of *terminals*, $\mathcal{N}$ such that $\mathcal{T} \cap \mathcal{N} = \varnothing$ is the alphabet of *nonterminals*, $\overline{S} \in \mathcal{N}$ is the *start symbol* (or *axiom*) and $\mathscr{R} \in \wp(\mathcal{N} \times \mathcal{V}^\star)$ is the finite set of *rules* written $A \to \sigma$ where the *lefthand side* $A \in \mathcal{N}$ is a nonterminal and the *righthand side* $\sigma \in \mathcal{V}^\star$ is a possibly empty sentence over the *vocabulary* $\mathcal{V} \triangleq \mathcal{T} \cup \mathcal{N}$. By convention, $\epsilon \notin \mathcal{V}$.

3   Transitional Semantics of Context-Free Grammars

Pushdown automata (PDA) and context-free grammars are equivalent [8, Sect. 8.2]. Inspired by PDA, we define the transitional semantics of grammars by labelled transition systems where states are stacks, labels encode the structure of sentences and transitions are small steps in the recursive derivation of sentences.

Stacks. Given a grammar $\mathcal{G} = \langle \mathcal{T}, \mathcal{N}, \overline{S}, \mathscr{R} \rangle$, we let *stacks* $\varpi \in \mathcal{S} \triangleq (\mathscr{R}^{\textbf{.}} \cup \mathcal{M})^\star$ be sentences over *rule states* $\mathscr{R}^{\textbf{.}} \triangleq \{[A \to \sigma\textbf{.}\sigma'] \mid A \to \sigma\sigma' \in \mathscr{R}\}$ specifying the state of the derivation (σ' is still to be derived) and markers $\mathcal{M} = \{\vdash, \dashv\}$ where $\vdash$ (resp. $\dashv$) marks the beginning (resp. the end) of a sentence. The *height* of a stack ϖ is its length $|\varpi|$.

Example 1. A stack ϖ for the grammar $A \to AA$, $A \to a$ is $\dashv[A \to AA\textbf{.}][A \to A\textbf{.}A][A \to a\textbf{.}]$. It records the ancestors in an infix traversal of a parse tree, as shown opposite.

$$\begin{array}{l} \dashv \\ [A \to AA\textbf{.}] \\ [A \to A\textbf{.}A] \\ [A \to a\textbf{.}] \end{array}$$

□

Labels. We let $\mathscr{P} \triangleq \mathcal{O} \cup \mathcal{C}$ be the set of *parentheses* where $\mathcal{O} \triangleq \{(\!|A \mid A \in \mathcal{N}\}$ is the set of *opening parentheses* while $\mathcal{C} \triangleq \{A|\!) \mid A \in \mathcal{N}\}$ is the set of *closing parentheses*. We let *labels* $\ell \in \mathscr{L}$ be parentheses or terminals so that $\mathscr{L} \triangleq \mathscr{P} \cup \mathcal{T}$. A pair of parentheses $(\!|A \ldots A|\!)$ delimits the structure of a sentence deriving from nonterminal $A \in \mathcal{N}$ while terminals describe elements of the sentence.

Labelled Transition System. Given a grammar $\mathcal{G} = \langle \mathcal{T}, \mathcal{N}, \overline{S}, \mathscr{R} \rangle$, we define a *labelled transition system* $\mathsf{S}^t[\![\mathcal{G}]\!] \triangleq \langle \mathcal{S}, \mathscr{L}, \longrightarrow, \vdash \rangle$ where the initial state is $\vdash$ and the labelled transition relation $\overset{\ell}{\longrightarrow}$, $\ell \in \mathscr{L}$ is

$$\vdash \xrightarrow{(\!(A} \dashv [A \to \boldsymbol{.}\sigma], \qquad\qquad A \to \sigma \in \mathscr{R} \tag{1}$$

$$\varpi[A \to \sigma\boldsymbol{.}a\sigma'] \xrightarrow{a} \varpi[A \to \sigma a\boldsymbol{.}\sigma'], \qquad A \to \sigma a\sigma' \in \mathscr{R} \tag{2}$$

$$\varpi[A \to \sigma\boldsymbol{.}B\sigma'] \xrightarrow{(\!(B} \varpi[A \to \sigma B\boldsymbol{.}\sigma'][B \to \boldsymbol{.}\varsigma], \quad A \to \sigma B\sigma' \in \mathscr{R} \wedge B \to \varsigma \in \mathscr{R} \tag{3}$$

$$\varpi[A \to \sigma\boldsymbol{.}] \xrightarrow{A)\!)} \varpi, \qquad\qquad A \to \sigma \in \mathscr{R}\,. \tag{4}$$

4   Maximal Derivations

The *maximal derivation semantics* of a grammar is the set of all possible maximal derivations for this grammar where a *maximal derivation* is a finite labelled trace of maximal length generated by the transitional semantics.

Example 2. The maximal derivation for the sentence a of the grammar $\langle\{a\}$, $\{A\}, A, \{A \to AA, A \to a\}\rangle$ is $\vdash \xrightarrow{(\!(A} \dashv [A \to \boldsymbol{.}a] \xrightarrow{a} \dashv [A \to a\boldsymbol{.}] \xrightarrow{A)\!)} \dashv$ while for the sentence aa it is $\vdash \xrightarrow{(\!(A} \dashv [A \to \boldsymbol{.}AA] \xrightarrow{(\!(A} \dashv [A \to A\boldsymbol{.}A][A \to \boldsymbol{.}a] \xrightarrow{a}$ $\dashv [A \to A\boldsymbol{.}A][A \to a\boldsymbol{.}] \xrightarrow{A)\!)} \dashv [A \to A\boldsymbol{.}A] \xrightarrow{(\!(A} \dashv [A \to AA\boldsymbol{.}][A \to \boldsymbol{.}a] \xrightarrow{a} \dashv$ $[A \to AA\boldsymbol{.}][A \to a\boldsymbol{.}] \xrightarrow{A)\!)} \dashv [A \to AA\boldsymbol{.}] \xrightarrow{A)\!)} \dashv$. $\square$

Traces. Formally a *trace* $\theta \in \Theta^n$ of length $|\theta| = n+1$, $n \geqslant 0$, has the form $\theta = \varpi_0 \xrightarrow{\ell_0} \varpi_1 \ldots \varpi_{n-1} \xrightarrow{\ell_{n-1}} \varpi_n$ whence it is a pair $\theta = \langle \underline{\theta}, \overline{\theta} \rangle$ where $\underline{\theta} \in [0, n] \mapsto S$ is a nonempty finite sequence of stacks $\underline{\theta}_i = \varpi_n$, $i = 0, \ldots, n$ and $\overline{\theta} \in [0, n-1] \mapsto \mathscr{L}$ is a finite sequence of labels $\overline{\theta}_j = \ell_j$, $j = 0, \ldots, n-1$. Traces $\theta \in \Theta$ are nonempty, finite, of any length so $\Theta \overset{\Delta}{=} \bigcup_{n \geqslant 0} \Theta^n$.

Again concatenation is denoted by juxtaposition and extended to sets. We respectively identify a single state ϖ and a transition $\varpi \xrightarrow{\ell} \varpi'$ with the corresponding traces containing only the single state ϖ and the transition $\varpi \xrightarrow{\ell} \varpi'$. By abuse of notation, a trace $\varpi_0 \xrightarrow{\ell_0} \varpi_1 \ldots \varpi_{n-1} \xrightarrow{\ell_{n-1}} \varpi_n$ is also understood as the concatenation of ϖ_0, $\xrightarrow{\ell_0}$, ϖ_1, $\ldots$, ϖ_{n-1}, $\xrightarrow{\ell_{n-1}}$, ϖ_n which, informally, *matches the trace pattern* $\varsigma_0 \varpi_1 \ldots \varsigma_{n-1} \varpi_n \varsigma_n$ by letting $\varsigma_0 = \varpi_0 \xrightarrow{\ell_0}$, $\ldots$, $\varsigma_{n-1} = \varpi_{n-1} \xrightarrow{\ell_{n-1}}$ and $\varsigma_n = \epsilon$. We also need the *junction* of sets of traces, as follows

$$T \,\S\, T' \overset{\Delta}{=} \{\theta \xrightarrow{\ell} \varpi \xrightarrow{\ell'} \theta' \mid \theta \xrightarrow{\ell} \varpi \in T \wedge \varpi' \xrightarrow{\ell'} \theta' \in T' \wedge \varpi = \varpi'\}\,.$$

The *selection* of the traces in T for nonterminal B is denoted $T.B$ defined as

$$T.B \overset{\Delta}{=} \{\varpi \xrightarrow{(\!(B} \theta \mid \varpi \xrightarrow{(\!(B} \theta \in T\}\,.$$

For the recursive *incorporation* of a derivation $\vdash \xrightarrow{\ell_0} \dashv\varpi_1 \ldots \dashv\varpi_{n-1} \xrightarrow{\ell_{n-1}} \dashv$ into another one, we need the operation

$$\langle \varpi, \varpi' \rangle \uparrow \vdash \xrightarrow{\ell_0} \dashv\varpi_1 \ldots \dashv\varpi_{n-1} \xrightarrow{\ell_{n-1}} \dashv \overset{\Delta}{=} \varpi \xrightarrow{\ell_0} \varpi'\varpi_1 \ldots \varpi'\varpi_{n-1} \xrightarrow{\ell_{n-1}} \varpi'$$

$$\langle \varpi, \varpi' \rangle \uparrow T \overset{\Delta}{=} \{\langle \varpi, \varpi' \rangle \uparrow \tau \mid \tau \in T\}\,.$$

Example 3. We have $\langle \dashv[A \to .AA], \dashv[A \to A.A]\rangle \uparrow \vdash \xrightarrow{(\!A} \dashv[A \to .a] \xrightarrow{a}$ $\dashv[A \to a.] \xrightarrow{A)\!} \dashv = \dashv[A \to .AA] \xrightarrow{(\!A} \dashv[A \to A.A][A \to .a] \xrightarrow{a} \dashv[A \to A.A][A \to$ $a.] \xrightarrow{A)\!} \dashv[A \to A.A]$ which we can recognize as the replacement of the first A deriving into a in the derivation for the sentence aa in **Ex. 2**. □

A *derivation* of grammar $\mathcal{G}$ is a trace $\varpi_0 \xrightarrow{\ell_0} \varpi_1 \dots \varpi_{n-1} \xrightarrow{\ell_{n-1}} \varpi_n$, $n \geqslant 0$ generated by the transition system $\mathsf{S}^t[\![\mathcal{G}]\!]$ that is $\forall i \in [0, n-1] : \varpi_i \xrightarrow{\ell_i} \varpi_{i+1}$. A *prefix derivation* of grammar $\mathcal{G}$ is a derivation of grammar $\mathcal{G}$ starting with an initial state $\varpi_0 = \vdash$. A *suffix derivation* of grammar $\mathcal{G}$ is derivation of grammar $\mathcal{G}$ ending with an final state $\forall \varpi \in S : \forall \ell \in \mathcal{L} : \neg(\varpi_n \xrightarrow{\ell} \varpi)$, so that $\varpi_n = \dashv$ by def. (1–4) of $\longrightarrow$. A *maximal derivation* of grammar $\mathcal{G}$ is both a prefix and a suffix derivation of the grammar $\mathcal{G}$.

Derivations are well-parenthesized so that the grammatical structure of sentences can be described by trees. Let us define the *parenthesis abstraction* α^p for a stack ϖ by $\alpha^p(\varpi\varpi') \triangleq \alpha^p(\varpi')\alpha^p(\varpi)$, $\alpha^p(\vdash) = \alpha^p(\dashv) = \epsilon$ and $\alpha^p([A \to \sigma.\sigma']) \triangleq A)\!$, for a label, $\alpha^p(a) \triangleq \epsilon$ for all $a \in \mathcal{T}$, $\alpha^p((\!A) \triangleq (\!A$ and $\alpha^p(A)\!) \triangleq A)\!$, and for a trace $\alpha^p(\varpi_0 \xrightarrow{\ell_0} \varpi_1 \xrightarrow{\ell_1} \dots \varpi_{n-1} \xrightarrow{\ell_{n-1}} \varpi_n) \triangleq \alpha^p(\ell_0)\alpha^p(\ell_1)\dots\alpha^p(\ell_{n-1})\alpha^p(\varpi_n)$.

Lemma 4. *For any prefix derivation θ of a grammar $\mathcal{G}$, $\alpha^p(\theta) \in \mathbb{D}_{\mathcal{P},\varnothing}$ is a pure Dyck language. A maximal derivation $\theta = \vdash \xrightarrow{\ell_0} \varpi_1 \xrightarrow{\ell_1} \dots \varpi_{n-1} \xrightarrow{\ell_{n-1}} \dashv$ of $\mathcal{G}$ is well-parenthesized in that $\alpha^p(\theta) = \alpha^p(\ell_0)\alpha^p(\ell_1)\dots\alpha^p(\ell_{n-1}) \in \mathbb{D}_{\mathcal{P},\varnothing}$ is a pure Dyck language.* □

5   Prefix Derivation Semantics

The *prefix derivation semantics* $\mathsf{S}^{\vec{\partial}}[\![\mathcal{G}]\!]$ of a grammar $\mathcal{G} = \langle \mathcal{T}, \mathcal{N}, \overline{S}, \mathcal{R}\rangle$ is the set of all prefix derivations for the labelled transition system $\langle S, \mathcal{L}, \longrightarrow, \vdash\rangle$, that is

$$\mathsf{S}^{\vec{\partial}}[\![\mathcal{G}]\!] \triangleq \{\varpi_0 \xrightarrow{\ell_0} \varpi_1 \dots \varpi_{n-1} \xrightarrow{\ell_{n-1}} \varpi_n \mid n > 0 \wedge \varpi_0 = \vdash \wedge$$
$$\forall i \in [0, n-1] : \varpi_i \xrightarrow{\ell_i} \varpi_{i+1}\} \ .$$

Lemma 5. *If the prefix derivation semantics $\mathsf{S}^{\vec{\partial}}[\![\mathcal{G}]\!]$ of a grammar $\mathcal{G} = \langle \mathcal{T}, \mathcal{N}, \overline{S}, \mathcal{R}\rangle$ contains a prefix derivation $\theta_1 \varpi \theta_2$ then*

- *either $\varpi = \vdash$ if and only if $\theta_1 = \epsilon$*
- *or the stack ϖ has the form $\varpi = \dashv[A_1 \to \eta_1 A_2.\eta'_1][A_2 \to \eta_2 A_3.\eta'_2]\dots[A_n \to \eta_n.\eta'_n]$ where $A_i \to \eta_i A_{i+1}\eta'_i \in \mathcal{R}$ and $A_n \to \eta_n\eta'_n \in \mathcal{R}$ are grammar rules and $\theta_1 = \vdash \xrightarrow{(\!A_1} \theta'_1$.*
- *Moreover if $\theta_1 \varpi \theta_2 \in \mathsf{S}^{\vec{\partial}}[\![\mathcal{G}]\!].A$ then necessarily $A_1 = A$.* □

It has been shown in the more general context of [12, **Th. 11**] that we have the following fixpoint characterization of the prefix derivation semantics

Theorem 6

$$\mathsf{S}^{\vec{\partial}}\,\llbracket \mathcal{G}\rrbracket = \mathit{lfp}^{\subseteq}\,\mathsf{F}^{\vec{\partial}}\,\llbracket \mathcal{G}\rrbracket = \mathit{gfp}^{\subseteq}\,\mathsf{F}^{\vec{\partial}}\,\llbracket \mathcal{G}\rrbracket$$

where $\mathsf{F}^{\vec{\partial}}\,\llbracket \mathcal{G}\rrbracket \in \wp(\Theta) \mapsto \wp(\Theta)$ is a complete $\cup$ and $\cap$ morphism defined as

$$\mathsf{F}^{\vec{\partial}}\,\llbracket \mathcal{G}\rrbracket \triangleq \lambda X \cdot \{\vdash\} \cup X_{\S} \longrightarrow \;.$$ ☐

6   Transitional Maximal Derivation Semantics

The *maximal derivation semantics* $\mathsf{S}^{\hat{d}}\llbracket \mathcal{G}\rrbracket \in \wp(\Theta)$ of a grammar $\mathcal{G} = \langle \mathscr{T}, \mathscr{N}, \overline{S}, \mathscr{R}\rangle$ is the set of maximal derivations for the labelled transition system $\mathsf{S}^{t}\llbracket \mathcal{G}\rrbracket \triangleq \langle \mathcal{S}, \mathscr{L}, \longrightarrow, \vdash\rangle$.

$$\mathsf{S}^{\hat{d}}\llbracket \mathcal{G}\rrbracket \triangleq \{\varpi_0 \xrightarrow{\ell_0} \varpi_1 \ldots \varpi_{n-1} \xrightarrow{\ell_{n-1}} \varpi_n \mid n > 0 \wedge \varpi_0 = \vdash \wedge \tag{5}$$
$$\forall i \in [0, n-1] : \varpi_i \xrightarrow{\ell_i} \varpi_{i+1} \wedge \forall \varpi \in \mathcal{S} : \forall \ell \in \mathscr{L} : \neg(\varpi_n \xrightarrow{\ell} \varpi)\}\;.$$

Lemma 7. *A maximal derivation of the transition system* $\mathsf{S}^{t}\llbracket \mathcal{G}\rrbracket$ *has the form* $\vdash \xrightarrow{\langle\!\langle A} \dashv[A \to .\sigma] \xrightarrow{\ell_1} \dashv\varpi_2 \ldots \dashv\varpi_{n-1} \xrightarrow{A\rangle\!\rangle} \dashv$ *where* $\varpi_{n-1} \neq \epsilon$. ☐

7   Bottom-Up Fixpoint Maximal Derivation Semantics

The maximal derivation semantics (5) can be expressed in fixpoint form.

Example 8. For the grammar $\mathcal{G} = \langle\{a, b\}, \{A\}, A, \{A \to aA, A \to b\}\rangle$, we have $\mathsf{S}^{\hat{d}}\llbracket \mathcal{G}\rrbracket = \mathit{lfp}^{\subseteq}\,\widehat{\vec{\mathsf{F}}}^{\hat{d}}\llbracket \mathcal{G}\rrbracket$ where

$$\widehat{\vec{\mathsf{F}}}^{\hat{d}}(T) \triangleq \vdash \xrightarrow{\langle\!\langle A} \dashv[A \to .b] \xrightarrow{b} \dashv[A \to b.] \xrightarrow{A\rangle\!\rangle} \dashv \cup$$
$$\vdash \xrightarrow{\langle\!\langle A} (\dashv[A \to .aA]) \xrightarrow{a} ((\dashv[A \to a.A], \dashv[A \to aA.]) \uparrow T.A) \,\S\, (\dashv[A \to aA.]) \xrightarrow{A\rangle\!\rangle} \dashv.$$

The first iterates of $\widehat{\vec{\mathsf{F}}}^{\hat{d}}\llbracket \mathcal{G}\rrbracket$ from $\widehat{\vec{\mathsf{F}}}^{\hat{d}}_0 = \varnothing$ are

$$\widehat{\vec{\mathsf{F}}}^{\hat{d}}_1 = \{\vdash \xrightarrow{\langle\!\langle A} \dashv[A \to .b] \xrightarrow{b} \dashv[A \to b.] \xrightarrow{A\rangle\!\rangle} \dashv\}$$
$$\widehat{\vec{\mathsf{F}}}^{\hat{d}}_2 = \{\vdash \xrightarrow{\langle\!\langle A} \dashv[A \to .b] \xrightarrow{b} \dashv[A \to b.] \xrightarrow{A\rangle\!\rangle} \dashv,$$
$$\vdash \xrightarrow{\langle\!\langle A} \dashv[A \to .aA] \xrightarrow{a} \dashv[A \to a.A] \xrightarrow{\langle\!\langle A} \dashv[A \to aA.][A \to .b] \xrightarrow{b}$$
$$\dashv[A \to aA.][A \to b.] \xrightarrow{A\rangle\!\rangle} \dashv[A \to aA.] \xrightarrow{A\rangle\!\rangle} \dashv\}$$
$$\cdots \quad \cdots$$
$$\widehat{\vec{\mathsf{F}}}^{\hat{d}}_{\omega} = \mathit{lfp}^{\subseteq}\,\widehat{\vec{\mathsf{F}}}^{\hat{d}}\llbracket \mathcal{G}\rrbracket$$ ☐

More generally, let us define the set of traces bottom-up transformer $\overrightarrow{\hat{\mathsf{F}}}^{\hat{d}}[\![\mathcal{G}]\!] \in$
$\wp(\Theta) \mapsto \wp(\Theta)$ as

$$\overrightarrow{\hat{\mathsf{F}}}^{\hat{d}}[\![\mathcal{G}]\!] \triangleq \lambda T \cdot \bigcup_{A \to \sigma \in \mathscr{R}} \vdash \xrightarrow{(\!A} \overrightarrow{\hat{\mathsf{F}}}^{\hat{d}}[A \to \bullet\sigma]T \xrightarrow{A)} \dashv \qquad (6)$$

where $\overrightarrow{\hat{\mathsf{F}}}^{\hat{d}}[A \to \sigma\bullet\sigma'] \in \wp(\Theta) \mapsto \wp(\Theta)$ is defined as

$$\overrightarrow{\hat{\mathsf{F}}}^{\hat{d}}[A \to \sigma\bullet a\sigma'] \triangleq \lambda T \cdot (\dashv[A \to \sigma\bullet a\sigma']) \xrightarrow{a} \overrightarrow{\hat{\mathsf{F}}}^{\hat{d}}[A \to \sigma a\bullet\sigma']T \qquad (7)$$

$$\overrightarrow{\hat{\mathsf{F}}}^{\hat{d}}[A \to \sigma\bullet B\sigma'] \triangleq \lambda T \cdot (\langle\dashv[A \to \sigma\bullet B\sigma'], \dashv[A \to \sigma B\bullet\sigma']\rangle \uparrow T.B) \,\S\, \overrightarrow{\hat{\mathsf{F}}}^{\hat{d}}[A \to \sigma B\bullet\sigma']T \qquad (8)$$

$$\overrightarrow{\hat{\mathsf{F}}}^{\hat{d}}[A \to \sigma\bullet] \triangleq \lambda T \cdot (\dashv[A \to \sigma\bullet]) \,. \qquad (9)$$

Observe that $\overrightarrow{\hat{\mathsf{F}}}^{\hat{d}}[\![\mathcal{G}]\!]$ is upper-continuous.

Lemma 9. *If all traces in $T \subseteq \Theta$ are derivations of the transition system $\mathsf{S}^t[\![\mathcal{G}]\!]$ then all traces in $\overrightarrow{\hat{\mathsf{F}}}^{\hat{d}}[A \to \sigma\bullet\sigma']T$ are generated by the transition system $\mathsf{S}^t[\![\mathcal{G}]\!]$, start in state $(\dashv[A \to \sigma\bullet\sigma'])$ and end in state $(\dashv[A \to \sigma\sigma'\bullet])$. It follows that all traces in $\overrightarrow{\hat{\mathsf{F}}}^{\hat{d}}[\![\mathcal{G}]\!]T$ are derivations of the transition system $\mathsf{S}^t[\![\mathcal{G}]\!]$.*

The derivation semantics of a grammar $\mathcal{G}$ can be expressed in fixpoint form as

Theorem 10. $\mathsf{S}^{\hat{d}}[\![\mathcal{G}]\!] = \mathit{lfp}^{\subseteq} \overrightarrow{\hat{\mathsf{F}}}^{\hat{d}}[\![\mathcal{G}]\!] \,.$ $\square$

8   Protoderivations

Prototraces (formally defined below) are traces in construction containing nonterminal variables which are placeholders for unknown prototraces to be substituted for the nonterminal variables. Protoderivations are prototraces generated by the grammar, initially a nonterminal variable (such as the grammar axiom), obtained by top-down replacement of a nonterminal on the lefthand side of a grammar rule by the corresponding righthand side, until no nonterminal variable is left.

Example 11. A prototrace derivation for the grammar $\mathcal{G} = \langle\{a\}, \{A\}, A, \{A \to AA, A \to a\}\rangle$ is (the prototrace derivation relation is written $\boxed{D}\!\!\Longrightarrow_{\mathcal{G}}$)

$$\vdash \xrightarrow{\boxed{A}} \dashv$$

$$\boxed{D}\!\!\Longrightarrow_{\mathcal{G}} \vdash \xrightarrow{(\!A} \dashv[A \to \bullet AA] \xrightarrow{\boxed{A}} \dashv[A \to A\bullet A] \xrightarrow{\boxed{A}} \dashv[A \to AA\bullet] \xrightarrow{A)} \dashv$$

$$\boxed{D}\!\!\Longrightarrow_{\mathcal{G}} \vdash \xrightarrow{(\!A} \dashv[A \to \bullet AA] \xrightarrow{\boxed{A}} \dashv[A \to A\bullet A] \xrightarrow{(\!A} \dashv[A \to AA\bullet][A \to \bullet a] \xrightarrow{a}$$
$$\dashv[A \to AA\bullet][A \to a\bullet] \xrightarrow{A)} \dashv[A \to AA\bullet] \xrightarrow{A)} \dashv$$

$$\boxed{D}\!\!\Longrightarrow_{\mathcal{G}} \vdash \xrightarrow{(\!A} \dashv[A \to \bullet AA] \xrightarrow{(\!A} \dashv[A \to A\bullet A][A \to \bullet a] \xrightarrow{a} \dashv[A \to A\bullet A][A \to$$
$$a\bullet] \xrightarrow{A)} \dashv[A \to A\bullet A] \xrightarrow{(\!A} \dashv[A \to AA\bullet][A \to \bullet a] \xrightarrow{a} \dashv[A \to AA\bullet][A \to$$
$$a\bullet] \xrightarrow{A)} \dashv[A \to AA\bullet] \xrightarrow{A)} \dashv \,. \qquad \square$$

Prototraces. The set of nonterminal variables is $\mathcal{N}^{\square} \triangleq \{\boxed{A} \mid A \in \mathcal{N}\}$. A *prototrace* $\pi \in \Pi^n$ of length $|\pi| = n+1$, $n \geqslant 0$, has the form $\pi = \varpi_0 \xrightarrow{\kappa_0} \varpi_1 \ldots$ $\varpi_{n-1} \xrightarrow{\kappa_{n-1}} \varpi_n$ whence is a pair $\pi = \langle \underline{\pi}, \overline{\pi} \rangle$ where $\underline{\pi} \in [0,n] \mapsto \mathcal{S}$ is a nonempty finite sequence of stacks $\underline{\pi}_i = \varpi_n$, $i = 0, \ldots, n$ and $\overline{\pi} \in [0, n-1] \mapsto (\mathcal{L} \cup \mathcal{N}^{\square})$ is a finite sequence of labels or nonterminal variables $\overline{\pi}_j = \kappa_j$, $j = 0, \ldots, n-1$. Prototraces $\pi \in \Pi$ are nonempty, finite, of any length so $\Pi \triangleq \bigcup_{n \geqslant 0} \Pi^n$ and $\Theta \subseteq \Pi$.

Again prototrace pattern matching, prototrace concatenation, set of prototraces concatenation, the assimilation of a single state ϖ and a transition $\varpi \xrightarrow{\ell} \varpi'$ with the corresponding prototraces, the junction $\S$ of sets of prototraces, the selection $P.B$ of the prototraces in P for nonterminal B and the stack incorporation in a prototrace $\langle \varpi, \varpi' \rangle \uparrow \pi$ or a set T of prototraces $\langle \varpi, \varpi' \rangle \uparrow T$ are defined as for traces and sets of traces.

Prototrace Derivation. The *prototrace generated by a grammar rule* $A \to \sigma \in \mathcal{R}$ is $\check{\mathsf{R}}^{\check{D}}[A \to \sigma]$ where $\check{\mathsf{R}}^{\check{D}} \in \mathcal{R} \mapsto \Pi$ is

$$\check{\mathsf{R}}^{\check{D}}[A \to \sigma] \triangleq \vdash \xrightarrow{(\!(A}} \check{\mathsf{F}}^{\check{D}}[A \to .\sigma] \xrightarrow{A)\!)} \dashv \tag{10}$$

$$\check{\mathsf{F}}^{\check{D}}[A \to \sigma.a\sigma'] \triangleq \dashv[A \to \sigma.a\sigma'] \xrightarrow{a} \check{\mathsf{F}}^{\check{D}}[A \to \sigma a.\sigma']$$

$$\check{\mathsf{F}}^{\check{D}}[A \to \sigma.B\sigma'] \triangleq \dashv[A \to \sigma.B\sigma'] \xrightarrow{\boxed{B}} \check{\mathsf{F}}^{\check{D}}[A \to \sigma B.\sigma']$$

$$\check{\mathsf{F}}^{\check{D}}[A \to \sigma.] \triangleq \dashv[A \to \sigma.] \; .$$

The *prototrace derivation* relation $\boxed{\mathbb{D}}\!\!\Longrightarrow_{\mathcal{G}} \in \wp(\Pi \times \Pi)$ for a grammar $\mathcal{G} = \langle \mathcal{T}, \mathcal{N}, \overline{\mathcal{S}}, \mathcal{R} \rangle$ consists in replacing one or several nonterminal variables by the prototrace generated by a grammar rule for that nonterminal.

$$\pi \; \boxed{\mathbb{D}}\!\!\Longrightarrow_{\mathcal{G}} \pi' \tag{11}$$

$$\triangleq \exists n > 0, \varsigma_1, \ldots, \varsigma_{n+1}, \varpi_1, \ldots, \varpi_{n+1} \in \mathcal{S}, A_1, \ldots, A_n \in \mathcal{N}, \sigma_1, \ldots, \sigma_n \in \mathcal{V}^* :$$

$$\pi = \varsigma_1 \varpi_1 \xrightarrow{\boxed{A_1}} \varpi_2 \varsigma_2 \ldots \varsigma_n \varpi_n \xrightarrow{\boxed{A_n}} \varpi_{n+1} \varsigma_{n+1} \wedge \forall i \in [1,n] : A_i \to \sigma_i \in \mathcal{R} \wedge$$

$$\pi' = \varsigma_1 \langle \varpi_1, \varpi_2 \rangle \uparrow \check{\mathsf{R}}^{\check{D}}[A_1 \to \sigma_1] \varsigma_2 \ldots \varsigma_n \langle \varpi_n, \varpi_{n+1} \rangle \uparrow \check{\mathsf{R}}^{\check{D}}[A_n \to \sigma_n] \varsigma_{n+1} \; .$$

9   Maximal Protoderivation Semantics

The *top-down maximal protoderivation semantics* $\mathsf{S}^{\check{D}}[\![\mathcal{G}]\!] \in \mathcal{N} \mapsto \wp(\Pi)$ of a context-free grammar $\mathcal{G}$ is

$$\mathsf{S}^{\check{D}}[\![\mathcal{G}]\!] \triangleq \lambda A \cdot \{\pi \in \Pi \mid (\vdash \xrightarrow{\boxed{A}} \dashv) \; \boxed{\mathbb{D}}\!\!\Longrightarrow_{\mathcal{G}}^* \pi\} \; . \tag{12}$$

where r^n, $n \in \mathbb{N}$ are the powers of relation r, $r^{n\star} \triangleq \bigcup_{i < n} r^i$ (so that $r^{0\star} \triangleq \bigcup \varnothing = \varnothing$), r^+ (resp. r^*) is the transitive closure (resp. reflexive transitive closure) of r.

10   Top-Down Fixpoint Maximal Protoderivation Semantics

The protoderivation semantics can be expressed in fixpoint form, as follows (where post $\in \wp(\Sigma) \mapsto \wp(\Sigma)$ is post$[r]X \triangleq \{s' \in \Sigma \mid \exists s \in X : \langle s, s' \rangle \in r\}$)

Theorem 12. $S^{\breve{D}}[\mathcal{G}] = lfp^{\dot{\subseteq}} \breve{F}^{\breve{D}}[\mathcal{G}]$ *where* $\dot{\subseteq}$ *is the pointwise extension of* $\subseteq$ *and the set of prototraces transformer* $\breve{F}^{\breve{D}}[\mathcal{G}] \in (\mathcal{N} \mapsto \wp(\Pi)) \mapsto (\mathcal{N} \mapsto \wp(\Pi))$ *is*

$$\breve{F}^{\breve{D}}[\mathcal{G}] \triangleq \lambda\phi \cdot \lambda A \cdot \{\vdash \xrightarrow{\boxed{A}} \dashv\} \cup \text{post}[\boxtimes\!\!\Longrightarrow_{\mathcal{G}}]\phi(A) \ . \qquad \square$$

11   Abstraction of the Top-Down Protoderivation Semantics into the Bottom-Up Derivation Semantics

The trace derivations $\theta \in S^{\hat{d}}[\mathcal{G}].A$ for a nonterminal A can be constructed top-down using the prototrace derivation $\boxtimes\!\!\xrightarrow{*}_{\mathcal{G}}$ as $(\vdash \xrightarrow{\boxed{A}} \dashv) \boxtimes\!\!\xrightarrow{*}_{\mathcal{G}} \theta$.

Lemma 13. *If* $T = \{\pi \in \Theta \mid \exists A \in \mathcal{N} : (\vdash \xrightarrow{\boxed{A}} \dashv) \boxtimes\!\!\xrightarrow{n*}_{\mathcal{G}} \pi\}$ *then* $\hat{\vec{F}}^{\hat{d}}[A \to \sigma_{\bullet}\sigma'](T) = \{\pi \in \Theta \mid \breve{F}^{\breve{D}}[A \to \sigma_{\bullet}\sigma'] \boxtimes\!\!\xrightarrow{n*}_{\mathcal{G}} \pi\}$. $\qquad \square$

Lemma 14. *Let* $\hat{\vec{F}}^{\hat{d}}{}_n$ *be the iterates of* $\hat{\vec{F}}^{\hat{d}}[\mathcal{G}]$ *from* $\hat{\vec{F}}^{\hat{d}}{}_0 = \varnothing$. *We have*

$$\hat{\vec{F}}^{\hat{d}}{}_n = \{\pi \in \Theta \mid \exists A \in \mathcal{N} : (\vdash \xrightarrow{\boxed{A}} \dashv) \boxtimes\!\!\xrightarrow{(n+1)*}_{\mathcal{G}} \pi\} \qquad \square$$

Theorem 15. $S^{\hat{d}}[\mathcal{G}] = \{\pi \in \Theta \mid \exists A \in \mathcal{N} : (\vdash \xrightarrow{\boxed{A}} \dashv) \boxtimes\!\!\xrightarrow{*}_{\mathcal{G}} \pi\}$. $\qquad \square$

Let us define the abstraction $\alpha^{\breve{D}\hat{d}} \triangleq \lambda P \cdot \lambda A \cdot P(A) \cap \Theta$ which collects the terminal traces (without nonterminal variables) among prototraces. This abstraction defines a Galois connection [13] $\langle \mathcal{N} \mapsto \wp(\Pi), \dot{\subseteq} \rangle \xrightleftharpoons[\alpha^{\breve{D}\hat{d}}]{\gamma^{\breve{D}\hat{d}}} \langle \mathcal{N} \mapsto \wp(\Theta), \dot{\subseteq}\rangle$. The restriction of the top-down maximal protoderivation semantics is the maximal derivation semantics.

Theorem 16. $\alpha^{\breve{D}\hat{d}}(S^{\breve{D}}[\mathcal{G}]) = \lambda A \cdot S^{\hat{d}}[\mathcal{G}].A$. $\qquad \square$

12   The Hierarchy of Grammar Semantics

Th. 16 shows that the bottom-up derivation semantics $S^{\hat{d}}[\mathcal{G}]$ of a grammar $\mathcal{G}$ is, up to an isomorphism, an abstraction of the top-down protoderivation semantics $S^{\breve{D}}[\mathcal{G}] \triangleq \lambda A \cdot \{\pi \in \Pi \mid (\vdash \xrightarrow{\boxed{A}} \dashv) \boxtimes\!\!\Longrightarrow_{\mathcal{G}} \pi\}$ by the abstraction $\alpha^{\breve{D}\hat{d}}$. We now introduce a hierarchy of abstractions of the protoderivation semantics $S^{\breve{D}}[\mathcal{G}]$, as given in **Fig. 1**. The various semantics and abstractions in **Fig. 1** (apart from $S^{\breve{D}}[\mathcal{G}]$, $S^{\hat{d}}[\mathcal{G}]$, and $\alpha^{\breve{D}\hat{d}}$) are described below.

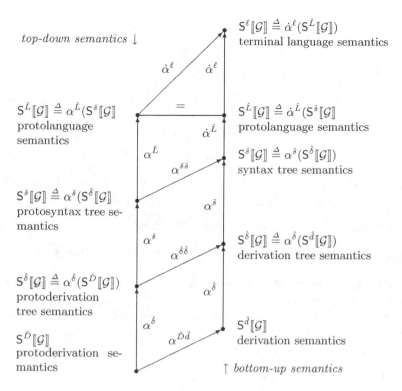

$$S^\ell[\mathcal{G}] \triangleq \dot{\alpha}^\ell(S^{\check{L}}[\mathcal{G}])$$
terminal language semantics

top-down semantics ↓

$\dot{\alpha}^\ell \quad \dot{\alpha}^\ell$

$$S^{\check{L}}[\mathcal{G}] \triangleq \alpha^{\check{L}}(S^{\check{s}}[\mathcal{G}])$$
protolanguage
semantics

$=$

$$S^L[\mathcal{G}] \triangleq \dot{\alpha}^L(S^s[\mathcal{G}])$$
protolanguage semantics

$\dot{\alpha}^{\check{L}}$

$\alpha^{\check{L}}$

$\alpha^{\check{s}\hat{s}}$

$$S^s[\mathcal{G}] \triangleq \alpha^s(S^{\hat{s}}[\mathcal{G}])$$
syntax tree semantics

$$S^{\check{s}}[\mathcal{G}] \triangleq \alpha^{\check{s}}(S^{\check{\delta}}[\mathcal{G}])$$
protosyntax tree se-
mantics

$\alpha^{\hat{s}}$

$\alpha^{\check{s}}$

$\alpha^{\check{\delta}\hat{\delta}}$

$$S^{\hat{\delta}}[\mathcal{G}] \triangleq \alpha^{\hat{\delta}}(S^{\hat{d}}[\mathcal{G}])$$
derivation tree semantics

$$S^{\check{\delta}}[\mathcal{G}] \triangleq \alpha^{\check{\delta}}(S^{\check{D}}[\mathcal{G}])$$
protoderivation
tree semantics

$\alpha^{\hat{\delta}}$

$\alpha^{\check{\delta}}$

$\alpha^{\check{D}\hat{d}}$

$$S^{\hat{d}}[\mathcal{G}]$$
derivation semantics

$$S^{\check{D}}[\mathcal{G}]$$
protoderivation se-
mantics

↑ *bottom-up semantics*

Fig. 1. The hierarchy of bottom-up grammar semantics

[Proto]Derivation Tree Abstraction $\alpha^{\check{\delta}}$ and $\alpha^{\hat{\delta}}$. [Proto]derivations can
be described by [proto]derivation trees where internal nodes are labelled with
nonterminals, leafs are labelled with terminals [or nonterminal variables] and
branches are decorated with rule states.

Example 17. One possible protoderivation tree for the protosentence
AaA of the grammar $\langle\{a\}, \{A\}, A,$
$\{A \rightarrow AA, A \rightarrow a\}\rangle$ is given on the
right. It can be represented in paren-
thesized form through an infix traversal
as $(A[A \rightarrow .AA]\ \boxed{A}\ [A \rightarrow A.A](A[A \rightarrow$
$.AA](A[A \rightarrow .a]a[A \rightarrow a.]A)[A \rightarrow$
$A.A]\boxed{A}[A \rightarrow AA.]A)[A \rightarrow AA.]A)$.

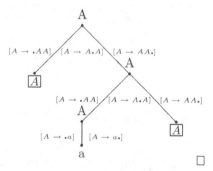

We let $\check{\mathcal{U}} \triangleq \mathcal{T} \cup \mathcal{N}^\square \cup \mathcal{R}^\bullet$ and $\check{\mathcal{D}} \triangleq (\mathcal{P} \cup \check{\mathcal{U}})^\star$. A *protoderivation tree* $\check{\delta}$ is
represented by a well-parenthesized sentence over $\check{\mathcal{U}}$ so that $\check{\delta} \in \mathbb{P}_{\mathcal{P},\check{\mathcal{U}}} \subseteq \check{\mathcal{D}}$. We
extend the selection to $\wp(\check{\mathcal{D}})$ whence $\wp(\mathbb{P}_{\mathcal{P},\check{\mathcal{U}}})$ as $D.A \triangleq \{(B\sigma B) \in D \mid B =$
$A\} \cup \{\boxed{B} \in D \mid B = A\}$ so that $D.A$ is the set of protoderivation trees in D
rooted at $A \in \mathcal{N}$.

The *protoderivation tree abstraction* $\alpha^{\breve{\delta}} \in \Pi \mapsto \breve{\mathcal{D}}$ of protoderivations is

$$\alpha^{\breve{\delta}}(\varpi \xrightarrow{\kappa} \tau) \triangleq \alpha^{\breve{\delta}}(\varpi)\kappa\alpha^{\breve{\delta}}(\tau) \qquad \alpha^{\breve{\delta}}(\dashv) \triangleq \epsilon$$
$$\alpha^{\breve{\delta}}(\epsilon) \triangleq \epsilon \qquad\qquad \alpha^{\breve{\delta}}(s_1 \dots s_n) \triangleq s_n, \quad s_1 \dots s_n \in \mathcal{S},$$
$$\alpha^{\breve{\delta}}(\vdash) \triangleq \epsilon \qquad\qquad\qquad\qquad\qquad n > 0, \text{otherwise}$$

which is extended elementwise to $\alpha^{\breve{\delta}} \in \wp(\Pi) \mapsto \wp(\breve{\mathcal{D}})$ as $\alpha^{\breve{\delta}}(T) \triangleq \{\alpha^{\breve{\delta}}(\pi) \mid \pi \in T\}$ so that we get the Galois connection $\langle \wp(\Pi), \subseteq \rangle \xleftarrow[\alpha^{\breve{\delta}}]{\gamma^{\breve{\delta}}} \langle \wp(\breve{\mathcal{D}}), \subseteq \rangle$, further extended pointwise to $\alpha^{\breve{\delta}} \in (\mathcal{N} \mapsto \wp(\Pi)) \mapsto (\mathcal{N} \mapsto \wp(\breve{\mathcal{D}}))$ as $\alpha^{\breve{\delta}}(\phi) \triangleq \lambda A \cdot \alpha^{\breve{\delta}}(\phi(A))$. The restriction of $\alpha^{\breve{\delta}}$ to derivation trees $\hat{\mathcal{D}} \triangleq (\mathcal{P} \cup \hat{\mathcal{U}})^\star$ where $\hat{\mathcal{U}} \triangleq \mathcal{T} \cup \mathcal{R}^{\scriptscriptstyle\bullet}$ is written $\alpha^{\hat{\delta}}$ so that $\langle \wp(\Theta), \subseteq \rangle \xleftarrow[\alpha^{\hat{\delta}}]{\gamma^{\hat{\delta}}} \langle \wp(\hat{\mathcal{D}}), \subseteq \rangle$. A *derivation tree* $\hat{\delta}$ is represented by a well-parenthesized sentence over $\hat{\mathcal{U}}$ so that $\hat{\delta} \in \mathbb{P}_{\mathcal{P}, \hat{\mathcal{U}}} \subseteq \hat{\mathcal{D}}$.

[Proto]Syntax Tree Abstraction $\alpha^{\breve{s}}$ and $\alpha^{\hat{s}}$. [Proto]syntax trees are [proto]-derivation trees denuded of the rule states decorating the branches. We represent [proto]syntax trees in parenthesized form through an infix traversal. We let $\breve{\mathcal{T}} \triangleq (\mathcal{P} \cup \mathcal{T} \cup \mathcal{N}^{\scriptscriptstyle\square})^\star$. A *protosyntax tree* $\breve{\tau}$ is represented by a well-parenthesized sentence over $(\mathcal{T} \cup \mathcal{N}^{\scriptscriptstyle\square})$ so that $\breve{\tau} \in \mathbb{P}_{\mathcal{P}, (\mathcal{T} \cup \mathcal{N}^{\scriptscriptstyle\square})} \subseteq \breve{\mathcal{T}}$.

Example 18. One possible protosyntax tree for the protosentence AaA of the grammar $\langle \{a\}, \{A\}, A, \{A \to AA, A \to a\} \rangle$ is given on the right and represented as $(\![A\boxed{A}(\![A(\![AaA]\!)\boxed{A}A]\!)A]\!)$.

The *protosyntax tree abstraction* $\alpha^{\breve{s}} \in \breve{\mathcal{D}} \mapsto \breve{\mathcal{T}}$ of protoderivation trees is ($A \in \mathcal{N}, \ell \in \mathcal{L}$)

$$\alpha^{\breve{s}}(\sigma(\![A\sigma') \triangleq \alpha^{\breve{s}}(\sigma)(\![A\alpha^{\breve{s}}(\sigma') \qquad \alpha^{\breve{s}}(\sigma[A \to \varsigma_{\scriptscriptstyle\bullet}\varsigma']\sigma') \triangleq \alpha^{\breve{s}}(\sigma)\alpha^{\breve{s}}(\sigma')$$
$$\alpha^{\breve{s}}(\sigma A]\!)\sigma') \triangleq \alpha^{\breve{s}}(\sigma)A]\!)\alpha^{\breve{s}}(\sigma') \qquad\qquad \alpha^{\breve{s}}(\sigma\ell\sigma') \triangleq \alpha^{\breve{s}}(\sigma)\ell\alpha^{\breve{s}}(\sigma')$$
$$\alpha^{\breve{s}}(\sigma\boxed{A}\sigma') \triangleq \alpha^{\breve{s}}(\sigma)\boxed{A}\alpha^{\breve{s}}(\sigma') \qquad\qquad \alpha^{\breve{s}}(\epsilon) \triangleq \epsilon$$

extended elementwise to $\alpha^{\breve{s}} \in \wp(\breve{\mathcal{D}}) \mapsto \wp(\breve{\mathcal{T}})$ as $\alpha^{\breve{s}}(D) \triangleq \{\alpha^{\breve{s}}(\breve{\delta}) \mid \breve{\delta} \in D\}$ so that we get a Galois connection $\langle \wp(\breve{\mathcal{D}}), \subseteq \rangle \xleftarrow[\alpha^{\breve{s}}]{\gamma^{\breve{s}}} \langle \wp(\breve{\mathcal{T}}), \subseteq \rangle$ which can be extended pointwise to $(\mathcal{N} \mapsto \wp(\breve{\mathcal{D}})) \mapsto (\mathcal{N} \mapsto \wp(\breve{\mathcal{T}}))$ as $\alpha^{\breve{s}}(\phi) \triangleq \lambda A \cdot \alpha^{\breve{s}}(\phi(A))$. The restriction $\alpha^{\hat{s}}$ to syntax trees $\hat{\mathcal{T}} \triangleq (\mathcal{P} \cup \mathcal{T})^\star$ is such that $\langle \wp(\hat{\mathcal{D}}), \subseteq \rangle \xleftarrow[\alpha^{\hat{s}}]{\gamma^{\hat{s}}} \langle \wp(\hat{\mathcal{T}}), \subseteq \rangle$. A *syntax tree* $\hat{\tau}$ is represented by a well-parenthesized sentence over $\mathcal{T}$ so that $\hat{\tau} \in \mathbb{P}_{\mathcal{P}, \mathcal{T}} \subseteq \hat{\mathcal{T}}$.

Protosentence Abstraction $\alpha^{\breve{L}}$ and $\dot{\alpha}^{\hat{L}}$. The *protolanguage* of a grammar $\mathcal{G} = \langle \mathcal{T}, \mathcal{N}, \overline{S}, \mathcal{R} \rangle$ with $\mathcal{V} \triangleq \mathcal{T} \cup \mathcal{N}$ is the set of protosentences deriving from the grammar axiom $\overline{S}$ where *protosentences* $\eta \in \mathscr{V}^\star$ contain both terminals in $\mathscr{T}$ and nonterminals in $\mathscr{N}$ and the derivation consists in replacing a nonterminal A by the righthand side σ of a grammar rule $A \to \sigma \in \mathscr{R}$.

The *protolanguage abstraction* $\alpha^{\check{L}} \in \check{T} \mapsto \mathscr{V}^\star$ of protosyntax trees is defined as (we follow the tradition of confusing nonterminals A denoting the grammatical structure and nonterminal variables $\boxed{A}$ for protosentence substitution)

$$\alpha^{\check{L}}(\sigma (\!| A\sigma')) \triangleq \alpha^{\check{L}}(\sigma)\alpha^{\check{L}}(\sigma'), \quad A \in \mathscr{N} \qquad \alpha^{\check{L}}(\sigma a\sigma') \triangleq \alpha^{\check{L}}(\sigma)a\alpha^{\check{L}}(\sigma'), \quad a \in \mathscr{T}$$

$$\alpha^{\check{L}}(\sigma A |\!)\sigma') \triangleq \alpha^{\check{L}}(\sigma)\alpha^{\check{L}}(\sigma') \qquad\qquad \alpha^{\check{L}}(\epsilon) \triangleq \epsilon$$

$$\alpha^{\check{L}}(\sigma \boxed{A}\sigma') \triangleq \alpha^{\check{L}}(\sigma)A\alpha^{\check{L}}(\sigma')$$

extended elementwise to $\alpha^{\check{L}} \in \wp(\check{T}) \mapsto \wp(\mathscr{V}^\star)$ as $\alpha^{\check{L}}(D) \triangleq \{\alpha^{\check{L}}(\check{\tau}) \mid \check{\tau} \in D\}$ so that we get a Galois connection $\langle \wp(\check{T}), \subseteq \rangle \xrightleftharpoons[\alpha^{\check{L}}]{\gamma^{\check{L}}} \langle \wp(\mathscr{V}^\star), \subseteq \rangle$ which can be extended pointwise to $\alpha^{\check{L}} \in (\mathscr{N} \mapsto \wp(\check{T})) \mapsto (\mathscr{N} \mapsto \wp(\mathscr{V}^\star))$ as $\alpha^{\check{L}}(\phi) \triangleq \lambda A \cdot \alpha^{\check{L}}(\phi(A))$.

Example 19. For the protosyntax tree in **Ex. 18** of the grammar $\langle \{a\}, \{A\}, A, \{A \to AA, A \to a\}\rangle$, we have $\alpha^{\check{L}}((\!| A\boxed{A}(\!| A(\!| AaA|\!)\boxed{A}A|\!)A|\!)A)) = AaA$. □

For syntax trees, we define the flattener $\alpha^{\hat{L}} \in \hat{T} \mapsto \wp(\mathscr{V}^\star)$ as

$$\alpha^{\hat{L}}((\!| A\sigma A|\!)\sigma') \triangleq (\{A\} \cup \alpha^{\hat{L}}(\sigma))\alpha^{\hat{L}}(\sigma') \qquad \alpha^{\hat{L}}(a\sigma') \triangleq \{a\}\alpha^{\hat{L}}(\sigma') \qquad \alpha^{\hat{L}}(\epsilon) \triangleq \{\epsilon\}$$

extended elementwise to $\alpha^{\hat{L}} \in \wp(\hat{T}) \mapsto \wp(\mathscr{V}^\star)$ as $\alpha^{\hat{L}}(\Sigma) \triangleq \bigcup\{\alpha^{\hat{L}}(\sigma) \mid \sigma \in \Sigma\}$ and pointwise to $\dot{\alpha}^{\hat{L}} \in \wp(\hat{T}) \mapsto (\mathscr{N} \mapsto \wp(\mathscr{V}^\star))$ as $\dot{\alpha}^{\hat{L}}(S) \triangleq \lambda A \cdot \alpha^{\hat{L}}(S.A)$ so that we get the Galois connection $\langle \wp(\hat{T}), \subseteq \rangle \xrightleftharpoons[\dot{\alpha}^{\hat{L}}]{\dot{\gamma}^{\hat{L}}} \langle \mathscr{N} \mapsto \wp(\mathscr{V}^\star), \dot{\subseteq} \rangle$.

Terminal Sentence Abstraction $\dot{\alpha}^{\ell}$. Terminal sentence abstraction eliminates the sentences of a protolanguage which are not terminal. Let us define the eraser $\alpha^{\ell} \in \mathscr{V}^\star \mapsto \wp(\mathscr{T}^\star)$ as

$$\alpha^{\ell}(A\sigma) \triangleq \varnothing \qquad \alpha^{\ell}(a\sigma) \triangleq a\alpha^{\ell}(\sigma) \qquad \alpha^{\ell}(\epsilon) \triangleq \epsilon$$

extended to $\alpha^{\ell} \in \wp(\mathscr{V}^\star) \mapsto \wp(\mathscr{T}^\star)$ as $\alpha^{\ell}(\Sigma) \triangleq \bigcup\{\alpha^{\ell}(\sigma) \mid \sigma \in \Sigma\} = \Sigma \cap \mathscr{T}^\star$ so that we get a Galois connection $\langle \wp(\mathscr{V}^\star), \subseteq \rangle \xrightleftharpoons[\alpha^{\ell}]{\gamma^{\ell}} \langle \wp(\mathscr{T}^\star), \subseteq \rangle$ which can be extended pointwise to $\dot{\alpha}^{\ell} \in (\mathscr{N} \mapsto \wp(\mathscr{V}^\star)) \mapsto (\mathscr{N} \mapsto \wp(\mathscr{T}^\star))$ as $\dot{\alpha}^{\ell}(\rho) \triangleq \lambda A \cdot \alpha^{\ell}(\rho(A))$.

13   Fixpoint Bottom-Up Abstract Semantics

All bottom-up semantics $S^{\sharp}[\![\mathcal{G}]\!] \in \hat{D}^{\sharp}$ of context-free grammars $\mathcal{G}$ are instances of the following abstract interpreter (which generalizes the bottom-up grammar flow analysis of [8, Def. 8.2.18]).

$$S^{\natural}[\![\mathcal{G}]\!] = \mathbf{lfp}^{\sqsubseteq} \, \vec{\hat{F}}^{\natural}[\![\mathcal{G}]\!] \tag{13}$$

where $\langle \hat{D}^{\natural}, \sqsubseteq, \bot, \sqcup \rangle$ is a cpo/complete lattice and the transformer $\vec{\hat{F}}^{\natural}[\![\mathcal{G}]\!] \in \hat{D}^{\natural} \mapsto \hat{D}^{\natural}$ is

$$\vec{\hat{F}}^{\natural}[\![\mathcal{G}]\!] \triangleq \lambda \rho \cdot \bigsqcup_{A \to \sigma \in \mathscr{R}} A^{\natural}(\vec{\hat{F}}^{\natural}[A \to {\boldsymbol{.}}\sigma]\rho) \tag{14}$$

$$\vec{\hat{F}}^{\natural}[A \to \sigma{\boldsymbol{.}}a\sigma'] \triangleq \lambda \rho \cdot [A \to \sigma{\boldsymbol{.}}a\sigma']^{\natural} \,{}_{\circ}^{\natural}\, \vec{\hat{F}}^{\natural}[A \to \sigma a{\boldsymbol{.}}\sigma']\rho$$

$$\vec{\hat{F}}^{\natural}[A \to \sigma{\boldsymbol{.}}B\sigma'] \triangleq \lambda \rho \cdot [A \to \sigma{\boldsymbol{.}}B\sigma']^{\natural}(\rho, B) \,{}_{\S}^{\natural}\, \vec{\hat{F}}^{\natural}[A \to \sigma B{\boldsymbol{.}}\sigma']\rho$$

$$\vec{\hat{F}}^{\natural}[A \to \sigma{\boldsymbol{.}}] \triangleq \lambda \rho \cdot [A \to \sigma{\boldsymbol{.}}]^{\natural}$$

where the abstract rooting is $A^{\natural} \in \hat{D}^{\natural} \mapsto \hat{D}^{\natural}$, $[A \to \sigma{\boldsymbol{.}}a\sigma']^{\natural} \in \hat{D}^{\natural}$, the abstract concatenation is ${}_{\circ}^{\natural} \in (\hat{D}^{\natural} \times \hat{D}^{\natural}) \mapsto \hat{D}^{\natural}$, $[A \to \sigma{\boldsymbol{.}}B\sigma']^{\natural} \in (\hat{D}^{\natural} \times \mathscr{N}) \mapsto \hat{D}^{\natural}$, the abstract junction is ${}_{\S}^{\natural} \in (\hat{D}^{\natural} \times \hat{D}^{\natural}) \mapsto \hat{D}^{\natural}$, and $[A \to \sigma{\boldsymbol{.}}]^{\natural} \in \hat{D}^{\natural}$.

The existence of the least fixpoint is guaranteed by the following

Hypothesis 20. *For all* $[A \to \sigma{\boldsymbol{.}}\sigma'] \in \mathscr{R}^{\boldsymbol{.}}$, $\vec{F}^{\natural}[A \to \sigma{\boldsymbol{.}}\sigma'] \in (\mathscr{N} \mapsto L) \longmapsto L$ *is upper continuous for the ordering* $\sqsubseteq$ *on* $\hat{D}^{\natural 3}$. $\qquad\square$

Hyp. 20 is guaranteed by the following local continuity conditions

Lemma 21. *If* $A^{\natural}$ *is continuous,* ${}_{\circ}^{\natural}$ *is continuous in its second argument,* $[A \to \sigma{\boldsymbol{.}}B\sigma']^{\natural}$ *is continuous in its first argument,* ${}_{\S}^{\natural}$ *is continuous then* **Hyp. 20** *holds.* $\qquad\square$

The hierarchy of semantics discussed in **Sect. 12** is obtained by the instances of the bottom-up abstract semantics (13) given in **Fig. 2**. Classical semantics and flow analyzes also have the same form given in **Fig. 3** (where $\mathbb{B} \triangleq \{\mathrm{ff}, \mathrm{tt}\}$).

We can define the soundness of an abstract interpreter $S^{\natural}[\![\mathcal{G}]\!]$ with respect to a concrete interpreter $S^{\natural}[\![\mathcal{G}]\!]$ as $\alpha(S^{\natural}[\![\mathcal{G}]\!]) = S^{\natural}[\![\mathcal{G}]\!]$ using a Galois connection $\langle L^{\natural}, \sqsubseteq^{\natural} \rangle \xleftrightarrow[\alpha]{\gamma} \langle L^{\natural}, \sqsubseteq^{\natural} \rangle$. This global soundness condition on the abstraction is implied by the *rule soundness condition*

$$\alpha(A^{\natural}(\vec{\hat{F}}^{\natural}[A \to {\boldsymbol{.}}\sigma]\rho)) = A^{\natural}(\vec{\hat{F}}^{\natural}[A \to {\boldsymbol{.}}\sigma]\alpha(\rho)) \tag{15}$$

which is itself implied by the *local soundness conditions* on the abstract operators (for all $x, y, \rho \in L^{\natural}$)

$$\alpha(A^{\natural}(x)) = A^{\natural}(\alpha(x)), \qquad\qquad \alpha([A \to \sigma{\boldsymbol{.}}B\sigma']^{\natural}(\rho, B)) = [A \to \sigma{\boldsymbol{.}}B\sigma']^{\natural}(\alpha(\rho), B),$$

$$\alpha([A \to \sigma{\boldsymbol{.}}a\sigma']^{\natural}) = [A \to \sigma{\boldsymbol{.}}a\sigma']^{\natural}, \qquad\qquad \alpha(x \,{}_{\S}^{\natural}\, y) = \alpha(x) \,{}_{\S}^{\natural}\, \alpha(y),$$

$$\alpha(x \,{}_{\circ}^{\natural}\, y) = \alpha(x) \,{}_{\circ}^{\natural}\, \alpha(y), \qquad\qquad \alpha([A \to \sigma{\boldsymbol{.}}]^{\natural}) = [A \to \sigma{\boldsymbol{.}}]^{\natural}.$$

---

[3] Indeed monotony is sufficient [14].

Abstract semantics $\mathsf{S}^{\natural}[\mathcal{G}]$	Maximal derivation $\mathsf{S}^{d}[\mathcal{G}]$	Derivation tree $\mathsf{S}^{s}[\mathcal{G}]$	Syntax tree $\mathsf{S}^{\hat{s}}[\mathcal{G}]$	Proto-language $\mathsf{S}^{L}[\mathcal{G}]$
$\hat{D}^{\natural}$	$\wp(\Theta)$	$\wp(\hat{D})$	$\wp(\hat{T})$	$\mathcal{N} \mapsto \wp(\mathcal{V}^{\star})$
$\sqsubseteq$	$\subseteq$	$\subseteq$	$\subseteq$	$\dot{\subseteq}$
$\bot$	$\varnothing$	$\varnothing$	$\varnothing$	$\dot{\varnothing}$
$\sqcup$	$\cup$	$\cup$	$\cup$	$\dot{\cup}$
$A^{\natural}(X)$	$\vdash \xrightarrow{(A} X \xrightarrow{A)} \dashv$	(AXA)	(AXA)	$A^{L}(X)$
$[A \to \sigma\bullet a\sigma']^{\natural}$	$(\dashv[A \to \sigma\bullet a\sigma']) \xrightarrow{a}$	$[A \to \sigma\bullet a\sigma']a$	a^{4}	$\lambda\,A' \cdot a$
$\overset{\natural}{\circ}$	5	$\cdot$	$\cdot$	$\cdot$
$[A \to \sigma\bullet B\sigma']^{\natural}(\rho, B)$	$[A \to \sigma\bullet B\sigma']^{d}(\rho, B)$	$[A \to \sigma\bullet B\sigma']\,\rho.B$	$\rho.B$	$\lambda\,A' \cdot \{B\} \cup \rho(B)$
$\overset{\natural}{\S}$	$\S$	$\cdot$	$\cdot$	$\cdot$
$[A \to \sigma\bullet]^{\natural}$	$\dashv[A \to \sigma\bullet]$	$[A \to \sigma\bullet]$	ϵ	$\lambda\,A' \cdot \epsilon$

where $A^{L}(X) \triangleq \lambda\,A' \cdot (A' = A \mathbin{?} \{A\} \cup X(A) \mathbin{\S} \varnothing)^{6}$ and $[A \to \sigma\bullet B\sigma']^{d}(\rho, B) \triangleq \langle \dashv[A \to \sigma\bullet B\sigma'], \dashv[A \to \sigma B\bullet\sigma'] \rangle \uparrow \rho.B$.

Fig. 2. Semantic instances of the abstract bottom-up grammar semantics (13)

Theorem 22. *The above local soundness conditions imply the soundness and completeness of the abstract interpreter* $\alpha(\mathsf{S}^{\natural}[\mathcal{G}]) = \mathsf{S}^{\natural}[\mathcal{G}]$. $\qquad\square$

For example, the terminal language semantics $\mathsf{S}^{\ell}[\mathcal{G}]$ defines the classical equational definition of the language generated by a grammar [15,16].

Theorem 23 (Ginsburg, Rice, Schützenberger). $\mathsf{S}^{\ell}[\mathcal{G}] = \mathit{lfp}^{\overset{\subseteq}{\,}} \overrightarrow{\hat{\mathsf{F}}}^{\ell}[\mathcal{G}]$.

Example 24. For the grammar $\mathcal{G} = \langle \{(,)\}, \{A\}, A, \{A \to (A)A, A \to \epsilon\}\rangle$, the fixpoint equation $\rho = \overrightarrow{\hat{\mathsf{F}}}^{\ell}[\mathcal{G}](\rho)$ or equivalently $\rho(A) = \overrightarrow{\hat{\mathsf{F}}}^{\ell}[\mathcal{G}](\rho)(A)$ is $\rho(A) = (\rho(A))\rho(A)\cup\epsilon$, which defining $\mathcal{X} = \rho(A)$, is $\mathcal{X} = \{(\}\mathcal{X}\{)\}\mathcal{X}\cup\{\epsilon\}$ which generates the Dyck language over parentheses $\{(,)\}$ that is, by iteration, $\{\epsilon\} \cup \{()\} \cup \{(()), ()()\} \cup \ldots$. $\qquad\square$

14   Extension of the Bottom-Up Structural Abstract Semantics to Grammar Rule States

When $\hat{D}^{\natural}$ is of the form $\mathcal{N} \mapsto L$, the abstract semantics $\mathsf{S}^{\natural}[\mathcal{G}] \in \mathcal{N} \mapsto L$ can be extended to grammar rule states $\overset{\leftrightarrow}{\mathsf{S}}^{\natural}[\mathcal{G}] \in \mathscr{R}^{\bullet} \mapsto L$ as

---

[4] Recall that a (and ϵ) is a shorthand for $\{a\}$ (and $\{\epsilon\}$).

[5] Sentence and language concatenation . is denoted by juxtaposition, extended pointwise.

[6] $(\mathsf{tt} \mathbin{?} a \mathbin{\S} b) = a$, $(\mathsf{ff} \mathbin{?} a \mathbin{\S} b) = b$, $(\mathsf{ff} \mathbin{?} a \parallel \mathsf{tt} \mathbin{?} b \mathbin{\S} c) = b$, $(\mathsf{ff} \mathbin{?} a \parallel \mathsf{ff} \mathbin{?} b \mathbin{\S} c) = c$, etc.

Abstract semantics $\mathsf{S}^\sharp[\mathcal{G}]$	Terminal language $\mathsf{S}^\ell[\mathcal{G}]$	First $\mathsf{S}^1[\mathcal{G}]$	ϵ–Productivity $\mathsf{S}^\epsilon[\mathcal{G}]$	Nonterminal productivity $\mathsf{S}^\circledast[\mathcal{G}]$
$\hat{\mathsf{D}}^\sharp$	$\mathcal{N} \mapsto \wp(\mathcal{T}^*)$	$\mathcal{N} \mapsto \wp(\mathcal{T} \cup \{\epsilon\})$	$\mathcal{N} \mapsto \mathbb{B}$	$\mathcal{N} \mapsto \mathbb{B}$
$\sqsubseteq$	$\dot{\subseteq}$	$\dot{\subseteq}$	$\dot{\Longrightarrow}$	$\dot{\Longrightarrow}$
$\bot$	$\dot{\varnothing}$	$\dot{\varnothing}$	$\lambda N \cdot \mathrm{ff}$	$\lambda N \cdot \mathrm{ff}$
$\sqcup$	$\dot{\cup}$	$\dot{\cup}$	$\dot{\vee}$	$\dot{\vee}$
$A^\sharp(X)$	$A^\ell(X)$	$A^1(X)$	$A^\epsilon(X)$	$A^\circledast(X)$
$[A \to \sigma.a\sigma']^\sharp$	$\lambda A' \cdot a$	$\lambda A' \cdot a$	$\lambda A' \cdot \mathrm{ff}$	$\lambda A' \cdot \mathrm{tt}$
$\circ^\sharp$	$\cdot$	$\dot{\oplus}^1$	$\dot{\wedge}$	$\dot{\wedge}$
$[A \to \sigma.B\sigma']^\sharp(\rho, B)$	$\lambda A' \cdot \rho(B)$	$\lambda A' \cdot \rho(B)$	$\lambda A' \cdot \rho(B)$	$\lambda A' \cdot \rho(B)$
$\S^\sharp$	$\cdot$	$\dot{\oplus}^1$	$\dot{\wedge}$	$\dot{\wedge}$
$[A \to \sigma.]^\sharp$	$\lambda A' \cdot \epsilon$	$\lambda A' \cdot \epsilon$	$\lambda A' \cdot \mathrm{tt}$	$\lambda A' \cdot \mathrm{tt}$

where $A^\ell(X) = A^1(X) \triangleq \lambda A' \cdot (A' = A \;?\; X(A) \;\S\; \varnothing)$, $A^\epsilon(X) = A^\circledast(X) \triangleq \lambda A' \cdot (A' = A \;?\; X(A) \;\S\; \mathrm{ff})$, the first abstraction $\oplus^1$ of language concatenation is defined in **Lem. 29**, and $\dot{\oplus}^1$ is its pointwise extension.

Fig. 3. Flow analysis instances of the abstract bottom-up grammar semantics (13)

$$\hat{\overline{\mathsf{S}}}^{\hat{\sharp}}[\mathcal{G}][A \to \sigma.\sigma'] \triangleq \hat{\overline{\mathsf{F}}}^{\hat{\sharp}}[A \to \sigma.\sigma'](\mathsf{S}^\sharp[\mathcal{G}]) \tag{16}$$

where $\hat{\overline{\mathsf{F}}}^{\hat{\sharp}}[\mathcal{G}] \in (\mathscr{R}^\bullet \mapsto L) \mapsto (\mathscr{R}^\bullet \mapsto L)$ is

$$\hat{\overline{\mathsf{F}}}^{\hat{\sharp}}[\mathcal{G}]\rho[A \to \sigma.a\sigma'] \triangleq [A \to \sigma.a\sigma']^\sharp \mathbin{\hat{\circ}^\sharp} \hat{\overline{\mathsf{F}}}^{\hat{\sharp}}[\mathcal{G}]\rho[A \to \sigma a.\sigma'] \tag{17}$$

$$\hat{\overline{\mathsf{F}}}^{\hat{\sharp}}[\mathcal{G}]\rho[A \to \sigma.B\sigma'] \triangleq [A \to \sigma.B\sigma']^\sharp(\bigsqcup_{C \to \varsigma \in \mathscr{R}} C^\sharp(\hat{\overline{\mathsf{F}}}^{\hat{\sharp}}[C \to .\varsigma](\rho)), B) \mathbin{\S^\sharp}$$

$$\hat{\overline{\mathsf{F}}}^{\hat{\sharp}}[\mathcal{G}]\rho[A \to \sigma B.\sigma']$$

$$\hat{\overline{\mathsf{F}}}^{\hat{\sharp}}[\mathcal{G}]\rho[A \to \sigma.] \triangleq [A \to \sigma.]^\sharp$$

with the following fixpoint characterization

Theorem 25

$$\hat{\overline{\mathsf{S}}}^{\hat{\sharp}}[\mathcal{G}] = \mathit{lfp}^{\sqsubseteq} \hat{\overline{\mathsf{F}}}^{\hat{\sharp}}[\mathcal{G}] \;. \qquad \qquad \Box$$

The relationship between the abstract semantics $\mathsf{S}^\sharp[\mathcal{G}]$ and its extension $\hat{\overline{\mathsf{S}}}^{\hat{\sharp}}[\mathcal{G}]$ to grammar rule states is given by (16) and the following

Theorem 26. *If* $\mathcal{G} = \langle \mathcal{T}, \mathcal{N}, \overline{S}, \mathscr{R} \rangle$ *is a grammar then*

$$\mathsf{S}^\sharp[\mathcal{G}] = \bigsqcup_{A \to \sigma \in \mathscr{R}} A^\sharp(\hat{\overline{\mathsf{S}}}^{\hat{\sharp}}[\mathcal{G}][A \to .\sigma]) \;. \qquad \qquad \Box$$

15   Fixpoint Top-Down Abstract Semantics

The top-down semantics in the hierarchy of **Sect. 12** can all be viewed as instances of an abstract interpreter generalizing the top-down flow analysis of [8, Def. 8.2.19]. For brevity, we consider only the *protolanguage semantics* $\mathsf{S}^{\check{L}}[\![\mathcal{G}]\!] \in \mathcal{N} \mapsto \wp(\mathcal{V}^\star)$ of a context-free grammar $\mathcal{G} = \langle \mathcal{T}, \mathcal{N}, \overline{S}, \mathcal{R} \rangle$, which is the protolanguage generated by the grammar $\mathcal{G}$ for each nonterminal. It is defined as

$$\mathsf{S}^{\check{L}}[\![\mathcal{G}]\!] \triangleq \alpha^{\check{L}}(\alpha^{\check{s}}(\alpha^{\check{\delta}}(\mathsf{S}^{\check{D}}[\![\mathcal{G}]\!]))) . \tag{18}$$

Let us define the *protolanguage derivation* $\Longmapsto_{\mathcal{G}}$ for a grammar $\mathcal{G} = \langle \mathcal{T}, \mathcal{N}, \overline{S}, \mathcal{R} \rangle$ ($\Longmapsto$ when $\mathcal{G}$ is understood)

$$\eta \Longmapsto_{\mathcal{G}} \eta' \tag{19}$$
$$\triangleq \exists n > 0, \varsigma_1, \ldots, \varsigma_{n+1}, A_1, \ldots, A_n, \sigma_1, \ldots, \sigma_n : \eta = \varsigma_1 A_1 \varsigma_2 \ldots \varsigma_n A_n \varsigma_{n+1} \wedge$$
$$\forall i \in [1, n] : A_i \to \sigma_i \in \mathcal{R} \wedge \eta' = \varsigma_1 \sigma_1 \varsigma_2 \ldots \varsigma_n \sigma_n \varsigma_{n+1} .$$

This is [8, Def. 8.2.2] for $n = 1$, the difference being that we allow several simultaneous substitutions.

The protolanguage semantics can be defined in fixpoint form as
Theorem 27

$$\mathsf{S}^{\check{L}}[\![\mathcal{G}]\!] = \mathit{lfp}^{\subseteq} \check{\mathsf{F}}^{\check{L}}[\![\mathcal{G}]\!]$$
$$\textit{where}\quad \check{\mathsf{F}}^{\check{L}}[\![\mathcal{G}]\!] \triangleq \boldsymbol{\lambda}\phi \cdot \boldsymbol{\lambda} A \cdot \{A\} \cup \mathrm{post}[\Longmapsto_{\mathcal{G}}]\phi(A) . \qquad \square$$

As a corollary of this proof and (12), it follows that

$$\boldsymbol{\lambda} A \cdot \{\alpha^{\check{L}}(\alpha^{\check{s}}(\alpha^{\check{\delta}}(\pi))) \mid (\vdash \xrightarrow{\boxed{A}} \dashv) \boxed{\scriptstyle\blacksquare}\xRightarrow{*}_{\mathcal{G}} \pi\} = \boldsymbol{\lambda} A \cdot \{\eta \mid A \Longmapsto_{\mathcal{G}} \eta\} \tag{20}$$

so that we also have the classical definition of the protolanguage generated by a grammar [8, Def. 8.2.3]

$$\mathsf{S}^{\check{L}}[\![\mathcal{G}]\!] = \boldsymbol{\lambda} A \cdot \{\eta \in \mathcal{V}^\star \mid A \xLongmapsto{*}_{\mathcal{G}} \eta\} . \tag{21}$$

Applying the terminal language abstraction, we get the classical definition of the terminal language generated by a grammar [8, Def. 8.2.3]

Theorem 28. $\mathsf{S}^{\ell}[\![\mathcal{G}]\!] \triangleq \dot{\alpha}^{\ell}(\mathsf{S}^{\hat{L}}[\![\mathcal{G}]\!]) = \boldsymbol{\lambda} A \cdot \{\sigma \in \mathcal{T}^\star \mid A \xLongmapsto{*}_{\mathcal{G}} \sigma\}.$ $\quad\square$

The protolanguage semantics $\mathsf{S}^{\check{L}}[\![\mathcal{G}]\!] \in \mathcal{N} \mapsto \wp(\mathcal{V}^\star)$ can be extended to grammar rule states $\hat{\overline{\mathsf{S}}}^{\check{L}}[\![\mathcal{G}]\!] \in \mathcal{R}^\cdot \mapsto \wp(\mathcal{V}^\star)$ as follows

$$\hat{\overline{\mathsf{S}}}^{\check{L}}[\![\mathcal{G}]\!][A \to \sigma \cdot a\sigma'] \triangleq a\, \hat{\overline{\mathsf{S}}}^{\check{L}}[\![\mathcal{G}]\!][A \to \sigma a \cdot \sigma'] \tag{22}$$
$$\hat{\overline{\mathsf{S}}}^{\check{L}}[\![\mathcal{G}]\!][A \to \sigma \cdot B\sigma'] \triangleq \mathsf{S}^{\check{L}}[\![\mathcal{G}]\!](B)\, \hat{\overline{\mathsf{S}}}^{\check{L}}[\![\mathcal{G}]\!][A \to \sigma B \cdot \sigma']$$
$$\hat{\overline{\mathsf{S}}}^{\check{L}}[\![\mathcal{G}]\!][A \to \sigma \cdot] \triangleq \epsilon$$

so that

$$\hat{\overline{\mathsf{S}}}^{\check{L}}[\![\mathcal{G}]\!][A \to \sigma \cdot \sigma'] = \{\varsigma \in \mathcal{V}^\star \mid \sigma' \xLongmapsto{*}_{\mathcal{G}} \varsigma\} . \tag{23}$$

16   Bottom-Up Grammar Analysis

Classical grammar analysis algorithms such as FIRST [8, Sect. 8.2.8], nonterminal productivity [8, Sect. 8.2.4], and ϵ-productivity ϵ-PROD [8, Sect. 8.2.3] are abstractions of the bottom-up grammar semantics and are instances of the bottom-up abstract interpreter (13).

16.1   First

The *first abstraction* $\alpha^1 \in \mathscr{T}^\star \mapsto \wp(\mathscr{T} \cup \{\epsilon\})$ of a terminal sentence is the first terminal of this sentence or ϵ for empty sentences. $\alpha^1 \triangleq \lambda \sigma \cdot \{a \in \mathscr{T} \mid \exists \sigma' \in \mathscr{T}^\star : \sigma = a\sigma'\} \cup \{\epsilon \mid \sigma = \epsilon\}$. It is extended to terminal languages $\alpha^1 \in \wp(\mathscr{T}^\star) \mapsto \wp(\mathscr{T} \cup \{\epsilon\})$ in order to collect the first terminals of the sentences of these languages $\alpha^1 \triangleq \lambda \Sigma \cdot \bigcup_{\sigma \in \Sigma} \alpha^1(\sigma)$ and finally extended pointwise $\dot{\alpha}^1 \in (\mathscr{N} \mapsto \wp(\mathscr{T}^\star)) \mapsto (\mathscr{N} \mapsto \wp(\mathscr{T} \cup \{\epsilon\}))$ on terminal languages derived for nonterminals as $\dot{\alpha}^1 \triangleq \lambda L \cdot \lambda A \cdot \alpha^1(L(A))$.

The first abstraction of language concatenation is

Lemma 29. *For all* $\Sigma, \Sigma' \in \wp(\mathscr{T}^\star)$ *and* $F, F' \in \wp(\mathscr{T})$,

$$\alpha^1(\Sigma\Sigma') = \alpha^1(\Sigma) \oplus^1 \alpha^1(\Sigma')$$

$$\textit{where} \quad F \oplus^1 F' \triangleq \big(F' \neq \varnothing \,?\, (F \setminus \{\epsilon\}) \cup \big(\epsilon \in F \,?\, F' \,\text{\textreferencemark}\, \varnothing\big) \,\text{\textreferencemark}\, \varnothing\big)$$

$$\textit{and} \quad \{a\} \oplus^1 F' \triangleq \big(F' \neq \varnothing \,?\, \{a\} \,\text{\textreferencemark}\, \varnothing\big) . \qquad \square$$

The first concatenation is monotone (hence upper-continuous since $\mathscr{T}$ is finite)

Lemma 30. *If* $F_1 \subseteq F_1'$ *and* $F_2 \subseteq F_2'$ *then* $F_1 \oplus^1 F_2 \subseteq F_1' \oplus^1 F_2'$. $\qquad \square$

The *first semantics* $\mathsf{S}^1[\![\mathcal{G}]\!] \in \mathscr{N} \mapsto \wp(\mathscr{T} \cup \{\epsilon\})$ of a grammar $\mathcal{G}$ is

$$\mathsf{S}^1[\![\mathcal{G}]\!] \triangleq \dot{\alpha}^1(\mathsf{S}^\ell[\![\mathcal{G}]\!]) . \tag{24}$$

The classical definition of the FIRST derivation of a grammar [8, Def. 8.2.33] is

Theorem 31

$$\mathsf{S}^1[\![\mathcal{G}]\!] = \lambda A \cdot \{a \in \mathscr{T} \mid \exists \sigma \in \mathscr{T}^\star : A \overset{*}{\Longmapsto}_{\mathcal{G}} a\sigma\} \cup \{\epsilon \mid A \overset{*}{\Longmapsto}_{\mathcal{G}} \epsilon\} . \qquad \square$$

For parsing, the input sentence is often assumed to be followed by the final mark $\dashv$, so it is useful to extend $\mathsf{S}^1[\![\mathcal{G}]\!]$ to $\mathsf{S}^{1\dashv}[\![\mathcal{G}]\!] \in \mathscr{N} \mapsto \wp(\mathscr{T} \cup \{\dashv\})$ as

$$\mathsf{S}^{1\dashv}[\![\mathcal{G}]\!] \triangleq \lambda A \cdot \{a \in \mathscr{T} \mid \exists \sigma \in \mathscr{T}^\star : A \overset{*}{\Longmapsto}_{\mathcal{G}} a\sigma\} \cup \{\dashv \mid A \overset{*}{\Longmapsto}_{\mathcal{G}} \epsilon\} . \tag{25}$$

The FIRST algorithm [8, **Fig. 8.11**] is indeed a fixpoint computation $\mathsf{S}^1[\![\mathcal{G}]\!] = \mathbf{lfp}^{\subseteq} \overset{\rightarrow}{\mathsf{F}}^1[\![\mathcal{G}]\!]$ where the bottom-up transformer $\overset{\rightarrow}{\mathsf{F}}^1[\![\mathcal{G}]\!]$ is (14) instantiated as given in **Sect. 13**[7].

---

[7] The classical definition [8, **Fig. 8.11**] is simpler since all grammar nonterminals are assumed to be productive.

16.2 ϵ-Productivity

The classical definition of ϵ-PROD [8, Sect. 8.2.3] provides information on which nonterminals can be empty. The corresponding abstraction is $\alpha^\epsilon \triangleq \lambda \varSigma \cdot (\!|\epsilon \in \varSigma \,?\, \mathrm{tt} \,\colon\, \mathrm{ff})\!|$ extended pointwise to $\alpha^\epsilon \triangleq \lambda L \cdot \lambda A \cdot \alpha^\epsilon(L(A))$ so that $\langle \mathcal{N} \mapsto \wp(\mathcal{T}^\star), \subseteq \rangle \xleftarrow[\alpha^\epsilon]{\dot{\gamma}^\epsilon} \langle \mathcal{N} \mapsto \mathbb{B}, \Longrightarrow \rangle$. The ϵ-productivity semantics $\mathsf{S}^\epsilon[\![\mathcal{G}]\!] \triangleq \alpha^\epsilon(\mathsf{S}^\ell[\![\mathcal{G}]\!]) = \alpha^\epsilon(\mathsf{S}^1[\![\mathcal{G}]\!])$ since $\alpha^\epsilon = \alpha^\epsilon \circ \dot{\alpha}^1$ and $\mathsf{S}^1[\![\mathcal{G}]\!] = \dot{\alpha}^1(\mathsf{S}^\ell[\![\mathcal{G}]\!])$. This is the classical definition of ϵ-productivity for a grammar [8, Sect. 8.2.9] since $\mathsf{S}^\epsilon[\![\mathcal{G}]\!] = \lambda A \cdot A \overset{\star}{\Longmapsto}_\mathcal{G} \epsilon$. The ϵ-PRODUCTIVITY iterative computation [8, **Fig. 8.14**] is indeed a fixpoint computation $\mathsf{S}^\epsilon[\![\mathcal{G}]\!] = \mathbf{lfp}^{\overrightarrow{\Longrightarrow}} \overrightarrow{\mathsf{F}}^\epsilon[\![\mathcal{G}]\!]$ where the bottom-up transformer $\overrightarrow{\mathsf{F}}^\epsilon[\![\mathcal{G}]\!]$ is (14) instantiated as given in **Sect. 13**.

16.3   Nonterminal Productivity

The classical definition of *nonterminal productivity* [8, Sect. 8.2.4] provides information on which nonterminals of the grammar can produce a non-empty terminal language. The nonterminal productivity semantics of a context-free grammar is indeed an abstraction of its first semantics $\mathsf{S}^\circledast[\![\mathcal{G}]\!] \triangleq \dot{\alpha}^\circledast(\mathsf{S}^\ell[\![\mathcal{G}]\!]) = \dot{\alpha}^\circledast(\mathsf{S}^1[\![\mathcal{G}]\!])$ where the *nonterminal productivity abstraction* is defined pointwise on terminal languages derived for nonterminals $\dot{\alpha}^\circledast \triangleq \lambda L \cdot \lambda A \cdot \alpha^\circledast(L(A))$ as true if the nonterminal can produce a non-empty terminal language and false otherwise $\alpha^\circledast \triangleq \lambda \varSigma \cdot (\!|\varSigma \neq \varnothing \,?\, \mathrm{tt} \,\colon\, \mathrm{ff})\!|$ so that $\langle \mathcal{N} \mapsto \wp(\mathcal{T}^\star), \subseteq \rangle \xleftarrow[\dot{\alpha}^\circledast]{\dot{\gamma}^\circledast} \langle \mathcal{N} \mapsto \mathbb{B}, \Longrightarrow \rangle$. The productivity iterative fixpoint computation [8, **Ex. 8.2.12**] is $\mathsf{S}^\circledast[\![\mathcal{G}]\!] = \mathbf{lfp}^{\overrightarrow{\Longrightarrow}} \overrightarrow{\mathsf{F}}^\circledast[\![\mathcal{G}]\!]$ where the bottom-up transformer $\overrightarrow{\mathsf{F}}^\circledast[\![\mathcal{G}]\!]$ is (14) instantiated as given in **Sect. 13**.

17   Top-Down Grammar Analysis

17.1   Follow

The classical definition of FOLLOW [8, Sect. 8.2.8] provides information on the possible right context of nonterminals during syntax analysis. The *follow abstraction* $\alpha^f \in \mathcal{V}^\star \mapsto (\mathcal{N} \mapsto \wp(\mathcal{T} \cup \{\dashv\}))$ is

$$\alpha^f(\eta) \triangleq \lambda A \cdot \{a \in \mathcal{T} \mid \exists \eta', \eta'' : \eta = \eta' A \eta'' \wedge \exists \eta''' \in \mathcal{T}^\star : \eta'' \overset{\star}{\Longmapsto}_\mathcal{G} a\eta'''\} \cup$$
$$\{\dashv \mid \exists \eta', \eta'' : \eta = \eta' A \eta'' \wedge \eta'' \overset{\star}{\Longmapsto}_\mathcal{G} \epsilon\}$$

where we use the classical convention that sentences derived from the grammar axiom $\overline{S}$ are assumed to be followed by the extra symbol $\dashv \notin \mathcal{V}$ ($\dashv$ is # in [8, Sect. 8.2.8]). This is extended to $\alpha^f(\varSigma) \in \wp(\mathcal{V}^\star) \mapsto (\mathcal{N} \mapsto \wp(\mathcal{T} \cup \{\dashv\}))$ as $\alpha^f(\varSigma) \triangleq \lambda A \cdot \bigcup_{\eta \in \varSigma} \alpha^f(\eta) A$ so that $\langle \wp(\mathcal{V}^\star), \subseteq \rangle \xleftarrow[\alpha^f]{\gamma^f} \langle \mathcal{N} \mapsto \wp(\mathcal{T} \cup \{\dashv\}), \subseteq \rangle$. The definition of FOLLOW [8, Def. 8.2.22] can also use that of FIRST since

Theorem 32. $\alpha^f(\Sigma) = \lambda A \cdot \bigcup_{\eta'A\eta''\in\Sigma} \hat{\vec{S}}^{\mathsf{T}}[\![\mathcal{G}]\!](\eta'')[\epsilon/\dashv]$ *where* $X[a/b] \triangleq (X \setminus \{a\}) \cup \{b \mid a \in X\}$. □

The *follow semantics* $\mathsf{S}^f[\![\mathcal{G}]\!]$ of a grammar $\mathcal{G}$ is $\mathsf{S}^f[\![\mathcal{G}]\!] \triangleq \alpha^f(\mathsf{S}^{\check{L}}[\![\mathcal{G}]\!](\overline{S}))$ so that we get [8, Def. 8.2.22]

Theorem 33. $\mathsf{S}^f[\![\mathcal{G}]\!] = \lambda A \cdot \{a \in \mathcal{T} \mid \exists \eta, \eta' : \overline{S} \overset{*}{\Longmapsto}_{\mathcal{G}} \eta A a \eta'\} \cup \{\dashv \mid \exists \eta : \overline{S} \overset{*}{\Longmapsto}_{\mathcal{G}} \eta A\}$.

By abstraction of the fixpoint characterization **Th. 27** of $\mathsf{S}^{\check{L}}[\![\mathcal{G}]\!]$, we get the classical FOLLOW algorithm as an iterative fixpoint computation [8, **Fig. 8.13**]

Theorem 34. $\mathsf{S}^f[\![\mathcal{G}]\!] \subseteq lfp^{\subseteq} \check{\mathsf{F}}^f[\![\mathcal{G}]\!]$ *where*

$$\check{\mathsf{F}}^f[\![\mathcal{G}]\!] \triangleq \lambda \phi \cdot \lambda A \cdot \{\dashv \mid A = \overline{S}\} \cup$$

$$\bigcup_{B \to \sigma A \sigma' \in \mathcal{R}} (\hat{\vec{S}}^{\mathsf{T}}[\![\mathcal{G}]\!](\sigma') \setminus \{\epsilon\}) \cup \left(\epsilon \in \hat{\vec{S}}^{\mathsf{T}}[\![\mathcal{G}]\!](\sigma') \; ? \; \phi(B) \; \vdots \; \varnothing \right) .$$

and $\subseteq$ *denotes* $=$ *if all nonterminals in* $\mathcal{G}$ *are productive (as defined in* **Sect. 16.3***) else* $\subseteq$ *denotes* $\subseteq$. □

17.2 Nonterminal Accessibility

The classical definition of *accessible nonterminals* [8, Def. 8.2.4] provides information on which nonterminals of the grammar are used in the definition of the language generated for the grammar axiom. The *accessibility abstraction* is $\alpha^a \triangleq \lambda \Sigma \cdot \lambda A \cdot \left(\exists \sigma, \sigma' \in \mathcal{V}^\star : \sigma A \sigma' \in \Sigma \; ? \; \mathsf{tt} \; \vdots \; \mathsf{ff} \right)$ so that $\langle \mathcal{N} \mapsto \wp(\mathcal{V}^\star), \subseteq \rangle \xleftrightarrow[\alpha^a]{\gamma^a} \langle \mathcal{N} \mapsto \mathbb{B}, \Longrightarrow \rangle$. The *nonterminal accessibility semantics* is $\mathsf{S}^a[\![\mathcal{G}]\!] \triangleq \alpha^a(\mathsf{S}^{\check{L}}[\![\mathcal{G}]\!](\overline{S}))$. This is the classical definition [8, Def. 8.2.4] since

Theorem 35. $\mathsf{S}^a[\![\mathcal{G}]\!] = \lambda A \cdot \exists \sigma, \sigma' \in \mathcal{V}^\star : \overline{S} \overset{*}{\Longmapsto}_{\mathcal{G}} \sigma A \sigma'$. □

The accessibility semantics $\mathsf{S}^a[\![\mathcal{G}]\!]$ has the following fixpoint characterization

Theorem 36. $\mathsf{S}^a[\![\mathcal{G}]\!] = lfp^{\subseteq} \check{\mathsf{F}}^a[\![\mathcal{G}]\!]$ *where* $\check{\mathsf{F}}^a[\![\mathcal{G}]\!]\phi A \triangleq (A = \overline{S}) \vee \bigvee_{B \to \sigma A \sigma' \in \mathcal{R}} \phi(B)$. □

The accessibility semantics is an abstraction of the follow semantics since, if all nonterminals are productive (as defined in **Sect. 16.3**), a nonterminal is accessible if and only if it has a non-empty follow set.

Theorem 37. *(All nonterminals are productive)* $\implies \left(\mathsf{S}^a[\![\mathcal{G}]\!] = \alpha^{\circledast}(\mathsf{S}^f[\![\mathcal{G}]\!]) \right)$. □

18 Grammar Problem

Knuth's *grammar problem* [1], a generalization of the single-source shortest-path problem, is to compute the minimum-cost derivation of a terminal string from each non-terminal of a given *superior grammar* that is a context-free grammar, with rules of the form $A \rightarrow g(A_1, \ldots, A_n), n \geqslant 0$ (where 'g', '(', ',', and ')' are terminals), equipped with a cost function val such that the cost of a derivation is $\text{val}(A \rightarrow g(A_1, \ldots, A_n)) = \text{val}(g)(\text{val}(A_1), \ldots, \text{val}(A_n))$ and $\text{val}(g) \in \mathbb{R}_+^n \mapsto \mathbb{R}_+$, $\mathbb{R}_+ \triangleq \{x \in \mathbb{R} \mid x \geqslant 0\} \cup \{\infty\}$, is a so-called *superior* function [1], a condition weakened in [2] where Knuth's algorithm is also given an incremental version.

Knuth's grammar problem [1] can be generalized to any bottom-up abstract grammar semantics $\mathsf{S}^{\sharp}[\mathcal{G}]$ by considering $\alpha(\mathsf{S}^{\sharp}[\mathcal{G}])$ where $\langle \hat{\mathsf{D}}^{\sharp}, \sqsubseteq \rangle \xrightarrow[\alpha]{\gamma} \langle \mathbb{R}_+, \geqslant \rangle$ is a Galois connection and $\langle \mathbb{R}_+, \geqslant, \infty, 0, \min, \max \rangle$ is a complete lattice.

Knuth considers the particular case when $\mathsf{S}^{\sharp}[\mathcal{G}] = \mathsf{S}^{\ell}[\mathcal{G}]$ and $\langle \hat{\mathsf{D}}^{\sharp}, \sqsubseteq \rangle = \langle \wp(S), \subseteq \rangle$ where S is a set (indeed $S = \wp(\mathcal{T}^\star)$ in [1,2]) with $\alpha(X) \triangleq \min\{\text{val}(x) \mid x \in X\}$ and $\gamma(m) \triangleq \{x \in S \mid \text{val}(x) \geqslant m\}$. Since α is antitone, the corresponding abstract semantics is taken in terms of greatest fixpoints for $\leqslant$ [2]. Knuth's monotony hypothesis [1,2] ensures the existence of the greatest fixpoint. The rule soundness condition (15) then amounts to Knuth's hypothesis that for every nonterminal A, every string in $\mathsf{S}^{\ell}[\mathcal{G}]A$ is a composition of superior functions $\alpha(g(x_1, \ldots, x_n)) = \text{val}(g)(\alpha(x_1), \ldots, \alpha(x_n))$.

Knuth superiority condition [1] and its variant [2] ensure that the greatest fixpoint can be computed by an elimination algorithm (generalizing Dijkstra's algorithm to solve shortest path problems [17]). However in general one must resort to an infinite fixpoint iteration as shown with the choice of $S = \wp(\mathcal{T}^\star)$, $\text{val}(x) = \frac{1}{|x|}$ so that $\text{val}(g)() = \frac{1}{3}$ and $\text{val}(g)(x_1, \ldots, x_n) = \frac{1}{\frac{1}{x_1} + \ldots + \frac{1}{x_n} + n + 2}$ which, for the grammar $A \rightarrow a()$, $A \rightarrow b(A, A)$ requires an infinite iteration and a passage to the limit 0.

Our generalization also copes with implicit abstractions of a grammar considered by [1,2] where a grammar is "recoded" into a superior grammar, which can indeed be defined by an appropriate α.

19   Bottom-Up Parsing

Given a grammar $\mathcal{G} = \langle \mathcal{T}, \mathcal{N}, \overline{S}, \mathcal{R} \rangle$ and an input $\sigma = \sigma_1 \sigma_2 \ldots \sigma_n \in \mathcal{T}^\star, n \geq 0$, *parsing* consists in proving either $\sigma \in \mathsf{S}^{\ell}[\mathcal{G}](\overline{S})$ or $\sigma \notin \mathsf{S}^{\ell}[\mathcal{G}](\overline{S})$, that is, by **Th. 28**, providing an algorithmic answer to the question $\overline{S} \overset{*}{\Longrightarrow}_{\mathcal{G}} \sigma$?

Bottom-up parsing is an abstraction of a bottom-up grammar semantics by restriction to a given input sentence. This is illustrated with the Cocke-Younger-Kasami or CYK algorithm [4, Sect. 4.2.1] attributed by [18] to John Cocke, [19,20]). It is traditionally restricted to grammars $\mathcal{G} = \langle \mathcal{T}, \mathcal{N}, \overline{S}, \mathcal{R} \rangle$ in *Chomsky normal form* with rules of the form $A \rightarrow BC$ and $A \rightarrow a$ where $A, B, C \in \mathcal{N}$ and $a \in \mathcal{T}$. We now design CYK by calculus for arbitrary grammars.

CYK is an abstract interpretation of the terminal language semantics $\mathsf{S}^{\ell}[\mathcal{G}]$ by

$$\alpha^{CYK} \triangleq \boldsymbol{\lambda}\sigma \cdot \boldsymbol{\lambda} X \cdot \{\langle i, j \rangle \in \hat{\mathsf{D}}^{CYK}(\sigma) \mid \sigma_i \ldots \sigma_{i+j-1} \in X\} \qquad (26)$$

where

$$\hat{\mathsf{D}}^{CYK} \triangleq \boldsymbol{\lambda}\sigma \cdot \{\langle i, j\rangle \mid i \in [1, |\sigma|+1] \wedge j \in [0, |\sigma|] \wedge i + j \leq |\sigma| + 1\}$$

so that $\langle i, j\rangle$ denotes the subsentence of length j from position i in σ (in particular $\langle|\sigma|+1, 0\rangle$ denotes the empty sentence ϵ after $\sigma = \sigma\epsilon$). Given $\sigma \in \mathscr{T}^\star$, we have

$$\langle\wp(\mathscr{T}^\star), \subseteq\rangle \xrightleftharpoons[\alpha^{CYK}(\sigma)]{\gamma^{CYK}(\sigma)} \langle\wp(\hat{\mathsf{D}}^{CYK}(\sigma)), \subseteq\rangle .$$

The pointwise extension to $\mathscr{N}$ is

$$\alpha^{CYK} \triangleq \boldsymbol{\lambda}\sigma \cdot \boldsymbol{\lambda}X \cdot \boldsymbol{\lambda}A \cdot \alpha^{CYK}(X(A)) \tag{27}$$

so that

$$\langle\mathscr{N} \mapsto \wp(\mathscr{T}^\star), \dot{\subseteq}\rangle \xrightleftharpoons[\alpha^{CYK}(\sigma)]{\gamma^{CYK}(\sigma)} \langle\mathscr{N} \mapsto \wp(\hat{\mathsf{D}}^{CYK}(\sigma)), \dot{\subseteq}\rangle .$$

The correctness of this parsing approach is proved by the following

Theorem 38. $\sigma \in \mathsf{S}^\ell[\![\mathcal{G}]\!](\overline{S}) \Longleftrightarrow \langle 1, |\sigma|\rangle \in \alpha^{CYK}(\sigma)(\mathsf{S}^\ell[\![\mathcal{G}]\!])(\overline{S})$.   □

The CYK algorithm is derived by abstracting the fixpoint definition **Th. 23** of $\mathsf{S}^\ell[\![\mathcal{G}]\!] = \mathbf{lfp}^{\subseteq} \vec{\hat{\mathsf{F}}}^\ell[\![\mathcal{G}]\!]$ by α^{CYK}.

Theorem 39

$$\alpha^{CYK}(\sigma)(\mathsf{S}^\ell[\![\mathcal{G}]\!])(\overline{S}) = \mathbf{lfp}^{\subseteq} \vec{\hat{\mathsf{F}}}^{CYK}[\![\mathcal{G}]\!](\sigma)$$

where

$$\vec{\hat{\mathsf{F}}}^{CYK}[\![\mathcal{G}]\!] \in \wp(\hat{\mathsf{D}}^{CYK}) \mapsto \wp(\hat{\mathsf{D}}^{CYK})$$

$$\vec{\hat{\mathsf{F}}}^{CYK}[\![\mathcal{G}]\!] \triangleq \boldsymbol{\lambda}\rho \cdot \boldsymbol{\lambda}A \cdot \bigcup_{A \to \sigma \in \mathscr{R}} \vec{\hat{\mathsf{F}}}^{CYK}[A \to .\sigma]\rho$$

$$\vec{\hat{\mathsf{F}}}^{CYK}[A \to \sigma.a\sigma'] \triangleq \boldsymbol{\lambda}\rho \cdot \{\langle i, j\rangle \in \hat{\mathsf{D}}^{CYK}(\sigma) \mid \sigma_i = a \wedge$$
$$\langle i+1, j-1\rangle \in \vec{\hat{\mathsf{F}}}^{CYK}[A \to \sigma a.\sigma']\rho\}$$

$$\vec{\hat{\mathsf{F}}}^{CYK}[A \to \sigma.B\sigma'] \triangleq \boldsymbol{\lambda}\rho \cdot \{\langle i, j\rangle \in \hat{\mathsf{D}}^{CYK}(\sigma) \mid \exists k : 0 \leqslant k \leqslant j : \langle i, k\rangle \in \rho(B)$$
$$\wedge \langle i+k, j-k\rangle \in \vec{\hat{\mathsf{F}}}^{CYK}[A \to \sigma B.\sigma']\rho\}$$

$$\vec{\hat{\mathsf{F}}}^{CYK}[A \to \sigma.] \triangleq \boldsymbol{\lambda}\rho \cdot \{\langle i, 0\rangle \mid 1 \leqslant i \leqslant |\sigma|\}$$ □

Because the abstract domain $\langle\mathscr{N} \mapsto \wp(\hat{\mathsf{D}}^{CYK}(\sigma)), \dot{\subseteq}\rangle$ is finite, the iterative computation of $\mathbf{lfp}^{\subseteq} \mathsf{F}^{CYK}[\![\mathcal{G}]\!](\sigma)$ terminates whence by **Th. 39** and **Th. 38** so does the CYK parsing algorithm. The CYK dynamic programming algorithm organizes the computation of the pairs $\langle i, j\rangle \in \hat{\mathsf{D}}^{CYK}(\sigma)$ in order to avoid repetition of work already done.

20   Top-Down Parsing

20.1   Nonrecursive Predictive Parser

A nonrecursive predictive parser is formally derived from the prefix derivation semantics $\mathsf{S}^{\vec{\partial}}\llbracket\mathcal{G}\rrbracket$ of **Sect. 5** by applying the abstraction

$$\alpha^{LL} \triangleq \boldsymbol{\lambda}\,\overline{S}\cdot\boldsymbol{\lambda}\,\sigma\cdot\boldsymbol{\lambda}\,X\cdot\{\langle i,\,\varpi\rangle \mid \exists\theta = \varpi_0 \xrightarrow{\ell_0} \varpi_1\ldots\varpi_{m-1} \xrightarrow{\ell_{m-1}} \varpi_m \in X.\overline{S}:$$
$$i\in[0,|\sigma|]\wedge\alpha^\tau(\theta)=\sigma_1\ldots\sigma_i\wedge\varpi=\varpi_m\}$$

where the *terminal abstraction* $\alpha^\tau\in\Theta\mapsto\mathcal{T}^*$ collects terminal labels of derivations, as follows

$$\alpha^\tau(\theta_1 \xrightarrow{(\!A} \theta_2) \triangleq \alpha^\tau(\theta_1)\alpha^\tau(\theta_2) \qquad\qquad \alpha^\tau(\varpi) \triangleq \epsilon,\quad \varpi\in\mathcal{S}$$

$$\alpha^\tau(\theta_1 \xrightarrow{A)\!\!\!|} \theta_2) \triangleq \alpha^\tau(\theta_1)\alpha^\tau(\theta_2) \qquad\qquad \alpha^\tau(\vdash) \triangleq \epsilon$$

$$\alpha^\tau(\theta_1 \xrightarrow{a} \theta_2) \triangleq \alpha^\tau(\theta_1)a\alpha^\tau(\theta_2),\quad a\in\mathcal{T} \qquad \alpha^\tau(\dashv) \triangleq \epsilon\,.$$

Let us write $\wp_1(S) \triangleq \{\{x\} \mid x\in S\}$ for the set of singletons of a set S and let $\alpha^\bullet\in\wp_1(S)\mapsto S$ be $\alpha^\bullet(\{x\})\triangleq x$. We have

Lemma 40. $\forall\theta\in\Theta_{()} : \alpha^\tau(\theta) = \alpha^\bullet\circ\alpha^\ell\circ\alpha^{\hat{L}}\circ\alpha^{\hat{s}}\circ\alpha^{\hat{\delta}}(\theta).$

The interpretation of the pair $\langle i,\,\varpi_i\rangle$ is that in the left-to-right scanning of the input sentence σ up to position i, the prefix $\sigma_1\ldots\sigma_i$ (ϵ when $i=0$) has been recognized by a prefix derivation from the start symbol $\overline{S}$. The stack ϖ_i allows for the recognition of the rest of the sentence, if possible. Fixing the start symbol $\overline{S}$ and the input sentence σ, we have a Galois connection

$$\langle\wp(\Theta),\,\subseteq\rangle \xrightleftharpoons[\alpha^{LL}(\overline{S})(\sigma)]{\gamma^{LL}(\overline{S})(\sigma)} \langle\wp([0,|\sigma|]\times\mathcal{S}),\,\subseteq\rangle$$

The correctness of this parsing approach is proved by the following

Theorem 41. $\sigma\in\mathsf{S}^\ell\llbracket\mathcal{G}\rrbracket(\overline{S}) \Longleftrightarrow \langle|\sigma|,\,\dashv\rangle\in\alpha^{LL}(\overline{S})(\sigma)(\mathsf{S}^{\vec{\partial}}\llbracket\mathcal{G}\rrbracket).$ $\square$

To get a correct parsing algorithm, it remains

- to express $\alpha^{LL}(\overline{S})(\sigma)(\mathsf{S}^{\vec{\partial}}\llbracket\mathcal{G}\rrbracket)$ in fixpoint form by abstraction of the fixpoint definition **Th. 6** of $\mathsf{S}^{\vec{\partial}}\llbracket\mathcal{G}\rrbracket$ (as shown in **Th. 42**), and
- to prove the termination of the fixpoint iteration (as shown in **Th. 44** for non left-recursive grammars).

Theorem 42. $\alpha^{LL}(\overline{S})(\sigma)(\mathsf{S}^{\vec{\partial}}\llbracket\mathcal{G}\rrbracket) = \boldsymbol{lfp}^\subseteq\,\mathsf{F}^{LL}\llbracket\mathcal{G}\rrbracket(\sigma)$ *where*

$$\mathsf{F}^{LL}\llbracket\mathcal{G}\rrbracket(\sigma)\in\wp([0,|\sigma|]\times\mathcal{S})\mapsto\wp([0,|\sigma|]\times\mathcal{S})$$

$$\mathsf{F}^{LL}\llbracket\mathcal{G}\rrbracket(\sigma) = \boldsymbol{\lambda}\,X\cdot\{\langle 0,\vdash\rangle\}\cup\{\langle 0,\dashv[\overline{S}\rightarrow\boldsymbol{.}\eta]\rangle \mid \langle 0,\vdash\rangle\in X\wedge\overline{S}\rightarrow\eta\in\mathcal{R}\}\cup$$
$$\{\langle i+1,\,\varpi[A\rightarrow\eta a\boldsymbol{.}\eta']\rangle \mid \langle i,\,\varpi[A\rightarrow\eta\boldsymbol{.}a\eta']\rangle\in X\wedge a=\sigma_{i+1}\}\cup$$
$$\{\langle i,\,\varpi[A\rightarrow\eta B\boldsymbol{.}\eta'][B\rightarrow\boldsymbol{.}\varsigma]\rangle \mid \langle i,\,\varpi[A\rightarrow\eta\boldsymbol{.}B\eta']\rangle\in X\wedge B\rightarrow\varsigma\in\mathcal{R}\}$$
$$\cup\,\{\langle i,\,\varpi\rangle \mid \langle i,\,\varpi[A\rightarrow\eta\boldsymbol{.}]\rangle\in X\}\,.$$ $\square$

$\mathbf{lfp}^{\subseteq} \, \mathsf{F}^{LL}[\![\mathcal{G}]\!](\sigma)$ is exactly the set of reachable states of the transition system $\langle [0, |\sigma|] \times \mathcal{S}, \xrightarrow{\text{LL}} \rangle$ where

$$\langle 0, \vdash \rangle \xrightarrow{\text{LL}} \langle 0, \dashv [\overline{S} \to \mathbf{.}\eta] \rangle \qquad\qquad \overline{S} \to \eta \in \mathcal{R} \qquad (28)$$

$$\langle i, \varpi[A \to \eta \mathbf{.}\sigma_{i+1}\eta'] \rangle \xrightarrow{\text{LL}} \langle i+1, \varpi[A \to \eta\sigma_{i+1}\mathbf{.}\eta'] \rangle \qquad (29)$$

$$\langle i, \varpi[A \to \eta \mathbf{.}B\eta'] \rangle \xrightarrow{\text{LL}} \langle i, \varpi[A \to \eta B\mathbf{.}\eta'][B \to \mathbf{.}\varsigma] \rangle \quad B \to \varsigma \in \mathcal{R} \qquad (30)$$

$$\langle i, \varpi[A \to \eta \mathbf{.}] \rangle \xrightarrow{\text{LL}} \langle i, \varpi \rangle \qquad (31)$$

with initial state $\langle 0, \vdash \rangle$. By **Th. 41**, parsing is therefore reduced to proving that the final state $\langle |\sigma|, \dashv \rangle$ is reachable (which can be done by computing the iterates of $\mathsf{F}^{LL}[\![\mathcal{G}]\!](\sigma)$ or equivalently by exploring the descendants of the transition relation $\xrightarrow{\text{LL}}$ with backtracking when reaching a dead-end [4, Alg. 4.1, Sect. 4.1.3]).

Example 43. Consider the grammar $\mathcal{G} = \langle \{a, b\}, \{A\}, A, \{A \to A, A \to a\} \rangle$. For the input sentence $\sigma = a$ we have

$$\langle 0, \vdash \rangle \qquad\qquad\qquad\qquad \langle \text{initial state} \rangle$$
$$\xrightarrow{\text{LL}} \quad \langle 0, \dashv [A \to \mathbf{.}a] \rangle \qquad\qquad\qquad \langle \text{by (28) with rule } A \to a \rangle$$
$$\xrightarrow{\text{LL}} \quad \langle 1, \dashv [A \to a\mathbf{.}] \rangle \qquad\qquad\qquad \langle \text{by (29) since } \sigma_1 = a \rangle$$
$$\xrightarrow{\text{LL}} \quad \langle 1, \dashv \rangle \qquad\qquad\qquad\qquad \langle \text{by (31), which is a final state .} \rangle$$

On the other hand, the transitions for $\sigma = b$ either lead to dead ends or do not terminate

$$\langle 0, \vdash \rangle \qquad\qquad\qquad\qquad\qquad\qquad\qquad\qquad \langle \text{initial state} \rangle$$
$$\xrightarrow{\text{LL}} \quad \langle 0, \dashv [A \to \mathbf{.}A] \rangle \qquad \langle \text{by (28) with rule } A \to A \text{ since } A \to a \text{ would lead to a dead end because } \sigma_1 = b \neq a \rangle$$
$$\xrightarrow{\text{LL}} \quad \langle 0, \dashv [A \to \mathbf{.}A][A \to \mathbf{.}A] \rangle \qquad \langle \text{by (30) with rule } A \to A \text{ since } A \to a \text{ would lead to a dead end because } \sigma_1 = b \neq a \rangle$$
$$\xrightarrow{\text{LL}} \quad \langle 0, \dashv [A \to \mathbf{.}A][A \to \mathbf{.}A][A \to \mathbf{.}A] \rangle \qquad \langle \text{by (30) with rule } A \to A \text{ since } A \to a \text{ would lead to a dead end because } \sigma_1 = b \neq a \rangle$$
$$\xrightarrow{\text{LL}} \quad \ldots \qquad \langle \text{etc, ad infinitum, without any possibility of success or failure in a blocking state.} \rangle \qquad \square$$

Theorem 44. *The nonrecursive predictive parsing algorithm for a grammar* $\mathcal{G} = \langle \mathcal{T}, \mathcal{N}, \overline{S}, \mathcal{R} \rangle$ *terminates (i.e. the transition relation* $\xrightarrow{\text{LL}}$ *has no infinite trace for all input sentences* $\sigma \in \mathcal{T}^\star$*) if and only if the grammar* $\mathcal{G}$ *has no left recursion (that is* $\exists A \in \mathcal{N} : \exists \eta \in \mathcal{V}^\star : A \xLongrightarrow{+}_{\mathcal{G}} A\eta$*).* $\qquad \square$

20.2   Nonrecursive Predictive Parsing with Lookahead

The nondeterminism in predictive parsing can be reduced by driving the right context in derivations (as approximated using FIRST and FOLLOW). We start by elucidating the rôle of the right context in derivations.

Given a stack $\varpi = \dashv [A_1 \to \eta_1.\eta_1'] \ldots [A_p \to \eta_p.\eta_p']$, $p \geqslant 0$ where $\varpi = \dashv$ when $p = 0$, we define the *right context* $\varpi^\triangle$ of ϖ as

$$\varpi^\triangle \triangleq \eta_p' \eta_{p-1}' \ldots \eta_2' \eta_1'$$

with $\eta_p' \eta_{p-1}' \ldots \eta_2' \eta_1' = \epsilon$ when $p = 0$.

Theorem 45. *Let* $\varpi_0 \xrightarrow{\ell_0} \varpi_1 \ldots \varpi_{i-1} \xrightarrow{\ell_{i-1}} \varpi_i \xrightarrow{\ell_i} \varpi_{i+1} \ldots \varpi_{n-1} \xrightarrow{\ell_{n-1}} \varpi_n \in$
$\mathsf{S}^{\hat{d}}[\mathcal{G}]$ *be a maximal derivation of the grammar* $\mathcal{G} = \langle \mathcal{T}, \mathcal{N}, \overline{S}, \mathcal{R} \rangle$ *with* $i > 0$.
Then

$$\varpi_i{}^\triangle \overset{*}{\Longmapsto}_\mathcal{G} \alpha^\tau (\varpi_i \xrightarrow{\ell_i} \varpi_{i+1} \ldots \varpi_{n-1} \xrightarrow{\ell_{n-1}} \varpi_n) \qquad \square$$

We call $\alpha^\tau (\varpi_i \xrightarrow{\ell_i} \varpi_{i+1} \ldots \varpi_{n-1} \xrightarrow{\ell_{n-1}} \varpi_n)$ the *terminal right context* of ϖ_i.

In order to approximate the right contexts in derivations by their first symbol, we define

$$\hat{\overline{\mathsf{S}}}^{\mathsf{T}}[\mathcal{G}][A \to \eta.\eta'] \tag{32}$$
$$\triangleq \hat{\overline{\mathsf{S}}}^{\mathsf{T}}[\mathcal{G}](\eta') \oplus^1 \mathsf{S}^f[\mathcal{G}](A)$$
$$= \left(\mathsf{S}^f[\mathcal{G}](A) \neq \varnothing \mathbin{?} (\hat{\overline{\mathsf{S}}}^{\mathsf{T}}[\mathcal{G}](\eta') \setminus \{\epsilon\}) \cup \left(\epsilon \in \hat{\overline{\mathsf{S}}}^{\mathsf{T}}[\mathcal{G}](\eta') \mathbin{?} \mathsf{S}^f[\mathcal{G}](A) \mathbin{\S} \varnothing \right) \mathbin{\S} \varnothing \right)$$
$$= \left(\mathsf{S}^f[\mathcal{G}](A) \neq \varnothing \mathbin{?} (\hat{\overline{\mathsf{S}}}^{\mathsf{T}}[\mathcal{G}](\eta') \setminus \{\epsilon\}) \cup \left(\hat{\overline{\mathsf{S}}}^\epsilon[\mathcal{G}](\eta') \mathbin{?} \mathsf{S}^f[\mathcal{G}](A) \mathbin{\S} \varnothing \right) \mathbin{\S} \varnothing \right).$$

Corollary 46. *Let* $\varpi_0 \xrightarrow{\ell_0} \varpi_1 \ldots \varpi_{i-1} \xrightarrow{\ell_{i-1}} \varpi_i \xrightarrow{\ell_i} \varpi_{i+1} \ldots \varpi_{n-1} \xrightarrow{\ell_{n-1}} \varpi_n \in$
$\mathsf{S}^{\hat{d}}[\mathcal{G}].\overline{S}$, $i > 0$ *be a maximal derivation of the grammar* $\mathcal{G} = \langle \mathcal{T}, \mathcal{N}, \overline{S}, \mathcal{R} \rangle$
from the grammar start symbol $\overline{S}$. *Then*

$$\alpha^\tau (\varpi_i \xrightarrow{\ell_i} \varpi_{i+1} \ldots \varpi_{n-1} \xrightarrow{\ell_{n-1}} \varpi_n) \dashv = a\sigma$$

where $\varpi_i = \varpi_i'[A \to \eta.\eta']$, $a \in \mathcal{T} \cup \{\dashv\}$, $\sigma \in (\mathcal{T} \cup \{\dashv\})^*$ *and*

$$a \in \hat{\overline{\mathsf{S}}}^{\mathsf{T}}[\mathcal{G}][A \to \eta.\eta'] . \qquad \square$$

If the input sentence σ derives from the start symbol $\overline{S}$ then the right context $\varpi^\triangle$ of the stack ϖ in $\langle i, \varpi \rangle$ should derive in the rest $\sigma_{i+1} \ldots \sigma_n$ of the input sentence. In order to introduce a lookahead, this can be approximated by the fact that, according to **Cor. 46**, the first symbol of this right context should be σ_{i+1} (which, by definition, is $\dashv$ when $i = n$ so that $\sigma_{|\sigma|+1} \triangleq \dashv$).

$$\alpha^{LL(1)} \triangleq \lambda \overline{S} \cdot \lambda \sigma \cdot \lambda X \cdot \{ \langle i, \varpi \rangle \mid \exists \theta = \varpi_0 \xrightarrow{\ell_0} \varpi_1 \ldots \varpi_{m-1} \xrightarrow{\ell_{m-1}} \varpi_m \in X.\overline{S} :$$
$$i \in [0, |\sigma|] \wedge \alpha^\tau(\theta) = \sigma_1 \ldots \sigma_i \wedge \varpi = \varpi_m \wedge \forall \varpi' \in \mathcal{S}, A \to \eta\eta' \in \mathcal{R} :$$
$$(\varpi = \varpi'[A \to \eta.\eta'] \wedge i \leqslant |\sigma|) \Longrightarrow (\sigma_{i+1} \in \hat{\overline{\mathsf{S}}}^{\mathsf{T}}[\mathcal{G}][A \to \eta.\eta']) \} .$$

The correctness of the nonrecursive predictive parser with lookahead is established by the following

Theorem 47

$$\sigma \in S^{\ell}[\mathcal{G}](\overline{S}) \Longleftrightarrow \langle |\sigma|, \dashv \rangle \in \alpha^{LL(1)}(\overline{S})(\sigma)(S^{\vec{\partial}}[\mathcal{G}]) \ . \qquad \Box$$

The nonrecursive predictive parser with lookahead is obtained by expressing the abstract semantics in fixpoint form

Theorem 48

$$\alpha^{LL(1)}(\overline{S})(\sigma)(S^{\vec{\partial}}[\mathcal{G}]) = \mathbf{lfp}^{\subseteq} \, \mathsf{F}^{LL(1)}[\mathcal{G}](\sigma)$$

where $\mathsf{F}^{LL(1)}[\mathcal{G}](\sigma) \in \wp([0,|\sigma|] \times \mathcal{S}) \mapsto \wp([0,|\sigma|] \times \mathcal{S})$ *is*

$$\mathsf{F}^{LL(1)}[\mathcal{G}](\sigma) = \boldsymbol{\lambda} X \bullet \{\langle 0, \vdash \rangle\} \cup \tag{33}$$
$$\{\langle 0, \dashv[\overline{S} \to \bullet\eta]\rangle \mid \langle 0, \vdash \rangle \in X \wedge \overline{S} \to \eta \in \mathcal{R} \wedge$$
$$\sigma_1 \in \hat{\overline{S}}^{\mathsf{T}}[\mathcal{G}][\overline{S} \to \bullet\eta]\} \cup$$
$$\{\langle i+1, \varpi[A \to \eta a \bullet \eta']\rangle \mid \langle i, \varpi[A \to \eta \bullet a\eta']\rangle \in X \wedge$$
$$a = \sigma_{i+1} \wedge \sigma_{i+2} \in \hat{\overline{S}}^{\mathsf{T}}[\mathcal{G}][A \to \eta a \bullet \eta']\} \cup$$
$$\{\langle i, \varpi[A \to \eta B \bullet \eta'][B \to \bullet\varsigma]\rangle \mid \langle i, \varpi[A \to \eta \bullet B\eta']\rangle \in X \wedge$$
$$B \to \varsigma \in \mathcal{R} \wedge \sigma_{i+1} \in \hat{\overline{S}}^{\mathsf{T}}[\mathcal{G}][B \to \bullet\varsigma]\} \cup$$
$$\{\langle i, \varpi \rangle \mid \langle i, \varpi[A \to \eta \bullet]\rangle \in X\} \ . \qquad \Box$$

Again, observe that $\mathbf{lfp}^{\subseteq} \, \mathsf{F}^{LL(1)}[\mathcal{G}](\sigma)$ is exactly the set of reachable states of the transition system $\langle [0,|\sigma|] \times \mathcal{S}, \xrightarrow{\text{LL}(1)} \rangle$ where

$$\langle 0, \vdash \rangle \xrightarrow{\text{LL}(1)} \langle 0, \dashv[\overline{S} \to \bullet\eta]\rangle \qquad\qquad \overline{S} \to \eta \in \mathcal{R} \wedge \tag{34}$$
$$\sigma_1 \in \hat{\overline{S}}^{\mathsf{T}}[\mathcal{G}][\overline{S} \to \bullet\eta]$$

$$\langle i, \varpi[A \to \eta \bullet \sigma_{i+1}\eta']\rangle \xrightarrow{\text{LL}(1)} \langle i+1, \varpi[A \to \eta\sigma_{i+1} \bullet \eta']\rangle \tag{35}$$
$$\sigma_{i+2} \in \hat{\overline{S}}^{\mathsf{T}}[\mathcal{G}][A \to \eta a \bullet \eta']$$

$$\langle i, \varpi[A \to \eta \bullet B\eta']\rangle \xrightarrow{\text{LL}(1)} \langle i, \varpi[A \to \eta B \bullet \eta'][B \to \bullet\varsigma]\rangle \ B \to \varsigma \in \mathcal{R} \wedge \tag{36}$$
$$\sigma_{i+1} \in \hat{\overline{S}}^{\mathsf{T}}[\mathcal{G}][B \to \bullet\varsigma]\}$$

$$\langle i, \varpi[A \to \eta \bullet]\rangle \xrightarrow{\text{LL}(1)} \langle i, \varpi \rangle \tag{37}$$

with initial state $\langle 0, \vdash \rangle$. This is essentially the algorithm suggested at the end of [4, Sect. 4.1.4] to speed up top-down nondeterministic parsing.

Indeed the lookahead may been done freely between the two extremes of everywhere in **Th. 47** and nowhere **Th. 41**, as follows

Corollary 49. *If* $\mathsf{F}^{LL(1)}[\mathcal{G}](\sigma) \subseteq \mathsf{F}[\mathcal{G}](\sigma) \subseteq \mathsf{F}^{LL}[\mathcal{G}](\sigma)$ *then*

$$\sigma \in S^{\ell}[\mathcal{G}](\overline{S}) \Longleftrightarrow \langle |\sigma|, \dashv \rangle \in \mathbf{lfp}^{\subseteq} \, \mathsf{F}[\mathcal{G}](\sigma) \ .$$

The iterative computation of $\mathbf{lfp}^{\subseteq} \, \mathsf{F}[\mathcal{G}](\sigma)$ *terminates for all* σ *if and only if the grammar* $\mathcal{G}$ *has no left recursion.* $\qquad \Box$

Our presentation of LL(1) parsing differs from the classical introduction in [8], mainly because, for practical efficiency and simplicity reasons, only the table-driven deterministic case is classically considered.

21   Conclusion

Many meanings assigned to grammars (such as syntax tree, protolanguage or terminal language generation) and grammar manipulation algorithms (such as grammar flow analyses or parsers) have quite similar structures. We have shown that this is because they are all abstract interpretations of a grammar small-step operational semantics to derive sentences together with their structure.

Future work should include the extension of the approach to context-free grammars such as *contextual grammars* [21] or to mildly context-sensitive grammars attempting to express the formal power needed to define the syntax of natural languages by tree rewriting such as (multicomponent) tree adjoining grammars or, more generally, *range concatenation grammars* [22].

Acknowledgements. We thank Tom Reps for drawing our attention to [1,2].

References

1. Knuth, D.: A generalization of Dijkstra's algorithm. Inf. Process. Lett. **6**(1) (Feb. 1977) 1–5
2. Ramalingam, G., Reps, T.: An incremental algorithm for a generalization of the shortest-path problem. J. Algorithms **21**(2) (Sep. 1996) 267–305
3. Bar-Hillel, J., Perles, M., Shamir, E.: On formal properties of simple phrase structure grammars. Z. Phonetik. Sprachwiss. Kommunikationforsch. **14** (1961) 143–172
4. Aho, A., Ullman, J.: Parsing. Volume 1 of The Theory of Parsing, Translation and Compiling. Prentice-Hall (1972)
5. Möncke, U., Wilhelm, R.: Iterative algorithms on grammar graphs. In Schneider, H., Gottler, H., eds.: Proc. 8th Conf. on Graphtheoretic Concepts in Computer Science (WG'82), Hanser Verlag (1982) 177–194
6. Möncke, U.: Generierung von Systemen zur Transformation attributierter Operatorbäume; Komponenten des Systems und Mechanismen der Generierung. Diplomarbeit, Universität des Saarlandes, Saarbrücken (1985)
7. Möncke, U., Wilhelm, R.: Grammar flow analysis. In Alblas, H., Melichar, B., eds.: Attribute Grammars, Applications and Systems, Intl. Summer School SAGA, Prague, CZ, 4–13 June , 1991, Proc. Volume 545 of LNCS., Springer (1991) 151–186
8. Wilhelm, R., Maurer, D.: Übersetzerbau. Theorie, Konstruktion, Generierung. Springer (1992)
9. Cousot, P., Cousot, R.: Abstract interpretation: a unified lattice model for static analysis of programs by construction or approximation of fixpoints. In: 4th POPL, Los Angeles, CA, ACM Press (1977) 238–252
10. Chomsky, N.: Three models for the description of language. IEEE Trans. Information Theory **2**(3) (1956) 113–124
11. Chomsky, N.: Syntactic Structures. Mouton, de Gruyter (1957)

12. Cousot, P.: Constructive design of a hierarchy of semantics of a transition system by abstract interpretation. Theoret. Comput. Sci. **277**(1—2) (2002) 47–103
13. Cousot, P., Cousot, R.: Systematic design of program analysis frameworks. In: 6th POPL, San Antonio, TX, ACM Press (1979) 269–282
14. Cousot, P., Cousot, R.: Constructive versions of Tarski's fixed point theorems. Pacific J. Math. **82**(1) (1979) 43–57
15. Ginsburg, S., Rice, G.: Two families of languages related to ALGOL. J. ACM **9** (1962) 350–371
16. Schützenberger, M.: On a theorem of R. Jungen. Proc. Amer. Math. Soc. **13** (1962) 885–889
17. Dijkstra, E.: A note on two problems in connexion with graphs. Numer. Math. **1** (1959) 269–271
18. Hays, D.: Introduction to Computational Linguistics. Amer. Elsevier (1967)
19. Younger, D.: Recognition and parsing of context-free languages in time n^3. Inform. and Control **10**(2) (1967) 609–617
20. Kasami, T.: An efficient recognition and syntax analysis algorithm for context-free languages. Technical report, Air Force Cambridge Research Laboratory, Bedford, MA, US (Aug. 1965)
21. Ehrenfeucht, A., Päun, G., Rozenberg, G.: Contextual grammars and formal languages. In Rozenberg, G., Salomaa, A., eds.: Handbook of Formal Languages. Volume 2. Springer (1997) 237–293
22. Boullier, P.: From contextual grammars to range concatenation grammars. ENTCS **53** (Apr. 2001) 41–52 http://www.elsevier.nl/locate/entcs/volume53.html.

Ensuring Properties of Interaction Systems

G. Gössler[1], S. Graf[2], M. Majster-Cederbaum[3,*], M. Martens[3], and J. Sifakis[2]

[1] INRIA Rhône-Alpes, Montbonnot, France
gregor.goessler@inria.fr
[2] VERIMAG, Grenoble, France
{graf,sifakis}@imag.fr
[3] University of Mannheim, Mannheim, Germany
mcb@informatik.uni-mannheim.de

Abstract. We propose results ensuring properties of a component-based system from properties of its interaction model and of its components. We consider here deadlock-freedom and local progress of subsystems. This is done in the framework of interaction systems, a model for component based modelling described in [9]. An interaction system is the superposition of two models: a behavior model and an interaction model. The behavior model describes the behavior of individual components. The interaction model describes the way the components may interact by introducing connectors that relate actions from different components. We illustrate our concepts and results with examples.

1 Introduction

Component-based design techniques are important for mastering design complexity. Nevertheless, for these techniques to be useful, it is essential that they guarantee more than syntax-based interface compatibilities. Methods based on the assume-guarantee paradigm [15] or similarly on the more recent interface automata [4] are useful for the verification of safety properties provided that they can be easily decomposed into a conjunction of component properties.

We show how one can discuss properties such as (global) deadlock-freedom and progress of a subset of components in a framework for component-based modelling by making use of compositional methods in various ways. Given that violations of safety properties can be expressed as deadlocks, these results can be also applied for general safety properties.

In previous papers [8,9,7,16], a framework for component-based modelling was proposed which clearly separates interaction from behavior. An **interaction model** describes how system components can interact. A **behavior model** is used to describe the behavior of individual components. The aim of this framework is twofold. One is to allow compositional verification. The second aim is to provide a composition framework with a flexible means for controlling the collaboration of a set of components. A general framework for defining such

---

* While working on this paper the author was a guest at and supported by the Ecole Polytechnique in Palaiseau.

T. Reps, M. Sagiv, and J. Bauer (Eds.): Wilhelm Festschrift, LNCS 4444, pp. 201–224, 2007.

glue operators was presented in [16] and its main ingredients are the interaction model presented here and priority rules, which are not considered in this paper.

Here, we generalize the initial results of [9] for proving deadlock freedom and local progress, 1) to apply to a broader class of systems and 2) to apply to subsystems. In addition, we adapt the framework to support bottom-up system development. Hence, we may start with some interaction systems that exhibit certain desirable properties. These can be combined to build more complex systems. We may now ask under which conditions the desirable properties can be ensured for the composed system.

We present and illustrate here the central notions and results concerning deadlock-freedom and progress on a simple version of the framework without variables.

2   Connectors, Interaction Models and Interaction Systems

We consider a framework where components i in a set K of components together with their port sets $\{A_i\}_{i \in K}$ are the basic building blocks. Components can interact, that is cooperate. A set C of connectors controls the cooperation. A connector is a set of ports with at most one port of each component, and an interaction is a subset of a connector. As an example, we consider a system with three components 1, 2, 3 and an interaction $\alpha = \{a, b, c\}$, where a is a port of component 1, b a port of component 2 and c a port of component 3. The interaction α describes a step of the system where a, b, and c are performed simultaneously. Each component i may constrain the order in which interactions on its ports can take place. We consider here these constraints to be given in the form of a transition system with edges labelled by elements in the port set.

Definition 1
A component system $CS = (K, \{A_i\}_{i \in K})$ consists of a set K of components and has for each component $i \in K$ a port set A_i, that is disjoint from the port set of every other component. Ports are also referred to as actions.

The union $A = \bigcup_{i \in K} A_i$ of all port sets is the port set of K. A finite nonempty subset c of A is called a connector for CS, if it contains at most one port of each component $i \in K$. A connector set is a set C of connectors for CS that covers all ports, and where no connector contains any other:

a) $\bigcup_{c \in C} c = A$
b) $c \subseteq c' \Rightarrow c = c'$ *for all $c, c' \in C$.*

If c is a connector, $I(c)$ denotes the set of all nonempty subsets of c and is called the set of interactions of c. For a set C of connectors,

$$I(C) = \bigcup_{c \in C} I(c)$$

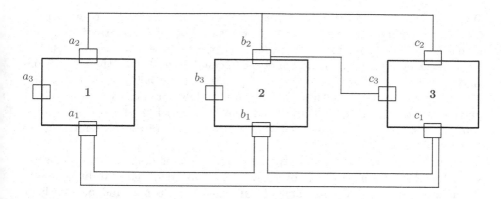

Fig. 1. Example of connectors

is the set of interactions of C. If C is a connector set, it is clear by the above that the connectors $c \in C$ are the maximal elements in $I(C)$. For component i and interaction α, we put $i(\alpha) = A_i \cap \alpha$. We say that component i participates in α, if $i(\alpha) \neq \emptyset$.

Remark 1
A connector $c = \{a\}$, $a \in A_i$, consisting of a single action, can be identified with this action. It models the situation that a is considered as internal action of component i that takes place independently of the environment.

In the following, we always assume that $K = \{1, ..., n\}$ for some $n \in \mathbb{N}$ or that K is countably infinite.

Example 1
We consider three components $1, 2, 3$ with port sets $A_1 = \{a_1, a_2, a_3\}$, $A_2 = \{b_1, b_2, b_3\}$, and $A_3 = \{c_1, c_2, c_3\}$. The connector set

$$C = \{\{a_1, b_1\}, \{b_1, c_1\}, \{a_1, c_1\}, \{a_2, b_2, c_2\}, \{a_3\}, \{b_3\}, \{b_2, c_3\}\}$$

describes a situation where any two systems may cooperate via their first port or they cooperate all via their second port. Components 1 and 2 may act individually via their third port. Finally component 2 may cooperate with the third port of component 3 via its second port. This situation can be graphically displayed by Figure 1 where a connector c with $|c| > 1$ is represented by a line connecting its ports.

Remark 2
Please note, that connectors allow a very liberal form of cooperation. One action may cooperate with m_1 other actions in one connector whereas it cooperates with m_2 actions in a different connector. In the above example this is the case for action b_2.

When we have specified for a component system (by choosing a connector set C) how the components can interact, we want to state which interactions should be considered independent of the availability of actions of other components.

In the example above, one design decision could be to declare the interactions $\{a_2\}$ and $\{b_1\}$ independent. That is, no matter if the actions occurring in a connector involving one of these actions are available or not, a_2 respectively b_1 may be performed independently of the environment, i. e. the status of other components. For this purpose, we introduce the notion of *complete* interactions and *interaction model*.

An *interaction model* for a component system CS is defined by a connector set C together with a set $Comp$ of interactions that are declared to be *complete*. If an interaction is declared *complete*, it can be performed independently of the environment. By environment we mean the other components and potential extensions of the system. In [9] it is required that all supersets of a complete interaction in $I(C)$ should also be complete[1], that is, $Comp$ has to be closed with respect to $I(C)$ in the following sense.

Definition 2
Let U, T be sets of sets, $U \subseteq T$. Then U is closed w.r.t. T, if for any $u \in U$ it contains all supersets $t \in T$ of u. The closure of U w.r.t. T, $cl(U, T)$, is the smallest set that contains U and is closed w.r.t. T.

Definition 3
Let C be a connector set for the component system CS. If $Comp \subseteq I(C)$ is closed with respect to $I(C)$, then

$$IM = (C, Comp)$$

is called an interaction model for CS. The elements of $Comp$ are called complete interactions.

Example 1 continued
By choosing

$$Comp = cl(\{\{a_2\}, \{b_1\}\}, I(C)) =$$

$$\{\{a_2\}, \{a_2, b_2\}, \{a_2, c_2\}, \{a_2, b_2, c_2\}, \{b_1\}, \{a_1, b_1\}, \{b_1, c_1\}\}$$

we model the situation described above.

As we stated before, we assume in this paper that the local behavior of each component $i \in K$ of a component system is given by a transition system T_i. When the connector set C is fixed, the *global behavior* of the system is given by allowing in each global state those transitions that correspond to interactions in $I(C)$.

---

[1] Please note, that most results carry over to a situation where we drop this condition. The results in Section 5 have to be slightly modified if we work in this more general setting.

Definition 4

Let $CS = (K, \{A_i\}_{i \in K})$ be a component system and $IM = (C, Comp)$ an interaction model for CS.

Let for each component $i \in K$ a transition system $T_i = (Q_i, A_i, \rightarrow_i)$ be given, where $\rightarrow_i \subseteq Q_i \times A_i \times Q_i$. We write $q \xrightarrow{a}_i q'$ for $(q, a, q') \in \rightarrow_i$. We suppose that $Q_i \cap Q_j = \emptyset$ for $i \neq j$.

The induced interaction system is given by

$$Sys = (CS, IM, T),$$

where the global behavior $T = (Q, I(C), \rightarrow)$ is obtained from the behaviors of individual components, given by transition systems T_i, in a straightforward manner:

- $Q = \prod_{i \in K} Q_i$, the cartesian product of the Q_i, which we consider to be order independent. We denote states by tuples $(q_1, ..., q_j, ...)$ and call them global states.
- the relation $\rightarrow \subseteq Q \times I(C) \times Q$, defined by
  $$\forall \alpha \in I(C) \, \forall q, q' \in Q : [\, q = (q_1, ..., q_j, ...) \xrightarrow{\alpha} q' = (q'_1, ..., q'_j, ...) \text{ iff}$$
  $$\forall i \in K \ (q_i \xrightarrow{i(\alpha)}_i q'_i \text{ if } i \text{ participates in } \alpha \text{ and } q'_i = q_i \text{ otherwise})].$$

A state $q_i \in Q_i$, resp. a global state $q \in Q$, is called complete, if there is some interaction $\alpha \in C \cup Comp$ and some q'_i with $q_i \xrightarrow{\alpha}_i q'_i$, resp. some q' with $q \xrightarrow{\alpha} q'$. Otherwise it is called incomplete.

Note that a global state $q = (q_1, q_2, ...)$ is complete if q_i is complete for some i. But q may be complete even if all q_i are incomplete.

Please also note that we allow edges to be labelled by elements that are neither maximal nor complete in the definition of T. For Sys itself we will only be interested in transitions labelled with $\alpha \in C \cup Comp$ as those are independent of the environment. When, however, we compose interaction systems as described in Section we will need the information about the transitions labelled with elements in $I(C)$.

Remark 3

A connector $c = \{a_1, ..., a_l\}$ specifies a degree of cooperation. For this connector to be performed in the global system, all l partners have to cooperate. As different connectors may have different size and involve different components, the degree of cooperation and the involved partners vary in the system. For instance, in one global state m_1 components may cooperate via one connector and alternatively m_2 components may cooperate via some other connector. In another state yet another type of cooperation is possible. Also, one port may cooperate in different connectors with different partners and different degrees of cooperation. Note that this is a very interesting feature of the model which allows for great flexibility and distinguishes our framework from others, for example process algebras or I/O-automata [10]. In process calculi such flexibility is either not realizable or can be achieved only in a clumsy way.

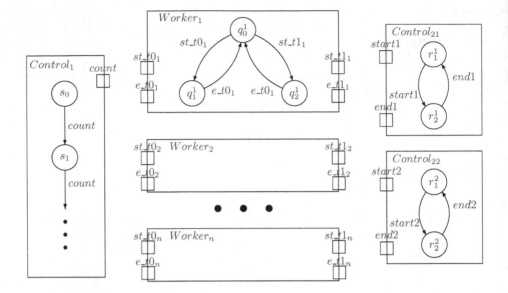

Fig. 2. Worker example: components with ports and component behavior

Example 2

Consider a set of components $Worker_i$, $1 \leq i \leq n$, that may choose between the execution of two tasks, $t0_i$ and $t1_i$. Each component $Worker_i$ can do its task $t0_i$ independently of the others, but has to cooperate with component $Control_1$ counting the number of tasks $t0$ already started. For executing the task $t1_i$, the component $Worker_i$ needs the collaboration of $Control_{21}$ or of $Control_{22}$ for the whole duration of the execution of $t1_i$. As the execution of a task may have some duration such that during its execution other interactions may take place, each task execution is represented by a corresponding $start$ and end event. The definition of the components together with the local transition systems is provided in Figure 2.

In order to achieve the collaboration of these components, we consider the interaction model $IM_1 = (C, Comp)$ with the connector set

$$C = \{conn_{1i}, conn_{2i}, conn_{3si}, conn_{3ei}, conn_{4si}, conn_{4ei} | 1 \leq i \leq n\}$$

and $Comp = \emptyset$. Here

$$conn_{1i}: \{count, st\_t0_i\}, \text{ for all } i \in \{1...n\}$$
$$conn_{2i}: \{e\_t0_i\}, \text{ for all } i \in \{1...n\}$$
$$conn_{3si}: \{start1, st\_t1_i\}, \text{ for all } i \in \{1...n\}$$
$$conn_{3ei}: \{end1, e\_t1_i\}, \text{ for all } i \in \{1...n\}$$
$$conn_{4si}: \{start2, st\_t1_i\}, \text{ for all } i \in \{1...n\}$$
$$conn_{4ei}: \{end2, e\_t1_i\}, \text{ for all } i \in \{1...n\}$$

All connectors represent binary rendezvous or local actions, which can easily be expressed in process algebra. However, the actions representing the start and end of execution of task $t1_i$ can synchronize either with $Control_{21}$ due to the connectors $conn_3$ or with $Control_{22}$ due to the connectors $conn_4$. This can not be directly expressed in CCS- or $TCSP$-style process algebra. Also, a third control unit $Control_{23}$ for improving the performance of the system, could be added without changing the behavior of the worker components. In this interaction system e.g. any global state q containing q_1^i, for some i, as well as $(s_l, q_2^1, ..., q_2^n, r_1^1, r_2^2)$ is complete for any l, whereas e.g. the states $(s_l, q_2^1, ..., q_2^n, r_1^1, r_1^2)$ are incomplete for any l. We can modify this system $Sys = (CS, IM_1, T)$ in various ways. One may modify the local behavior while maintaining the interaction model. Or one may conceive a different scheme for the interaction. For example, instead of interleaving the terminations of the tasks $t0_i$, we may also allow executing them in cooperation; this can be done by replacing the n connectors $conn_{2i}$ by a single connector $conn_2$, leading to interaction model IM_2:

$$conn_2 : \{e\_t0_1, e\_t0_2, ..., e\_t0_n\}$$

and declare each individual action to be complete. In this modelling when any number of workers is ready to terminate they may do so simultaneously.

3   Properties of Interaction Systems

We consider in the following two essential properties of interaction systems and show in the next sections how they can be established by either testing the property using a graph criterion or by deriving the property from properties of subsystems. In what follows, we consider a system

$$Sys = (CS, IM, T) \text{ with}$$

$$CS = (K, \{A_i\}_{i \in K}) \text{ and } IM = (C, Comp) \text{ and } T = (Q, I(C), \rightarrow).$$

where T is constructed from given transition systems T_i, $i \in K$, as described in Definition 4.

The first property under consideration is (global) deadlock-freedom. A system is considered to be (globally) deadlock-free if in every global state it may perform a maximal or complete interaction, in other words, if every global state is complete. This definition is justified by the fact that both for complete and maximal interactions there is no need to wait for other components to participate. In the case of maximal interactions there do not exist such components, in the case of complete interactions this holds true by the definition of an interaction model. If a maximal or complete interaction is enabled in a global state q, it may be performed right-away. A global state q where neither a maximal or complete interaction may be performed means that every component needs some other components' cooperation which do not provide the needed ports in q.

Definition 5
An interaction system Sys is called deadlock-free if for every state $q \in Q$ there is a transition $q \xrightarrow{\alpha} q'$ with $\alpha \in C \cup Comp$.

In many systems there is a designated start-state q_0 and one is only interested in the states that can be reached from q_0. To model this and similar situations we introduce a notion of P-deadlock-freedom in [6], where P is a predicate on the state space and the existence of a transition labelled by some $\alpha \in C \cup Comp$ is only requested for states satisfying P. For $P = true$ we obtain the above notion of deadlock-freedom.

Deadlock-freedom is an important property of a system. But it does not provide any information about the progress that an individual component $i \in K$ may achieve. Hence, it is interesting to consider the property of (individual) progress of component i, i.e. the property that at any point of any run of the system, there is an option to proceed in such a way that i will eventually participate in some interaction, which means that a clever scheduler can achieve progress of component i.

Definition 6
Let Sys be a deadlock-free interaction system. A run of Sys is an infinite sequence σ

$$q_0 \xrightarrow{\alpha_0} q_1 \xrightarrow{\alpha_1} q_2 \cdots$$

with $q_l \in Q$ and $\alpha_l \in C \cup Comp$. For $n \in \mathbb{N}$, σ_n denotes the prefix

$$q_0 \xrightarrow{\alpha_0} q_1 \xrightarrow{\alpha_1} q_2 \cdots \xrightarrow{\alpha_{n-1}} q_n$$

We define here a notion of progress of subsets $K' \subseteq K$ of components in two ways. In the first case, we just guarantee that the system may always proceed in such a way that some component of K' participates in some interaction. In the second case, it may proceed in such a way that every component $i \in K'$ participates in some interaction.

Definition 7
Let Sys be a deadlock-free interaction system. Let $K' \subseteq K$.

- *K' may progress in Sys, if for any run σ of Sys and for any $n \in \mathbb{N}$ there exists σ' such that $\sigma_n \sigma'$ is a run of Sys and for some $i \in K'$, i participates in some interaction α of σ'.*
- *K' may strongly progress in Sys, if for any run σ of Sys and for any $n \in \mathbb{N}$ there exists σ' such that $\sigma_n \sigma'$ is a run of Sys such that every $i \in K'$ participates in some interaction α of σ'.*

If a set K' of components *may progress* in Sys then a clever scheduler can guarantee that a *run is chosen* where infinitely often some interaction with participation of the subsystem K' is performed.

If $|K'| = 1$ then the two notions coincide and yield the special case presented in [9]. As for deadlock-freedom one may generalize the progress properties to P-progress.

In the following example, we look at some of the properties defined above. For this example, we introduce the following rule of maximal progress.

Definition 8

The maximal progress rule *restricts the transition relation for Sys to maximal transitions, i.e. to those transitions such that $q \xrightarrow{\alpha} q'$, implies that there is no β, q'' with $\alpha \subsetneq \beta$ and $q \xrightarrow{\beta} q''$.*

Example 3

We consider a system of n identical tasks that have to be scheduled, differently to the preceding example, by allowing preemption and without explicit representation of a scheduler or a controller. In our framework, we achieve this by collaboration of the n tasks with an appropriate interaction model.

We consider a set of tasks i $(i \in K = \{1, ..., n\})$ that compete for some resource in mutual exclusion. The transition system T_i of each task i is given in Figure 3 and needs not to be further explained. Let the set of ports of component i be:

$$A_i = \{activate_i, start_i, resume_i, preempt_i, finish_i, reset_i\}$$

We want to guarantee mutual exclusion with respect to the exec state, i.e. no two tasks should be in this state at the same time, in the sense that this is an inductive invariant [2]. Mutual exclusion, in this sense, can be achieved using the rule of maximal progress and the interaction model $IM = (C, Comp)$ with the connector set $C = \{conn_1^i, conn_2^{ij}, conn_3^{ij}, conn_g\}$, where

$$conn_1^i: \{activate_i\}, i \in K$$
$$conn_2^{ij}: \{preempt_i, start_j\}, i, j \in K, i \neq j$$
$$conn_3^{ij}: \{resume_i, finish_j\}, i, j \in K, i \neq j$$
$$conn_g: \{reset_1, ..., reset_n\}$$

and $Comp = cl(\{\{start_j\}, \{finish_j\} | 1 \le j \le n\}, I(C))$.

Mutual exclusion is guaranteed because whenever component j enters $exec_j$, either by $start_j$ or $resume_j$, then either there is no other task in its exec-state or the component i that is in the state $exec_i$ must leave this state. The following items explain why this is the case for each of the two transitions entering the exec-state:

– for $resume_j$, the reason is that $resume_j$ can never happen alone. It can only be executed together with the $finish_i$ action if component i is currently in the critical state $exec_i$.

---

[2] Whenever a global state satisfies this condition then any successor state should satisfy it as well.

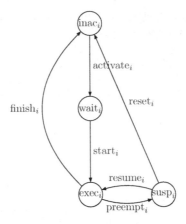

Fig. 3. Transition system of task i

- for $start_j$, which is complete, the reason is the rule of maximal progress: when component i is in the critical state $exec_i$, it can execute the $preempt_i$ action. Therefore, $start_j$ cannot be executed alone as also the pair $\{preempt_i, start_j\}$ is enabled. On the other hand, if there is no process in the critical section, component j can enter it by executing $start_j$ alone.

We now consider the properties of deadlock-freedom and progress. The interaction system $Sys = (CS, IM, T)$ as defined above, where we first ignore the rule of maximal progress, is deadlock-free as the only incomplete state in each local transitions system T_i is the state $susp_i$. But the global state in which all components are in state $susp_i$ admits the interaction $conn_g = \{reset_1, ..., reset_n\} \in C$ and hence does not cause any problems. Each component i may progress.

When a finite interaction system is deadlock-free, then it is also deadlock-free when we apply the rule of maximal progress. This is the case because, even if we disallow some transitions in a global state q, as they are not maximal there is always at least one transition with a label in $C \cup Comp$ left. Hence, our example is deadlock-free under the rule of maximal progress. Also every component may progress under the rule of maximal progress. As all components have identical behavior it suffices to consider one of them, say component 1. The only situation in which component 1 cannot proceed by itself is when it is in state $susp_1$. We have to show that we can reach a global state where it can perform a transition:

- case 1) all other components are in the state $susp$. Then $conn_g$ can happen and component 1 has proceeded.
- case 2) at least one component j is in the state $exec_j$. Then $\{resume_1, finish_j\}$ may happen.
- case 3) not all other components are in state $susp$ and none is in state $exec$. Then there must be one component j that is in state $inac_j$ or $wait_j$. If it is in state $inac_j$ then it performs the complete action $activate_j$ and reaches state $wait_j$. As there is no component in state $exec$ there is no $preempt$

action available and $start_j$ may be performed alone even under the rule of maximal progress. Now, $\{resume_1, finish_j\}$ may happen and component 1 has made progress.

In this example, we enforced deadlock-freedom by introducing the connector $conn_g$, i.e., by solving the problem on the level of the interaction model. An alternative way is to consider an invariant on the state space, namely the one expressing that not all local states are $susp$-states. One then shows that if we start in a state that satisfies this invariant then all successor states satisfy the invariant too. Hence, the problematic state is never reached from a good state.

In [6] we introduce further properties of interaction systems, in particular local deadlock-freedom, liveness, fairness, and robustness of properties with respect to failure of ports/components.

4   Testing Deadlock-Freedom and Progress

The definition of deadlock-freedom and other properties of interaction systems are conditions on the global state space and hence cannot be tested directly in an efficient way. In [13] it was shown that deciding deadlock-freedom in interaction systems is NP-hard. In [12] it was shown that deciding liveness is NP-hard. Therefore it is desirable to establish (stronger) conditions that are easier to test and entail the desired properties. In [6] we present a condition that can be tested in polynomial time and ensures liveness of a set of components. In [11] we gave a parameterized condition that can be tested in polynomial time and ensures (local) deadlock-freedom of an interaction system. Here we present a generalization of a criterion developed in [9] that ensures deadlock-freedom and give a condition that guarantees local progress of a set of components.

In what follows, we assume for simplicity that the local transition systems T_i have the property that they offer *at least one action* in every state. The general case can be reduced to this case by introducing idle actions or by adapting the definitions and results below to include this situation.

In [9], a condition for deadlock-freedom of Sys (called interaction safety there) was presented that uses a directed graph with labels in $A = \bigcup A_i$. The set of nodes is given by

$$V = K \cup H$$

where K is the set of components and H is some subset of $C \times Comp$. The edges relate nodes in K with nodes in H and vice versa. The non-existence of certain cycles in the graph ensures deadlock-freedom of the system. We propose here another graph called G_{Sys} that is simpler and smaller. One can exhibit a system with n components where the graph of [9] contains $O(n^3)$ nodes and $\Omega(n^3)$ edges independently of the structure of the transition systems. In contrast to this G_{Sys} has n nodes and - depending on the local transition systems - possibly no edges. Based on G_{Sys} we establish a criterion involving a notion of refutability that

- allows classifying a larger set of systems as deadlock-free
- is suitable to give a characterization of all deadlock-free systems.

In the following we define the labelled directed graph G_{Sys}. The nodes of this graph are the components of Sys. There are two kinds of labels for the edges. An edge (i, c, j), where $c \in C$, means that there is an incomplete state $q_i \in Q_i$ such that $i(c)$ is enabled in q_i and j participates in c. Similarly an edge $(i, (c, \alpha), j)$ means that there is an incomplete state $q_i \in Q_i$ such that $i(c)$ is enabled in q_i and j participates in α. Both edges mean that it might happen in some global state $(\ldots, q_i, \ldots)$ that i has to wait for j.

Definition 9
Let Sys be an interaction system. The dependency graph for Sys is a labelled directed graph

$$G_{Sys} = (V, E)$$

where the set of nodes is $V = K$ and the set of labels is $L = L_1 \cup L_2$, with

$$L_1 = \{c \in C \mid \not\exists \alpha \in Comp : \alpha \subseteq c\}$$

and

$$L_2 = \{(c, \alpha) \mid c \in C, \alpha \in Comp, \alpha \subseteq c \text{ and } \not\exists \beta \in Comp : \beta \subsetneq \alpha\}$$

and the set of edges is $E \subseteq V \times L \times V$ such that

a) $(i, c, j) \in E$, where $c \in L_1$, iff

$\exists q_i \in Q_i$, q_i incomplete, $\exists q_i' \in Q_i$ such that $q_i \overset{i(c)}{\rightarrow} q_i'$ and $j(c) \neq \emptyset$

b) $(i, (c, \alpha), j) \in E$, where $(c, \alpha) \in L_2$, iff

$\exists q_i \in Q_i$, q_i incomplete, $\exists q_i' \in Q_i$ such that $q_i \overset{i(c)}{\rightarrow} q_i'$ and $j(\alpha) \neq \emptyset$.

In addition to G_{Sys}, resp. subgraphs G of G_{Sys}, we will refer to snapshots of G_{Sys}, resp. G, with respect to a global state $q = (q_1, q_2, \ldots, q_i, \ldots) \in Q$

$$G_{Sys}(q) = (V, E(q))$$

where $E(q) \subseteq E$ such that

a) $(i, c, j) \in E(q)$, where $c \in L_1$, iff

q_i is incomplete and $\exists q_i' \in Q_i$ such that $q_i \overset{i(c)}{\rightarrow} q_i'$

b) $(i, (c, \alpha), j) \in E(q)$, where $(c, \alpha) \in L_2$, iff

q_i is incomplete and $\exists q_i' \in Q_i$ such that $q_i \overset{i(c)}{\rightarrow} q_i'$

Moreover, we introduce the snapshot $G_{Sys}^a(q) = (V, E^a(q))$ relative to q and $a = (a_1, \ldots, a_i, \ldots)$ with $a_i \in A_i$. $G_{Sys}^a(q)$ contains those edges (i, c, j), resp. $(i, (c, \alpha), j)$, of $G_{Sys}(q)$, where $a_i = i(c)$ and we apply the same constructions to subgraphs of G_{Sys}.

Remark 4
Note that for the construction of the graph we inspect each local transition system T_i separately and hence avoid the combinatorial complexity of global state analysis. In the finite case, i.e. $K = n$, A_i finite and T_i finite for $i = 1, \ldots, n$,

the graph G_{Sys} can be constructed in cost polynomial in $|C|$, $|Comp|$, and the sum of the sizes of the local transition systems.

In the following we will use predicates on global states that are conjunctions of predicates on local states.

Notation 1
Let for $i \in K$ $pred_i$ be a state predicate on Q_i. We say $q = (q_1, q_2, \ldots) \in Q$ satisfies $pred_i$ if q_i satisfies $pred_i$.

We use the following predicates on states. $en(a_i)$ describes all states of component i where action a_i is enabled. $cond(e)$ for edge $e = (i, c, j)$ describes all global states $q = (q_1, \ldots, q_i, \ldots)$ such that $i(c)$ is enabled in q_i and there is some action a_k in c that is not enabled in the respective local state of q. $inc(i)$ yields all incomplete states of component i.

Definition 10
For $a_i \in A_i, i \in K$: $en(a_i) = \{q_i \in Q_i \mid q_i \overset{a_i}{\rightarrow} q_i'$ for some $q_i'\}$.
For $e = (i, c, j) \in E$: $cond(e) = en(i(c)) \wedge (\exists x \in c : \neg en(x))$.
For $e = (i, (c, \alpha), j) \in E$: $cond(e) = en(i(c)) \wedge (\exists x \in \alpha : \neg en(x))$.
For $i \in K$: $inc(i) = \{q_i \in Q_i \mid q_i$ is incomplete$\}$.
If $p = e_1, \ldots, e_r$ is a path in G_{Sys}, then we put $cond(p) = \bigwedge_{i=1}^{r} cond(e_i)$.

In the next definition the notion of critical path is introduced. A critical cycle describes a situation where cyclic waiting of components could arise.

Definition 11
A path p in G_{Sys} is called critical, if $(cond(p) \wedge \bigwedge_{i \in p} inc(i)) \not\equiv false$, where $i \in p$ means that node i is the start of some edge of p. A path p in $G_{Sys}(q)$ is called critical if $(cond(p) \wedge \bigwedge_{i \in p} inc(i))$ $(q) \neq false$. A path that is not critical is called non-critical.

Certain paths can immediately be singled out as non-critical.

Lemma 1
If $c \in L_1$ occurs $|c|$-times as a label on path p in G_{Sys}, where for any two edges $e = (i, c, k)$, $e' = (j, c, l)$ we have $i \neq j$, then $cond(p) \equiv false$. (Analogously for the label (c, α)).

Definition 12
Let p be a critical cycle in a finite successor-closed subgraph G_f of G_{Sys}, $q = (q_1, q_2, \ldots)$ a global state. p is said to be refutable, if, whenever p lies in $G_f(q)$, where q_i is incomplete for every i, then there is a non-critical path $\hat{p}$ in $G_f(q)$ such that for every edge $e = (i, c, j)$, resp. $e = (i, (c, \alpha), j)$, on that path $en(i(c))(q_i)$ holds.

There are some simpler but stronger conditions that guarantee refutability.

Lemma 2

Let p be a critical cycle in a finite successor-closed subgraph G_f of G_{Sys}. p is refutable, if one of the following conditions holds:

a) *whenever p lies in $G_f^a(q)$ then there is a non-critical path $\hat{p}$ in $G_f^a(q)$ with $i \in \hat{p} \Rightarrow i \in p$.*

b) *whenever p lies in $G_f(q)$ then there is a non-critical path $\hat{p}$ in $G_f(q)$ such that for every edge $e = (i, c, j)$, resp. $e = (i, (c, \alpha), j)$, on that path $en(i(c))(q_i)$ holds if q_i is incomplete.*

As the next theorem shows, a system is deadlock-free if there is a successor-closed subgraph of G_{Sys} that does not contain any critical cycle. One can show that a system satisfies this condition iff it satisfies the condition of [9]. In addition, the theorem states that, if there is no such subgraph, we have the option to check if there is a subgraph in which the critical cycles can be *refuted*. The second part of the theorem is more of theoretical interest and gives a characterization of of deadlock-free systems in terms of snapshots of the graph.

Theorem 1

Let Sys be an interaction system as above.

1) *If there is a finite nonempty successor-closed subgraph G_f of G_{Sys} such that every critical cycle in G_f is refutable, then Sys is deadlock-free.*

2) *Sys is deadlock-free iff $\forall q \in Q$ the following holds*
   a) *either $G_{Sys}(q)$ has a node with out-degree 0*
   b) *or there is $\alpha \in L_1$ resp. $(c, \alpha) \in L_2$ such that $\alpha = \{a_{i_1}, ..., a_{i_r}\}$, $a_{i_j} \in A_{i_j}$ and $G_{Sys}(q)$ has a simple cycle with the nodes $i_1, ..., i_r$ where all labels are α, resp. (c, α) and for every such cycle p $cond(p)(q) = false$.*

Proof: See Appendix.

Remark 5

If $|c| \leq 2$ for all $c \in C$ then the condition in 1) can be tested in polynomial time. The theorem can be formulated analogously for the notion of P-deadlock-freedom.

Example 3 continued: G_{Sys} has no proper successor-closed subgraphs, so we have to check G_{Sys} for critical cycles. We discuss the case $n = 3$. In this case G_{Sys} is given in Figure 4.

Here $l_{ij} = (conn_3^{ij}, \{finish_j\})$ where $conn_3^{ij} = \{resume_i, finish_j\}$. We have omitted the label $conn_g$ for better reading, so all edges without label carry the label $conn_g$. Let us consider the cycle

$$p = (1, (\{resume_1, finish_2\}, \{finish_2\}), 2), (2, (\{resume_2, finish_1\}, \{finish_1\}), 1).$$

This cycle is critical as in $q = (susp_1, susp_2, q_3)$ with $q_3 \in \{inac_3, wait_3, exec_3, susp_3\}$

$$cond(p) = (en(resume_1) \wedge \neg en(finish_2)) \wedge (en(resume_2) \wedge \neg en(finish_1))$$

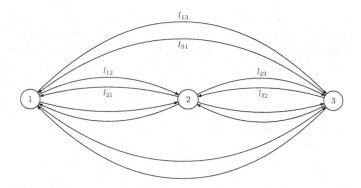

Fig. 4. The graph G_{Sys} for the scheduling example, $n = 3$

is satisfied and q_i is incomplete for $i = 1, 2$. This cycle, however, can be refuted. If the last state is complete, i.e. $\neq susp_3$, then we consider the path $\hat{p} = (3, l_{32}, 2)$. The path $\hat{p}$ is non-critical and satisfies condition b) of Lemma 2. If the last state is incomplete, i.e. $= susp_3$ then the path $\hat{p} = (1, conn_g, 2)$ is non-critical as

$$cond(\hat{p}) = en(reset_1) \wedge (\neg en(reset_2) \vee \neg en(reset_3))$$

is false in the state $(susp_1, susp_2, susp_3)$. The other cycles in the graph are treated analogously.

The graph that we use to determine deadlock-freedom of a system can also be used to determine if a subsystem $K' \subseteq K$ may progress. For this we construct the restriction $IM[K']$ of the interaction model IM to K' as given in the **Appendix** and define when K' is controllable with respect to an interaction $\alpha \in I(C[K'])$, that is a potential partner for an interaction in $I(C) \setminus Comp$, which means that we may ensure that the subsystem defined by K' will be able to provide α, when it is needed.

Definition 13
Let $Sys = ((K, \{A_i\}_{i \in K}), IM, T)$ *be an interaction system,* $K' \subseteq K$. *Let* $Sys[K'] = ((K', \{A_i\}_{i \in K'}), IM[K'], T[K'])$ *be the induced system where*

$$T[K'] = (Q[K'], I(C[K']), \to'), \quad Q[K'] = \prod_{i \in K'} Q_i$$

is given by Definition 4.
A state $q \in Q[K']$ *is called complete in* $Sys[K']$ *if* $\exists q' \; \exists \alpha \in Comp[K'] \cup$
$C[K']: q \overset{\alpha}{\to}' q'$. *For* $X \subseteq Q[K']$ *define* $pre(X) \subseteq Q[K']$ *such that* $q \in pre(X)$ *if*

a) $q \in Q[K']$ *is complete in* $Sys[K']$ *then* $\exists \alpha \in Comp[K'] \; \exists q' : q \overset{\alpha}{\to}' q' \wedge q' \in X$
b) $q \in Q[K']$ *is incomplete in* $Sys[K']$ *then*

$$\forall q' \in Q[K'] \; \forall \alpha \in (I(C[K']) \setminus Comp[K']) : (q \overset{\alpha}{\to}' q' \implies q' \in X)$$

For $Q_0 \subseteq Q[K']$, we denote by $PRE(Q_0)$ the least solution of $X = Q_0 \cup pre(X)$. $PRE(Q_0)$ is the set of states from which we can reach a state in Q_0 along a path in $T[K']$ by always performing complete interactions whenever a state is complete in $Sys[K']$.

Definition 14

Let Sys be a deadlock-free interaction system.
K is controllable with respect to $\alpha \in I(C)$, if $PRE(en(\alpha)) = Q$.
$K' \subseteq K$ is controllable with respect to IM, if $\forall \alpha' \in I(C[K'])$

$(\exists \alpha \in I(C) \setminus Comp : (\alpha \cup \alpha' \in I(C) \implies$
K' is controllable with respect to α' in the induced subsystem $Sys[K'])$.

We can now present a condition ensuring that a subsystem induced by K' may strongly progress, i.e. for every run σ we may at any point continue with a run σ' such that every component of K' will participate at some time in the run σ'.

Theorem 2

Let Sys be a deadlock-free interaction system. Let $K' \subseteq K$ finite or infinite. K' may strongly progress in Sys, if the following two conditions hold

a) $\forall i \in K' \; \exists$ a finite successor-closed subgraph $G_{f,i}$ of G_{Sys} that contains i and does not contain any critical cycle.
b) $\forall i \in K' \; \forall \alpha \in C[K'']$ $owners(\alpha)$ is controllable with respect to IM, where K'' is the set of components of $G_{f,i}$, and $owners(\alpha) = \{k \in K \mid k(\alpha) \neq \emptyset\}$.

Proof: See Appendix.

In an analogous way, we can treat the concept of may progress.

5   Composition of Systems

5.1   Composition of Interaction Models and Systems

In this section, we explain how interaction systems can be constructed bottom up from smaller interaction systems. In contrast to other bottom up techniques composition is performed in such a way that the individual components remain visible after composition. The composition operator can be also used as a basis for a different approach to tackle the problem of NP-hardness of deciding the properties introduced above. In order to establish a desirable property for a composite system we might try to establish the property for the subsystems and infer the property for the composite system. In Section 5.2 we display some first conditions under which such a procedure can be applied.

Our view of composition is given in the following. Composition is determined on the level of the *interaction models*. We start with two (or more) disjoint interaction models, say $IM_i = (C_i, Comp_i)$ for finite component systems $(K_i, \{A_j\}_{j \in K_i})$, $i = 1, 2$. We then decide how these two models should be able to interact by providing a new set S of connectors that relate an interaction of one model with an interaction of the other. We always assume that S contains only **maximal** elements with respect to set inclusion, in analogy to the definition of a connector set. In addition, we may declare a set $BComp$ of new complete elements. For those we request that they **must** be *new* interactions in $I(S)$. This condition guarantees that by putting systems together, we do not interfere with the structure of the sub-models.

The following proposition explains how to compose in general two interaction models with respect to a given set S of new connectors and a set $BComp$ of new complete elements.

Notation 2

Let X, Y be sets of port sets. Then $X \bowtie Y := \{x \cup y \mid x \in X \wedge y \in Y\}$. $maxel(X)$ denotes the set of maximal elements of X with respect to set inclusion.

Proposition 1

Let $CS_1 = (K_1, \{A_i\}_{i \in K_1})$, $CS_2 = (K_2, \{A_i\}_{i \in K_2})$ be two component systems such that K_1, K_2 are disjoint and the elements in $\{A_i\}_{i \in K_1 \cup K_2}$ are pairwise disjoint. Let $IM_i = (C_i, Comp_i)$ be interaction models for CS_i, $i = 1, 2$. Let

- $S \subseteq I(C_1) \bowtie I(C_2)$ be the set of new connectors,
- $BComp \subseteq I(S) \cap (I(C_1) \bowtie I(C_2))$ be the set of new complete elements.

We put

- $C = maxel(C_1 \cup C_2 \cup S)$,
- $Comp = cl(Comp_1 \cup Comp_2 \cup BComp, I(C))$.

Then

a) C is a connector set for $(K_1 \cup K_2, \{A_i\}_{i \in K_1 \cup K_2})$ with $S \subseteq C$ and $I(C) = I(C_1) \cup I(C_2) \cup I(S)$
b) $IM = (C, Comp)$ is an interaction model for $(K_1 \cup K_2, \{A_i\}_{i \in K_1 \cup K_2})$.

Definition 15

Under the conditions of Proposition 1, the interaction model $IM = (C, Comp)$ is said to be obtained by composition from IM_1 and IM_2 and we write

$$IM = IM_1 \bigcup_{S, BComp} IM_2.$$

When composing interaction models IM_i and IM_j for some i, j using a set S of new connectors we use the notation S_{ij} to denote S, where it is understood that $S_{ij} = S_{ji}$. Analogously, $BComp_{ij}$ is used to denote the set of new complete elements and it is understood that $BComp_{ij} = BComp_{ji}$.

The composition of interaction models defined above is obviously commutative. One can show that it is **associative**. Associativity is an important property that allows composing systems incrementally without regarding the order in which subsystems are added. In process calculi, interaction is modelled by parallel operators that enforce restriction as in some versions of CSP [5] or a general parallel operator in combination with a restriction operator as e.g. in CCS. Associativity is generally not given for process calculus type parallel constructs.

Remark 6
The composition operator defined in Definition 15 is binary. If we want to compose systems from more than two subsystems then we can exploit the associativity of the operator. For example consider systems Sys_i, where $1 \leq i \leq 3$. We want to compose these systems by introducing a connector $c = \alpha_1 \cup \alpha_2 \cup \alpha_3$ where $\alpha_i \in I(C_i)$ and another connector $c' = \beta_1 \cup \beta_3$ where $\beta_i \in I(C_i)$. To achieve this we first compose Sys_1 with Sys_3 using the connectors $\alpha_1 \cup \alpha_3$ and c'. Then we compose the resulting system with Sys_2 using the connector $(\alpha_1 \cup \alpha_3) \cup \alpha_2 = c$. Similarly we may handle the interactions that we want to declare complete.

When the composition of the interaction models is defined, the interaction systems are now composed in a straightforward manner to yield a more complex system.

Definition 16
Let $Sys_i = ((K_i, \{A_j\}_{j \in K_i}), IM_i, T_i)$, $i = 1, 2$, be interaction systems, $S_{12} \subseteq I(C_1) \bowtie I(C_2)$ a set of new connectors and $BComp_{12} \subseteq I(S_{12}) \cap (I(C_1) \bowtie I(C_2))$, then

$$Sys_1 \big\| Sys_2$$
$$\scriptstyle S_{12}, BComp_{12}$$

is the system given by

$$Sys = ((K_1 \cup K_2, \{A_j\}_{j \in K_1 \cup K_2}), IM_1 \bigcup_{S_{12}, BComp_{12}} IM_2, T) \text{ where}$$

$T = (Q_1 \times Q_2, I(C_{12}), \rightarrow_{12})$ *and* $\rightarrow_{12}$ *is the least relation satisfying*

1. if $q_1 \xrightarrow{\alpha_1}_1 q_1'$ then $(q_1, q_2) \xrightarrow{\alpha_1}_{12} (q_1', q_2)$
2. if $q_2 \xrightarrow{\alpha_2}_2 q_2'$ then $(q_1, q_2) \xrightarrow{\alpha_2}_{12} (q_1, q_2')$
3. if $q_1 \xrightarrow{\alpha_1}_1 q_1'$, $q_2 \xrightarrow{\alpha_2}_2 q_2'$, $\alpha_1 \cup \alpha_2 \in I(S_{12})$ then $(q_1, q_2) \xrightarrow{\alpha_1 \cup \alpha_2}_{12} (q_1', q_2')$.

From the associativity for composition of interaction models, it is straightforward to see that the so defined parallel operator on interaction systems is associative and Remark 6 applies analogously.

5.2   Ensuring Deadlock-Freedom and Progress by Construction

In this section we rise the question under which conditions desirable properties of subsystems can be lifted to composed systems. As an example we treat deadlock-freedom and progress of a component. In the following, we consider two interaction systems $Sys_i = (CS_i, IM_i, T_i)$, $i = 1, 2$ that are composed by introducing a new set of connectors S_{12}. We assume that all conditions that are necessary to compose systems are fulfilled, as required in Proposition 1. We first consider deadlock-freedom.

Proposition 2

Let Sys_i $i = 1, 2$ be interaction systems. If one of the following conditions is satisfied

a) Let Sys_1 be deadlock-free and $C_1 \subseteq Comp_1$ and let $S_{12} \subseteq I(C_1) \bowtie I(C_2)$ be arbitrary.

b) Sys_1 is deadlock-free and $S_{12} \subseteq (I(C_1) \setminus C_1) \bowtie I(C_2)$

c) Sys_1 is deadlock-free or Sys_2 is deadlock-free and

$$S_{12} \subseteq (Comp_1 \bowtie (I(C_2) \setminus C_2)) \cup ((I(C_1) \setminus C_1) \bowtie Comp_2)$$

then

$$Sys_1 \big\| Sys_2$$
$$\scriptstyle S_{12}, BComp_{12}$$

is deadlock-free for any $BComp_{12} \subseteq I(S_{12}) \cap (I(C_1) \bowtie I(C_2))$.

Sketch of proof for b): in this case the connectors of the deadlock-free system Sys_1 remain maximal after composition and as the complete elements of Sys_1 remain complete by definition every state in $Sys_1 \big\|_{S_{12}, BComp_{12}} Sys_2$ offers a complete or maximal interaction in $I(C)$.

These are only some examples for conditions that can be put on the level of the interaction models. Further conditions, as well as conditions imposing restrictions on the local transition systems, and conditions involving the graph criterion of Theorem 1 are being elaborated.

Example 4

We consider the following two component systems CS_1 and CS_2. The components of CS_1 are 1 and 2 those of CS_2 are 3 and 4. The port sets of 1 and 2 are given by $A_1 = \{a_1, a_2, a_3\}$ and $A_2 = \{c_1, c_2, c_3\}$. The port sets of the other two components are given by $A_3 = \{b_1, b_2, b_3\}$ and $A_4 = \{d_1, d_2\}$. We define $IM_i = (C_i, Comp_i)$ for CS_i where $C_1 := \{\{a_1, c_1\}, \{a_2, c_2\}, \{a_3\}, \{c_3\}\}$ and $Comp_1 := \{\{a_2\}, \{a_2, c_2\}, \{c_3\}\}$ respectively $C_2 := \{\{b_1\}, \{b_2, d_1\}, \{d_2\}, \{b_3\}\}$ and $Comp_2 := \{\{b_1\}\}$. The behavior of the second system Sys_2 is given by the two local transition systems of Figure 5. It is clear that Sys_2 is deadlock-free. Now let the behavior of the first system be given by any transition system that is labelled with interactions from $I(C_1)$. Composing the two systems according to $S_{12} := \{\{b_2, a_2, c_2\}, \{b_2, c_3\}\} \cup \{\{b_1, a_1\}, \{b_1, c_1\}\}$ and arbitrary $BComp_{12}$ yields a deadlock-free system according to Proposition 2 c).

We now consider the question under which conditions a component k that may progress in Sys_1 will still have this property when Sys_1 is composed with some other system. We present here two examples for conditions that are similar to those that ensure deadlock-freedom for the composite system.

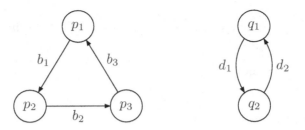

Fig. 5. Local Transition Systems

Proposition 3
Let Sys_i, $i = 1, 2$, be interaction systems and let Sys_1 be deadlock-free and let $k \in K_1$ be a component that may progress in Sys_1. If one of the following conditions is satisfied

a) $S_{12} \subseteq (I(C_1) \setminus C_1) \bowtie I(C_2)$
b) $S_{12} \subseteq Comp_1 \bowtie I(C_2)$

then k may progress in $Sys_1 \underset{S_{12}, BComp_{12}}{\big\|} Sys_2$ for any $BComp_{12} \subseteq I(S_{12}) \cap (I(C_1) \bowtie$

$I(C_2))$.

Sketch of proof for a): the reason is that the maximal and complete interactions of Sys_1 are still so in $Sys_1 \underset{S_{12}, BComp_{12}}{\big\|} Sys_2$.

6   Discussion and Related Work

The paper proposes results ensuring properties of component-based systems from properties of its interaction model and its components in the framework of interaction systems encompassing heterogeneous interaction presented in [9]. The following features of the framework are instrumental for developing our results:

- the separation of behavior and coordination, where coordination is not expressed by another behavior, but by an interaction model. We hope that the small examples illustrate the flexibility of this framework for coordinating a set of components at a high level of abstraction without interfering with the components' behaviors.
- the associativity of the framework which is the basis for well-defined incremental construction of systems.

An important motivation for introducing a clean theoretical framework for interaction and control is the hope that this will provide means for proving properties – which in general have to be shown on global models – in an incremental manner and as independently as possible from the behavior models of components. It has been shown in [13] that deciding deadlock-freedom in interaction systems is NP-hard. A similar result exists for liveness of a set of components [12]. This motivates the focus on conditions for establishing such properties. Our examples show the usefulness of these results. More such results are still needed, and can probably be obtained when some specificities of an application domain are exploited.

Related methods for showing absence of deadlocks or mutual waiting have been studied in various settings, for example in the context of data base transactions in a more restricted form [18,14] or operating systems for dynamic deadlock avoidance [17].

More recently, in [2], absence of interlocking has been studied for a framework of communicating processes where processes interact in all their interactions with the same fixed set of other processes. In [1] a condition under which a composed system is deadlock-free is given in a CSP-like setting. In [3] a condition for the deadlock-freedom of a component-system with two components is given.

Extended versions of our framework, including local variables of components and priority rules as an additional control layer, are presently being implemented. The implementation in the context of the Prometheus tool focusses on verification, in particular verification of SystemC specifications. A second implementation, called BIP, focusses on the efficient execution of systems and includes also timed specifications.

The work presented here shows some typical results that can be established in this framework. Further properties such as liveness, fairness and robustness as well as a result presenting a condition that can be tested in polynomial time and ensures liveness can be found in [6]. There is work in progress that is concerned with robustness and further exploits compositionality. Moreover first steps to incorporate probabilities have been taken in order to eventually be able to make quantitative propositions about the properties presented here. For example we want be able to prove statements like "with probability p no deadlock occurs". The notion of a component can be extended with various additional information including invariants [9], but also observability criteria and associated equivalence relations are of interest. Other possible interesting extensions concern introduction of time, as well as dynamic reconfiguration.

References

1. Robert Allen and David Garlan. A Formal Basis for Architectural Connection. *ACM Trans. Softw. Eng. Methodol.*, 6(3):213–249, 1997.
2. P.C. Attie and H. Chockler. Efficiently verifiable conditions for deadlock-freedom of large concurrent programs. In R. Cousot, editor, *proc. VMCAI'05*, volume 3385 of *LNCS*, pages 465–481, 2005.
3. Hubert Baumeister, Florian Hacklinger, Rolf Hennicker, Alexander Knapp, and Martin Wirsing. A Component Modell for Architectural Programming. In *Proceedings of FACS 2005*. ENTCS, 2005.
4. Luca de Alfaro and Thomas A. Henzinger. Interface automata. In *Proceedings of the 8th European Software Engineering Conference, Vienna*, pages 109–120, 2001.

5. N. Francez, C.A.R. Hoare, D.J. Lehmann, and W.P. de Roever. Semantics of non-determinism, concurrency and communication. *Journal of Computer Science*, 19:290–308, 1979.
6. G. Gössler, S. Graf, M. Majster-Cederbaum, M. Martens, and J. Sifakis. An Approach to Modelling and Verification of Component Based Systems. In *Proceedings of the 33rd International Conference on Current Trends in Theory and Practice of Computer, Science SOFSEM07*, volume 4362 of *LNCS*, 2007.
7. Gregor Gßler and Joseph Sifakis. Component-based construction of deadlock-free systems. In *proceedings of FSTTCS 2003, Mumbai, India*, LNCS 2914, pages 420–433, 2003.
8. Gregor Gßler and Joseph Sifakis. Priority systems. In *proceedings of FMCO'03*, LNCS 3188, 2004.
9. Gregor Gßler and Joseph Sifakis. Composition for component-based modeling. *Sci. Comput. Program.*, 55(1-3):161–183, 2005.
10. Nancy A. Lynch and Mark R. Tuttle. An introduction to input/output automata. *CWI-Quarterly*, 2(3):219–246, September 1989.
11. Mila Majster-Cederbaum, Moritz Martens, and Christoph Minnameier. A Polynomial-Time Checkable Sufficient Condition for Deadlock-Freedom of Component-Based Systems. In *Proceedings of the 33rd International Conference on Current Trends in Theory and Practice of Computer, Science SOFSEM07*, volume 4362 of *LNCS*, 2007.
12. Moritz Martens, Christoph Minnameier, and Mila Majster-Cederbaum. Deciding Liveness in Component-Based Systems is NP-hard. Technical report TR-2006-017, Universität Mannheim, 2006.
13. Christoph Minnameier. Deadlock-Detection in Component-Based Systems is NP-hard. Technical report TR-2006-015, Universität Mannheim, 2006. also submitted for publication elsewhere.
14. Christos H. Papadimitriou. *The Theory of Database Concurrency Control*. Computer Science Press, 1986.
15. A. Pnueli. In transition from global to modular temporal reasoning about programs. In *Logics and Models for Concurrent Systems*. NATO, ASI Series F, Vol. 13, Springer Verlag, 1985.
16. Joseph Sifakis. A framework for component-based construction. In *3rd IEEE International Conference on Software Engineering and Formal Methods*, volume Key note talk, Koblenz, 2005.
17. A.S. Tanenbaum. *Modern Operating Sytems*. Prentice Hall, 2001.
18. Jeffrey D. Ullman. *Data Base and Knowledge-Base Systems, vol.1*. Computer Science Press, 1988.

A   Appendix

A.1   Subsystems

In order to be able to talk about subsystems, we define a notion of restriction of an interaction model to a subset of components.

Definition 17

Let $CS = (K, \{A_i\}_{i \in K})$ be a component system, $IM = (C, Comp)$ an interaction model for CS and $K' \subseteq K$. Denote by

$$C[K'] := \{c' \subseteq A[K'] \mid \exists\, c \in C : \ c' = c \cap A[K'] \land \nexists\, \bar{c} \in C : \ c' \subsetneq \bar{c} \cap A[K']\}$$

the restriction of the connectors in C to K' where $A[K'] = \bigcup_{i \in K'} A_i$.

We put $Comp[K'] = I(C[K']) \cap Comp$.

If $C[K']$ is a connector set for $CS[K'] = (K', \{A_i\}_{i \in K'})$, then the induced interaction model for $CS[K']$ is given by: $IM[K'] := (C[K'], Comp[K'])$ which is also called the restriction of IM to K'.

Remark 7

Note that in the case of a system with infinitely many components it might occur that $C[K']$ does not satisfy the conditions for a connector set. In particular, $C[K']$ might be empty for infinite systems. For finite systems $C[K']$ is always a connector set for $CS[K'] = (K', \{A_i\}_{i \in K'})$ and $I(C[K']) = \{\alpha \cap A[K'] \mid \alpha \in I(C)\}$.

A.2   Proofs

Proof of Theorem 1

The proof of part 1) is an extension of the proof of the corresponding theorem in [9] if there is a successor-closed subgraph that does not contain any critical. In addition one has to show that refutability will do if there are critical cycles. We give here the proof of part 2):

Let Sys be deadlock-free and $q = (q_1, q_2, \ldots)$ a state in Q.

Case 1: There exists i such that q_i is complete.
Then the node i has out-degree 0 in $G_{Sys}(q)$.
Case 2: $\forall i$ q_i is incomplete.

As Sys is deadlock-free, there is some $\beta \in C \cup Comp$ $q \xrightarrow{\beta} q'$ for some q'.
Case 2.1: β is a minimal element in $C \cup Comp$.
Case 2.1.1: $\beta = \{a_{i_1}, \ldots, a_{i_r}\} \in C$, $r > 1$
Hence $\beta \in L_1$, then choose $\alpha = \beta$. Hence (i_j, α, i_k) is an edge in $G_{Sys}(q)$, $j \neq k$, $j, k = 1, \ldots, r$. I.e. we obtain edges labelled with α between any two nodes in $\{i_1, \ldots, i_r\}$. In particular there is the cycle $i_1 \xrightarrow{\alpha} i_2 \cdots \cdots \xrightarrow{\alpha} i_r \xrightarrow{\alpha} i_1$. For any such cycle p between these nodes $cond(p)(q) = false$.
Case 2.1.2: $\beta = \{a_{i_1}, \ldots, a_{i_r}\} \in Comp \setminus C$, $r > 1$
Let c be a connector with $\beta \subset c$. Put $\alpha = \beta$. Then $(c, \alpha) \in L_2$. Hence we get edges $(i_j, (c, \alpha), i_k)$ in $G_{Sys}(q)$, $j \neq k$, $j, k = 1, \ldots, r$ and for all cycles p over all these nodes labelled with (c, α) $cond(p)(q) = false$.
Case 2.2: β is not minimal in $C \cup Comp$
Then there is some minimal $\alpha \in Comp$ with $\alpha \subset \beta$. As there is some transition $q \xrightarrow{\beta} q'$ for some q' in T, we also have a transition $q \xrightarrow{\alpha} q''$ for some q''. Let $\alpha = \{a_{i_1}, \ldots, a_{i_r}\}$, $r > 1$. We now proceed as in Case 2.1.2.

Let *conversely* each state q satisfy a) or b). Let q be an arbitrary state. We have to show that there is some $\alpha \in C \cup Comp$ with $q \xrightarrow{\alpha} q'$ for some q'.

If a) is satisfied then let i be the node in $G_{Sys}(q)$ with out-degree 0. In this case q_i is complete and the statement is obvious.

If b) is satisfied then there is $\alpha \in L_1$ or $(c, \alpha) \in L_2$ such that $\alpha = \{a_{i_1}, ..., a_{i_r}\}$ whith $a_{i_j} \in A_{i_j}$ and $G_{Sys}(q)$ has a simple cycle with the nodes $i_1, ..., i_r$ where all labels are α, resp. (c, α) and for every such cycle we have $cond(p)(q) = false$.

Case 1: Label α. Let w.l.o.g. $i_1 \overset{\alpha}{\to} i_2 ...... \overset{\alpha}{\to} i_r \overset{\alpha}{\to} i_1$ be a simple cycle with $cond(p)(q) = false$. Then there must be one edge e with $cond(e) = false$, hence for some j $(en(a_{i_j}) \wedge \exists x \in \alpha, x \neq a_{i_j} : \neg en(x))(q) = false$. But this edge is only in $G_{Sys}(q)$ if $en(a_{i_j})(q_{i_j}) = true$, hence $\alpha \in C$ can be performed in state q.

Case 2: Label (c, α): analogously.

Proof of Theorem 2

One shows in a first step that, under the conditions of the theorem, every $k \in K'$ may progress in Sys. This can be done in a similar way as in [9] and is hence omitted here. In a second step we conclude that for finite K', K' may strongly progress and finally we show how to obtain the result for infinite K'. Let K' be finite, $K' = \{k_1, k_2 ..., k_n\}$. Let $\sigma = q_0 \overset{\alpha_0}{\to} q_1 \overset{\alpha_1}{\to} q_2 ...$ be a run of Sys and $n \in \mathbb{N}$. As k_1 may progress in Sys there exists σ' such that $\sigma(1) = \sigma_n \sigma'$ is a run of Sys and k_1 participates in some interaction of σ'. Let σ'_{l_1} be a prefix of σ' of length l_1 such that k_1 participates in some interaction of this prefix. Set $n_1 = n + l_1$ then there must be some σ'' such that $\sigma(2) = \sigma(1)_{n_1} \sigma''$ is a run of Sys and component k_2 participates in some interaction of σ''. As K' is finite this process terminates and we have a run in which finally every component participates in some interaction. We now assume that K' is countable. We consider the set R of all runs of Sys and introduce a metric $d : R \times R \to \{0, 1\}$ on R by $d(\sigma, \hat{\sigma}) = inf\{1/2^n : \sigma_n = \hat{\sigma}_n\}$. (R, d) is a complete metric space by standard arguments, hence every Cauchy-sequence converges in R. We now proceed as above and construct for every $m \in \mathbb{N}$ a run $\sigma(m)$ such that every element $\{1, 2, ..., m\}$ participates in some interaction of $\sigma(m)$ by maintaining the prefix that has participation of $\{1, ..., m\}$ when constructing the run that has participation of $\{1, ..., m + 1\}$. In such a way we construct a Cauchy-sequence of runs $\sigma(1), \sigma(2), ...$ The limit of this sequence is the desired run that has the prefix σ_n and then contains for every $k \in K'$ an interaction in which k participates.

On the Expressive Power of
Live Sequence Charts*

Werner Damm, Tobe Toben, and Bernd Westphal

Carl von Ossietzky Universität Oldenburg, 26111 Oldenburg, Germany
{damm,toben,westphal}@informatik.uni-oldenburg.de

Abstract. The Live Sequence Charts (LSC) language is a formally rig-
orous variant of the well-known scenario language Message Sequence
Charts (MSC). LSCs yield expressive power by means to distinguish
mandatory and scenario behaviour, means to characterise by another
scenario the context in which a specification applies, and means to distinguish required from possible progress, i.e. to require liveness.

From the original proposal by Damm & Harel [1], two slightly different
dialects emerged, one in the context of LSC play-in and -out [2] and one
for the use of LSCs as formal requirements specification language in
formal, model-based approaches to software development [3].

In this paper, we investigate the expressive power of LSCs in the sense
of [3]. That is, we first (constructively) show that for each LSC there is
an equivalent CTL* formula. Complementing existing work, we show
that the containment is strict, that is, not each CTL* formula has an
equivalent LSC. To complete the discussion, we present for the first time
a way back, from a syntactically characterised fragment of CTL* to the
subset of bonded LSC specifications, thereby establishing an equivalence.

1 Introduction

Scenario-based approaches are an adequate approach to the formal specification
of requirements on systems that are composed of different components [4,5]. The
common idea of scenario-based specification is to formally yet comprehensibly
describe all interactions between system components, and their interaction with
the environment, that are necessary to accomplish a certain task. This is, for
example, in contrast to temporal logic patterns [6,7], which also claim comprehensibility but only provide rather atomic templates for action/response pairs
of which many have to be used to cover more complex tasks.

The Live Sequence Charts (LSC) language is a particular formalism that supports the scenario-based approach. It has been introduced by Damm & Harel in [1]
as a conservative extension of the well-known ITU-standard Message Sequence
Charts (MSC) [8] and in the meantime gained wide adoption [9,10,11,12,13].

In the following, we give a brief example to recall the scenario-based approach
and the LSC language. Although the LSC language is graphical and intuitive,

---

* This work was partly supported by the German Research Council (DFG) in SFB/TR
14 AVACS and in project DA 206/7-3 (USE), SPP 1064.

T. Reps, M. Sagiv, and J. Bauer (Eds.): Wilhelm Festschrift, LNCS 4444, pp. 225–246, 2007.
© Springer-Verlag Berlin Heidelberg 2007

there is no complete introduction possible within a page or two. For a more thorough introduction, the reader is referred to [1,3,2].

Consider the design of the software of a level-crossing system. There might be a central controller 'CrossingCtrl' and separate controllers 'LightsCtrl' and 'BarrierCtrl' for the traffic lights and the barriers. One requirement on the system is clearly to secure the crossing on a request '*secreq*' by the environment. Then the central controller shall finally trigger the lights and barrier controller by sending appropriate messages. If the lights controller is operational at that point in time, it shall continue to switch on the red traffic lights and report back success while the barrier controller simultaneously initiates lowering of the barrier and finally reports back success. The barrier moving up in between the latter two events would be an error. After both sub-controllers reported success, it would be kind (but not necessary) if the central controller reported success back to the environment.

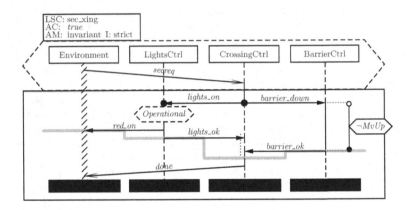

Fig. 1. Live Sequence Chart for a system of level-crossing controllers

This prosaic specification can be formalised using scenarios by the LSC shown in Figure 1. There is one (vertical) instance line for each sub-controller labelled accordingly and one for the environment, as indicated by the diagonal lines. The large dashed hexagon is called *pre-chart* and characterises the activation of the scenario, that is, the situations in which the remainder (or *main chart*) of the chart is supposed to be observed. In the example, this is the single *asynchronous message*, i.e. receipt occurs strictly after sending, '*secreq*' from the environment, which requests securing. To express that the central controller shall *finally* send the following two *instantaneous messages* '*lights_on*' and '*barrier_down*', we can use the LSC feature that instance line segments have a temperature. Temperature *hot*, graphically indicated by a solid line segment, enforces progress, while *cold*, indicated by a dashed line segment, doesn't. The segment of the 'CrossingCtrl' instance line starting at the top of the main-chart is hence solid.

Black circles on instance lines are *simultaneous regions*, which enforce simultaneity. Thus messages '*lights_on*' and '*barrier_down*' should be sent (and received) simultaneously.

The smaller hexagon on the 'LightsCtrl' instance line is a *condition*, which requires that the controller shall be operational at the point in time when '*lights_on*' is received. Note that conditions in LSC are treated differently than MSC conditions. First of all, they are semantically significant in LSCs, while in MSCs they are merely comments. And secondly they may also have a temperature, either hot or cold, which is graphically indicated by solid or dashed outline. The semantics of cold conditions is that if they hold when evaluated, then in order to satisfy the LSC one has to adhere to the remainder of the scenario; and if they don't hold, the whole scenario is immediately considered to be satisfied. Thus cold conditions can be used to provide *legal exits* to a scenario. In practice, scenarios with legal exits are typically complemented by another scenario which shares the same prefix and continues after the complementary condition with the actions to take in the complementary case. Thus in our example, there should be another chart which specifies the system behaviour in case the lights controller is *not* operational when receiving '*lights_on*'.

To indicate that a condition is supposed to hold for a span of time, we can use the LSC feature *local invariant*. In Figure 1, there is a local invariant that starts *exclusively* with the receipt of '*barrier_down*' and ends *inclusively* with the sending of '*barrier_ok*' as denoted by the unfilled and filled circles. It requires that the barrier shall not move up from (strictly after) the point in time where '*barrier_down*' has been received up to (and including) the point in time where '*barrier_ok*' is sent. The solid outline of the condition hexagon indicates that its temperature is hot, that is, if the condition is violated during a system run that matched the scenario up to this point, then the system violates the LSC.

As we don't care in which order the subsidiary controllers reported back to the central controller, the order on messages '*lights_ok*' and '*barrier_ok*' is explicitly relaxed by enclosing them in a *coregion*, graphically indicated by the dotted line in parallel to the 'CrossingCtrl' instance line. Both messages may be observed in either order or even simultaneously.

Note that progress is enforced up to the configuration or cut (cf. 2.2) indicated by the horizontal gray line, as there are hot instance line segments at the participating instances. Below the gray line, all instance line segments are cold, that is, progress is no longer enforced. In other words, the message '*done*' *may* be sent, but need not.

In addition to locations and conditions, the whole chart also has a temperature, either hot or cold, which is graphically indicated by the box enclosing the *main chart*, which complements the pre-chart. In order to satisfy a hot (or *universal*) chart as in the example, a system has to satisfy the main chart *whenever* the pre-chart is observed. In contrast, a cold (or *existential*) chart is already satisfied if there exists a single system run that adheres to the concatenation of pre- and main-chart.

The last aspect of Figure 1 to discuss is the *header*, the small box on top of the pre-chart. It assigns the chart a name, chooses an interpretation, and may further restrict activation. Namely, the pre-chart is only considered, if the *activation condition* (AC) holds. That is, if the activation holds at some point in time and *from there on* the pre-chart is observed, than the main-chart has to be considered. The *activation mode* (AM) denotes the candidates for evaluation of the activation condition. If it is *invariant*, then any point in time is considered while if it is *initial*, only the initial states of the system are. A third mode, *iterative*, is similar to invariant but excludes overlapping activation. If the LSC is non-reactivating, that is, if the pre-chart is not a sub-sequence of the main-chart, then the iterative mode is equivalent to the invariant mode. If the LSC is reactivating, then the LSC has not even an equivalent in CTL* thus we will exclude this mode from the discussion in the following sections. Finally, the *interpretation* (I) determines the significance of additional occurrences of messages. In the *strict* interpretation, additional occurrences are considered to be violations, thus an implementation of 'LightsCtrl' that sends '*red_on*' twice before reporting back success violates Figure 1. In the *weak* (or *tolerant* [2]) interpretation, additional occurrences of messages are ignored.

Having introduced the most common features of the LSC language, we can summarise that the most significant differences between LSCs and MSCs are

- *modalities* for
  - the whole chart, distinguishing example scenarios from universal ones,
  - locations, possibly indicating liveness,
  - conditions, providing for legal exits and anti-scenarios, and
  - messages (cf. [1,3,2]),
- precise characterisation of the activation time by pre-charts, activation condition, and activation mode, and
- semantical significance of conditions.

These additions make LSCs significantly more powerful than MSCs in the sense that more behaviour is distinguishable with LSCs than with MSCs (cf. [1] for details) whereas the graphical appeal and intuitive comprehensibility of MSCs is preserved by indicating the modalities graphically.

In order to understand the relation of this work to [14,15], note that after the original introduction of LSCs by Damm & Harel [1], two slightly different dialects, motivated by different application domains, emerged.

The LSC language of Harel & Marelly [2] is tailored for the so called play-out approach. They employ a tool called play-engine to execute LSC specifications, i.e. sets of LSCs. Thereby there needn't be an implementation of the intra-object behaviour of the system under design; the set of LSCs *is* the implementation. To this end, they added elements like actions to modify the state of the system, loops, and sub-charts to [1]. The semantics is given using the linearisation of partial orders [2].

The LSC language of Damm & Klose [3], which is the subject of this paper, is tailored to complement the model-based development of the intra-object behaviour of a system using, e.g., Statemate state-charts or UML state-machines. The model can then formally be checked for whether it adheres to the LSC specification, for example employing model-checking techniques as discussed in [16] and demonstrated in [13] for Statemate and in [17] for Rhapsody/UML.[1] To this

---

[1] Statemate and Rhapsody are trademarks of i-Logix, Inc.

end, they added local invariants and the activation mode [1]. The semantics is given by a variant of Büchi Automata [18,3].

The motivation of this work is also rooted in the latter application domain. As MSCs and LSCs are, in contrast to other graphical formalisms, not simply graphical representations of more fundamental and well-understood formalisms like Temporal Logic but have been designed driven by the needs of the application domain, with an intuition of the semantics in mind, which has then been formalised. In order to understand the potentials and limitations of the LSC language, it is necessary to compare its expressive power to more fundamental formalisms like temporal logic. Pragmatically, a translation from LSCs to temporal logic makes it possible to employ any of the many temporal logic model-checkers for formal verification of LSCs against given system models.

The first result of our paper is similar to [14,15] where the relation of a small subset of the LSCs of [2] to CTL* has already been established. We consider the different LSC dialect of [3] and obtain the result in a different way. Using the automaton based semantics of LSCs [3], we can employ older results for the translation from particular automata to temporal logic by [19]. In addition, we already convey a first comparison of both dialects on the common level of temporal logic; a full comparison will be possible with the full version of [15] that proposes to discuss a larger subset of the LSCs of [2]. Furthermore, we not only provide an embedding of LSCs into temporal logic but can more precisely characterise a fragment of first-order CTL* that comprises the subset of LSCs we consider via an inductive syntactical definition (similar to the syntactical characterisation of the common fragment of LTL and CTL* [20]).

As a second result, we obtain for the first time a description of an *equivalent* fragment of first-order CTL* for the slightly smaller but most commonly used subset of *bonded LSCs*, i.e. where conditions and local invariants only appear in simultaneous regions with messages. The equivalence is shown constructively by providing a translation back from formulae to LSCs.

A minor original contribution of this paper is the full version of a closed formalisation of the syntax and the semantics of the LSCs of [3], including the interpretations weak and strict. It turned out to be necessary to introduce an alternative formalisation, since [3,18] give the semantics of LSCs only in form of an imperative unwinding algorithm that iteratively constructs the automaton for a given LSC. Our formalisation allowed to establish the results presented here and in [21,16]. We expect it to be useful in further research on both dialects of LSCs since we are confident that it is extendable to the LSCs of [2].

2   Core Live Sequence Charts

For a (slightly clearer) presentation, in the following we introduce a subset of the LSCs of [3] which we call *core* LSCs. Core LSCs are missing three features that are out of the scope of this paper. Firstly, we discuss activation only by an *activation condition* and not the general case of pre-charts. An activation condition can be used if the activation only depends on properties of a single system state and not on a whole scenario. For the translation to temporal logic, pre-charts can be treated similar to [15] as an implication from the formula of the pre-chart to the formula of concatenation of pre- and main-chart.

Secondly, we only consider *un-timed* LSCs, that is, we exclude timer-set and -reset and timeout elements as well as timing intervals which LSCs inherit from MSCs. General timed LSCs require a timed Temporal Logic. They can be treated similar to the Real time Symbolic Timing Diagrams (RSTD) in [22] since they use the same kind of automata that we use for LSCs [3].

And thirdly, we consider only hot asynchronous messages, i.e. sending *and* receipt has to be observed in contrast to cold asynchronous messages, which admit that the message is lost. Cold asynchronous messages add irregular transitions to the Symbolic Automaton, which are tedious to consider but effectively don't harm the automaton properties we use in the proofs. The translation to temporal logic extends directly to possible asynchronous messages, for the translation back we might need to exclude them.

The new representation of the abstract syntax of LSCs we introduce in the following Section 2.1 is equivalent to the one used in [3] in that it is closely related to the actual graphical charts like the one shown in Figure 1, but it is much more concise than [3]. Note that for our purpose, it is not sufficient to use a more abstract notion of abstract syntax like, for instance, partial orders on the set of LSC elements as demonstrated by [14]. The reason is that the proof of equivalence between a fragment of first-order prenex CTL* (cf. Section 3) and a subset of LSCs in Section 3.2 inductively constructs an LSC, and to this end needs a rather detailed abstract syntax.

As mentioned in the introduction, our definition of the LSC semantics in Section 2.2 is equivalent to the one of [3] but closed, instead of in terms of a translation algorithm, and thus much more appropriate to our needs.

2.1 Syntax

Formally, annotations of messages, conditions, and local invariants of an LSC are boolean expressions, i.e. core LSCs are defined over a signature. A *signature* $\mathcal{S} = (\mathcal{V}, \mathcal{P}, \chi)$ comprises a set of variables $\mathcal{V}$, a set $\mathcal{P}$ of predicates, and – in addition to the standard definition – a partial function $\chi : \mathcal{P} \rightharpoonup \mathcal{P}$ with $\text{dom}(\chi) \cap \text{ran}(\chi) = \emptyset$ that partitions $\mathcal{P}$ into the three sets of *message send predicates* $\mathcal{P}_{snd} := \text{dom}\,\chi$, *message receive predicates* $\mathcal{P}_{rcv} := \text{ran}\,\chi$, and *non-message predicates* $\mathcal{P}_{cnd} := \mathcal{P} \setminus \mathcal{P}_{msg}$, where $\mathcal{P}_{msg} = \mathcal{P}_{snd} \,\dot\cup\, \mathcal{P}_{rcv}$. This separation of predicates is the key to identify messages and conditions in the formula when considering the translation back to LSCs. The *boolean expressions* over $\mathcal{S}$, denoted by $Expr_{\mathcal{S}}$, are defined by the grammar $\psi ::= true \mid p_0 \mid p(x_1, \ldots, x_n) \mid \neg \psi_1 \mid \psi_1 \vee \psi_2$ where p_0 is a 0-ary predicate and p of arity $n > 0$. We shall use the common abbreviations *false*, $\wedge$, $\rightarrow$, and $\leftrightarrow$. A tuple $\mathcal{M} = (\mathcal{U}, \mathcal{I})$ is called *structure* of $\mathcal{S}$ if $\mathcal{U}$ is a non-empty set called *universe* and $\mathcal{I}$ is an interpretation of the predicates in $\mathcal{P}$. A function $\sigma : \mathcal{V} \rightarrow \mathcal{U}$ is called *valuation* of $\mathcal{V}$. The semantics of $\psi \in Expr_{\mathcal{S}}$ is standard given a structure $(\mathcal{U}, \mathcal{I})$ and a valuation from $Val_{\mathcal{U}}(\mathcal{S})$, the set of all valuations of $\mathcal{V}$.

A central piece of information in the concrete syntax of an LSC as given in Figure 1 is the order of elements along a single instance line as their order shall be preserved unless relaxed by coregions. As coregions mustn't be nested, the order of elements is actually a scenario order as defined in the following. An LSC instance line is then simply a set equipped with a scenario order and a function that assigns each element a temperature from $Temp := \{hot, cold\}$.

Definition 1 (LSC Instance Line). *Let A be a finite, non-empty set. The tuple $(A, \prec)$ is called* instance line *if and only if $\prec \subseteq A \times A$ is a scenario order (or* direct predecessor relation*) on A, that is, if and only if*

(i) $\exists! \, a^\perp \in A \; \forall a \in A : a^\perp \prec^* a$ (Unique Minimum)
     where $\prec^*$ denotes the reflexive transitive closure of $\prec$.

(ii) $\forall a, a_1, a_2 \in A : a \prec a_1 \wedge a \prec a_2 \implies a_1 \not\bowtie^* a_2$ (Unordered Successors)
     where $a_1 \not\bowtie^* a_2$ denotes that a_1, a_2 are unordered*, i.e. $a_1 \not\prec^* a_2$ and $a_2 \not\prec^* a_1$.*

(iii) $\forall a_1, a_2 \in A : (\exists a_0 \in A : a_0 \prec a_1 \wedge a_0 \prec a_2)$
     $\implies (\forall a_3 \in A : a_1 \prec a_3 \implies a_2 \prec a_3)$. (Diamond Property)

A triple $(A, \prec, \vartheta)$ with $\vartheta : A \to Temp$ is called LSC instance line *if and only if $(A, \prec)$ is an instance line. The elements $a \in A$ are then called (tempered) atoms. When dealing with multiple instance lines, we use $a_1 \bowtie a_2$ to denote that the atoms a_1 and a_2 belong to the same instance line.*   ◇

The following definition of core LSCs captures the essence of an LSC picture like Figure 1, in particular the set of elements and their order on the instance lines. Formally, a core LSC is structured into the body and the information found in the head and given by the frame around the body, namely the activation condition, the activation mode, the interpretation, and the quantification. The body is further structured and comprises a set of LSC instance lines together with three sets of the elements: messages, conditions, and local invariants (cf. Figure 2). Messages in addition have a synchroneity from $Sync := \{inst, asyn\}$, conditions and local invariants are equipped with an *obligation* from $Obl := \{mand, poss\}$ (the formal names for *hot* and *cold*), and a local invariant start- and end-atom has a *containedness* from $Cont =: \{incl, excl\}$.

Definition 2. *Let $S = (\mathcal{V}, \mathcal{P}, \chi)$ be a signature. A* core LSC *over S is a tuple $L = (\ell, ac, am, int, quant)$ with activation condition $ac \in Expr_S$, activation mode $am \in \{initial, invariant, iterative\}$, interpretation $int \in \{strict, weak\}$, quantification $quant \in \{existential, universal\}$, and body*

$$\ell = (\{(A_1, \prec_1, \vartheta_1), \ldots, (A_n, \prec_n, \vartheta_n)\}, Msg_L, Cond_L, LocInv_L), n \geq 1, \; where$$

– $\{(A_1, \prec_1, \vartheta_1), \ldots, (A_n, \prec_n, \vartheta_n)\}$ *is a set of disjoint LSC instance lines.*
     We set $Inst(L) := \{1, \ldots, n\}$, $A_L := \bigcup_{i \in Inst(L)} A_i$, $\prec_L := \bigcup_{i \in Inst(L)} \prec_i$, and $\vartheta_L := \bigcup_{i \in Inst(L)} \vartheta_i$. We denote by $a_i^\perp$ the minimum of $\prec_i$, $i \in Inst(L)$, also called instance head*, and set $A_L^\perp := \{a_i^\perp \mid i \in Inst(L)\}$. By $A|_i := A \cap A_i$ we denote the projection of a set $A \subseteq A_L$ onto instance $i \in Inst(L)$.*
     If the LSC L is clear by context we shall simply write, e.g., $\prec$ instead of $\prec_L$.

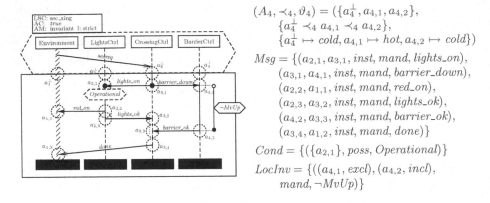

$(A_4, \prec_4, \vartheta_4) = (\{a_4^{\perp}, a_{4,1}, a_{4,2}\},$
$\{a_4^{\perp} \prec_4 a_{4,1} \prec_4 a_{4,2}\},$
$\{a_4^{\perp} \mapsto cold, a_{4,1} \mapsto hot, a_{4,2} \mapsto cold\})$

$Msg = \{(a_{2,1}, a_{3,1}, inst, mand, lights\_on),$
$(a_{3,1}, a_{4,1}, inst, mand, barrier\_down),$
$(a_{2,2}, a_{1,1}, inst, mand, red\_on),$
$(a_{2,3}, a_{3,2}, inst, mand, lights\_ok),$
$(a_{4,2}, a_{3,3}, inst, mand, barrier\_ok),$
$(a_{3,4}, a_{1,2}, inst, mand, done)\}$

$Cond = \{(\{a_{2,1}\}, poss, Operational)\}$

$LocInv = \{((a_{4,1}, excl), (a_{4,2}, incl),$
$mand, \neg MvUp)\}$

Fig. 2. Abstract syntax of the LSC from Figure 1. For brevity, we only consider the LSC body, give the order and temperature only for the right-most instance line, and in messages omit the receive expressions as they are equal to the send expressions.

– ($m \in$) Msg_L is a set of messages,

$$m = (a_s, a_r, \varsigma, \psi_s, \psi_r) \in A \times A \times Sync \times Expr_{\mathcal{S}} \times Expr_{\mathcal{S}},$$

each comprising the message send and receive atoms a_s and a_r, the message synchroneity ς, and the message send and receive expressions $\psi_s = p(x_1, .., x_n)$ with $p \in \mathcal{P}_{snd}$ and $\psi_r = \chi(p)(x_1, .., x_n)$, $n \geq 0$, $x_i \in \mathcal{V}$. By $Msg_{inst}(L) := \{m \in Msg(L) \mid \varsigma(m) = inst\}$ and $Msg_{asyn}(L) := \{m \in Msg(L) \mid \varsigma(m) = asyn\}$ we denote the sets of instantaneous and asynchronous messages of L and set $atoms(m) := \{a_s, a_r\}$;

– ($c \in$) $Cond_L$ is a set of conditions,

$$c = (A_c, \kappa, \psi_c) \in \left(2^A \setminus \{\emptyset\}\right) \times Obl \times Expr_{\mathcal{S}},$$

each comprising the set of condition atoms A_c with at most one atom per instance line[2], i.e. $|(A_c|_i)| \leq 1$ for $i \in Inst(L)$, the condition mode κ, and the condition expression ψ_c. We set $atoms(c) := A_c(c)$;

– ($l \in$) $LocInv_L$ is a set of local invariants,

$$l = ((a_s, \gamma_s), (a_e, \gamma_e), \kappa, \psi) \in (A \times Cont) \times (A \times Cont) \times Obl \times Expr_{\mathcal{S}},$$

each comprising the local invariant start and end atoms a_s and a_e with containedness γ_s and γ_e, the local invariant mode κ, and the local invariant expression ψ. We set $atoms(l) := \{a_s, a_e\}$.

---

[2] In general, conditions are not limited to single instance lines as shown in Figure 1, but may span multiple instance lines; a condition spanning multiple instance lines synchronises the participating components.

The set $elems(L) := Msg_L \cup Cond_L \cup LocInv_L$ *is called the set of* elements of L. *To denote the components of a given element we use functional notations, like* $a_s(m)$ *for a message* m, *etc. These functions and 'atoms' are canonically extended from single elements to subsets of* $elems(L)$ *yielding sets of components and atoms, respectively, and we set* $atoms(L) := atoms(elems(L))$.

A core LSC is called closed *if and only if* $atoms(elems(L)) \cup A_L^\perp = A_L$, *i.e. if there are no atoms not used by elements except for instance heads. In the following we will only consider closed core LSCs.* ◇

Note that all expressions in an LSC may use variables from $\mathcal{V}$. Thereby we cover dynamic binding of core LSCs as introduced in [23,24] as an extension of the static binding core LSCs in [3]. The example in Figure 1 is statically bound. To extend it, for example, to cover systems with four barriers, each having its own barrier controller, we would write '$barrier\_down(b)$' where b is a free variable ranging over the identities of barrier controllers in the system.

Definition 3 (LSC Specification). *Let* $Lsc = \{L_1, \ldots, L_n\} \neq \emptyset$ *be a set of core LSCs over signature* S. Lsc *is then called* core LSC specification *over* S. ◇

2.2 Semantics

The central concept of the LSC semantics of [3] is the *cut* that represents how far each instance line has been observed. If the LSC has been activated and no element has been observed yet, then the cut is empty. Any other cut comprises at least one atom per instance line. It may comprise multiple atoms from one instance line if they all belong to the same coregion.

Definition 4 (Cut). *Let* S *be a signature and* L *a core LSC over* S. *A set of atoms* $\alpha \subseteq atoms(L)$ *is called* cut *if and only if*

(i) $\alpha \neq \emptyset \Longrightarrow \forall i \in Inst(L) : \alpha|_i \neq \emptyset$ *and (ii)* $\forall a_1, a_2 \in \alpha : a_1 \bowtie a_2 \Longrightarrow a_1 \not\prec^* a_2$.

We call $\alpha_0 := \emptyset$ *the* initial cut, $\alpha_\perp(L) := A_L^\perp$ *the* instance heads cut, *and* $\alpha_{fin}(L)$, *the maximal cut* α *with* $\forall a \in \alpha \; \forall a' \in atoms(L) : a \prec^* a' \Longrightarrow a' = a$, *the* final cut. *The temperature of* α, *denoted by* $\vartheta(\alpha)$, *is 'cold' if* $\alpha = \alpha_{fin}(L)$ *or* $\forall a \in \alpha : \vartheta(a) = cold$ *and 'hot' otherwise.* $Cuts(L)$ *is the set of all cuts of* L. ◇

The unit by which a cut can be advanced is the *simultaneous class* (*simclass* for short). Simultaneity is transitively induced by synchronous messages and by conditions that span multiple instance lines. All atoms of these elements are supposed to be observed at the same point in time.

Definition 5 (Simclass). *Let* S *be a signature and* L *a core LSC over* S. *Two atoms* $a_1, a_2 \in atoms(L)$ *are called* simultaneous, *denoted by* $a_1 \sim a_2$, *if and only if*

(i) $a_1 = a_2$, *or*   *(iii)* $\exists e \in Cond(L) \cup Msg_{inst}(L) : \{a_1, a_2\} \subseteq atoms(e)$, *or*
(ii) $\{a_1, a_2\} \subseteq A_L^\perp$, *or (iv)* $\exists a_3 \in atoms(L) : a_1 \sim a_3 \wedge a_3 \sim a_2$.

For each $a \in atoms(L)$, $[a] := \{a' \in atoms(L) \mid a' \sim a\}$ denotes the equivalence class of 'a' with respect to $\sim$. The elements of the set $Simclass(L) := atoms(L)/\sim$ of all equivalence classes of atoms from $atoms(L)$ are called sim-classes.

By $elems(scl) := \{e \in elems(L) \mid atoms(e) \cap scl \neq \emptyset\}$ we denote the set of LSC elements that share an atom from the simclass $scl \in Simclass(L)$. $\Diamond$

A cut α can be advanced by observing a set of *enabled* simclasses. A simclass scl is enabled by a cut α if each atom in scl has all of its direct predecessors in α or belongs to a coregion and there is at least one other atom from the same coregion in α. The intuition of asynchronous messages is explicitly added by saying that a simclass is only enabled if for each asynchronous message receive atom in scl the sending has been observed in α or earlier. The *step function* formalises the advancement of α by a non-empty set of enabled simclasses. We note without a proof that $Step_L$ yields a proper cut if applied to a cut and a non-empty set of enabled simclasses, and that it strictly advances the cut.

Definition 6 (Ready-set and $Step_L$). *Let L be a core LSC over signature S, $\alpha \in Cuts(L)$, and $scl \in Simclass(L)$. We say α enables scl, denoted $\alpha \rhd scl$, if and only if*

$$(\forall\, a' \in scl : prereq(a') \subseteq \alpha \lor \exists a \in \alpha : a \bowtie a' \land a \not\prec^* a')$$
$$\land (\forall\, m \in Msg_{asyn}(L) \cap elems(scl) : a_r(m) \in scl \implies \exists a \in \alpha : a_s(m) \prec^* a)$$

where $prereq(a) := \{a' \in atoms(L) \mid a' \prec a\}$ is the prerequisite of a.

A non-empty set of simclasses $Scl \subseteq Simclass(L)$ such that each simclass $scl \in Scl$ is enabled by α, i.e. $\alpha \rhd scl$, is called fired-set *of α. The set $Ready_L(\alpha)$ of all fired-sets of α is called the* ready-set *of α.*

For $\emptyset \neq \{scl_1, \ldots, scl_n\} \subseteq Simclass(L)$, the step function *of L is defined as $Step_L(\alpha, \{scl_1, \ldots, scl_n\}) := Max(\alpha \cup scl_1 \cup \cdots \cup scl_n)$ where $Max(A) := A \setminus \{a \in A \mid \exists a' \in A : a \prec^+ a'\}$.* $\Diamond$

The semantics of an LSC L is defined in terms of $\mathcal{A}_L$, the Symbolic Automaton of its body. Symbolic Automata are a variant of Büchi automata whose transitions are labelled by expressions over a signature S instead of by elements of an alphabet. They accept sequences of interpretations of the predicates in S on a fixed universe and under a fixed valuation of the variables in S.

Definition 7 (Symbolic Automata). *A Symbolic Automaton over signature S is a tuple $\mathcal{A} = (Q, q_s, \rightsquigarrow, F)$ comprising a finite set of states Q, the initial state $q_s \in Q$, the transition relation $\rightsquigarrow \subseteq Q \times Expr_S \times Q$, and the accepting states $F \subseteq Q$. We write $q_i \rightarrow q_j$ if and only if $(q_i, \psi, q_j) \in \rightsquigarrow$ for some ψ and $q_i \overset{\rightarrow}{\rightarrow} q_j$ if and only if $q_i \rightarrow q_j$ and $q_i \neq q_j$.*

$\mathcal{A}$ is called partially ordered, *or POSA, if the reflexive transitive closure of $\rightarrow$ is antisymmetric. It is called* deterministic *if $(q, \psi_1, q_1) \in \rightsquigarrow$ and $(q, \psi_2, q_2) \in \rightsquigarrow$, $q_1 \neq q_2$, implies $\mathcal{M}, \sigma \models \neg(\psi_1 \land \psi_2)$ for any $\mathcal{M}$ and σ.*

For a universe $\mathcal{U}$, $\overrightarrow{Int}_\mathcal{U}(S)$ is the set of all interpretation sequences, i.e. sequences $\vec{\iota} = \iota_0 \iota_1 \iota_2 \ldots$ of interpretations ι_i of the predicates $\mathcal{P}$ in S. By

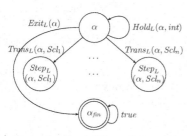
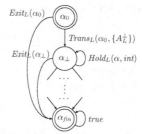

(a) Outgoing transitions from state α.   (b) Overall structure of $\mathcal{A}_L$.

Fig. 3. Structure of the LSC body automaton. Double lined states are in F.

$\bar{\iota}/k := \iota_k\iota_{k+1}\ldots$ *we denotes the suffix of* $\bar{\iota}$ *starting at position* k *and set* $\bar{\iota}^k := \iota_k$.

An infinite sequence $r = q_0\,q_1\,q_2\,\ldots$ *of states* $q_i \in Q$ *is called a* run *of* $\mathcal{A}$ *over* $\bar{\iota}$ *under* σ *if and only if* $q_0 = q_s$ *and for* $i \in \mathbb{N}_0$ *there is a* $(q_i, \psi, q_{i+1}) \in\leadsto$ *such that* $(\mathcal{U}, \iota_i), \sigma \models \psi$.

The set of runs of $\mathcal{A}$ *over* $\bar{\iota}$ *under* σ *is denoted by* $\Pi^{\bar{\iota}}_\sigma(\mathcal{A})$. *The language accepted by* $\mathcal{A}$ *is* $\mathcal{L}_\sigma(\mathcal{A}) := \{\bar{\iota} \in \overrightarrow{Int}_\mathcal{U}(\mathcal{P}) \mid \exists\, r \in \Pi^{\bar{\iota}}_\sigma(\mathcal{A}) : inf(r) \cap F \neq \emptyset\}$ *where* $inf(r)$ *is the set of states occurring infinitely often in* r. $\diamond$

The states of $\mathcal{A}_L$ are the cuts of L and each state gets three kinds of outgoing transitions, a self-loop, progress transitions to the following cuts, and a legal exit transition if possible conditions have to be considered (cf. Figure 3).

To construct the transition annotations, we use a number of abbreviations. The following five abbreviations select relevant elements from a simclass and, point-wise extended, from sets of simclasses.

$$Cond(scl) := Cond(L) \cap elems(scl), \quad Msg(scl) := Msg(L) \cap elems(scl),$$

$$Cond_{poss}(scl) := \{c \in Cond(scl) \mid \kappa(c) = poss\}, \quad Msg_{snd}(scl) :=$$

$$\{m \in Msg(scl) \mid a_s(m) \in scl\}, \quad Msg_{rcv}(scl) := \{m \in Msg(scl) \mid a_r(m) \in scl\}.$$

A local invariant $l \in LocInv(L)$ affects the transition annotation of a cut α if it is *active beyond* α, i.e. $\exists\, a, a' \in \alpha : a_s(l) \prec^* a \wedge a' \prec^+ a_e(l)$ or if it is *active at* α, i.e. it ends inclusively at α or it is active beyond α and not starting exclusively at α. By $ali_{L,=}(\alpha)$ ($ali_{L,>}(\alpha)$) we denote all local invariants *active at (beyond)* α and by $ali^{poss}_{L,=}(\alpha)$ ($ali^{poss}_{L,>}(\alpha)$) those $l \in ali_{L,=}(\alpha)$ ($ali_{L,>}(\alpha)$) with $\kappa(l) = poss$.

The expression

$$A_{\{scl_1,\ldots,scl_n\}} := \bigwedge(\psi_s(Msg_{snd}(scl_1 \cup \cdots \cup scl_n)) \cup \psi_r(Msg_{rcv}(scl_1 \cup \cdots \cup scl_n)))$$

characterise the simultaneous occurrence of all messages of simclasses $scl_1, \ldots, scl_n$ and

$$N_{\{scl_1,\ldots,scl_n\}} := \neg\bigvee(\psi_s(Msg_{snd}(scl_1 \cup \cdots \cup scl_n)) \cup \psi_r(Msg_{rcv}(scl_1 \cup \cdots \cup scl_n)))$$

the absence of these messages where $\bigvee\{\psi_1, \ldots, \psi_n\} := (\psi_1 \vee \cdots \vee \psi_n)$, $\bigvee\emptyset := false$, $\bigwedge\{\psi_1, \ldots, \psi_n\} := (\psi_1 \wedge \cdots \wedge \psi_n)$, and $\bigwedge\emptyset := true$.

The first kind of transitions is labelled with a *hold predicate*

$$Hold_L(\alpha, int) := N_{ExclMsg(int)} \wedge \bigwedge \psi(ali_{L,>}(\alpha))$$

which allows the automaton to remain in a state α while none of the awaited messages is observed and all local invariants active beyond α hold. The progress transitions are labelled with *transition predicates*

$$Trans_L(\alpha, int, Scl) := A_{Scl} \wedge N_{ExclMsg(int)\setminus Scl}$$
$$\wedge \bigwedge \psi_c(Cond(Scl)) \wedge \bigwedge \psi(ali_{L,=}(Step_L(\alpha, Scl)))$$

where $ExclMsg(weak) = \{scl \in Simclass(L) \mid \exists Scl \in Ready_L(\alpha) : scl \in Scl\}$ and $ExclMsg(strict) = Simclass(L)$, and $F = \{\alpha \in Cuts(L) \mid \vartheta(\alpha) = cold\}$, allows a transition from α to $\alpha' = Step_L(\alpha, Scl)$ if all messages required by the fired-set Scl and none of the messages from any other fired-set in the ready-set are observed and if the conditions co-located with the relevant messages and the local invariants active in α' hold. And legal exit transitions with *exit predicates*

$$Exit_L(\alpha, int) := \bigvee_{\substack{scl \in \\ Ready_L(\alpha)}} \left[N_{\{scl\}} \wedge \neg \bigvee \psi\left(ali_{L,>}^{poss}(\alpha)\right) \vee A_{\{scl\}} \wedge \right.$$
$$\left. \left(\neg \bigwedge \psi_c(Cond_{poss}(scl)) \vee \neg \bigwedge \psi\left(ali_{L,=}^{poss}(Step_L(\alpha, scl))\right)\right)\right]$$

which allow to the take the legal exit from α if a possible local invariant is violated while the awaited messages are not yet observed or if a possible condition or local invariant at a target cut is violated when observing the relevant messages. The disjunction over the complete ready-set avoids parallel exit edges in the automaton.

Definition 8. *Given a core LSC L over signature S with interpretation 'int', the* Symbolic Automaton *of L is $\mathcal{A}_L := (Q, q_s, \leadsto, F)$ with $Q = Cuts(L)$, $q_s = \alpha_0$,*

$$\leadsto = \{(\alpha, Hold_L(\alpha, int), \alpha) \mid \alpha \in Cuts(L) \setminus \{\alpha_0\}\}$$
$$\cup \{(\alpha, Exit_L(\alpha, int), \alpha_{fin}(L)) \mid \alpha \in Cuts(L),$$
$$\nexists Scl \in Ready_L(\alpha) : Step_L(\alpha, Scl) = \alpha_{fin}(L)\} \setminus \{\alpha_{fin}(L)\}$$
$$\cup \{(\alpha, Trans_L(\alpha, int, Scl), \alpha') \mid \alpha \in Cuts(L),$$
$$Scl \in Ready_L(\alpha), \alpha' = Step_L(\alpha, Scl) \neq \alpha_{fin}(L)\}$$
$$\cup \{(\alpha, Trans_L(\alpha, int, Scl) \vee Exit_L(\alpha, int), \alpha') \mid \alpha \in Cuts(L),$$
$$Scl \in Ready_L(\alpha), \alpha' = Step_L(\alpha, Scl) = \alpha_{fin}(L)\}.$$

Figure 4 shows the automaton $\mathcal{A}_L$ of the body of the LSC from Figure 1 according to Definition 8, omitting the exit transitions annotated with *false* and all states not reachable from the Vinitial cut.

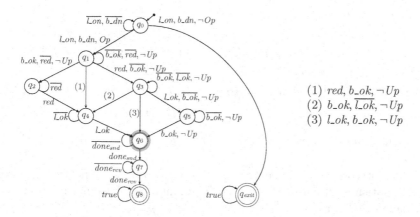

Fig. 4. For lack of space, message and condition names are abbreviated, negation of message-observation predicates is expressed by over-lining, and a comma is used for conjunction. E.g. q_0's loop fires if neither '*lights_on*' nor '*barrier_down*' are observed.

Note that the interpretation *strict* or *weak* (called *tolerant* in [2]) has no effect on the structure of the automaton but only on the annotations. A *strict* LSC restricts the occurrence of the messages used in the LSC to exactly those points in time where they are supposed to occur according to the scenario. For example, if a level-crossing system sends '*red_on*' twice (to play safe) then the system wouldn't satisfy Figure 1 in the strict interpretation. In the *weak* interpretation, the specification is satisfied if each necessary message occurs at least once where it is supposed to.

By the following Lemma, the Symbolic Automaton of a (bonded) LSC is a (deterministic) POSA. We provide the rather technical proof in the appendix.

Lemma 1 (POSA). *Let L be a core LSC over signature S. Then $\mathcal{A}_L$ is a POSA. If L is bonded, i.e. if all condition and local invariant atoms in L are co-located with at least one message atom, then $\mathcal{A}_L$ is a deterministic POSA.*

In practice, LSCs are nearly always bonded. Non-bonded LSCs, i.e. those with loose conditions, are highly counter-intuitive and it is significantly harder to understand counter-examples obtained from model-checking because $\mathcal{A}_L$ runs of a given counter-example need not be unique. Already [3] explicitly recommends to avoid loose conditions.

The semantics of a complete LSC L is obtained by quantifying the interpretation sequences accepted by its $\mathcal{A}_L$ according to the activation mode and quantification.

Definition 9 (LSC Semantics). *Let $L = (\ell, ac, am, int, quant)$ be a core LSC over signature S and $\mathcal{U}$ a universe. A set of interpretation sequences $\vec{I} \subseteq \overrightarrow{Int}_{\mathcal{U}}(S)$ is said to* satisfy *L, denoted $\vec{I} \models_{LSC} L$, if and only if*

- $quant = existential$ and

$$\exists\, \vec{\imath} \in \vec{I}\, \exists\, \sigma \in Val_\mathcal{U}(\mathcal{S}) : am = initial \land \left((\mathcal{U}, \vec{\imath}^{\,0}), \sigma \models ac \land \vec{\imath}/0 \in \mathcal{L}_\sigma(\mathcal{A}_L)\right)$$
$$\lor\, am = invariant \land \left(\exists\, k \in \mathbb{N}_0 : (\mathcal{U}, \vec{\imath}^{\,k}), \sigma \models ac \land \vec{\imath}/k \in \mathcal{L}_\sigma(\mathcal{A}_L)\right)$$

- $quant = universal$ and

$$\forall\, \vec{\imath} \in \vec{I}\, \forall\, \sigma \in Val_\mathcal{U}(\mathcal{S}) : am = initial \land \left((\mathcal{U}, \vec{\imath}^{\,0}), \sigma \models ac \implies \vec{\imath}/0 \in \mathcal{L}_\sigma(\mathcal{A}_L)\right)$$
$$\lor\, am = invariant \land \left(\forall\, k \in \mathbb{N}_0 : (\mathcal{U}, \vec{\imath}^{\,k}), \sigma \models ac \implies \vec{\imath}/k \in \mathcal{L}_\sigma(\mathcal{A}_L)\right).$$

The language accepted by L is $\mathcal{L}(L) := \{\vec{I} \subseteq \overrightarrow{Int}_\mathcal{U}(\mathcal{P}) \mid \vec{I} \models_{LSC} L\}$. $\Diamond$

A set $\vec{I}$ of interpretation sequences satisfies a core LSC specification Lsc if and only if it satisfies all core LSCs in Lsc. The language of Lsc is the intersection of the languages of the core LSCs in Lsc.

3   The Temporal Logics of Core LSCs

In order to cover symbolic LSCs with free variables, the temporal logic has to provide first-order quantification over logical variables. And in order to cover both, existential and universal LSCs, LTL is not sufficient but quantification over paths is necessary. Consequently, we basically use first-order CTL* as the destination temporal logic.

For convenience, the following definition already introduces a fragment of CTL* which we call FOP-CTL* (first-order prenex CTL*). Its expressive power is sufficient for our purposes since LSCs only need top-level path and logical quantifiers and the semantics (which is standard) can be explained using a set of (system) runs instead of a computation tree for general CTL*.

Definition 10 (FOP-CTL*). *The set of first-order prenex CTL* (FOP-CTL*) formulae over signature $\mathcal{S}$ is defined by the grammar*

$$\varphi ::= \varphi^{\exists\forall} \mid \neg\varphi \mid \varphi_1 \lor \varphi_2 \qquad \varphi^{\exists\forall} ::= \varphi^{EA} \mid \exists\, x\,.\, \varphi^{\exists\forall} \mid \forall\, x\,.\, \varphi^{\exists\forall}$$
$$\varphi^{EA} ::= \phi \mid \mathsf{E}\,\phi \mid \mathsf{A}\,\phi \qquad\qquad \phi ::= \psi \mid \neg\phi \mid \phi_1 \lor \phi_2 \mid \phi_1\,\mathsf{U}\,\phi_2 \mid \mathsf{X}\,\phi$$

where $\psi \in Expr_\mathcal{S}$. We shall use the abbreviations $\land$, $\rightarrow$, $\leftrightarrow$, F, G, and W.

The formulae we construct for core LSCs in Section 3.1 are in FOP-CTL* but we can identify further structure. We will find that general core LSCs translate to formulae from the FOP-CTL* fragment CSCTL and the bonded ones translate to DCSCTL. Formulae of the latter fragment even provide enough information to establish a way back to LSCs (cf. Section 3.2).

Definition 11 (CSCTL, DCSCTL). *The set of* communication sequence *FOP-CTL* (CSCTL) formulae over signature $\mathcal{S}$ is*

$$
\begin{array}{ll}
\zeta ::= \xi_E \mid \xi_A \mid \zeta \land \zeta & \xi_E ::= \mathsf{E}\,(\psi \rightarrow \pi) \mid \mathsf{E}\,\mathsf{G}\,(\psi \rightarrow \pi) \mid \exists\, x\,.\, \xi_E \\[4pt]
\pi ::= \eta\,\mathsf{U}\,\hat{\pi} \mid \eta\,\mathsf{W}\,\hat{\pi} & \xi_A ::= \mathsf{A}\,(\psi \rightarrow \pi) \mid \mathsf{A}\,\mathsf{G}\,(\psi \rightarrow \pi) \mid \forall\, x\,.\, \xi_A \\[4pt]
\eta ::= \neg\mu \land \eta \mid \psi & \hat{\pi} ::= \hat{\pi}_1 \lor \hat{\pi}_2 \mid \tau \land \mathsf{X}\,\pi \mid false \\[4pt]
\tau ::= \neg\mu \land \tau \mid \mu \land \tau \mid \psi & \mu ::= p_{msg}(x_1, \ldots, x_n) \qquad\qquad (1)
\end{array}
$$

where $\psi \in Expr_{\mathcal{S}}$, $x_i \in \mathcal{V}$, $1 \leq i \leq n$, and $p_{msg} \in \mathcal{P}_{msg}$ is a message predicate.

Deterministic *CSCTL (DCSCTL) comprises the formulae obtained from grammar (1) with the $\hat{\pi}$ production changed to*

$$\hat{\pi} ::= \tau \vee \phi \mid (\tau \wedge \mathsf{X}\,\pi) \vee \phi, \phi ::= false \mid \tau \mid \phi_1 \vee \phi_2,$$

that satisfy

(i) *occurrences of $p \in \mathcal{P}_{snd}$ and $\chi^{-1}(p)$ in ξ_E and ξ_A are injectively related,*

(ii) *if $\neg\mu_1$ and μ_2 occur on both sides of an U or W, then $\mu_1 = \mu_2$, and*

(iii) *in each $\hat{\pi}$, any μ in τ is disjoint to ϕ, i.e. $\models \neg(\mu \wedge \phi)$.* $\Diamond$

3.1 From Core LSCs to Temporal Logic...

Lemma 2 (Schlör [19]). *Let $\mathcal{A} = (Q, q_s, \leadsto, F)$ be a POSA over signature $\mathcal{S}$, $\mathcal{U}$ a universe, and $\sigma \in Val_{\mathcal{U}}(\mathcal{S})$ a valuation. Then there is an LTL formula $\phi_{\mathcal{A}}$ over $\mathcal{S}$ with $\bar{\imath} \in \mathcal{L}_{\sigma}(\mathcal{A}) \iff \bar{\imath}, \sigma \models \phi_{\mathcal{A}}$.* $\Diamond$

The proof is by induction over the distance of states from the states whose only outgoing transitions are self-loops, in case of $\mathcal{A}_L$ this is only $\alpha_{fin}(L)$. The POSA property ensures that the sequence of the sets of states with distance $1, 2, \ldots$ is ascending with respect to $\subseteq$. The formula constructed in the course of the proof is recursively defined as $\phi_{\mathcal{A}} := \phi_{q_s}$ with

$$\phi_q := \psi(q, q)\ U_q \bigvee_{q \hat{\rightarrow} q'} \left(\psi(q, q') \wedge \mathsf{X}\,\phi_{q'} \right)$$

for $q \in Q$ where $\psi(q_1, q_2)$ denotes the (well-defined) transition predicate of a transition $q_1 \rightarrow q_2$ between locations $q_1, q_2 \in Q$. The temporal operator U_q is W (unless or weak until) if $q \in F$ and U (until or strong until) otherwise.

As an example consider the outgoing transitions of a typical automaton state as shown in Figure 3(a).We may stay at state α as long as the hold condition $Hold_L(\alpha, int)$ holds and may leave α if any of the outgoing transitions can fire. Then, recursively, we may stay at the destination state as long as the destination state's hold condition holds etc. The formula directly follows this structure (cf. Figure 5).

Theorem 1. *Let L be a core LSC over signature $\mathcal{S}$. There is a CSCTL formula ϕ_L over $\mathcal{S}$ with $\mathcal{L}(L) = \mathcal{L}(\phi_L)$. If L is bonded, then there is an equivalent formula in DCSCTL.* $\Diamond$

$$\phi_\alpha = Hold_L(\alpha, int)\ \mathsf{U}\ \big((Trans_L(\alpha, Scl_1) \wedge \mathsf{X}\,\phi_{Step_L(\alpha, Scl_1)}) \vee \cdots \vee$$
$$(Trans_L(\alpha, Scl_n) \wedge \mathsf{X}\,\phi_{Step_L(\alpha, Scl_n)}) \vee (Exit_L(\alpha) \wedge \mathsf{X}\,\phi_{\alpha_{fin}}) \big)$$

Fig. 5. Schlör formula of the location α shown in Figure 3(a)

By Lemma 1, we can apply Lemma 2 to the automaton $\mathcal{A}_L$ of an LSC, which represents the LSC body. Adding path and variable quantifiers according to the LSC activation mode and quantification completes the proof of the first claim. For example, an LSC $L = (\ell, ac, am, int, quant)$ with $am = invariant$ and $quant = universal$ over a signature $\mathcal{S} = (\{x_1, \ldots, x_n\}, \mathcal{P}, \chi)$ becomes $\phi_L ::= \forall x_1 \ldots \forall x_n \,.\, \mathsf{A}\,\mathsf{G}\,(ac \rightarrow \phi_{\mathcal{A}_L})$. The second claim is established by a result of [19] that transforms the CSCTL formula to the desired DCSCTL form if the transition expressions, here $\psi(q, q')$, are mutually disjoint which is the case by Lemma 1. The finer structure of DCSCTL formulae is obtained by close examination of the construction of the translation relation $\rightsquigarrow$ for $\mathcal{A}_L$. Theorem 1 extends to an LSC specification Lsc by conjoining the formulae of all LSCs in Lsc.

As a first observation, the formula for bonded LSCs is actually in deterministic ACTL, and thus in LTL, as also observed in [15]. They also claim that non-bonded LSCs in their interpretation are in LTL which is not the case for ours as non-bonded LSCs introduce non-determinism via self-loops annotated only with *true*. Restricted to messages, the core LSCs studied here and the kernel LSCs studied in [15] coincide (as expected).

LSCs are strictly weaker than general first-order CTL* as they can't express alternating path quantifiers [15]. The following lemma shows that there are simpler patterns not expressible by core (and kernel) LSCs. Intuitively, core (and kernel) LSCs only consider non-temporal properties as hold-conditions, i.e. before the "until" operator. Thus they can in general not express that some sub-scenario shall be repeated until the main-scenario continues. In contrast to [3], the LSC dialect of [2] provides (bounded and unbounded) loops, so the full version of [15] will show whether that extension is sufficient to make LSCs equivalent to LTL.

Lemma 3. *FOP-CTL* over $\mathcal{S}$ is strictly more expressive than core LSCs.* $\quad \diamond$

Proof. Assume there were an equivalent LSC for the formula $\varphi = (\mathsf{X}\,\mathsf{X}\,p)\,\mathsf{U}\,q$ from the LTL fragment of CTL*. The interpretation sequence $\vec{\imath} = \bar{p}\bar{q}\,\bar{p}\bar{q}\,pq\,p\ldots$ satisfies φ. Then ϕ_L, a formula equivalent to L, has by Theorem 1 a conjunctive term of the form $\mathsf{A}\,(\psi \rightarrow \eta\,\mathsf{U}\,\hat{\pi})$ or $\mathsf{A}\,(\psi \rightarrow \eta\,\mathsf{W}\,\hat{\pi})$ that is satisfied by $\vec{\imath}$. This implies $\bar{p}\bar{q} \rightarrow \psi$ and $\bar{p}\bar{q} \rightarrow \eta$ since ψ and η don't comprise temporal operators. Consequently $\vec{\imath}' \models L$ with $\vec{\imath}' = \bar{p}\bar{q}\,\bar{p}\bar{q}\,\bar{p}\bar{q}\,\bar{p}\bar{q}\ldots$ but $\vec{\imath}' \not\models \varphi$ in contradiction to the equivalence assumption. $\qquad \square$

3.2   ...and Back

Theorem 2. *Let ζ be a DCSCTL formula over signature $\mathcal{S}$. There exists a bonded LSC specification Lsc over $\mathcal{S}$ such that $\mathcal{L}(Lsc) = \mathcal{L}(\zeta)$.* $\quad \diamond$

The constructive proof exploits that ζ is a DCSCTL formula, i.e. has the properties (i)–(iii) from Definition 11. Intuitively, a sub-formula of ζ of the form

$$\pi = \underbrace{\neg\mu}_{\eta} \wedge \psi_1 \,\mathsf{U}\,((\underbrace{\mu \wedge \psi_2}_{\tau} \wedge \mathsf{X}\,\pi_1) \vee \phi)$$

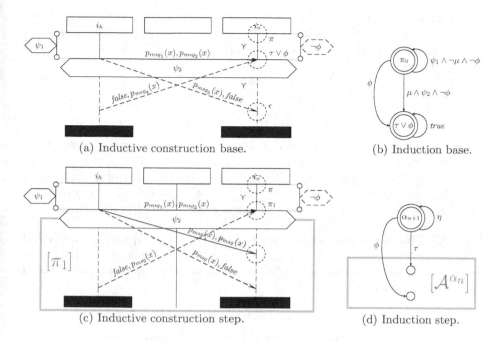

(a) Inductive construction base. (b) Induction base.

(c) Inductive construction step. (d) Induction step.

Fig. 6. Construction of an LSC from a DCSCTL formula and its automaton structure

says that η is supposed to hold until either τ is observed and the (system) run continues as required by π_1, *or* ϕ holds which indicates that the current (system) run exhibits a different message order than the one accepted by π. If this different message order is legal, then there is another sub-formula of ζ that is satisfied by the (system) run. Transferring this intuition to LSCs, we inductively construct a core LSC specification of bonded core LSCs with (for convenience) two instance lines i_h and i_o. Each LSC accepts one particular message order, the atoms are pairs of the instance line name and the sub-formula that is observed up to this location. For example, the instance head atoms are (i_h, π) and (i_o, π).

The expression ψ_1 in π becomes a mandatory local-invariant that is required to hold until τ, one or more messages co-located with a condition ψ_2, is observed, unless a parallel cold local-invariant with expression $\neg\phi$ is violated, indicating that this core LSC can not accept the (system) run (cf. Figure 6(a) and 6(c)).

We omit the (tedious) formal inductive construction, but focus on the proof of language equivalence to the formula.

Proof. Part 2. Without loss of generality we assume that ζ accepts exactly one message order since the general case is a conjunction of such formulae. Let L be the core LSC specification constructed for ζ by the procedure described above. By construction, all instantaneous messages and conditions in L either share all atoms or none, so all simclasses and all consistent cuts (see below) are of the form $\{(i_h, \pi), (i_o, \pi)\}$.

We define the *nesting depth* of a formula by $dep(\eta \, U \, \tau \vee \phi) = 0$ and $dep(\eta \, U \, \tau \wedge \pi \vee \phi) = n + 1$ if $dep(\pi) = n$ with $U \in \{\, U, W \,\}$. There is at most one consistent cut $\{(i_h, \pi), (i_o, \pi)\} \in Cuts(L)$ with $dep(\pi) = n$. A cut is called *consistent* if $\forall a \in \alpha, a' \in [a] \, \exists a'' \in \alpha : a' \prec^* a''$.

Let $\mathcal{A}_L = (Q, q_s, \leadsto, F)$ be the automaton of L. The sequence $(T_n)_{n \in \mathbb{N}_0}$ with $T_n := \{q \in Q \mid dep(q) \leq n \wedge q \text{ consistent}\}$ is monotone. We prove by induction

$$\forall n \in \mathbb{N}_0 \; \forall \alpha_n \in T_n \; \forall \sigma \in Val_{\mathcal{U}}(\mathcal{S}), \; \vec{\imath} \in \overrightarrow{Int_{\mathcal{U}}}(\mathcal{P}) : \vec{\imath} \in \mathcal{L}_\sigma(\mathcal{A}_L^{\alpha_n}) \iff \vec{\imath}, \sigma \models \varphi_{\alpha_n},$$

where $\mathcal{A}_L^q := (Q, q, \leadsto, F)$ is the automaton that coincides with $\mathcal{A}_L$ except for the start location $q \in Q$ and where $\varphi_{\alpha_n} := \pi$ if $\alpha_n = \{(i_h, \pi), (i_o, \pi)\}$.

Let N be the nesting depth of the largest π sub-formula of ζ. Then $\pi = \varphi_{\alpha_N}$. Examining the quantifiers in ζ and in the semantics of L according to Definition 9, we obtain the desired equivalence between L and ζ.

Induction base. T_0 comprises only the cut $\{(i_h, \pi_0), (i_o, \pi_0)\}$ with $\pi_0 = \eta \, W \, (\tau \vee \phi) = (\neg \mu \wedge \psi_1) \, W \, (\mu \wedge \psi_2 \vee \phi)$ (the until ('U') case follows analogously). The automaton $\mathcal{A}_L^{\alpha_0}$ is depicted in Figure 6(b). Its corresponding formula $\phi_{\mathcal{A}_L^{\alpha_0}}$ obtained by the construction of Lemma 2 is

$$\phi_{\mathcal{A}_L^{\alpha_0}} = (\neg \mu \wedge \psi_1 \wedge \neg \phi) \, W \, (\mu \wedge \psi_2 \wedge X \, (true \, W \, false) \vee \phi \wedge X \, (true \, W \, false))$$
$$\iff (\neg \mu \wedge \psi_1 \wedge \neg \phi) \, W \, (\mu \wedge \psi_2 \vee \phi) \iff (\neg \mu \wedge \psi_1) \, W \, (\mu \wedge \psi_2 \vee \phi) = \pi_0.$$

Induction step. Now let $\alpha_{n+1} = \{(i_h, \pi), (i_o, \pi)\} \in T_{n+1}$ with

$$\pi = \eta \, W \, (\tau \wedge X \, (\pi_1) \vee \phi) = (\neg \mu \wedge \psi_1) \, W \, (\mu \wedge \psi_2 \wedge X \, (\pi_1) \vee \phi)$$

('U' case analogously). By construction of $\prec_L$, the only simclass that can possibly be enabled by α_{n+1} is $scl := \{(i_h, \pi_1), (i_o, \pi_1)\}$. It is actually enabled since all its prerequisites are obviously part of α_{n+1} and all the sendings of asynchronous receptions lie strictly before α_{n+1} by definition of DCSCTL (Definition 11.(i)) and construction of L. By definition of the $Step_L$ function, α_{n+1} has a unique successor cut, namely $Step_L(\alpha_{n+1}, \{scl\}) = scl = \alpha_n$ with $dep(\varphi_{\alpha_n}) = n$.

The automaton $\mathcal{A}_L^{\alpha_{n+1}}$ is shown in Figure 6(d). The τ transition leads to the state $Step_L(\alpha_{n+1}, \{scl\})$ which we just identified to lie in T_n and the ϕ transition leads to the final cut that lies in T_0 by definition. Hence we can use the induction hypothesis as follows, where (∗) exploits the style of outgoing transitions of α_{n+1}:

$$\vec{\imath}, \sigma \models \varphi_{\alpha_{n+1}} \leftrightarrow \vec{\imath}, \sigma \models \eta \, W \, (\tau \wedge X \, (\varphi_n) \vee \phi)$$
$$\leftrightarrow \vec{\imath}, \sigma \models G \, (\eta) \vee (\eta \, U \, (\tau \wedge X \, (\varphi_n) \vee \phi))$$
$$\leftrightarrow \forall j \in \mathbb{N}_0 : \vec{\imath}^j \models \eta \vee (\exists k \in \mathbb{N}_0 : (\forall 0 \leq j < k : \vec{\imath}^j, \sigma \models \eta)$$
$$\wedge (\vec{\imath}^{k+1}, \sigma \models \phi \vee \vec{\imath}^{k+1}, \sigma \models \tau \wedge \vec{\imath}/k + 2, \sigma \models \varphi_{\alpha_n}))$$
$$\leftrightarrow (\exists r \in \Pi_\sigma^{\vec{\imath}}(\mathcal{A}_L^{\alpha_{n+1}}) : r = \alpha_{n+1} \, \alpha_{n+1} \, \alpha_{n+1} \cdots$$
$$\vee (\exists \tilde{r} \in \Pi_\sigma^{\vec{\imath}}(\mathcal{A}_L^{\alpha_{fin}(L)}) \, \exists k > 0 : r = \alpha_{n+1}^k \tilde{r} \wedge \inf(\tilde{r}) \cap F \neq \emptyset)$$
$$\vee (\exists \tilde{r} \in \Pi_\sigma^{\vec{\imath}}(\mathcal{A}_L^{\alpha_n}) \, \exists k > 0 : r = \alpha_{n+1}^k \tilde{r} \wedge \inf(\tilde{r}) \cap F \neq \emptyset))$$
$$\overset{(*)}{\leftrightarrow} \exists r \in \Pi_\sigma^{\vec{\imath}}(\mathcal{A}_L^{\alpha_{n+1}}) : \inf(r) \cap F \neq \emptyset \leftrightarrow \vec{\imath} \in \mathcal{L}_\sigma(\mathcal{A}_L^{\alpha_{n+1}}) \qquad \square$$

Recall that intuitively the translation considers single paths through the LSC specification, that is a translation back and forth yields as many LSCs as there are paths through the original ones. Thus the back-translation makes the possible paths and combinations of conditions and local invariants explicitly visible and thus may help in the debugging of LSC specifications. But in presence of concurrency introduced, for instance, by independent parts or coregions, a single original LSC can be exponentially more succinct then the back and forth translation.

4   Conclusion

Our new concise formalisation of the LSCs of [3] makes it possible to compare these LSCs to temporal logic. General core LSCs are at most as powerful as the fragment CSCTL of FOP-CTL* for which we provided a syntactical characterisation. The practically relevant set of *bonded* core LSCs is exactly as powerful as the smaller fragment DCSCTL because we can construct an LSC specification for a given formula. The embedding into first-order prenex CTL* is strict even without resorting to nesting of path quantifiers [15].

These results have a number of applications. Section 3.1 formally justifies the practice of LSC model-checking using formulae [3] and allows to compare both dialects of LSCs that emerged from the original proposal [1]. Section 3.2 provides for the first time an instrument to decide whether a given formula has an equivalent LSC specification. This is useful since experts in formal methods sometimes easier come up with a formula for a given requirement while for discussion within a more general audience it is highly desirable to present the requirement in form of LSCs. Another aspect stems from the observation of [25] that their distributed LTL model-checker performs extraordinarily well on formulae that are a chain of right-nested "Until" operators without noticing that this is exactly the structure of (D)CSCTL. Section 3 would justify a restriction of their input language to (D)CSCTL, thus obtaining an LSC model-checker, and raise the question whether this restriction could yield further speedup. Finally, the fact that we use results from the theory of Symbolic Timing Diagrams [19,22] (STD) raises the question whether STDs also qualify as a scenario language and, for example, whether they can be played out [26].

Further work comprises the extension to the full LSC language of [3], that is, pre-charts, real-time, and possible asynchronous messages, as outlined in the introduction of Section 2.

Acknowledgements. The authors want to express their gratitude to Matthias Brill and Hartmut Wittke for clarifying discussions on the intricacies of LSCs, sharing of expertise, and valuable hints on related literature.

Note. An abridged version of this paper appeared at the SofSem'06 poster session [27].

References

1. Damm, W., Harel, D.: LSCs: Breathing Life into Message Sequence Charts. Formal Methods in System Design **19** (2001) 45–80
2. Harel, D., Marelly, R.: Come, Let's Play: Scenario-Based Programming Using LSCs and the Play-Engine. Springer (2003)
3. Klose, J.: Live Sequence Charts: A Graphical Formalism for the Specification of Communication Behavior. PhD thesis, C. v. O. Universität Oldenburg (2003)
4. Weidenhaupt, K., Pohl, K., Jarke, M., Haumer, P.: Scenarios in system development: Current practice. IEEE Software **15** (1998) 34–45
5. Amyot, D., Eberlein, A.: An evaluation of scenario notations and construction approaches for telecommunication systems development. Telecommunications Systems Journal **24** (2003) 61–94
6. Dwyer, M.B., Avrunin, G.S., Corbett, J.C.: Patterns in property specifications for finite-state verification. In: ICSE'99. Proceedings of the 1999 International Conference on Software Engineering, May 16-22, 1999, Los Angeles, CA, USA., ACM (1999) 411–420
7. Bitsch, F.: Safety patterns - the key to formal specification of safety requirements. In Voges, U., ed.: Computer Safety, Reliability and Security, 20th International Conference, SAFECOMP 2001, Budapest, Hungary, September 26-28, 2001, Proceedings. Volume 2187 of Lecture Notes in Computer Science., Springer (2001) 176–190
8. ITU-T: ITU-T Rec. Z.120: Message Sequence Chart (MSC). ITU-T, Geneva (1999)
9. Knieke, C., Huhn, M., Goltz, U.: Modelling and simulation of an automotive system using LSCs. In Houmb, S.H., Jürjens, J., eds.: Proc. CSDUML'2005, TUM (2005) 0–0 TUM-TR.
10. Combes, P., Harel, D., Kugler, H.: Modeling and verification of a telecommunication application using Live Sequence Charts and the Play-Engine tool. In: Proc. ATVA 2005. Number 3707 in LNCS (2005)
11. Bunker, A., Gopalakrishnan, G., Slind, K.: Live Sequence Charts applied to hardware requirements specification and verification: A VCI bus interface model. Software Tools for Technology Transfer **7** (2004) 341–350
12. Bontemps, Y., Heymans, P., Kugler, H.: Applying LSCs to the specification of an air traffic control system. In: Proc. SCESM'03. (2003)
13. Bohn, J., Damm, W., Wittke, H., Klose, J., Moik, A.: Modelling and validating train system applications using statemate and live sequence charts. In: Proc. IDPT 2002, Society for Design and Process Science (2002)
14. Bontemps, Y.: Relating Inter-Agent and Intra-Agent Specifications. PhD thesis, University of Namur (Belgium) (2005)
15. Kugler, H., Harel, D., Pnueli, A., Lu, Y., Bontemps, Y.: Temporal logic for scenario-based specifications. In Halbwachs, N., Zuck, L.D., eds.: Proc. TACAS 2005. Volume 3440 of LNCS. (2005)
16. Klose, J., Toben, T., Westphal, B., Wittke, H.: Check it out: On the efficient formal verification of Live Sequence Charts. In Ball, T., Jones, R.B., eds.: Proc. CAV 2006. Volume 4144 of Lecture Notes in Computer Science., Springer-Verlag (2006) 219–233
17. Schinz, I., Toben, T., Mrugalla, C., Westphal, B.: The Rhapsody UML Verification Environment. In Cuellar, J.R., Liu, Z., eds.: Proc. SEFM 2004. (2004) 174–183
18. Klose, J., Wittke, H.: An automata based interpretation of Live Sequence Charts. In Margaria, T., Yi, W., eds.: Proc. TACAS 2001. Number 2031 in LNCS (2001) 512–527

19. Schlör, R.C.: Symbolic Timing Diagrams: A Visual Formalism for Model Verification. PhD thesis, C.v.O. Universität Oldenburg (2000)
20. Maidl, M.: The common fragment of ctl and ltl. In: IEEE Symp. on Foundations of Computer Science. (2000) 643–652
21. Westphal, B., Toben, T.: The good, the bad and the ugly: Well-formedness of Live Sequence Charts. In Baresi, L., Heckel, R., eds.: Proc. FASE 2006. Volume 3922 of Lecture Notes in Computer Science., Springer-Verlag (2006) 230–246
22. Feyerabend, K., Josko, B.: A visual formalism for real time requirement specification. In Bertran, M., Rus, T., eds.: Proc. ARTS'97. Volume 1231 of LNCS. (1997) 158–168
23. Klose, J., Westphal, B.: Relating LSC specifications to UML models. In Ehrig, H., Grosse-Rhode, M., eds.: Proc. INT'02. (2002)
24. Damm, W., Westphal, B.: Live and let die: LSC-based verification of UML-models. Science of of Computer Programming **55** (2005) 117–159
25. Barnat, J.: Distributed Memory LTL Model Checking. PhD thesis, Faculty of Informatics, Masaryk University Brno (2004)
26. Harel, D.: personal communication (2005)
27. Toben, T., Westphal, B.: On the expressive power of LSCs. In Wiedermann, J., Tel, G., Pokorný, J., Bieliková, M., Štuller, J., eds.: Proc. SofSem 2006. Volume 2., Institute of Computer Science AS CR, Prague (2006) 33–43

Appendix

Definition 12. *Let L be a core LSC over signature $\mathcal{S}$ and $\alpha, \alpha' \in Cuts(L)$. The cut α' is said to be larger than α, denoted by $\alpha \sqsubset \alpha'$, if and only if*

$$\forall i \in Inst(L) \ \forall a \in \alpha|_i \ \exists a' \in \alpha'|_i :$$

$$a \prec^* a' \wedge \exists i \in Inst(L) : \alpha|_i \subsetneq \alpha'|_i \vee \alpha' \neq \emptyset \wedge \forall a \in \alpha|_i, a' \in \alpha'|_i : a \prec^+ a'.$$

Note that $\sqsubset$ is a strict partial order (irreflexive, asymmetric, and transitive). ◊

Proof of Lemma 1

Part 1. Let $\mathcal{A}_L = (Q, q_s, \leadsto, F)$. We have to prove antisymmetry of $\to^*$, i.e. $(q \to^* q') \wedge (q' \to^* q) \implies q = q'$ for $q, q' \in Q$. Consider the interesting case where $q \neq \alpha_{fin}(L) \neq q'$. Then there is a minimal $n \in \mathbb{N}_0$ such that

$$q_0 \to \cdots \to q_{k-1} \to q_k \to q_{k+1} \to \cdots \to q_n$$

with $q_0 = q_n = q$ and $q_k = q'$ and none of the transitions is a self-loop, i.e. $q_k \neq q_{k+1}$, $0 \leq k < n$.

Also none of the transitions is an exit loop, i.e. a transition annotated by $Exit_L$, since then one of intermediate states were the final cut $\alpha_{fin}(L)$, thus $q = \alpha_{fin}(L)$ by $(*)$ in contradiction to the assumption.

Thus all transitions are by regular transitions defined by $Step_L$, i.e. there are fired-sets $Scl_k \in Ready_L(q_k)$ such that $q_{k+1} = Step_L(q_k, Scl_k)$, $0 \leq k < n$. Since $Step_L$ strictly advances the cut, we have $q_k \sqsubset q_{k+1}$, $0 \leq k < n$ and thus

$$q = q_0 \sqsubset q_1 \sqsubset \cdots \sqsubset q_{n-1} \sqsubset q_n = q$$

in contradiction to the fact that the cut order is a strict partial order.

Part 2. If L is bonded, i.e. $\forall e \in Cond \cup LocInv \; \forall a \in atoms(e) \exists m \in Msg :$ $\kappa(m) = mand \wedge [a] \cap atoms(m) \neq \emptyset$, we have that every simclass Scl contains at least one message send or message receive atom.

To prove determinism of $\mathcal{A}_L$, we have to show for all $\alpha \in Q$

(i) $\models \neg(Hold_L(\alpha, int) \wedge Trans_L(\alpha, , intf))$,

(ii) $\models \neg(Trans_L(\alpha, int, f_1) \wedge Trans_L(\alpha, int, f_2))$,

(iii) $\models \neg(Hold_L(\alpha, int) \wedge Exit_L(\alpha, int))$, and

(iv) $\models \neg(Exit_L(\alpha, int) \wedge Trans_L(\alpha, int, f))$

for arbitrary $f, f_1, f_2 \in Ready_L(\alpha)$ with $f_1 \neq f_2$. Most of the cases can be proved by exploiting the observation that $\models \neg(A_{\{Scl\}} \wedge N_{\{Scl\}})$ if $Msg_{snd}(Scl) \cup Msg_{rcv}(Scl) \neq \emptyset$. In the other cases, the condition and local invariant expressions ensure the mutual disjointness of the transition predicates. $\qquad\square$

Refinement-Based Verification for Possibly-Cyclic Lists*

Alexey Loginov[1],**, Thomas Reps[2], and Mooly Sagiv[3]

[1] IBM T.J. Watson Research Center
alexey@us.ibm.com
[2] Comp. Sci. Dept., University of Wisconsin
reps@cs.wisc.edu
[3] School of Comp. Sci., Tel-Aviv University
msagiv@post.tau.ac.il

Abstract. In earlier work, we presented an abstraction-refinement mechanism that was successful in verifying automatically the partial correctness of *in-situ* list reversal when applied to an acyclic linked list [10]. This paper reports on the automatic verification of the *total correctness* (partial correctness and termination) of the same list-reversal algorithm, when applied to a *possibly-cyclic* linked list. A key contribution that made this result possible is an extension of the *finite-differencing* technique [14] to enable the maintenance of reachability information for a restricted class of possibly-cyclic data structures, which includes possibly-cyclic linked lists.

1 Introduction

Reinhard Wilhelm has long been associated with the Dagstuhl Seminars on Computer Science. In March of 2003, the Dagstuhl Seminar "Reasoning about Shape" was dedicated to one of the subjects that benefited from important contributions on the part of Reinhard Wilhelm. During that seminar, Richard Bornat posed an interesting challenge problem to the authors. The challenge concerns the application of the *in-situ* list reversal procedure `Reverse` to a *panhandle list*, i.e., a linked list that contains a cycle but in which at least the head of the list is not part of the cycle. (The lists shown in Fig. 1 are examples of panhandle lists.) Richard Bornat challenged us to use our techniques to demonstrate that, when applied to a panhandle list, `Reverse` produces a list in which the orientation of the successor edges in the panhandle (the acyclic part of the list) is as it was in the input list, while the orientation of the successor edges on the cycle is reversed.

In [10], we presented an abstraction-refinement mechanism for use in static analyses based on 3-valued logic [17], where the semantics of statements and the query of interest are expressed using logical formulas. Our abstraction-refinement mechanism introduces additional *instrumentation relations* (defined via logical formulas over *core relations*, which capture the basic properties of memory configurations). Instrumentation relations record auxiliary information in a logical structure, thus providing a mechanism to fine-tune an abstraction: an instrumentation relation captures a property that

---

* Supported by ONR (N00014-01-1-{0708,0796}) and NSF (CCR-9986308 and CCF-{0524051,0540955}).
** The work was performed while Loginov was at the University of Wisconsin.

T. Reps, M. Sagiv, and J. Bauer (Eds.): Wilhelm Festschrift, LNCS 4444, pp. 247–272, 2007.

an individual memory cell may or may not possess. In general, the introduction of additional instrumentation relations refines an abstraction into one that is prepared to track finer distinctions among stores. This allows more properties of the program's stores to be identified. The abstraction-refinement mechanism made possible the automatic verification of a number of interesting properties, including the partial correctness of *in-situ* list reversal when applied to an *acyclic* linked list.

In our context, the semantics of statements is expressed using logical formulas that describe changes to core-relation values. When instrumentation relations have been introduced to refine an abstraction, the challenge is to reflect the changes in core-relation values in the values of the instrumentation relations. To address this challenge, the authors presented *finite differencing*, a technique that constructs automatically *instrumentation-relation maintenance formulas*, the part of abstract transformers that deals with instrumentation relations [14].

A key aspect of the finite-differencing technique is its handling of reachability instrumentation relations, i.e., relations defined via the transitive-closure operator. In [14], we adapted a result by Dong and Su [2] to enable the maintenance of reachability information for acyclic data structures purely in first-order logic, i.e., without the recomputation of transitive closure, which generally results in a loss of precision.

In this paper, we reduce the problem of reachability maintenance for possibly-cyclic lists, e.g., panhandle lists, to the problem of reachability maintenance in acyclic data structures. The essential problem is that all nodes in the cyclic part of a panhandle list "look the same" in some sense, and the key to a solution is finding a way to break the symmetry of the cycle. (This is discussed further in §3.) The key idea—inspired by a similar idea used by William Hesse in his Ph.D. thesis—is to "break" each cycle: we define a binary instrumentation relation sfe_n to include all edges of the data structure, except one designated edge on each cycle. We define an additional instrumentation relation, sfp_n, to be the reflexive transitive closure of the acyclic relation sfe_n.[1] The relation sfp_n can be maintained using our prior results for acyclic reachability maintenance. Reachability information in the actual (possibly-cyclic) data structure can then be computed based on sfp_n.

This reduction addresses the shortcoming of finite differencing that prevented our techniques from establishing interesting properties of programs that manipulate possibly-cyclic linked lists. We show that, equipped with the extended finite-differencing technique, the abstraction-refinement mechanism is capable of introducing instrumentation relations that are sufficient to encode the key properties of `Reverse` when applied to possibly-cyclic linked lists. The contributions of this paper can be summarized as follows:

- We present an extension of finite differencing that allows first-order-logic maintenance of reachability information in possibly-cyclic linked lists. This is achieved via a reduction to the problem of reachability maintenance in acyclic data structures.
- We demonstrate the use of a *Data-Structure Constructor* for constructing an abstract representation of all possibly-cyclic linked lists, including panhandle lists.

---

[1] As discussed later, sfe_n and sfp_n stand for "spanning-forest edge" and "spanning-forest path", respectively.

- We demonstrate the use of automatic abstraction refinement for introducing the instrumentation relations that are sufficient for verifying the partial correctness of `Reverse` when applied to any possibly-cyclic linked list.
- We present a simple progress monitor that allows the analysis to establish the termination of `Reverse` on any possibly-cyclic linked list.

The contributions fall into two categories: (i) extending the scope of finite differencing so that reachability information can be maintained for possibly-cyclic lists, and (ii) the application of abstraction refinement for verifying properties of `Reverse`. The former contribution category is discussed in §3. The latter contribution category is discussed in §6.

An advantage of our abstract-interpretation approach is that it does not require the use of a theorem prover. This is particularly beneficial in our setting because our logic is undecidable [5].

2   Program Analysis Using 3-Valued Logic

In this section, we give a brief overview of the framework of parametric shape analysis via 3-valued logic. For more details, the reader is referred to [17].

Program states are represented using *first-order logical structures*,

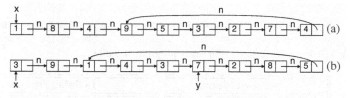

Fig. 1. Possible stores for *panhandle* linked lists. (a) A panhandle list pointed to by x. We will refer to lists of this shape as type-*X* lists. (b) A panhandle list pointed to by x with y pointing into the middle of the cycle. We will refer to lists of this shape as type-*XY* lists.

which consist of a collection of *individuals*, together with an *interpretation* for a finite vocabulary of finite-arity relation symbols, $\mathcal{R}$. An interpretation is a truth-value assignment for each relation symbol for every appropriate-arity tuple of individuals. To ensure termination, the framework puts a bound on the number of distinct logical structures that can arise during analysis by grouping individuals that are indistinguishable according to a special subset of unary relations, $\mathcal{A}$. The grouping of nodes is referred to as *canonical abstraction* and the set $\mathcal{A}$ is referred to as the set of *abstraction relations*.

The application of canonical abstraction typically transforms a logical structure S into a *3-valued logical structure* $S^{\#}$, in which the third value, $1/2$, denotes the possibility of having either 0 (false) or 1 (true) in S. A program state is updated and queried via logical formulas, which are interpreted over the 3-valued structure $S^{\#}$ using a straightforward extension of Kleene's 2-valued semantics.

Because of canonical abstraction, an individual in a 3-valued structure can represent more than one individual in a given 2-valued structure; such an individual is referred to as a *summary individual*. In general, a 3-valued logical structure can represent an infinite set of 2-valued structures.

Table 1. (a) Declaration of a linked-list datatype in C; (b) core relations used for representing the stores manipulated by programs that use type List

```
typedef struct node {
    struct node *n;
    int data;
} *List;
```

Relation	Intended Meaning
$x(v)$	Does pointer variable x point to memory cell v?
$n(v_1, v_2)$	Does the n field of v_1 point to v_2?

(a)   (b)

Program states are encoded in terms of *core relations*, $C \subseteq R$. Core relations are part of the underlying semantics of the language to be analyzed; they record atomic properties of stores. For instance, Tab. 1 gives the definition of a C linked-list datatype, and lists the core relations that would be used to represent the stores manipulated by programs that use type List, such as the stores in Fig. 1. Unary relations represent pointer variables, and binary relation n represents the n field of a List cell. Fig. 2(a) shows 2-valued structure S_2, which represents the store of Fig. 1(a) using the relations of Tab. 1.

Table 2. Defining formulas of instrumentation relations commonly employed in analyses of programs that use type List. The relation name is_n abbreviates "is-shared". There is a separate reachability relation $r_{n,x}$ for every program variable x.

p	Intended Meaning	Defining Formula
$is_n(v)$	Do n fields of two or more list nodes point to v?	$\exists v_1, v_2 : n(v_1, v) \wedge n(v_2, v) \wedge v_1 \neq v_2$
$r_{n,x}(v)$	Is v reachable from pointer variable x along n fields?	$\exists v_1 : x(v_1) \wedge n^*(v_1, v)$
$c_n(v)$	Is v on a directed cycle of n fields?	$n^+(v, v)$

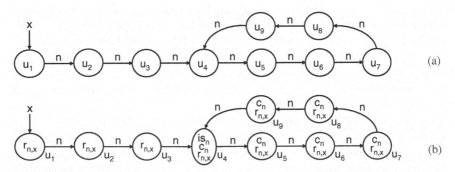

Fig. 2. A logical structure S_2 that represents the store shown in Fig. 1(a) in graphical form: (a) S_2 with relations of Tab. 1; (b) S_2 with relations of Tabs. 1 and 2

The abstraction function on which an analysis is based, and hence the precision of the analysis defined, can be tuned by (i) choosing to equip structures with additional *instrumentation relations* to record derived properties, and (ii) varying which of the unary core and unary instrumentation relations are used as the set of abstraction relations. The set of instrumentation relations is denoted by $\mathcal{I}$. Each arity-k relation symbol is defined by an *instrumentation-relation defining formula* with k free variables. Instrumentation-relation symbols may appear in the defining formulas of other instrumentation relations as long as there are no circular dependences.

Tab. 2 lists some instrumentation relations that are important for the analysis of programs that use type `List`. Instrumentation relations that involve reachability properties, such as relation $r_{n,x}(v)$, often play a crucial role in the definitions of abstractions. These relations have the effect of keeping disjoint sublists summarized separately. Fig. 2(b) shows 2-valued structure S_2, which represents the store of Fig. 1(a) using the core relations of Tab. 1, as well as the instrumentation relations of Tab. 2.

If all unary relations are abstraction relations, the canonical abstraction of 2-valued logical structure S_2 is S_3, shown in Fig. 3, with list nodes corresponding to u_2 and u_3 in S_2 represented by the summary individual u_2 of S_3 and list nodes corresponding to $u_5, \ldots, u_9$ in S_2 represented by the summary individual u_4 of S_3. S_3 represents any type-X panhandle list with at least two nodes in the panhandle and at least two nodes in the cycle. The following graphical notation is used for depicting 3-valued logical structures:

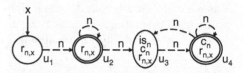

Fig. 3. A 3-valued structure S_3 that is the canonical abstraction of structure S_2. In addition to S_2, S_3 represents any type-X panhandle list with at least two nodes in the panhandle and at least two nodes in the cycle.

– Individuals are represented by circles containing (non-0) values for unary relations. Summary individuals are represented by double circles.
– A unary relation p corresponding to a pointer-valued program variable is represented by a solid arrow from p to the individual u for which $p(u) = 1$, and by the absence of a p-arrow to each node u' for which $p(u') = 0$. (If $p = 0$ for all individuals, the relation name p is not shown.)
– A binary relation q is represented by a solid arrow labeled q between each pair of individuals u_i and u_j for which $q(u_i, u_j) = 1$, and by the absence of a q-arrow between pairs u'_i and u'_j for which $q(u'_i, u'_j) = 0$.
– Relations with value $1/2$ are represented by dotted arrows.

For each kind of statement in the programming language, the concrete semantics is defined by *relation-update formulas* for core relations. The structure transformers for the abstract semantics are defined by the same relation-update formulas for core relations and *relation-maintenance formulas* for instrumentation relations. The latter are generated automatically via *finite differencing* [14]. Abstract interpretation collects a set of 3-valued structures at each program point. It is implemented as an iterative procedure that finds the least fixed point of a certain set of equations [17]. When the fixed point is reached, the structures that have been collected at a program point describe a superset of all the execution states that can arise there.

Not all logical structures represent admissible stores. To exclude structures that do not, we impose integrity constraints. For instance, relation $x(v)$ of Tab. 1 captures whether pointer variable x points to memory cell v; x would be given the attribute "unique", which imposes the integrity constraint that x can hold for at most one individual in any structure: $\forall v_1, v_2 : x(v_1) \wedge x(v_2) \Rightarrow v_1 = v_2$. This formula evaluates to 1 in any 2-valued logical structure that corresponds to an admissible store. Integrity constraints contribute to the concretization function (γ) for our abstraction [18]. Integrity constraints are enforced by *coerce*, a clean-up operation that may "sharpen" a 3-valued logical structure by setting an indefinite value $(1/2)$ to a definite value (0 or 1), or discard a structure entirely if an integrity constraint is definitely violated by the structure (e.g., if the structure cannot represent any admissible store).

3   Reachability Maintenance in Possibly-Cyclic Linked Lists

Unfortunately, the relations defined in Tabs. 1 and 2 do not permit precise maintenance of reachability information, such as relation $r_{n,x}$, in possibly-cyclic lists. A difficulty arises when reachability information has to be updated to reflect the deletion of an n edge on a cycle (e.g., as a result of statement y->n = NULL). With the relations defined in Tabs. 1 and 2, such an update requires the recomputation of a transitive-closure formula, which generally results in a drastic loss of precision in the presence of abstraction.

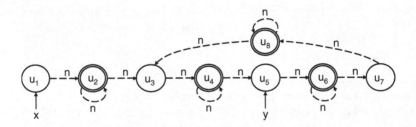

Fig. 4. Logical structure S_4 that represents type-XY panhandle lists, such as the store of Fig. 1(b). The relations of Tab. 2 are omitted to reduce clutter. Their values are as expected for a type-XY list: $r_{n,x}$ holds for all nodes, $r_{n,y}$ and c_n hold for all nodes on the cycle, and is_n holds for u_3.

We demonstrate the issue on panhandle lists represented by the abstract structure S_4 shown in Fig. 4, i.e., lists of type XY. Statement y->n = NULL has the effect of deleting the n edge leaving u_5, thus making the nodes represented by u_6, u_7, and u_8 unreachable from x.[2] Note that a first-order-logic formula over the relations of Tabs. 1 and 2 cannot distinguish the list nodes represented by u_4 from those represented by u_6, u_7, and u_8: all of those nodes are reachable from both x and y, none of those nodes are shared, and all of them lie on a cycle. Our inability to characterize the group of nodes represented by u_4 via a first-order formula requires the maintenance formula for the reachability relation $r_{n,x}$ to recompute some transitive-closure information, e.g., the transitive-closure subformula of the definition of $r_{n,x}$, namely, $n^*(v_1, v)$. However, in the presence of abstraction, recomputing transitive-closure formulas often

---

[2] Clearly, all nodes except u_5 also become unreachable from y.

yields $1/2$. For instance, in S_4, formula $n^*(v_1, v)$ evaluates to $1/2$ under the assignment $[v_1 \mapsto u_1, v \mapsto u_4]$ because of the many $1/2$ values of relation n (see the dashed edges connecting u_1 with u_2, for example).

The essence of a solution that enables maintaining reachability relations for possibly-cyclic lists in first-order logic is to find a way to break the symmetry of each cycle. The basic idea for a solution was suggested to us by William Hesse and Neil Immerman. It consists of maintaining a spanning-tree representation of a possibly-cyclic list. Reachability in such a representation can be maintained using first-order-logic formulas. Reachability in the actual list can be expressed in first-order logic based on the spanning-tree representation. We now explain our approach and highlight some differences with the approach taken by Hesse [4].

Our approach relies on the introduction of additional core and instrumentation relations. We extend the set of core relations (Tab. 1) with unary relation roc_n, which designates one node on each cycle to be the representative of the cycle. (We refer to such a node as a roc_n node.) Relation roc_n is used for tracking a unique *cut edge* on each cycle, which allows the maintenance of a spanning tree. Fig. 5(a) shows 2-valued structure S_5, which represents the store of Fig. 1(a) using the extended set of core relations. Here, we let u_7 be the roc_n node. In general, we simply require that exactly one node on each cycle be designated as a roc_n node. Later in this section we describe how we ensure this.

Tab. 3 lists the extended set of instrumentation relations. Note that relation roc_n is not part of the semantics of the language. A natural question is whether $roc_n(v)$ can be defined as an instrumentation relation. For instance, we can try to define it using the following defining formula:

$$c_n(v) \land \exists v_1 \colon n(v_1, v) \land \neg c_n(v_1) \tag{1}$$

Formula (1) identifies nodes that lie on a cycle but have a predecessor that does not. There are three problems with this approach. First, this definition works for panhandle lists but not for cyclic lists without a panhandle. (In general, no other definition can work for cyclic lists without a panhandle because if one existed, it would need to choose one list node among identical-looking nodes that lie on each cycle.) Second, because the cyclicity relation c_n is defined in terms of roc_n (and sfp_n), the definition of roc_n has a circular dependence, which is disallowed. (This circularity cannot be avoided, if we want all reachability relations to benefit from the precise maintenance of one transitive-closure relation—here, sfp_n.) The third problem with introducing roc_n as an instrumentation relation is discussed later in the section (in footnote 3).

We divide our description of the abstraction based on the new set of relations into three parts, which describe (i) how the relations of Tab. 3 define *directed* spanning forests, (ii) how we maintain precision on a cycle in the presence of abstraction, and (iii) how we generate maintenance formulas for instrumentation relations *automatically*. The three parts highlight the differences between our approach and that of Hesse.

Defining Directed Spanning Forests. Instrumentation relation sfe_n—*sfe* stands for spanning-forest edge—is used to maintain the set of edges that form a spanning forest of list nodes. In Hesse's work, the spanning-forest edges retain the direction of the n edges. As a result, he maintains spanning forests, in which the edges lead to the roots of

Table 3. Defining formulas of instrumentation relations. The sharing relation is_n is defined as in Tab. 2. Relations $r_{n,x}$ and c_n are redefined via first-order-logic formulas in terms of other relations.

p	Intended Meaning	Defining Formula
$is_n(v)$	Do n fields of two or more list nodes point to v?	$\exists v_1, v_2 \colon n(v_1, v) \wedge n(v_2, v) \wedge v_1 \neq v_2$
$sfe_n(v_1, v_2)$	Is there an n edge from v_2 to v_1 (assuming that v_2 is not a roc_n node)	$n(v_2, v_1) \wedge \neg roc_n(v_2)$
$sfp_n(v_1, v_2)$	Is v_2 reachable from v_1 along sfe_n edges?	$sfe_n^*(v_1, v_2)$
$t_n(v_1, v_2)$	Is v_2 reachable from v_1 along n fields?	$sfp_n(v_2, v_1) \vee$ $\exists u, w \colon \begin{pmatrix} sfp_n(u, v_1) \wedge \\ roc_n(u) \wedge n(u, w) \\ \wedge sfp_n(v_2, w) \end{pmatrix}$
$r_{n,x}(v)$	Is v reachable from pointer variable x along n fields?	$\exists v_1 \colon x(v_1) \wedge t_n(v_1, v)$
$c_n(v)$	Is v on a directed cycle of n fields?	$\exists v_1, v_2 \colon roc_n(v_1) \wedge n(v_1, v_2)$ $\wedge sfp_n(v, v_2)$
$pr_x(v)$	Does v lie on an sfe_n path from x (does v precede x on an n-path to a roc_n node)?	$\exists v_1 \colon x(v_1) \wedge sfp_n(v_1, v)$
$pr_{is}(v)$	Does v lie on an sfe_n path from a shared node (does v precede a shared node on an n-path to a roc_n node)?	$\exists v_1 \colon is_n(v_1) \wedge sfp_n(v_1, v)$

the spanning forest, which are designated as roc_n nodes in our abstraction. For clarity of presentation, we define sfe_n to be the reverse of n edges (all but the edges leaving roc_n nodes). The graph defined by the sfe_n relation then defines a *directed* spanning forest with roc_n nodes as spanning-forest roots and with the usual orientation of spanning-forest edges.

Instrumentation relation sfp_n—*sfp* stands for spanning-forest **p**ath—is used to maintain the set of paths in the spanning forest of list nodes. Binary reachability in the actual lists (see relation t_n in Tab. 3) can be defined in terms of n, roc_n, and sfp_n using a first-order-logic formula: v_2 is reachable from v_1 if there is a spanning-forest path from v_2 to v_1 or there is a pair of spanning-forest paths, one from the source of a cut edge (a roc_n node) to v_1 and the other from v_2 to the target of the cut edge (the n-successor of the same roc_n node).

Unary reachability relations $r_{n,x}$ and the cyclicity relation c_n can be defined via first-order formulas, as well. We defined $r_{n,x}$ in terms of binary reachability relation t_n. While we could define c_n in terms of t_n, as well, we chose another simple definition by observing that a node lies on a cycle if and only if there is a spanning-forest path from it to the target of a cut edge (the n-successor of a roc_n node).

Fig. 5(b) shows 2-valued structure S_5, which represents the store of Fig. 1(a) using the extended set of core and instrumentation relations. The relations pr_x and pr_{is} will be explained shortly.

Preserving Node Ordering on a Cycle in the Presence of Abstraction. The fact that our techniques need to be applicable in the presence of abstraction introduces a

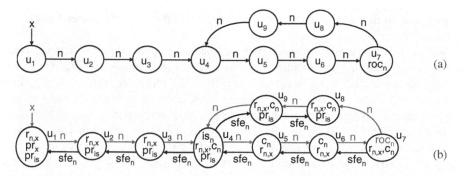

(a)

(b)

Fig. 5. A logical structure S_5 that represents the store shown in Fig. 1(a) in graphical form: (a) S_5 with the extended set of core relations.(b) S_5 with the extended set of core and instrumentation relations (core relations appear in grey). Transitive-closure relations sfp_n and t_n have been omitted to reduce clutter. The values of the transitive-closure relations can be readily seen from the graphical representation of relations sfe_n and n. For instance, node u_5 is related via the sfp_n relation to itself and all nodes appearing to the left or above it in the pictorial representation.

complication that is not present in the setting studied by Hesse. His concern was with the expressibility of certain properties within the confines of a logic with certain syntactic restrictions. Our concern is with the ability to maintain precision in the framework of canonical abstraction.

Unary reachability relations $r_{n,x}$ (one for every program variable x) play a crucial role in the analysis of programs that manipulate acyclic linked lists. In addition to keeping disjoint lists summarized separately, they keep list nodes that have been visited during a traversal summarized separately from nodes that have not been visited: if x is the pointer used to traverse the list, then the nodes that have been visited will have value 0 for relation $r_{n,x}$,

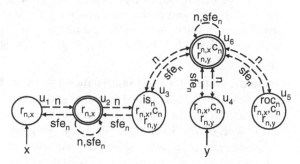

Fig. 6. A 3-valued structure S_6 that is the canonical abstraction of structure S_4 if relations pr_x and pr_{is} are not added to $\mathcal{A}$ and node u_7 is the roc_n node

while the nodes that have not been visited will have value 1. If a list contains a cycle, then all nodes on the cycle are reachable from the same set of variables, namely, all variables that point to any node in that list. As a result, the instrumentation relations discussed thus far cannot prevent nodes u_4, u_6, and u_8 of S_4 shown in Fig. 4 from being summarized together. Thus, assuming that u_7 is the roc_n node, the canonical abstraction of S_4 is the 3-valued structure S_6 shown in Fig. 6. The nodes represented by u_4, u_6, and u_8 of S_4 are represented by the single summary individual u_6 in S_6. The symmetry hides all information about the order of traversal via pointer variable y. Moreover, the values of the sfp_n relation (not shown in Fig. 6) lose precision because ancestors of the shared node in the spanning tree are summarized together with its descendants in the spanning tree.

We break the symmetry of the nodes on a cycle using a general mechanism via unary properties akin to unary reachability relations $r_{n,x}$. In the definitions of relations pr_x of Tab. 3, full reachability (relation t_n) has been replaced with spanning-forest reachability (relation sfp_n). The relations pr_x distinguish nodes according to whether or not they are reachable from program variable x along spanning-forest edges. The relation pr_{is} is defined similarly but using instrumentation relation is_n; pr_{is} partitions the nodes of a panhandle list into ancestors and descendants of the shared node in the spanning tree. Fig. 7 shows structure S_7 that is the canonical abstraction of S_4 of Fig. 4, assuming that u_7 is the roc_n node. In S_7, each of the nodes u_4, u_6, and u_8 has a distinct vector of values for the relations pr_y and pr_{is}, thus breaking the symmetry.

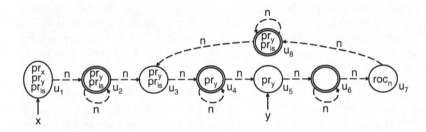

Fig. 7. A 3-valued structure S_7 that is the canonical abstraction of structure S_4 if node u_7 is the roc_n node. S_7 represents panhandle lists of type XY, such as the store of Fig. 1(b). The only instrumentation relations shown in the figure are pr_x, pr_y, and pr_{is}. As in structure S_4 shown in Fig. 4, $r_{n,x}$ holds for all nodes, $r_{n,y}$ and c_n hold for all nodes on the cycle, and is_n holds for u_3.

Automatic Generation of Maintenance Formulas for Instrumentation Relations. In his thesis, Hesse gives hand-specified update formulas for a collection of relations that are used for maintaining a spanning-forest representation of possibly-cyclic linked lists. Instead of specifying them by hand, we rely on finite differencing to generate relation-maintenance formulas for all instrumentation relations. Finite-differencing-generated maintenance formulas have been effective in maintaining all relations defined via first-order-logic formulas, i.e., all relations of Tab. 3 except sfp_n. Additionally, under certain conditions, finite-differencing-generated maintenance formulas have been effective in maintaining relations defined via the reflexive transitive closure of binary relations. The necessary conditions for this technique to be applicable for the maintenance of relation sfp_n are:

Acyclicity condition: The graph defined by sfe_n needs to be acyclic;
Unit-size-change condition: The change to the graph effected by any program statement needs to be a single-edge addition or deletion (but not both).

The acyclicity condition applies in our setting because the graph defined by sfe_n defines a spanning forest. The unit-size-change condition requires some discussion.

The relation sfe_n is defined in terms of n and roc_n. While we have not yet discussed the relation-update formulas for core relation roc_n, it should be clear that the value of the relation roc_n should only change in response to a change in the value of a node's n field. There are two types of statements that change the value of the n field and thus may have an effect that should be reflected in the value of the sfe_n relation, namely, statements of the forms x->n = NULL and x->n = y. The former destroys the n edge leaving the node pointed to by x, and the latter creates a new n-connection from the node pointed to by x to the node pointed to by y. While both of these statements add or remove a single edge of the n relation, it is not necessarily the case that they add or remove a single edge of the sfe_n relation. When interpreted on logical structure S_7 of Fig. 7, statement y->n = NULL has the effect of deleting the n edge leaving u_5, an action that should result in the deletion of the sfe_n edge entering u_5 (not shown in the figure). However, to preserve the spanning-forest representation, we need to ensure that roc_n holds only for nodes that lie on a cycle and that sfe_n represents spanning-forest edges. This requires setting the value of roc_n for u_7 to 0 and adding an sfe_n edge from u_8 to u_7. Because, as this example illustrates, a language statement may result in the deletion of one sfe_n edge and the addition of another, our technique for maintaining instrumentation relations defined via the transitive-closure operator does not apply.

To work around this problem, we apply each transformer associated with statements x->n = NULL and x->n = y in two phases. In one phase, we apply the part of the transformer that corresponds to the relation n and reflect it in the values of all instrumentation relations. In the other phase, we apply the part of the transformer that corresponds to the relation roc_n and reflect it in the values of all instrumentation relations. As we explain below, each phase of the two transformers satisfies the requirement that the change adds a single edge or removes a single edge of the sfe_n relation.[3] Additionally, by paying attention to the order of phases, we ensure that the graph defined by the relation sfe_n remains acyclic throughout the application of the transformers.

To preserve the acyclicity condition in the case of statement x->n = NULL, we apply the part of the transformer that corresponds to the relation n first:

$$n'(v_1, v_2) = n(v_1, v_2) \land \neg x(v_1). \tag{2}$$

Unless x points to a roc_n node (or x->n is NULL), this phase results in the deletion of the sfe_n edge that enters the node pointed to by x. In the second phase, we apply the part of the transformer that corresponds to the relation roc_n:

$$roc'_n(v) = roc_n(v) \land \exists v_1 : n(v, v_1) \land sfp_n(v, v_1) \tag{3}$$

This phase sets the roc_n property of the source n_s of a cut edge to 0, if there is no longer a spanning-forest path from n_s to the target n_t of the same cut edge. When this happens and x does not point to n_s, i.e., the cut edge is not being deleted, this phase results in the addition of an sfe_n edge from n_t to n_s.

To preserve the acyclicity condition in the case of statement x->n = y, we apply the part of the transformer that corresponds to the relation roc_n first:

$$roc'_n(v) = roc_n(v) \lor (x(v) \land \exists v_1 : y(v_1) \land sfp_n(v, v_1)) \tag{4}$$

---

[3] The third problem with defining roc_n as an instrumentation relation (alluded to earlier in the section) is that we would lose the ability to apply the two parts of a transformer separately: the change in the values of n would immediately trigger a change in the values of roc_n. The resulting transformer would not be able to satisfy the unit-size-change condition.

If there is a spanning-forest path from node n_x, pointed to by x, to node n_y, pointed to by y, the statement creates a new cycle in the data structure. The update of Formula (4) sets the roc_n property of n_x to 1, thus making n_x the source of a new cut edge and n_y the target of the cut edge. Because there was no n edge from n_x to n_y prior to the execution of this statement,[4] this phase results in no change to the sfe_n relation. In the second phase, we apply the part of the transformer that corresponds to the relation n:

$$n'(v_1, v_2) = n(v_1, v_2) \vee (x(v_1) \wedge y(v_2)) \tag{5}$$

Unless the node pointed to by x became a roc_n node in the first phase, this phase results in the addition of an sfe_n edge from n_y to n_x.

The break-up of the transformers corresponding to statements x->n = NULL and x->n = y into two phases, as described above, ensures that the sfe_n relation remains acyclic throughout the analysis (the acyclicity condition) and that the change to the sfe_n relation effected by each phase is a unit-size change (the unit-size-change condition).[5] Thus, it is sound to maintain sfp_n ($= sfe_n^*$) via the techniques described in [14]. Additionally, it is also sound to maintain the remaining instrumentation relations via those techniques because the remaining relations are defined by first-order-logic formulas. Soundness guarantees that the stored values of instrumentation relations agree with the relations' defining formulas throughout the analysis. However, the stored values may not agree with the relations' *intended meanings*. For instance, if the n-transfer phase of the transformer for statement x->n = NULL removes a non-cut n edge on a cycle, the sfe_n relation will temporarily not span the entire list. However, as long as we do not query the results of abstract interpretation between the phases of a two-phase transformer, the stored values of instrumentation relations agree with the relations' intended meanings, as well as their defining formulas.

Optimized Maintenance of Relation sfp_n. By demonstrating that the acyclicity and unit-size-change conditions hold for relation sfe_n, we were able to rely on the techniques of [14] to maintain the relation sfp_n. Note, however, that the definition of sfe_n ensures that the graph defined by sfe_n is not only acyclic but is tree-shaped. This knowledge has no bearing on the maintenance formulas that reflect a positive unit-size change $\Delta^+[sfe_n]$ to the sfe_n relation in the values of the sfp_n relation (see [14, Formula 8]). However, it allows a negative unit-size change $\Delta^-[sfe_n]$ to the sfe_n relation to be reflected in the values of the sfp_n relation in a more efficient manner. In a tree-shaped graph, there exists at most one path between a pair of nodes; if that path goes through the sfe_n edge to be deleted, it should be removed (cf. [14, Formula 10]):

$$sfp'_n(v_1, v_2) = sfp_n(v_1, v_2) \\ \wedge \neg(\exists v'_1, v'_2 : sfp_n(v_1, v'_1) \wedge \Delta^-[sfe_n](v'_1, v'_2) \wedge sfp_n(v'_2, v_2)). \tag{6}$$

---

[4] By normalizing procedures to include a statement of the form x->n = NULL prior to a statement of the form x->n = y, we ensure that x->n is always NULL prior to the latter assignment.

[5] Ensuring the unit-size-change condition requires answering a question that is in general undecidable. However, we found that a conservative approximation based on a syntactic analysis of logical formulas suffices for the types of analyses we have performed so far [14].

We extended our finite-differencing technique with the optimized schema for maintaining the transitive closure of a tree-shaped binary relation in response to a negative unit-size change in the relation. We will refer to the method of [14] as *acyclic-sfe$_n$ maintenance* and the optimized method as *tree-shaped-sfe$_n$ maintenance*.

4   Expressing Properties of Transformations

When discussing properties of Reverse, we are interested in making assertions that compare the state of a store at the end of the procedure with its state at the start. For instance, we may be interested in checking that all tree nodes reachable from variable x at the start of the procedure are guaranteed to be reachable from x at the end. To allow the user to make such assertions, we double the vocabulary: for each relation p, we extend the program-analysis specification with a *history* relation, p^0, which serves as an indelible record of the state of the store at the entry point. We will use the term history relations to refer to the latter kind of relations, and the term *active* relations to refer to the relations from the original vocabulary. We can now express the property mentioned above:

$$\forall v\colon r_{n,x}(v) \Leftrightarrow r_{n,x}^0(v). \tag{7}$$

If Formula (7) evaluates to 1, then the elements reachable from x after the procedure executes are exactly the same as those reachable at the beginning of the procedure.

In addition to history relations, we introduce a collection of nullary instrumentation relations that track whether active relations have changed from their initial values. For each active relation $p(v_1, \ldots, v_k)$, the relation $same_p()$ is defined by formula $\forall v_1, \ldots, v_k\colon p(v_1, \ldots, v_k) \Leftrightarrow p^0(v_1, \ldots, v_k)$. We can now use $same_{r_{n,x}}()$ in place of Formula (7). Additionally, we introduce a unary relation ch_n which tracks the changes to the sole binary core relation, n. The relation ch_n is defined by the formula $ch_n(v) = \neg \forall v_1\colon n(v, v_1) \Leftrightarrow n^0(v, v_1)$; it is *not* part of the set of abstraction relations, $\mathcal{A}$.

5   In-Situ List-Reversal Algorithm

Fig. 8 shows the list-reversal algorithm that we analyze. The algorithm performs the reversal in place using three pointer variables, x, y, and t. The n field of list nodes is reversed on lines [7] and [8]. During the execution of the statements on those lines, x points to the next node to be processed, y points to the node whose n field is reversed, and t points to the predecessor of that node.

First, let us consider how Reverse processes an acyclic list L_a with head u_1, pointed to by x. Fig. 9 shows a logical structure S_9 that represents a store that arises before line [7] during the application of Reverse to L_a. At this

```
[1]    void reverse(List *x)
[2]    { List *y = NULL;
[3]        while (x != NULL) {
[4]            t = y;
[5]            y = x;
[6]            x = x->n;
[7]            y->n = NULL;
[8]            y->n = t;
[9]        }
[10]       x = y;
[11]   }
```

Fig. 8. In-situ list reversal algorithm

point the n edges of nodes $u_1, \ldots, u_3$ have been reversed, while the remaining edges retain their original orientation. The statements on lines [7] and [8] replace the n edge from u_4 to u_5 with an n edge from u_4 to u_3. The traversal continues until, on the last loop iteration, t is set to point to u_7's predecessor in the input list, y is set to point to u_7, and x is set to NULL. The subsequent execution of lines [7] and [8] reverses the remaining n edge. The head of the reversed list is u_7, pointed to by y. As in the input list, no node lies on a cycle. The last statement of the procedure (the assignment on line [10]) restores x as the head pointer. The transformation described above can be stated formally using history relations as follows:

$$same_{r_{n,x}}() \wedge same_{c_n}() \wedge \forall v_1, v_2 : n(v_1, v_2) \Leftrightarrow n^0(v_2, v_1). \qquad (8)$$

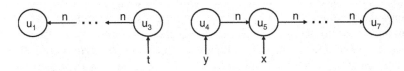

Fig. 9. Logical structure S_9 that represents a store that arises prior to line [7] of Reverse when the algorithm is applied to an acyclic list

Let us consider how Reverse processes a list L_c that consists of a single cycle without a panhandle, such as the acyclic list L_a discussed above, but with an additional n edge from u_7 to u_1. The behavior of Reverse on list L_c is nearly identical to its behavior on list L_a. The outgoing n edges are reversed one at a time until, on the last iteration, t is set to point to u_7, y is set to point to u_1, and x is set to NULL. The subsequent execution of lines [7] and [8] reverses the remaining n edge from u_7 to u_1. The head of the reversed list remains u_1, pointed to by y. Every list node still lies on a cycle. The last statement of the procedure (the assignment on line [10]) restores x as the head pointer. The transformation of lists such as L_c also obeys the property specified in Formula (8).

Now, we discuss how Reverse processes a panhandle list L_p. Initially, the procedure advances the three pointer variables, x, y, and t, down the panhandle, reversing the n edges out of y. After the panhandle is processed, the algorithm proceeds with the processing of the cycle. Fig. 10(a) shows a logical structure that represents a store that arises prior to line [7] while Reverse processes nodes that lie on the cycle. Until Reverse completes the processing of the cycle, the steps are identical to the steps taken during the processing of lists L_a and L_c. Note that the orientation of the n edges in the panhandle is reversed when the loop body is executed with x pointing to u_5 (while reversing the backedge at the end of processing the cycle). As a result, the algorithm proceeds along the reversed n edges down the panhandle, reestablishing the original orientation of those edges. Fig. 10(b) shows a logical structure that represents a store that arises prior to line [7] while Reverse processes panhandle nodes for the second time. Instead of reversing every n edge in the list, as it does for lists L_a and L_c,[6] the

---

[6] Reversing every n edge of a panhandle list is not possible because it requires the shared node (u_5 in Fig. 10) to have two outgoing n edges.

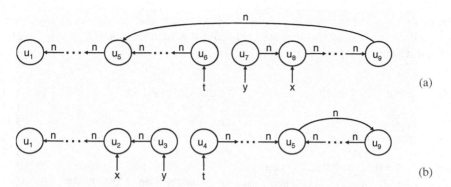

Fig. 10. Logical structures that represent stores that arise prior to line [7] of `Reverse` when the algorithm is applied to a panhandle list. (a) Logical structure that represents a store that arises while `Reverse` processes nodes that lie on the cycle, i.e., after processing nodes that lie in the panhandle once. (b) Logical structure that represents a store that arises while `Reverse` processes nodes that lie on the panhandle for the second time, i.e., after processing nodes that lie on the cycle.

algorithm reverses the direction of every n edge on the cycle but reestablishes the original direction of the n edges in the panhandle. The cyclicity property of all nodes remains as it was on input. The head of the output list remains u_1, pointed to by y. The last statement of the procedure (the assignment on line [10]) restores x as the head pointer. The transformation described above can be stated formally using history relations as follows:

$$\forall v_1, v_2: \begin{array}{c} same_{r_{n,x}}() \wedge same_{c_n}() \wedge \\ (c_n^0(v_1) \wedge c_n^0(v_2)) \wedge (n(v_1, v_2) \Leftrightarrow n^0(v_2, v_1)) \\ \vee \neg(c_n^0(v_1) \wedge c_n^0(v_2)) \wedge (n(v_1, v_2) \Leftrightarrow n^0(v_1, v_2)). \end{array} \quad (9)$$

Note that while the behavior of `Reverse` on lists consisting of a cycle without a panhandle can be described by Formula (8), as we mentioned above, it can also be described by Formula (9). (The case described by formula $\neg(c_n^0(v_1) \wedge c_n^0(v_2))$ never arises.)

6 Establishing Properties of `Reverse`

In this section we describe how the abstraction-refinement mechanism presented in [10] can be used to verify automatically that `Reverse` obeys the properties described in the previous section.

Constructing All Valid Inputs for `Reverse`. To verify that `Reverse` satisfies the properties discussed in the previous section, we need a collection of 3-valued abstract input structures that represent all valid inputs to the procedure. Our methodology for obtaining values for abstract input structures is to perform an abstract interpretation on a loop that nondeterministically constructs the family of all valid inputs to the program (we call such a loop a **Data-Structure Constructor**, or **DSC**). This allows the values of instrumentation relations to be maintained (as input structures are manufactured from the empty store) rather than computed; in general, this results in more precise values for the instrumentation relations without requiring the user to specify input 3-valued logical structures.

```
[1]   List *x = NULL;          List *x, *y, *h;              [1]
                               x = y = h = NULL;             [2]
[3]   int sz =                 int sz =                      [3]
[4]      sizeof(List);            sizeof(List);              [4]
[5]   while (?) {              while (?) {                   [5]
[6]      List *t = malloc(sz);    List *t = malloc(sz);      [6]
                                  // save the last node      [7]
                                  if (y == NULL) y = t;      [8]
                                  // save a node (or NULL)   [9]
                                  if (?) h = t;             [10]
[11]     t->n = x;                t->n = x;                 [11]
[12]     x = t;                   x = t;                    [12]
[13]  }                        }                            [13]
                               // if y and h are non-NULL,  [14]
                               // this will create a cycle  [15]
                               if (y != NULL) y->n = h;     [16]

          (a)                            (b)
```

Fig. 11. (a) The Data-Structure Constructor for acyclic linked lists. (b) The Data-Structure Constructor for possibly-cyclic linked lists (including acyclic and panhandle lists). The differences between the two versions appear in bold.

Two examples of our methodology are depicted in Fig. 11. The loop on the left non-deterministically constructs an acyclic linked list pointed to by x: a list is constructed from tail to head (i.e., most deeply nested node first); the loop exits after some number of nodes have been added at the front of the list. The slight modification shown on the right nondeterministically constructs a (cyclic or acyclic) linked list pointed to by x. This is achieved by setting y to point to the last list node on line [8], nondeterministically setting h to point to some list node (or NULL) on line [10], and setting y->n to point to h on line [16] if y is non-NULL (possibly completing a cycle). If h is NULL, the DSC constructs an acyclic list. If h points to the head of the list, the DSC constructs a list consisting of a cycle with no panhandle. If h is neither NULL nor points to the head of the list, the DSC constructs a panhandle list.

Abstract interpretation of the DSC of Fig. 11(b) constructs an abstract representation of all linked lists pointed to by x. When testing the application of a procedure to acyclic lists, we select only those structures collected at the exit of the DSC that satisfy the following formula:

$$(\exists v: r_{n,x}(v)) \wedge (\forall v: r_{n,x}(v) \Rightarrow \neg c_n(v)) \tag{10}$$

We will refer to input abstractions satisfying Formula (10) as *type Acyclic*. When testing the application of a procedure to cyclic lists without a panhandle, we select only those structures collected at the exit of the DSC that satisfy the following formula:

$$(\exists v: r_{n,x}(v)) \wedge (\forall v: r_{n,x}(v) \Rightarrow c_n(v)) \tag{11}$$

We will refer to input abstractions satisfying Formula (11) as *type Cyclic*. When testing the application of a procedure to panhandle lists, we select only those structures collected at the exit of the DSC that satisfy the following formula:

$$(\exists v_1 : r_{n,x}(v_1) \wedge \neg c_n(v_1)) \wedge (\exists v_2 : r_{n,x}(v_2) \wedge c_n(v_2)) \tag{12}$$

We will refer to input abstractions satisfying Formula (12) as *type Panhandle*. Note that Formulas (10)–(12) ensure that each of the input types admits only non-empty lists. Note also that the three types represent disjoint collections of data structures. Additionally, the cross product of the set of lists represented by type *Acyclic* and the set of lists represented by type *Cyclic* is in a one-to-one correspondence with the set of lists represented by type *Panhandle:* the acyclic-list component corresponds to the panhandle of a panhandle list and the cyclic-list component corresponds to its cycle. We will make use of these facts in §7.

In addition to constructing the valid inputs prior to the first analysis of Reverse, the DSC is used for constructing *refined* inputs on every iteration of abstraction refinement: after abstraction refinement introduces additional instrumentation relations, the abstract interpretation of the DSC is performed using an extended vocabulary that contains the new relation symbols; the 3-valued structures collected at the exit node of the DSC become the abstract input to the original procedure for the subsequent abstract interpretation of the procedure.

Note that history relations (such as $r_{n,x}^0(v)$ from §4) are intended to record the state of the store at the entry point to the procedure or, equivalently, at the exit from the DSC. To make sure that these relations have appropriate values, they are maintained in tandem with their active counterparts during abstract interpretation of the DSC. When abstract input refinement is completed, values of history relations are frozen in preparation for the abstract interpretation that is about to be performed on the procedure proper.

Abstraction-Refinement Steps. After an abstraction of the appropriate valid input is constructed by analyzing the DSC, the abstract interpretation collects all structures that arise at all program points of Reverse. To check if Reverse satisfies the expected properties, we check if all structures collected at the exit of Reverse satisfy the appropriate query (Formula (8) when testing the application of the procedure to lists represented by type *Acyclic* and Formula (9) when testing the application of the procedure to lists represented by type *Panhandle*; we can check either query when testing the application of the procedure to lists represented by type *Cyclic*).

Both queries (Formulas (8) and (9)) contain formula $n(v_1, v_2) \Leftrightarrow n^0(v_2, v_1)$ as a subformula. Because this formula evaluates to $1/2$ under any assignment that maps v_1 and v_2 to the same summary individual with a $1/2$-valued self-loop for the relation n, it should come as no surprise that the first run of abstract interpretation returns an indefinite answer, whether we are checking Formula (8) or Formula (9).

In [10], we introduced *subformula-based refinement*, which analyzes the sources of imprecision in the evaluation of the query in a structure collected at the exit of a procedure, and chooses how to define new instrumentation relations using subformulas of the query that contribute to the indefinite answer. Tab. 4 shows the instrumentation relations that are introduced by subformula-based refinement after Formula (8) evaluates to $1/2$ on a structure collected at the exit of `Reverse`, given an input abstraction of either type *Acyclic* or *Cyclic*. Column 2 of Tab. 4 shows the imprecise subformulas that are used to define new instrumentation relations. To gain precision improvements from storing and maintaining the new instrumentation relations all occurrences of the defining formulas for the new instrumentation relations in the query and in the definitions of other instrumentation relations are replaced with the use of the corresponding new instrumentation-relation symbols. Here, the use of Formula (8) in the query is replaced with the use of the stored value $rev_1()$. Then the definitions of all instrumentation relations are scanned for occurrences of the defining formulas for $rev_1, \ldots, rev_6$. These occurrences are replaced with the names of the six relations. In this case, only the new relations' definitions are changed, yielding the definitions given in Column 3 of Tab. 4.

Table 4. Instrumentation relations created by subformula-based refinement when the application of `Reverse` is checked against the query expressed in Formula (8) on an input abstraction of either type *Acyclic* or *Cyclic*

Relation	Imprecise Subformula	Defining formula
$rev_1()$	$same_{r_{n,x}}() \wedge same_{c_n}() \wedge$ $\forall v_1, v_2 : n(v_1, v_2) \Leftrightarrow n^0(v_2, v_1)$	$same_{r_{n,x}}() \wedge same_{c_n}() \wedge rev_2()$
$rev_2()$	$\forall v_1, v_2 : n(v_1, v_2) \Leftrightarrow n^0(v_2, v_1)$	$\forall v_1 : rev_3(v_1)$
$rev_3(v_1)$	$\forall v_2 : n(v_1, v_2) \Leftrightarrow n^0(v_2, v_1)$	$\forall v_2 : rev_4(v_1, v_2)$
$rev_4(v_1, v_2)$	$n(v_1, v_2) \Leftrightarrow n^0(v_2, v_1)$	$rev_5(v_1, v_2) \wedge rev_6(v_2, v_1)$
$rev_5(v_1, v_2)$	$n(v_1, v_2) \Rightarrow n^0(v_2, v_1)$	$n(v_1, v_2) \Rightarrow n^0(v_2, v_1)$
$rev_6(v_2, v_1)$	$n^0(v_2, v_1) \Rightarrow n(v_1, v_2)$	$n^0(v_2, v_1) \Rightarrow n(v_1, v_2)$

Tab. 5 shows the instrumentation relations that are introduced by subformula-based refinement after Formula (9) evaluates to $1/2$ on a structure collected at the exit of `Reverse`, given an input abstraction of either type *Panhandle* or *Cyclic*. Column 2 of Tab. 5 shows the imprecise subformulas that are used to define new instrumentation relations. Note that subformulas of $acycSame(v_1, v_2)$, i.e., $\neg(c_n^0(v_1) \wedge c_n^0(v_2)) \wedge (n(v_1, v_2) \Leftrightarrow n^0(v_1, v_2))$ were not introduced. This is because refinement was triggered by imprecise evaluation on a structure that had a single concrete individual in the panhandle. However, relation rev_3 is capable of maintaining the key property of nodes in the panhandle with enough precision, so that another refinement iteration is not required. Column 3 of Tab. 5 gives the definitions of the new instrumentation relations after all occurrences of the defining formulas of new instrumentation relations in the query and in the definitions of other instrumentation relations have been replaced with the use of the corresponding new instrumentation-relation symbols. Again, only the query and new relations' definitions are changed.

After the introduction of the new instrumentation relations (Tab. 4 or 5, depending on the query being verified), the abstract interpretation of the DSC is performed using an

Table 5. Instrumentation relations created by subformula-based refinement when the application of `Reverse` is checked against the query expressed in Formula (9) on an input abstraction of either type *Panhandle* or *Cyclic*. For compactness, we refer to formula $(c_n^0(v_1) \wedge c_n^0(v_2)) \wedge (n(v_1, v_2) \Leftrightarrow n^0(v_2, v_1))$ as $cycRev(v_1, v_2)$ and to formula $\neg(c_n^0(v_1) \wedge c_n^0(v_2)) \wedge (n(v_1, v_2) \Leftrightarrow n^0(v_1, v_2))$ as $acycSame(v_1, v_2)$.

Relation	Imprecise Subformula	Defining formula
$rev_1()$	$same_{r_{n,x}}() \wedge same_{c_n}() \wedge$ $\forall v_1, v_2: cycRev(v_1, v_2) \vee acycSame(v_1, v_2)$	$same_{r_{n,x}}() \wedge same_{c_n}() \wedge rev_2()$
$rev_2()$	$\forall v_1, v_2: cycRev(v_1, v_2) \vee acycSame(v_1, v_2)$	$\forall v_1 : rev_3(v_1)$
$rev_3(v_1)$	$\forall v_2: cycRev(v_1, v_2) \vee acycSame(v_1, v_2)$	$\forall v_2 : rev_4(v_1, v_2)$
$rev_4(v_1, v_2)$	$cycRev(v_1, v_2) \vee acycSame(v_1, v_2)$	$rev_5(v_1, v_2) \vee acycSame(v_1, v_2)$
$rev_5(v_1, v_2)$	$cycRev(v_1, v_2)$	$(c_n^0(v_1) \wedge c_n^0(v_2)) \wedge rev_6(v_2, v_1)$
$rev_6(v_1, v_2)$	$n(v_1, v_2) \Leftrightarrow n^0(v_2, v_1)$	$rev_7(v_1, v_2) \wedge rev_8(v_2, v_1)$
$rev_7(v_1, v_2)$	$n(v_1, v_2) \Rightarrow n^0(v_2, v_1)$	$n(v_1, v_2) \Rightarrow n^0(v_2, v_1)$
$rev_8(v_2, v_1)$	$n^0(v_2, v_1) \Rightarrow n(v_1, v_2)$	$n^0(v_2, v_1) \Rightarrow n(v_1, v_2)$

extended vocabulary that contains the new instrumentation-relation symbols. The subsequent abstract interpretation of `Reverse` succeeds: in all of the structures collected at the exit, $rev_1() = 1$.

Establishing that `Reverse` Terminates. We can establish that `Reverse` terminates using a few unary core relations and a simple progress monitor. We introduce a collection of unary core *state relations*, $state_0(v)$, $state_1(v)$, and $state_2(v)$.[7] Every time the reversal of the n pointer of the list node pointed to by y is completed (after line [8] of Fig. 8), the node's state is changed to the next state. (The state relations carry no semantics with respect to the pointer values of nodes; they simply record the "visit counts" for each node.) For each state relation s, we create a copy of s, which is used to save the values of relation s at the start of the currently-processed loop iteration (after line [3] of Fig. 8). We give the new relations the superscript *lh* to indicate that they hold the *loop-head* values. The first abstract operation of each iteration of the loop takes a snapshot of the current states of nodes: $state_i^{lh}(v) \leftarrow state_i(v)$, for each $i \in [0..2]$ and each assignment of v to an individual in the abstract structure being processed. Additionally, it asserts that x does not point to a list node in state 2 at the head of the loop (at that point, x points to the node whose n edge is about to be reversed). The last operation of every loop iteration performs a progress test by asserting the following formula:

$$\exists v: \left(state_0^{lh}(v) \wedge state_1(v) \vee state_1^{lh}(v) \wedge state_2(v) \right)$$
$$\wedge \forall v_1 \neq v: \bigwedge_{i \in [0..2]} \left(state_i^{lh}(v_1) \Leftrightarrow state_i(v_1) \right)$$

The assertion ensures that one node's state makes forward progress (the first line of the assertion) and that no other node changes state (the second line of the assertion). Together with the assertion that x does not point to a list node in state 2 at the start of the loop, the above progress monitor establishes that each list node is visited at most twice, thus establishing that the algorithm terminates.

---

[7] The state relations are *not* added to the set of abstraction relations, $\mathcal{A}$.

7 Performance

The tables shown in Fig. 12 give execution times that were collected on a 3GHz Linux PC. The rows indicate the type of data structures assumed as input, and the columns indicate the query to be verified. In each case, one round of abstraction refinement was required to obtain the definite answer 1 to the query. In other words, two rounds of analysis were performed for both the DSC and Reverse: the first analysis round of the DSC and Reverse used the initial abstraction (the core relations of Tab. 1, core relation roc_n, the instrumentation relations of Tab. 3, and the history relations of §4), while the second round used the final abstraction, which additionally included the relations of Tab. 4 or 5, depending on the query. For a given abstraction, the cost of the DSC analysis is nearly identical for all input types because the general DSC of Fig. 11(b) constructs an abstraction of all input types, from which structures that represent the chosen input type are selected at the end using Formula (10), (11), or (12). To gain a better understanding of the cost of verifying Reverse proper, the tables also include the execution times for the last analysis round (using the final abstraction) of Reverse, excluding the analysis time for the DSC.

The tables of Fig. 12 show that the use of tree-shaped-sfe_n maintenance in place of acyclic-sfe_n maintenance for maintaining the relation sfp_n results in a reduction of the total analysis time by a factor in the range of 2.8-4.8. The highest-cost analyses are those that include type *Panhandle* as input. Using tree-shaped-sfe_n maintenance, the last iteration of the analysis of Reverse with the input abstraction of type *Panhandle/Cyclic* takes approximately 2.5 minutes (the total execution time is approximately 4.5 minutes). The last iteration of the analysis of Reverse when the input abstraction is of any other type takes under 13 seconds. The majority of the total analysis cost in those cases is due to the use of the general DSC, which could be specialized to produce input abstractions of type *Acyclic* or *Cyclic* more efficiently (e.g., using the DSC shown in Fig. 11(a)).

The two tables of Fig. 12 share many qualitative characteristics. Below we draw some conclusions from Fig. 12(b), but all of the conclusions can be drawn from Fig. 12(a) equally well. As expected, the cost of the last run of the analysis of Reverse when the input abstraction is of type *Acyclic/Cyclic* is close to the sum of the cost when the input abstraction is of type *Acyclic* and the cost when the input abstraction is of type *Cyclic*. Similarly, the cost of the last run of the analysis of Reverse when the input abstraction is of type *Panhandle/Cyclic* is close to the sum of the cost when the input abstraction is of type *Panhandle* and the cost when the input abstraction is of type *Cyclic*. Curiously, the total cost of the analysis when the input abstraction is of type *Panhandle* is slightly higher than the total cost when the input abstraction is of type *Panhandle/Cyclic*. The reason is that a structure of type *Cyclic* triggers the refinement process at an earlier point. The resulting shorter execution of the first run of the analysis of Reverse explains the counterintuitive relation of total execution times. The cost of the analysis when the input abstraction is of type *Cyclic* (both total cost and the cost of the last iteration of the analysis of Reverse) is similar for the two queries. The panhandle query (Formula (9)) results in the introduction of a more complex

Input Type	Query	
	acyclic total/last	panhandle total/last
Acyclic	161.2/11.8	
Cyclic	208.1/28.2	232.9/34.6
Acyclic/Cyclic	219.7/38.6	
Panhandle		1320.3/782.3
Panhandle/Cyclic		1249.3/810.3

(a)

Input Type	Query	
	acyclic total/last	panhandle total/last
Acyclic	57.1/4.6	
Cyclic	65.6/8.4	71.5/9.0
Acyclic/Cyclic	69.1/12.5	
Panhandle		277.1/147.8
Panhandle/Cyclic		268.1/154.9

(b)

Fig. 12. Execution times in seconds using (a) acyclic-sfe_n maintenance for maintaining the relation sfp_n; (b) tree-shaped-sfe_n maintenance for maintaining the relation sfp_n. In row labels, input types "*Acyclic/Cyclic*" and "*Panhandle/Cyclic*" denote an abstraction that represents lists of either type. The label of column 2 (query "acyclic") denotes the query of Formula (8). The label of column 3 (query "panhandle") denotes the query of Formula (9). Empty cells indicate inappropriate input/query combinations. The first number in each column represents the total execution time for all iterations of the analysis (on both the DSC and Reverse). The second number represents the execution time for only the last iteration of the analysis of Reverse (and not the DSC).

abstraction (cf. Tabs. 5 and 4), so the costs in column 3 of Fig. 12(b) are slightly higher.

The cost of verifying that Reverse terminates is negligible (when compared to the cost of verifying the query) because the progress monitor does not increase the size of the reachable state space.

The three analyses represented by column 3 of Fig. 12(a), i.e., analyses using the panhandle query (Formula (9)) and acyclic-sfe_n maintenance, used a maximum of approximately 170 MB of memory, as reported by the Java Runtime. All other analyses required significantly less memory.

As a sanity check, we studied the number of distinct 3-valued structures collected at all points of Reverse during the last run of the analysis. As we expected, that information is identical when the analysis relies on acyclic-sfe_n maintenance and when it relies on tree-shaped-sfe_n maintenance, thus providing a cross-validation of the implementation of the two methods. The structure counts are shown in Tab. 6. The table shows that when the input abstraction is of type *Cyclic*, the same number of structures is collected with either query. Also, the number of structures collected when the input abstraction is of type *Acyclic/Cyclic* is the sum of the number when the input abstraction is of type *Acyclic* and the number when the input abstraction is of type *Cyclic*. Similarly, the number of structures collected when the input abstraction is of type *Panhandle/Cyclic* is the sum of the number when the input abstraction is of type *Panhandle* and the number when the input abstraction is of type *Cyclic*.

Additionally, we used the data collected in our experiments to answer an instance of the following general question: "Can we predict how much work needs to be done for analysis X when we know how much work is done for related analyses Y and Z?" Given the correspondence of lists represented by type *Panhandle* with combinations of lists represented by type *Acyclic* and lists represented by type *Cyclic*, we made a prediction about the number of structures collected during the analysis of `Reverse` when the input abstraction is of type *Panhandle* (using the panhandle query) based on the number of structures collected during the analyses of `Reverse` when the input abstraction is of types *Acyclic* and *Cyclic* (using the acyclic query). Let a_n, c_n, and p_n, represent the numbers of structures collected at CFG node n during the analysis of `Reverse` when the input abstraction is of type *Acyclic*, *Cyclic*, and *Panhandle*, respectively. For a CFG node n that lies outside the loop of `Reverse`, we expect that $p_n = a_n * c_n$. For a CFG node n that lies inside the loop, we expect that

Table 6. The number of distinct 3-valued structures collected during the last iteration of the analysis of `Reverse` (and not the DSC). Rows and columns have the same meaning as in Fig. 12.

Input Type	Query	
	acyclic	panhandle
Acyclic	103	
Cyclic	162	162
Acyclic/Cyclic	265	
Panhandle		921
Panhandle/Cyclic		1083

$$p_n = c_{entry} * a_n + a_{exit} * c_n + c_{exit} * a_n, \tag{13}$$

where c_{entry} is the number of structures at the entry node of `Reverse` when the input abstraction is of type *Cyclic*, a_{exit} is the number of structures collected at the exit of `Reverse` when the input abstraction is of type *Acyclic*, and c_{exit} is the number of structures collected at the exit of `Reverse` when the input abstraction is of type *Cyclic*. The intuition behind the first summand of Formula (13) is that every acyclic structure collected at n (when the input abstraction is of type *Acyclic*) can be extended to c_{entry} panhandle structures at n. These structures represent the states in which the panhandle is being reversed before the cycle is entered. The intuition behind the second summand of Formula (13) is that every cyclic structure collected at n (when the input abstraction is of type *Cyclic*) can be extended to a_{exit} panhandle structures. These structures represent the states in which the cycle is being reversed after the panhandle has been reversed. Finally, the intuition behind the third summand of Formula (13) is that every acyclic structure collected at n can be extended to c_{exit} panhandle structures. These structures represent the states in which the panhandle is being un-reversed after the cycle has been reversed. The summation of predicted values for p_n over the nodes n of `Reverse` gives 858 structures. This prediction is a little short of the actual number (921). This relatively small discrepancy is probably due to the fact that our prediction for a run using the panhandle query (which leads to the abstraction of Tab. 5) is based on numbers for the right-hand side quantities of Formula (13) gathered from runs that use a slightly different abstraction, namely, Tab. 4. The more complex abstraction introduced when verifying the panhandle query apparently creates a few additional intermediate structures.

Note that the sum of the numbers of structures collected during the analyses when the input abstraction is of types *Acyclic* and *Cyclic* is much lower than the number of structures collected during the analysis when the input abstraction is of type *Panhandle*. The sum of the execution times of the analyses when the input abstraction is of types *Acyclic* and *Cyclic* is also much lower than the execution time of the analysis when the input abstraction is of type *Panhandle*. A possible extension of this work is to infer properties of Reverse when applied to input abstraction of type *Panhandle* from properties of Reverse when applied to input abstractions of types *Acyclic* and *Cyclic*. To make this possible, we need to find a way to infer properties of heap configurations from properties of components of those configurations. The concept of *local heaps* introduced by Rinetzky et al. is relevant in this line of research [16].

8   Related Work

In §3, we compared our work with that of William Hesse, which is closest in spirit to what is reported here. Prior work that is related to the general concept of finite differencing has been discussed in [14]. Work related to the abstraction-refinement mechanism has been discussed in [10]. In this section, we discuss a few approaches that bear resemblance to ours in that they attempt to translate or simulate a data structure that cannot be handled by some core techniques into one that can.

The idea of using spanning-tree representations for specifying or reasoning about data structures that are "close to trees" is not new. Klarlund and Schwartzbach introduced *graph types*, which can be used to specify some common non-tree-shaped data structures in terms of a spanning-tree *backbone* and regular expressions that specify where non-backbone edges occur within the backbone [7]. Examples of data structures that can be specified by graph types are doubly-linked lists and threaded trees. A panhandle list cannot be specified by a graph type because in a graph type the location of each non-backbone edge has to be defined in terms of the backbone using a regular expression, and a regular expression cannot be used to specify the existence of a backedge to *some* node that occurs earlier in the list. In the PALE project [12], which incorporates work on graph types, automated reasoning about programs that manipulate data structures specified as graph types can be carried out using a decision procedure for monadic second-order logic. Unfortunately, the decision procedure has non-elementary complexity. Additionally, the decision procedure cannot handle 2-vocabulary structures, which the present paper uses to express data-structure transformations (the second vocabulary consists of history relations p^0). An advantage of our approach over that of PALE is that we do not rely on the use of a decision procedure.

Immerman et al. presented *structure simulation*, a technique that broadens the applicability of decision procedures to a larger class of data structures [6]. Under certain conditions, it allows data structures that cannot be reasoned about using decidable logics to be translated into data structures that can, with the translation expressed as a first-order-logic formula. Unlike graph types, structure simulation is capable of specifying panhandle lists. However, this technique shares a limitation of graph types because it relies on decision procedures for automated reasoning about programs.

Manevich et al. specified abstractions (in canonical-abstraction and predicate-abstraction forms) for showing safety properties of programs that manipulate possibly-cyclic linked lists [11]. By maintaining reachability within list segments that are not *interrupted* by nodes that are shared or pointed to by a variable, they are able to break the symmetry of a cycle. The definition of several key instrumentation relations in that work makes use of transitive-closure formulas that cannot be handled precisely by finite differencing. As a result, a drawback of that work is the need to define some relation-maintenance formulas by hand. Another drawback is the difficulty of reasoning about reachability (in a list) from a program variable (see reachability relations $r_{n,x}$ of Tab. 3). Because in [11] reachability in a list has to be expressed in terms of reachability over a sequence of uninterrupted segments, a formula that expresses the reachability of node v from program variable x in a list has to enumerate all permutations of other program variables that may act as interruptions on a path from x to v in the list.

A number of past approaches to the analysis of programs that manipulate linked lists relied on first-order axiomatizations of reachability information. All of these approaches involved the use of first-order-logic decision procedures. While our approach does not have this limitation, it is instructive to compare our work with those approaches that included mechanisms for breaking the symmetry on a cycle. Nelson defined a set of first-order axioms that describe the ternary reachability relation $r_n(u, v, w)$, which has the meaning: w is reachable from u along n edges without encountering v [13]. The use of this relation alone is not sufficient in our setting because in the presence of abstraction we require unary distinctions (such as the relations pr_x and pr_{is} of §3) to break the symmetry. Additionally, the maintenance of ternary relations is more expensive than the maintenance of binary relations. Lahiri and Qadeer specify a collection of first-order axioms that are sufficient to verify properties of procedures that perform a single change to a cyclic list, e.g., the removal of an element [8]. They also verify properties of in-situ list reversal, albeit under the assumption that the input list is acyclic. (We verify properties of Reverse when applied to any linked list, including cyclic and panhandle lists.) They break the symmetry of cycles in a similar fashion to how it is done in [11]: the *blocking cells* of [8] are a subset of the interruptions of [11]. The blocking cells include only the set of *head variables*—program variables that act as heads of lists used in the program. This set has to be maintained carefully by the user to (i) satisfy the system's definition of acceptable (*well-founded*) lists, (ii) allow the system to verify useful postconditions, and (iii) avoid falling prey to the difficulty— that arises in [11]—of expressing reachability in the list. The current mechanism of [8] is insufficient for reasoning about panhandle lists because the set of blocking cells does not include shared nodes. This limitation can be partially addressed by generalizing the set of blocking cells to mimic interruptions of [11] more faithfully. However, this may make it more difficult to satisfy points (ii) and (iii) stated above. As in our work, Lahiri and Qadeer rely on the insight that reachability information can be maintained in first-order logic. They use a collection of manually-specified update formulas that define how their relations are affected by the statements of the language and the (user-inserted) statements that manage the set of head variables.

Gotsman et al. present an interprocedural shape-analysis algorithm that is capable of checking some properties of programs that manipulate possibly-cyclic linked lists [3]. This algorithm is based on a novel abstract domain that consists of formulas in a decidable fragment of Separation Logic [1,15]. The analysis relies on carefully hand-crafted inductive predicates and axioms to evaluate some properties of possibly-cyclic linked lists precisely and efficiently. However, because the formulas allowed in the analysis need to come from a decidable fragment of Separation Logic and, furthermore, need to make up a finite abstract domain, the set of properties that can be tested is limited. For instance, their analysis of `Reverse` when applied to a panhandle list verifies memory safety and the absence of memory leaks, but shows neither the partial correctness (the property described by Formula (9)), nor the termination of the algorithm. Although our analysis is also based on logic, our abstract domain consists of sets of (abstracted) logical structures. An advantage of our approach is the ability to test more general properties. Additionally, our approach does not rely on decision procedures.[8]

Lee et al. defined a shape-analysis algorithm that extends the shape graphs of Sagiv et al. [17] with grammars [9]. Grammars are employed in place of instrumentation relations for expressing and maintaining derived properties of data structures. The meaning of a grammar is given by an inductive predicate of Separation Logic. An important connection of that work with ours is the cutting of one edge on each cycle for modeling some cyclic structures by acyclic ones. Lee et al. define a *cut* rule, which removes one edge from each cycle and stores information about the edge in the grammar that corresponds to the data structure. Their mechanism is sufficiently precise to represent cyclic and panhandle lists. While Lee et al. do not discuss the application of their techniques to `Reverse`, their techniques should be capable of ensuring that the program has no unsafe memory operations or memory leaks when applied to a cyclic or a panhandle list. However, their analysis has no mechanism for relating the input and output data structures—a mechanism required for showing the total correctness of the algorithm.

Acknowledgments

The authors would like to thank the anonymous reviewers for their insightful comments, as well as Hongseok Yang for important clarifications on the power and limitations of grammar-based shape analysis [9].

References

1. D Distefano, P O'Hearn, and H Yang. Interprocedural shape analysis with separated heap abstractions. In *Tools and Algs. for the Construction and Analysis of Systems*, pages 287–302, March 2006.
2. G. Dong and J. Su. Incremental maintenance of recursive views using relational calculus/SQL. *SIGMOD Record*, 29(1):44–51, 2000.
3. A. Gotsman, J. Berdine, and B. Cook. Interprocedural shape analysis with separated heap abstractions. In *Static Analysis Symp.*, pages 240–260, August 2006.
4. W. Hesse. *Dynamic Computational Complexity*. PhD thesis, Dept. of Computer Science, University of Massachusetts, June 2003.
5. N. Immerman, A. Rabinovich, T. Reps, M. Sagiv, and G. Yorsh. The boundary between decidability and undecidability for transitive closure logics. In *Workshop on Computer Science Logic*, pages 160–174, September 2004.
6. N. Immerman, A. Rabinovich, T. Reps, M. Sagiv, and G. Yorsh. Verification via structure simulation. In *Computer-Aided Verification*, pages 281–294, July 2004.
7. N. Klarlund and M. Schwartzbach. Graph types. In *Symp. on Principles of Programming Languages*, January 1993.

---

[8] In fact, the logic that we use is not decidable.

8. S. Lahiri and S. Qadeer. Verifying properties of well-founded linked lists. In *Symp. on Principles of Programming Languages*, pages 115–126, January 2006.

9. O. Lee, H. Yang, and K. Yi. Automatic verification of pointer programs using grammar-based shape analysis. In *European Symp. On Programming*, pages 124–140, April 2005.

10. A. Loginov, T. Reps, and M. Sagiv. Abstraction refinement via inductive learning. In *Computer-Aided Verification*, pages 519–533, July 2005.

11. R. Manevich, E. Yahav, G. Ramalingam, and M. Sagiv. Predicate abstraction and canonical abstraction for singly-linked lists. In *Verification, Model Checking, and Abstract Interpretation*, pages 181–198, January 2005.

12. A. Møller and M. Schwartzbach. The pointer assertion logic engine. In *Conf. on Programming Language Design and Impl.*, pages 221–231, June 2001.

13. G. Nelson. Verifying reachability invariants of linked structures. In *Symp. on Principles of Programming Languages*, pages 38–47, January 1983.

14. T. Reps, M. Sagiv, and A. Loginov. Finite differencing of logical formulas for static analysis. In *European Symp. On Programming*, pages 380–398, April 2003.

15. J. Reynolds. Separation Logic: A logic for shared mutable data structures. In *Symp. on Logic in Computer Science*, pages 55–74, July 2002.

16. N. Rinetzky, J. Bauer, T. Reps, M. Sagiv, and R. Wilhelm. A semantics for procedure local heaps and its abstractions. In *Symp. on Principles of Programming Languages*, pages 296–309, January 2005.

17. M. Sagiv, T. Reps, and R. Wilhelm. Parametric shape analysis via 3-valued logic. *Trans. on Programming Languages and Systems (TOPLAS)*, 24(3):217–298, 2002.

18. G. Yorsh, T. Reps, M. Sagiv, and R. Wilhelm. Logical characterizations of heap abstractions. To appear in *ACM Transactions on Computational Logic (TOCL)*.

Abstract Counterexample-Based Refinement
for Powerset Domains

R. Manevich[1,*], J. Field[2], T.A. Henzinger[3,**],
G. Ramalingam[4,***], and M. Sagiv[1]

[1] Tel Aviv University
{rumster,msagiv}@tau.ac.il
[2] IBM T.J. Watson Research Center
jfield@watson.ibm.com
[3] EPFL
tah@epfl.ch
[4] Microsoft Research India
grama@microsoft.com

Abstract. Counterexample-guided abstraction refinement (CEGAR) is a powerful technique to scale automatic program analysis techniques to large programs. However, so far it has been used primarily for model checking in the context of predicate abstraction. We formalize CEGAR for general powerset domains. If a spurious abstract counterexample needs to be removed through abstraction refinement, there are often several choices, such as which program location(s) to refine, which abstract domain(s) to use at different locations, and which abstract values to compute. We define several plausible preference orderings on abstraction refinements, such as refining as "late" as possible and as "coarse" as possible. We present generic algorithms for finding refinements that are optimal with respect to the different preference orderings. We also compare the different orderings with respect to desirable properties, including the property if locally optimal refinements compose to a global optimum. Finally, we point out some difficulties with CEGAR for non-powerset domains.

1 Introduction

The CEGAR (Counterexample-guided Abstraction Refinement) paradigm [1,3] has been the subject of a significant body of work in the automatic verification community. The basic idea is as follows. First, we statically analyze a program using a given abstraction. When an error is discovered, the analyzer generates an abstract counterexample, and checks whether the error occurs in the corresponding concrete execution path. If so, the execution path is presented to the user. Otherwise, the analyzer examines the spurious abstract counterexample and refines the abstraction to remove it. The analyzer continues refining iteratively, driven by abstract counterexamples, until it either reaches a fixpoint or runs out of resources.

---

* This research is partially supported by the Clore Fellowship Programme.
** Supported in part by the Swiss National Science Foundation.
*** Work done while author was at IBM T.J. Watson Research Center.

T. Reps, M. Sagiv, and J. Bauer (Eds.): Wilhelm Festschrift, LNCS 4444, pp. 273–292, 2007.

Our motivation for creating a general model for the abstract counterexample-based refinement problem is twofold. First, given a spurious abstract counterexample, there may be more than one abstraction refinement that eliminates it. Indeed, in some situations the set of suitable refinements is infinite. However, two refinements that remove the same spurious abstract counterexample may differ significantly in their cost to compute, or in their effect on the number of subsequent refinement steps required to reach convergence. Until now, we had no way to cleanly separate refinement strategies from the abstractions that use them; this in turn made it difficult to compare and contrast the cost and effectiveness of different CEGAR techniques, or to mix and match abstraction constructions and refinement strategies. Second, most abstraction refinement techniques have heretofore been based on predicate abstractions. We would like to extend the applicability of automatic refinement to other domains, in particular to expensive domains such as the ones used for shape analysis [12], in order to achieve scalability. Although in this paper we do not demonstrate how to instantiate our framework for abstract domains not based on predicate abstraction, we hope that the framework can be used as a first step in this direction.

In the remainder of this paper, we lay out a framework for counterexample-guided abstraction refinement for arbitrary abstract domains, place existing work in this framework, define various "preference orderings" that may be used to select among candidate abstraction refinements, and compare and contrast the consequences of various refinement strategies that use these orderings. For example, we show that for certain preference orderings, computing optimal refinements for each counterexample path iteratively does not necessarily compose to a globally optimal abstraction.

Our focus is on a single refinement step within the CEGAR method: how to refine the abstraction in order to remove one abstract counterexample. We present a theoretical framework for refining abstractions in order to remove spurious abstract counterexamples. Our framework is based on the theory of abstract interpretation [4], making it possible to extend the problem beyond predicate abstraction. Inspired by the concept of "parsimonious abstractions" [7], we allow different abstractions to be associated with different control flow locations. Furthermore, we consider a parametric variant of refinement. In this setting, rather than computing refinements over the space of all abstractions of a concrete domain, we assume we are given as a parameter a lattice of predefined abstractions, e.g., because its values are computationally cheap to manipulate.

During the investigation of the problem, we discovered that the refinement of powerset domains[1] is simpler than refinement of non-powerset domains. In the latter case, refinement may need to be done for a set of control flow paths simultaneously, and special underapproximation techniques may have to be devised (see Appendix A for further details). We therefore focus on refinement of powerset domains.

---

[1] An abstract domain is a powerset domain if it is closed under unions. For example, predicate abstractions yield relational domains.

The main results of this paper are as follows:

Refinement Orderings. For a given spurious counterexample, there may be many possible refinements that eliminate it. We identify and focus on three dimensions[2] in the space of refinements: (i) the abstract domain at the control flow locations along the trace, (ii) the set of control flow locations where refinement occurs, and (iii) the abstract elements that appear along the refined trace at those locations. We use these dimensions to define preference orders on the space of refinements.

Refinement Procedures. We present new refinement procedures that provide optimal refinements with respect to a given preference order and we identify, along the way, a set of abstract domain operations that can be used for refining abstract counterexamples.

Constrained Problem Settings. We modify the initial idealized setting of the problem to consider a more realistic situation where refinement of an abstract domain is done by adding abstract values from a given lattice of abstract values.

Local Optima vs. Global Optima. We consider the question of whether proving a property by refining abstract counterexamples in a locally optimal way provides globally optimal solutions (w.r.t. the orderings we define). We show that the answer depends on the given ordering, and that for two of the orderings the answer is negative, and for one it is positive.

Running Example. Consider the simple program shown in Table 1. The goal is to prove the assertion at label 5, which is true, since the variable x is assigned the values $0, 1, 2, 3$ at labels $2, 3, 4, 5$, respectively. The initial abstract domain A has the following overapproximations available for these values at the corresponding program labels: $2:\{x < 7\}$, $3:\{x = 1\}$, $4:\{x = 0\}$, and $5:\{x = 2\}$. Using a sound (overapproximate) abstract semantics, the analysis determines that x can have any value at labels 4 and 5 (since the abstract values $\{x = 0\}$ and $\{x = 2\}$ cannot be used to approximate the values of x at labels 4 and 5), which is insufficient to prove the assertion.

We can eliminate the abstract counterexample by adding new (more precise) abstract values to the abstraction at the corresponding program labels, resulting in the abstract domain U. One such refinement adds the following abstract values at the corresponding labels: $2:\{x = 0\}$, $4:\{x = 2\}$, and $5:\{x = 3\}$. The refined abstract semantics produces the sequence of values $2:\{x = 0\}$, $3:\{x = 1\}$, $4:\{x = 2\}$, and $5:\{x = 3\}$, which proves the assertion, since $\{x = 3\} \subseteq \{x < 10\}$. Another refinement that eliminates the abstract counterexample adds the following values to the abstractions at the corresponding labels: $3:\{x < 8\}$, $4:\{x < 9\}$, and $5:\{x < 10\}$. We denote the refined abstract domain by W. The refined abstract semantics produces the sequence of values $2:\{x < 7\}$,

---

[2] In this paper, we use the term dimension loosely to talk about properties of refinements. The properties are in fact inter-related.

3:$\{x < 8\}$, 4:$\{x < 9\}$, and 5:$\{x < 10\}$, which proves the assertion, since $\{x < 10\} \subseteq \{x < 10\}$.

Notice that the two refinements discussed here refine at different sets of labels (the first refines at $\{2, 4, 5\}$, and the second refines at $\{3, 4, 5\}$). They use different abstract values to perform the refinement, and the "shape" of the abstract values is different — the first refinement uses rather simple abstract values, of the form $\{x = a\}$, where a is a constant, whereas the second refinement uses values of the form $\{x < a\}$. This shows that the same problem can have solutions with different characteristics. We will look at several characteristics of the set of possible refinements and explain how to favor some refinements over others, according to these characteristics.

Table 1. Program label and statement; Val_A:initial sequence of abstract values; Val_U:sequence of abstract values with abstract domain U; and Val_W:sequence of abstract values using abstract domain W. In every row, the values correspond to the label before the statement.

label: statement	Val_A	Val_U	Val_W
1: x=0	$\{x \in \mathbb{N}\}$	$\{x \in \mathbb{N}\}$	$\{x \in \mathbb{N}\}$
2: x=x+1	$\{x < 7\}$	$\{x = 0\}$	$\{x < 7\}$
3: x=x+1	$\{x \in \mathbb{N}\}$	$\{x = 1\}$	$\{x < 8\}$
4: x=x+1	$\{x \in \mathbb{N}\}$	$\{x = 2\}$	$\{x < 9\}$
5: assert(x<10)	$\{x \in \mathbb{N}\}$	$\{x = 3\}$	$\{x < 10\}$

Outline. In Sec. 2, we present a theoretical framework for the abstract counterexample refinement problem, based on abstract interpretation. In Sec. 3, we characterize the space of solutions for the problem, and define axes and preference orders on the set of solutions. In Sec. 4, we present refinement procedures that produce optimal solutions for the preference orders we define. In Sec. 5, we consider a constrained variant of the problem. In Sec. 6, we investigate the relation between locally optimal solutions and globally optimal solutions for different optimality criteria. Sec. 7 discusses related work and concludes the paper.

2   Abstract Counterexample-Based Refinement

Throughout the paper, we fix the abstract counterexample refinement problem to be $\langle P, C, \phi, \overline{A}, \pi \rangle$ where: P is a program, C is a concrete domain (with a fixed concrete semantics), ϕ is a property we wish to prove, $\overline{A}$ is the initial *compound* abstract domain, and $\pi \doteq l_1, \dots, l_k$ is a sequence of program location representing the abstract counterexample with the associated abstract values $a_1, \dots, a_k$. We now explain each element of these elements in detail.

Program. The program P is represented by a control flow graph (CFG). The vertices of the CFG are program locations $\{entry = l_1, \dots, l_m = exit\}$. The edges of the CFG are labeled by program statements using the notation $st_{i,j}$ to denote the statement on the edge (l_i, l_j).

Concrete Domain and Concrete Semantics. Let $STATES$ be the set of all possible concrete states that may occur at any program location (the states do not include the program counter). The complete lattice C is the powerset of $STATES$, ordered by the subset relation. A concrete operational semantics assigns a forward meaning to each program statement st, $\mathsf{post}(st) : C \to C$.[3] The *entry* location is associated with an initial value *init*, which is the set of concrete states that program execution may begin with.

Property. The *exit* location is associated with a safety property ϕ—a set of concrete states—which defines the set of legal program executions. A concrete execution that ends at the *exit* location with a concrete state $\sigma \in STATES$ is considered legal when $\sigma \in \phi$.

Localized Abstractions and Abstract Semantics. Every program location l_i is associated with a powerset abstract domain in the form of a complete sublattice $A_i \subseteq C$ such that A_i is given by an upper closure operator[4], $\rho_i : C \to C$, i.e., $A_i \doteq \{\rho_i(c) \mid c \in 2^{STATES}\}$. Thus, the elements of our abstract domains are sets of concrete states. This is not a limiting assumption, since every Galois Connection is isomorphic to one such abstract domain with a corresponding upper closure operator. We use this assumption purely to simplify the presentation.

The initial abstraction for P is a *compound abstract domain* $\overline{A} \doteq \langle A_1, \dots, A_m \rangle$. We say that an abstract domain A is more precise than B if $B \subseteq A$. We use the point-wise extension of this order to compare the precision of two compound abstract domains.

The abstract semantics of a statement $st_{i,j}$ is given by $\mathsf{post}^{\sharp}(st_{i,j}) \doteq \rho_j \circ \mathsf{post}(st_{i,j})$ where A_j is obtained via the upper closure operator ρ_j.

Abstract Counterexample. We define a *trace* to be a sequence of program locations $l_1, \dots, l_k$ (with possible repetitions of locations) that form a path in the CFG. For a given abstraction $\overline{A}$ such that A_i is the abstract domain at location l_i, given by the upper-closure operator ρ_i, we define the sequence of abstract values associated with the trace by: $a_1 \doteq \rho_1(init)$, and $a_{i+1} \doteq \mathsf{post}^{\sharp}(st_i)(a_i)$ for every $i = 1 \dots k - 1$, where st_i is the statement between l_i and l_{i+1}. We will use this notation as a convention for other abstract domains and corresponding sequences of abstract values along a trace. The trace and associated abstract values together make an abstract counterexample if $a_k \not\subseteq \phi$.

There are two different cases. The abstract counterexample is a *real counterexample* if $(\mathsf{post}(st_k) \circ \dots \circ \mathsf{post}(st_1))(init) \not\subseteq \phi$. Otherwise, we say that the abstract counterexample is a *spurious counterexample*.

---

[3] Notice that the statements are interpreted directly over sets of concrete states, since we are using the collecting semantics [11].

[4] $\rho : C \to C$ is an upper closure operator if it is monotone ($x \subseteq y$ implies $\rho(x) \subseteq \rho(y)$), extensive ($x \subseteq \rho(x)$), and idempotent ($\rho(x) = \rho(\rho(x))$). In particular, this means that for every $x \in C$, $\rho(x)$ is the best overapproximation of x in $\{\rho(y) \mid y \in C\}$.

Goal. The goal of the problem is to first differentiate between real counterexamples and spurious counterexamples. Second, in the case of a spurious counterexample, a solution is a compound abstract domain $\overline{A'} \doteq \langle A'_1, \ldots, A'_m \rangle$, which we call a a *refinement*, such that: (i) $A'_i \supseteq A_i$ for every $i = 1, \ldots, k$ (i.e., A'_i is as least as precise as A_i), and (ii) $(\mathsf{post}^{\sharp'}(st_{k-1}) \circ \ldots \circ \mathsf{post}^{\sharp'}(st_1) \circ \rho'_1)(init) \subseteq \phi$, where $\mathsf{post}^{\sharp'}(st_i) \doteq \rho'_j \circ \mathsf{post}(st_i)$.

Additional Definitions and Notations. We shall refer to the operations $\mathsf{pre}(st, c)$ and $\mathsf{post}(st, c)$, which supply the semantic weakest-precondition and strongest-postcondition of the statement st and set of concrete states c, respectively. We shall also refer to the curried versions of the pre and post operators, i.e., $\mathsf{pre}(st) = \lambda c \in C . \mathsf{pre}(st, c)$ and $\mathsf{post}(st) = \lambda c \in C . \mathsf{post}(st, c)$.

For a powerset domain A, the operation $\rho(c)$, which is not standard in abstract interpretation, supplies the best, i.e., the tightest, under-approximation for a set of concrete states c. This operation can be defined by $\underline{\rho}_A(c) \doteq \bigcup_{a \in A, a \subseteq c} a$. The resulting abstract element is in the abstract domain since the domain is closed under union.

Given a powerset domain A, the best transformer for a statement st is given by $\overline{\mathsf{post}}_A(st) \doteq \rho_A \circ \mathsf{post}(st)$. The best underapproximation of the backward meaning of a statement is given by $\underline{\mathsf{pre}}_A(st) \doteq \underline{\rho}_A \circ \mathsf{pre}(st)$.

The operation $U \sqcap_{Rel} W$ accepts two powerset domains and gives the coarsest, i.e., most abstract, powerset domain that is more precise than U and W (App. B supplies further details on this operation). For a set of concrete states $S \in STATES$, $\mathcal{D}(S) \doteq \{S, \top_C\}$, where $\top_C = STATES$, is the coarsest abstract domain containing the element S. For sets of concrete states $S_1, \ldots, S_b$, the notation $\mathcal{D}(S_1, \ldots, S_b) \doteq \sqcap_{Rel}(\mathcal{D}(S_1), \ldots, \mathcal{D}(S_k))$ denotes the coarsest abstract domain containing the sets. The notation $\mathcal{D}_\top$ stands for the abstract domain $\{\top_C\}$.

Limitations of the Model. There are certain features in static analyses that are not handled in this paper:

- We consider only the problem of refining abstract counterexamples along a fixed number of iterations over loops. This simplification does not affect the correctness of a solution, only its "quality". That is, the resulting solution eliminates a spurious counterexample but may be sub-optimal with respect to the preference orderings we define.
- We assume that all of the abstract domains are powerset domains. This assumption allows us to refine different control-flow paths independently and also to define unique optimal refinements for the orderings we define.
- The model considered above assumes that the analysis does not use widening operators, which are sometimes used by static analyses to accelerate least-fixpoint computations.
- We ignore scoping mechanisms, e.g., procedures and objects.

These limitations do not affect the applicability of the model but may affect its effectiveness in real applications.

3   Refinement Orderings

The problem defined in Sec. 2 does not lead, in general, to a unique refinement, as shown by the running example.

We denote by $Ref(\overline{A})$ the set of solutions to the given abstract counterexample refinement problem $\langle P, C, \phi, \overline{A}, \pi \rangle$, i.e., the set of compound powerset domains that refine $\overline{A}$ and remove the abstract counterexample.

Notice that a trivial refinement $\overline{A'} \doteq \langle A'_1 = C, \ldots, A'_k = C \rangle$ (i.e., the concrete domain at every position) eliminates any spurious counterexample along a given path. However, this defeats the purpose of counterexample-based refinement, which is an attempt to refine the given abstraction only as much as needed to achieve the verification goal. Since there are potentially many refinements, we would like to be able to evaluate them according to some quality ordering, and favor refinements of high quality. In this section, we define interesting properties of refinements, allowing us define the orderings.

Definition 1 (Refinement Dimensions). *Let $\langle P, C, \phi, \overline{A}, \pi \rangle$ be an instance of the abstract counterexample refinement problem, and let $\overline{B} \doteq \langle B_1, \ldots, B_k \rangle$ be in $Ref(\overline{A})$.*

Domains Dimension. The coordinate of the refinement along the domain dimension is the vector $\langle B_1, \ldots, B_k \rangle$.

Values Dimension. The forward abstract interpretation of the trace $l_1, \ldots, l_k$ with $\overline{B}$ yields the sequence of abstract values $b_1 \doteq \rho_{B_1}(init)$, and $b_{i+1} \doteq \overline{post}_{B_{i+1}}(st_i, b_i)$. We define $Val_B \doteq \langle b_1, \ldots, b_k \rangle$.

Indices Dimension. We define $Ind_B \doteq \{i \mid A_i \subset B_i\}$ to be the set of indices where $\overline{B}$ refines $\overline{A}$.

In the running example, $Ind_U = \{2, 4, 5\}$ and $Ind_W = \{3, 4, 5\}$; and the refined domains and corresponding abstract values are shown in Table 2.

In the rest of this section, we define a preference ordering for each dimension and establish lower and upper bounds for each ordering.

Table 2. Label; initial abstraction $\overline{A}$ and abstract values; a refinement $\overline{U}$; abstract values Val_U; a refinement $\overline{W}$; abstract values Val_W. In every row, the abstract domains and values correspond to the label before the statement.

lab.	A	Val_A	U	Val_U	W	Val_W
1	$\mathcal{D}_\top$	$\top_C$	$\mathcal{D}_\top$	$\top_C$	$\mathcal{D}_\top$	$\top_C$
2	$\mathcal{D}(\{x < 7\})$	$\{x < 7\}$	$\mathcal{D}(\{x < 7\}, \{x = 0\})$	$\{x = 0\}$	$\mathcal{D}(\{x < 7\})$	$\{x < 7\}$
3	$\mathcal{D}(\{x = 1\})$	$\top_C$	$\mathcal{D}(\{x = 1\})$	$\{x = 1\}$	$\mathcal{D}(\{x = 1\}, \{x < 8\})$	$\{x < 8\}$
4	$\mathcal{D}(\{x = 0\})$	$\top_C$	$\mathcal{D}(\{x = 0\}, \{x = 2\})$	$\{x = 2\}$	$\mathcal{D}(\{x = 0\}, \{x < 9\})$	$\{x < 9\}$
5	$\mathcal{D}(\{x = 2\})$	$\top_C$	$\mathcal{D}(\{x = 2\}, \{x = 3\})$	$\{x = 3\}$	$\mathcal{D}(\{x = 2\}, \{x < 10\})$	$\{x < 10\}$

3.1   A Preference Ordering on the Domains Dimension

We consider the following preference ordering on the domains dimension.

Definition 2 (Domain Coarseness Ordering). *For two compound abstract domains $\overline{U}$ and $\overline{W}$, we write $\overline{U} \preceq_{dom} \overline{W}$ if $W_i \subseteq U_i$ for every $i = 1 \ldots k$. That is, $\overline{W}$ is less precise than $\overline{U}$.*

In the running example, $\overline{U}$ and $\overline{W}$ are incomparable by the domain coarseness ordering.

A refinement can extend the abstract domains along the trace by adding "useless" abstract values, i.e., values that are not needed in order to eliminate the given abstract counterexample. It is possible to remove useless abstract values to obtain an *equivalent* refinement that is maximal w.r.t. the ordering $\preceq_{dom}$. We now formalize this.

Definition 3. *For two compound abstract domains $\overline{U}$ and $\overline{W}$, we write $\overline{U} \sim_{val} \overline{W}$ when $Val_U = Val_W$.*

It is straightforward to verify that $\sim_{val}$ is an equivalence relation. We now show that every equivalence class of $\sim_{val}$ contains a maximal element (w.r.t. $\preceq_{dom}$).

Definition 4. *Let $\pi \doteq l_1, \ldots, l_k$ be a sequence of program locations and let $\overline{A} \doteq \langle A_1, \ldots, A_k \rangle$ be the initial abstraction. Let $\overline{U} \doteq \langle U_1, \ldots, U_k \rangle$ be a compound abstract domain with the associated sequence of abstract values $u_1, \ldots, u_k$. We define the compound abstract domain $\widehat{\overline{U}}$ by $\widehat{\overline{U}}_i \doteq A_i \sqcap_{Rel} \mathcal{D}(u_i)$, i.e., $\widehat{\overline{U}}$ minimally refines A_i with the abstract value computed at location l_i by the abstract semantics with the compound abstraction $\overline{U}$.*

The following proposition shows that for every refinement there is a unique maximal refinement with respect to $\preceq_{dom}$.

Proposition 1. *For every compound domain $\overline{U} \in Ref(\overline{A})$: (i) $\overline{U} \sim_{val} \widehat{\overline{U}}$, (ii) $\widehat{\overline{U}} \in Ref(\overline{A})$, and (iii) for every $\overline{W} \in Ref(\overline{A})$, if $\overline{W} \sim_{val} \overline{U}$ then $\overline{W} \preceq_{dom} \widehat{\overline{U}}$.*

The refinement algorithm of Ball et el. [1] works in two phases. The first phase computes a set of predicates that can be added to the abstract domain to eliminate a spurious counterexample. The second phase tries to remove redundant predicates, i.e., predicates that are not needed to eliminate the counterexample. In our framework, the second phase can be seen as an attempt to maximize with respect to the ordering $\preceq_{dom}$.

In the sequel, we consider only members of $\sim_{val}$-equivalence classes that are maximal w.r.t. $\preceq_{dom}$.

3.2   A Preference Ordering on the Values Dimension

We now define an ordering on the abstract values dimension.

Definition 5 (Value Coarseness Ordering). *For two compound abstract domains $\overline{U}, \overline{W} \in \text{Ref}(\overline{A})$, we write $\overline{U} \preceq_{val} \overline{W}$ when the corresponding sequences of abstract values $u_1, \ldots, u_k$ and $w_1, \ldots, w_k$ are such that $u_i \subseteq w_i$ for $i = 1, \ldots, l$.*

In the running example, $\overline{U} \preceq_{val} \overline{W}$.

In order to define optimal refinements for the value coarseness ordering, we use the following definition, which establishes lower and upper bounds for this ordering.

Definition 6. *[Extremal Values] Let $\pi \doteq l_1, \ldots, l_k$ be a trace. We define and fix three sequence of abstract values.*

The lower envelope *is the sequence of abstract values: $f_1 \doteq init$, and $f_{i+1} \doteq \text{post}(st_i, f_i)$, for $i = 1, \ldots, k - 1$.*

The sequence of abstract values computed by a backward analysis, using weakest-precondition is $b_k \doteq \phi$ and $b_j \doteq \text{pre}(st_j, b_{j+1})$, for $j = 1 \ldots k - 1$.

The upper envelope *is the sequence of abstract values: $h_i \doteq a_i \cap b_i$ (recall that a_i is the abstract value at location l_i computed with $\overline{A}$).*

The following lemma uses the extremal values to supply a constructive way to differentiate between real and spurious abstract counterexamples.

Lemma 1. *Let $\langle P, C, \phi, \overline{A}, \pi \rangle$ be an instance of the abstract counterexample refinement problem. Then: (i) π is spurious if and only if $f_1 = init \subseteq h_1$, and (ii) if $f_1 \subseteq h_1$ then $f_i \subseteq h_i$, for every $i = 1, \ldots, k$.*

The next lemma establishes lower and upper bounds for the value coarseness ordering.

Lemma 2. *Let $\overline{U}$ be a compound abstract domain in $\text{Ref}(\overline{A})$ with the sequence of abstract values $\{u_i\}_{i=1}^k$. Let $\{a_i\}_{i=1}^k$ be the sequence of abstract values for the initial abstraction $\overline{A}$ and let $\{f_i\}_{i=1}^k$, $\{b_i\}_{i=1}^k$, and $\{h_i\}_{i=1}^k$ be the sequences defined Def. 6. Then, the following holds for every $i = 1, \ldots, k$: $f_i \subseteq u_i \subseteq h_i$.*

The first phase of the refinement algorithm of Ball et el. [1] finds refinement predicates using strongest postconditions, i.e., it computes the abstract values of the lower envelope. In our framework, this can be seen as an attempt to minimize with respect to the ordering $\preceq_{val}$. The refinement algorithm of Henzinger et al. [8] computes the weakest-precondition to find the abstract values used for refinement. In our framework, this can be seen as an attempt to maximize with respect to the ordering $\preceq_{val}$.

3.3 A Preference Ordering on the Indices Dimension

Notice that in the running example, $\overline{U}$ and $\overline{W}$ refine at different sets of control flow locations, except for locations 4 and 5. We now ask ourselves whether there exists a minimal set of indices where refinement is necessary for every refinement. This gives a lower bound along the indices dimension. Formally, we are interested in the set

$$Ind_{min} \doteq \bigcap \{Ind_U \mid \overline{U} \in \text{Ref}(\overline{A})\} .$$

The following proposition gives such a lower bound.

Proposition 2. *Let* $\langle P, C, \phi, \overline{A}, \pi \rangle$ *be an instance of the abstract counterexample refinement problem such that* π *is spurious, and let* $\{f_i\}_{i=1}^k$ *and* $\{h_i\}_{i=1}^k$, *be the lower and upper envelope values, respectively. The set* Ind_{min}, *defined above, can be constructively defined as follows:* $Ind_{min} = \{i \mid \rho_i(f_i) \not\sqsubseteq h_i\}$.

In the running example, $Ind_{min} = \{4, 5\}$.

We say that a set $I \subseteq \{1, \ldots, k\}$ is *sufficient* (to eliminate a spurious abstract counterexample) if there exists a refinement that extends the abstract domains only at the locations in I. Although the set Ind_{min} is included in the set of indices of every refinement, it is not always sufficient. In the running example, it is not enough to refine at just the control flow locations in $Ind_{min} = \{4, 5\}$.

Intuitively, we would like to favor refinements that extend the abstract domains at as few locations as possible.

We would like to find a minimal set of locations, with respect to the subset relation, where refinement is sufficient to remove a spurious counterexample. The intuition is that refining fewer abstract domains could lead to a cheaper analysis.

We define an ordering on the indices dimension. The ordering aims to minimize the set of locations where refinement occurs by choosing the locations that have the highest indices.

Definition 7 (Lazy Indices Ordering). *For two compound abstract domains* $\overline{U}, \overline{W} \in Ref(\overline{A})$, *we write* $\overline{U} \preccurlyeq_{lazy} \overline{W}$ *if* $Ind_U \subseteq Ind_W$, *or when* Ind_U *is lexicographically greater than or equal to* Ind_W.

In the running example, $\overline{W} \preccurlyeq_{lazy} \overline{U}$.

The lazy indices ordering has certain interesting properties. First, the set of indices is minimal in the sense that it is not possible to remove any location from the set and remain with a set of locations that are sufficient to remove a spurious counterexample. Second, the first index is as far as possible from the beginning of the trace. The refinement method in [8] starts refining as late as possible in order to reduce the amount of re-computation in subsequent refinement iteration steps. Some refinement techniques (e.g., [1] and [7]) refine at every location along the trace, aiming to eliminate as many spurious counterexamples as possible that share a common prefix with the given counterexample; this can be seen as a method that attempts to maximize with respect to the ordering $\preccurlyeq_{lazy}$.

From Def. 7 it immediately follows that the set of refinements that are minimal with respect to the lazy refinement ordering determine a unique set of indices. We denote this set by Ind_{lazy}. In the next section we present a procedure for finding Ind_{lazy}. The upper bound on the indices dimension, for the lazy indices ordering, is given by the set of indices $1, \ldots, k$.

3.4   Combining Preference Orderings

We combine preference orderings as follows. For an ordering $\preccurlyeq$, let $\succcurlyeq$ denote its reversed version. A combined ordering $\langle a, b \rangle$, where $a \in \{\preccurlyeq_{lazy}, \succcurlyeq_{lazy}\}$ and

$b \in \{\preccurlyeq_{val}, \succcurlyeq_{val}\}$, compares two compound abstract domains lexicographically, first by the ordering a and then by the ordering b. We also consider the combined ordering $\langle b, a \rangle$.

4 Refinement Procedures

In this section, we provide refinement procedures that yield optimal solutions for the preference orderings defined in the previous section. We describe the procedures and state the corresponding correctness and optimality claims.

We first describe two helper procedures: Fig. 1(a) shows a procedure for finding the abstract values found by backward propagation of the property, by using weakest preconditions, and for finding the abstract values of the upper envelope, according to Lem. 2; and Fig. 1(b) is used to detect real counterexamples before attempting to apply any refinement procedure. If $init \not\subseteq b_1$, then executing the concrete semantics with any value in $init \setminus b_1$ yields a concrete counterexample.

Proposition 3. *Given an instance of the abstract counterexample refinement problem $\langle P, C, \phi, \overline{A}, \pi \rangle$, the procedure in Fig. 1(b) detects whether π is a real counterexample or a spurious counterexample.*

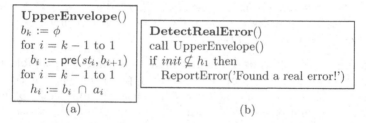

Fig. 1. (a) A procedure that computes the upper envelope values, according to Lem. 2; (b) A procedure for detecting real counterexamples

4.1 Refining with the Most Concrete Values/Most Abstract Values

The refinement procedures for the preference orderings $\{\preccurlyeq_{val}, \succcurlyeq_{val}\}$ are shown in Fig. 2. These procedures use Lem. 2 in order to choose the values with which to refine. Applying **RefineMostConcrete** to the running example yields the refinement $\overline{U}$, and applying **RefineMostAbstract** yields the refinement $\overline{W}$.

Theorem 1. *Given an instance of the abstract counterexample refinement problem $\langle P, C, \phi, \overline{A}, \pi \rangle$ where π is a spurious counterexample, the procedures shown in Fig. 2 output the optimal refinements for the orderings $\langle \succcurlyeq_{val}, b \rangle$ and $\langle \preccurlyeq_{val}, b \rangle$, respectively. That is, they result with refinements that have the most concrete values*

(Fig. 2(a)) or the most abstract values (Fig. 2(b)), regardless of the ordering on the indices, b. (This is because the optimums are unique and thus exactly determine the locations where refinement occurs.)

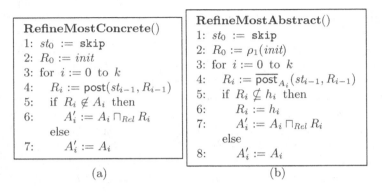

Fig. 2. (a) A procedure that refines with the most concrete values (the lower envelope values $\{f_i\}_{i=1}^{k}$); and (b) A procedure that refines with the most abstract values (the upper envelope values $\{h_i \doteq a_i \cap b_i\}_{i=1}^{k}$)

4.2   Computing Ind_{lazy}

Theorem 2. *Given an instance of the abstract counterexample refinement problem $\langle P, C, \phi, \overline{A}, \pi \rangle$ where π is a spurious counterexample, the procedure in Fig. 3(a) outputs the sequence of indices Ind_{lazy}.*

The procedure in Fig. 3(a) uses the approximations that are available in the abstract domains when they are contained in the upper envelope. Otherwise, it does not overapproximate the values, in order to increase the opportunity of finding appropriate approximations in the domains at the subsequent locations. Applying the procedure to the running example result in locations $\{3, 4, 5\}$.

4.3   Adapting the Refinement for the Most Concrete Values/Most Abstract Values

Theorem 3. *Given an instance of the abstract counterexample refinement problem $\langle P, C, \phi, \overline{A}, \pi \rangle$ where π is a spurious counterexample, and a set of indices $I \subseteq \{1, \dots, k\}$ that are sufficient for refinement, the procedures in Fig. 3(b) and Fig. 3(c) output the refinements with the most concrete abstract values and the most coarse abstract values, respectively.*

The advantage of having the indices as an additional parameter is that we can use the same procedures with different orderings on the indices, not just the lazy indices ordering. Applying **RefineHigh** to the running example with the indices $\{3, 4, 5\}$ yields the refinement $\overline{W}$.

We combine the procedures to produce optimal refinements for a combined ordering $\langle a, b \rangle$. The procedure is shown in Fig. 4.

IndLazy()	**RefineLow**(I : indices)	**RefineHigh**(I : indices)
$Ind_{lazy} := \{\}$	$st_0 := \texttt{skip}$	$st_k := \texttt{skip}$
$st_0 := \texttt{skip}$	$R_0 := init$	$R_{k+1} := \phi$
$R_0 := init$	for $i := 0$ to k	for $i := k$ to 1
for $i := 1$ to k	$\quad L_i := \mathsf{post}(st_{i-1}, R_{i-1})$	$\quad H_i := \mathsf{pre}(st_i, R_{i+1})$
$\quad L_i := \mathsf{post}(st_{i-1}, R_{i-1})$	$\quad H_i := \rho_i(L_i)$	$\quad L_i := \underline{\rho}_i(H_i)$
$\quad H_i := \rho_i(L_i)$	$\quad$ if $i \in I$ then	$\quad$ if $i \in I$ then
$\quad$ if $H_i \subseteq h_i$ then	$\quad\quad R_i := H_i$	$\quad\quad R_i := H_i$
$\quad\quad R_i := H_i$	$\quad\quad A_i' := A_i \sqcap_{Rel} R_i$	$\quad\quad A_i' := A_i \sqcap_{Rel} R_i$
$\quad$ else	$\quad$ else	$\quad$ else
$\quad\quad R_i := L_i$	$\quad\quad R_i := L_i$	$\quad\quad R_i := L_i$
$\quad\quad Ind_{lazy} := Ind_{lazy} \cup \{i\}$	$\quad\quad A_i' := A_i$	$\quad\quad A_i' := A_i$
(a)	(b)	(c)

Fig. 3. (a) A procedure for finding Ind_{lazy}; (b) A procedure for refining at a specified set of control flow locations with the most precise abstract values; and (c) A procedure for refining at a specified set of control flow locations with the coarsest abstract values

RefineIndVal($\langle a, b \rangle$: ordering)
if a is $\preccurlyeq_{lazy}$
$\quad I := \text{IndLazy}()$
else // a is $\succcurlyeq_{lazy}$
$\quad I := [1, \ldots, k]$
if b is $\preccurlyeq_{val}$
$\quad$ RefineHigh(I)
else // b is $\succcurlyeq_{val}$
$\quad$ RefineLow(I)

Fig. 4. A procedure for the optimal refinement for the preference ordering $\langle a, b \rangle$

Theorem 4. *Given an instance of the abstract counterexample refinement problem $\langle P, C, \phi, \overline{A}, \pi \rangle$ where π is a spurious counterexample, and a combined ordering $\langle a, b \rangle$, the procedure in Fig. 4 outputs the optimal refinement w.r.t. $\langle a, b \rangle$.*

5   Constrained Problem Settings

In previous sections, we considered the abstraction refinement problem over the entire space of abstractions of the concrete domain. In this section, we constrain the set of possible abstractions in the following way. For a concrete domain C, we assume that an abstract domain $D \subseteq C$ is given as a parameter. Intuitively, D is rather precise but possibly very expensive for static analysis. We consider the lattice of abstractions that weaken D:

$$Weak(D) \doteq \{D' \mid \rho \text{ is an upper-closure operator and } D' = \rho(D)\} \ .$$

(As an example for a lattice of abstractions consider the set of abstractions obtained by choosing different subsets from a fixed set of predicates.) Essentially, the domain D establishes a lower bound on the precision of the refinement. This can be used both to guide the refinement process in the abstract values it chooses, and to limit the number of refinement iterations (by the height of the lattice D). Although it is possible to use different lattices of abstractions at different locations, we use the same lattice in every location to simplify things. Generalizing to different lattices of abstractions at different locations is straightforward.

We now rephrase the goal of the abstraction refinement problem in the modified settings. The goal of the refinement procedure is to check whether it is possible to refine the compound abstract domain $\overline{A} \doteq \langle A_1, \ldots, A_m \rangle$ into $\overline{A'} \doteq \langle A'_1, \ldots, A'_m \rangle$, where A_i and A'_i are in $Weak(D)$ for every $i = 1, \ldots, m$, such that $(\mathsf{post}^{\sharp'}(st_{k-1}) \circ \ldots \circ \mathsf{post}^{\sharp'}(st_1) \circ \rho'_1)(init) \subseteq \phi$, where $\mathsf{post}^{\sharp'}(st_i) = \rho'_j \circ \mathsf{post}(st_i)$ for every $i = 1 \ldots k - 1$. If this is impossible (with $A'_i = D_i$ for $i = 1, \ldots, n$) then report that D is insufficiently precise to prove that ϕ holds on the path.

The refinement procedures from the previous section can be adapted to the new setting by replacing $\mathsf{post}(st)$ with $\mathsf{post}_D(st) \doteq \rho_D \circ \mathsf{post}(st)$, and replacing $\mathsf{pre}(st)$ with $\underline{\mathsf{pre}}_D(st) \doteq \underline{\rho}_D \circ \mathsf{pre}(st)$.

We note that in this setting, the optimality of the refinement procedures is used in a narrower sense than in the previous sections. Here, optimality is given with respect to the lattice $Weak(D)$ (not $Weak(C)$).

Cost-based Preference Orderings. It is possible to define more sophisticated preference orderings by assigning costs to abstract values. For example, the abstract values used in the running example by the refinement U are simpler than the values used by the refinement W, and thus may be assigned lower costs. A very simple technique to find cheap refinements is to first try refining with a low cost elements, and if this fails try refining with more costly elements. We plan to investigate the issue of cost-based ordering in future work.

6   Local Optima vs. Global Optima

Until now, we have focused on a single step within the CEGAR framework — refining along a given path. The analyzer starts with an initial abstraction and then iteratively applies the refinement step to individual paths in the CFG in order to prove the property. When this process converges, it yields a final abstraction, i.e., a compound abstract domain for the entire CFG, and set of abstract values (stored in each control flow location). For a given preference ordering, let us call the final abstraction (and abstract values) that result by applying an optimal refinement in each refinement step a *locally optimal solution*. We continue by defining preference orderings on entire CFGs, which allow us to define *globally optimal solutions*. We then compare the two types of solutions.

The dimensions defined in Sec. 3 do not depend on having the locations set on a path. Therefore, they extend immediately to an entire CFG. Thus, we can extend the domain coarseness ordering by point-wise comparison of the abstract domains in all CFG locations. Similarly, we can extend the values ordering by point-wise comparison of the fixpoint values computed with the two abstractions. The ordering on indices depends on a "natural" order on the locations along a path. We therefore consider an extension only for acyclic CFGs, by fixing a topological order on the locations.

We say that a refinement is *globally optimal* if it is precise enough to prove the property and optimal with respect to a given preference ordering.

label: statement		A	Val_A
1:	x = 0	$\mathcal{D}_\top$	$\top_C$
	if (...)		
2t:	x = x + 1	$\mathcal{D}(\{x = 0\})$	$\{x = 0\}$
	else		
2f:	x = x + 5	$\mathcal{D}(\{x = 0\})$	$\{x = 0\}$
3:	x = x + 1	$\mathcal{D}(\{x < 5\})$	$\{x < 8\}$
4:	x = x + 1	$\mathcal{D}(\{x = 2\}, \{x = 6\})$	$\top_C$
5:	assert(x < 10)	$\mathcal{D}(\{x < 10\})$	$\top_C$

```
1:   x = 3
2:   y = 3
     if (...)
3t:      x = x + 1
     else
3f:      y = y + 1
4:   assert(x == 4 || y == 4)
```

(a)   (b)

Fig. 5. (a) An example program for the domain coarseness order; (b) An example program for the lazy indices order; initial abstraction; corresponding abstract values

Domain Coarseness Order. We now show that for the domain coarseness ordering the globally optimal solution can be better than a locally optimal solution. This is not surprising. Iterative refinement might refine at a given location numerous times (for different spurious counterexamples) until reaching the final abstraction $\overline{U}$. On the other hand, it is possible to use Def. 4 to produce a coarser abstraction that suffices to prove the property by refining with at most one abstract value at every location. The next example shows this gap.

Example 1. Assume we are given the program fragment shown in Fig. 5(a) with an empty initial abstraction and that we wish to verify that the assertion in line 4 holds. There are two control flow paths $(1, 2, 3t, 4)$ and $(1, 2, 3f, 4)$, which we first consider separately:

- For the path $(1, 2, 3t, 4)$, we compute the weakest-precondition $p_{3t} : x = 3 \vee y = 4$ at location 3t, $p_2 : x = 3$ at location 2, and $p_1 : true$ at location 1.
- For the path $(1, 2, 3f, 4)$, we compute the weakest-precondition $p_{3f} : x = 4 \vee y = 3$ at location 3f, $p_2 : true$ at location 2, and $p_1 : true$ at location 1.

By refining the abstraction for each path separately, we get the abstract domain $\mathcal{D}(\{(x = a, y = b) \mid a = 3 \vee b = 4\}) \wedge \mathcal{D}(\{(x = a, y = b) \mid a = 4 \vee b = 3\})$, which includes all of the points from both of the individual abstract domains.

However, if we compute the weakest-precondition over the two control flow paths together, we get the set of states $\{(x = a, y = b) \mid (a = 3 \vee b = 4) \wedge (a = 4 \vee b = 3)\} = \{(x = 3, y = 3), (x = 4, y = 4)\}$. This allows us to obtain a coarser abstraction than before, representing only two concrete states. $\square$

Lazy Indices Order. The following example shows that the globally optimal solution, with respect to the lazy indices order, can be better than a locally optimal solution. Consider the program shown in Fig. 5(b). The globally optimal solution contains the single location $\{3\}$, since it is possible to refine the domain at location 3 to $\mathcal{D}(\{x < 5\}, \{x = 1\}, \{x = 2\})$ and prove the property. This solution is obtained by modifying the procedure **IndLazy** to operate simultaneously on sets of acyclic paths.

If the analysis first refines the trace $(1, 2\mathrm{t}, 3, 4, 5)$, the lazy indices order gives us the set of locations $\{4\}$ (e.g., it is possible to refine the trace with the abstract domain $\mathcal{D}(\{x = 2\}, \{x = 6\}, \{x < 6\})$). However, no matter how we refine at location 4 (either with the most precise value $\{x = 1\}$, or with the most abstract value $\{x < 6\}$), the trace $(1, 2\mathrm{f}, 3, 4, 5)$ still needs to be refined at location 3 (say, with the value $\{x = 5\}$). Thus, the locations where refinement occurs are $\{3, 4\} \preccurlyeq_{lazy} \{3\}$, which shows the optimality gap.

Abstract Values Order. We now state a positive optimality result. Intuitively, this optimality result holds because the global optimum for the values order, at every location, is given by the intersection of the upper envelope values for the set of all program traces at that location.

Theorem 5. *An analysis that iteratively refines spurious counterexamples using the procedure **RefineMostAbstract** produces the globally optimal solution.*

7   Related Work and Conclusions

Gulavani and Rajamani [6] describe and implement an algorithm for refining widening operators to joins and join operators to disjunctions for non-powerset domains, which our model does not handle. However, their method does not refine powerset domains, which we consider here. Therefore, their work is orthogonal to ours.

Giacobazzi and Quintarelli [5] use a procedure that iteratively refines the abstract domain in order to achieve completeness of the abstract interpretation. They show that in the limit, a complete abstract interpretation removes all spurious counterexamples. This gives a semi-algorithm that can be applied to a given path to remove the abstract counterexample, albeit indirectly. The algorithm is guaranteed to converge for finite concrete domains. Our framework is geared towards eliminating a given counterexample directly using a different set of operations, and since our refinement procedure does not require completeness of the abstract interpretation it always terminates.

Loginov et al. [10] use inductive learning to refine abstractions for 3-valued shape analysis. Their refinement is not guided by abstract counterexamples but rather by imprecisions detected during the analysis itself.

Beyer et al. [2] integrate the TVLA system [9] into the BLAST software model checker [8] and use information from counterexamples to refine 3-valued structures in order to make shape analysis more scalable. Their technique is one application of abstract-counterexample refinement that goes beyond predicate abstraction.

In this paper, we present a theoretical framework for refinement of powerset domains in order to eliminate spurious counterexamples. We describe operations on abstract domains and generic algorithms that can be used as a starting point for applying counterexample-guided refinement in new settings, e.g., shape analysis. Using the framework, we are able to define different optimality criteria and compare locally optimal refinements with globally optimal refinements, which was not done until now.

References

1. T. Ball and S. K. Rajamani. The slam project: Debugging system software via static analysis. In *POPL '02: Proceedings of the 29th ACM SIGPLAN-SIGACT symposium on Principles of programming languages*, pages 1–3, New York, NY, USA, 2002. ACM Press.
2. D. Beyer, T. A. Henzinger, and G. Théoduloz. Lazy shape analysis. In *Proceedings of the 18th International Conference on Computer-Aided Verification (CAV)*, volume 4144 of *LNCS*, pages 532–546. Springer Verlag, 2006.
3. E.M. Clarke, O. Grumberg, S. Jha, Y. Lu, and H. Veith. Counterexample-guided abstraction refinement. In *Proc. Computer Aided Verification*, pages 154–169, 2000.
4. P. Cousot and R. Cousot. Abstract interpretation: A unified lattice model for static analysis of programs by construction of approximation of fixed points. In *Proc. Symp. on Principles of Prog. Languages*, pages 238–252, New York, NY, 1977. ACM Press.
5. R. Giacobazzi and E. Quintarelli. Incompleteness, counterexamples, and refinements in abstract model-checking. In P. Cousot, editor, *Static Analysis: 8th International Symposium, SAS 2001*, pages 356–373. Springer-Verlag GmbH, July 2001.
6. B. S. Gulavani and S. K. Rajamani. Counterexample driven refinement for abstract interpretation. In *Appeared in the 12th. International Conference on Tools and Algortihms for the Construction and Analysis of Systems, TACAS'06*, pages 474–488. Springer-Verlag, Mar 2006.
7. T. A. Henzinger, R. Jhala, R. Majumdar, and K. L. McMillan. Abstractions from proofs. In *POPL '04: Proceedings of the 31st ACM SIGPLAN-SIGACT symposium on Principles of programming languages*, pages 232–244, 2004.
8. T.A. Henzinger, R. Jhala, R. Majumdar, and G. Sutre. Lazy abstraction. In *Symposium on Principles of Programming Languages*, pages 58–70, 2002.
9. T. Lev-Ami and M. Sagiv. TVLA: A framework for Kleene based static analysis. In *Proc. Static Analysis Symp.*, volume 1824 of *LNCS*, pages 280–301. Springer-Verlag, 2000.
10. A. Loginov, T. Reps, and M. Sagiv. Abstraction refinement via inductive learning. In *Proceedings of the 17th International Conference on Computer-Aided Verification (CAV)*, LNCS, pages 519–533. Springer Verlag, 2005.

11. F. Nielson, H.R. Nielson, and C. Hankin. *Principles of Program Analysis.* Springer-Verlag, 2001.
12. M. Sagiv, T. Reps, and R. Wilhelm. Parametric shape analysis via 3-valued logic. *ACM Transactions on Programming Languages and Systems (TOPLAS)*, 24(3):217–298, 2002.

A   The Challenges of Refining Non-powerset Domains

Inter-Path Dependencies. We now show that in the face of non-powerset abstract domains, it is not always possible to remove spurious counterexample by refining single control flow paths independently. Consider the C program fragment shown in Fig. 6(a) and assume that the abstract domain used to verify the property in the assertion statement is the constant propagation domain, or *ICP*, shown in Fig. 6(b). The verification fails, since the abstract value propagated after the statement x=2 is $x = 2$, the abstract value propagated after the statement x=4 is $x = 4$, and the join of the values is $x = \top$, which is not precise enough to prove the property, even though the property holds on every concrete execution.

Now, if we consider each control flow path through the if statement separately, we discover that the abstract domain is precise enough to verify the property: we get $x = 2$ for the path the follows the positive branch and $x = 4$ for the path that follows the negative branch, both of which satisfy the property. The loss of imprecision is due to the join operator, which approximates the set of values $\{2, 4\}$ from the two paths with $\top$. This shows that in order to remove spurious counterexamples, the analysis needs to consider both control flow paths.

Non-Existence of Best Underapproximations. It is known that for an abstract domain, every concrete state $c \in C$ has the best overapproximation in A, given by $\rho(c)$. However, this is not generally true for underapproximation, as stated by the next lemma.

Lemma 3. *For a concrete domain C and an abstract domain A, the best underapproximation in A of every concrete element in C is ensured to exist only when A is a powerset domain.*

Proof. We first give an example showing that when A is a non-powerset domain the best underapproximation does not exist. Consider the concrete domain given by the powerset of integers and its abstraction by the ICP lattice. The set $\{2, 3\}$ can be underapproximated in the ICP domain by either 2 or 3. Both of these underapproximations are tight, yet they are incomparable.

Let c be an element in C. We claim that $\underline{\rho}_A(c) \equiv \bigcup_{a \in A, a \subseteq c} a$ is the best underapproximation of c in A[5].

---

[5] In this case, $\underline{\rho}_A$ is a lower closure operator, and A is a complete sublattice of C.

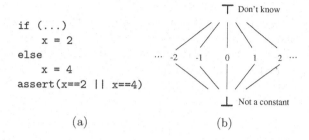

```
if (...)
    x = 2
else
    x = 4
assert(x==2 || x==4)
```

(a)   (b)

Fig. 6. An example for inter-path dependency: (a) A program fragment; (b) The Constant Propagation Lattice

First, since every $x \in A$ such that $x \subseteq c$ contains only states in c, $\underline{\rho}_A(c) \subseteq c$ is an underapproximation. Furthermore, since A is a powerset domain, $\underline{\rho}_A(c) \in A$ is an underapproximation in A. Now, if $x' \in A$ is an underapproximation of c then $x \subseteq \bigcup_{x \in A, x \subseteq c} x$, and therefore $\underline{\rho}_A(c)$ is the tightest underapproximation. □

As seen in this paper, best underapproximations are very useful for abstract counterexample refinement. They are used both to determine in which control flow location to refine and how to refine (which abstract values to use).

B   Abstract Domain Refinement

In this section, we discuss the operations used for refinement in the general abstract domains setting and in the setting of powerset abstract domains in particular. We use Fig. 7 as an illustrative example.

Let $C \doteq 2^{STATES}$ be a concrete domain containing all subsets of concrete states as its elements with set inclusion as an ordering relation. Given two abstract domains A and B (given by upper closure operators), the reduced product operation of A and B, denoted by $A \sqcap B$, is the simplest (i.e., most abstract) abstract domain containing $A \cup B$. In the context of this paper, A is an initial abstraction of C, and B is a simple domain containing the elements we wish to be included in the refined abstract domain. The reduced product operation is natural here, since it does the minimal amount of refinement needed to add the new elements. As an example, Fig. 7(a) and Fig. 7(b) show to abstract domain, and Fig. 7(c) shows their reduced product.

Notice that the domains in Fig. 7(a) and Fig. 7(b) are powerset domains. However, their reduced product is not, since, for example, the element $\{1, 2, 3\}$ is missing. In this paper, we focus only on powerset abstract domains. We would like an operation that takes as input two powerset abstract domains and gives the simplest powerset abstract domain that includes its operands. Therefore, the reduced product operation in itself is inappropriate for this kind of abstract domain refinement. To fix this, we need to extend the result of the reduced product in order to achieve closure under set union. The abstract domain operation that achieves this is called *disjunctive completion*. We denote by $A \sqcap_{Rel} B$ the operation that accepts two powerset abstract domains and returns the simplest powerset abstract domain that is more precise than A and B. Fig. 7(d) shows the result of applying this operation to the abstract domains in Fig. 7(a) and Fig. 7(b).

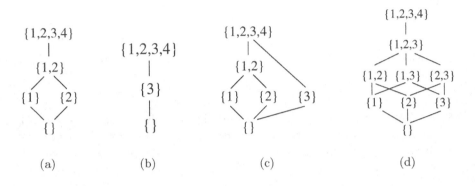

(a)   (b)   (c)   (d)

Fig. 7. Abstractions of $C = 2^{\{1,2,3\}}$: (a) A powerset abstract domain A^1; (b) A powerset abstract domain A^2; (c) The reduced product $A = A^1 \sqcap A^2$; and (d) The disjunctive completion of A

Types from Control Flow Analysis

Flemming Nielson and Hanne Riis Nielson

Informatics and Mathematical Modelling, Richard Petersens Plads bldg. 321,
Technical University of Denmark, DK-2800 Kongens Lyngby, Denmark
{nielson|riis}@imm.dtu.dk

Abstract. Control flow analysis is a powerful method for analysing which functions are applied to which arguments. However, many users find the information more understandable if the information is presented in the form of types rather than sets of function abstractions. We therefore show how to translate the result of the control flow analysis into the syntax of types (to be called *observed types*).

To compare our approach with the more traditional approach using type systems (to be called *inferred types*) we develop the subtyping relations in both approaches; in particular we show that covariant subtyping is the appropriate choice for observed types whereas contravariant subtyping is appropriate choice for inferred types. This serves as a technical underpinning of our main thesis that observed types should merely record how the entity *has been used* in the program at hand whereas inferred types should indicate how the entity *can be used* in all possible contexts.

1 Introduction

Data flow analysis is a powerful method for analysing the behaviour of many programming languages. In the interprocedural case it is based on control flow analysis for determining which functions, procedures or methods are applied at which program points. This information can be represented in a number of ways suitable for the internal operation of a compiler, e.g. the set of function abstractions that reach a given call site. However, in cases where this information needs to be presented to the user it is important to match the expectations of the user. Some users will be mostly familiar with types and this motivates the study of the present paper where we show how to translate the result of the control flow analysis into the syntax of types.

We start by introducing our simple functional programming language in Section 2 together with its call-by-name operational semantics.

We then develop a control flow analysis in Section 3 by means of a syntax-directed generation of constraints in Horn Clauses with Sharing [11]. We show the semantic correctness of the analysis by means of a subject-reduction result and we review the theory guaranteeing the existence of least solutions.

In Section 4 we then present our main contribution which is to develop *observed types* from the result of the control flow analysis. This approach is "descriptive" in that we aim to express how the entity under study has been used in

T. Reps, M. Sagiv, and J. Bauer (Eds.): Wilhelm Festschrift, LNCS 4444, pp. 293–310, 2007.

the program at hand. We first introduce the *syntax* of types and next *axiomatise* when a set of values can be described by a given type; in the case of values being function abstractions this makes use of the result of the control flow analysis. Next we develop the *observed types* and in particular we formulate the subtyping rule which turns out to be *covariant* in line with considerations in previous work on subtyping object-types and set-based analysis. Finally we show how to automatically construct the optimal type for describing a given set of values; since the control flow analysis can be computed in cubic time this provides a cubic time algorithm for calculating *observed types* of a given depth.

To compare our approach with the more traditional approach using type systems we develop *inferred types* in Section 5. This approach is "prescriptive" in that we aim to express how the entity under study can be used in all possible contexts. As expected the subtyping rule needs to be *contravariant* and we establish some of the usual theoretical results including subject-reduction. We conclude with giving a deeper comparison of *observed types* and *inferred types*: this includes showing a sufficient condition for when the type system for observed types strictly includes that of inferred types.

We provide an additional perspective and concluding remarks in Section 6.

Related work. There have been many papers studying the interplay between types and flow analysis. Some papers have focussed on showing their close relationship culminating in the ability to provide a type system equivalent to flow analysis [2,13,14] and vice versa. Other papers have shown that the framework of Abstract Interpretation [5] is able to describe type systems as abstractions of the semantics (typically in the form of a collecting semantics tracing all possible executions) [4,9]; our own favourite is Chapter 5 of [10] that shows in Proposition 5.12 that the judgements of a type and effect system indeed constitute a Moore family (and hence fall within the developments of Abstract Interpretation). Yet other papers have shown how to incorporate flow analysis into the formulation of type systems [3,6,7]; this is especially direct in the case of type and effect systems where the control flow information takes the form of effects on the function types.

Somehow these developments fail to be fully convincing in capturing the distinction between intensionality and extensionality inherent in traditional approaches to type systems and control and data flow analysis. Indeed, while the concepts of flow analysis and type systems can be massaged so as to coincide [2,13,14] our thesis is that flow analysis and type systems capture related but somehow distinct features of programs. In this paper we intend to capture some of those distinctions amid the many strong relationships that exist.

2   Preliminaries

We start by introducing a simple functional language and its operational semantics. The syntax is given by

Table 1. Small-step operational semantics: $e_1^l \longrightarrow e_2^l$

$$\frac{e_1^{l_1} \longrightarrow e_1'^{\,l_1}}{(e_1^{l_1} + e_2^{l_2})^l \longrightarrow (e_1'^{\,l_1} + e_2^{l_2})^l} \qquad \frac{e_2^{l_2} \longrightarrow e_2'^{\,l_2}}{(n_1^{l_1} + e_2^{l_2})^l \longrightarrow (n_1^{l_1} + e_2'^{\,l_2})^l}$$

$$(n_1^{l_1} + n_2^{l_2})^l \longrightarrow n^l \quad \text{if } n = n_1 + n_2$$

$$\frac{e_1^{l_1} \longrightarrow e_1'^{\,l_1}}{(e_1^{l_1} = e_2^{l_2})^l \longrightarrow (e_1'^{\,l_1} = e_2^{l_2})^l} \qquad \frac{e_2^{l_2} \longrightarrow e_2'^{\,l_2}}{(n_1^{l_1} = e_2^{l_2})^l \longrightarrow (n_1^{l_1} = e_2'^{\,l_2})^l}$$

$$(n_1^{l_1} = n_2^{l_2})^l \longrightarrow \mathsf{tt}^l \quad \text{if } n_1 = n_2 \qquad (n_1^{l_1} = n_2^{l_2})^l \longrightarrow \mathsf{ff}^l \quad \text{if } n_1 \neq n_2$$

$$\frac{e_1^{l_1} \longrightarrow e_1'^{\,l_1}}{(e_1^{l_1} \; e_2^{l_2})^l \longrightarrow (e_1'^{\,l_1} \; e_2^{l_2})^l} \qquad ((\lambda x.e_0^{l_0})^{l_1} \; e_2^{l_2})^l \longrightarrow (e_0[e_2/x])^l$$

$$(\mu f \, x.e_0^{l_0})^l \longrightarrow (\lambda x.(e_0[\mu f \, x.e_0^{l_0}/f])^{l_0})^l$$

$$\frac{e_0^{l_0} \longrightarrow e_0'^{\,l_0}}{(\text{if } e_0^{l_0} \text{ then } e_1^{l_1} \text{ else } e_2^{l_2})^l \longrightarrow (\text{if } e_0'^{\,l_0} \text{ then } e_1^{l_1} \text{ else } e_2^{l_2})^l}$$

$$(\text{if } \mathsf{tt}^{l_0} \text{ then } e_1^{l_1} \text{ else } e_2^{l_2})^l \longrightarrow e_1^l \qquad (\text{if } \mathsf{ff}^{l_0} \text{ then } e_1^{l_1} \text{ else } e_2^{l_2})^l \longrightarrow e_2^l$$

$$
\begin{aligned}
e^l \quad ::= \quad & \mathsf{tt}^l \quad | \quad \mathsf{ff}^l \quad | \quad n^l \quad | \quad x^l \quad | \quad (e_1^{l_1} + e_2^{l_2})^l \quad | \quad (e_1^{l_1} = e_2^{l_2})^l \quad | \\
& (\lambda x.e_0^{l_0})^l \quad | \quad (\mu f x.e_0^{l_0})^l \quad | \quad (e_1^{l_1} e_2^{l_2})^l \quad | \quad (\text{if } e_0^{l_0} \text{ then } e_1^{l_1} \text{ else } e_2^{l_2})^l
\end{aligned}
$$

where e^l ranges over labelled expressions, n denotes integers and x denotes variables. Addition and equality are intended to work only on integers and $(\mu f x.e_0^{l_0})^l$ denotes a recursive variant of the λ-abstraction $(\lambda x.e_0^{l_0})^l$ where the body $e_0^{l_0}$ is allowed to be recursive by reference to f. The labels, denoted l, have no semantic significance but will serve as useful placeholders when developing the control flow analysis; we shall allow to dispense with them in examples when they do not add clarity.

The operational semantics is defined as a small-step semantics in Table 1. For simplicity of presentation it is a call-by-name semantics but this is of no consequence for the development. It is intended to operate on *closed* expressions only, i.e. expressions with no free variables.

Example 1. Consider the following example program:

$$((\lambda x.(x^1 x^2)^3)^4 (\lambda y.(y^5 y^6)^7)^8)^9$$

This program will call $(\lambda y.(yy))$ repeatedly upon itself and never terminate.

Example 2. Consider the following example program:

$$((\lambda x.(\lambda z.(x^1 x^2)^3)^4)^5 (\lambda y.(\lambda z.(y^6 y^7)^8)^9)^{10})^{11}$$

This function will consume all parameters supplied to it and return the function $\lambda z.((\lambda y.(\lambda z.(yy)))(\lambda y.(\lambda z.(yy))))$.

3   Control Flow Analysis

We now develop a control flow analysis for the functional language together with a review of the theory that admits solutions in at most cubic time.

3.1   Correct Specification

A control flow analysis keeps track of which values (mainly lambda abstractions but for a higher order language also rudimentary information about truth values and integers) that reach which points in the program. We formalise it using these predicates:

$C(l, v)$ indicates that the value v may reach a subexpression labelled l,

$R(x, v)$ indicates that the value v may be bound to the variable x,

$P(l, v)$ indicates that the value v may be an actual parameter to a λ-abstraction whose body is labelled l,

$B(v)$ indicates that v is used where a boolean value is expected,

$I(v)$ indicates that v is used where an integer value is expected,

$A(l)$ indicates that l labels the body of a λ-abstraction used in the program.

The values v belong to an unspecified universe $\mathcal{U}$ of constants. The contants include the boolean values tt, ff, the token int (representing arbitrary integers) and all labels in the program. A lambda abstraction $\lambda x.e^l$ will be represented by the label l.

For each subprogram of a given program we then generate clauses as shown in Table 2. The overall clause generated for the entire program is the conjunction of all the clauses recursively generated using the method of Table 2; we shall write $[\![e^l]\!]$ for the clause generated from e^l. Finally we shall write $(A, B, C, I, P, R) \models [\![e^l]\!]$ to mean that the predicates A, B, C, I, P, R satisfy the overall clause generated from e^l. We shall allow to abbreviate A, B, C, I, P, R to ρ and write $\rho(A)$, $\rho(B)$, $\rho(C)$, $\rho(I)$, $\rho(P)$ and $\rho(R)$ for its components.

We next state the key result showing the consistency of the control flow analysis; it takes the form of a *subject-reduction* result:

Lemma 1. *If $\rho \models [\![e^l]\!]$ and $e^l \longrightarrow e'^l$ then $\rho \models [\![e'^l]\!]$.*

Proof. The proof exploits the following substitution result (that can be proved by structural induction on e^l):

If $\rho \models [\![e^l]\!]$ and $\rho \models [\![e_0^{l_0}]\!]$ and furthermore $\forall v : \rho(C)(l_0, v) \Rightarrow \rho(R)(x, v)$ then $\rho \models [\![e[e_0/x]^l]\!]$.

The Lemma is then proved by induction on $e^l \longrightarrow e'^l$.   □

Table 2. The generation of clauses for control flow analysis: $[\![e^l]\!]$

$$
\begin{aligned}
\mathsf{tt}^l &\mapsto C(l,\mathsf{tt}) \wedge B(\mathsf{tt}) \\
\mathsf{ff}^l &\mapsto C(l,\mathsf{ff}) \wedge B(\mathsf{ff}) \\
n^l &\mapsto C(l,\mathsf{int}) \wedge I(\mathsf{int}) \\
x^l &\mapsto \forall v : R(x,v) \Rightarrow C(l,v) \\
(e_1^{l_1} + e_2^{l_2})^l &\mapsto \begin{cases} \forall u : C(l_1,u) \Rightarrow I(u)\wedge \\ \forall u : C(l_2,u) \Rightarrow I(u)\wedge \\ C(l,\mathsf{int}) \wedge I(\mathsf{int}) \end{cases} \\
(e_1^{l_1} = e_2^{l_2})^l &\mapsto \begin{cases} \forall u : C(l_1,u) \Rightarrow I(u)\wedge \\ \forall u : C(l_2,u) \Rightarrow I(u)\wedge \\ C(l,\mathsf{tt}) \wedge C(l,\mathsf{ff}) \wedge B(\mathsf{tt}) \wedge B(\mathsf{ff}) \end{cases} \\
(\lambda x.e_0^{l_0})^l &\mapsto C(l,l_0) \wedge A(l_0) \wedge \forall v : P(l_0,v) \Rightarrow R(x,v) \\
(\mu f\, x.e_0^{l_0})^l &\mapsto \begin{cases} C(l,l_0) \wedge A(l_0) \wedge \forall v : P(l_0,v) \Rightarrow R(x,v)\wedge \\ \forall w : C(l,w) \Rightarrow R(f,w) \end{cases} \\
(e_1^{l_1} e_2^{l_2})^l &\mapsto \begin{cases} \forall u : C(l_1,u) \Rightarrow A(u)\wedge \\ \forall u : C(l_1,u) \Rightarrow ((\forall v : C(l_2,v) \Rightarrow P(u,v))\wedge \\ \quad (\forall w : C(u,w) \Rightarrow C(l,w))) \end{cases} \\
(\text{if } e_0^{l_0} \text{ then } e_1^{l_1} \text{ else } e_2^{l_2})^l &\mapsto \begin{cases} \forall u : C(l_0,u) \Rightarrow B(u)\wedge \\ \forall v : (C(l_1,v) \vee C(l_2,v)) \Rightarrow C(l,v) \end{cases}
\end{aligned}
$$

Example 3. Consider the example program $((\lambda x.(x^1 x^2)^3)^4 (\lambda y.(y^5 y^6)^7)^8)^9$ from Example 1. The predicates A, B, C, I, P, R given by

$$
\begin{aligned}
B &= I = \emptyset \\
A &= \{3,7\} \\
P &= \{(3,7),(7,7)\} \\
R &= \{(x,7),(y,7)\} \\
C &= \{(1,7),(2,7),(4,3),(5,7),(6,7),(8,7)\}
\end{aligned}
$$

correctly describe the behaviour of the program as follows from checking the truth of $(A, B, C, I, P, R) \models [\![((\lambda x.(x^1 x^2)^3)^4 (\lambda y.(y^5 y^6)^7)^8)^9]\!]$.

Example 4. Consider the program $((\lambda x.(\lambda z.(x^1 x^2)^3)^4)^5 (\lambda y.(\lambda z.(y^6 y^7)^8)^9)^{10})^{11}$ of Example 2. The predicates A, B, C, I, P, R given by

$$
\begin{aligned}
B &= I = \emptyset \\
A &= \{3,4,8,9\} \\
P &= \{(4,9),(9,9)\} \\
R &= \{(x,9),(y,9)\} \\
C &= \{(1,9),(2,9),(4,3),(5,4),(6,9),(7,9),(9,8),(10,9),(11,3)\}
\end{aligned}
$$

correctly describe the behaviour of the program as follows from checking the truth of $(A, B, C, I, P, R) \models [\![((\lambda x.(\lambda z.(x^1 x^2)^3)^4)^5 (\lambda y.(\lambda z.(x^6 x^7)^8)^9)^{10})^{11}]\!]$.

Table 3. Semantics of preconditions and clauses

$$
\begin{array}{lll}
(\rho,\sigma)\vdash R\,(x_1,\cdots,x_n) & \text{iff} & (\sigma(x_1),\cdots,\sigma(x_n))\in\rho(R) \\
(\rho,\sigma)\vdash \mathrm{pre}_1\wedge\mathrm{pre}_2 & \text{iff} & (\rho,\sigma)\vdash\mathrm{pre}_1 \ \text{ and } \ (\rho,\sigma)\vdash\mathrm{pre}_2 \\
(\rho,\sigma)\vdash \mathrm{pre}_1\vee\mathrm{pre}_2 & \text{iff} & (\rho,\sigma)\vdash\mathrm{pre}_1 \ \text{ or } \ (\rho,\sigma)\vdash\mathrm{pre}_2 \\
(\rho,\sigma)\vdash \exists x:\mathrm{pre} & \text{iff} & (\rho,\sigma[x\mapsto a])\vdash\mathrm{pre} \ \text{ for some } a\in\mathcal{U} \\[4pt]
(\rho,\sigma)\vdash R\,(x_1,\cdots,x_n) & \text{iff} & (\sigma(x_1),\cdots,\sigma(x_n))\in\rho(R) \\
(\rho,\sigma)\vdash 1 & \text{iff} & \text{true} \\
(\rho,\sigma)\vdash cl_1\wedge cl_2 & \text{iff} & (\rho,\sigma)\vdash cl_1 \ \text{ and } \ (\rho,\sigma)\vdash cl_2 \\
(\rho,\sigma)\vdash \forall x:cl & \text{iff} & (\rho,\sigma[x\mapsto a])\vdash cl \ \text{ for all } a\in\mathcal{U} \\
(\rho,\sigma)\vdash \mathrm{pre}\Rightarrow cl & \text{iff} & (\rho,\sigma)\vdash cl \ \text{ whenever } \ (\rho,\sigma)\vdash\mathrm{pre}
\end{array}
$$

3.2   Least Solutions

The clauses generated by Table 2 turn out to be Horn Clauses with Sharing and hence have least solutions:

Definition 2 (From [11]). *Given a set of variables X (ranged over by x) and an alphabet of predicate symbols $\mathcal{R}$ (ranged over by R), we define the set of Horn Clauses with Sharing, cl, and preconditions, pre, by the grammar:*

$$
\begin{array}{llllllll}
\mathrm{pre} & ::= & R\,(x_1,\cdots,x_n) & \mid & \mathrm{pre}_1\wedge\mathrm{pre}_2 & \mid & \mathrm{pre}_1\vee\mathrm{pre}_2 & \mid \quad \exists x:\mathrm{pre} \\
cl & ::= & R\,(x_1,\cdots,x_n) & \mid & 1 & \mid & cl_1\wedge cl_2 & \mid \quad \forall x:cl \quad \mid \quad \mathrm{pre}\Rightarrow cl
\end{array}
$$

Semantics. We interpret the logic over a universe $\mathcal{U}$ of constants. Given interpretations ρ and σ for predicate symbols and variables, respectively, we define in Table 3 the satisfaction relations:

$$
(\rho,\sigma)\vdash\mathrm{pre} \quad \text{and} \quad (\rho,\sigma)\vdash cl
$$

We are mainly interested in *closed* clauses cl, i.e. clauses that have no free variables. Hence we can fix an arbitrary interpretation σ_0 and we shall say that an interpretation ρ is a *solution* to the clause cl, written $\rho\models cl$, provided that $(\rho,\sigma_0)\vdash cl$.

Proposition 3 (Corollary of [12]). *Given a closed clause cl the solution set $\Delta_{cl}=\{\rho\mid\rho\models cl\}$ forms a Moore family, i.e. it is closed under greatest lower bounds (w.r.t. the ordering $\rho_1\sqsubseteq\rho_2$ given by $\rho_1(R)\subseteq\rho_2(R)$ for all R).*

Proof. In [12] a similar result is proved for the Alternation-free fragment of Least Fixpoint Logic. As Least Fixpoint Logic amounts to Horn Clauses with Sharing extended with the ability to use universal quantifiers in preconditions as well as negations (subject to a notion of stratification and a more complex definition of the partial order) the proof carries over. $\qquad\square$

In the sequel we shall only be interested in the least solution ρ as guaranteed by the above proposition; indeed, this is the solution computed by the Succinct Solver [12]. From the construction of the Succinct Solver, and in analogy with

Kleene's fixpoint construction, it follows that it can be characterised *inductively*: from initially empty estimates of the predicates we gradually enlarge them by inserting tuples as required by the clauses until ρ is obtained. We shall make use of this characterisation in the proof of Theorem 18 in Section 5.

Returning to the control flow analysis of Subsection 3.1 we shall take it for granted that the sets $\{\mathsf{tt}, \mathsf{ff}\}$, $\{\mathsf{int}\}$ and $\{l \mid l \text{ is a label}\}$ are mutually disjoint. We can then define the following desirable property of solutions; intuitively it says that a clash-free solution records no attempt to add or compare values other than integers, to perform tests in conditionals on values other than booleans, or to apply entities other than functions in function applications.

Definition 4. *We say that ρ is* clash-free *whenever $\rho(\mathrm{B}) \subseteq \{\mathsf{tt}, \mathsf{ff}\}$, $\rho(\mathrm{I}) \subseteq \{\mathsf{int}\}$ and $\rho(\mathrm{A}) \subseteq \{l \mid l \text{ is a label}\}$.*

It is worth pointing out that Proposition 3 does *not* guarantee the existence of a *clash-free* solution and indeed that there are clauses (and programs) that have no clash-free solutions. We shall return to this in Subsection 5.2.

Since the nesting depth of quantifiers is at most two it follows from Proposition 1 in [11] that the least solution to the control flow analysis can be calculated in time at most cubic in the size of the program because both the size of the clause generated and the size of the universe is bounded by the size of the program.

4   Observed Types

We are now ready for showing how to translate the result of the control flow analysis into the syntax of types. This will give rise to defining a judgement $\rho \models e^l : t$ meaning that the type t is consistent with the information that ρ gives about the label l. Furthermore, we shall show that the observed types of a given depth are computable in cubic time.

There are many choices of the syntax of types; what will turn out to be essential is that we include a universal top type (denoted $\top$). This is because our use of types is "descriptive" rather than "prescriptive" in that all programs, including the nonsencical ones, should have a type. (This is similar to the viewpoint of *soft* types as opposed to *strong* types.)

Definition 5. *The syntax of types $t \in \mathcal{T}$ is given by the grammar:*

$$t \; ::= \; \mathsf{B} \; \mid \; \mathsf{I} \; \mid \; t_1 \to t_2 \; \mid \; \bot \; \mid \; \top$$

Here B is the type of booleans, I is the type of integers, $t_1 \to t_2$ is a function type, $\bot$ is a type indicating non-reachability (including non-termination), and $\top$ is a universal top type.

4.1   Observed Types from Control Flow Estimates

Our first goal is to consider a set of values $V \subseteq \mathcal{U}$ and to determine whether or not those values are described by some type t.

Clearly a value like tt should have the type B but since ⊤ is a universal top type it should have ⊤ as type as well. Similarly if n is an integer it should have the types I and ⊤. If we consider a set of "incompatible" values like $\{tt, n\}$ our only option is to give it the type ⊤.

Next consider an abstraction $\lambda x.e^l$ and the type $t_1 \rightarrow t_2$ to be given to it (actually to the label l). This is intended to express that throughout the entire computation $\lambda x.e^l$ has only been applied to arguments described by t_1 and has only produced results described by t_2. How do we determine what has happened during the entire computation? We simply inspect the information supplied by the solution ρ which by Lemma 1 applies to the entire computation. If the function is only applied to the boolean tt it would have the type B → B but also (as discussed above) B → ⊤. However, it would *not* have any of the types ⊥ → ⊤ or I → ⊤ because the argument tt is described by neither ⊥ nor I. If the function is not applied at all it will have the type $t_1 \rightarrow t_2$ for all choices of t_1 and t_2. Clearly they cannot all be optimal — only ⊥ → ⊥ is. But it is in keeping with the philosophy of Abstract Interpretation always to admit "more approximative" descriptions of sets of values.

For the formal definition we define the judgement

$$\rho \models V : t$$

by the following[1] inductive definition:

$$\rho \models V : \mathsf{B} \text{ iff } V \subseteq \rho(B)$$
$$\rho \models V : \mathsf{I} \text{ iff } V \subseteq \rho(I)$$
$$\rho \models V : t_1 \rightarrow t_2 \text{ iff } \begin{cases} V \subseteq \rho(A) \wedge \\ \rho \models \{v \mid u \in V \wedge (u,v) \in \rho(P)\} : t_1 \wedge \\ \rho \models \{w \mid u \in V \wedge (u,w) \in \rho(C)\} : t_2 \end{cases}$$
$$\rho \models V : \bot \text{ iff } V \subseteq \emptyset$$
$$\rho \models V : \top \text{ iff } V \subseteq \mathcal{U}$$

Often we are specially interested in the values that may arise at the label l and we shall write

$$\rho@l = \{v \mid (l,v) \in \rho(C)\}$$

to denote this. This faciliates introducing a more readable notation for when a program has some observed type and for restating the subject-reduction result:

Definition 6. *We write* $\rho \models e^l : t$ *as a shorthand for* $\rho \models [\![e^l]\!] \wedge \rho \models \rho@l : t$.

Lemma 7. *If* $\rho \models e^l : t$ *and* $e \longrightarrow e'$ *then* $\rho \models e'^l : t$.

Proof. This is a trivial consequence of Lemma 1.   □

---

[1] An alternative would be to substitute $\{tt, ff\}$ for $\rho(B)$, $\{int\}$ for $\rho(I)$ and finally $\{l \mid l \text{ is a label}\}$ for $\rho(A)$; these definitions are essentially equivalent for clash-free solutions ρ.

Table 4. The covariant rules for subtyping: $t_1 \preceq t_2$

$$\frac{t \in \mathcal{T}}{t \preceq t} \qquad \frac{t \in \mathcal{T}}{\bot \preceq t} \qquad \frac{t \in \mathcal{T}}{t \preceq \top} \qquad \frac{t_1 \preceq t_1' \quad t_2 \preceq t_2'}{t_1 \rightarrow t_2 \preceq t_1' \rightarrow t_2'}$$

Example 5. Recall the program $((\lambda x.(x^1 x^2)^3)^4 (\lambda y.(y^5 y^6)^7)^8)^9$ from Example 3 and let us denote by ρ the analysis estimate defined there. The overall program has type $\bot$ as should be quite natural given that it does not terminate. More formally, this is evidenced by

$$\rho \models ((\lambda x.(x^1 x^2)^3)^4 (\lambda y.(y^5 y^6)^7)^8)^9 : \bot$$

using the notation introduced above.

Example 6. Consider the program $((\lambda x.(\lambda z.(x^1 x^2)^3)^4)^5 (\lambda y.(\lambda z.(y^6 y^7)^8)^9)^{10})^{11}$ from Example 4 and let us denote by ρ the analysis estimate defined there. We already stated that it evaluates to $\lambda z.((\lambda y.(\lambda z.(yy)))(\lambda y.(\lambda z.(yy))))$ and it should therefore be intuitively clear that it has a type t_∞ that is somehow equivalent to $\bot \rightarrow t_\infty$; the choice of $\bot$ is because the argument z is never instantiated to any arguments.

We cannot express t_∞ succinctly using the types of Definition 5 because we do not allow recursive types, but we can give a number of "upper" approximations:

$$
\begin{aligned}
t_0 &= \top \\
t_1 &= \bot \rightarrow t_0 = \bot \rightarrow \top \\
t_2 &= \bot \rightarrow t_1 = \bot \rightarrow (\bot \rightarrow \top) \\
&\vdots \\
t_i &= \bot \rightarrow t_{i-1} = \cdots
\end{aligned}
$$

More formally, this is evidenced by

$$\rho \models ((\lambda x.(\lambda z.(x^1 x^2)^3)^4)^5 (\lambda y.(\lambda z.(y^6 y^7)^8)^9)^{10})^{11} : t_i$$

(for all i) using the notation introduced above.

4.2   Covariant Subtyping

Our next goal will be to define an ordering $\preceq$ on types such that we can obtain a subtyping result of the form $\rho \models e^l : t \wedge t \preceq t' \implies \rho \models e^l : t'$. Inspecting the inductive definition of $\rho \models V : t$ it is quite natural to define it as in Table 4.

It is worthwhile noting that in the case of function types we have adopted a fully *covariant* definition: $t_1 \rightarrow t_2 \preceq t_1' \rightarrow t_2'$ demands that $t_1 \preceq t_1' \wedge t_2 \preceq t_2'$ rather than $t_1' \preceq t_1 \wedge t_2 \preceq t_2'$. This is indeed necessary in order to establish the subtyping result:

Lemma 8. *If $\rho \models V : t$, $V' \subseteq V$ and $t \preceq t'$ then $\rho \models V' : t'$; in particular, if $\rho \models e^l : t$ and $t \preceq t'$ then $\rho \models e^l : t'$.*

Proof. It is immediate to show by structural induction on t that $\rho \models V : t$ and $V' \subseteq V$ suffice for deducing that $\rho \models V' : t$. Next it is immediate to show by induction on the inference tree for $t \preceq t'$ that $\rho \models V : t$ and $t \preceq t'$ suffice for establishing $\rho \models V : t'$. □

Looking ahead to the development of Section 5 where a contravariant subtype relation $t \leq t'$ is defined in Table 6 it is worth stating that Lemma 8 would fail if $t \leq t'$ was used instead of $t \preceq t'$. As an example consider the program $(\lambda x.x^l)$ tt and the least solution ρ as guaranteed by Proposition 3. It is immediate to see that $\rho \models \{l\} : B \to B$ and that $B \to B \leq \bot \to \top$ whereas $\rho \models \{l\} : \bot \to \top$ fails because $\rho \models \{tt\} : \bot$ fails.

The next few results explore the properties of the partial order $\preceq$.

Lemma 9. $(\mathcal{T}, \preceq)$ *is a lattice.*

Proof. It is straightforward to show that $\preceq$ is reflexive, transitive and antisymmetric and hence a partial order. Next binary least upper bounds $\smile$ and binary greatest lower bounds $\frown$ are defined in a mostly pointwise fashion:

$\frown$	$\bot$	B	I	$t_1 \to t_2$	$\top$
$\bot$	$\bot$	$\bot$	$\bot$	$\bot$	$\bot$
B	$\bot$	B	$\bot$	$\bot$	B
I	$\bot$	$\bot$	I	$\bot$	I
$t'_1 \to t'_2$	$\bot$	$\bot$	$\bot$	$(t'_1 \frown t_1) \to (t'_2 \frown t_2)$	$t'_1 \to t'_2$
$\top$	$\bot$	B	I	$t_1 \to t_2$	$\top$

$\smile$	$\bot$	B	I	$t_1 \to t_2$	$\top$
$\bot$	$\bot$	B	I	$t_1 \to t_2$	$\top$
B	B	B	$\top$	$\top$	$\top$
I	I	$\top$	I	$\top$	$\top$
$t'_1 \to t'_2$	$t'_1 \to t'_2$	$\top$	$\top$	$(t'_1 \smile t_1) \to (t'_2 \smile t_2)$	$\top$
$\top$	$\top$	$\top$	$\top$	$\top$	$\top$

It is straightforward to prove that this defines the lattice operators. □

It is immediate that all programs have a type, e.g. $\rho_\top \models e^l : \top$ where $\rho_\top$ maps all predicates of arity k to $\mathcal{U}^k$. Furthermore, $\rho \models e^l : t_1$ and $\rho \models e^l : t_2$ suffice for establishing $\rho \models e^l : t_1 \smile t_2$. This naturally leads to establishing the following result for $t_1 \frown t_2$:

Lemma 10. *Consider an analysis estimate ρ that is clash-free. If $\rho \models V : t$ and $\rho \models V : t'$ then $\rho \models V : t \frown t'$; in particular, if $\rho \models e^l : t$ and $\rho \models e^l : t'$ then $\rho \models e^l : t \frown t'$.*

Proof. By induction on $t \frown t'$. Intuitively, clash-free ensures that whenever the validations of $\rho \models V : t$ and $\rho \models V : t'$ make different choices, one can equally well make the choice needed for validating $\rho \models V : t \frown t'$. □

In applications of Abstract Interpretation [5,10] it is quite customary to prove stronger versions of Lemmas 9 and 10: that $(\mathcal{T}, \preceq)$ is a complete lattice and that $\{t \mid \rho \models V : t\}$ constitutes a Moore family. However, the latter result fails as shown by Example 7 below.

Example 7. In Example 6 we identified the sequence of types $t_0 = \top$, $t_1 = \bot \to \top$, $\cdots$, $t_i = \bot \to t_{i-1}$, $\cdots$ that all described the type of the program $((\lambda y.(\lambda z.(yy)))(\lambda y.(\lambda z.(xx))))$. It is immediate that they form a strictly decreasing chain

$$t_0 \succ t_1 \succ t_2 \succ t_3 \succ \cdots \succ t_i \succ \cdots$$

and that $\bot$ is a lower bound. In fact one can show that $\bot$ is the only lower bound and hence the greatest lower bound. It is therefore important to observe that $\bot$ is *not* a valid type for the program; indeed, $\rho \models ((\lambda y.(\lambda z.(yy)))(\lambda y.(\lambda z.(xx)))) : \bot$ clearly is false.

In the absence of the Moore family result we shall instead show that optimal types exist among types of a given *depth*. Here a type t is said to have depth k if k is the maximum nesting depth of the function type constructor; e.g. $\bot \to (\bot \to \top)$ and $(\mathsf{I} \to \mathsf{B}) \to (\mathsf{I} \to \mathsf{B})$ both have depth 2.

Lemma 11. *Consider an estimate ρ that is clash-free. The set of observed types $\{t \mid \rho \models V : t$ and t has depth at most $k\}$ constitutes a Moore family (w.r.t. the ordering $\preceq$); in particular, $\{t \mid \rho \models e^l : t$ and t has depth at most $k\}$ constitutes a Moore family.*

Proof. From Lemma 9 it follows that $(\{t \in \mathcal{T} \mid t$ has depth at most $k\}, \preceq)$ is a complete lattice because there are only finitely many types of depth at most k. Furthermore, the Moore family property follows from $\rho \models V : \top$ and Lemma 10. A more constructive proof will be given in Subsection 4.3.   □

4.3   Optimal Observed Types

We conclude by giving a more constructive proof of Lemma 11 with a view to defining the optimal type (of a given depth) of an abstraction occurring in some program.

Definition 12. *The* canonical type $\llbracket V \rrbracket_k^\rho$ *of depth at most $k \geq 0$ of a set of values V is defined by:*

$$\llbracket V \rrbracket_k^\rho = \quad \textit{if } V \subseteq \emptyset \textit{ then } \bot \textit{ else}$$
$$\textit{if } V \subseteq \rho(\mathsf{B}) \textit{ then } \mathsf{B} \textit{ else}$$
$$\textit{if } V \subseteq \rho(\mathsf{I}) \textit{ then } \mathsf{I} \textit{ else}$$
$$\textit{if } V \subseteq \rho(\mathsf{A}) \wedge k > 0 \textit{ then}$$
$$\llbracket \{v \mid u \in V \wedge (u,v) \in \rho(\mathsf{P})\} \rrbracket_{k-1}^\rho \to \llbracket \{w \mid u \in V \wedge (u,w) \in \rho(\mathsf{C})\} \rrbracket_{k-1}^\rho$$
$$\textit{else } \top$$

Lemma 13. $[\![V]\!]_k^\rho$ *has depth at most* k *and satisfies* $\rho \models V : [\![V]\!]_k^\rho$.

Proof. We proceed by induction on k and then perform a case analysis on V (more precisely, on the outcome of the tests $V \subseteq \emptyset$, $V \subseteq \rho(B)$ etc.).   □

Lemma 14. *Consider a clash-free estimate* ρ. *The type* $[\![V]\!]_k^\rho$ *is least (wrt.* $\preceq$*) among all types* t *of depth at most* k *that satisfy* $\rho \models V : t$.

Proof. We proceed by induction on k and then perform case analysis on V.   □

Since the control flow analysis can be computed in cubic time the development above provides a cubic time algorithm (for fixed choices of k) for calculating optimal *observed types*.

Definition 15. *The optimal observed type of depth* k *for an expression* $\lambda x.e^l$ *occurring in some program* $e' = \cdots \lambda x.e^l \cdots$ *is defined by*

$$[\![\{l\}]\!]_k^\rho \quad where \; \rho = \sqcap\{\rho' \mid \rho' \models [\![e']\!]\}$$

and is denoted $[\![l \mid e']\!]_k$.

In the case of ρ being clash-free the type will be optimal in the sense of Lemma 14. If $[\![l \mid e']\!]_k$ contains no occurrences of $\top$ it will in fact be optimal also for larger values of k.

Example 8. The optimal type of $((\lambda x.(x^1 x^2)^3)^4(\lambda y.(y^5 y^6)^7)^8)^9$ is $\bot$.

Example 9. The optimal type (of depth k) of the program

$$((\lambda x.(\lambda z.(x^1 x^2)^3)^4)^5(\lambda y.(\lambda z.(y^6 y^7)^8)^9)^{10})^{11}$$

is t_k as defined in Example 6; it has no type that is optimal for all values of k.

5   Inferred Types

In this section we investigate the relationship between the approach of observed types of Section 4 and the more traditional approach of types inferred using a type system [1,8,15].

5.1   Contravariant Subtyping

To facilitate the development we shall base the type system on the syntax of types displayed in Definition 5. The judgement $\Gamma \vdash e^l : t$ says that the expression e^l has type t in the type environment Γ; it is defined in Table 5 and makes use of the standard notation for type environments. The type system has the flavour of a system for *strong typing* rather than *soft typing* because of the insistence that only integers are added or compared, only booleans are used in conditionals and

Table 5. The traditional type system of inferred types: $\Gamma \vdash e^l : t$

$$\frac{}{\Gamma \vdash \mathsf{tt}^l : \mathsf{B}} \qquad \frac{}{\Gamma \vdash \mathsf{ff}^l : \mathsf{B}} \qquad \frac{}{\Gamma \vdash n^l : \mathsf{I}} \qquad \frac{\Gamma(x) = t}{\Gamma \vdash x^l : t}$$

$$\frac{\Gamma \vdash e_1^{l_1} : \mathsf{I} \quad \Gamma \vdash e_2^{l_2} : \mathsf{I}}{\Gamma \vdash (e_1^{l_1} + e_2^{l_2})^l : \mathsf{I}} \qquad \frac{\Gamma \vdash e_1^{l_1} : \mathsf{I} \quad \Gamma \vdash e_2^{l_2} : \mathsf{I}}{\Gamma \vdash (e_1^{l_1} = e_2^{l_2})^l : \mathsf{B}}$$

$$\frac{\Gamma[x : t] \vdash e_0^{l_0} : t_0}{\Gamma \vdash (\lambda x.e_0^{l_0})^l : t \to t_0} \qquad \frac{\Gamma[f : t \to t_0][x : t] \vdash e_0^{l_0} : t_0}{\Gamma \vdash (\mu f x.e_0^{l_0})^l : t \to t_0} \qquad \frac{\Gamma \vdash e_1^{l_1} : t_2 \to t \quad \Gamma \vdash e_2^{l_2} : t_2}{\Gamma \vdash (e_1^{l_1} e_2^{l_2})^l : t}$$

$$\frac{\Gamma \vdash e_0^{l_0} : \mathsf{B} \quad \Gamma \vdash e_1^{l_1} : t \quad \Gamma \vdash e_2^{l_2} : t}{\Gamma \vdash (\mathsf{if}\ e_0^{l_0}\ \mathsf{then}\ e_1^{l_1}\ \mathsf{else}\ e_2^{l_2})^l : t} \qquad \frac{\Gamma \vdash e^l : t_1 \quad t_1 \leq t_2}{\Gamma \vdash e^l : t_2}$$

Table 6. The contravariant rules for subtyping: $t_1 \leq t_2$

$$\frac{t \in \mathcal{T}}{t \leq t} \qquad \frac{t \in \mathcal{T}}{\bot \leq t} \qquad \frac{t \in \mathcal{T}}{t \leq \top} \qquad \frac{t_1' \leq t_1 \quad t_2 \leq t_2'}{t_1 \to t_2 \leq t_1' \to t_2'}$$

only functions are applied. This choice makes the comparison somewhat more complex but also more interesting.

The type system of Table 5 uses subtyping as defined in Table 6. As is customary for type systems the rule for function type is covariant in the result type but *contravariant* in the argument type. It may be instructive to give a simple example showing why this needs to be the case. Considering the function $\lambda x.x$ we would expect it to have a type like $\mathsf{B} \to \mathsf{B}$ and it seems semantically correct to allow subtyping to massage the type to $\mathsf{B} \to \top$ whereas $\top \to \mathsf{B}$ does not seem right: indeed $(\lambda x.x)\,7$ would then be well-typed with type B whereas 7 clearly is not well-typed with type B. At the more technical level the consistency of the type system (Lemma 16 below) would fail. Using contravariant subtyping as in Table 6 allows us to massage the type of $\lambda x.x$ to the less problematic $\bot \to \mathsf{B}$ and indeed we can establish the consistency of the type system by means of a *subject-reduction* result:

Lemma 16. *If* $[\,] \vdash e^l : t$ *and* $e^l \longrightarrow e'^l$ *then* $[\,] \vdash e''^l : t$.

Proof. The proof exploits the following substitution result (that can be proved by structural induction on e^l):

If $\Gamma[x : t_0'] \vdash e^l : t'$ and $\Gamma \vdash e_0^{l_0} : t_0$ and $t_0 \leq t_0'$ and $t' \leq t$ then $\Gamma \vdash e[e_0/x]^l : t$.

The Lemma is then proved by induction on $e^l \longrightarrow e''^l$. □

Next we state an analogy of Lemma 9 for exploring the properties of the partial order $\leq$.

Lemma 17. $(\mathcal{T}, \leq)$ *is a lattice.*

Proof. It is straightforward to show that $\leq$ is reflexive, transitive and anti-symmetric and hence a partial order. Next binary least upper bounds $\vee$ and binary greatest lower bounds $\wedge$ are defined in a mostly pointwise fashion:

$\wedge$	$\bot$	B	I	$t_1 \to t_2$	$\top$
$\bot$	$\bot$	$\bot$	$\bot$	$\bot$	$\bot$
B	$\bot$	B	$\bot$	$\bot$	B
I	$\bot$	$\bot$	I	$\bot$	I
$t'_1 \to t'_2$	$\bot$	$\bot$	$\bot$	$(t'_1 \vee t_1) \to (t'_2 \wedge t_2)$	$t'_1 \to t'_2$
$\top$	$\bot$	B	I	$t_1 \to t_2$	$\top$

$\vee$	$\bot$	B	I	$t_1 \to t_2$	$\top$
$\bot$	$\bot$	B	I	$t_1 \to t_2$	$\top$
B	B	B	$\top$	$\top$	$\top$
I	I	$\top$	I	$\top$	$\top$
$t'_1 \to t'_2$	$t'_1 \to t'_2$	$\top$	$\top$	$(t'_1 \wedge t_1) \to (t'_2 \vee t_2)$	$\top$
$\top$	$\top$	$\top$	$\top$	$\top$	$\top$

It is straightforward to prove that this defines the lattice operators. □

Example 10. The example program $((\lambda x.(x^1 x^2)^3)^4 (\lambda y.(y^5 y^6)^7)^8)^9$ of Example 1 has no type in the type system of Tables 5 and 6:

$$\neg \exists t : [\,] \vdash ((\lambda x.(x^1 x^2)^3)^4 (\lambda y.(y^5 y^6)^7)^8)^9 : t$$

To show this we proceed by contradiction and suppose that there does exist a type judgement. We first observe that proof trees for type judgements can be normalised so that all applications of the rule for subtyping follows immediately after one of the other rules or axioms. Furthermore, in order to determine typability it suffices to use the rule for subtyping only on the argument type in the rule for application.

Given a type judgement this allows us to introduce the following types: t_x for the type assigned to the formal parameter x, t_y for the type assigned to the formal parameter y, t_X for the type assigned to the body $(x^1 x^2)^3$ and t_Y for the type assigned to the body $(y^5 y^6)^7$. These must satisfy

$$t_x \leq t_x \to t_X \leq t_y \leq t_y \to t_Y$$

from which $t_x \leq t_y \leq t_y$ is immediate and $t_y \leq t_y \leq t_x$ follows using $t_x \to t_X \leq t_y \to t_Y$. Using Lemma 17 we have $t_x = t_y$ and hence

$$t_x = t_x \to t_X$$

which can be shown to be impossible (by induction on the size of t_x).

It is an immediate consequence of the rule for subtyping in Table 6 and Lemma 17 that $\Gamma \vdash e^l : t_1$ and $\Gamma \vdash e^l : t_2$ suffice for establishing $\Gamma \vdash e^l : t_1 \vee t_2$. However, it is easy to show that $\Gamma \vdash e^l : t_1$ and $\Gamma \vdash e^l : t_2$ do *not* suffice for establishing $\Gamma \vdash e^l : t_1 \wedge t_2$; as an example take $e = \lambda x.x$ and $t_1 = \mathsf{B} \to \mathsf{B}$ and $t_2 = \mathsf{I} \to \mathsf{I}$ where $t_1 \wedge t_2 = \top \to \bot$. This is unlike the situation in Section 4.

5.2   Comparison of Inferred Versus Observed Types

We shall conclude by a new way of presenting the usual slogan for type systems: that well-typed programs do not go wrong. Usually the correctness of an inferred type system is formalised with respect to the operational semantics; here it will be formalised with respect to the control flow analysis (which is itself formalised with respect to the operational semantics). It says that well-typed programs produce clash-free solutions and that the types carry over from the inferred types to the observed types.

Due to the difference between the partial orders $\leq$ and $\preceq$ we shall introduce the partial orders $\leq^\circ$ and $\preceq^\circ$ indicating that they have been used in covariant position [2] only. It is immediate that $t_1 \leq^\circ t_2$ is equivalent to $t_1 \preceq^\circ t_2$ and implies $t_1 \leq t_2$ as well as $t_1 \preceq t_2$. In order to ensure that the partial orders are used in covariant position only it suffices to use $t_1 = t_1'$ in the rules for function types in Tables 4 and 6. In the statement of the theorem $[] \vdash e^l : \top$ merely says that e^l has some type in the type system (and hence should not lead to any run-time errors.).

Theorem 18. *Consider a program e^l that is uniquely labelled and α-renamed apart. If $[] \vdash e^l : \top$ (using only $\leq^\circ$ for subtyping) there exists ρ such that $\rho \models e^l : \top$ and ρ is clash-free.*

Proof. Let ρ be the least solution to $\rho \models \llbracket e^l \rrbracket$ as guaranteed by Proposition 3 and as can be constructed *inductively* as a sequence of estimates $\bot = \rho_0, \rho_1, \rho_2, \rho_3, \cdots, \rho_n = \rho$ as explained after Proposition 3 in Section 3.

Since the program e^l is uniquely labelled and α-renamed apart there is a unique correspondence between labels and variables on the one hand and program points and defining occurrences of variables on the other. In particular there is a unique correspondence between the binding occurrence of a variable x (of the form $(\lambda x.e_0^{l_0})^l$ or $(\mu f x.e_0^{l_0})^l$) and the label l_x of the body of the abstraction (l_0 in both cases). In analogy with the definition of $\rho@l$ we shall then define

$$\rho@x = \{v \mid (x, v) \in \rho(R) \ \lor \ (l_x, v) \in \rho(P)\}$$

to denote the set of values associated with the variable x in ρ. We use both R and P because the control flow analysis of Table 2 promotes actual parameters to formal parameters in two steps: $C(l, v) \implies P(l_x, v) \implies R(x, v)$ and hence the entry (l, v) in $\rho_i(C)$ shows up as (l_x, v) in $\rho_{i+1}(P)$ but as (x, v) only in $\rho_{i+2}(R)$.

> We shall prove for all i and all type judgements $\Gamma \vdash e^{l'} : t'$ occurring in the inference tree for $[] \vdash e^l : \top$ (using only $\leq^\circ$ for subtyping) that ρ_i is clash-free and that $\forall x \in \text{dom}(\Gamma) : \rho \models \rho_i@x : \Gamma(x)$ implies that $\rho \models \rho_i@l' : t'$.

---

[2] The program $(\lambda x.\text{if tt then } x\, 7 \text{ else } x\, \text{ff})(\lambda y.5)$ illustrates some of the subtleties. It is natural to type x as $\top \to I$ and then after then then-branch (resp. the else-branch) it can be subtyped to the larger (w.r.t $\leq$ but not $\leq^\circ$) type $I \to I$ (resp. $B \to I$) which contradicts the induction hypothesis of Theorem 18. It remains future work to possibly strengthen the result by omitting the restriction to $\leq^\circ$.

We proceed by induction on i and the base case is immediate so consider the induction step. For this we proceed by induction over the inference tree for $[] \vdash e^l : \top$ where for each judgement we inspect the clauses generated by $[\![e^l]\!]$ of Table 2 for the expression of the judgement.

By inspection of the relevant clause generated by $[\![e^l]\!]$ of Table 2 it is clear that no such clash is forced. In the case of subtyping we use Lemma 8 and that $t_1 \leq^\circ t_2$ implies $t_1 \preceq^\circ t_2$.   □

It follows from Examples 5 and 10 that the converse result does not hold (as indeed the solution in Example 3 is clash-free). As other examples of interest note that we have $\rho_\top \models 3 + \mathsf{tt} : \top$ (where $\rho_\top$ is clearly not clash-free) whereas we do not have $[] \vdash 3 + \mathsf{tt} : \top$. Similarly we have $\rho_\top \models 7\,8 : \top$ (where $\rho_\top$ once more is not clash-free) whereas we do not have $[] \vdash 7\,8 : \top$.

6   Conclusion

In this paper we have shown how to express the results of control flow analysis in the form of type systems. At the same time we have developed our thesis that flow analysis and type systems capture related but somehow distinct features of programs:

- The approach of *observed types* based on control flow analysis is "descriptive" in that we aim to express how the entity under study has been used in program at hand. This has the flavour of a "whole-program" analysis where no unknown variables can occur. It seems the right concept for program debugging and program understanding.
- The approach of *inferred types* based on type systems is "prescriptive" in that we aim to express how the entity under study can be used in all possible contexts. This has the flavour of a "partial-program" analysis where indeed unknown variables can occur. It seems the right concept for program construction.

Although we do not consider recursive types in this paper we expect our thesis to hold in this more general setting as well.

An intriguing point of this development is the need for using *covariant subtyping* in the case of *observed types* and *contravariant subtyping* in the case of *inferred types*. We already illustrated in Section 4 that Lemma 8 would fail if using contravariant subtyping instead of covariant subtyping. Similarly we said in Section 5 that Lemma 16 would fail if using covariant subtyping rather than contravariant subtyping. This dichotomy between when to use covariant subtyping and when to use contravariant subtyping has also emerged in the work on record types.

To shed further light on this point let us reformulate the definition of $\rho \models e^l : t$ in the case of function types:

$$\rho \models e^l : t_1 \to t_2 \text{ iff } \begin{cases} \rho@l \subseteq \rho(A) \wedge \\ \rho \models \{v \mid u \in \rho@l \wedge (u,v) \in \rho(P)\} : t_1 \wedge \\ \rho \models \{w \mid u \in \rho@l \wedge (u,w) \in \rho(C)\} : t_2 \end{cases}$$

Instead of establishing the consistency of the type system by means of a subject-reduction result we could instead have explored a more semantic approach where we defined a satisfaction relation $\Vdash e^l : t$ which in the case of function types would be:

$$\Vdash e^l : t_1 \rightarrow t_2 \text{ iff } \forall v, w : \begin{cases} \Vdash v : t_1 \quad \wedge \quad e^l \, v \longrightarrow^* w \\ \quad \Downarrow \\ \Vdash w : t_2 \end{cases}$$

Here it is clear that the use of *logical relations* for the type system enforces the need for *contravariance* in the subtyping relation whereas the opposite is needed for the observed types based on control flow analysis.

A similar comparison can be given in the case of soft type systems where the simple type system no longer demands that the absence of internal clashes; in terms of the observed types we then dispense with the consideration of clash-free solutions. Frequently control flow analyses contain reachability components or are dependent on context in which case the increased strength of observed types would be more manifest.

Acknowledgements. This work has been supported by the Danish Natural Science Research Council projects LoST (21-02-0507) and SiES (2059-03-0011) and by the EU-IST-FETPI project SENSORIA (FP6-016004).

The thesis that control flow analysis naturally leads to the use of covariant subtyping seems to be somewhat controversial. We wish to thank Fritz Henglein, Jens Palsberg and the referees for their views on the topic — they have helped to improve the presentation of the thesis.

References

1. M. Abadi, L. Cardelli, B. C. Pierce, and G. D. Plotkin. Dynamic typing in a statically typed language. In *Proc. POPL'89*, pages 213–227. ACM, 1989.
2. T. Amtoft and F. Turbak. Faithful translations between polyvariant flows and polymorphic types. In *Proc. ESOP'00*, pages 26–40. Springer, 2000.
3. A. Banerjee. A modular, polyvariant, and type-based closure analysis. In *Proc. ICFP '97*, pages 1–10. ACM Press, 1997.
4. P. Cousot. Types as abstract interpretations. In *Proc. POPL '97*, pages 316–331. ACM Press, 1997.
5. P. Cousot and R. Cousot. Abstract Interpretation: a Unified Lattice Model for Static Analysis of Programs by Construction or Approximation of Fixpoints. In *Proc. POPL '77*, pages 238–252. ACM Press, 1977.
6. K.-F. Faxén. Polyvariance, polymorphism, and flow analysis. In *Proc. Analysis and Verification of Multiple-Agent Languages*, volume 1192 of *Lecture Notes in Computer Science*, pages 260–278. Springer, 1997.
7. N. Heintze. Control-flow analysis and type systems. In *Proc. SAS '95*, volume 983 of *Lecture Notes in Computer Science*, pages 189–206. Springer, 1995.
8. F. Henglein. Global Tagging Optimization by Type Inference. In *Proc. LFP '92*, pages 205–215. ACM Press, 1992.

9. B. Monsuez. Polymorphic types and widening operators. In *Proc. Static Analysis (WSA '93)*, volume 724 of *Lecture Notes in Computer Science*, pages 267–281. Springer, 1993.
10. F. Nielson, H. R. Nielson, and C. L. Hankin. *Principles of Program Analysis*. Springer, 1999.
11. F. Nielson and H. Seidl. Control-flow analysis in cubic time. In *Proc. ESOP'01*, number 2028 in Lecture Notes in Computer Science, pages 252–268. Springer, 2001.
12. F. Nielson, H. Seidl, and H. Riis Nielson. A Succinct Solver for ALFP. *Nordic Journal of Computing*, 9:335–372, 2002.
13. J. Palsberg and P. O'Keefe. A type system equivalent to flow analysis. *ACM Transactions on Programming Languages and Systems*, 17(4):576–599, 1995.
14. J. Palsberg and C. Pavlopoulou. From polyvariant flow information to intersection and union types. In *Proc. POPL'98*, pages 197–208. ACM, 1998.
15. S. Thatte. Type inference with partial types. In *Proc. ICALP'88*, number 317 in Lecture Notes in Computer Science, pages 615–629. Springer, 1988.

Data Flow Analysis for CCS

Hanne Riis Nielson and Flemming Nielson

Informatics and Mathematical Modelling, Richard Petersens Plads bldg. 321,
Technical University of Denmark, DK-2800 Kongens Lyngby, Denmark
{riis|nielson}@imm.dtu.dk

Abstract. Data Flow Analysis as expressed by Monotone Frameworks
is often associated with classical imperative programming languages and
has played a crucial role in the efficient implementation of these languages. Robin Milner's Calculus of Communicating Systems, CCS, is
concerned with modelling concurrent systems and has mainly been anal-
ysed using types and control flow analyses. In the present paper we
present an instance of a Monotone Framework together with a novel
worklist algorithm for more precisely approximating the flow-sensitive
control structure of even infinitary processes expressed in CCS.

1 Introduction

There are many approaches to static analysis of programming languages and
calculi. In [11] we developed four of these in some depth: Data Flow Analysis building on transfer functions associated with program blocks; Control Flow
Analysis taking a specification oriented approach to formulating constraints on
the set of functions reaching given application points; Abstract Interpretation
presenting a semantics based method for calculating and subsequently approximating static analyses; and finally Type and Effect Systems for expressing the
behaviour of functions by means of syntactic expressions in a monomorphic or
polymorphic type system.

Recent years have seen an increased interest in applying static analysis techniques to highly concurrent languages, in particular a variety of process calculi
allowing concurrent processes to interact by means of synchronisation or communication. The majority of approaches have aimed at adapting type systems from
mainly functional and object-oriented languages to express meaningful properties, e.g. [8,10,18]. Together with our coauthors we have been active in developing Control Flow Analysis for a variety of process calculi including the
π-calculus [3], the spi-calculus [4,13], mobile ambients [12,14,15] and our own
calculus LySa [2,6].

One drawback of simple control flow analyses of the 0CFA variety is their
lack of context-sensitivity; however, it is often possible to add a suitable notion
of constext using ideas from kCFA, e.g. [16]. Another drawback of of simple
control flow analyses is their lack of flow-sensitivity; indeed for massively parallel
languages like most process algebras it is hard to determine the effect of each local
program point (in each concurrent thread) without an exponential growth in the

T. Reps, M. Sagiv, and J. Bauer (Eds.): Wilhelm Festschrift, LNCS 4444, pp. 311–327, 2007.

number of global program points (having one component for each concurrent thread).

To get some progress on the latter problem we focus on the classical approach of Data Flow Analysis where transfer functions associated with basic blocks are often specified as a Bitvector Framework or, more generally, as a Monotone Framework. What these analyses have in common is that there are ways of *removing* analysis information when no longer appropriate. We give the first account of an instance of an analysis problem for CCS, the Calculus of Communicating Systems [9], where the bitvectors (which correspond to finite sets) are generalised to so-called extended multisets. This involves the development of suitable generalisations of the *gen* and *kill* components of Monotone Frameworks are used to construct transfer functions that:

> provide finitary information about the control structure of configurations arising dynamically during computation.

Unlike the classical scenario it does not suffice to simply solve the particular Monotone Framework over a given flow graph. Here we also need to dynamically construct the nodes to be part of the resulting finite graph for describing a given process even in the case where its transition system is infinite. To ensure that the graph remains finite and that the algorithm terminates even for infinitary processes we shall use a so-called granularity function and a suitable widening operator.

The overall motivation of the work presented here came from our work on improving the analysis information obtained from analysing communication protocols; we conclude with a simple worked example based on the Ingemarsson-Tang-Wong Key Agreement Protocol [5].

2   Setting the Scene

Programming Languages versus Process Calculi. Before undertaking to adapt methods and techniques from programming languages to process calculi it is important to understand the similarities and differences between these paradigms. In doing so we shall focus on the nature of statements versus processes and disregard more high-level notions like recursive procedures versus recursive processes (which especially in the case of process calculi are important for obtaining the desired expressive power).

Starting with a simple non-procedural imperative programming language we often represent it by means of a flow graph with basic blocks containing statements. This corresponds roughly to the two main operations of sequencing (denoted $\langle ; \rangle$) and branching out of conditionals (denoted $\langle \vee \rangle$) leaving the corresponding join of branches implicit. Clearly a concurrency construct may be added to this setup (denoted $\langle \| \rangle$) but only few static analyses have been developed for this scenario; examples include analyses of low-level VHDL programs [17].

Turning to process calculi usually the sequencing construct $\langle ; \rangle$ is replaced by a prefixing construct $\langle . \rangle$; in practice this does not seem to limit the expressive power although it simplifies the technical development since there is no issue of prefixed axioms dead-locking or not terminating. Also all process calculi contain a concurrency construct $\langle | \rangle$. This suffices for some process calculi like mobile ambients and LySa whereas others additionally have a choice-construct. However, there are some variations as to the precise details of how this construct behaves. The *internal choice* (also denoted $\langle \lor \rangle$) is characterised by the choice being taken outside of our control; from the static analysis point of view this is rather comparable to the branching out of conditionals in that we usually are not able to determine which branch is taken. The alternative *external choice* (denoted $\langle + \rangle$) is characterised by the choice being taken when some other process (or the environment) wishes to communicate. Generally speaking the use of external choice gives fewer "false" executions than the use of internal choice.

It follows that programming languages tend to use features like $\langle ;\lor \rangle$ or sometimes $\langle ;\lor | \rangle$; process calculi, on the other hand, tend to use $\langle . | \rangle$ or $\langle .+ | \rangle$ or even $\langle .\lor + | \rangle$. As for developing the static analyses, the change from $\langle ; \rangle$ to $\langle . \rangle$ does not give rise to any complications (at most some simplifications) whereas the change from $\langle \lor \rangle$ to $\langle + \rangle$ should be considered carefully.

Internal versus External Choice. As an example consider the specification of a (unary) semaphore S; in CCS syntax it can be written:

$$S \triangleq g.p.S$$

First the process offers the action g, then the action p after which it starts all over again. Assume that it operates in parallel with a process Q given by

$$Q \triangleq \bar{g}.\tau.Q + \bar{p}.Q$$

that it is willing to either perform the action $\bar{g}$ (that will synchronise with a g action) or the action $\bar{p}$ (that will synchronise with a p action). After the $\bar{g}$ action some internal action τ is performed and then the process recurses; after the $\bar{p}$ action the process recurses immediately. Now assume that the sum operation is interpreted as an *internal* choice. Then the system $S \mid Q$ may silently move into one of the two configurations $S \mid \bar{p}.Q$ or $S \mid \bar{g}.\tau.Q$ and only in the latter case will it be able to proceed and become $p.S \mid \tau.Q$ and subsequently $p.S \mid Q$. This and the subsequent interactions are illustrated by the figure:

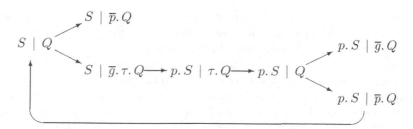

However, if the sum is interpreted as *external* choice then the ability of S to perform the g action will prevent Q from making the "wrong" choice so the process will simply become $p.\,S \mid \tau.\,Q$ and subsequently $p.\,S \mid Q$ and $S \mid Q$ as illustrated on the figure:

$$S \mid Q \longrightarrow p.\,S \mid \tau.\,Q \longrightarrow p.\,S \mid Q$$

The Essence of Data Flow Analysis. Both in the case of Bitvector Frameworks and Monotone Frameworks we attach *transfer functions* to the blocks of a data flow graph representing the program. In the case of a *forwards* Data Flow Analysis the transfer function describes how information entering the block is transformed so as to correspond to the exit of the block. In a Bitvector Framework formulated using finite sets the transfer function usually takes the simple form

$$f_{\mathsf{block}}(E) = (E \setminus \mathit{kill}_{\mathsf{block}}) \cup \mathit{gen}_{\mathsf{block}}$$

where we first remove the information invalidated by the block and next add the new information provided by the block. The classical examples of information E of interest are reaching definitions, available expressions, live variables and very busy expressions [1,11].

Overview. The analysis problem considered in the present paper is to provide finitary information about the control structure of configurations arising dynamically during computation. This is trivial in the case of traditional programming languages ($\langle ;\vee\rangle$) but it is non-trivial and interesting whenever we admit a concurrency construct – regardless of whether or not a choice construct is included.

We shall study the problem for CCS (reviewed in Section 3) which in addition to the concurrency construct incorporates silent actions as well as explicit external choice. Indeed, the presence of external choice and silent actions ($\langle +\tau\rangle$) allows to model internal choice ($\langle \vee\rangle$) as well.

The first part of the development (in Section 4) amounts to defining *transfer functions* for the individual actions occurring in some CCS process. We shall see that the labels of individual actions will correspond to the basic blocks of Data Flow Analysis but that there is a need to generalise from bitvectors to so-called extended multisets.

The second part of the development (in Section 5) is to devise a worklist algorithm for constructing a finite control flow graph for some CCS process. The nodes describe the exposed actions for the various configurations that may arise dynamically during execution whereas the edges capture the control structure telling how one configuration may evolve into another. Unlike the classical scenario it does not suffice to simply solve the particular Monotone Framework over a given flow graph. Here we also need to dynamically construct the nodes to be part of the resulting finite graph for describing a given process even in the case where its transition system is infinite. One concern is to bound the size of the graph to be constructed; this is achieved using a so-called granularity function for limiting the extent to which new nodes are created. Another concern is to ensure termination of the extended multiset computations; this is achieved using a widening [7] on extended multisets constructed from a rather standard widening operation over the integers. Since the choice of granularity function gives detailed control over the size of the graph we have deciced to let it be a user-selectable component unlike the widening for extended multisets that is fixed throughout the presentation.

As a worked example we consider (in Section 6) the Ingemarsson-Tang-Wong Key Agreement Protocol [5] and show the control graphs produced by our prototype implementation of our analysis. One application of such graphs is in the areas of program understanding; quite often security flaws in protocols are only discovered years after their conception at which time it may not be clear how a given software system implements the protocol or whether appropriate safe guards have already been taken.

3 Communicating Systems

The syntax of CCS [9] processes P and actions α is given by:

$$P ::= \mathsf{new}\, x\, P \mid P_1 \mid P_2 \mid \Sigma_{i \in I} \alpha_i^{\ell_i}.P_i \mid A$$
$$\alpha ::= x \mid \overline{x} \mid \tau$$

Here I is a finite indexing set; if $I = \emptyset$ we write 0 for the sum and if I is a singleton we simply write $\alpha^\ell.P$. Binary sums are written $\alpha_1^{\ell_1}.P_1 + \alpha_2^{\ell_2}.P_2$ and in the following we shall perform much of the development in this simple case; it is easily generalised to arbitrary guarded sums. The labels $\ell \in \mathbf{Lab}$ of the actions are added to prepare for the analysis to be presented shortly; they have no impact on the semantics. Actions and co-actions (x and $\overline{x}$) are constructed from names x; local names are introduced by the restriction construct $\mathsf{new}\, x\, P$. The construct A allow us to refer to named processes defined by (recursive) equations of the form $A \triangleq P$.

There are two main approaches to the semantics of the calculus [9]. Perhaps the simplest approach amounts to defining a reduction semantics (denoted $\rightarrow$) and a structural congruence (denoted $\equiv$); this will be the choice used here and we shall recall its definition below. The original approach was to define a labelled transition system (LTS); however, it is worth pointing out that the two semantics can be proved equivalent [9] and that the choice of semantics does not affect the development of the present paper.

The reduction semantics expresses that the τ-action is a *silent* action that elimitates potential alternatives in a summation:

$$\tau^\ell.P + Q \;\rightarrow\; P$$

This represents an *internal* choice. The action x together with its co-action $\overline{x}$ enforces a *synchronisation* between two parallel processes; again we express this in the case they are both binary summands:

$$(x^{\ell_1}.P_1 + Q_1) \mid (\overline{x}^{\ell_2}.P_2 + Q_2) \;\rightarrow\; P_1 \mid P_2$$

This represents an *external* choice and as above we observe that potential alternatives are eliminated. Further semantic rules (see [9]) ensures that the semantic transitions can occur arbitrarily deep within parallel subprocesses and restricted processes.

Example. To illustrate the semantics let us return to the process $S \mid Q$ considered earlier where we, for the sake of later reference, add labels:

$$S \triangleq g^1.\, p^2.\, S$$
$$Q \triangleq \overline{g}^3.\, \tau^4.\, Q + \overline{p}^5.\, Q$$

Using the formal semantics we can express the transitions of the system already illustrated graphically by

$$\begin{aligned}
S \mid Q &\equiv (g^1.\, p^2.\, S) \mid (\overline{g}^3.\, \tau^4.\, Q + \overline{p}^5.\, Q) \\
&\rightarrow (p^2.\, S) \mid (\tau^4.\, Q) \\
&\rightarrow (p^2.\, S) \mid Q \\
&\equiv (p^2.\, S) \mid (\overline{g}^3.\, \tau^4.\, Q + \overline{p}^5.\, Q) \\
&\rightarrow S \mid Q
\end{aligned}$$

where we have included the rewritings of processes due to applications of the structural congruence $\equiv$.

4   Transfer Functions

An *exposed action* is an action that *may* participate in the next interaction. The process S above only has g^1 as exposed action whereas the process Q has $\overline{g}^3$ as well as $\overline{p}^5$ as exposed actions. In general, a process may contain many occurrences of the same action (all identified by the same label) and it may be the case that several of them are ready to participate in the next interaction – this will for example be the case for a system like $S \mid S \mid Q$ where two parallel occurrences of the unary semaphore is used to model a binary semaphore. Actually there may be an infinite number of occurrences of the same action that are ready to interact – this is for example the case for the process $Q' \triangleq (\overline{g}^3.\tau^4.0 + \overline{p}^5.0) \mid Q'$ that is equivalent to an infinite number of parallel occurrences of the process $\overline{g}^3.\tau^4.0 + \overline{p}^5.0$.

To capture this we define an *extended multiset* M as an element of:

$$\mathfrak{M} = \mathbf{Lab} \rightarrow \mathbb{N} \cup \{\infty\}$$

The idea is that $M(\ell)$ records the number of occurrences of the label ℓ; there may be a finite number in which case $M(\ell) \in \mathbb{N}$ or an infinite number in which case $M(\ell) = \infty$. This domain will become a complete lattice when equipped with the ordering $\leq_{\mathfrak{M}}$ defined by $M \leq_{\mathfrak{M}} M'$ if and only if for all ℓ either $M(\ell) \leq M'(\ell)$ or $M'(\ell) = \infty$. The least element $\bot_{\mathfrak{M}}$ hence maps all labels to 0 and the greatest element $\top_{\mathfrak{M}}$ maps all labels to ∞. The least upper bound operation $\sqcup_{\mathfrak{M}}$ and the greatest lower bound operation $\sqcap_{\mathfrak{M}}$ will be the pointwise extension of, respectively, the minimum and the maximum operators on $\mathbb{N} \cup \{\infty\}$.

Calculating Exposed Actions. The key information of interest is the collection of extended multisets of exposed actions of the processes. Initially this is computed by an abstraction function $\mathcal{E}$. First consider the sum of two processes $\alpha_1^{\ell_1}.P_1 + \alpha_2^{\ell_2}.P_2$. Here both of the actions α_1 and α_2 are ready to interact but none of those of P_1 and P_2 are so we shall take:

$$\mathcal{E}[\![\alpha_1^{\ell_1}.P_1 + \alpha_2^{\ell_2}.P_2]\!] = \perp_{\mathfrak{M}}[\ell_1 \mapsto 1] +_{\mathfrak{M}} \perp_{\mathfrak{M}}[\ell_2 \mapsto 1]$$

Here $+_{\mathfrak{M}}$ is a pointwise addition operator so if the two labels happen to be equal then the overall count will become 2. It is straightforward to adapt the formula to the general guarded summation construct. Turning to parallel composition we shall use a similar formula for $\alpha_1^{\ell_1}.P_1 \mid \alpha_2^{\ell_2}.P_2$:

$$\mathcal{E}[\![\alpha_1^{\ell_1}.P_1 \mid \alpha_2^{\ell_2}.P_2]\!] = \perp_{\mathfrak{M}}[\ell_1 \mapsto 1] +_{\mathfrak{M}} \perp_{\mathfrak{M}}[\ell_2 \mapsto 1]$$

Again, both of the actions α_1 and α_2 are ready to interact but none of those of P_1 and P_2 are. In the general case the formula simply is:

$$\mathcal{E}[\![P_1 \mid P_2]\!] = \mathcal{E}[\![P_1]\!] +_{\mathfrak{M}} \mathcal{E}[\![P_2]\!]$$

The clause for the new $x\,P$ construct simply ignores the introduction of the new name thereby ignoring the scope of names. Clearly this may lead to imprecision; however, in the simple case where recursion is not involved a simple alpha renaming of bound names will solve the problem. Turning to the clause for A where $A \triangleq P$ we easily obtain a recursive equation of the form $\mathcal{E}[\![A]\!] = \mathcal{E}[\![P]\!]$ (where $\mathcal{E}[\![A]\!]$ may occur inside $\mathcal{E}[\![P]\!]$) and this can be reformulated as a monotone function over a complete lattice. Tarski's fixed point theorem then gives us a least fixed point and this will be the analysis result for A.

Example. Turning to the semaphore examples we get:

$$\mathcal{E}[\![S \mid Q]\!] = \perp_{\mathfrak{M}}[1 \mapsto 1, 3 \mapsto 1, 5 \mapsto 1]$$
$$\mathcal{E}[\![S \mid S \mid Q]\!] = \perp_{\mathfrak{M}}[1 \mapsto 2, 3 \mapsto 1, 5 \mapsto 1]$$
$$\mathcal{E}[\![S \mid Q']\!] = \perp_{\mathfrak{M}}[1 \mapsto 1, 3 \mapsto \infty, 5 \mapsto \infty]$$

Generated and Killed Actions. The abstraction function $\mathcal{E}$ only gives us the information of interest for the initial process and we shall now present auxiliary functions allowing us to approximate how the information evolves during the execution of the process. To be more precise we shall aim at constructing an over-approximation to the result of applying the abstraction function to the processes occurring during reduction.

Once an action has participated in an interaction some new actions may become exposed – and some may no longer be exposed. As an example consider the semaphore process S. Initially, the action g^1 is exposed but once it has been executed it will no longer be exposed (i.e. it is killed) and instead the action p^2 becomes exposed (i.e. it is generated).

We shall now introduce two functions $\mathcal{G}$ and $\mathcal{K}$ approximating this information for processes. The relevant information will be an element of

$$\mathfrak{T} = \mathbf{Lab} \to \mathfrak{M} \qquad (= \mathbf{Lab} \to (\mathbf{Lab} \to \mathbb{N} \cup \{\infty\}))$$

As for exposed actions it is not sufficient to use sets: there may be more than one occurrence of an action that is either generated or killed by another action.

Let us first consider prefixing as expressed in the process $\alpha^\ell.P$. Clearly, once α^ℓ has been executed it will no longer be exposed but those of $\mathcal{E}[\![P]\!]$ will become exposed. Thus a first suggestion may be to take $\mathcal{G}[\![\alpha^\ell.P]\!](\ell) = \mathcal{E}[\![P]\!]$ and $\mathcal{K}[\![\alpha^\ell.P]\!](\ell) = \bot_{\mathfrak{M}}[\ell \mapsto 1]$. However, to cater for the general case where the same label may occur several times in a process (ℓ may be used inside P) we have to modify these formulas sligthly. The function $\mathcal{G}$ must compute an *over*-approximation so we take

$$\mathcal{G}[\![\alpha^\ell.P]\!] = \bot[\ell \mapsto \mathcal{E}[\![P]\!]] \sqcup \mathcal{G}[\![P]\!]$$

where $\sqcup$ is the least upper bound operator on $\mathfrak{T}$ and $\bot$ is the least element of $\mathfrak{T}$. Similarly, the function $\mathcal{K}$ must compute an *under*-approximation so we take

$$\mathcal{K}[\![\alpha^\ell.P]\!] = \top[\ell \mapsto M] \sqcap \mathcal{K}[\![P]\!] \qquad \text{where } M = \bot_{\mathfrak{M}}[\ell \mapsto 1]$$

where $\sqcap$ is the greatest lower bound operator on $\mathfrak{M}$ and $\top$ is the greatest element of $\mathfrak{T}$.

We can now generalise these formulas to guarded sums and parallel composition. The function $\mathcal{G}$ is defined in a straightforward manner in that it simply combines information from the subprocesses using the least upper bound operation:

$$\mathcal{G}[\![P \mid P']\!] = \mathcal{G}[\![P]\!] \sqcup \mathcal{G}[\![P']\!]$$
$$\mathcal{G}[\![\alpha_1^{\ell_1}.P_1 + \alpha_2^{\ell_2}.P_2]\!] = \mathcal{G}[\![\alpha_1^{\ell_1}.P_1]\!] \sqcup \mathcal{G}[\![\alpha_2^{\ell_2}.P_2]\!]$$

For $\mathcal{K}$ we use the greatest lower bound operation in the case of parallelism but we can do better in the case of sums:

$$\mathcal{K}[\![P \mid P']\!] = \mathcal{K}[\![P]\!] \sqcap \mathcal{K}[\![P']\!]$$
$$\mathcal{K}[\![\alpha_1^{\ell_1}.P_1 + \alpha_2^{\ell_2}.P_2]\!] = \top[\ell_1 \mapsto M] \sqcap \mathcal{K}[\![P_1]\!] \sqcap \top[\ell_2 \mapsto M] \sqcap \mathcal{K}[\![P_2]\!]$$
$$\text{where } M = \bot_{\mathfrak{M}}[\ell_1 \mapsto 1] +_{\mathfrak{M}} \bot_{\mathfrak{M}}[\ell_2 \mapsto 1]$$

Here we exploit that *all* the exposed actions (denoted M) of a sum can be killed independently of which action is taken. As for $\mathcal{E}$ we shall ignore the introduction of new names and we shall rely on fixed point theory when analysing the recursive definitions.

Example. Turning to the semaphore example $S \mid Q$ we obtain the following information:

ℓ	$\mathcal{G}[\![\cdots]\!](\ell)$
1	$\bot_{\mathfrak{M}}[2 \mapsto 1]$
2	$\bot_{\mathfrak{M}}[1 \mapsto 1]$
3	$\bot_{\mathfrak{M}}[4 \mapsto 1]$
4	$\bot_{\mathfrak{M}}[3 \mapsto 1, 5 \mapsto 1]$
5	$\bot_{\mathfrak{M}}[3 \mapsto 1, 5 \mapsto 1]$

ℓ	$\mathcal{K}[\![\cdots]\!](\ell)$
1	$\bot_{\mathfrak{M}}[1 \mapsto 1]$
2	$\bot_{\mathfrak{M}}[2 \mapsto 1]$
3	$\bot_{\mathfrak{M}}[3 \mapsto 1, 5 \mapsto 1]$
4	$\bot_{\mathfrak{M}}[4 \mapsto 1]$
5	$\bot_{\mathfrak{M}}[3 \mapsto 1, 5 \mapsto 1]$

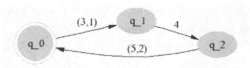

Fig. 1. The finite automaton for the process $S \mid Q$

Exactly the same information is obtained for $S \mid S \mid Q$ whereas for $S \mid Q'$ the information about generated actions needs to be modified:

ℓ	$\mathcal{G}[\![\cdots]\!](\ell)$
1	$\perp_{\mathfrak{M}}[2 \mapsto 1]$
2	$\perp_{\mathfrak{M}}[1 \mapsto 1]$
3	$\perp_{\mathfrak{M}}[4 \mapsto 1]$
4	$\perp_{\mathfrak{M}}$
5	$\perp_{\mathfrak{M}}$

ℓ	$\mathcal{K}[\![\cdots]\!](\ell)$
1	$\perp_{\mathfrak{M}}[1 \mapsto 1]$
2	$\perp_{\mathfrak{M}}[2 \mapsto 1]$
3	$\perp_{\mathfrak{M}}[3 \mapsto 1, 5 \mapsto 1]$
4	$\perp_{\mathfrak{M}}[4 \mapsto 1]$
5	$\perp_{\mathfrak{M}}[3 \mapsto 1, 5 \mapsto 1]$

Transfer Functions. Next consider a process P_s that in one step evolves into another process P_t because of an action labelled l_1 interacting with an action labelled l_2; this may be written $P_s \longrightarrow_{(l_1, l_2)} P_t$. Intuitively, the extended multiset of exploded labels in P_t should be obtained from those in P_s by removing those actions that are killed, i.e. $\mathcal{K}[\![P_s]\!][\ell_1] +_{\mathfrak{M}} \mathcal{K}[\![P_s]\!][\ell_2]$, and by adding those actions that are generated, i.e. $\mathcal{G}[\![P_s]\!][\ell_1] +_{\mathfrak{M}} \mathcal{G}[\![P_s]\!][\ell_2]$. Here $+_{\mathfrak{M}}$ is the pointwise addition operator and we write $-_{\mathfrak{M}}$ for the pointwise subtraction operator. This then suggests that one can prove that

$$\mathcal{E}[\![P_t]\!] \leq_{\mathfrak{M}} \mathcal{E}[\![P_s]\!] -_{\mathfrak{M}} (\ \mathcal{K}[\![P_s]\!][\ell_1] +_{\mathfrak{M}} \mathcal{K}[\![P_s]\!][\ell_2]\ ) +_{\mathfrak{M}} (\ \mathcal{G}[\![P_s]\!][\ell_1] +_{\mathfrak{M}} \mathcal{G}[\![P_s]\!][\ell_2]\ )$$

as is indeed the case.

This is not quite suitable for defining a transfer function as we should like it to remain stable during evaluation. We therefore use the fact that if an original process $P_\star$ is given and if P_s is a derivative of $P_\star$, i.e. $P_\star \longrightarrow^\star P_s$, then the generated actions described by $P_\star$ is an over-approximation of those described by P_s; similarly that the killed actions described by $P_\star$ is an under-approximation of those described by P_s. This motivates defining the transfer function as follows:

$$f_\star(E) = (E -_{\mathfrak{M}} (\ \mathcal{K}[\![P_\star]\!][\ell_1] +_{\mathfrak{M}} \mathcal{K}[\![P_\star]\!][\ell_2]\ )) +_{\mathfrak{M}} (\ \mathcal{G}[\![P_\star]\!][\ell_1] +_{\mathfrak{M}} \mathcal{G}[\![P_\star]\!][\ell_2]\ )$$

It follows that $\mathcal{E}[\![P_t]\!] \leq_{\mathfrak{M}} f_\star(\mathcal{E}[\![P_s]\!])$.

5   The Worklist Algorithm

Given a process $P_\star$ the development above gives information about which actions may be ready to interact, namely $\mathcal{E}[\![P_\star]\!]$. Furthermore, using $\mathcal{G}[\![P_\star]\!]$ and

$\mathcal{K}[\![P_\star]\!]$ we may approximate the actions that may be ready for interaction in the next step. The goal is to represent this information as a finite graph; Figure 1 illustrates this for the running example $S \mid Q$. Note that due to the simplicity of the example this is is very close to the transition graph displayed in Section 2.

The *nodes* of the graph will correspond to extended multisets of exposed actions thereby indicating those actions that are candidates for interaction in a given node. In the algorithm to be presented below we shall use a table E to record this information — for the above semaphore example we will have:

$$E[q_0] = \bot_{\mathfrak{m}}[1 \mapsto 1, 3 \mapsto 1, 5 \mapsto 1]$$
$$E[q_1] = \bot_{\mathfrak{m}}[2 \mapsto 1, 4 \mapsto 1]$$
$$E[q_2] = \bot_{\mathfrak{m}}[2 \mapsto 1, 3 \mapsto 1, 5 \mapsto 1]$$

Initially the table will consist of a single node q_0 with $E[q_0] = \mathcal{E}[\![P_\star]\!]$. No other information is associated with nodes except for the extended multisets of exposed actions as recorded by the table E. In particular a node does not contain any process expression; as indicated in the construction of the transfer function above the extended multiset of exposed actions together with knowledge of the original program $P_\star$ gives us all the information needed.

The *edges* of the graph records the potential transitions of the process: there will be an edge labelled (ℓ_1, ℓ_2) from q_s to q_t in the graph if (1) the actions labelled ℓ_1 and ℓ_2 are in $E[q_s]$ and they are enabled for interaction and (2) q_t describes the resulting set of exposed actions as determined by the transfer function. Thus the algorithm will set

$$E[q_t] = E[q_s] -_{\mathfrak{m}} (\, K[\ell_1] +_{\mathfrak{m}} K[\ell_2] \,) +_{\mathfrak{m}} (\, G[\ell_1] +_{\mathfrak{m}} G[\ell_2] \,)$$

where we write write G and K for the mappings $\mathcal{G}[\![P_\star]\!]$ and $\mathcal{K}[\![P_\star]\!]$, respectively.

The Algorithm. The graph is constructed using a simple worklist algorithm starting from the node q_0 and adding states and transitions using the ideas outlined above. The algorithm uses the data structures Nodes and Edges to contain the accumulated version of the graph while the worklist W keeps track of the nodes that still have to be processed. The worklist algorithm can now be described as follows (writing $G[\ell_1, \ell_2]$ for $G[\ell_1] +_{\mathfrak{m}} G[\ell_2]$ and similarly $K[\ell_1, \ell_2]$ for $K[\ell_1] +_{\mathfrak{m}} K[\ell_2]$):

$$
\begin{aligned}
&\text{Nodes} := \{q_0\}; E[q_0] := \mathcal{E}[\![P_\star]\!]; \\
&W := \{q_0\}; \text{Edges} := \emptyset; \\
&\text{while } W \neq \emptyset \text{ do} \\
&\qquad \text{select } q_s \text{ from } W; W := W \setminus \{q_s\}; \\
&\qquad \text{for each } \tilde{\ell} \in \text{enabled}(E[q_s]) \text{ do} \\
&\qquad\qquad \text{let } E = E[q_s] -_{\mathfrak{m}} K[\tilde{\ell}] +_{\mathfrak{m}} G[\tilde{\ell}] \\
&\qquad\qquad \text{in update}(q_s, \tilde{\ell}, E)
\end{aligned}
$$

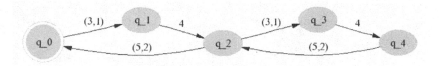

Fig. 2. The graph for the process $S \mid S \mid Q$

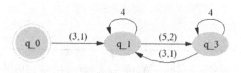

Fig. 3. The graph for the process $S \mid Q'$

The operation enabled(E) will return a set of potential interactions:

- if $E(\ell) \geq 1$ and ℓ is the label of a τ action then $\ell \in$ enabled(E) and
- if $E(\ell_1) \geq 1$ and $E(\ell_2) \geq 1$ and ℓ_1 and ℓ_2 are labels of actions of the form x and $\bar{x}$ for some x then $(\ell_1, \ell_2) \in$ enabled(E) (ensuring that they are in different parallel branches).

The operation update($q_s, \tilde{\ell}, E$) proceeds as follows:

- First it determines whether an existing node q_t needs to be reused (in order to guarantee that only finitely many nodes are generated). A simple choice is to reuse q_t in case the domain of $\mathsf{E}[q_t]$ equals that of E: $\{l \mid \mathsf{E}[q_t](l) > 0\} = \{l \mid E(l) > 0\}$.
- If an existing node q_t must be reused then we join the information of $\mathsf{E}[q_t]$ with that of E.
- If no existing node should be reused then we introduce a new node q_t with $\mathsf{E}[q_t] = E$.
- Finally, in both cases the edge relation Edges is updated with $(q_s, \tilde{\ell}, q_t)$ and q_t is added to the worklist.

The algorithm as presented so far has three shortcomings. One is that the condition for when to reuse nodes is a bit inflexible. For this we use a so-called *granularity function* for determining whether an existing state must be reused; a useful family of acceptable granularity functions have the form

$$H_L^k(E) = \{\ell \in L \mid 0 < E(\ell) \leq k\}$$

where L is a any finite subset of the labels and k is any element of $\mathbb{N} \cup \{\infty\}$. A state q_t then must be reused if $H_L^k(\mathsf{E}[q_t]) = H_L^k(E)$. The special case where $L = \mathbf{Lab}$ and $k = \infty$ corresponds to the simple choice mentioned above.

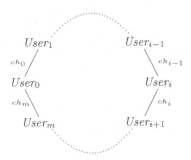

Fig. 4. The Ingemarsson-Tang-Wong key agreement protocol with m users

Another shortcoming is that the algorithm may loop even though we have guarded against infinitely often choosing new nodes. This is because the lattice

$$\mathfrak{M} = \mathbf{Lab} \to \mathbb{N} \cup \{\infty\}$$

of extended multisets has infinitely increasing chains. To overcome this problem we shall use a suitable *widening operator* ∇ for joining the old and the new information associated with the node. Hence we shall be setting the new value $\mathsf{E}[q_t]$ of a reused node q_t to be $\mathsf{E}[q_t]\nabla E$.

A third shortcoming of the algorithm is that the resulting graph may have nodes that are not reachable from the initial node q_0; this is simply solved by performing a *reachability analysis*.

Example. The algorithm will construct the graphs of Figure 1 when applied to the semaphore process $S \mid Q$ using a granularity function of the form $H_{\mathbf{Lab}}$. Figures 2 and 3 show the graphs obtained for $S \mid S \mid Q$ and $S \mid Q'$.

Implementation. The graphs shown in this paper have been produced by an implementation carried out in Moscow ML. First the auxiliary information of $\mathcal{E}$, $\mathcal{G}$ and $\mathcal{K}$ is computed using a straightforward fixed point iteration. In the case of $\mathcal{E}$ and $\mathcal{G}$ this results in ascending chains and termination is then guaranteed because the main operations are addition and maximum, respectively; in the case of $\mathcal{K}$ the iteration gives rise to descending chains and hence termination is guaranteed. The implementation of the worklist algorithm follows the theoretical development and is parameterised on the granularity function. Finally the implementation makes use of the Graphviz tool[1] to display the analysis result.

---

[1] See http://www.graphviz.org/.

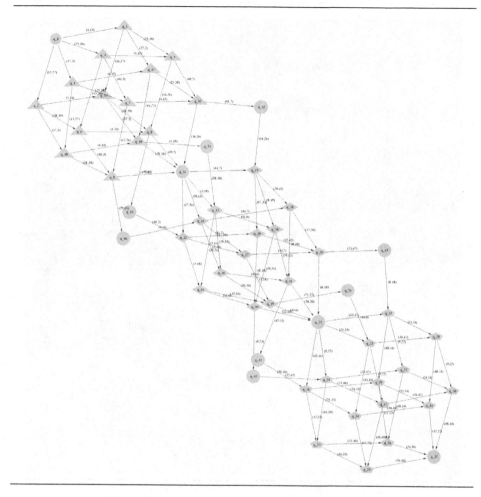

Fig. 5. Four users complete one run of the protocol

6   Worked Example: A Key Agreement Protocol

To illustrate the use of the analysis we shall consider the Ingemarsson-Tang-Wong key agreement protocol [5]. It is a generalisation of the Diffie-Hellman key agreement protocol for establishing a joint secret key between a number of users. The idea is as follows: m users $User_1, \cdots , User_m$ are organised in a ring so that $User_i$ only receives messages from $User_{i-1}$ and only sends messages to $User_{i+1}$ (with indices calculated modulo m); this is illustrated in Figure 4. Initially, all the users have agreed upon a generator constant g that will be used to construct the shared key. The protocol then proceeds in $m - 1$ rounds. In the first round each of the users selects a random number r_i, raises g to the power of r_i and

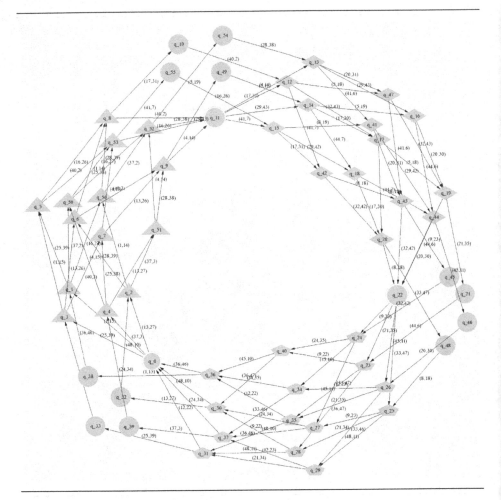

Fig. 6. Four users complete any number of runs of the protocol

sends it to its neighbour. Thus, in the first round $User_i$ will receive $g^{r_{i-1}}$ from $User_{i-1}$ and send g^{r_i} to $User_{i+1}$. In the second round $User_i$ will then raise the received value $g^{r_{i-1}}$ to the power of r_i to construct $g^{r_{i-1}r_i}$ and send it to $User_{i+1}$; obviously he will receive a value constructed in a similar manner from $User_{i-1}$ and this is the value he will use in the next round. This process is repeated for $m-1$ rounds after which each user will know $g^{r_1\cdots r_m}$; this value will then serve as the joint secret key.

To comply with the syntax of CCS we shall focus on the synchronisation structure of the protocol and hence ignore the calculations performed by the users and the actual values being communicated; this suffices for getting some understanding of the operation of the protocol. The users $User_i$ and $User_{i+1}$ (modulo m) synchronize over channels ch_i and in each round they may interact with their neighbours in any order. Thus the code for $User_i$ in round n (for $n < m$) may be written as:

$$User_i^n \triangleq ch_{i-1}.\ \overline{ch_i}.\ User_i^{n+1} + \overline{ch_i}.\ ch_{i-1}.\ User_i^{n+1}$$

Let us first consider the case where the users only complete one run of the protocol; so we simply have $User_i^m = 0$. In the case of four users the analysis constructs the automaton displayed in Figure 5. The initial state q_0 is shown on the top left and final state q_{32} is shown on the bottom right. Any path between these two states corresponds to a possible run of the protocol; the multitude of paths reflects the many possible interleavings that are made possible by the use of the summation in the definition of $User_i^n$ above. In the "doubly circled" states (to be called q_0, q_{11}, q_{22} and q_{32}) *all* the users are ready to start on a new round (or, equivalently, have just finished a round). However, the automaton also shows that there are runs where the users do not synchronise in that way. In the two groups of "singly circled" states (to the lower left and the upper right of the two internal "doubly circled" states q_{11} and q_{22} on the figure) one pair of users has started on the next round before the other pair has finished the previous round. The remaining states fall into three groups (shown as "triangles", "diamonds" and "pentagons" on the figure) and in these states all the users participate in the same round.

Let us modify the scenario in which the protocol is used so that the users recursively initiate a new run of a protocol as soon as the current run has been completed; this corresponds to defining $User_i^m$ to be equal to $User_i^1$. In the case of four users we obtain the automaton displayed in Figure 6. We see that the overall structure of Figure 5 is preserved except that the graph has become fully connected. In general terms this is achieved by feeding the final state (the state q_{32} occurring on the bottom right) of Figure 5 into the initial state (the state q_0 occurring on the top left) of Figure 5; to be a bit more precise the interaction between the two states gives rise to the same pattern of five "circled" states seen between the three groups of Figure 5.

7   Conclusion

Often static analysis is used to capture properties of the *configurations* arising during the execution of programs or processes — the analysis presented in this paper goes one step further and focusses on the *transitions* between configurations.

The presence of communicating concurrent processes in itself makes this a non-trivial task and for CCS it is further complicated by the fact that new processes may arise dynamically just as they may cease to exist. To handle this complex scenario we first introduced extended multisets of exposed actions; they are used to model the configurations of the systems. To capture the dynamic nature of processes we then performed a detailed analysis of how the extended multisets will grow and shrink with the execution of the processes; this was inspired by the classical kill/gen functions of Monotone Frameworks. For construction of the finite automaton the classical worklist algorithm plays a key role but in order to ensure termination we rely on our notion of granularity function as well as the widening operators of Abstract Interpretation. The finite automaton amounts to a finite graph that represents the potentially infinite transition systems of processes. It is important to stress that proper use of granularity functions ensure that we always obtain a finite automation and that the construction always terminates. In future work we intend to explore the use of narrowing to further increase the precision of the automaton and collapsing functions for presenting "projections" of it that may be more useful for program understanding.

In the development of this paper the actions themselves (the x's of the syntax) only play a minor role — they are only consulted when determining whether or not two exposed actions might indeed synchronise. The setting becomes far more complicated when turning to process calculi like the π-calculus where synchronisation is replaced by communication of names over channels which are themselves names. This adds substantial expressivity and adds further complications to the analysis concerning the proper binding of names. In future work we intend to investigate the challenges posed by name-passing calculi; this will be useful for a more detailed study of communication protocols.

Acknowledgements. This work has been supported by the Danish Natural Science Research Council project LoST (21-02-0507), by the Danish Natural Science Research Council project Security in Embedded Systems (2059-03-0011) and by the EU-IST-FET project SENSORIA (FP6-016004).

References

1. A. V. Aho, M. S. Lam, R. Sethi, and J. D. Ullman. *Compilers: Principles, Techniques, and Tools.* Addison Wesley, 2006.
2. C. Bodei, M. Buchholtz, P. Degano, F. Nielson, and H. Riis Nielson. Static validation of protocol narration. *Journal of Computer Security*, 13:347–390, 2005.
3. C. Bodei, P. Degano, F. Nielson, and H. Riis Nielson. Static analysis for the π-calculus with applications to security. *Information and Computation*, 168:68–92, 2001.
4. C. Bodei, P. Degano, H. Riis Nielson, and F. Nielson. Flow logic for Dolev-Yao secrecy in cryptographic processes. *FGCS*, 18(6):747–756, 2002.
5. C. Boyd and A. Mathuria. *Protocols for authentication and key establishment.* Springer, 2003.
6. M. Buchholz, H. Riis Nielson, and F. Nielson. A calculus for control flow analysis of security protocols. *International Journal of Information Security*, 2:145–167, 2004.
7. P. Cousot and R. Cousot. Systematic design of program analysis frameworks. In *Symposium on Principles of Programming Languages*, page 269282. ACM Press, 1979.
8. K. Honda, V. T. Vasconcelos, and M. Kubo. Language primitives and type discipline for structured communication-based programming. In *Programming Languages and Systems (ESOP)*, volume 1381 of *Lecture Notes in Computer Science*, pages 122–138. Springer, 1998.
9. R. Milner. *Communicating and Mobile Systems: The pi-Calculus.* Cambridge University Press, 1999.

10. M. Neubauer and P. Thiemann. An implementation of session types. In *Practical Aspects of Declarative Languages (PADL)*, volume 3057 of *Lecture Notes in Computer Science*, pages 56–70. Springer, 2004.

11. F. Nielson, H. Riis Nielson, and C. L. Hankin. *Principles of Program Analysis*. Springer, 1999. Second printing, 2005.

12. F. Nielson, H. Riis Nielson, and R. R. Hansen. Validating firewalls using flow logics. *Theoretical Computer Science*, 283(2):381–418, 2002.

13. F. Nielson, H. Riis Nielson, and H. Seidl. Cryptographic analysis in cubic time. *Electronic Notes of Theoretical Computer Science*, 62:7–23, 2002.

14. H. Riis Nielson and F. Nielson. Shape analysis for mobile ambients. *Nordic Journal of Computing*, 8:233–275, 2001.

15. H. Riis Nielson, F. Nielson, and M. Buchholtz. Security for Mobility. In R. Focardi and R. Gorrieri, editors, *Foundations of Security Analysis and Design II*, volume 2946 of *Lecture Notes in Computer Science*, pages 207–266. Springer, 2004.

16. H. Riis Nielson, F. Nielson, and H. Pilegaard. Spatial analysis of BioAmbients. In *Proc. SAS'04*, Lecture Notes in Computer Science. Springer, 2004.

17. T. K. Tolstrup, F. Nielson, and H. Riis Nielson. Information flow analysis for VHDL. In *Proc. PaCT'05*, Lecture Notes in Computer Science. Springer, 2005.

18. V. T. Vasconcelos, A. Ravara, and S. J. Gay. Session types for functional multithreading. In *CONCUR - Concurrency Theory*, volume 3170 of *Lecture Notes in Computer Science*, pages 497–511. Springer, 2004.

Towards a Source Level Compiler: Source Level Modulo Scheduling

Yosi Ben-Asher and Danny Meisler

Computer Sci. dep.
Haifa University, Haifa
dmeisler@cs.haifa.ac.il

Abstract. Modulo scheduling is a major optimization of high performance compilers wherein The body of a loop is replaced by an overlapping of instructions from different iterations. Hence the compiler can schedule more instructions in parallel than in the original option. Modulo scheduling, being a scheduling optimization, is a typical backend optimization relying on detailed description of the underlying CPU and its instructions to produce a good schedule. This work considers the problem of applying modulo scheduling at source level as a loop transformation, using only general information of the underlying CPU architecture. By doing so it is possible: a) Create a more retargeble compiler as modulo scheduling is now applied at source level, b) Study possible interactions between modulo scheduling and common loop transformations. c) Obtain a source level optimizer whose output is readable to the programmer, yet its final output can be efficiently compiled by a relatively "simple" compiler.

Experimental results show that source level modulo scheduling can improve performance also when low level modulo scheduling is applied by the final compiler, indicating that high level modulo scheduling and low level modulo scheduling can co-exist to improve performance. An algorithm for source level modulo scheduling modifying the abstract syntax tree of a program is presented. This algorithm has been implemented in an automatic parallelizer (Tiny). Preliminary experiments yield runtime and power improvements also for the ARM CPU for embedded systems.

1   Introduction

This work considers the problem of implementing Modulo Scheduling (MS) [16] at software level rather than implementing it at machine level, as is usually done in modern compilers [12]. The main motivation in doing so is to allow users to view the effect of modulo scheduling at source level, allowing possible interaction with other loop transformations and manual improvements. During experiments, it turned out that in many cases, Source Level Modulo Scheduling (SLMS) improved the execution times even when the underlying compiler used "exact" machine level MS. Consequently, SLMS and machine level MS should co-exist even in a high performance compiler. Thus SLMS is used for two different tasks: optimizing programs at source level along with other loop transformations and as a stand alone optimization complementary to machine level MS.

T. Reps, M. Sagiv, and J. Bauer (Eds.): Wilhelm Festschrift, LNCS 4444, pp. 328–360, 2007.

Basically, MS is one type of solution to the problem of extracting parallelism from loops by "pipelining" the loop's iterations as follows:

$$
\begin{array}{ll}
& S1_0: \quad t = A[0] * B[0]; \\
for(i = 0; i < n; i++) & for(i = 0; i < n-1; i++) \\
\{ & \{ \\
S1_i: \quad t = A[i] * B[i]; \longrightarrow & S2_i: \quad s = s + t; \\
S2_i: \quad s = s + t; & S1_{i+1}: \quad t = A[i+1] * B[i+1]; \\
\} & \} \\
& S2_{n-1}: \quad s = s + t;
\end{array}
$$

Note that after this "pipelining" the dependency between $S1_i$ and $S2_i$ has been eliminated and the new statements $S2_i$ and $S1_{i+1}$ can be executed in parallel (denoted by $S2_i || S1_{i+1}$). [1]

Many techniques have been proposed to approximate the solution to the problem of optimal pipelining of loops iterations by eliminating the maximal number of inter iteration dependencies [3,23].

A common technique to illustrate MS (very schematically) puts consecutive iterations $i, i+1, \ldots$ shifted by a fixed size (called the Initiation Interval or II [16]) in a 2D table of "rows". The instructions of iteration $i + k$ ($k = 0, 1, 2, \ldots$) are placed in the k'th column of this table, starting at the $II * k$ row. Let $I_0, \ldots, I_{n-1}$ be the assignments or instructions in the loop's body, then rows $n - II, \ldots, n - 1$ will repeat themselves i.e., the instructions in rows $n - II, \ldots, n - 1$ will be identical to the instructions in rows $n, \ldots n + II - 1$ and so forth. This repeated II rows form the kernel of the new loop. The first $n - II$ rows form the prologue used to initialize the "iterations pipe" and the last $n - II$ rows (if we put only $2n - II$ iterations) from the epilogue that drains the pipe. The II is valid if the resulting kernel does not violate any data dependency of the original loop. Figure 1 depicts this basic form of MS.

In modern compilers, MS is executed at machine level after the machine depended optimization level. It is natural since in this case the machine instructions of the loop's body fill the columns of the MS table, which forms a schedule of the new loop's instructions. Every row of the table corresponds to instructions that can be executed in parallel:

- For VLIW architectures such as TI, each row of the kernel is a VLS (compound instruction).
- For super scalar architectures such as the Pentium, each row contains instructions that can be executed in parallel by the different pipeline units of the CPU.

Consequently, each row of the MS table should be valid, in terms of the data dependencies, as well as in order not to violate the amount of hardware resources (and possibly encoding restrictions). For example, if the hardware allows only

---

[1] This parallel execution $S2_i || S1_{i+1}$ is valid under the assumption that in a parallel execution the load of t in $S2_i$ is not affected by the update of t in $S1_{i+1}$. Such a claim is true for most VLIW machines and other models.

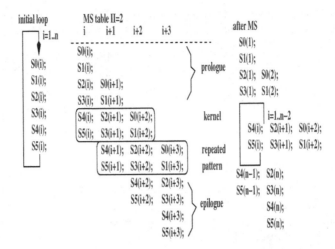

Fig. 1. Using the MS table

two parallel additions, any row with more than two additions implies that either the II is wrong or the instructions in the kernel's rows should be rearranged. In addition, MS is also used to minimize the amount of pipeline stalls between the consecutive rows (VLSs in VLIW architectures) of the resulting kernel. Figure 2 depicts MS of a simple loop after it has been compiled to machine code. In this case, the hardware allows VLSs with up to two load/store instructions and up to two additions. The MS table was filled by using $II = 1$ and $(r0), (r0 + 1)$, $(r0 + 2), \ldots$ as the iteration index.

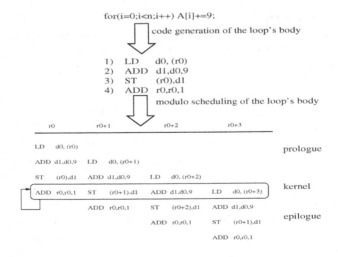

Fig. 2. Machine level MS

This work considers another possibility of implementing MS, namely to implement it as a source level loop transformation. The goal is to develop eventually a Source Level Compiler (SLC) that will combine SLMS and known loop transformations such as peeling, fusion, and tiling as described in [4]. A program is first compiled by using the SLC and then the resulting optimized program is compiled to the target architecture by using a regular compiler (called the final compiler).

Figure 3 depicts how SLMS is applied. After SLMS the final compiler applies code-generation, register allocation and list scheduling of basic blocks to create VLIW instructions. The outcome in this case is as efficient as the one would have obtained by using machine level MS. Remark: some MS algorithms such as Iterative MS [17] use modified versions of List scheduling to schedule the kernel after the II has been computed. In this respect, it may be possible to view SLMS as moving the first part of MS to the front-end (computing the II and generating the prologue, kernel and epilogue) leaving the actual scheduling of the kernel to the List scheduling of the backend.

```
source code            source level               loop's body
                       modulo scheduling           after code generation
                                                   and list scheduling
for(i = 0 ; i < n ; i++){   int d0,d1;             [
   A[i] = A[i] + 1;         d0 = A[0];                ADD r0,r0,2  ||
}                           d1 = d0+9;   d0 = A[1];   ST  (r0),d  ||
                            for(i = 0 ; i < n-2 ; i++){   ADD d1,d0,9 ||
                               A[i] = d1;             LD  d0,(r0+2)
                               d1 = d0 + 9;          ]
                               d0 = A[i+2];
                            }
                            A[n-2] = d1;  d1 = d0+9;
                            A[n-1] = d1;
```

Fig. 3. Using SLMS followed by List scheduling

2 Source Level Compiler Scheme

We show that the SLC can improve final performances of programs (by using advanced array analysis and source level transformations) as follows:

- Based on the interaction with the SLC, the user can modify parts of its code producing new opportunities for the SLC (e.g, replacing while-loops by fixed range for-loops or using arrays instead of pointers/records). The user can acknowledge speculative operations of the SLC such as allowing SLMS to use II that violates some data dependency. The proposed SLMS algorithm is designed to minimize the changes to the original program thus, preserving the readability of the optimized code.
- SLMS is a powerful optimization that can potentially improve the execution times even if the underlying final compiler includes a machine level MS. Thus, the SLC can potentially improve execution times of modern compilers or cover the lack of a given optimization (e.g., MS) in the backend of the final compiler.

– The combination of SLMS and loop transformations can be, in some cases, more effective when it is implemented at source level (as shown later on several possible combinations).

Figure 4 presents a block diagram of the SLC scheme. The programmer interacts with the SLC to improve the performance of his code.

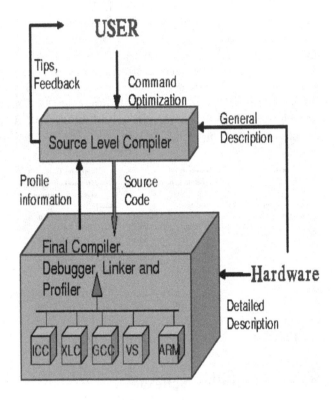

Fig. 4. Source Level Compiler Interaction with the User, Final Compiler and HW

Figure 5 is an example of how the SLC can improve the register allocation of the final compiler. This is done in the following steps:

1. The original loop is given as input to the SLC
2. The SLC tips the user that the life-times of loop-variants (a,b and c) can be reduced.
3. Than the user marks the code that does not depend on those variables.
4. SLC re-arranges the source code such that the life-times are reduced.
5. The loop is than compiled by the final compiler resulting a better register allocation scheme.

Note that this optimization is usually done by the register allocation of the compiler, apart from cases where the compiler is not able to move instruction

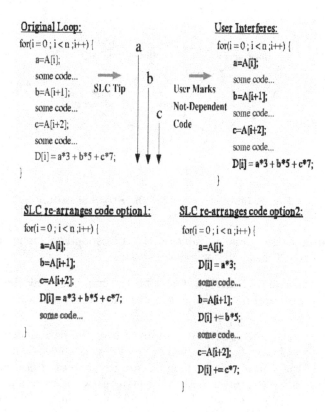

Fig. 5. Source Level Compiler can improve register allocation

due to possible dependencies with the rest of the code. For example of the code after $a = A[i]$ contains a call to a function that may change the value of a than only the user can hint the SLC that $a = a[i]$ can be safely move after this call.

3   Basic Operations Used by the SLMS Algorithm

In the following subsections, are listed shortly the elementary operations used by the proposed SLMS algorithm. Some of these operations are known and were used in other MS algorithms. Initially, the loops are represented by their abstract syntax tree (AST) [2]. In addition, the dependencies (including the iteration-distances) between array references and scalar variables in the AST are given as directed labeled edges between the AST nodes. For example, the body of the loop $for(i = 0; i < n; i + +)A[i]+ = A[i - 1];$ is depicted in figure 6. The input AST is logically partitioned to "multi-instructions"(MI), corresponding to assignments, function-calls or to elementary if-statements. For example the AST in figure 6 contains a single MI.

Next, we describe the concept of the minimum initiation interval (MII) [16] and how it is computed. The minimum initiation interval is the one for which

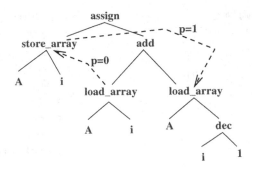

Fig. 6. Input structure for the SLMS algorithm

a valid schedule exists. Smaller values of II correspond to higher throughput. Calculation of the II accounts for two constrains:

1. Resource constraint (RMII). Let $r(i)$ be the number of available resources (e.g. add units) and $n(i)$ the number of times the resource i is used in the code. $RMII = max_i \lceil \frac{r(i)}{n(i)} \rceil$.
2. Recurrence constraint (PMII) is computed over the data dependency graph G of the loop's body [4]. For a given cycle of dependencies C_i in G let pm_i be the ratio of the sum of delays along C_i and the sum of "iteration-distances" in C_i. The delay (for machine level) between two instructions is basically the number of pipeline stalls that occur if the two instruction are executed one after the other. For SLMS a different notion of delays will be defined as pipeline stalls has no meaning at source level.

   The "iteration-distance" indicates the number of iterations that separate the "define" and "use" of a value (e.g., the iteration-distance between $A[i] = x$ and $y = A[i - 3]$) is three).
3. The value of MII is set to $MII = Max\{PMII, RMII\}$.

The MS algorithm first attempts to obtain a valid schedule of with $II = MII$ MIs. In case that such a schedule is not possible the MS algorithm tries larger values of II until such a schedule is obtained.

3.1   Source Level If-Conversion

MS algorithms are basically designed to work on simple loops without conditional branches. The algorithms that do handle conditional branches usually use predicated instructions to eliminate the conditional branches [19]. In case that the underlying machine does not have predication, the reverse if-conversion is used to restore conditional branches after MS was applied [21]. This work, uses predication at source level. If-statements of the AST are predicated with Boolean variables, similar to the if-conversion operation performed in assembly mode.

For example, the if-statement $if(x < y)x = x + 1; A[i]+ = x;\ elsey = y + 1;$ is converted to

$$c = (x < y);$$
$$if(c)\ x = x + 1;$$
$$if(c)\ A[i]+ = x;$$
$$if(not(c))\ y = y + 1;$$

Remark: apart from the use of if-conversion in MS there have been other proposals for MS of loops with conditional statements. For example, Lam [10] uses a sequence of hierarchical reductions of strongly connected components to MS a loop with conditional statements.

3.2 Decomposition of MIs

This operation divides a complex "large" MI to a set of "smaller" MIs, e.g., $A[i] = a + b * c;$ may be divided to $t = b * c;\ A[i] = a + t;$. As explained before, in SLMS the resulting code must be as similar as possible to the original code. Hence, we are seeking to minimize the number of decompositions of MIs needed to obtain a valid SLMS. Finding a minimal decomposition of MIs is a key problem in SLMS and the implemented algorithm uses the following two types of operations:

1. Break a self data dependency edge inside the AST of the MI, e.g. the one between $A[i]+ = A[i-1];$.
2. Reduces the number of resources (arithmetic operations and load/store operations) in the MI. For example the MI $x = A[i] + B[i] + C[i] + D[i];$ contains four load operations and four additions. In assumption that the underlying CPU is a VLIW machine allowing up to two additions and two load/store operation in a multi-instruction (VLS), it is better to decompose $x = A[i] + B[i] + C[i] + D[i];$ to $t = A[i] + B[i];$ and $x = t + C[i] + D[i].$

Decomposition is needed for two reasons:

1. In case that the original loop contains only one MI, at least two are needed to perform MS.
2. In case a loop-carried self dependency prevents finding the MI (section 5).

Consider the loop:

$$for(i = 0; i < N; i + +)\{$$
$$A[i] = A[i-1] + A[i-2] + A[i+1] + A[i+2];\ \}$$

This loop does not have a valid schedule for $II = 1$, because there is only one MI and because of the loop-carried self dependency between $A[i], A[i-1]$. First, we select one load array reference $A[i+1]$ with no flow dependence with the store operation $A[i] =$. By using this selected array reference we create two MIs using a temporary variable as follows:

$$for(i = 0; i < (N-2); i + +)\{$$
$$reg1 = A[i+2];$$
$$A[i] = A[i-1] + A[i-2] + A[i+1] + reg1;$$
$$\}$$

The data dependency of $reg1 = \ldots$ and $A[i-2] + reg1+$ will be eliminated by applying Modulo Variable Expansion (MVE), described in section 3.3. At this stage SLMS can be applied with $II = 1$ as follows:

$$reg1 = A[2];$$
$$for(i = 0; i < (N-3); i++)\{$$
$$\quad A[i] = A[i-1] + A[i-2] + A[i+1] + reg1; \parallel$$
$$\quad reg1 = A[i+3];$$
$$\}$$
$$A[i] = A[i-1] + A[i-2] + A[i+1] + reg1;$$

The symbol $\parallel$ is used between multi instructions that can be totally parallelized by the final compiler/hardware in terms of not violating any data dependencies.

Remark: SLMS assumes that the backend compiler shall use a register for the new local variable "reg1".

3.3   Modulo Variable Expansion

The SLMS operation, as explained so far can introduce new data dependencies between MIs, such as the dependency between $\ldots a[i-2] + reg1 + a[i+2]\ldots$ and $\ldots reg1 = a[i+2];$ in the last code example of subsection 3.2. Such dependencies may prevent the underlying scheduler (the scheduler of the final compiler) or the hardware (in case of a Super scalar CPU) to extract parallelism. Modulo variable expansion (MVE) [10] is used to eliminate such dependencies. Basically, MVE of a variable (say $reg1$) is performed by unrolling [2] the kernel, and renaming the variable such that the data dependency inside each unrolled copy of the kernel is removed.

$$reg1 = a[2];$$
$$for(i = 0; i < (N-4); i+= 2)\{$$
$$\quad a[i] = a[i-1] + a[i-2] + a[i+1] + reg1; \parallel$$
$$\quad\quad reg2 = a[i+3];$$
$$\quad a[i+1] = a[i] + a[i-1] + a[i+2] + reg2; \parallel$$
$$\quad\quad reg1 = a[i+4];$$
$$\}$$
$$a[i] = a[i-1] + a[i-2] + a[i+1] + reg1;$$

Note that after MVE the MIs of each copy (in the unroll operation) can be executed in parallel forming a source level "parallel set of MIs" (indicated by the $\parallel$ symbol in each row).

The following example (see figure 7) presents an application of SLMS and MVE. In this example the original loop contained a loop variant named scal. The first MI of the loop was decomposed by SLMS generating a second loop variant named reg. MVE was applied separately for each loop variant, generating two registers for each variant.

---

[2] The number of times we need to unroll the loop depends on the lifetime of each variable in the loop as described in [10].

```
for(i=1;i<N-1;i++){        reg1 = A[2];
  reg = A[i+1];        ➡   A[1] = A[0] + reg1;  ||  reg2 = A[3];
  A[i] = A[i-1] + reg;        scal1 = B[1] / 2;    ||  A[2] = A[1] + reg2;  ||  reg1 = A[4];
  scal = B[i] / 2;
  C[i] = scal * 3;           for(i = 1 ; i < N - 5; i += 2) {
}                              C[i] = scal1 * 3;   || scal2 = B[i+1] / 2; || A[i+2] = A[i+1] + reg1; || reg2 = A[i+4];
                               C[i+1] = scal2 * 3; || scal1 = B[i+2] / 2; || A[i+3] = A[i+2] + reg2; || reg1 = A[i+5];
                             }


                             C[i] = scal1 * 3;   ||  scal2 = B[i+1] / 2; || A[i+2] = A[i+1] + reg1;
                             C[i+1] = scal2 * 3; ||  scal1 = B[i+2] / 2;
                             C[i+2] = scal1 * 3;


                             Complete last Iteration;
```

Fig. 7. SLMS decomposition and original loop scalar

3.4   Scalar Expansion

Another possibility to remove data dependencies caused by scalar variables is to use scalar expansion [4] and replace the scalar variable by a sequence of array references. For example, instead of applying MVE on the loop of section 3.2 scalar expansion can be applied by replacing $reg1$ by $regArr[i]$ so that the SLMS will be:

$$regArr[2] = a[2];$$
$$for(i = 0; i < (N - 3); i + +)\{$$
$$\quad a[i] = a[i - 1] + a[i - 2] + a[i + 1] + regArr[i + 2];$$
$$\quad || \ regArr[i + 3] = a[i + 3];$$
$$\}$$
$$a[i] = a[i - 1] + a[i - 2] + a[i + 1] + regArr[i + 2];$$

This operation removed the anti-dependence caused by $reg1$ and enables the parallel execution of the two expressions indicated by $||$.

3.5   Delay Calculations

For SLMS the delay between two MIs must be defined in general terms related to the source code rather than the hardware. The delay of a data dependency edge (see figure 6) has been defined so, that the sum of delays along every cycle of dependencies will be greater or equal the number of edges in that cycle. If this condition is not met, some dependency will be violated in the resulting kernel. Let MI_i, MI_j be two MIs connected by a dependency edge $e_{i,j}$ then the $delay(MI_i, MI_j)$ is defined as follows:

1. $delay(MI_i, MI_j) = 1$ if $i = j$ (loop-carried self dependency).
2. $delay(MI_i, MI_{i+1}) = 1$.

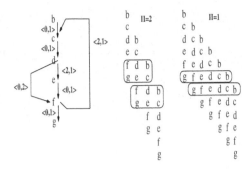

Fig. 8. Delays between MIs

3. $delay(MI_i, MI_j) = k$ if $e_{i,j}$ is a forward edge and k is the maximal delay along any path from MI_i to MI_j. Note: j is sequentially ordered after i $i < j$.
4. $delay(MI_i, MI_j) = 1$ if $e_{i,j}$ is a back edge.

Figure 8 depicts a data dependency graph whose edges are labeled by pairs of $< itr\_distance, delay >$ yielding two cycles: $C1 = c \rightarrow d \rightarrow e \rightarrow f \rightarrow c$ and $C2 = c \rightarrow d \rightarrow f \rightarrow c$. The MII due to $C1$ is $(1 + 1 + 1 + 1)/(2 + 2) = 1$ while the MII due to $C2$ is $(1 + 2 + 1)/2 = 2$. Indeed (as depicted in figure 8), a feasible schedule is obtained for $MII = 2$ and not for $MII = 1$ which violates the backedge from f to c.

3.6   Computing the MII

In SLMS the MII accounts only for recurrence constraint (PMII [16]). The computation of the MII is a complex task since the MII is computed over all cycles of dependencies. The Iterative Shortest Path algorithm presented in [3,23] has been selected for two reasons.

1. First, its simplicity and its ability to naturally handle the case where each dependency edge has several pairs of $< iteration - distance, delay >$. This case is frequent in SLMS as each MI may contain more than one array reference, e.g., the edge connecting $MI_i : A[i] = B[i-1]+y$; to $MI_j : B[i] = A[i-2] + A[i-3]$ has two iteration distances one for $A[i-2] \longrightarrow A[i]$ and one for $A[i-3] \longrightarrow A[i]$.
2. Second, it does not use the resource MII which is an advantage for SLMS.

4   Filtering Bad-Cases

Filtering "bad cases" where SLMS reduces performance is the first phase of the SLMS algorithm. This phase has to includes various types of heuristics that are specific for both the final compiler and target machine. An example of such a filter is given.

In order to "skip" bad cases, where SLMS reduce performances we compared the ratio between the number of load/store operations (LS) and the arithmetic operations (AO) in the loop's body $\frac{LS}{LS+AO}$. This ratio is termed as the memory-ref ratio. High values of memory-ref implies that overlapping of iterations may lead to too many parallel load store operations in one "row". In that case, SLMS might cause stalls due to memory reference pressure. Experimentaly, it turned out that many such "bad cases" can be eliminated if we require that the above ratio will be less than 0.85. For example, the following loop has $LS = 6$ and $AO = 1$ and ratio 0.857 and thus SLMS will not be applied here.

$$for(k = 0; k < n; k + +)\{$$
$$CT = X[k, i];$$
$$X[k, i] = X[k, j] * 2;$$
$$X[k, j] = CT;$$
$$\}$$

Note that if we have several arithmetic operations per each load/store operation then the scheduler can probably hide memory delays (such L1-cache misses) using these arithmetic computations. Remark: Although not tested on other machines, we assume that the memory-ref ratio is machine-specific, and that this ratio depends on the machine's capacity to perform parallel memory operations and the delay of an L1-cache miss. An alternative way of filtering bad cases would have been to estimate the expected number of cycles of the loop's body after SLMS length of the critical path Other factors that can affect this ratio include: penalty of L1-cache misses,

Following is an example showing how SLMS may increase the number of memory references due to overlapping of successive iterations. In the following simplified loop, most array references can be replaced by a register. But, after applying SLMS, the array references must be implemented by separate load/store operations.

$$for(i = 0; i < n; i + +)\{ \quad prologue$$
$$a[i]+ = i; \qquad\qquad for(i = 0; i < n - 2; i + +)\{$$
$$a[i]* = 6; \quad \longrightarrow \quad a[i] - -; \ ||a[i + 1]* = 6; \ ||a[i + 2]+ = i;$$
$$a[i] - -; \qquad\qquad \}$$
$$\} \qquad\qquad\qquad epilogue$$

5 The SLMS Algorithm

The Overall structure of the SLMS algorithm is as follows.

1. A test to filter bad cases where SLMS will probably degrade performances is applied (explained in section 4).
2. Apply software if-conversion.
3. Generate all the MIs in the loop's body, following the order of execution in the source code. Re-name multi defined-used scalars.
4. Find the MII.
   (a) Dependency edges are "raised" to the root of each MI (section 3.6).
   (b) Obtain the delays of the data dependencies edges (section 3.5).
   (c) Compute the MII (section 3.6).

5. If there is no valid MII, then repeat the following until a valid II is obtained or a failure occurs:
   (a) Select[3] a MI and decompose it (section 3.2) based on data dependency analysis. If there are no MIs that can be decomposed then a failure occurs.
   (b) Re-compute delays and MII.
6. If the MII was found, then:
   (a) Update registers lifetime (used for MVE 3.3), save the maximum lifetime.
   (b) Build the prologue kernel and epilogue.
   (c) For each decomposed MI, MVE (section 3.3) or Scalar Expansion (section 3.4) is applied to eliminate dependencies caused by the decomposition. MVE or Scalar Expansion may also be activate to eliminate false dependencies caused by the use of scalars in the loop. The choice between MVE and Scalar Expansion is given to the user as MVE implies loop unrolling and code expansion while Scalar Expansion uses temporary arrays.

Computing MII is performed as follows.

1. Initialize the difMin Matrix [3], and obtain delay and flow or anti data dependencies between MIs. Edges connecting memory reference nodes are propagated up to the parent MI.
2. Activate the Iterative Shortest Path algorithm [23] with increasing values of II until a valid II is found and returned, or II is equal to the number of MI in the loop, in this case return error.

Note, SLMS defines a **valid II** as one that yields a better schedule then the sequential one, e.g. $II < number\ of\ sequential\ MIs$.

Consider the following loop for finding the maximum of an array:

$$max = arr[0];$$
$$for(i = 0; i < n; i + +)$$
$$if(max < arr[i])max = arr[i];$$

Using source level if-conversion and MVE, the following SLMS was obtained:

$$max0 = arr[0];$$
$$max1 = max0;$$
$$pred0 = (max0 < arr[1]);$$
$$for(i = 1; i < n - 2; i+ = 2)\{$$
$$\quad if(pred0)max0 = arr[i]; \|$$
$$\quad\quad pred1 = (max1 < arr[i + 1]);$$
$$\quad if(pred1)max1 = arr[i + 1]; \|$$
$$\quad\quad pred0 = (max0 < arr[i + 2]);$$
$$\}$$
$$if(pred0)\ max0 = arr[i];$$
$$if(max0 > max1)\ max = max0;\ else\ max = max1;$$

Note: The last line was added manually.

---

[3] Selection of a MI can be done by sequential order or by data dependence analysis.

Some loops don't require decomposition of MI nor MVE, such loops have more than one MI and no loop variants. The following example demonstrates such a case. In this loop the lack of loop-carried dependence edges generated a MS with $MII = 1$.

$$for(ky = 1; ky < n; k++)\{$$
$$DU1[ky] = U1[ky + 1] - U1[ky - 1];$$
$$DU2[ky] = U2[ky + 1] - U2[ky - 1];$$
$$DU3[ky] = U3[ky + 1] - U3[ky - 1];$$
$$U1[ky + 101] = U1[ky] + 2 * DU1[ky] + 2 * DU2[ky] + 2 * DU3[ky];$$
$$U2[ky + 101] = U2[ky] + 2 * DU1[ky] + 2 * DU2[ky] + 2 * DU3[ky];$$
$$U3[ky + 101] = U3[ky] + 2 * DU1[ky] + 2 * DU2[ky] + 2 * DU3[ky];$$
$$\}$$

SLMS transformation removed inter-iteration sequential dependencies allowing parallel execution of all MIs within one iteration.

Epilogue...;

$$for(ky = 1; ky < n - 5; ky++)\{$$

$$U3[ky + 101] = U3[ky] + 2 * DU1[ky] + 2 * DU2[ky] + 2 * DU3[ky]; \ ||$$

$$U2[ky + 1 + 101] = U2[ky + 1] + 2 * DU1[ky + 1] + 2 * DU2[ky + 1] + 2 * DU3[ky + 1]; \ ||$$

$$U1[ky + 2 + 101] = U1[ky + 2] + 2 * DU1[ky + 2] + 2 * DU2[ky + 2] + 2 * DU3[ky + 2]; \ ||$$

$$DU3[ky + 3] = U3[ky + 3 + 1] - U3[ky + 3 - 1]; \ ||$$

$$DU2[ky + 4] = U2[ky + 4 + 1] - U2[ky + 4 - 1]; \ ||$$

$$DU1[ky + 5] = U1[ky + 5 + 1] - U1[ky + 5 - 1]; \ ||$$

$$\}$$

6   SLMS and Other Loop Transformations

SLMS can be combined with other loop reordering and restructuring transformations [4]. At source level, MS can be applied both before or after other loop transformations. The first form of combining is to apply SLMS after loop transformations to extract the parallelism exposed by these transformations. For example, SLMS can not be directly applied to the following inner loop due to the dependency of $a[i, j + 1] = t$; and $t = a[i, j + 1]$; as depicted by the following erroneous kernel obtained by using $II = 1$:

```
for(i = 0; i < n; i++)
    for(j = 0; j < n; j++){        t = a[i][j];
    t = a[i][j];            ⟶   a[i][j + 1] = t; || t = a[i][j + 1];
    a[i][j + 1] = t;                a[i][j + 2] = t;
    }
```

Using loop interchange [4] to replace the innermost loop from $'j'$ to $'i'$ yields a legal kernel with $II = 1$. Note that the dependence on the temporary variable t is resolved by using MVE. This allows the parallel execution of MI separated by ||.

$$for(j = 0; j < n; j + +)\{$$
$$\quad for(i = 0; i < n; i + +)\{$$
$$\quad\quad t \ = \ a[i, j];$$
$$\quad\quad a[i, j + 1] = t;$$
$$\}$$

$\longrightarrow$

$$for(j = 0; j < n; j + +)\{$$
$$\quad t1 = a[0, j];$$
$$\quad for(i = 0; i < n - 2; i+ = 2)\{$$
$$\quad\quad a[i, j + 1] = t1; \ || \ t2 = a[i + 1, j];$$
$$\quad\quad a[i + 1, j + 1] = t2; \ || \ t1 = a[i + 2, j];$$
$$\quad\}$$
$$\quad a[i, j + 1] = t1;$$
$$\}$$

Performing MS at source level enables its application also before other loop transformations. Another example where loop transformations allow us to apply SLMS is loop fusion [4]. Each of the following two loops can not be SLMSed due to the dependency between the first statement of the next iterations and the last statement of the current iteration. After loop fusion we get a single loop, now SLMS can be applied obtaining a valid scheduling with $II = 3$ as follows:

$$for(i = 1; i < n; i + +)\{$$
$$\quad t = A[i - 1];$$
$$\quad B[i] = B[i] + t;$$
$$\quad A[i] = t + B[i];$$
$$\}$$
$$//second \ loop$$
$$for(i = 1; i < n; i + +)\{$$
$$\quad q = C[i - 1];$$
$$\quad B[i] = B[i] + q;$$
$$\quad C[i] = q * B[i];$$
$$\}$$
$$TR$$

$$for(i = 1; i < n; i + +)\{$$
$$\quad t = A[i - 1];$$
$$\quad B[i] = B[i] + t;$$
$$\quad A[i] = t + B[i];$$
$$\quad q = C[i - 1];$$
$$\quad B[i] = B[i] + q;$$
$$\quad C[i] = q * B[i];$$
$$\}$$

$$t = A[i - 1];$$
$$B[i] = B[i] + t;$$
$$A[i] = t + B[i];$$
$$q = C[i - 1]; \quad ||t = A[i];$$
$$B[i] = B[i] + q; ||B[i + 1] = B[i + 1] + t;$$
$$C[i] = q * B[i]; \ ||A[i + 1] = t + B[i + 1];$$
$$q = C[i];$$
$$B[i + 1] = B[i + 1] + q;$$
$$C[i + 1] = q * B[i + 1];$$

Consider two loops, applying SLMS separately to each loop followed by Fusion of the two loops will generate a different schedule than first applying Fusion and then SLMS to the fused loop. The example depicted in figure 9 demonstrates this case.

SLMS can also be used to enable the application of loop transformations. For example, the following two loops can not be joined by loop fusion. Usually, this example is solved using a complex combination of loop peeling + loop reversal, however one application of SLMS (as depicted in figure 10) will allow loop fusion.

Loop unrolling is used to resolve cases where the II is to high (close to the number of MI). Also, in some cases, unrolling the kernel of an SLMSed loop can improve resource utilization. In conclusion, clearly there are cases where the combination of loop transformations and SLMS is useful.

Original Loops

```
for( i = 1; i <, N-1 ; i++){
    a[i] = a[i-1] * 2 + a[i+1] * 2;
}

for( i = 1; i <, N-1 ; i++){
    b[i] = b[i-1] * 2 + b[i+1] * 2;
}
```

SLMS -> Fusion

```
reg1 = a[2];
reg3 = b[2];
for( i = 1; i < N-3 ; i+=2){
    a[i] = a[i-1]*2+reg1*2;  || reg2 = a[i+2];
    a[i+1] = a[i]*2+reg2*2 ; || reg1 = a[i+3];
    b[i] = b[i-1]*2+reg3*2;  || reg4 = b[i+2];
    b[i+1] = b[i]*2+reg4*2;  || reg3 = b[i+3];
}
a[i] = a[i-1]*2+reg1*2;
b[i] = b[i-1]*2+reg3*2;
```

Fusion -> SLMS

```
a[1] = a[0]*2+a[2]*2;
for( i = 1; i < N-2 ; i++){
    b[i] = b[i-1]*2+b[i+1]*2; ||
    a[i+1] = a[i]*2+a[i+2]*2;
}
b[i] = b[i-1]*2+b[i+1]*2;
```

Fig. 9. The order of transformations changes the final scheduling

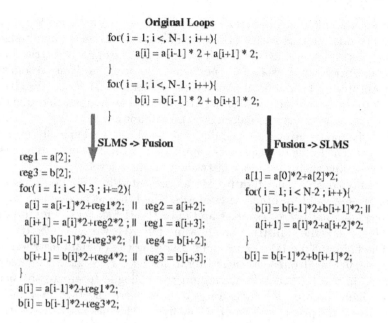

Fig. 10. SLMS allows loop fusion

7 Cases Where SLMS Optimizes Better Than the Lower Level MS

In here we consider possible explanations of why SLMS can in some cases obtain better schedulings than the underlying lower level MS. First it is important to understand the difference between optimizing at source level mode and at machine level mode. At machine level the optimization can use exact knowledge of the CPU resources and obtained optimized scheduling. The opposite is true for source level optimization which is actually performed ignoring hardware resources constrains, optimizing for maximal parallelism at source level. This "disadvantage" can work to the benefit of a SLMS. In particular, it can happen that due to hardware resource constrains the underlying MS will not optimize a given loop while after SLMS a more optimized scheduling will be obtained. Typically, even an elementary list scheduling of basic blocks applied after SLMS can in some cases find better scheduling than the more constrained machine level MS.

We mainly consider the Iterative MS as presented in [18] (IMS) however the following is also valid for other types of MS. The IMS has a complete knowledge of the available hardware resources and once the II has been computed it tries to schedule the kernel's instructions in a modulo reservation table (RT) with II rows. The filling of the RT rows is done following the original instruction order mixing instructions from consecutive iterations $i, i + 1, i + 2, \ldots$ The instruction are placed in the RT "as is" relaying on the epilogue to create the necessary pipeline chain. Figure 11 demonstrates a case where the IMS may fail due to increased register pressure. The DDG in figure 11 contains three instructions x, y, z and is frequently found in loop accessing arrays. For example the long delay between x and y can be the result of a more complex arithmetic operation such as floating multiplication, while the dependency cycle between y and z can be easily generated by the index increment of array accesses ($y = \ldots z[i-1]$) or by an accumulator instruction ($y+ = z[i]$). In this case $II = 2$ and we assume the the IMS is able to build the corresponding kernel (figure 11 left). The use of such a kernel implies that the last four values of x must be held in four different registers since they must remain alive to be used by later iterations of this kernel. As explained before, modulo variable expansion will unroll the kernel four times in order to let the value computed by the x instruction stay alive during the next four iterations. This unrolling increases the register pressure and may lead to performance degradation or the compiler will prevent from using the code generated by the IMS+Modulo-variable-expansion. On the other hand SLMS can be applied to this loop leading to the kernel $[z||x]; [y]$ which can be safely schedule (figure 11). Basically the SLMS in this example was used only to expose the possible parallelism of $[z||x]$.

Another drawback of the IMS is that it can not explicitly correct the indexes of instructions that are placed in the RT. Note that when the k'th instruction is scheduled in a RT with $II < k$ rows it is assumed to belong to the $i + \lfloor k/II \rfloor$ iteration where i marks the iteration of the first instruction. Hence the IMS can not violate the order of the instruction scheduling. The code in the example in figure 12 is taken from [18] where it is used to show how IMS fails to schedule $A3$ and $A4$ in a RT with $II = 4$ rows (figure 12 left). Since SLMS ignores the issue of hardware resources is will produce the kernel $[A3_i||A1_{i+1}]; [A4_i||A2_{i+1}]$ which can be schedule (using list scheduling) in a RT with 4 rows (as depicted in figure figure 12 right). Technically the IMS failed since $A3$ and $A4$ must be

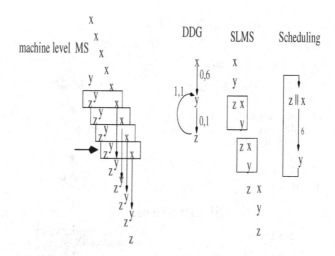

Fig. 11. Failure due to register pressure

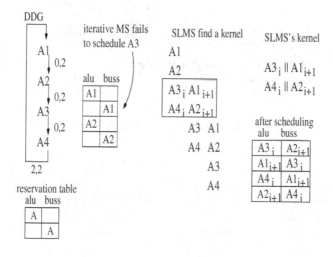

Fig. 12. Failure due to in ability indexing of instruction during sheduling

scheduled to the rows already occupied by $A1$ and $A2$. Note that even if the IMS would have considered mixed solutions such as the one described in figure 12 (right) it lacks the ability of changing the indexing of $A1$ $A2$ from i to $i+1$. Thus this failure of the IMS is not a technical issue it follows from the fact that unlike IMS, SLMS can change the index of instructions while scheduling them in the II rows of the kernel, e.g., from $A1 : r1 = r0 + x[i]$ to $A1 : r1 = r0 + A[i+1]$.

Finally, SLMS usually changes the data dependencies of the loop's body compare to the original code thus allowing different (possibly better) schedulings not

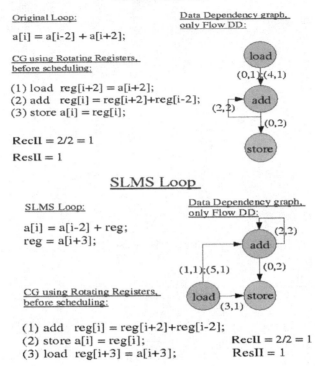

Fig. 13. SLMS changes the DD graph thus enabling other scheduling options

available in the original code. As an example consider the loop $a[i] = a[i - 2] + a[i+2]$; of figure 13 where the code generation used rotating registers [9] to create the loop's code. The underlying MS parallelizes the loop ($MII = RecII = 1$) due to, the dependency cycle between the "load" and the "add". Note, that the "add" was assigned a delay of 2 cycles. The Data Dependency (DD) edges between the "load" and the "add" and not between the "load" and the "store" are due to the use of rotating registers. In addition, redundant "load" optimization was applied (no need to "load" $a[i-2]$). Next, SLMS was applied before code generation obtaining the loop $a[i] = a[i - 2] + reg$; $reg = a[i + 3]$;. Due to simplicity MVE was not applied. After SLMS, the DD graph for the SLMSed loop (we present only "flow" DD arcs) changes. The MII calculated by the underlying MS remains 1. But since the DD graph changed, the underlying scheduler can generate a different schedule for that loop. Since the scheduler has now more options,the new schedule can be better than the original one. However, note that, any form of parallelization obtained by a machine level MS is clearly obtainable using SLMS, as SLMS is less restricted than machine level MS (limited from resource constrains).

Apart from this ability of SLMS to find optimized scheduling by first ignoring resource constrains, there are some technical factors working in favor of SLMS.

1. It is common that compilers restrict MS to small size loops such as loops with less than 50 instructions. Thus SLMS can optimize and parallelize even large size loops improving their final scheduling however there is no special benefit in applying loop unrolling before SLMS.
2. SLMS works at source level thus can directly determine the exact dependencies between each two array references. Though a compiler can also obtain these dependencies at the front-end/AST level it may fail to transfer them to the machine level representation (RTL) of the back-end. Thus, MS operations such as replacing $A[2*i]$ by $A[2*(i+1)]$ are more complicated to implement in RTL/machine level than at source level.

8   Working with the Source Level Compiler

In here we shortly demonstrate how the user can use the source level compiler (SLC) to on-line improve its source code such that SLMS can be applied. Consider the following loop for which the SLMS obtained a MS with $II = 2$. Based on the outcome, the user can determine that $II = 1$ was not obtained due to a dependency cycle with $temp-=x[lw]*y[j]$ of the next iteration and $lw++$ of the current iteration.

$$lw = 6;$$
$$for(j = 4; j < n; j = j+2)$$
$$\{$$
$$\quad temp-=x[lw]*y[j];$$
$$\quad lw++;$$
$$\}$$

$\longrightarrow$

$$lw = 6;$$
$$reg1 = y[4];$$
$$temp = temp - x[lw]*reg1;$$
$$for(j = 4; j < n-1; j = j+2)$$
$$\{$$
$$\quad lw++; \;||\; reg1 = y[j+1];$$
$$\quad temp = temp - x[lw]*reg1;$$
$$\}$$
$$lw++;$$

The user can fix this problem by moving the $lw++$ before the first MI allowing the MVE to operate replacing lw by two variables $lw1, lw2$. The outcome is that SLMS now obtains a schedule with $II = 1$ increasing the parallelism:

$$lw = 5;$$
$$for(j = 4; j < n; j = j+2)$$
$$\{$$
$$\quad lw++;$$
$$\quad temp-=x[lw]*y[j];$$
$$\}$$

$\longrightarrow$

$$lw1 = 4;$$
$$lw2 = 5;$$
$$lw1++;$$
$$for(j = 4; j < n-2; j = j+4)$$
$$\{$$
$$\quad temp-=x[lw1]*y[j]; \;||\; lw2++;$$
$$\quad temp-=x[lw2]*y[j+2]; \;||\; lw1++;$$
$$\}$$
$$temp-=x[lw1]*y[j];$$

An even better improvement would have been obtained had the user decided to apply manual decomposition of $temp- = x[lw] * y[j]$ before moving $lw + +$. Since the lifetime of lw after SLMS is two iterations, then MVE will unroll twice and use renaming to obtain the following code.

$$
\begin{aligned}
&lw = 5; \\
&for(j = 4; j < n; j = j + 2) \\
&\{ \\
&\quad lw + +; \\
&\quad reg1 = y[j]; \\
&\quad temp- = x[lw] * reg1; \\
&\}
\end{aligned}
\quad \longrightarrow \quad
\begin{aligned}
&lw1 = 4;\ lw2 = 6;\ lw3 = 4; \\
&lw1 + +;\ reg1 = y[4]; \\
&for(j = 4; j < n - 6; j = j + 6) \\
&\{ \\
&\quad temp- = x[lw1] * reg1;\ ||\ reg2 = y[j + 2];\ ||\ lw3+ = 3; \\
&\quad temp- = x[lw2] * reg2;\ ||\ reg1 = y[j + 4];\ ||\ lw1+ = 3; \\
&\quad temp- = x[lw3] * reg1;\ ||\ reg2 = y[j + 6];\ ||\ lw2+ = 3; \\
&\} \\
&temp- = x[lw1] * reg1;\ ||\ reg2 = y[j + 2]; \\
&temp- = x[lw2] * reg2;
\end{aligned}
$$

9   Experimental Results

SLMS was implemented in Wolfe's Tiny system [22] enhanced by the Omega test [14]. Tiny, was chosen, due to its support in source-to-source transformations and its support of array analysis. Tiny is a loop restructuring and research tool which interacts with the user. Tiny's GUI allows the user to select which transformation to apply, it includes among others, Distribution, Interchange, Fusion, Unroll and SLMS. The following benchmarks were used to test SLMS: The NAS [5] benchmark, Livermore [11] loops, Linpack [6] loops, and the STONE benchmark. The benchmarks were compiled and tested using several commercial compilers and machines: Intel's ICC-ia64(V 9.1) and GCC-ia64 over Itanium II (IA64), IBM's XLC over Power 4 Regata, and GCC over ARM simulator. We have also tested SLMS with GCC over superscalar processor Pentium(R). The Experimental results are divided into three subsections: the first describes the results with GCC and the second describes the results obtained using ICC and XLC, and the third describes results for embedded systems. The GCC has a weak Swing MS and thus modeling the use of a general source level compiler optimizing the program (with SLMS) before it is compiled by the relatively weak compiler. ICC and XLC are high performance compilers with advanced machine level MS, their results support the claim that SLMS is a separate optimization that can be used before low level MS is applied. Remarks: (1) in all the following graphs, the Y axes represents the speedup obtained by SLMSed loop vs. non SLMSed loops. In all tests both SLMSed and non SLMSed loops are compiled with the same compilation flags. (2) SLMS was tested with and without source level MVE, the presented results show the best time obtained. (3) In ia-64 architecture, improvement can be measured by counting the number of bundles in the loop body, a bundle can be viewed as a VLS regarding for explicit instruction level parallelism.

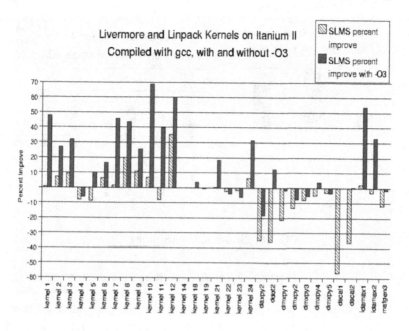

Fig. 14. Livermore & Linpack over GCC

9.1 Experimental Results over a Relatively Weak Compiler

As explained in the introduction, SLMS is considered as part of a potential SLC. Thus, showing that SLMS improves execution times over GCC supports the claim that a SLC can be used to improve execution times over relatively weak final compilers. The following graphs 14 and 15, present speedups obtained using GCC (IA64) over Itanium II with and without $-O3$. Analyzing GCC's assembly for $-O3$ revealed that scheduling optimizations such as MVE and Unrolling where not performed. In some successful cases such as ddot2 the application of those transformations at source level compensated for the lack of them in the final compiler. Another successful loop is kernel 8, this loop has a big loop body without loop-carried dependency edges and contains only array references. For this kind of loop, SLMS doesn't need to decompose and in this case $MII = 1$. The application of SLMS released the intra-iteration sequential dependency between MI and revealed the parallelism between them, thus enabling the generation of less bundles. Indeed before SLMS GCC's assembly contained 23 bundles and after SLMS 16 bundles.

Regarding bad cases, most of them are within the Linpack loops. Most of those loops contain one long MI and use intensive floating point calculations. The negative results can be explained by the level of parallelism of floating point operations in the Itanium processor. To prove this, we replaced all the floating point variables with integer ones and re-run the test. The results where reversed in favor of SLMS. Another prove is by the fact that those same loops have better speedups on Pentium(R) and Power4-Regata. Filtering bad cases is an

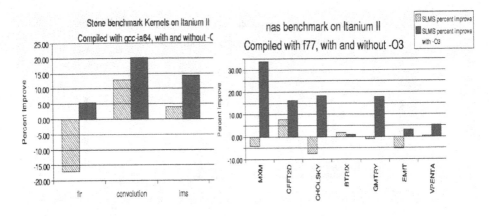

Fig. 15. Stone and NAS over GCC

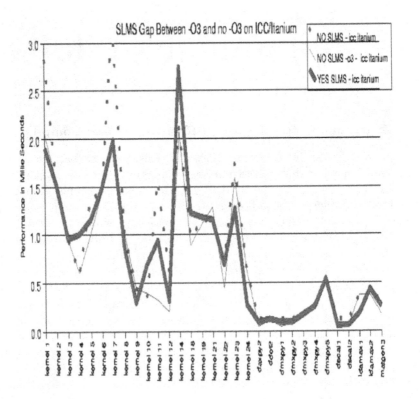

Fig. 16. SLMS can be used to close the gap between using and not using -O3

important issue in SLMS. Bad cases can be identified at source level by general high level characteristics, experimental results prove that they are specific for the pair compiler/hardware.

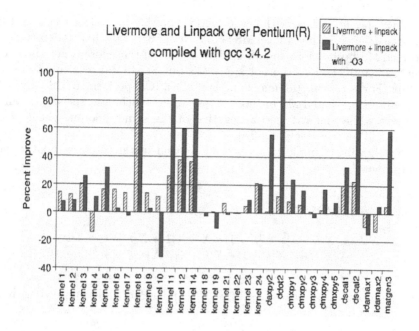

Fig. 17. SLMS can improve performance over superscalar processor

Another interesting experiment is to see how SLMS as a SLC can be used to close the gap between using and not using -O3 for example in the ICC compiler. If SLMS can cover a significant part of this gap, it can cover up cases where the underlying final compiler fails to optimize for new architectures. Thus increasing the retargibility of the underlying final compiler. In order to see this, we have compared how SLMS without -O3 can bridge the gap between using -O3 and the relative weak compiler obtained when -O3 is not used. Figure 16 depicts the results over ICC+Itanium, showing that using SLMS without -O3 as a SLC can "close" the gap between a good highly optimizing compiler and a relative weak compiler.

We also tested SLMS on a superscalar processor (Pentium(R)) where all the parallelism is obtained by the HW pipeline. Figure 17 depicts the results, the loops where compiled using GCC with and without −O3. The results show that SLMS was successful in exposing the parallelism in most of the loops. One example for which SLMS had a negative impact is kernel 10. Kernel 10 contains several loop-variants and a big loop body causing SLMS's MVE to use 35 register, apparently causing spilling since Pentium(R) has much less registers.

9.2 Experimental Results over Highly Optimizing Compilers

The following graphs 18, 19 and 20, present speedups obtained using ICC (IA64) over Itanium II and XLC over Power 4 Regata. Showing that SLMS improves performance over highly optimizing compilers and powerful machines, proving that SLMS should co-exist with low level MS. Another indication to the fact that SLMS can co-exist with low level MS is that out of 31 loops that were tested, ICC performed MS both before and after SLMS for 26 of those loops. For three loops (kernels 2,7 and 24), ICC did not apply MS but SLMS did resulting in positive speedups. For two loops (idamax2 and kernel 8), ICC performed MS only before SLMS. SLMS prevented MS of those loops, kernel 8 achieved speedup of almost 15 percent while idamax2 had a negative of the same amount. Showing that SLMS should be selectively applied.

In the following example we analyze a loop that has an intensive floating point computation.

$$float\ k[n];$$
$$for(k = 1; k < n; k + +)$$
$$\{$$
$$\quad X[k] = X[k-1] * X[k-1] * X[k-1] * X[k-1] * X[k-1]+$$
$$\quad\quad X[k+1] * X[k+1] * X[k+1] * X[k+1] * X[k+1];$$
$$\}$$

The loop was transformed using SLMS and MVE and compiled with ICC $-O3$ over ItaniumII.

$$float\ k[n];$$
$$reg1 = X[1];$$
$$for(k = 1; k < n - 3; k+ = 2)$$
$$\{$$
$$\quad X[k] = X[k-1] * X[k-1] * X[k-1] * X[k-1] * X[k-1]+$$
$$\quad\quad reg1 * reg1 * reg1 * reg1 * reg1;\quad ||\quad reg2 = X[k+2];$$
$$\quad X[k+1] = X[k+1] * X[k+1] * X[k+1] * X[k+1] * X[k+1]+$$
$$\quad\quad reg2 * reg2 * reg2 * reg2 * reg2;\quad ||\quad reg1 = X[k+3];$$
$$\}$$
$$X[k] = X[k-1] * X[k-1] * X[k-1] * X[k-1] * X[k-1]+$$
$$reg1 * reg1 * reg1 * reg1 * reg1;$$

Since the ItaniumII has two floating point units, and can concurrently execute two bundles, each bundle can contain one fma.s (floating multiply and add) instruction. For the original loop ICC unrolled the kernel 8 times until maximum resource utilization was achieved, ICC achieved 5.8 bundles per iteration. SLMS aided ICC to produced a compact and optimized code with 4 bundles per iteration. For both loops ICC performed MS, but the II for the SLMS loop was much smaller than the one for the original loop. This example shows that SLMS can aid the low level MS to find a better solution. This specific example is also relevant for improvement of floating point numeric applications. Livermore kernel 24 contains a condition branch. For both loops (original and SLMSed) ICC did not unroll nor performed MS. For the original loop ICC generated 5 bundles per iteration and for the SLMS loop it generated 3.5 bundles per iteration. This improvement was because SLMS transformed the loop in a way that gave ICC other scheduling options. Apparently, unrolling and mixing iterations enabled ICC to better utilize resources.

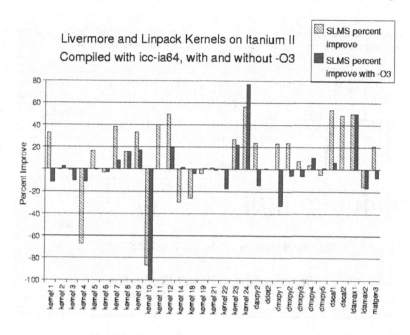

Fig. 18. Livermore & Linpack over ICC

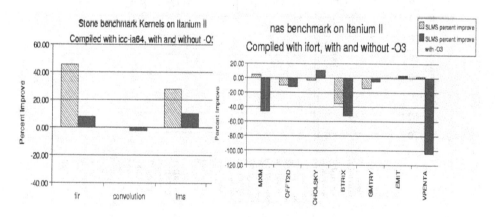

Fig. 19. Stone and NAS over ICC

9.3 Experimental Results for Embedded Systems

In order to test the effectiveness of SLMS for embedded systems, one should test the power consumption gain/loss involved with SLMS. Moreover, the comparison should be made over a classic embedded core such as the ARM or over a VLIW machine.[4] The effectiveness of SLMS for VLIW machines has been demonstrated

---

[4] SLMS has a very minor effect on the code size, and thus this aspect of embedded systems has not been considered.

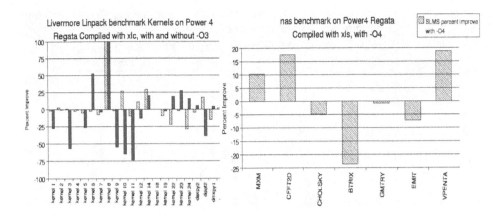

Fig. 20. Livermore & Linpack + NAS over XLC

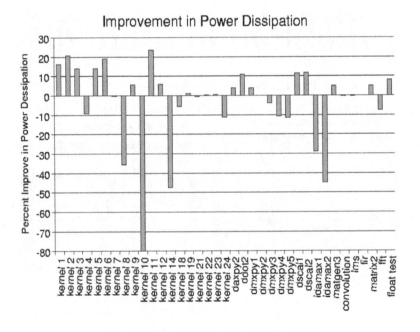

Fig. 21. Power dissipation for the ARM

by the experiments over the IA-64. The Panalyzer system [1] with the simple-scalar tool chain for ARM is used to measure the effect of SLMS on the power dissipation of the ARM 7TDMI processor. Figure 21 depict the improvements obtained in the overall power dissipation including caches and memories. The results show that SLMS can indeed improve the power dissipation, but not in all cases, hence SLMS must be applied selectively. Similar, results where also

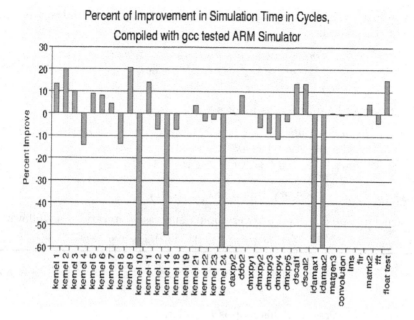

Fig. 22. Total number of cycles for the ARM

obtained for cycle count figure 22. There is a clear correlation between the bad cases of the power consumption and the cycle count. in addition the results over the ARM are worse than those obtained over other architectures. The main reason is that the ARM does not use Instruction Level Parallelism using basically one ALU operation per cycle. Consequently, the parallelism that SLMS created could only be used for hiding memory latencies and pipeline stalls (compare to the IA64 where it was used to fill empty slots). Thus, the results of figure 21 should be regarded as a success, provided that SLMS will be used selectively.

10   Possible Extensions

In here possible extensions to SLMS are considered, showing its generality of handling more complex cases than the simple loops presented so far. These extensions include applying SLMS to while-loops and applying SLMS to loops with conditional statements. The potential of SLMS to handle while-loops and conditional statements is only demonstrated via examples, full implementation of these extensions is beyond the scope of this work.

It is well known [8] that in some cases while-loops can be unrolled in spite of the fact that their iteration count is not fixed. The ability to unroll while-loops suggests that SLMS can also be applied to while-loops. Following are two examples showing how SLMS can be applied to while-loops.

In the first example, the loop finds the first element in a linked list, whose value equal a given key.

$$for(p = head; p = null; p = p-> next)\{$$
$$if(p-> key == KEY)\ break;$$
$$\}$$

This loop can be unrolled as follows.

$$for(p = head; p = null\ \&\&\ p-> next = null; p = p-> next-> next)\{$$
$$if(p-> key == KEY) break;$$
$$if(p-> next-> key == KEY) break;$$
$$\}$$
$$p = (p-> key == KEY)?p : p-> next;$$

A kernel can be obtained by overlapping successive iterations as follows.

iteration i	iteration $i+1$	iteration $i+2$
$c = (p-> key == Key)$	$if(c)break;$	$(c = p-> next-> next) == Key$ $if(c)break;$

The final SLMS version of this loop is as follows.

$(c1 = head) = nuu?head-> key == KEY\ :\ false;$
$for(p = head; p = null; p = p-> next-> next)\{$
    $[if(c1)break;\ ||\ c2 = (p-> nextSLMS = null)?\ p-> next-> key == KEY\ :\ true;]$
    $[if(c2)break;\ ||\ c1 = (p-> next-> next = null)?\ p-> next-> next-> key == KEY\ :\ true;]$
$\}$
$if(c2)\ result\ =\ p-> next;$
$else\ if(c1)\ result\ =\ (head-> key == KEY)?head\ :\ p;$
$else\ result\ =\ null;$

In the second example, the loop performs a shifted copy of a string.

$$i = 0;$$
$$while(a[i + 2])\{$$
$$a[i] = a[i + 2];$$
$$i + +;$$
$$\}$$

This loop can be unrolled as follows.

$$i = 0;$$
$$startUpCode();$$
$$while(a[i + 2]\ \&\&\ a[i + 3])\{$$
$$a[i] = a[i + 2];$$
$$a[i + 1] = a[i + 3];$$
$$i+ = 2;$$
$$\}$$
$$closeUpCode();$$

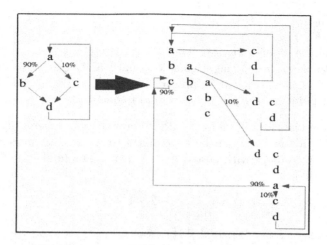

Fig. 23. Schematic representation of SLMS that is focused on the most frequent path

The SLMS version after decomposition is as follows.

$$i = 0; j = 1;$$
$$startUpCode();$$
$$reg1 = a[i + 2];$$
$$a[i] = reg1; \;\| \; reg2 = a[j + 2];$$
$$while(a[j + 3] \; \&\& \; a[i + 3])\{$$
$$\quad i+ = 2; \;\| \; a[j] = reg2; \;\| \; reg1 = a[j + 3];$$
$$\quad j+ = 2; \;\| \; a[i] = reg1; \;\| \; reg2 = a[i + 3];$$
$$\}$$
$$closeUpCode();$$

Note: this outcome is better (in terms of extracted parallelism) than the unrolled version.

The second extension is to apply SLMS to loops with conditional if-statements. The solution of section 3.1 using source level if-conversion is not very efficient as it adds conditional checks before every statement of the if-then/if-else body. Instead we can use the following idea (to the best of our knowledge a novel one but there is some similarity to the work of [20]):

- Let L be a simple loop with an if-statement $L = for(i = 0; i < n; i + +)\{if(A_i)B_i \; else \; C_i; \; D_i; \}$.
- Assume that we can identify (via profile information or static analysis) that $Pf = A_i; B_i; D_i$ is the most frequent path.
- We can chose the II according to Pf assuming that it is executed repeatedly many times. By overlapping successive iterations of Pf a kernel $KPf = D_i \; \|B_{i+1}\|A_{i+2}$ may be obtained. Note that KPf can be repeatedly executed as long as A_{i+2} is evaluated to true.

- Thus, when A_{i+2} is false we must:
  - exit KPf.
  - drain the pipeline by executing $D_{i+1}; C_{i+2}; D[i+2]$.
  - continue executing the original loop until KPf can be re-started.
- Note that the less efficient fix-up code for draining the pipeline and locating a restart point for KPf is not executed frequently.

The process of transforming a loop with if-statements is schematically depicted in figure 23. This method can be generalized to loops with more than one if-statements and to loops with nested if-statements. The final code for the loop's kernel is a s follows.

$$
\begin{aligned}
&for(i = 0; i < n - 2; i + +)\{ \\
&\quad D[1]; \; B[i + 1]; \\
&\quad if(!A[i + 2])\{ \\
&\qquad D[i + 1]; \quad C[i + 2]; \quad D[i + 2]; \\
&\qquad for(i = i + 3; i < n; i + +)\{ \\
&\qquad\quad if(!A[i])\{ C[i]; \quad D[i]; \} \\
&\qquad\quad else \; \{ \\
&\qquad\qquad B[i]; \\
&\qquad\qquad if(a[i + 1])\{ \\
&\qquad\qquad\quad i - -; \\
&\qquad\qquad\quad break; \\
&\qquad\qquad \} \; else \; \{ \\
\\
&\qquad\qquad\quad D[i]; \\
&\}\}\}\}\}
\end{aligned}
$$

11   Conclusions

In this work a method for source level modulo scheduling (SLMS) has been developed and implemented in the Tiny parallelizer. In spite of its relative simplicity it obtained good speedups over the GCC (with and without the Swing MS), ICC and XLC as-well improvements of power-dissipation on ARM. Experimental results show that SLMS can have a different effect depending on the compiler and architecture hence SLMS must be applied selectively. The bad cases of performance degradation can be attributed to the additional array references inserted by the SLMS transformation. It turned out that by applying SLMS to loops with more than six arithmetic operations per each array references almost all of these bad cases can be eliminated.

To the best of our knowledge this is the first time SLMS has been demonstrated and implemented. This work, also presents two possible extensions to SLMS. An extended solution to loops with if-statements, and a partial solution to while-loops. The development of these extension will enable the application of SLMS to complex loops, thus allowing SLMS to use the full power of source level transformations. Register pressure (a critical issue with machine level MS) basically did not occurred in our experiments (except for kernel 10), in spite of the extensive parallelism obtained by the SLMS. This also may be attributed to the fact that register allocation and code generation are executed after SLMS.

The relation between SLMS and known loop transformations has been considered and demonstrated. The fact that SLMS is a source level optimization implies that it can be easily combined with other loop transformations to form a source level compiler (SLC) (a tool currently developed at Haifa University). Though, the relation of SLCs and SLMS is not the focus of this work, it is an important usage of SLMS. Other compilers such as Polaris [7] that apply loop transformations and are able to generate C source code should not be considered as SLC as they produce C code from machine level intermediate representation. More related are real SLCs such as the LoopTool [15] interactively applying controlled loop fusion and unroll-and-jam to optimize programs at source level. Finally automatic parallelizers acting as a SLC such as the Parafrase system [13] can also benefit from using SLMS.

SLMS is useful for two tasks: as an addition to the arsenal of loop transformations for a source level compiler and as a preliminary optimization that differs from machine MS. We have proved, via examples and experiments that SLMS can lead to different scheduling results than machine level MS. Thus, SLMS can be also used as a regular optimization.

References

1. Sim-panalyzer: http://www.eecs.umich.edu/panalyzer/.
2. J. Ullman. A. Aho, R. Sethi. *Compilers: Principles, Techniques and Tools*. Addison-Wesley, 1986.
3. V. H. Allan, R. B. Jones, R. M. Lee, and S. J. Allan. Software pipelining. *ACM Computing Surveys*, 27(3):367–432, 1995.
4. D. F. Bacon, S. L. Graham, and O. J. Sharp. Compiler transformations for high-performance computing. *ACM Computing Surveys*, 26(4):345–420, 1994.
5. David Bailey. Nas kernel benchmark program: http://www.netlib.org/benchmark/nas.
6. J. Dongarra, P. Luszczek, and A. Petitet. The linpack benchmark: Past, present, and future: http://www.netlib.org/utk/jackdongarra.
7. K. A. Faigin, S. A. Weatherford, J. P. Hoeflinger, D. A. Padua, and P. M. Petersen. The Polaris internal representation. *International Journal of Parallel Programming*, 22(5):553–586, 1994.
8. J. Huang and T. Leng. Generalized loop-unrolling: a method for program speed-up, 1997.
9. Sverre Jarp. Optimizing IA-64 performance. *Journal of Software tools*, 26(7):21–22, 24, 26, July 2001.
10. M. Lam. Software pipelining : an effective scheduling technique for vliw machines. In *PLDI*, pages 318–328, 1988.
11. F. H. McMahon. Lawrence livermore national laboratory fortrn kernel:mflops.
12. V. R. North. Ia-64 code generation: http://citeseer.ist.psu.edu/385244.html.

13. C. D. Polychronopoulos, M. B. Gikar, M. R. Haghighat, C. L. Lee, B. P. Leung, and D. A. Schouten. The structure of parafrase-2: an advanced parallelizing compiler for c and fortran. In *Selected papers of the second workshop on Languages and compilers for parallel computing*, pages 423–453, 1990.

14. W. Pugh. The omega test: a fast and practical integer programming algorithm for dependence analysis. In *Supercomputing*, pages 4–13, 1991.

15. A. Qasem, G. Jin, and J. Mellor-Crummey. Improving performance with integrated program transformations. Technical Report TR03-419, Rice University, 2003.

16. B. R. Rau and C. D. Glaese. Some scheduling techniques and an easily schedulable horizontal architecture for high performance scientific computing. In *Proceeding of the 14th Annual Workshop on Microprogramming*, pages 183–198, October 1981.

17. B. Ramakrishna Rau. Iterative modulo scheduling: An algorithm for software pipelining loops. In *MICRO*, pages 63–74, 1994.

18. B. Ramakrishna Rau. Iterative-modulo-scheduling. In *HPL-94-115*, November 22,1995.

19. Warter, Lavery, and Wwu (1993). The benefit of predicated execution for software pipelining. In *HICSS-26 Conference Proceedings*, page Vol. 1, January 1993.

20. N. J. Warter, J. W. Bockhaus, G. E. Haab, and K. Subramanian. Enhanced modulo scheduling for loops with conditional branches. In *The 25th Annual International Symposium on Microarchitecture*, Portland, Oregon, 1992. ACM and IEEE.

21. N. J. Warter, S. A. Mahlke, W. W. Hwu, and B. R. Rau. Reverse if-conversion. *SIGPLAN Not.*, 28(6):290–299, 1993.

22. M. Wolfe. The tiny loop restructuring research tool. In *Proceedings of the International Conference on Parallel Processing*, 1991.

23. A. M. Zaky. *Efficient Static Scheduling of Loops on Synchronous Multiprocessors.* PhD thesis, Ohio State University, OH, 1989.

Author Index

Printing: Mercedes-Druck, Berlin
Binding: Stein+Lehmann, Berlin

Lecture Notes in Computer Science

For information about Vols. 1–4322

please contact your bookseller or Springer

Vol. 4370: P.P Lévy, B. Le Grand, F. Poulet, M. Soto, L. Darago, L. Toubiana, J.-F. Vibert (Eds.), Pixelization Paradigm. XV, 279 pages. 2007.

Vol. 4369: M. Umeda, A. Wolf, O. Bartenstein, U. Geske, D. Seipel, O. Takata (Eds.), Declarative Programming for Knowledge Management. X, 229 pages. 2006. (Sublibrary LNAI).

Vol. 4368: T. Erlebach, C. Kaklamanis (Eds.), Approximation and Online Algorithms. X, 345 pages. 2007.

Vol. 4367: K. De Bosschere, D. Kaeli, P. Stenström, D. Whalley, T. Ungerer (Eds.), High Performance Embedded Architectures and Compilers. XI, 307 pages. 2007.

Vol. 4366: K. Tuyls, R. Westra, Y. Saeys, A. Nowé (Eds.), Knowledge Discovery and Emergent Complexity in Bioinformatics. IX, 183 pages. 2007. (Sublibrary LNBI).

Vol. 4364: T. Kühne (Ed.), Models in Software Engineering. XI, 332 pages. 2007.

Vol. 4362: J. van Leeuwen, G.F. Italiano, W. van der Hoek, C. Meinel, H. Sack, F. Plášil (Eds.), SOFSEM 2007: Theory and Practice of Computer Science. XXI, 937 pages. 2007.

Vol. 4361: H.J. Hoogeboom, G. Păun, G. Rozenberg, A. Salomaa (Eds.), Membrane Computing. IX, 555 pages. 2006.

Vol. 4360: W. Dubitzky, A. Schuster, P.M.A. Sloot, M. Schroeder, M. Romberg (Eds.), Distributed, High-Performance and Grid Computing in Computational Biology. X, 192 pages. 2007. (Sublibrary LNBI).

Vol. 4358: R. Vidal, A. Heyden, Y. Ma (Eds.), Dynamical Vision. IX, 329 pages. 2007.

Vol. 4357: L. Buttyán, V. Gligor, D. Westhoff (Eds.), Security and Privacy in Ad-Hoc and Sensor Networks. X, 193 pages. 2006.

Vol. 4355: J. Julliand, O. Kouchnarenko (Eds.), B 2007: Formal Specification and Development in B. XIII, 293 pages. 2006.

Vol. 4354: M. Hanus (Ed.), Practical Aspects of Declarative Languages. X, 335 pages. 2006.

Vol. 4353: T. Schwentick, D. Suciu (Eds.), Database Theory – ICDT 2007. XI, 419 pages. 2006.

Vol. 4352: T.-J. Cham, J. Cai, C. Dorai, D. Rajan, T.-S. Chua, L.-T. Chia (Eds.), Advances in Multimedia Modeling, Part II. XVIII, 743 pages. 2006.

Vol. 4351: T.-J. Cham, J. Cai, C. Dorai, D. Rajan, T.-S. Chua, L.-T. Chia (Eds.), Advances in Multimedia Modeling, Part I. XIX, 797 pages. 2006.

Vol. 4349: B. Cook, A. Podelski (Eds.), Verification, Model Checking, and Abstract Interpretation. XI, 395 pages. 2007.

Vol. 4348: S.T. Taft, R.A. Duff, R.L. Brukardt, E. Ploedereder, P. Leroy (Eds.), Ada 2005 Reference Manual. XXII, 765 pages. 2006.

Vol. 4347: J. Lopez (Ed.), Critical Information Infrastructures Security. X, 286 pages. 2006.

Vol. 4346: L. Brim, B. Haverkort, M. Leucker, J. van de Pol (Eds.), Formal Methods: Applications and Technology. X, 363 pages. 2007.

Vol. 4345: N. Maglaveras, I. Chouvarda, V. Koutkias, R. Brause (Eds.), Biological and Medical Data Analysis. XIII, 496 pages. 2006. (Sublibrary LNBI).

Vol. 4344: V. Gruhn, F. Oquendo (Eds.), Software Architecture. X, 245 pages. 2006.

Vol. 4342: H. de Swart, E. Orłowska, G. Schmidt, M. Roubens (Eds.), Theory and Applications of Relational Structures as Knowledge Instruments II. X, 373 pages. 2006. (Sublibrary LNAI).

Vol. 4341: P.Q. Nguyen (Ed.), Progress in Cryptology - VIETCRYPT 2006. XI, 385 pages. 2006.

Vol. 4340: R. Prodan, T. Fahringer, Grid Computing. XXIII, 317 pages. 2007.

Vol. 4339: E. Ayguadé, G. Baumgartner, J. Ramanujam, P. Sadayappan (Eds.), Languages and Compilers for Parallel Computing. XI, 476 pages. 2006.

Vol. 4338: P. Kalra, S. Peleg (Eds.), Computer Vision, Graphics and Image Processing. XV, 965 pages. 2006.

Vol. 4337: S. Arun-Kumar, N. Garg (Eds.), FSTTCS 2006: Foundations of Software Technology and Theoretical Computer Science. XIII, 430 pages. 2006.

Vol. 4336: V.R. Basili, D. Rombach, K. Schneider, B. Kitchenham, D. Pfahl, R.W. Selby, Empirical Software Engineering Issues. XVII, 193 pages. 2007.

Vol. 4335: S.A. Brueckner, S. Hassas, M. Jelasity, D. Yamins (Eds.), Engineering Self-Organising Systems. XII, 212 pages. 2007. (Sublibrary LNAI).

Vol. 4334: B. Beckert, R. Hähnle, P.H. Schmitt (Eds.), Verification of Object-Oriented Software. XXIX, 658 pages. 2007. (Sublibrary LNAI).

Vol. 4333: U. Reimer, D. Karagiannis (Eds.), Practical Aspects of Knowledge Management. XII, 338 pages. 2006. (Sublibrary LNAI).

Vol. 4332: A. Bagchi, V. Atluri (Eds.), Information Systems Security. XV, 382 pages. 2006.

Vol. 4331: G. Min, B. Di Martino, L.T. Yang, M. Guo, G. Ruenger (Eds.), Frontiers of High Performance Computing and Networking – ISPA 2006 Workshops. XXXVII, 1141 pages. 2006.

Vol. 4330: M. Guo, L.T. Yang, B. Di Martino, H.P. Zima, J. Dongarra, F. Tang (Eds.), Parallel and Distributed Processing and Applications. XVIII, 953 pages. 2006.

Vol. 4329: R. Barua, T. Lange (Eds.), Progress in Cryptology - INDOCRYPT 2006. X, 454 pages. 2006.

Vol. 4328: D. Penkler, M. Reitenspiess, F. Tam (Eds.), Service Availability. X, 289 pages. 2006.

Vol. 4327: M. Baldoni, U. Endriss (Eds.), Declarative Agent Languages and Technologies IV. VIII, 257 pages. 2006. (Sublibrary LNAI).

Vol. 4326: S. Göbel, R. Malkewitz, I. Iurgel (Eds.), Technologies for Interactive Digital Storytelling and Entertainment. X, 384 pages. 2006.

Vol. 4325: J. Cao, I. Stojmenovic, X. Jia, S.K. Das (Eds.), Mobile Ad-hoc and Sensor Networks. XIX, 887 pages. 2006.

Vol. 4323: G. Doherty, A. Blandford (Eds.), Interactive Systems. XI, 269 pages. 2007.